THE BIBLE
A Literary Survey

The Dragon, the Beast, and the False Prophet Are Cast into Hell. From an early fourteenth-century manuscript of the Apocalypse. New York, The Metropolitan Museum of Art—The Cloisters.

THE BIBLE
A Literary Survey

edited by
Charles W. Harwell
and
Daniel McDonald

THE BOBBS-MERRILL COMPANY, INC.
INDIANAPOLIS

Copyright © 1975 by The Bobbs-Merrill Company, Inc.
Printed in the United States of America

The Bobbs-Merrill Company, Inc.
4300 West 62nd Street
Indianapolis, Indiana 46268

First Edition
First Printing 1975
Designed by Andrée Coers

Library of Congress Cataloging in Publication Data

Bible. English. Authorized. Selections. 1975.
  The Bible: a literary survey.

  I. Harwell, Charles W., 1934–   , comp.
II. McDonald, Daniel Lamont, comp.
BS391.2.H33   809′.935′22   74–13465
ISBN 0-672-63278-0 (pbk.)

CONTENTS

ILLUSTRATIONS

ACKNOWLEDGMENTS

We are indebted to Rev. James Yamauchi, S.J., for his thoughts on *Revelation*; to Rev. Jerome Neyrey, S.J., for his insights into *Mark*; and to Mrs. Irene McDonald for her counsel in areas involving definition. All three are members of the faculty at Spring Hill College.

We thank the administration of the University of South Alabama for acts of generosity relating to this book.

We are grateful to our students, whose questions and comments pointed out specific problems which needed attention.

Mobile, Alabama
July, 1974

CHARLES W. HARWELL
DANIEL MCDONALD

The Just Upright Man Is Laughed to Scorn. William Blake, 1826. Reproduced by permission of The Huntington Library, San Marino, California.

INTRODUCTION

No other book possesses the literary and religious sweep of the Bible. Tracing mankind from an idyllic garden to a celestial city, it records the follies, passions, and hopes of people as they scheme, love, and worship. Its influence on the course of history cannot be measured; its impact on the lives of individuals cannot be measured.

This edition presents selections from Scripture—including thirteen books in their entirety—and discusses the works as examples of literary types. In these works, the devout will find divine reassurance in times of confusion and distress. And the skeptical must surely be impressed by examples of faith, commitment, vulnerability, and tenacity which define the human condition.

Some textual matters should be mentioned. A careful reader will note occasional italicized words or phrases in the Old and New Testaments. These italics indicate a gloss, i.e., a word or phrase omitted in the original Hebrew or Greek but included in the KJV to clarify the translation. Furthermore, in the Apocrypha, proper names have been given Latinized spelling instead of transliteration from the Greek, e.g., *Nineveh* rather than *Nineve, Nebuchadnezzar* rather than *Nabuchodonosor, Assyria* rather than *Assur*, and so on. Finally, some of the more important names have been changed to reflect a more accurate textual consensus: e.g., *Sarchedonus* for *Esarhaddon, Enemessar* for *Shalmaneser, Achiacharus* for *Ahikar*.

The present text is taken from the King James translation (1611). As the Authorized Version, it has prevailed through the centuries and remains a foundation of English literature. Errors and obscurities are clarified in the footnotes, some of which quote from twentieth-century translations of the Scriptures.

Modern Bibles can be more accurate than the Authorized Version because the King James translators did not have access to the most ancient Hebrew and Greek manuscripts. They based their New Testament, for example, on Erasmus' *Novum Instrumentum* (1516), a Greek edition which relied heavily on a single twelfth-century manuscript. Modern translators have some forty-five hundred Greek New Testaments from which to establish a text, and they draw especially from the fifth-century Alexandrian manuscript, which did not reach England until 1628, and from the fourth-century Sinaitic and Vatican codices, which were not available to scholars until the nineteenth century. Modern translators also benefit from Greek papyri unearthed in Egypt since 1900, from the Dead Sea Scrolls discovered in 1947, and from major advances in understanding the grammar, syntax, and idiom of the Biblical languages.

The new translations clarify obscurities found in the King James Version. Some of these occurred because the translators, in their reverence for the sacred documents, expressed the idiom of the language rather than its meaning. (Thus, in *Luke* 17:8, a master's command to his slave becomes "Make ready wherewith I may sup.") Most difficulties arise, however, because the English language has changed. The King James Version was essentially a revision of existing English Bibles, and these derived in large measure from the translation of William Tyndale (1535). Tyndale's eloquent language and dignified style—already dated in 1611—were retained to create a kind of sanctified English appropriate to the Bible. This sanctified English remains one of the glories of the Authorized Version. Generations have treasured lines like "I prevented the dawning of the morning" (*Psalms* 119:147), "man goeth to his long home" (*Ecclesiastes* 12:5), "Let the dead bury their dead" (*Luke* 12:60), and "I am become as sounding brass, or a tinkling cymbal" (*I Corinthians* 13:1). But the modern reader can be excused for not knowing what they mean.

In this book, a difficult passage in the Authorized Version is related in a footnote to a modern reading of the line. This serves not only to clarify the passage and to introduce the reader to twentieth-century Bibles but also to reveal general problems of text and translation.

Because we could not explain every complex passage, we chose to footnote verses where obscurity would confuse or impede a general reading of the work. We also footnoted passages which illustrate the different kinds of problems that occur in reading the Bible.

CHRONOLOGY

Almost all Biblical dates are educated conjecture. For specific works, the dates suggest time of origin, not the time to which a book refers.

THE OLD TESTAMENT

2000–1700 B.C.
The Patriarchal Period

1700–1300 B.C.
The Hebrews in Egypt

1300–1200 B.C.
The Exodus
Song of Lamech (*Genesis* 4:23-24)
Song of Miriam (*Exodus* 15:21)

1200–1000 B.C.
The Settlement in Canaan
Curse of Canaan (*Genesis* 9:25-27)
Song of Deborah (*Judges* 5)
The Book of the Covenant (*Exodus* 20:23–23:19)

1000–900 B.C.
The United Monarchy
The Early Source history of the Kingdom
David's Lament (*II Samuel* 1:17-27)
The Late Source history of the Kingdom
J source of the Pentateuch

900–700 B.C.
The Kingdom Divided / The Collapse of Israel
E source of the Pentateuch
Amos

700–600 B.C.
The Collapse of Judah
Judges

600–400 B.C.
The Exile and Return
P source of the Pentateuch
Job

400–200 B.C.
Foreign Domination by Persia and Greece

Jonah
Ruth
Song of Songs
Ecclesiastes
Psalms (final compilation)

THE APOCRYPHA

200–4 B.C.
The Maccabean Priest-Kings
Roman Rule of Palestine
Tobit
Susanna
Bel and the Dragon
Judith

THE NEW TESTAMENT

4 B.C. to A.D. 30
The Life of Jesus

A.D. 30–65
The Prominence of Paul
Galatians
II Corinthians

A.D. 65–70
Roman Persecution of Christians
Mark

A.D. 70–150
Emergence of the Church
Matthew
Luke
John
Revelation

KEY TO
BIBLICAL TRANSLATIONS CITED

BARCLAY *The Revelation of John*, 2 vols., translated, with an introduction and interpretation, by William Barclay. Westminster Press, 1959.

BECK *The New Testament in the Language of Today*, translated by William F. Beck. Concordia Publishing House, 1963.

BERKELEY *The Modern Language Bible: The New Berkeley Version*, translated by Gerrit Verkuyl. Zondervan Publishing House, 1969.

GOODSPEED *The Bible: An American Translation.* The Old Testament translated by Alexander R. Gordon, Theophile J. Meek, J. M. Powis Smith, and Leroy Waterman; the New Testament translated by Edgar J. Goodspeed. University of Chicago Press, 1935.
The Apocrypha: An American Translation, translated by Edgar J. Goodspeed. University of Chicago Press, 1938.

IB *The Interpreter's Bible*, 12 vols. Abingdon Press, 1954.

JB *The Jerusalem Bible.* Doubleday and Company, 1966.

KINGDOM *The Kingdom Interlinear Translation of the Greek Scriptures*, produced by the New World Bible Translation Committee. Watchtower Bible and Tract Society of New York, Inc., 1969.

KJV *The Holy Bible*, containing the Old and New Testaments in the Authorized (King James) Version. Westminster Press, 1948.

KNOX *The Holy Bible.* A translation from the Latin Vulgate in the light of the Hebrew and Greek originals, by Monsignor Ronald Knox. Sheed & Ward, Inc., 1956.

LATTIMORE *The Revelation of John*, translated by Richmond Lattimore. Harcourt, Brace & World, 1962.

MEEK *The Bible: An American Translation.* (See GOODSPEED.)

MOFFATT *The Bible*, translated by James Moffatt. Harper & Row, 1964.

NAB *The New American Bible.* Translated from the original languages with critical use of all the ancient sources, by members of the Catholic Biblical Association of America. St. Anthony Guild Press, 1970.

NEB *The New English Bible: With the Apocrypha.* Oxford University Press, 1971.

PHILLIPS *The New Testament in Modern English*, translated by J. B. Phillips. The Macmillan Company, 1958.

Four Prophets: A Translation into Modern English, by J. B. Phillips. The Macmillan Company, 1969.

RIEU   *The Four Gospels.* A new translation from the Greek by E. V. Rieu. Penguin Books, 1953.

RSV   *The Oxford Annotated Bible with the Apocrypha*: Revised Standard Version. Oxford University Press, 1965.

SCHONFIELD   *The Authentic New Testament*, translated by Hugh J. Schonfield. New American Library of World Literature, 1956.

SMITH   *The Bible: An American Translation.* (See GOODSPEED.)

TCNT   *The Twentieth Century New Testament.* Moody Press, 1961.

TEV   *Good News for Modern Man: The New Testament and Psalms in Today's English Version.* American Bible Society, 1970.

TORAH   *The Torah: The Five Books of Moses.* A new translation of the Holy Scriptures according to the Masoretic text. The Jewish Publication Society of America, 1962.

WATERMAN   *The Bible: An American Translation.* (See GOODSPEED.)

WEYMOUTH   *The New Testament in Modern Speech.* Translated by Richard Francis Weymouth. Revised by James Alexander Robertson. Harper & Brothers, Publishers, 1929.

WILLIAMS   *The New Testament in the Language of the People*, translated by Charles B. Williams. Moody Press, 1965.

THE OLD TESTAMENT

The Fall. Hugo van der Goes, about 1470. Vienna, Kunsthistorisches Museum.

Introduction to the Old Testament

The thirty-nine books which constitute the King James Version of the Old Testament testify to the variety and vitality of ancient Jewish literature. A catalogue of genres would include myth, legend, saga, epic, folk tale, biography, poetry, prophecy, and parable. Some of the writing is dated as early as 1200 B.C.—e.g., Lamech's Song (*Genesis* 4:23-24) and Miriam's Song (*Exodus* 15:21)—and some as late as 300–200 B.C.—e.g., *The Song of Songs*. During these thousand years, the Old Testament materials were told and retold, embellished and expanded, refined and recast, and eventually recorded, compiled, edited, and declared canonical.

The Rabbinical Council which convened at Jamnia, Palestine, in A.D. 90 declared the authority of the Scriptures. But this pronouncement merely affirmed the position which the Law, the Prophets, and the Writings already held in Judaism. Since about 350 B.C., the Law had been considered authoritative. Sometimes called the Books of Moses, it had defined and regulated Judaism since the days of King Josiah (ca. 640–609 B.C.). Consisting initially of a few chapters of *Deuteronomy*, the Law came to include all the material in *Genesis* through *Deuteronomy*. The message of the Prophets began with Amos (ca. 750 B.C.) and ended, according to the author of *Ezra*, around 400 B.C. Through the following years, these works were sifted and mellowed so that by 200 B.C., the Prophets were considered on a level with the Law. The remaining books of the Scripture, the Writings, had achieved special status in the synagogues of Palestine through years of use. The Council of Jamnia, after some debate concerning *The Song of Songs* and *Ecclesiastes*, accepted the Writings and, in one official act, established the Hebrew canon.

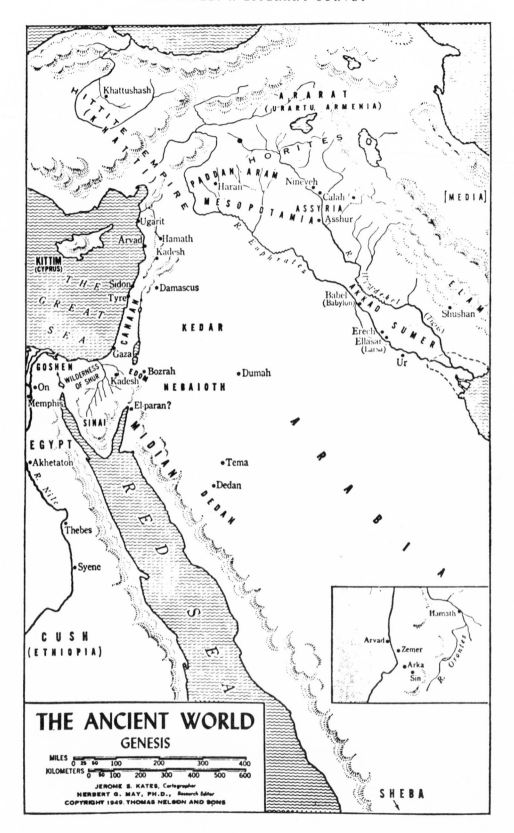

THE ANCIENT WORLD
GENESIS

MILES
KILOMETERS

JEROME S. KATES, Cartographer
HERBERT G. MAY, PH.D., Research Editor
COPYRIGHT 1949. THOMAS NELSON AND SONS

Introduction to
GENESIS

"Now the Lord has said unto Abram, 'Get thee out of thy country, and from thy kindred, and from thy father's house, unto a land that I will show thee: And I will make of thee a great nation, and I will bless thee, and make thy name great; and thou shalt be a blessing.'"

Genesis, the book of beginnings, expresses man's curiosity regarding origins. Moving from the creation of the world to the death of Joseph, it records the origin of Jewish history, customs, rites, and institutions. It presents myths, legends, and sagas composed and compiled over a 600-year period (1000–400 B.C.) by unknown writers whom modern textual scholars have designated as J, E, and P.

Myth is a powerful genre, for it combines a compelling narrative with elements of cultural belief. At a time when neither science nor philosophy existed, myths interpreted the world to man. Thus, the early chapters of *Genesis* explain day and night, the creation of the world, man's superiority over animals, and the place of woman. They tell why men must labor, why women endure childbirth pains, why snakes crawl and are universally despised, and why people speak different languages. They comment on local traditions concerning a great flood.

It is in the interpretation of myths that *Genesis* is unique. The authors were undoubtedly familiar with the recorded myths of other and older cultures. Parallels exist between the Babylonian *Enuma elish* (ca. 1500 B.C.) and the first account of creation; between the Babylonian *Gilgamesh Epic* (ca. 2000 B.C.), the Akkadian myth of Adapa (ca. 1300 B.C.), and the story of the Fall; between the *Gilgamesh Epic* and the narrative of the flood. The parallels are overshadowed, however, by the Hebrew interpretations of these tales. *Genesis* emphasizes God's beneficent attitude toward man, man's responsibility to obey God and to relate positively to others, and God's justifiable punishment of wickedness and arrogance. No contemporary literature described such a relationship between God and man.

Attention shifts from God as protagonist to man as protagonist when one moves from myth to legend. While legends retain an interest in origins, the areas explored are less universal. The dramatic narratives following the flood, for example, explain the migration of the Jewish people, the establishment of famous sanctuaries at Bethel and Beer-Sheba, and a great catastrophe said to have befallen a remote city near the Dead Sea. The stories emphasize Israel's rights in Canaan by showing a legal purchase and by repeating a divine promise. They demonstrate Israel's moral precedence by exposing the inferior origins of the Canaanites (Ham), the Ammonites and Moabites (Lot and his daughters), the Ishmaelites (Ishmael), and the Edomites (Esau).

The legends concerning Abraham, Isaac, Sarah, Lot, and Ishmael circulated orally for centuries before they were recorded. And oral transmission shaped some

3

of their literary characteristics. There are, for example, the separate, usually brief, episodes; the minimum number of characters; the simple descriptions which tease the hearer's imagination; and the suspense concerning the final resolution. To these characteristics must be added elements of historical fact. While it is impossible to reconstruct exact history from these stories, many scholars would affirm the observation of Norman K. Gottwald (*A Light to the Nations*, 1959): "Legends survive because they retain a kernel of historicity."

The factual base is heavier in saga, which can be defined as the traditional history of important families. Developing the covenant promise made to Abraham, *Genesis* records the sagas of Jacob and Joseph. These are enlivened by the substantial use of dialogue, by careful characterization which exposes both the strength and weaknesses of the heroes, and by a keen sense of dramatic tension. The sagas still partake of legendary material, but they seldom show the direct hand of God in events, and they present features (the migrations, the establishment of religious centers, the rise of foreigners to power in Egypt) which can be related to historical evidence.

Continuing the emphasis on origins, the sagas explain how the tribes got their names and why some fared better than others. The story of the birth of twins tells why one baby is named Esau (red) and the other Jacob (heel-grabber). Another story shows the birth of Jacob's eleven sons amid circumstances which account for their names. (See footnote 47.) The family histories tell why tribes descending from first sons failed to maintain preeminence: Esau sold his birthright; Reuben slept with his father's concubine; Manasseh did not receive Jacob's blessing. The tales also explain why the tribes of Simeon and Levi faded away; why those of Judah and Joseph rose to power; and why new clans—Manasseh and Ephraim—came to have full tribal status.

Further, the sagas describe and affirm a singular characteristic of the family heroes. While Jacob, Joseph, and the others are presented as great and holy men, the quality which unifies the family history is a craftiness bordering on guile. The trait appeared earlier when Abraham prospered by passing his wife as his sister and when he negotiated shrewdly first to save Sodom and later to purchase a burial site for Sarah. Such actions are central in the sagas. Jacob buys Esau's birthright and disguises himself to gain Isaac's blessing. Laban tricks Jacob into wedding Leah and working an extra seven years for Rachel. Jacob outwits Laban and wins most of his sheep and goats. Rachel steals Laban's household gods and conceals them during his search. Jacob, with artful prudence, arranges his goods to meet Esau's possible vengeance. Dinah's brothers persuade the Shechemites to be circumcized, then attack them while they are weak from the loss of blood. Tamar poses as a temple-prostitute to get Judah to father a child. Joseph cleverly negotiates with Pharaoh to win Goshen for the Israelites. After Jacob's death, his sons create a death-bed story to keep Joseph from taking revenge on them. Through these stories, it is clear that people prevail because God favors their cause. But there remains the meaningful implication that God is with individuals who can take care of themselves.

Genesis, like *Exodus* and the other books of the Law, shows evidence of multiple authorship. Scholars have identified at least three separate authors by their vocabulary, their conceptions of God, and their primary interests.

The earliest of these author-compiler-editors is called J. This writer—more probably, this school of writers—regularly refers to God as "Yahweh" (*Lord* in KJV) and is known as the Yahwist. He lived in Judah, the Southern Kingdom, between 950 and 850 B.C. J begins his narrative with the creation of the world and continues it until the chosen people enter into Canaan. His concept of God is anthropomorphic, e.g., Yahweh talks to Adam, strolls in the garden in the cool of the evening, and asks Cain about his brother Abel. The Yahwist is concerned with all of Israelite life, not just religious matters. He portrays patriarchal figures in all their vulnerable humanness. Some of the most memorable narratives of the Old Testament—Jacob's deception of Isaac, Joseph and Potiphar's wife, the plagues of Egypt—are attributed to J.

The second author, E, is identified by his regular use of "Elohim" (God in KJV) as the name for deity. This author, or group of authors, lived in Ephraim in the Northern Kingdom around 750 B.C. His narrative begins with the call of Abraham and ends with the Hebrew people still in the wilderness. His God is less anthropomorphic, tending to communicate with the patriarchs in dreams, through visions, and by angelic messengers. The Elohist emphasizes the origin of ritual acts (e.g., Jacob wrestles with the angel), and he glosses over the imperfections of ancient figures (e.g., Abraham allows Abimelech to take Sarah, but the king does not touch her). E is credited with the vivid descriptions of the sacrifice of Isaac, the reunion of Joseph with his brothers, and the birth of Moses.

The third author, P, is distinguished by his concern for the religious institutions of Judaism. P—a group comprising the Priestly school of authors and editors—begins the Old Testament, shaping a creation story which emphasizes the seventh day as the sabbath. He is concerned with covenants and records those of Noah (the rainbow), Abraham (circumcision), and Moses (the Passover). He is responsible for the exhaustive genealogies which unify the books. Thought to have written between 550 and 450 B.C., P is given much of the credit for the present arrangement of J and E materials.

In its final form, *Genesis*, the book of beginnings, describes a great and resourceful people and a profound affirmation of faith. In its literary variety and vitality, it remains a book for all times.

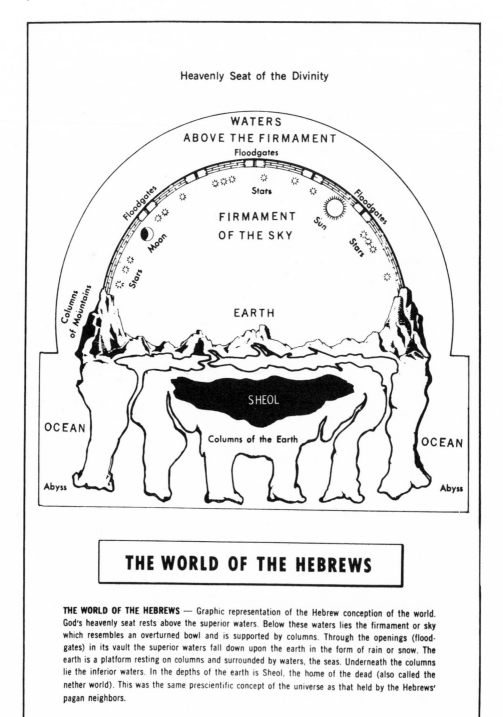

THE WORLD OF THE HEBREWS — Graphic representation of the Hebrew conception of the world. God's heavenly seat rests above the superior waters. Below these waters lies the firmament or sky which resembles an overturned bowl and is supported by columns. Through the openings (floodgates) in its vault the superior waters fall down upon the earth in the form of rain or snow. The earth is a platform resting on columns and surrounded by waters, the seas. Underneath the columns lie the inferior waters. In the depths of the earth is Sheol, the home of the dead (also called the nether world). This was the same prescientific concept of the universe as that held by the Hebrews' pagan neighbors.

From the *New American Bible*, St. Anthony Guild Edition, reprinted with permission of Catholic Book Publishing Corp.

GENESIS

THE BEGINNINGS

Creation

1 In the beginning God created the heaven and the earth.[1] 2 And the earth was without form, and void; and darkness *was* upon the face of the deep. And the Spirit of God moved upon the face of the waters. 3 And God said, "Let there be light": and there was light. 4 And God saw the light, that *it was* good: and God divided the light from the darkness. 5 And God called the light Day, and the darkness he called Night. And the evening and the morning were the first day.

6 And God said, "Let there be a firmament in the midst of the waters, and let it divide the waters from the waters." 7 And God made the firmament, and divided the waters which *were* under the firmament from the waters which *were* above the firmament: and it was so. 8 And God called the firmament Heaven. And the evening and the morning were the second day.

9 And God said, "Let the waters under the heaven be gathered together unto one place, and let the dry *land* appear": and it was so. 10 And God called the dry *land* Earth; and the gathering together of the waters called he Seas: and God saw that *it was* good. 11 And God said, "Let the earth bring forth grass, the herb yielding seed, *and* the fruit tree yielding fruit after his kind, whose seed *is* in itself, upon the earth": and it was so. 12 And the earth brought forth grass, *and* herb yielding seed after his kind, and the tree yielding fruit, whose seed *was* in itself, after his kind: and God saw that *it was* good. 13 And the evening and the morning were the third day.

14 And God said, "Let there be lights in the firmament of the heaven to divide the day from the night; and let them be for signs, and for seasons, and for days, and years: 15 And let them be for lights in the firmament of the heaven to give light upon the earth": and it was so. 16 And God made two great lights; the greater light to rule the day, and the lesser light to rule the night: *he made* the stars also.[2] 17 And God set them in the firmament of the heaven to give light upon the earth, 18 And to rule over the day and over the night, and to divide the light from the darkness:

and God saw that *it was* good. 19 And the evening and the morning were the fourth day.

20 And God said, "Let the waters bring forth abundantly the moving creature that hath life, and fowl *that* may fly above the earth in the open firmament of heaven." 21 And God created great whales, and every living creature that moveth, which the waters brought forth abundantly, after their kind, and every winged fowl after his kind: and God saw that *it was* good. 22 And God blessed them, saying, "Be fruitful, and multiply, and fill the waters in the seas, and let fowl multiply in the earth." 23 And the evening and the morning were the fifth day.

24 And God said, "Let the earth bring forth the living creature after his kind, cattle, and creeping thing, and beast of the earth after his kind": and it was so. 25 And God made the beast of the earth after his kind, and cattle after their kind, and every thing that creepeth upon the earth after his kind: and God saw that *it was* good.

26 And God said, "Let us make man in our image, after our likeness:[3] and let them have dominion over the fish of the sea, and over the fowl of the air, and over the cattle, and over all the earth, and over every creeping thing that creepeth upon the earth." 27 So God created man in his *own* image, in the image of God created he him; male and female created he them. 28 And God blessed them, and God said unto them, "Be fruitful, and multiply, and replenish the earth, and subdue it: and have dominion over the fish of the sea, and over the fowl of the air, and over every living thing that moveth upon the earth."

29 And God said, "Behold, I have given you every herb bearing seed, which *is* upon the face of all the earth, and every tree, in the which *is* the fruit of a tree yielding seed; to you it shall be for meat. 30 And to every beast of the earth, and to every fowl of the air, and to every thing that creepeth upon the earth, wherein *there is* life, *I have given* every green herb for meat": and it was so. 31 And God saw every thing that he had made, and, behold, *it was* very good. And the evening and the morning were the sixth day.

2 Thus the heavens and the earth were finished, and all the host of them. 2 And on the seventh day God ended his work which he had made; and

---

1. (1:1–2:1) This account of creation, attributed to P, reflects an ancient conception of the world. See the illustration on the facing page.
2. Other ancient peoples deified the sun, moon, and stars. For the Hebrews, with their all-powerful God, these were merely lights.
3. The "us" and "our" may refer to members of a divine council. They may refer simply to God, who is using the royal plural. (See also 3:22.)

he rested on the seventh day from all his work which he had made. 3 And God blessed the seventh day, and sanctified it: because that in it he had rested from all his work which God created and made.

Another Account of Creation [4]

4 These *are* the generations of the heavens and of the earth when they were created, in the day that the LORD God made the earth and the heavens, 5 And every plant of the field before it was in the earth, and every herb of the field before it grew: for the LORD God had not caused it to rain upon the earth, and *there was* not a man to till the ground. 6 But there went up a mist from the earth, and watered the whole face of the ground. 7 And the LORD God formed man *of* the dust of the ground, and breathed into his nostrils the breath of life; and man became a living soul.

8 And the LORD God planted a garden eastward in Eden; and there he put the man whom he had formed. 9 And out of the ground made the LORD God to grow every tree that is pleasant to the sight, and good for food; the tree of life also in the midst of the garden, and the tree of knowledge of good and evil. 10 And a river went out of Eden to water the garden; and from thence it was parted, and became into four heads. 11 The name of the first *is* Pison: that *is* it which compasseth the whole land of Havilah, where *there is* gold; 12 And the gold of that land *is* good: there *is* bdellium and the onyx stone. 13 And the name of the second river *is* Gihon: the same *is* it that compasseth the whole land of Ethiopia. 14 And the name of the third river *is* Hiddekel: that *is* it which goeth toward the east of Assyria. And the fourth river *is* Euphrates. 15 And the LORD God took the man, and put him into the garden of Eden to dress it and to keep it. 16 And the LORD God commanded the man, saying, "Of every tree of the garden thou mayest freely eat: 17 But of the tree of the knowledge of good and evil, thou shalt not eat of it: for in the day that thou eatest thereof thou shalt surely die."

18 And the LORD God said, "*It is* not good that the man should be alone; I will make him a help meet for him." 19 And out of the ground the LORD God formed every beast of the field, and every fowl of the air; and brought *them* unto Adam to see what he would call them: and whatsoever Adam called every living creature, that *was* the name thereof. 20 And Adam gave names to all cattle, and to the fowl of the air, and to every

beast of the field;[5] but for Adam there was not found a help meet for him. 21 And the LORD God caused a deep sleep to fall upon Adam, and he slept; and he took one of his ribs, and closed up the flesh instead thereof. 22 And the rib, which the LORD God had taken from man, made he a woman, and brought her unto the man. 23 And Adam said, "This *is* now bone of my bones, and flesh of my flesh: she shall be called Woman, because she was taken out of man." 24 Therefore shall a man leave his father and his mother, and shall cleave unto his wife: and they shall be one flesh. 25 And they were both naked, the man and his wife, and were not ashamed.

The Fall

3 Now the serpent was more subtile than any beast of the field which the LORD God had made.[6] And he said unto the woman, "Yea, hath God said, 'Ye shall not eat of every tree of the garden'?" 2 And the woman said unto the serpent, "We may eat of the fruit of the trees of the garden: 3 But of the fruit of the tree which *is* in the midst of the garden, God hath said, 'Ye shall not eat of it, neither shall ye touch it, lest ye die.' " 4 And the serpent said unto the woman, "Ye shall not surely die: 5 For God doth know that in the day ye eat thereof, then your eyes shall be opened, and ye shall be as gods, knowing good and evil." 6 And when the woman saw that the tree *was* good for food, and that it *was* pleasant to the eyes, and a tree to be desired to make *one* wise, she took of the fruit thereof, and did eat, and gave also unto her husband with her; and he did eat. 7 And the eyes of them both were opened, and they knew that they *were* naked; and they sewed fig leaves together, and made themselves aprons. 8 And they heard the voice of the LORD God walking in the garden in the cool of the day: and Adam and his wife hid themselves from the presence of the LORD God amongst the trees of the garden.

9 And the LORD God called unto Adam, and said unto him, "Where *art* thou?" 10 And he said, "I heard thy voice in the garden, and I was afraid, because I *was* naked; and I hid myself." 11 And he said, "Who told thee that thou *wast* naked? Hast thou eaten of the tree, whereof I commanded thee that thou shouldest not eat?"

---

4. (2:4-25) In this account, attributed to J, man is created first, then plant life, animals, and woman. There is no seven-day sequence.

5. (2:19-20) This reflects the ancient belief that to know the name of a being is to have control over it. Adam (i.e., "man") is given dominion over the animals.

6. Ignatius Hunt (*The Book of Genesis*, 1960, Paulist/Newman Press) writes, "The 'serpent' was probably introduced as a subtle attack on the false forms of Chanaanite worship and the sexual abuses of the writer's time. . . . In the Chanaan of his own time, the image of the serpent had some part in pagan rites, most likely as a fertility symbol."

12 And the man said, "The woman whom thou gavest *to be* with me, she gave me of the tree, and I did eat." 13 And the LORD God said unto the woman, "What *is* this *that* thou hast done?" And the woman said, "The serpent beguiled me, and I did eat." 14 And the LORD God said unto the serpent, "Because thou hast done this, thou *art* cursed above all cattle, and above every beast of the field; upon thy belly shalt thou go, and dust shalt thou eat all the days of thy life: 15 And I will put enmity between thee and the woman, and between thy seed and her seed; it shall bruise thy head, and thou shalt bruise his heel." [7] 16 Unto the woman he said, "I will greatly multiply thy sorrow and thy conception; in sorrow thou shalt bring forth children; and thy desire *shall be* to thy husband, and he shall rule over thee."

17 And unto Adam he said, "Because thou hast hearkened unto the voice of thy wife, and hast eaten of the tree, of which I commanded thee, saying, 'Thou shalt not eat of it': cursed *is* the ground for thy sake; in sorrow shalt thou eat *of* it all the days of thy life; 18 Thorns also and thistles shall it bring forth to thee; and thou shalt eat the herb of the field: 19 In the sweat of thy face shalt thou eat bread, till thou return unto the ground; for out of it wast thou taken: for dust thou *art,* and unto dust shalt thou return." 20 And Adam called his wife's name Eve; because she was the mother of all living. 21 Unto Adam also and to his wife did the LORD God make coats of skins, and clothed them.

22 And the LORD God said, "Behold, the man is become as one of us, to know good and evil: and now, lest he put forth his hand, and take also of the tree of life, and eat, and live for ever": 23 Therefore the LORD God sent him forth from the garden of Eden, to till the ground from whence he was taken. 24 So he drove out the man: and he placed at the east of the garden of Eden cherubim, and a flaming sword which turned every way, to keep the way of the tree of life.

THE FAMILY OF MAN
Cain and Abel

4 And Adam knew Eve his wife; and she conceived, and bare Cain, and said, "I have gotten a man from the Lord." 2 And she again bare his brother Abel. And Abel was a keeper of sheep, but Cain was a tiller of the ground. 3 And in process of time it came to pass, that Cain brought of the fruit of the ground an offering unto the LORD. 4 And Abel, he also brought of the firstlings of his flock and of the fat thereof. And the LORD had respect unto Abel and to his offering: 5 But unto Cain and to his offering he had not respect. And Cain was very wroth, and his countenance fell. 6 And the LORD said unto Cain, "Why art thou wroth? and why is thy countenance fallen? 7 If thou doest well, shalt thou not be accepted? and if thou doest not well, sin lieth at the door: and unto thee *shall be* his desire, and thou shalt rule over him." [8] 8 And Cain talked with Abel his brother: and it came to pass, when they were in the field, that Cain rose up against Abel his brother, and slew him.

9 And the LORD said unto Cain, "Where *is* Abel thy brother?" And he said, "I know not: *Am* I my brother's keeper?" 10 And he said, "What hast thou done? the voice of thy brother's blood crieth unto me from the ground. 11 And now *art* thou cursed from the earth, which hath opened her mouth to receive thy brother's blood from thy hand. 12 When thou tillest the ground, it shall not henceforth yield unto thee her strength; a fugitive and a vagabond shalt thou be in the earth." 13 And Cain said unto the LORD, "My punishment *is* greater than I can bear. 14 Behold, thou hast driven me out this day from the face of the earth; and from thy face shall I be hid; and I shall be a fugitive and a vagabond in the earth; and it shall come to pass, *that* every one that findeth me shall slay me." 15 And the LORD said unto him, "Therefore whosoever slayeth Cain, vengeance shall be taken on him sevenfold." And the LORD set a mark upon Cain, lest any finding him should kill him.

16 And Cain went out from the presence of the LORD, and dwelt in the land of Nod, on the east of Eden.

Descendants of Cain and Seth

17 And Cain knew his wife; and she conceived, and bare Enoch: and he builded a city, and called the name of the city, after the name of his son, Enoch. 18 And unto Enoch was born Irad: and Irad begat Mehujael: and Mehujael begat Methusael: and Methusael began Lamech. 19 And Lamech took unto him two wives: the name of the one *was* Adah, and the name of the other Zillah. 20 And Adah bare Jabal: he was the father of such as dwell in tents, and *of such as have* cattle. 21 And his brother's name *was* Jubal: he was the father of all such as handle the harp and organ.

---

7. MEEK: "They shall attack you in the head, / And you shall attack them in the heel." The myth explains why men hate snakes.

8. NAB: "If you do well, you can hold up your head; but if not, sin is a demon lurking at the door: his urge is toward you, yet you can be his master."

22 And Zillah, she also bare Tubal-cain, an instructor of every artificer in brass and iron: and the sister of Tubal-cain *was* Naamah. 23 And Lamech said unto his wives,

> "Adah and Zillah, hear my voice;
> Ye wives of Lamech, hearken unto my
>   speech:
> For I have slain a man to my wounding,
> And a young man to my hurt.

24   If Cain shall be avenged sevenfold,
> Truly Lamech seventy and sevenfold." [9]

25 And Adam knew his wife again; and she bare a son, and called his name Seth: "For God," *said she,* "hath appointed me another seed instead of Abel, whom Cain slew." 26 And to Seth, to him also there was born a son; and he called his name Enos: then began men to call upon the name of the LORD.

5 This *is* the book of the generations of Adam.[10] In the day that God created man, in the likeness of God made he him; 2 Male and female created he them; and blessed them, and called their name Adam, in the day when they were created.

3 And Adam lived a hundred and thirty years, and begat *a son* in his own likeness, and his image; and called his name Seth: 4 And the days of Adam after he had begotten Seth were eight hundred years: and he begat sons and daughters: 5 And all the days that Adam lived were nine hundred and thirty years: and he died.[11]

6 And Seth lived a hundred and five years, and begat Enos: 7 And Seth lived after he begat Enos eight hundred and seven years, and begat sons and daughters: 8 And all the days of Seth were nine hundred and twelve years: and he died.

9 And Enos lived ninety years, and begat Cainan: 10 And Enos lived after he begat Cainan eight hundred and fifteen years, and begat sons and daughters: 11 And all the days of Enos were nine hundred and five years: and he died.

12 And Cainan lived seventy years, and begat Mahalaleel: 13 And Cainan lived after he begat Mahalaleel eight hundred and forty years, and begat sons and daughters: 14 And all the days of Cainan were nine hundred and ten years: and he died.

15 And Mahalaleel lived sixty and five years, and begat Jared: 16 And Mahalaleel lived after he begat Jared eight hundred and thirty years, and begat sons and daughters: 17 And all the days of Mahalaleel were eight hundred ninety and five years: and he died.

18 And Jared lived a hundred sixty and two years, and he begat Enoch: 19 And Jared lived after he begat Enoch eight hundred years, and begat sons and daughters: 20 And all the days of Jared were nine hundred sixty and two years: and he died.

21 And Enoch lived sixty and five years, and begat Methuselah: 22 And Enoch walked with God after he begat Methuselah three hundred years, and begat sons and daughters: 23 And all the days of Enoch were three hundred sixty and five years: 24 And Enoch walked with God: and he *was* not; for God took him.[12]

25 And Methuselah lived a hundred eighty and seven years, and begat Lamech: 26 And Methuselah lived after he begat Lamech seven hundred eighty and two years, and begat sons and daughters: 27 And all the days of Methuselah were nine hundred sixty and nine years: and he died.

28 And Lamech lived a hundred eighty and two years, and begat a son: 29 And he called his name Noah, saying, "This *same* shall comfort us concerning our work and toil of our hands, because of the ground which the LORD hath cursed." 30 And Lamech lived after he begat Noah five hundred ninety and five years, and begat sons and daughters: 31 And all the days of Lamech were seven hundred seventy and seven years: and he died. 32 And Noah was five hundred years old: and Noah begat Shem, Ham, and Japheth.

6 And it came to pass, when men began to multiply on the face of the earth, and daughters were born unto them, 2 That the sons of God saw the daughters of men that they *were* fair; and they took them wives of all which they chose. 3 And the LORD said, "My Spirit shall not always strive with man, for that he also *is* flesh: yet his days shall be a hundred and twenty years." 4 There were giants in the earth in those days; and also after that, when the sons of God came in unto the

---

9. (4:23-24) This song may be the oldest in the Bible. NAB offers a strong translation:
> "Adah and Zillah, hear my voice;
>   wives of Lamech, listen to my utterance;
> I have killed a man for wounding me,
>   a boy for bruising me.
> If Cain is avenged sevenfold,
>   then Lamech seventy-sevenfold."

10. (5:1-32) This genealogy, like others scattered through *Genesis* (10:1-32; 11:10-32; 22:20-24; 25:1-4, 12-18; and 36:1-42), need not be read as accurate history. The editor gathered up a body of ancient names and arranged them systematically. Genealogies are used to link episodes, to set the stage for coming events, and to explain tribal relationships.

11. (5:5-32) The ancient Hebrews did not believe in an eternal reward and thought the reward for righteousness was health, many children, and long life. Since they venerated the patriarchs, it followed that these figures had particularly long lives.

12. MOFFATT: "and then he disappeared, for God took him away." The perfection of Enoch's life is indicated by his life span; 365 was the number of perfection based on the solar year.

daughters of men, and they bare *children* to them, the same *became* mighty men which *were* of old, men of renown.[13]

The Flood

5 And GOD saw that the wickedness of man *was* great in the earth, and *that* every imagination of the thoughts of his heart *was* only evil continually. 6 And it repented the LORD that he had made man on the earth, and it grieved him at his heart. 7 And the LORD said, "I will destroy man whom I have created from the face of the earth; both man, and beast, and the creeping thing, and the fowls of the air; for it repenteth me that I have made them." 8 But Noah found grace in the eyes of the LORD.

9 These *are* the generations of Noah: Noah was a just man *and* perfect in his generations, *and* Noah walked with God. 10 And Noah begat three sons, Shem, Ham, and Japheth. 11 The earth also was corrupt before God; and the earth was filled with violence. 12 And God looked upon the earth, and, behold, it was corrupt; for all flesh had corrupted his way upon the earth.

13 And God said unto Noah, "The end of all flesh is come before me; for the earth is filled with violence through them; and, behold, I will destroy them with the earth. 14 Make thee an ark of gopher wood; rooms shalt thou make in the ark, and shalt pitch it within and without with pitch. 15 And this *is the fashion* which thou shalt make it *of:* The length of the ark *shall be* three hundred cubits, the breadth of it fifty cubits, and the height of it thirty cubits.[14] 16 A window shalt thou make to the ark, and in a cubit shalt thou finish it above; and the door of the ark shalt thou set in the side thereof; *with* lower, second, and third *stories* shalt thou make it. 17 And, behold, I, even I, do bring a flood of waters upon the earth, to destroy all flesh, wherein *is* the breath of life, from under heaven; *and* every thing that *is* in the earth shall die. 18 But with thee will I establish my covenant; and thou shalt come into the ark, thou, and thy sons, and thy wife, and thy sons' wives with thee. 19 And of every living thing of all flesh, two of every *sort* shalt thou

bring into the ark, to keep *them* alive with thee; they shall be male and female. 20 Of fowls after their kind, and of cattle after their kind, of every creeping thing of the earth after his kind; two of every *sort* shall come unto thee, to keep *them* alive. 21 And take thou unto thee of all food that is eaten, and thou shalt gather *it* to thee; and it shall be for food for thee, and for them." 22 Thus did Noah; according to all that God commanded him, so did he.

7 And the LORD said unto Noah, "Come thou and all thy house into the ark; for thee have I seen righteous before me in this generation. 2 Of every clean beast thou shalt take to thee by sevens, the male and his female: and of beasts that *are* not clean by two, the male and his female.[15] 3 Of fowls also of the air by sevens, the male and the female; to keep seed alive upon the face of all the earth. 4 For yet seven days, and I will cause it to rain upon the earth forty days and forty nights; and every living substance that I have made will I destroy from off the face of the earth." 5 And Noah did according unto all that the LORD commanded him.

6 And Noah *was* six hundred years old when the flood of waters was upon the earth. 7 And Noah went in, and his sons, and his wife, and his sons' wives with him, into the ark, because of the waters of the flood. 8 Of clean beasts, and of beasts that *are* not clean, and of fowls, and of every thing that creepeth upon the earth, 9 There went in two and two unto Noah into the ark, the male and the female, as God had commanded Noah. 10 And it came to pass after seven days, that the waters of the flood were upon the earth. 11 In the six hundredth year of Noah's life, in the second month, the seventeenth day of the month, the same day were all the fountains of the great deep broken up, and the windows of heaven were opened. 12 And the rain was upon the earth forty days and forty nights.

13 In the selfsame day entered Noah, and Shem, and Ham, and Japheth, the sons of Noah, and Noah's wife, and the three wives of his sons with them, into the ark; 14 They, and every beast after his kind, and all the cattle after their kind, and every creeping thing that creepeth upon the earth after his kind, and every fowl after his kind, every bird of every sort. 15 And they went in unto Noah into the ark, two and two of all flesh, wherein *is* the breath of life. 16 And they that went in, went in male and female of all flesh, as God had commanded him: and the LORD shut him in.

---

13. (6:1-4) This ancient fragment explains the Nephilim, a mythological race of giants. They were thought to derive from the union of divine beings with the daughters of men.

14. A cubit was 18 inches; thus, the dimensions of the ark are 450 by 75 by 45 feet. Robert Graves (*Hebrew Myths: The Book of Genesis*, 1963) notes, "The Ark's Biblical dimensions contravene the principles of ship-building: a wholly wooden three decker 450 feet long would have broken up even in a slight swell."

15. *Leviticus* 11 names the unclean animals: the camel, the rock badger, the hare, the pig, etc.

17 And the flood was forty days upon the earth; and the waters increased, and bare up the ark, and it was lifted up above the earth. 18 And the waters prevailed, and were increased greatly upon the earth; and the ark went upon the face of the waters. 19 And the waters prevailed exceedingly upon the earth; and all the high hills, that *were* under the whole heaven, were covered. 20 Fifteen cubits upward did the waters prevail; and the mountains were covered. 21 And all flesh died that moved upon the earth, both of fowl, and of cattle, and of beast, and of every creeping thing that creepeth upon the earth, and every man: 22 All in whose nostrils *was* the breath of life, of all that *was* in the dry *land,* died. 23 And every living substance was destroyed which was upon the face of the ground, both man, and cattle, and the creeping things, and the fowl of the heaven; and they were destroyed from the earth: and Noah only remained *alive,* and they that *were* with him in the ark. 24 And the waters prevailed upon the earth a hundred and fifty days.[16]

8 And God remembered Noah, and every living thing, and all the cattle that *was* with him in the ark: and God made a wind to pass over the earth, and the waters assuaged. 2 The fountains also of the deep and the windows of heaven were stopped, and the rain from heaven was restrained. 3 And the waters returned from off the earth continually: and after the end of the hundred and fifty days the waters were abated. 4 And the ark rested in the seventh month, on the seventeenth day of the month, upon the mountains of Ararat. 5 And the waters decreased continually until the tenth month: in the tenth *month,* on the first *day* of the month, were the tops of the mountains seen.

6 And it came to pass at the end of forty days, that Noah opened the window of the ark which he had made: 7 And he sent forth a raven, which went forth to and fro, until the waters were dried up from off the earth. 8 Also he sent forth a dove from him, to see if the waters were abated from off the face of the ground. 9 But the dove found no rest for the sole of her foot, and she returned unto him into the ark; for the waters *were* on the face of the whole earth. Then he put forth his hand, and took her, and pulled her in unto him into the ark. 10 And he stayed yet other seven days; and again he sent forth the dove out of the ark. 11 And the dove came in to him in the evening, and, lo, in her mouth *was* an olive leaf

plucked off: so Noah knew that the waters were abated from off the earth. 12 And he stayed yet other seven days, and sent forth the dove, which returned not again unto him any more.

13 And it came to pass in the six hundredth and first year, in the first *month,* the first *day* of the month, the waters were dried up from off the earth: and Noah removed the covering of the ark, and looked, and, behold, the face of the ground was dry. 14 And in the second month, on the seven and twentieth day of the month, was the earth dried.

15 And God spake unto Noah, saying, 16 "Go forth of the ark, thou, and thy wife, and thy sons, and thy sons' wives with thee. 17 Bring forth with thee every living thing that *is* with thee, of all flesh, *both* of fowl, and of cattle, and of every creeping thing that creepeth upon the earth; that they may breed abundantly in the earth, and be fruitful, and multiply upon the earth." 18 And Noah went forth, and his sons, and his wife, and his sons' wives with him: 19 Every beast, every creeping thing, and every fowl, *and* whatsoever creepeth upon the earth, after their kinds, went forth out of the ark.

20 And Noah builded an altar unto the LORD; and took of every clean beast, and of every clean fowl, and offered burnt offerings on the altar. 21 And the LORD smelled a sweet savor; and the LORD said in his heart, "I will not again curse the ground any more for man's sake; for the imagination of man's heart *is* evil from his youth:[17] neither will I again smite any more every thing living, as I have done. 22 While the earth remaineth, seedtime and harvest, and cold and heat, and summer and winter, and day and night shall not cease."

The Covenant with Noah

9 And God blessed Noah and his sons, and said unto them, "Be fruitful, and multiply, and replenish the earth. 2 And the fear of you and the dread of you shall be upon every beast of the earth, and upon every fowl of the air, upon all that moveth *upon* the earth, and upon all the fishes of the sea; into your hand are they delivered. 3 Every moving thing that liveth shall be meat for you; even as the green herb have I given you all things. 4 But flesh with the life thereof, *which is* the blood thereof, shall ye not eat. 5 And surely your blood of your lives will I require: at the hand of every beast will I require it, and at the hand of man; at the hand of every

16. (7:17-24) RSV footnotes: "Archeological evidence indicates that traditions of a prehistoric flood covering the whole earth are heightened versions of local inundations, e.g., in the Tigris-Euphrates basin."

17. MOFFATT: "though the bent of man's mind is indeed towards evil from his youth."

man's brother will I require the life of man. 6 Whoso sheddeth man's blood, by man shall his blood be shed: for in the image of God made he man. 7 And you, be ye fruitful, and multiply; bring forth abundantly in the earth, and multiply therein."

8 And God spake unto Noah, and to his sons with him, saying, 9 "And I, behold, I establish my covenant with you, and with your seed after you; 10 And with every living creature that *is* with you, of the fowl, of the cattle, and of every beast of the earth with you; from all that go out of the ark, to every beast of the earth. 11 And I will establish my covenant with you; neither shall all flesh be cut off any more by the waters of a flood; neither shall there any more be a flood to destroy the earth." 12 And God said, "This *is* the token of the covenant which I make between me and you, and every living creature that *is* with you, for perpetual generations: 13 I do set my bow in the cloud, and it shall be for a token of a covenant between me and the earth.[18] 14 And it shall come to pass, when I bring a cloud over the earth, that the bow shall be seen in the cloud: 15 And I will remember my covenant, which *is* between me and you and every living creature of all flesh; and the waters shall no more become a flood to destroy all flesh. 16 And the bow shall be in the cloud; and I will look upon it, that I may remember the everlasting covenant between God and every living creature of all flesh that *is* upon the earth." 17 And God said unto Noah, "This *is* the token of the covenant, which I have established between me and all flesh that *is* upon the earth."

The Curse on Canaan

18 And the sons of Noah, that went forth of the ark, were Shem, and Ham, and Japheth: and Ham *is* the father of Canaan. 19 These *are* the three sons of Noah: and of them was the whole earth overspread.

20 And Noah began *to be* a husbandman, and he planted a vineyard: 21 And he drank of the wine, and was drunken; and he was uncovered within his tent. 22 And Ham, the father of Canaan, saw the nakedness of his father, and told his two brethren without. 23 And Shem and Japheth took a garment, and laid *it* upon both their shoulders, and went backward, and covered the nakedness of their father; and their faces *were* backward, and they saw not their father's nakedness. 24 And Noah awoke from his wine, and

knew what his younger son had done unto him. 25 And he said,

"Cursed *be* Canaan;
A servant of servants shall he be unto his brethren."

26 And he said,

"Blessed *be* the Lord God of Shem;
And Canaan shall be his servant.

27   God shall enlarge Japheth,
And he shall dwell in the tents of Shem;
And Canaan shall be his servant." [19]

28 And Noah lived after the flood three hundred and fifty years. 29 And all the days of Noah were nine hundred and fifty years: and he died.

The Tower of Babel

10 Now these *are* the generations of the sons of Noah; Shem, Ham, and Japheth: and unto them were sons born after the flood. 2 The sons of Japheth; Gomer, and Magog, and Madai, and Javan, and Tubal, and Meshech, and Tiras. 3 And the sons of Gomer; Ashkenaz, and Riphath, and Togarmah. 4 And the sons of Javan; Elishah, and Tarshish, Kittim, and Dodanim. 5 By these were the isles of the Gentiles divided in their lands; every one after his tongue, after their families, in their nations.

6 And the sons of Ham; Cush, and Mizraim, and Phut, and Canaan. 7 And the sons of Cush; Seba, and Havilah, and Sabtah, and Raamah, and Sabtecha: and the sons of Raamah; Sheba, and Dedan. 8 And Cush begat Nimrod: he began to be a mighty one in the earth. 9 He was a mighty hunter before the Lord: wherefore it is said, "Even as Nimrod the mighty hunter before the Lord." 10 And the beginning of his kingdom was Babel, and Erech, and Accad, and Calneh, in the land of Shinar. 11 Out of that land went forth Asshur, and builded Nineveh, and the city Rehoboth, and Calah, 12 And Resen between Nineveh and Calah: the same *is* a great city. 13 And Mizraim begat Ludim, and Anamim, and Lehabim, and Naphtuhim, 14 And Pathrusim, and Casluhim, (out of whom came Philistim,) and Caphtorim.

15 And Canaan begat Sidon his firstborn, and Heth, 16 And the Jebusite, and the Amorite, and the Girgasite, 17 And the Hivite, and the Arkite, and the Sinite, 18 And the Arvadite, and the Zemarite, and the Hamathite: and afterward were the families of the Canaanites spread abroad. 19 And the border of the Canaanites was from Sidon, as thou comest to Gerar, unto Gaza; as

---

18. The ancients imagined lightning bolts to be arrows from God's bow. A rainbow seen in the heavens is a sign that God's wrath is abated, that he has laid his weapon aside.

19. (9:20-27) This tale, intended to demean Israel's enemies, is based on two differing accounts: in one, Ham is guilty; in the other, Canaan. Verse 24 suggests that the story is related to myths of castration.

thou goest unto Sodom, and Gomorrah, and Admah, and Zeboim, even unto Lasha. 20 These *are* the sons of Ham, after their families, after their tongues, in their countries, *and* in their nations.

21 Unto Shem also, the father of all the children of Eber, the brother of Japheth the elder, even to him were *children* born. 22 The children of Shem; Elam, and Asshur, and Arphaxad, and Lud, and Aram. 23 And the children of Aram; Uz, and Hul, and Gether, and Mash. 24 And Arphaxad begat Salah; and Salah begat Eber. 25 And unto Eber were born two sons: the name of one *was* Peleg; for in his days was the earth divided; and his brother's name *was* Joktan. 26 And Joktan begat Almodad, and Sheleph, and Hazarmaveth, and Jerah, 27 And Hadoram, and Uzal, and Diklah, 28 And Obal, and Abimael, and Sheba, 29 And Ophir, and Havilah, and Jobab: all these *were* the sons of Joktan. 30 And their dwelling was from Mesha, as thou goest unto Sephar, a mount of the east. 31 These *are* the sons of Shem, after their families, after their tongues, in their lands, after their nations.

32 These *are* the families of the sons of Noah, after their generations, in their nations: and by these were the nations divided in the earth after the flood.

11 And the whole earth was of one language, and of one speech. 2 And it came to pass, as they journeyed from the east, that they found a plain in the land of Shinar; and they dwelt there. 3 And they said one to another, "Go to, let us make brick, and burn them thoroughly." And they had brick for stone, and slime had they for mortar. 4 And they said, "Go to, let us build us a city, and a tower, whose top *may reach* unto heaven; and let us make us a name, lest we be scattered abroad upon the face of the whole earth."

5 And the LORD came down to see the city and the tower, which the children of man builded. 6 And the LORD said, "Behold, the people *is* one, and they have all one language; and this they begin to do: and now nothing will be restrained from them, which they have imagined to do. 7 Go to, let us go down, and there confound their language, that they may not understand one another's speech." 8 So the LORD scattered them abroad from thence upon the face of all the earth: and they left off to build the city. 9 Therefore is the name of it called Babel; because the LORD did there confound the language of all the earth: and from thence did the LORD scatter them abroad upon the face of all the earth.[20]

ABRAHAM

Genealogy and Call of Abram

10 These *are* the generations of Shem: Shem *was* a hundred years old, and begat Arphaxad two years after the flood: 11 And Shem lived after he begat Arphaxad five hundred years, and begat sons and daughters.

12 And Arphaxad lived five and thirty years, and begat Salah: 13 And Arphaxad lived after he begat Salah four hundred and three years, and begat sons and daughters.

14 And Salah lived thirty years, and begat Eber: 15 And Salah lived after he begat Eber four hundred and three years, and begat sons and daughters.

16 And Eber lived four and thirty years, and begat Peleg: 17 And Eber lived after he begat Peleg four hundred and thirty years, and begat sons and daughters.

18 And Peleg lived thirty years, and begat Reu: 19 And Peleg lived after he begat Reu two hundred and nine years, and begat sons and daughters.

20 And Reu lived two and thirty years, and begat Serug: 21 And Reu lived after he begat Serug two hundred and seven years, and begat sons and daughters.

22 And Serug lived thirty years, and begat Nahor: 23 And Serug lived after he begat Nahor two hundred years, and begat sons and daughters.

24 And Nahor lived nine and twenty years, and begat Terah: 25 And Nahor lived after he begat Terah a hundred and nineteen years, and begat sons and daughters.

26 And Terah lived seventy years, and begat Abram, Nahor, and Haran.

27 Now these *are* the generations of Terah: Terah begat Abram, Nahor, and Haran; and Haran begat Lot. 28 And Haran died before his father Terah in the land of his nativity, in Ur of the Chaldees. 29 And Abram and Nahor took them wives: the name of Abram's wife *was* Sarai; and the name of Nahor's wife, Milcah, the daughter of Haran, the father of Milcah, and the father of Iscah. 30 But Sarai was barren; she *had* no child. 31 And Terah took Abram his son, and Lot the son of Haran his son's son, and Sarai his daughter-in-law, his son Abram's wife; and they went forth with them from Ur of the Chaldees, to go into the land of Canaan; and they came unto Haran, and dwelt there. 32 And the days of Terah were two hundred and five years: and Terah died in Haran.

---

20. (11:1-9) The story is based on traditions concerning the temple-towers (ziggurats) of Babylonia. Probably some ruined or never-finished tower was interpreted as a divine response to human pride.

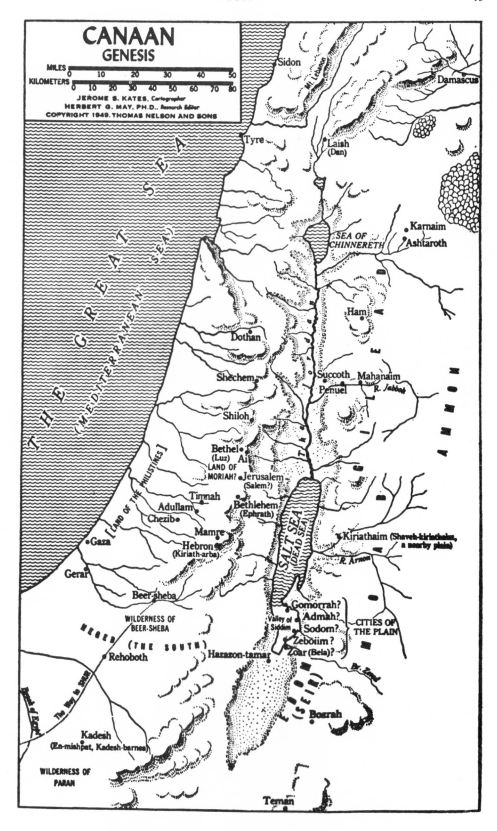

CANAAN
GENESIS

MILES
0   10   20   30   40   50
KILOMETERS
0   10   20   30   40   50   60   70   80

JEROME S. KATES, Cartographer
HERBERT G. MAY, PH.D., Research Editor
COPYRIGHT 1949, THOMAS NELSON AND SONS

Sidon

Damascus

Tyre

Laish
(Dan)

MT. Lebanon

Karnaim
Ashtaroth

SEA OF
CHINNERETH

Ham

THE GREAT SEA
(MEDITERRANEAN SEA)

Dothan

Shechem

Succoth   Mahanaim
Penuel   R. Jabbok

Shiloh

Bethel
(Luz)   Ai
LAND OF
MORIAH?   Jerusalem
(Salem?)

Timnah

Adullam   Bethlehem
(Ephrath)

Chezib

Mamre

Gaza

Hebron
(Kiriath-arba)

Kiriathaim (Shaveh-kiriathaim,
a nearby plain)

R. Arnon

Gerar

Beer-sheba

WILDERNESS OF
BEER-SHEBA

NEGEB

(THE SOUTH)

Rehoboth

Hazazon-tamar

Gomorrah?
Valley of   Admah?
Siddim   Sodom?
Zeboiim?
Zoar (Bela)?

CITIES OF
THE PLAIN

Bozrah

[LAND OF THE PHILISTINES]

SALT SEA
(DEAD SEA)

AMMON

Br. Zered

SEIR (EDOM)

The Way to Shur

Brook of Egypt

Kadesh
(En-mishpat, Kadesh-barnea)

WILDERNESS OF
PARAN

Teman

12 Now the LORD had said unto Abram, "Get thee out of thy country, and from thy kindred, and from thy father's house, unto a land that I will show thee: 2 And I will make of thee a great nation, and I will bless thee, and make thy name great; and thou shalt be a blessing: 3 And I will bless them that bless thee, and curse him that curseth thee: and in thee shall all families of the earth be blessed." 4 So Abram departed, as the LORD had spoken unto him; and Lot went with him: and Abram *was* seventy and five years old when he departed out of Haran. 5 And Abram took Sarai his wife, and Lot his brother's son, and all their substance that they had gathered, and the souls that they had gotten in Haran; and they went forth to go into the land of Canaan; and into the land of Canaan they came. 6 And Abram passed through the land unto the place of Sichem, unto the plain of Moreh. And the Canaanite *was* then in the land. 7 And the LORD appeared unto Abram, and said, "Unto thy seed will I give this land": and there builded he an altar unto the LORD, who appeared unto him. 8 And he removed from thence unto a mountain on the east of Beth-el, and pitched his tent, *having* Beth-el on the west, and Hai on the east: and there he builded an altar unto the LORD, and called upon the name of the LORD. 9 And Abram journeyed, going on still toward the south.

10 And there was a famine in the land: and Abram went down into Egypt to sojourn there; for the famine *was* grievous in the land. 11 And it came to pass, when he was come near to enter into Egypt, that he said unto Sarai his wife, "Behold now, I know that thou *art* a fair woman to look upon: 12 Therefore it shall come to pass, when the Egyptians shall see thee, that they shall say, 'This *is* his wife': and they will kill me, but they will save thee alive. 13 Say, I pray thee, thou *art* my sister: that it may be well with me for thy sake; and my soul shall live because of thee." 14 And it came to pass, that, when Abram was come into Egypt, the Egyptians beheld the woman that she *was* very fair. 15 The princes also of Pharaoh saw her, and commended her before Pharaoh: and the woman was taken into Pharaoh's house. 16 And he entreated Abram well for her sake: and he had sheep, and oxen, and he asses, and menservants, and maidservants, and she asses, and camels. 17 And the LORD plagued Pharaoh and his house with great plagues, because of Sarai, Abram's wife. 18 And Pharaoh called Abram, and said, "What *is* this *that* thou hast done unto me? why didst thou not tell me that she *was* thy wife? 19 Why saidst thou, 'She *is* my sister'? so I might have taken her to me to wife: now therefore behold thy wife, take *her,* and go thy way." 20 And Pharaoh commanded *his* men concerning him: and they sent him away, and his wife, and all that he had.[21]

Abram and Lot

13 And Abram went up out of Egypt, he, and his wife, and all that he had, and Lot with him, into the south. 2 And Abram *was* very rich in cattle, in silver, and in gold. 3 And he went on his journeys from the south even to Beth-el, unto the place where his tent had been at the beginning, between Beth-el and Hai; 4 Unto the place of the altar, which he had made there at the first: and there Abram called on the name of the LORD. 5 And Lot also, which went with Abram, had flocks, and herds, and tents. 6 And the land was not able to bear them, that they might dwell together: for their substance was great, so that they could not dwell together. 7 And there was a strife between the herdmen of Abram's cattle and the herdmen of Lot's cattle: and the Canaanite and the Perizzite dwelt then in the land. 8 And Abram said unto Lot, "Let there be no strife, I pray thee, between me and thee, and between my herdmen and thy herdmen; for we *be* brethren. 9 *Is* not the whole land before thee? separate thyself, I pray thee, from me: if *thou wilt take* the left hand, then I will go to the right; or if *thou depart* to the right hand, then I will go to the left." 10 And Lot lifted up his eyes and beheld all the plain of Jordan, that it *was* well watered every where, before the LORD destroyed Sodom and Gomorrah, *even* as the garden of the LORD, like the land of Egypt, as thou comest unto Zoar. 11 Then Lot chose him all the plain of Jordan; and Lot journeyed east: and they separated themselves the one from the other. 12 Abram dwelt in the land of Canaan, and Lot dwelt in the cities of the plain, and pitched *his* tent toward Sodom. 13 But the men of Sodom *were* wicked and sinners before the LORD exceedingly.

14 And the LORD said unto Abram, after that Lot was separated from him, "Lift up now thine eyes, and look from the place where thou art northward, and southward, and eastward, and westward: 15 For all the land which thou seest, to thee will I give it, and to thy seed for ever. 16 And I will make thy seed as the dust of the earth: so that if a man can number the dust of the earth, *then* shall thy seed also be numbered. 17 Arise, walk through the land in the length of it and in the breadth of it; for I will give it unto

---

21. (12:11-20) This tale of introducing one's wife as his sister is repeated in Chapter 20 (with Sarah) and in 26:1-16 (with Isaac and Rebekah). Later accounts seek to absolve the husband. (JB footnotes: "The story reflects a stage of moral development . . . when the husband's life meant more than his wife's honour.")

thee." 18 Then Abram removed *his* tent, and came and dwelt in the plain of Mamre, which *is* in Hebron, and built there an altar unto the LORD.

The Campaign of the Four Kings [22]

14 And it came to pass in the days of Amraphel king of Shinar, Arioch king of Ellasar, Chedorlaomer king of Elam, and Tidal king of nations; 2 *That these* made war with Bera king of Sodom, and with Birsha king of Gomorrah, Shinab king of Admah, and Shemeber king of Zeboiim, and the king of Bela, which is Zoar. 3 All these were joined together in the vale of Siddim, which is the salt sea. 4 Twelve years they served Chedorlaomer, and in the thirteenth year they rebelled. 5 And in the fourteenth year came Chedorlaomer, and the kings that *were* with him, and smote the Rephaim in Ashteroth Karnaim, and the Zuzim in Ham, and the Emim in Shaveh Kiriathaim, 6 And the Horites in their mount Seir, unto Elparan, which *is* by the wilderness. 7 And they returned, and came to En-mishpat, which *is* Kadesh, and smote all the country of the Amalekites, and also the Amorites, that dwelt in Hazezontamar. 8 And there went out the king of Sodom, and the king of Gomorrah, and the king of Admah, and the king of Zeboiim, and the king of Bela, (the same *is* Zoar;) and they joined battle with them in the vale of Siddim; 9 With Chedorlaomer the king of Elam, and with Tidal king of nations, and Amraphel king of Shinar, and Arioch king of Ellasar; four kings with five. 10 And the vale of Siddim *was full of* slime pits; and the kings of Sodom and Gomorrah fled, and fell there;[23] and they that remained fled to the mountain. 11 And they took all the goods of Sodom and Gomorrah, and all their victuals, and went their way. 12 And they took Lot, Abram's brother's son, who dwelt in Sodom, and his goods, and departed.

13 And there came one that had escaped, and told Abram the Hebrew; for he dwelt in the plain of Mamre the Amorite, brother of Eshcol, and brother of Aner: and these *were* confederate with Abram. 14 And when Abram heard that his brother was taken captive, he armed his trained *servants*, born in his own house, three hundred and eighteen, and pursued *them* unto Dan. 15 And he divided himself against them, he and his servants, by night, and smote them, and pursued them unto Hobah, which *is* on the left hand of Damascus. 16 And he brought back all the goods, and also brought again his brother Lot, and his goods, and the women also, and the people.

17 And the king of Sodom went out to meet him, after his return from the slaughter of Chedorlaomer and of the kings that *were* with him, at the valley of Shaveh, which *is* the king's dale. 18 And Melchizedek king of Salem brought forth bread and wine: and he *was* the priest of the most high God. 19 And he blessed him, and said,

"Blessed be Abram of the most high God,
Possessor of heaven and earth:
20 And blessed be the most high God,
Which hath delivered thine enemies into
thy hand."

And he gave him tithes of all. 21 And the king of Sodom said unto Abram, "Give me the persons, and take the goods to thyself." 22 And Abram said to the king of Sodom, "I have lifted up mine hand unto the LORD, the most high God, the possessor of heaven and earth, 23 That I will not *take* from a thread even to a shoe-latchet, and that I will not take any thing that *is* thine, lest thou shouldest say, 'I have made Abram rich': 24 Save only that which the young men have eaten, and the portion of the men which went with me, Aner, Eshcol, and Mamre; let them take their portion."

The Covenant with Abram

15 After these things the word of the LORD came unto Abram in a vision, saying, "Fear not, Abram: I *am* thy shield, *and* thy exceeding great reward." 2 And Abram said, "Lord GOD, what wilt thou give me, seeing I go childless, and the steward of my house *is* this Eliezer of Damascus?" 3 And Abram said, "Behold, to me thou hast given no seed: and, lo, one born in my house is mine heir." 4 And, behold, the word of the LORD *came* unto him, saying, "This shall not be thine heir; but he that shall come forth out of thine own bowels shall be thine heir." 5 And he brought him forth abroad, and said, "Look now toward heaven, and tell the stars, if thou be able to number them": and he said unto him, "So shall thy seed be." 6 And he believed in the LORD; and he counted it to him for righteousness. 7 And he said unto him, "I *am* the LORD that brought thee out of Ur of the Chaldees, to give thee this land to inherit it." 8 And he said, "Lord GOD, whereby shall I know that I shall inherit it?" 9 And he said unto him, "Take me a heifer of three years old, and a she goat of three years old,

---

22. Chapter 14 does not derive from the main sources of the Pentateuch. It is intended to add prominence to Abraham by describing him as a successful military commander.
23. TORAH: "Now the Valley of Sidim was dotted with bitumen pits; and the kings of Sodom and Gomorrah, in their flight, threw themselves into them."

and a ram of three years old, and a turtledove, and a young pigeon." 10 And he took unto him all these, and divided them in the midst, and laid each piece one against another: but the birds divided he not. 11 And when the fowls came down upon the carcasses, Abram drove them away. 12 And when the sun was going down, a deep sleep fell upon Abram; and, lo, a horror of great darkness fell upon him. 13 And he said unto Abram, "Know of a surety that thy seed shall be a stranger in a land *that is* not theirs, and shall serve them; and they shall afflict them four hundred years; 14 And also that nation, whom they shall serve, will I judge: and afterward shall they come out with great substance. 15 And thou shalt go to thy father in peace; thou shalt be buried in a good old age. 16 But in the fourth generation they shall come hither again: for the iniquity of the Amorites *is* not yet full." 17 And it came to pass, that, when the sun went down, and it was dark, behold a smoking furnace, and a burning lamp that passed between those pieces.[24]

18 In that same day the LORD made a covenant with Abram, saying, "Unto thy seed have I given this land, from the river of Egypt unto the great river, the river Euphrates: 19 The Kenites, and the Kenizzites, and the Kadmonites, 20 And the Hittites, and the Perizzites, and the Rephaim, 21 And the Amorites, and the Canaanites, and the Girgashites, and the Jebusites."

The Birth of Ishmael

16 Now Sarai, Abram's wife, bare him no children: and she had a handmaid, an Egyptian, whose name *was* Hagar. 2 And Sarai said unto Abram, "Behold now, the LORD hath restrained me from bearing: I pray thee, go in unto my maid; it may be that I may obtain children by her." [25] And Abram hearkened to the voice of Sarai. 3 And Sarai, Abram's wife, took Hagar her maid the Egyptian, after Abram had dwelt ten years in the land of Canaan, and gave her to her husband Abram to be his wife. 4 And he went in unto Hagar, and she conceived: and when she saw that she had conceived, her mistress was despised in her eyes. 5 And Sarai said unto Abram, "My wrong *be* upon thee: I have given

my maid into thy bosom; and when she saw that she had conceived, I was despised in her eyes: the LORD judge between me and thee." 6 But Abram said unto Sarai, "Behold, thy maid *is* in thy hand; do to her as it pleaseth thee." And when Sarai dealt hardly with her, she fled from her face.

7 And the angel of the LORD found her by a fountain of water in the wilderness, by the fountain in the way to Shur. 8 And he said, "Hagar, Sarai's maid, whence camest thou? and whither wilt thou go?" And she said, "I flee from the face of my mistress Sarai." 9 And the angel of the LORD said unto her, "Return to thy mistress, and submit thyself under her hands." 10 And the angel of the LORD said unto her, "I will multiply thy seed exceedingly, that it shall not be numbered for multitude." 11 And the angel of the LORD said unto her, "Behold, thou *art* with child, and shalt bear a son, and shalt call his name Ishmael; because the LORD hath heard thy affliction. 12 And he will be a wild man; his hand *will be* against every man, and every man's hand against him: and he shall dwell in the presence of all his brethren." 13 And she called the name of the LORD that spake unto her, "Thou God seest me": for she said, "Have I also here looked after him that seeth me?" [26] 14 Wherefore the well was called Beer-lahai-roi: behold, *it is* between Kadesh and Bered. 15 And Hagar bare Abram a son: and Abram called his son's name, which Hagar bare, Ishmael. 16 And Abram *was* fourscore and six years old, when Hagar bare Ishmael to Abram.

The Covenant of Circumcision

17 And when Abram was ninety years old and nine, the LORD appeared to Abram, and said unto him, "I *am* the Almighty God; walk before me, and be thou perfect. 2 And I will make my covenant between me and thee, and will multiply thee exceedingly." 3 And Abram fell on his face: and God talked with him, saying, 4 "As for me, behold, my covenant *is* with thee, and thou shalt be a father of many nations. 5 Neither shall thy name any more be called Abram, but thy name shall be Abraham; for a father of many nations have I made thee. 6 And I will make thee exceeding fruitful, and I will make nations of thee, and kings shall come out of thee. 7 And I will establish my covenant between me and thee and

24. (15:8-17) The covenant is sealed according to the ancient rite in which animals were killed and divided; the contracting parties passed between the pieces to show their readiness to die rather than fail the compact. Here, it is God alone, under the form of fire, who passes between the pieces.

25. Nuzi documents of the fifteenth century B.C. disclose that this practice was common for barren women. After the servant gave birth, the wife raised the child as her own.

26. TORAH: "And she called the Lord who spoke to her, 'You are El-roi,' by which she meant, 'Have I not gone on seeing after He saw me!' " Implicit here is the threat voiced by Yahweh in *Exodus* 33:20: "there shall no man see me, and live."

thy seed after thee in their generations, for an everlasting covenant, to be a God unto thee and to thy seed after thee. 8 And I will give unto thee, and to thy seed after thee, the land wherein thou art a stranger, all the land of Canaan, for an everlasting possession; and I will be their God." 9 And God said unto Abraham, "Thou shalt keep my covenant therefore, thou, and thy seed after thee in their generations. 10 This *is* my covenant, which ye shall keep, between me and you and thy seed after thee; Every man child among you shall be circumcised.[27] 11 And ye shall circumcise the flesh of your foreskin; and it shall be a token of the covenant betwixt me and you. 12 And he that is eight days old shall be circumcised among you, every man child in your generations, he that is born in the house, or bought with money of any stranger, which *is* not of thy seed. 13 He that is born in thy house, and he that is bought with thy money, must needs be circumcised: and my covenant shall be in your flesh for an everlasting covenant. 14 And the uncircumcised man child whose flesh of his foreskin is not circumcised, that soul shall be cut off from his people; he hath broken my covenant."

15 And God said unto Abraham, "As for Sarai thy wife, thou shalt not call her name Sarai, but Sarah *shall* her name *be.* 16 And I will bless her, and give thee a son also of her: yea, I will bless her, and she shall be *a mother* of nations; kings of people shall be of her." 17 Then Abraham fell upon his face, and laughed, and said in his heart, "Shall *a child* be born unto him that is a hundred years old? and shall Sarah, that is ninety years old, bear?" 18 And Abraham said unto God, "O that Ishmael might live before thee!" 19 And God said, "Sarah thy wife shall bear thee a son indeed; and thou shalt call his name Isaac: and I will establish my covenant with him for an everlasting covenant, *and* with his seed after him. 20 And as for Ishmael, I have heard thee: Behold, I have blessed him, and will make him fruitful, and will multiply him exceedingly; twelve princes shall he beget, and I will make him a great nation. 21 But my covenant will I establish with Isaac, which Sarah shall bear unto thee at this set time in the next year." 22 And he left off talking with him, and God went up from Abraham.

23 And Abraham took Ishmael his son, and all that were born in his house, and all that were bought with his money, every male among the men of Abraham's house; and circumcised the flesh of their foreskin in the selfsame day, as God had said unto him. 24 And Abraham *was* ninety years old and nine, when he was circumcised in the flesh of his foreskin. 25 And Ishmael his son *was* thirteen years old, when he was circumcised in the flesh of his foreskin. 26 In the selfsame day was Abraham circumcised, and Ishmael his son. 27 And all the men of his house, born in the house, and bought with money of the stranger, were circumcised with him.

The Lord Visits Abraham

18 And the LORD appeared unto him in the plains of Mamre: and he sat in the tent door in the heat of the day; 2 And he lifted up his eyes and looked, and, lo, three men stood by him: and when he saw *them,* he ran to meet them from the tent door, and bowed himself toward the ground, 3 And said, "My Lord,[28] if now I have found favor in thy sight, pass not away, I pray thee, from thy servant: 4 Let a little water, I pray you, be fetched, and wash your feet, and rest yourselves under the tree: 5 And I will fetch a morsel of bread, and comfort ye your hearts; after that ye shall pass on: for therefore are ye come to your servant." And they said, "So do, as thou hast said." 6 And Abraham hastened into the tent unto Sarah, and said, "Make ready quickly three measures of fine meal, knead *it,* and make cakes upon the hearth." 7 And Abraham ran unto the herd, and fetched a calf tender and good, and gave *it* unto a young man; and he hasted to dress it. 8 And he took butter, and milk, and the calf which he had dressed, and set *it* before them; and he stood by them under the tree, and they did eat. 9 And they said unto him, "Where *is* Sarah thy wife?" And he said, "Behold, in the tent." 10 And he said, "I will certainly return unto thee according to the time of life; and, lo, Sarah thy wife shall have a son." And Sarah heard *it* in the tent door, which *was* behind him. 11 Now Abraham and Sarah *were* old *and* well stricken in age; *and* it ceased to be with Sarah after the manner of women. 12 Therefore Sarah laughed within herself, saying, "After I am waxed old shall I have pleasure, my lord being old also?" 13 And the LORD said unto Abraham, "Wherefore did Sarah laugh, saying, 'Shall I of a surety bear a child, which am old?' 14 Is any thing too hard for the LORD? At the time appointed I will return unto thee, according to the time of life, and Sarah shall have a son." 15 Then Sarah denied, saying, "I

---

27. Circumcision was widely practiced in ancient religion. Originally it was part of an initiation rite by which a youth assumed his religious and civil responsibilities. For the Jews, it became a sign of God's covenant with Abraham.

28. NEB: "Sirs." Abraham believes the visitors are simply men and follows the semitic code of hospitality. He does not recognize their divine nature until verse 13, where the Lord shows his power by reading Sarah's thoughts.

laughed not"; for she was afraid. And he said, "Nay; but thou didst laugh."

Sodom and Gomorrah

16 And the men rose up from thence, and looked toward Sodom: and Abraham went with them to bring them on the way. 17 And the LORD said, "Shall I hide from Abraham that thing which I do; 18 Seeing that Abraham shall surely become a great and mighty nation, and all the nations of the earth shall be blessed in him? 19 For I know him, that he will command his children and his household after him, and they shall keep the way of the LORD, to do justice and judgment; that the LORD may bring upon Abraham that which he hath spoken of him." 20 And the LORD said, "Because the cry of Sodom and Gomorrah is great, and because their sin is very grievous, 21 I will go down now, and see whether they have done altogether according to the cry of it, which is come unto me; and if not, I will know." 22 And the men turned their faces from thence, and went toward Sodom: but Abraham stood yet before the LORD.

23 And Abraham drew near, and said, "Wilt thou also destroy the righteous with the wicked? 24 Peradventure there be fifty righteous within the city: wilt thou also destroy and not spare the place for the fifty righteous that *are* therein? 25 That be far from thee to do after this manner, to slay the righteous with the wicked; and that the righteous should be as the wicked, that be far from thee: Shall not the Judge of all the earth do right?" 26 And the LORD said, "If I find in Sodom fifty righteous within the city, then I will spare all the place for their sakes." 27 And Abraham answered and said, "Behold now, I have taken upon me to speak unto the Lord, which *am but* dust and ashes: 28 Peradventure there shall lack five of the fifty righteous: wilt thou destroy all the city for *lack of* five?" And he said, "If I find there forty and five, I will not destroy *it*." 29 And he spake unto him yet again, and said, "Peradventure there shall be forty found there." And he said, "I will not do *it* for forty's sake." 30 And he said *unto him,* "Oh let not the Lord be angry, and I will speak: Peradventure there shall thirty be found there." And he said, "I will not do *it,* if I find thirty there." 31 And he said, "Behold now, I have taken upon me to speak unto the Lord: Peradventure there shall be twenty found there." And he said, "I will not destroy *it* for twenty's sake." 32 And he said, "Oh let not the Lord be angry, and I will speak yet but this once: Peradventure ten shall be found there." And he said, "I will not destroy *it* for ten's sake." 33 And the LORD went his way, as soon as he had left

communing with Abraham: and Abraham returned unto his place.

19 And there came two angels to Sodom at even; and Lot sat in the gate of Sodom: and Lot seeing *them* rose up to meet them; and he bowed himself with his face toward the ground; 2 And he said, "Behold now, my lords, turn in, I pray you, into your servant's house, and tarry all night, and wash your feet, and ye shall rise up early, and go on your ways." And they said, "Nay; but we will abide in the street all night." 3 And he pressed upon them greatly; and they turned in unto him, and entered into his house; and he made them a feast, and did bake unleavened bread, and they did eat. 4 But before they lay down, the men of the city, *even* the men of Sodom, compassed the house round, both old and young, all the people from every quarter: 5 And they called unto Lot, and said unto him, "Where *are* the men which came in to thee this night? bring them out unto us, that we may know them." 6 And Lot went out at the door unto them, and shut the door after him, 7 And said, "I pray you, brethren, do not so wickedly. 8 Behold now, I have two daughters which have not known man; let me, I pray you, bring them out unto you, and do ye to them as *is* good in your eyes: only unto these men do nothing; for therefore came they under the shadow of my roof." 9 And they said, "Stand back." And they said *again,* "This one *fellow* came in to sojourn, and he will needs be a judge: now will we deal worse with thee than with them." And they pressed sore upon the man, *even* Lot, and came near to break the door. 10 But the men put forth their hand, and pulled Lot into the house to them, and shut to the door. 11 And they smote the men that *were* at the door of the house with blindness, both small and great: so that they wearied themselves to find the door. 12 And the men said unto Lot, "Hast thou here any besides? son-in-law, and thy sons, and thy daughters, and whatsoever thou hast in the city, bring *them* out of this place: 13 For we will destroy this place, because the cry of them is waxen great before the face of the LORD; and the LORD hath sent us to destroy it." 14 And Lot went out, and spake unto his sons-in-law, which married his daughters, and said, "Up, get you out of this place; for the LORD will destroy this city." But he seemed as one that mocked unto his sons-in-law.

15 And when the morning arose, then the angels hastened Lot, saying, "Arise, take thy wife, and thy two daughters, which are here; lest thou be consumed in the iniquity of the city." 16 And while he lingered, the men laid hold upon his hand, and upon the hand of his wife, and upon the hand of his two daughters; the LORD being

merciful unto him: and they brought him forth, and set him without the city. 17 And it came to pass, when they had brought them forth abroad, that he said, "Escape for thy life; look not behind thee, neither stay thou in all the plain; escape to the mountain, lest thou be consumed." 18 And Lot said unto them, "Oh, not so, my Lord: 19 Behold now, thy servant hath found grace in thy sight, and thou hast magnified thy mercy, which thou hast showed unto me in saving my life; and I cannot escape to the mountain, lest some evil take me, and I die: 20 Behold now, this city *is* near to flee unto, and it *is* a little one: O, let me escape thither, (*is* it not a little one?) and my soul shall live." 21 And he said unto him, "See, I have accepted thee concerning this thing also, that I will not overthrow this city, for the which thou hast spoken. 22 Haste thee, escape thither; for I cannot do any thing till thou be come thither." Therefore the name of the city was called Zoar.

23 The sun was risen upon the earth when Lot entered into Zoar. 24 Then the LORD rained upon Sodom and upon Gomorrah brimstone and fire from the LORD out of heaven; 25 And he overthrew those cities, and all the plain, and all the inhabitants of the cities, and that which grew upon the ground. 26 But his wife looked back from behind him, and she became a pillar of salt. 27 And Abraham gat up early in the morning to the place where he stood before the LORD: 28 And he looked toward Sodom and Gomorrah, and toward all the land of the plain, and beheld, and, lo, the smoke of the country went up as the smoke of a furnace.

29 And it came to pass, when God destroyed the cities of the plain, that God remembered Abraham, and sent Lot out of the midst of the overthrow, when he overthrew the cities in the which Lot dwelt.

30 And Lot went up out of Zoar, and dwelt in the mountain, and his two daughters with him; for he feared to dwell in Zoar: and he dwelt in a cave, he and his two daughters. 31 And the firstborn said unto the younger, "Our father *is* old, and *there is* not a man in the earth to come in unto us after the manner of all the earth: 32 Come, let us make our father drink wine, and we will lie with him, that we may preserve seed of our father." 33 And they made their father drink wine that night: and the firstborn went in, and lay with her father; and he perceived not when she lay down, nor when she arose. 34 And it came to pass on the morrow, that the firstborn said unto the younger, "Behold, I lay yesternight with my father: let us make him drink wine this night also; and go thou in, *and* lie with him, that we may pre-

serve seed of our father." 35 And they made their father drink wine that night also: and the younger arose, and lay with him; and he perceived not when she lay down, nor when she arose. 36 Thus were both the daughters of Lot with child by their father. 37 And the firstborn bare a son, and called his name Moab: the same *is* the father of the Moabites unto this day. 38 And the younger, she also bare a son, and called his name Ben-ammi: the same *is* the father of the children of Ammon unto this day.[29]

Abraham at Gerar

20 And Abraham journeyed from thence toward the south country, and dwelt between Kadesh and Shur, and sojourned in Gerar. 2 And Abraham said of Sarah his wife, "She *is* my sister": and Abimelech king of Gerar sent, and took Sarah. 3 But God came to Abimelech in a dream by night, and said to him, "Behold, thou *art but* a dead man, for the woman which thou hast taken; for she *is* a man's wife." 4 But Abimelech had not come near her: and he said, "LORD, wilt thou slay also a righteous nation? 5 Said he not unto me, 'She *is* my sister?' and she, even she herself said, 'He *is* my brother': in the integrity of my heart and innocency of my hands have I done this." 6 And God said unto him in a dream, "Yea, I know that thou didst this in the integrity of thy heart; for I also withheld thee from sinning against me: therefore suffered I thee not to touch her. 7 Now therefore restore the man *his* wife; for he *is* a prophet, and he shall pray for thee, and thou shalt live: and if thou restore *her* not, know thou that thou shalt surely die, thou, and all that *are* thine."

8 Therefore Abimelech rose early in the morning, and called all his servants, and told all these things in their ears: and the men were sore afraid. 9 Then Abimelech called Abraham, and said unto him, "What hast thou done unto us? and what have I offended thee, that thou hast brought on me and on my kingdom a great sin? thou hast done deeds unto me that ought not to be done." 10 And Abimelech said unto Abraham, "What sawest thou, that thou hast done this thing?" 11 And Abraham said, "Because I thought, Surely the fear of God *is* not in this place; and they will slay me for my wife's sake. 12 And yet indeed *she is* my sister; she *is* the daughter of my father, but not the daughter of my mother; and she became my wife. 13 And it came to pass, when God caused me to wander from my father's

---

29. (19:30-38) Hebrew morality condemned incest. This story was intended to malign Israel's neighbors, the Moabites and the Ammonites.

house, that I said unto her, 'This *is* thy kindness which thou shalt show unto me; at every place whither we shall come, say of me, "He *is* my brother." ' "   14 And Abimelech took sheep, and oxen, and menservants, and womenservants, and gave *them* unto Abraham, and restored him Sarah his wife.   15 And Abimelech said, "Behold, my land *is* before thee: dwell where it pleaseth thee." 16 And unto Sarah he said, "Behold, I have given thy brother a thousand *pieces* of silver: behold, he *is* to thee a covering of the eyes, unto all that *are* with thee, and with all *other*":[30] thus she was reproved.   17 So Abraham prayed unto God: and God healed Abimelech, and his wife, and his maidservants; and they bare *children*.   18 For the LORD had fast closed up all the wombs of the house of Abimelech, because of Sarah, Abraham's wife.

The Birth of Isaac

21 And the LORD visited Sarah as he had said, and the LORD did unto Sarah as he had spoken. 2 For Sarah conceived, and bare Abraham a son in his old age, at the set time of which God had spoken to him.   3 And Abraham called the name of his son that was born unto him, whom Sarah bare to him, Isaac.   4 And Abraham circumcised his son Isaac being eight days old, as God had commanded him.   5 And Abraham was a hundred years old, when his son Isaac was born unto him.   6 And Sarah said, "God hath made me to laugh, *so that* all that hear will laugh with me." 7 And she said, "Who would have said unto Abraham, that Sarah should have given children suck? for I have borne *him* a son in his old age."

Hagar and Ishmael[31]

8 And the child grew, and was weaned: and Abraham made a great feast the *same* day that Isaac was weaned.   9 And Sarah saw the son of Hagar the Egyptian, which she had borne unto Abraham, mocking.   10 Wherefore she said unto Abraham, "Cast out this bondwoman and her son: for the son of this bondwoman shall not be heir with my son, *even* with Isaac."   11 And the thing was very grievous in Abraham's sight because of his son.   12 And God said unto Abraham, "Let it not be grievous in thy sight because of the lad, and because of thy bondwoman; in all

30. This text is obscure. KNOX: "See, I am giving this brother of thine a thousand silver pieces; such amends will enable thee to look the world in the face, wherever thou goest."
31. (21:8-21) This is thought to be an E retelling of the J story of Hagar's expulsion (16:4-16). The second version is more sympathetic to Abraham.

that Sarah hath said unto thee, hearken unto her voice; for in Isaac shall thy seed be called. 13 And also of the son of the bondwoman will I make a nation, because he *is* thy seed."   14 And Abraham rose up early in the morning, and took bread, and a bottle of water, and gave *it* unto Hagar, putting *it* on her shoulder, and the child, and sent her away: and she departed, and wandered in the wilderness of Beer-sheba.   15 And the water was spent in the bottle, and she cast the child under one of the shrubs.   16 And she went, and sat her down over against *him* a good way off, as it were a bowshot: for she said, "Let me not see the death of the child." And she sat over against *him*, and lifted up her voice, and wept.   17 And God heard the voice of the lad; and the angel of God called to Hagar out of heaven, and said unto her, "What aileth thee, Hagar? fear not; for God hath heard the voice of the lad where he *is*. 18 Arise, lift up the lad, and hold him in thine hand; for I will make him a great nation."   19 And God opened her eyes, and she saw a well of water; and she went, and filled the bottle with water, and gave the lad drink.   20 And God was with the lad; and he grew, and dwelt in the wilderness, and became an archer.   21 And he dwelt in the wilderness of Paran: and his mother took him a wife out of the land of Egypt.

The Pact at Beer-sheba

22 And it came to pass at that time, that Abimelech and Phichol the chief captain of his host spake unto Abraham, saying, "God *is* with thee in all that thou doest: 23 Now therefore swear unto me here by God, that thou wilt not deal falsely with me, nor with my son, nor with my son's son: *but* according to the kindness that I have done unto thee, thou shalt do unto me, and to the land wherein thou hast sojourned."   24 And Abraham said, "I will swear."   25 And Abraham reproved Abimelech because of a well of water, which Abimelech's servants had violently taken away. 26 And Abimelech said, "I wot not who hath done this thing: neither didst thou tell me, neither yet heard I *of it*, but to-day."   27 And Abraham took sheep and oxen, and gave them unto Abimelech; and both of them made a covenant. 28 And Abraham set seven ewe lambs of the flock by themselves.   29 And Abimelech said unto Abraham, "What *mean* these seven ewe lambs which thou hast set by themselves?"   30 And he said, "For *these* seven ewe lambs shalt thou take of my hand, that they may be a witness unto me, that I have digged this well."   31 Wherefore he called that place Beer-sheba; because there they sware both of them.   32 Thus they made a covenant at Beer-sheba: then Abimelech rose up,

and Phichol the chief captain of his host, and they returned into the land of the Philistines. 33 And *Abraham* planted a grove in Beer-sheba, and called there on the name of the LORD, the everlasting God. 34 And Abraham sojourned in the Philistines' land many days.

The Sacrifice of Isaac

22 And it came to pass after these things, that God did tempt Abraham, and said unto him, "Abraham": and he said, "Behold, *here* I *am.*" 2 And he said, "Take now thy son, thine only *son* Isaac, whom thou lovest, and get thee into the land of Moriah; and offer him there for a burnt offering upon one of the mountains which I will tell thee of." 3 And Abraham rose up early in the morning, and saddled his ass, and took two of his young men with him, and Isaac his son, and clave the wood for the burnt offering, and rose up, and went unto the place of which God had told him. 4 Then on the third day Abraham lifted up his eyes, and saw the place afar off. 5 And Abraham said unto his young men, "Abide ye here with the ass; and I and the lad will go yonder and worship, and come again to you." 6 And Abraham took the wood of the burnt offering, and laid *it* upon Isaac his son; and he took the fire in his hand, and a knife; and they went both of them together. 7 And Isaac spake unto Abraham his father, and said, "My father": and he said, "Here *am* I, my son." And he said, "Behold the fire and the wood: but where *is* the lamb for a burnt offering?" 8 And Abraham said, "My son, God will provide himself a lamb for a burnt offering": so they went both of them together.

9 And they came to the place which God had told him of; and Abraham built an altar there, and laid the wood in order, and bound Isaac his son, and laid him on the altar upon the wood. 10 And Abraham stretched forth his hand, and took the knife to slay his son. 11 And the Angel of the LORD called unto him out of heaven, and said, "Abraham, Abraham": and he said, "Here *am* I." 12 And he said, "Lay not thine hand upon the lad, neither do thou any thing unto him: for now I know that thou fearest God, seeing thou hast not withheld thy son, thine only *son,* from me." 13 And Abraham lifted up his eyes, and looked, and behold behind *him* a ram caught in a thicket by his horns: and Abraham went and took the ram, and offered him up for a burnt offering in the stead of his son.[32] 14 And Abraham called

the name of that place Jehovah-jireh: as it is said *to* this day, In the mount of the LORD it shall be seen. 15 And the Angel of the LORD called unto Abraham out of heaven the second time, 16 And said, "By myself have I sworn, saith the LORD, for because thou hast done this thing, and hast not withheld thy son, thine only *son,* 17 That in blessing I will bless thee, and in multiplying I will multiply thy seed as the stars of the heaven, and as the sand which *is* upon the seashore; and thy seed shall possess the gate of his enemies; 18 And in thy seed shall all the nations of the earth be blessed; because thou hast obeyed my voice." 19 So Abraham returned unto his young men, and they rose up and went together to Beer-sheba; and Abraham dwelt at Beer-sheba.

20 And it came to pass after these things, that it was told Abraham, saying, "Behold, Milcah, she hath also borne children unto thy brother Nahor; 21 Huz his firstborn, and Buz his brother, and Kemuel the father of Aram, 22 And Chesed, and Hazo, and Pildash, and Jidlaph, and Bethuel." 23 And Bethuel begat Rebekah: these eight Milcah did bear to Nahor, Abraham's brother. 24 And his concubine, whose name *was* Reumah, she bare also Tebah, and Gaham, and Thahash, and Maachah.

The Burial of Sarah

23 And Sarah was a hundred and seven and twenty years old: *these were* the years of the life of Sarah. 2 And Sarah died in Kirjath-arba; the same *is* Hebron in the land of Canaan: and Abraham came to mourn for Sarah, and to weep for her. 3 And Abraham stood up from before his dead, and spake unto the sons of Heth, saying, 4 "I *am* a stranger and a sojourner with you: give me a possession of a buryingplace with you, that I may bury my dead out of my sight." 5 And the children of Heth answered Abraham, saying unto him, 6 "Hear us, my lord: thou *art* a mighty prince among us: in the choice of our sepulchres bury thy dead; none of us shall withhold from thee his sepulchre, but that thou mayest bury thy dead." 7 And Abraham stood up, and bowed himself to the people of the land, *even* to the children of Heth. 8 And he communed with them, saying, "If it be your mind that I should bury my dead out of my sight, hear me, and entreat for me to Ephron the son of Zohar, 9 That he may give me the cave of Machpelah, which he hath, which *is* in the end of his field; for as much money as it

32. Ignatius Hunt (*The Book of Genesis*, 1960, Paulist/Newman Press) writes: "The story . . . aims at the justification of the practice of redeeming the first-born, perhaps even attempts to assign an origin to this practice. The first-born belonged to God, but instead of taking their lives, their parents 'bought them back' from Him. The story also condemns Chanaanite practices of child-sacrifice and demonstrates the great faith of Abraham, here put to the supreme test."

is worth he shall give it me for a possession of a buryingplace amongst you." 10 And Ephron dwelt among the children of Heth: and Ephron the Hittite answered Abraham in the audience of the children of Heth, *even* of all that went in at the gate of his city, saying, 11 "Nay, my lord, hear me: the field give I thee, and the cave that *is* therein, I give it thee; in the presence of the sons of my people give I it thee: bury thy dead." 12 And Abraham bowed down himself before the people of the land. 13 And he spake unto Ephron in the audience of the people of the land, saying, "But if thou *wilt give it,* I pray thee, hear me: I will give thee money for the field; take *it* of me, and I will bury my dead there." 14 And Ephron answered Abraham, saying unto him, 15 "My lord, hearken unto me: the land *is worth* four hundred shekels of silver; what *is* that betwixt me and thee? bury therefore thy dead." 16 And Abraham hearkened unto Ephron; and Abraham weighed to Ephron the silver, which he had named in the audience of the sons of Heth, four hundred shekels of silver, current *money* with the merchant. 17 And the field of Ephron, which *was* in Machpelah, which *was* before Mamre, the field, and the cave which *was* therein, and all the trees that *were* in the field, that *were* in all the borders round about, were made sure 18 Unto Abraham for a possession in the presence of the children of Heth, before all that went in at the gate of his city. 19 And after this, Abraham buried Sarah his wife in the cave of the field of Machpelah before Mamre: the same *is* Hebron in the land of Canaan. 20 And the field, and the cave that *is* therein, were made sure unto Abraham for a possession of a buryingplace by the sons of Heth.[33]

Isaac and Rebekah

24 And Abraham was old, *and* well stricken in age: and the LORD had blessed Abraham in all things. 2 And Abraham said unto his eldest servant of his house, that ruled over all that he had, "Put, I pray thee, thy hand under my thigh: 3 And I will make thee swear by the LORD, the God of heaven, and the God of the earth, that thou shalt not take a wife unto my son of the daughters of the Canaanites, among whom I dwell: 4 But thou shalt go unto my country, and to my kindred, and take a wife unto my son Isaac." 5 And the servant said unto him, "Peradventure the woman will not be willing to follow me unto this land: must I needs bring thy son

again unto the land from whence thou camest?" 6 And Abraham said unto him, "Beware thou that thou bring not my son thither again. 7 The LORD God of heaven, which took me from my father's house, and from the land of my kindred, and which spake unto me, and that sware unto me, saying, 'Unto thy seed will I give this land'; he shall send his angel before thee, and thou shalt take a wife unto my son from thence. 8 And if the woman will not be willing to follow thee, then thou shalt be clear from this my oath: only bring not my son thither again." 9 And the servant put his hand under the thigh of Abraham his master, and sware to him concerning that matter.[34]

10 And the servant took ten camels of the camels of his master, and departed; for all the goods of his master *were* in his hand: and he arose, and went to Mesopotamia, unto the city of Nahor. 11 And he made his camels to kneel down without the city by a well of water at the time of the evening, *even* the time that women go out to draw *water.* 12 And he said, "O LORD God of my master Abraham, I pray thee, send me good speed this day, and show kindness unto my master Abraham. 13 Behold, I stand *here* by the well of water; and the daughters of the men of the city come out to draw water: 14 And let it come to pass, that the damsel to whom I shall say, 'Let down thy pitcher, I pray thee, that I may drink'; and she shall say, 'Drink, and I will give thy camels drink also': *let the same be* she *that* thou hast appointed for thy servant Isaac; and thereby shall I know that thou hast showed kindness unto my master." 15 And it came to pass, before he had done speaking, that, behold, Rebekah came out, who was born to Bethuel, son of Milcah, the wife of Nahor, Abraham's brother, with her pitcher upon her shoulder. 16 And the damsel *was* very fair to look upon, a virgin, neither had any man known her: and she went down to the well, and filled her pitcher, and came up. 17 And the servant ran to meet her, and said, "Let me, I pray thee, drink a little water of thy pitcher." 18 And she said, "Drink, my lord": and she hasted, and let down her pitcher upon her hand, and gave him drink. 19 And when she had done giving him drink, she said, "I will draw *water* for thy camels also, until they have done drinking." 20 And she hasted, and emptied her pitcher into the trough, and ran again unto the well to draw *water,* and drew for all his camels. 21 And the man wondering at her held his peace, to wit whether the LORD had made his journey prosperous or not. 22 And

---

33. (23:1-20) With this negotiation, the Jews first secured property rights in Canaan. God's promise to Abraham begins to be fulfilled.

34. This is a genital oath of extraordinary power; it combines both the origin of life and the bond of circumcision.

it came to pass, as the camels had done drinking, that the man took a golden earring of half a shekel weight, and two bracelets for her hands of ten *shekels* weight of gold; 23 And said, "Whose daughter *art* thou? tell me, I pray thee: is there room *in* thy father's house for us to lodge in?" 24 And she said unto him, "I *am* the daughter of Bethuel the son of Milcah, which she bare unto Nahor." 25 She said moreover unto him, "We have both straw and provender enough, and room to lodge in." 26 And the man bowed down his head, and worshipped the LORD. 27 And he said, "Blessed *be* the LORD God of my master Abraham, who hath not left destitute my master of his mercy and his truth: I *being* in the way, the LORD led me to the house of my master's brethren." 28 And the damsel ran, and told *them of* her mother's house these things.

29 And Rebekah had a brother, and his name *was* Laban: and Laban ran out unto the man, unto the well. 30 And it came to pass, when he saw the earring, and bracelets upon his sister's hands, and when he heard the words of Rebekah his sister, saying, "Thus spake the man unto me," that he came unto the man; and, behold, he stood by the camels at the well. 31 And he said, "Come in, thou blessed of the LORD; wherefore standest thou without? for I have prepared the house, and room for the camels." 32 And the man came into the house: and he ungirded his camels, and gave straw and provender for the camels, and water to wash his feet, and the men's feet that *were* with him. 33 And there was set *meat* before him to eat: but he said, "I will not eat, until I have told mine errand." And he said, "Speak on." 34 And he said, "I *am* Abraham's servant. 35 And the LORD hath blessed my master greatly, and he is become great: and he hath given him flocks, and herds, and silver, and gold, and menservants, and maidservants, and camels, and asses. 36 And Sarah my master's wife bare a son to my master when she was old: and unto him hath he given all that he hath. 37 And my master made me swear, saying, 'Thou shalt not take a wife to my son of the daughters of the Canaanites, in whose land I dwell: 38 But thou shalt go unto my father's house, and to my kindred, and take a wife unto my son.' 39 And I said unto my master, 'Peradventure the woman will not follow me.' 40 And he said unto me, 'The LORD, before whom I walk, will send his angel with thee, and prosper thy way; and thou shalt take a wife for my son of my kindred, and of my father's house: 41 Then shalt thou be clear from *this* my oath, when thou comest to my kindred; and if they give not thee *one,* thou shalt be clear from my oath.' 42 And I came this day

unto the well, and said, 'O LORD God of my master Abraham, if now thou do prosper my way which I go: 43 Behold, I stand by the well of water; and it shall come to pass, that when the virgin cometh forth to draw *water,* and I say to her, "Give me, I pray thee, a little water of thy pitcher to drink"; 44 And she say to me, "Both drink thou, and I will also draw for thy camels": *let* the same *be* the woman whom the LORD hath appointed out for my master's son.' 45 And before I had done speaking in mine heart, behold, Rebekah came forth with her pitcher on her shoulder; and she went down unto the well, and drew *water:* and I said unto her, 'Let me drink, I pray thee.' 46 And she made haste, and let down her pitcher from her *shoulder,* and said, 'Drink, and I will give thy camels drink also': so I drank, and she made the camels drink also. 47 And I asked her, and said, 'Whose daughter *art* thou?' And she said, 'The daughter of Bethuel, Nahor's son, whom Milcah bare unto him': and I put the earring upon her face, and the bracelets upon her hands. 48 And I bowed down my head, and worshipped the LORD, and blessed the LORD God of my master Abraham, which had led me in the right way to take my master's brother's daughter unto his son. 49 And now, if ye will deal kindly and truly with my master, tell me: and if not, tell me; that I may turn to the right hand, or to the left."

50 Then Laban and Bethuel answered and said, "The thing proceedeth from the LORD: we cannot speak unto thee bad or good. 51 Behold, Rebekah *is* before thee; take *her,* and go, and let her be thy master's son's wife, as the LORD hath spoken." 52 And it came to pass, that, when Abraham's servant heard their words, he worshipped the LORD, *bowing himself* to the earth. 53 And the servant brought forth jewels of silver, and jewels of gold, and raiment, and gave *them* to Rebekah: he gave also to her brother and to her mother precious things. 54 And they did eat and drink, he and the men that *were* with him, and tarried all night; and they rose up in the morning, and he said, "Send me away unto my master." 55 And her brother and her mother said, "Let the damsel abide with us *a few* days, at the least ten; after that she shall go." 56 And he said unto them, "Hinder me not, seeing the LORD hath prospered my way; send me away that I may go to my master." 57 And they said, "We will call the damsel, and inquire at her mouth." 58 And they called Rebekah, and said unto her, "Wilt thou go with this man?" And she said, "I will go." 59 And they sent away Rebekah their sister, and her nurse, and Abraham's servant, and his men. 60 And they blessed Rebekah, and said unto her,

"Thou *art* our sister;
Be thou *the mother* of thousands of mil-
lions,
And let thy seed possess the gate of those
which hate them." [35]

61 And Rebekah arose, and her damsels, and
they rode upon the camels, and followed the
man: and the servant took Rebekah, and went his
way. 62 And Isaac came from the way of the
well Lahai-roi; for he dwelt in the south country.
63 And Isaac went out to meditate in the field at
the eventide: and he lifted up his eyes, and saw,
and, behold, the camels *were* coming. 64 And
Rebekah lifted up her eyes, and when she saw
Isaac, she lighted off the camel. 65 For she *had*
said unto the servant, "What man *is* this that
walketh in the field to meet us?" And the servant
had said, "It *is* my master": therefore she took a
veil, and covered herself. 66 And the servant
told Isaac all things that he had done. 67 And
Isaac brought her into his mother Sarah's tent,
and took Rebekah, and she became his wife; and
he loved her: and Isaac was comforted after his
mother's *death.*

The Last Days of Abraham

25 Then again Abraham took a wife, and her
name *was* Keturah. 2 And she bare him Zimran,
and Jokshan, and Medan, and Midian, and Ish-
bak, and Shuah. 3 And Jokshan begat Sheba,
and Dedan. And the sons of Dedan were As-
shurim, and Letushim, and Leummim. 4 And
the sons of Midian; Ephah, and Epher, and Hanoch, and Abidah, and Eldaah. All these *were* the
children of Keturah.[36] 5 And Abraham gave all
that he had unto Isaac. 6 But unto the sons of
the concubines, which Abraham had, Abraham
gave gifts, and sent them away from Isaac his son,
while he yet lives, eastward, unto the east country. 7 And these *are* the days of the years of
Abraham's life which he lived, a hundred threescore and fifteen years. 8 Then Abraham gave
up the ghost, and died in a good old age, an old
man, and full *of years;* and was gathered to his
people. 9 And his sons Isaac and Ishmael buried
him in the cave of Machpelah, in the field of
Ephron the son of Zohar the Hittite, which *is* before Mamre; 10 The field which Abraham purchased of the sons of Heth: there was Abraham
buried, and Sarah his wife. 11 And it came to
pass after the death of Abraham, that God
blessed his son Isaac; and Isaac dwelt by the well
Lahai-roi.

12 Now these *are* the generations of Ishmael,
Abraham's son, whom Hagar the Egyptian, Sarah's handmaid, bare unto Abraham: 13 And
these *are* the names of the sons of Ishmael, by
their names, according to their generations: the
firstborn of Ishmael, Nebajoth; and Kedar, and
Adbeel, and Mibsam, 14 And Mishma, and
Dumah, and Massa, 15 Hadar, and Tema, Jetur,
Naphish, and Kedemah: 16 These *are* the sons
of Ishmael, and these *are* their names, by their
towns, and by their castles; twelve princes according to their nations. 17 And these *are* the
years of the life of Ishmael, a hundred and thirty
and seven years: and he gave up the ghost and
died, and was gathered unto his people. 18 And
they dwelt from Havilah unto Shur, that *is* before
Egypt, as thou goest toward Assyria: *and* he died
in the presence of all his brethren.

JACOB

The Birth of Esau and Jacob

19 And these *are* the generations of Isaac,
Abraham's son: Abraham begat Isaac: 20 And
Isaac was forty years old when he took Rebekah
to wife, the daughter of Bethuel the Syrian of
Padan-aram, the sister to Laban the Syrian.
21 And Isaac entreated the LORD for his wife, because she *was* barren: and the LORD was entreated of him, and Rebekah his wife conceived.
22 And the children struggled together within
her; and she said, "If *it be* so, why *am* I thus?" [37]
And she went to inquire of the LORD. 23 And
the LORD said unto her,
"Two nations *are* in thy womb,
And two manner of people shall be separated from thy bowels;
And *the one* people shall be stronger than
the other people;
And the elder shall serve the younger."
24 And when her days to be delivered were
fulfilled, behold, *there were* twins in her womb.
25 And the first came out red, all over like a hairy
garment; and they called his name Esau. 26 And
after that came his brother out, and his hand took
hold on Esau's heel; and his name was called
Jacob: and Isaac *was* threescore years old when
she bare them.

27 And the boys grew: and Esau was a cunning
hunter, a man of the field; and Jacob *was* a plain
man, dwelling in tents. 28 And Isaac loved Esau,
because he did eat of *his* venison: but Rebekah

---

35. NEB: "may your sons possess the cities of their enemies."
36. (25:1-4) These eponyms explain the origin of and affirm Israel's relation with certain Arabian tribes.

37. NEB: "what does this mean?" Recognizing her condition as
an omen, Rebekah seeks an oracular explanation. She goes
to a sanctuary, presumably the one at Beer-sheba.

loved Jacob. 29 And Jacob sod pottage: and Esau came from the field, and he *was* faint: 30 And Esau said to Jacob, "Feed me, I pray thee, with that same red *pottage;* for I *am* faint": therefore was his name called Edom. 31 And Jacob said, "Sell me this day thy birthright." 32 And Esau said, "Behold, I *am* at the point to die: and what profit shall this birthright do to me?" 33 And Jacob said, "Swear to me this day"; and he sware unto him: and he sold his birthright unto Jacob. 34 Then Jacob gave Esau bread and pottage of lentils; and he did eat and drink, and rose up, and went his way. Thus Esau despised *his* birthright.[38]

Isaac and Abimelech

26 And there was a famine in the land, besides the first famine that was in the days of Abraham. And Isaac went unto Abimelech king of the Philistines unto Gerar. 2 And the LORD appeared unto him, and said, "Go not down into Egypt; dwell in the land which I shall tell thee of. 3 Sojourn in this land, and I will be with thee, and will bless thee; for unto thee, and unto thy seed, I will give all these countries, and I will perform the oath which I sware unto Abraham thy father; 4 And I will make thy seed to multiply as the stars of heaven, and will give unto thy seed all these countries; and in thy seed shall all the nations of the earth be blessed: 5 Because that Abraham obeyed my voice, and kept my charge, my commandments, my statutes, and my laws."

6 And Isaac dwelt in Gerar. 7 And the men of the place asked *him* of his wife; and he said, "She *is* my sister." for he feared to say, "*She is* my wife"; lest, *said he,* "the men of the place should kill me for Rebekah"; because she *was* fair to look upon. 8 And it came to pass, when he had been there a long time, that Abimelech king of the Philistines looked out at a window, and saw, and, behold, Isaac *was* sporting with Rebekah his wife. 9 And Abimelech called Isaac, and said, "Behold, of a surety she *is* thy wife: and how saidst thou, 'She *is* my sister'?" And Isaac said unto him, "Because I said, 'Lest I die for her.'" 10 And Abimelech said, "What *is* this thou hast done unto us? one of the people might lightly have lain with thy wife, and thou shouldest have brought guiltiness upon us." 11 And Abimelech charged all *his* people, saying, "He that toucheth this man or his wife shall surely be put to death." 12 Then Isaac sowed in that land, and received in

the same year a hundredfold: and the LORD blessed him. 13 And the man waxed great, and went forward, and grew until he became very great: 14 For he had possession of flocks, and possession of herds, and great store of servants: and the Philistines envied him. 15 For all the wells which his father's servants had digged in the days of Abraham his father, the Philistines had stopped them, and filled them with earth.[39] 16 And Abimelech said unto Isaac, "Go from us; for thou art much mightier than we."

17 And Isaac departed thence, and pitched his tent in the valley of Gerar, and dwelt there. 18 And Isaac digged again the wells of water, which they had digged in the days of Abraham his father; for the Philistines had stopped them after the death of Abraham: and he called their names after the names by which his father had called them. 19 And Isaac's servants digged in the valley, and found there a well of springing water. 20 And the herdmen of Gerar did strive with isaac's herdmen, saying, "The water *is* ours": and he called the name of the well Esek; because they strove with him. 21 And they digged another well, and strove for that also: and he called the name of it Sitnah. 22 And he removed from thence, and digged another well; and for that they strove not: and he called the name of it Rehoboth; and he said, "For now the LORD hath made room for us, and we shall be fruitful in the land."

23 And he went up from thence to Beer-sheba. 24 And the LORD appeared unto him the same night, and said, "I *am* the God of Abraham thy father: fear not, for I *am* with thee, and will bless thee, and multiply thy seed for my servant Abraham's sake." 25 And he builded an altar there, and called upon the name of the LORD, and pitched his tent there: and there Isaac's servants digged a well.

26 Then Abimelech went to him from Gerar, and Ahuzzath one of his friends, and Phichol the chief captain of his army. 27 And Isaac said unto them, "Wherefore come ye to me, seeing ye hate me, and have sent me away from you?" 28 And they said, "We saw certainly that the LORD was with thee: and we said, 'Let there be now an oath betwixt us,' *even* betwixt us and thee, and let us make a covenant with thee; 29 That thou wilt do us no hurt, as we have not touched thee, and as we have done unto thee nothing but good, and have sent thee away in peace: thou *art* now the blessed of the LORD." 30 And he made them a feast, and they did eat and drink. 31 And

---

38. (25:29-34) The birthright, normally belonging to the eldest son, conveyed a position of family leadership and a double portion of the inheritance. When applied to nations, as it is here, it suggests superiority. ("Pottage" is usually translated "soup" or "stew.")

39. MOFFATT adds continuity by putting this after verse 17.

they rose up betimes in the morning, and sware one to another: and Isaac sent them away, and they departed from him in peace. 32 And it came to pass the same day, that Isaac's servants came, and told him concerning the well which they had digged, and said unto him, "We have found water." 33 And he called it Shebah: therefore the name of the city is Beer-sheba unto this day.

34 And Esau was forty years old when he took to wife Judith the daughter of Beeri the Hittite, and Bashemath the daughter of Elon the Hittite: 35 Which were a grief of mind unto Isaac and to Rebekah.

Jacob's Duplicity

27 And it came to pass, that when Isaac was old, and his eyes were dim, so that he could not see, he called Esau his eldest son, and said unto him, "My son": and he said unto him, "Behold, here am I." 2 And he said, "Behold now, I am old, I know not the day of my death: 3 Now therefore take, I pray thee, thy weapons, thy quiver and thy bow, and go out to the field, and take me some venison; 4 And make me savory meat, such as I love, and bring it to me, that I may eat; that my soul may bless thee before I die." [40]
5 And Rebekah heard when Isaac spake to Esau his son. And Esau went to the field to hunt for venison, and to bring it. 6 And Rebekah spake unto Jacob her son, saying, "Behold, I heard thy father speak unto Esau thy brother, saying, 7 'Bring me venison, and make me savory meat, that I may eat, and bless thee before the LORD before my death.' 8 Now therefore, my son, obey my voice according to that which I command thee. 9 Go now to the flock, and fetch me from thence two good kids of the goats; and I will make them savory meat for thy father, such as he loveth: 10 And thou shalt bring it to thy father, that he may eat, and that he may bless thee before his death." 11 And Jacob said to Rebekah his mother, "Behold, Esau my brother is a hairy man, and I am a smooth man: 12 My father peradventure will feel me, and I shall seem to him as a deceiver; and I shall bring a curse upon me, and not a blessing." 13 And his mother said unto him, "Upon me be thy curse, my son: only obey my voice, and go fetch me them." 14 And he went, and fetched, and brought them to his mother: and his mother made savory meat, such as his father loved. 15 And Rebekah took goodly raiment of her eldest son Esau, which were with

her in the house, and put them upon Jacob her younger son: 16 And she put the skins of the kids of the goats upon his hands, and upon the smooth of his neck: 17 And she gave the savory meat and the bread, which she had prepared, into the hand of her son Jacob.

18 And he came unto his father, and said, "My father": and he said, "Here am I; who art thou, my son?" 19 And Jacob said unto his father, "I am Esau thy firstborn; I have done according as thou badest me: arise, I pray thee, sit and eat of my venison, that thy soul may bless me." 20 And Isaac said unto his son, "How is it that thou hast found it so quickly, my son?" And he said, "Because the LORD thy God brought it to me." 21 And Isaac said unto Jacob, "Come near, I pray thee, that I may feel thee, my son, whether thou be my very son Esau or not." 22 And Jacob went near unto Isaac his father; and he felt him, and said, "The voice is Jacob's voice, but the hands are the hands of Esau." 23 And he discerned him not, because his hands were hairy, as his brother Esau's hands: so he blessed him.[41] 24 And he said, "Art thou my very son Esau?" And he said, "I am." 25 And he said, "Bring it near to me, and I will eat of my son's venison, that my soul may bless thee." And he brought it near to him, and he did eat: and he brought him wine, and he drank. 26 And his father Isaac said unto him, "Come near now, and kiss me, my son." 27 And he came near, and kissed him: and he smelled the smell of his raiment, and blessed him, and said,

> "See, the smell of my son
> Is as the smell of a field
> Which the LORD hath blessed:

28   Therefore God give thee
> Of the dew of heaven,
> And the fatness of the earth,
> And plenty of corn and wine:

29   Let people serve thee,
> And nations bow down to thee:
> Be lord over thy brethren,
> And let thy mother's sons bow down to
>   thee:
> Cursed be every one that curseth thee,
> And blessed be he that blesseth thee."

30 And it came to pass, as soon as Isaac had made an end of blessing Jacob, and Jacob was yet scarce gone out from the presence of Isaac his father, that Esau his brother came in from his hunting. 31 And he also had made savory meat, and brought it unto his father, and said unto his father, "Let my father arise, and eat of his son's

---

40. The deathbed blessing—or deathbed curse—was thought to convey power. It could not be retracted.

41. NEB: "that is why he blessed him." The blessing is not given until verse 27.

venison, that thy soul may bless me." 32 And Isaac his father said unto him, "Who *art* thou?" And he said, "I *am* thy son, thy firstborn, Esau." 33 And Isaac trembled very exceedingly, and said, "Who? where *is* he that hath taken venison, and brought *it* me, and I have eaten of all before thou camest, and have blessed him? yea, *and he* shall be blessed." 34 And when Esau heard the words of his father, he cried with a great and exceeding bitter cry, and said unto his father, "Bless me, *even* me also, O my father." 35 And he said, "Thy brother came with subtilty, and hath taken away thy blessing." 36 And he said, "Is not he rightly named Jacob? for he hath supplanted me these two times: he took away my birthright; and, behold, now he hath taken away my blessing." And he said, "Hast thou not reserved a blessing for me?" 37 And Isaac answered and said unto Esau, "Behold, I have made him thy lord, and all his brethren have I given to him for servants; and with corn and wine have I sustained him: and what shall I do now unto thee, my son?" 38 And Esau said unto his father, "Hast thou but one blessing, my father? bless me, *even* me also, O my father." And Esau lifted up his voice, and wept. 39 And Isaac his father answered and said unto him,

> "Behold, thy dwelling shall be the fatness
> of the earth,
> And of the dew of heaven from above;[42]
40 And by thy sword shalt thou live,
> And shalt serve thy brother:
> And it shall come to pass when thou shalt
> have the dominion,
> That thou shalt break his yoke from off
> thy neck."

41 And Esau hated Jacob because of the blessing wherewith his father blessed him: and Esau said in his heart, "The days of mourning for my father are at hand; then will I slay my brother Jacob." 42 And these words of Esau her elder son were told to Rebekah: and she sent and called Jacob her younger son, and said unto him, "Behold, thy brother Esau, as touching thee, doth comfort himself, *purposing* to kill thee. 43 Now therefore, my son, obey my voice; and arise, flee thou to Laban my brother to Haran;

44 "And tarry with him a few days, until thy brother's fury turn away; 45 Until thy brother's anger turn away from thee, and he forget *that* which thou hast done to him: then I will send,

and fetch thee from thence: why should I be deprived also of you both in one day?" [43]

Jacob Sent to Laban

46 And Rebekah said to Isaac, "I am weary of my life because of the daughters of Heth: if Jacob take a wife of the daughters of Heth, such as these *which are* of the daughters of the land, what good shall my life do me?"

28 And Isaac called Jacob, and blessed him, and charged him, and said unto him, "Thou shalt not take a wife of the daughters of Canaan. 2 Arise, go to Padan-aram, to the house of Bethuel thy mother's father; and take thee a wife from thence of the daughters of Laban thy mother's brother. 3 And God Almighty bless thee, and make thee fruitful, and multiply thee, that thou mayest be a multitude of people; 4 And give thee the blessing of Abraham, to thee, and to thy seed with thee; that thou mayest inherit the land wherein thou art a stranger, which God gave unto Abraham." 5 And Isaac sent away Jacob: and he went to Padan-aram unto Laban, son of Bethuel the Syrian, the brother of Rebekah, Jacob's and Esau's mother.

6 When Esau saw that Isaac had blessed Jacob, and sent him away to Padan-aram, to take him a wife from thence; and that as he blessed him he gave him a charge, saying, "Thou shalt not take a wife of the daughters of Canaan"; 7 And that Jacob obeyed his father and his mother, and was gone to Padan-aram; 8 And Esau seeing that the daughters of Canaan pleased not Isaac his father; 9 Then went Esau unto Ishmael, and took unto the wives which he had Mahalath the daughter of Ishmael Abraham's son, the sister of Nebajoth, to be his wife.

Jacob's Dream

10 And Jacob went out from Beer-sheba, and went toward Haran. 11 And he lighted upon a certain place, and tarried there all night, because the sun was set; and he took of the stones of that place, and put *them for* his pillows, and lay down in that place to sleep. 12 And he dreamed, and behold a ladder set up on the earth, and the top of it reached to heaven: and behold the angels of God ascending and descending on it. 13 And, behold, the Lord stood above it, and said, "I *am* the Lord God of Abraham thy father, and the God of Isaac: the land whereon thou liest, to thee will I give it, and to thy seed; 14 And thy seed

---

42. The KJV rendering is incorrect. Esau's blessing should begin:
   "Ah, far from the fertile earth
      shall be your dwelling;
      far from the dew of the heavens above!" [NAB]

43. There is an implicit irony in Rebekah's lines: once he leaves home, she never sees Jacob again.

shall be as the dust of the earth; and thou shalt spread abroad to the west, and to the east, and to the north, and to the south: and in thee and in thy seed shall all the families of the earth be blessed. 15 And, behold, I *am* with thee, and will keep thee in all *places* whither thou goest, and will bring thee again into this land; for I will not leave thee, until I have done *that* which I have spoken to thee of." 16 And Jacob awaked out of his sleep, and he said, "Surely the LORD is in this place; and I knew *it* not." 17 And he was afraid, and said, "How dreadful *is* this place! this *is* none other but the house of God, and this *is* the gate of heaven."

18 And Jacob rose up early in the morning, and took the stone that he had put *for* his pillows, and set it up *for* a pillar, and poured oil upon the top of it. 19 And he called the name of that place Beth-el: but the name of that city *was called* Luz at the first. 20 And Jacob vowed a vow, saying, "If God will be with me, and will keep me in this way that I go, and will give me bread to eat, and raiment to put on, 21 So that I come again to my father's house in peace; then shall the LORD be my God: 22 And this stone, which I have set *for* a pillar, shall be God's house: and of all that thou shalt give me I will surely give the tenth unto thee."

Jacob's Two Marriages

29 Then Jacob went on his journey, and came into the land of the people of the east. 2 And he looked, and behold a well in the field, and, lo, there *were* three flocks of sheep lying by it; for out of that well they watered the flocks: and a great stone *was* upon the well's mouth. 3 And thither were all the flocks gathered: and they rolled the stone from the well's mouth, and watered the sheep, and put the stone again upon the well's mouth in his place. 4 And Jacob said unto them, "My brethren, whence *be* ye?" And they said; "Of Haran *are* we." 5 And he said unto them, "Know ye Laban the son of Nahor?" And they said, "We know *him*." 6 And he said unto them, "*Is* he well?" And they said, "*He is* well: and, behold, Rachel his daughter cometh with the sheep." 7 And he said, "Lo, *it is* yet high day, neither *is it* time that the cattle should be gathered together: water ye the sheep, and go *and* feed *them*." 8 And they said, "We cannot, until all the flocks be gathered together, and *till* they roll the stone from the well's mouth; then we water the sheep." 9 And while he yet spake with them, Rachel came with her father's sheep: for she kept them. 10 And it came to pass, when Jacob saw Rachel the daughter of Laban his mother's brother, and the sheep of Laban his mother's

brother, that Jacob went near, and rolled the stone from the well's mouth, and watered the flock of Laban his mother's brother. 11 And Jacob kissed Rachel, and lifted up his voice, and wept. 12 And Jacob told Rachel that he *was* her father's brother, and that he *was* Rebekah's son: and she ran and told her father.

13 And it came to pass, when Laban heard the tidings of Jacob his sister's son, that he ran to meet him, and embraced him, and kissed him, and brought him to his house. And he told Laban all these things. 14 And Laban said to him, "Surely thou *art* my bone and my flesh." And he abode with him the space of a month. 15 And Laban said unto Jacob, "Because thou *art* my brother, shouldest thou therefore serve me for nought? tell me, what *shall* thy wages *be?*" 16 And Laban had two daughters: the name of the elder *was* Leah, and the name of the younger *was* Rachel. 17 Leah *was* tender eyed;[44] but Rachel was beautiful and well-favored. 18 And Jacob loved Rachel; and said, "I will serve thee seven years for Rachel thy younger daughter." 19 And Laban said, "*It is* better that I give her to thee, than that I should give her to another man: abide with me." 20 And Jacob served seven years for Rachel; and they seemed unto him *but* a few days, for the love he had to her.

21 And Jacob said unto Laban, "Give *me* my wife, for my days are fulfilled, that I may go in unto her." 22 And Laban gathered together all the men of the place, and made a feast. 23 And it came to pass in the evening, that he took Leah his daughter, and brought her to him;[45] and he went in unto her. 24 And Laban gave unto his daughter Leah Zilpah his maid *for* a handmaid. 25 And it came to pass, that in the morning, behold, it *was* Leah: and he said to Laban, "What *is* this thou hast done unto me? did not I serve with thee for Rachel? wherefore then hast thou beguiled me?" 26 And Laban said, "It must not be so done in our country, to give the younger before the firstborn. 27 Fulfil her week,[46] and we will give thee this also for the service which thou shalt serve with me yet seven other years." 28 And Jacob did so, and fulfilled her week: and he gave him Rachel his daughter to wife also. 29 And Laban gave to Rachel his daughter Bilhah his handmaid to be her maid. 30 And he went in also unto Rachel, and he loved also Rachel more than Leah, and served with him yet seven other years.

---

44. JB: "There was no sparkle in Leah's eyes."
45. The custom was to keep the bride veiled until the wedding night.
46. NEB: "Go through with the seven days' feast for the elder."

Jacob's Children [47]

31 And when the LORD saw that Leah *was* hated, he opened her womb: but Rachel *was* barren. 32 And Leah conceived, and bare a son; and she called his name Reuben: for she said, "Surely the LORD hath looked upon my affliction; now therefore my husband will love me." 33 And she conceived again, and bare a son; and said, "Because the LORD hath heard that I *was* hated, he hath therefore given me this *son* also": and she called his name Simeon. 34 And she conceived again, and bare a son; and said, "Now this time will my husband be joined unto me, because I have borne him three sons": therefore was his name called Levi. 35 And she conceived again, and bare a son; and she said, "Now will I praise the LORD: therefore she called his name Judah," and left bearing.

30 And when Rachel saw that she bare Jacob no children, Rachel envied her sister; and said unto Jacob, "Give me children, or else I die." 2 And Jacob's anger was kindled against Rachel; and he said, "*Am* I in God's stead, who hath withheld from thee the fruit of the womb?" 3 And she said, "Behold my maid Bilhah, go in unto her; and she shall bear upon my knees, that I may also have children by her." 4 And she gave him Bilhah her handmaid to wife: and Jacob went in unto her. 5 And Bilhah conceived, and bare Jacob a son. 6 And Rachel said, "God hath judged me, and hath also heard my voice, and hath given me a son": therefore called she his name Dan. 7 And Bilhah Rachel's maid conceived again, and bare Jacob a second son. 8 And Rachel said, "With great wrestlings have I wrestled with my sister, and I have prevailed": and she called his name Naphtali. 9 When Leah saw that she had left bearing, she took Zilpah her maid, and gave her Jacob to wife. 10 And Zilpah Leah's maid bare Jacob a son. 11 And Leah said, "A troop cometh": and she called his name Gad. 12 And Zilpah Leah's maid bare Jacob a second son. 13 And Leah said, "Happy am I, for the daughters will call me blessed": and she called his name Asher.

14 And Reuben went in the days of wheat harvest, and found mandrakes in the field, and brought them unto his mother Leah. Then Rachel said to Leah, "Give me, I pray thee, of thy son's mandrakes." 15 And she said unto her, "*Is it* a small matter that thou hast taken my husband? and wouldest thou take away my son's mandrakes also?" And Rachel said, "Therefore he shall lie with thee to-night for thy son's mandrakes." 16 And Jacob came out of the field in the evening, and Leah went out to meet him, and said, "Thou must come in unto me; for surely I have hired thee with my son's mandrakes." And he lay with her that night. 17 And God hearkened unto Leah, and she conceived, and bare Jacob the fifth son. 18 And Leah said, "God hath given me my hire, because I have given my maiden to my husband": and she called his name Issachar. 19 And Leah conceived again, and bare Jacob the sixth son. 20 And Leah said, "God hath endued me *with* a good dowry; now will my husband dwell with me, because I have borne him six sons": and she called his name Zebulun. 21 And afterward she bare a daughter, and called her name Dinah. 22 And God remembered Rachel, and God hearkened to her, and opened her womb. 23 And she conceived, and bare a son; and said, "God hath taken away my reproach": 24 And she called his name Joseph; and said, "The LORD shall add to me another son."

Jacob Outwits Laban

25 And it came to pass, when Rachel had borne Joseph, that Jacob said unto Laban, "Send me away, that I may go unto mine own place, and to my country. 26 Give *me* my wives and my children, for whom I have served thee, and let me go: for thou knowest my service which I have done thee." 27 And Laban said unto him, "I pray thee, if I have found favor in thine eyes, *tarry: for* I have learned by experience that the LORD hath blessed me for thy sake." 28 And he said, "Appoint me thy wages, and I will give *it*." 29 And he said unto him, "Thou knowest how I have served thee, and how thy cattle was with me. 30 For *it was* little which thou hadst before I *came,* and it is *now* increased unto a multitude; and the LORD hath blessed thee since my coming: and now, when shall I provide for mine own house also?" 31 And he said, "What shall I give thee?" And Jacob said, "Thou shalt not give me any thing: if thou wilt do this thing for me, I will again feed *and* keep thy flock. 32 I will pass through all thy flock to-day, removing from thence all the speckled and spotted cattle, and all the brown cattle among the sheep, and the spotted and speckled among the goats: and *of such* shall be my hire. 33 So shall my righteousness answer for me in time to come; when it shall come for my hire before thy face: every one that

---

47. (29:31–30:24) The story of the birth competition sought to explain the origin of the names of the Israelite tribes. In Hebrew *Reuben* means "see, a son"; *Simeon,* "hearing"; *Levi,* "union"; *Judah,* "praise"; *Dan,* "judge"; *Naphtali,* "trickery"; *Gad,* "good fortune"; *Asher,* "happy"; *Issachar,* "reward"; *Zebulun,* "prince"; and *Joseph,* either "he takes away" or "may he add."

is not speckled and spotted among the goats, and brown among the sheep, that shall be counted stolen with me." 34 And Laban said, "Behold, I would it might be according to thy word." [48] 35 And he removed that day the he goats that were ring-streaked and spotted, and all the she goats that were speckled and spotted, *and* every one that had *some* white in it, and all the brown among the sheep, and gave *them* into the hand of his sons. 36 And he set three days' journey betwixt himself and Jacob: and Jacob fed the rest of Laban's flocks.

37 And Jacob took him rods of green poplar, and of the hazel and chestnut tree; and pilled white streaks in them, and made the white appear which *was* in the rods. 38 And he set the rods which he had pilled before the flocks in the gutters in the watering troughs when the flocks came to drink, that they should conceive when they came to drink. 39 And the flocks conceived before the rods, and brought forth cattle ring-streaked, speckled, and spotted. 40 And Jacob did separate the lambs, and set the faces of the flocks toward the ring-streaked, and all the brown in the flock of Laban; and he put his own flocks by themselves, and put them not unto Laban's cattle. 41 And it came to pass, whensoever the stronger cattle did conceive, that Jacob laid the rods before the eyes of the cattle in the gutters, that they might conceive among the rods. 42 But when the cattle were feeble, he put *them* not in: so the feebler were Laban's, and the stronger Jacob's. 43 And the man increased exceedingly, and had much cattle, and maidservants, and menservants, and camels, and asses.

Jacob Returns Home

31 And he heard the words of Laban's sons, saying, "Jacob hath taken away all that *was* our father's; and of *that* which *was* our father's hath he gotten all this glory." 2 And Jacob beheld the countenance of Laban, and, behold, it *was* not toward him as before. 3 And the LORD said unto Jacob, "Return unto the land of thy fathers, and to thy kindred; and I will be with thee." 4 And Jacob sent and called Rachel and Leah to the field unto his flock, 5 And said unto them, "I see your father's countenance, that it *is* not toward me as before; but the God of my father hath been with me. 6 And ye know that with all my power I have served your father. 7 And your father hath deceived me, and changed my wages ten

times; but God suffered him not to hurt me. 8 If he said thus, 'The speckled shall be thy wages'; then all the cattle bare speckled: and if he said thus, 'The ring-streaked shall be thy hire'; then bare all the cattle ring-streaked. 9 Thus God hath taken away the cattle of your father, and given *them* to me. 10 And it came to pass at the time that the cattle conceived, that I lifted up mine eyes, and saw in a dream, and, behold, the rams which leaped upon the cattle *were* ring-streaked, speckled, and grizzled. 11 And the angel of God spake unto me in a dream, *saying,* 'Jacob': and I said, 'Here *am* I.' 12 And he said, 'Lift up now thine eyes, and see, all the rams which leap upon the cattle *are* ring-streaked, speckled, and grizzled: for I have seen all that Laban doeth unto thee. 13 I *am* the God of Beth-el, where thou anointedst the pillar, *and* where thou vowedst a vow unto me: now arise, get thee out from this land, and return unto the land of thy kindred.'" 14 And Rachel and Leah answered and said unto him, "*Is there* yet any portion or inheritance for us in our father's house? 15 Are we not counted of him strangers? for he hath sold us, and hath quite devoured also our money.[49] 16 For all the riches which God hath taken from our father, that *is* ours, and our children's: now then, whatsoever God hath said unto thee, do."

17 Then Jacob rose up, and set his sons and his wives upon camels; 18 And he carried away all his cattle, and all his goods which he had gotten, the cattle of his getting, which he had gotten in Padan-aram, for to go to Isaac his father in the land of Canaan. 19 And Laban went to shear his sheep: and Rachel had stolen the images that *were* her father's.[50] 20 And Jacob stole away unawares to Laban the Syrian, in that he told him not that he fled. 21 So he fled with all that he had; and he rose up, and passed over the river, and set his face *toward* the mount Gilead.

The Covenant with Laban

22 And it was told Laban on the third day, that Jacob was fled. 23 And he took his brethren with him, and pursued after him seven days' journey; and they overtook him in the mount Gilead. 24 And God came to Laban the Syrian in a dream by night, and said unto him, "Take heed that thou speak not to Jacob either good or

---

48. (30:31-34) In the near East, most sheep are white or light gray; most goats, black or dark brown. In promising the dark sheep and the speckled goats to Jacob, Laban seems to be making a shrewd agreement.

49. NEB: "he has sold us and spent on himself the whole of the money paid for us." MEEK; "he sold us, and has enjoyed the usufruct of our dowry as well."
50. NAB: "her father's household idols." These may have been statues used in divination. The author satirically disparages their worth in verses 34-35.

bad." [51] 25 Then Laban overtook Jacob. Now Jacob had pitched his tent in the mount: and Laban with his brethren pitched in the mount of Gilead. 26 And Laban said to Jacob, "What hast thou done, that thou hast stolen away unawares to me, and carried away my daughters, as captives *taken* with the sword? 27 Wherefore didst thou flee away secretly, and steal away from me; and didst not tell me, that I might have sent thee away with mirth, and with songs, with tabret, and with harp? 28 And has not suffered me to kiss my sons and my daughters? thou hast now done foolishly in *so* doing. 29 It is in the power of my hand to do you hurt: but the God of your father spake unto me yesternight, saying, 'Take thou heed that thou speak not to Jacob either good or bad.' 30 And now, *though* thou wouldest needs be gone, because thou sore longedst after thy father's house, *yet* wherefore hast thou stolen my gods?" 31 And Jacob answered and said to Laban, "Because I was afraid: for I said, Peradventure thou wouldest take by force thy daughters from me. 32 With whomsoever thou findest thy gods, let him not live: before our brethren discern thou what *is* thine with me, and take *it* to thee." For Jacob knew not that Rachel had stolen them.

33 And Laban went into Jacob's tent, and into Leah's tent, and into the two maidservants' tents; but he found *them* not. Then went he out of Leah's tent, and entered into Rachel's tent. 34 Now Rachel had taken the images, and put them in the camel's furniture, and sat upon them. And Laban searched all the tent, but found *them* not. 35 And she said to her father, "Let it not displease my lord that I cannot rise up before thee; for the custom of women *is* upon me." And he searched, but found not the images.

36 And Jacob was wroth, and chode with Laban: and Jacob answered and said to Laban, "What *is* my trespass? what *is* my sin, that thou hast so hotly pursued after me? 37 Whereas thou hast searched all my stuff, what hast thou found of all thy household stuff? set *it* here before my brethren and thy brethren, that they may judge betwixt us both. 38 This twenty years *have* I *been* with thee; thy ewes and thy she goats have not cast their young, and the rams of thy flock have I not eaten. 39 That which was torn *of beasts* I brought not unto thee; I bare the loss of it; of my hand didst thou require it, *whether* stolen by day, or stolen by night. 40 *Thus* I was; in the day the drought consumed me, and the frost by night; and my sleep departed from mine eyes. 41 Thus have I been twenty years in thy house: I served

thee fourteen years for thy two daughters, and six years for thy cattle; and thou hast changed my wages ten times. 42 Except the God of my father, the God of Abraham, and the fear of Isaac, had been with me, surely thou hadst sent me away now empty. God hath seen mine affliction and the labor of my hands, and rebuked *thee* yesternight."

43 And Laban answered and said unto Jacob, "*These* daughters *are* my daughters, and *these* children *are* my children, and *these* cattle *are* my cattle, and all that thou seest *is* mine: and what can I do this day unto these my daughters, or unto their children which they have borne? 44 Now therefore come thou, let us make a covenant, I and thou; and let it be for a witness between me and thee." 45 And Jacob took a stone, and set it up *for* a pillar. 46 And Jacob said unto his brethren, "Gather stones"; and they took stones, and made a heap: and they did eat there upon the heap. 47 And Laban called it Jegarsahadutha: but Jacob called it Galeed. 48 And Laban said, "This heap *is* a witness between me and thee this day." Therefore was the name of it called Galeed. 49 And Mizpah; for he said, "The Lord watch between me and thee, when we are absent one from another. 50 If thou shalt afflict my daughters, or if thou shalt take *other* wives beside my daughters, no man *is* with us; see, God *is* witness betwixt me and thee." 51 And Laban said to Jacob, "Behold this heap, and behold *this* pillar, which I have cast betwixt me and thee; 52 This heap *be* witness, and *this* pillar *be* witness, that I will not pass over this heap to thee, and that thou shalt not pass over this heap and this pillar unto me, for harm. 53 The God of Abraham, and the God of Nahor, the God of their father, judge betwixt us." And Jacob sware by the fear of his father Isaac. 54 Then Jacob offered sacrifice upon the mount, and called his brethren to eat bread: and they did eat bread, and tarried all night in the mount. 55 And early in the morning Laban rose up, and kissed his sons and his daughters, and blessed them: and Laban departed, and returned unto his place.

Preparation to Meet Esau

32 And Jacob went on his way, and the angels of God met him. 2 And when Jacob saw them, he said, "This *is* God's host": and he called the name of that place Mahanaim.

3 And Jacob sent messengers before him to Esau his brother unto the land of Seir, the country of Edom. 4 And he commanded them, saying, "Thus shall ye speak unto my lord Esau; 'Thy servant Jacob saith thus, "I have sojourned

---

51. The counsel is to let Jacob do as he wishes. Torah: "Beware of attempting anything with Jacob, good or bad."

with Laban, and stayed there until now: 5 And I have oxen, and asses, flocks, and menservants, and womenservants: and I have sent to tell my lord, that I may find grace in thy sight." ' "
6 And the messengers returned to Jacob, saying, "We came to thy brother Esau, and also he cometh to meet thee, and four hundred men with him." 7 Then Jacob was greatly afraid and distressed: and he divided the people that *was* with him, and the flocks, and herds, and the camels, into two bands; 8 And said, "If Esau come to the one company, and smite it, then the other company which is left shall escape."

9 And Jacob said, "O God of my father Abraham, and God of my father Isaac, the LORD which saidst unto me, 'Return unto thy country, and to thy kindred, and I will deal well with thee': 10 I am not worthy of the least of all the mercies, and of all the truth, which thou hast showed unto thy servant; for with my staff I passed over this Jordan; and now I am become two bands.[52] 11 Deliver me, I pray thee, from the hand of my brother, from the hand of Esau: for I fear him, lest he will come and smite me, *and* the mother with the children. 12 And thou saidst, 'I will surely do thee good, and make thy seed as the sand of the sea, which cannot be numbered for multitude.' "

13 And he lodged there that same night; and took of that which came to his hand a present for Esau his brother; 14 Two hundred she goats and twenty he goats, two hundred ewes and twenty rams, 15 Thirty milch camels with their colts, forty kine and ten bulls, twenty she asses and ten foals. 16 And he delivered *them* into the hand of his servants, every drove by themselves; and said unto his servants, "Pass over before me, and put a space betwixt drove and drove." 17 And he commanded the foremost, saying, "When Esau my brother meeteth thee, and asketh thee, saying, 'Whose *art* thou?' and 'whither goest thou?' and 'whose *are* these before thee?' 18 Then thou shalt say, '*They be* thy servant Jacob's; it *is* a present sent unto my lord Esau: and, behold, also he *is* behind us.' " 19 And so commanded he the second, and the third, and all that followed the droves, saying, "On this manner shall ye speak unto Esau, when ye find him. 20 And say ye moreover, 'Behold, thy servant Jacob *is* behind us.' " For he said, "I will appease him with the present that goeth before me, and afterward I will see his face; peradventure he will accept of me." 21 So went the present over before him; and himself lodged that night in the company. 22 And he rose up that night, and took his two wives, and his

two womenservants, and his eleven sons, and passed over the ford Jabbok. 23 And he took them, and sent them over the brook, and sent over that he had.

Jacob Wrestles with God

24 And Jacob was left alone; and there wrestled a man with him until the breaking of the day.[53] 25 And when he saw that he prevailed not against him, he touched the hollow of his thigh; and the hollow of Jacob's thigh was out of joint, as he wrestled with him. 26 And he said, "Let me go, for the day breaketh." And he said, "I will not let thee go, except thou bless me." 27 And he said unto him, "What *is* thy name?" And he said, "Jacob." 28 And he said, "Thy name shall be called no more Jacob, but Israel: for as a prince hast thou power with God and with men, and hast prevailed." 29 And Jacob asked *him*, and said, "Tell *me*, I pray thee, thy name." And he said, "Wherefore *is* it *that* thou dost ask after my name?" And he blessed him there. 30 And Jacob called the name of the place Peniel: "for I have seen God face to face, and my life is preserved." 31 And as he passed over Penuel the sun rose upon him, and he halted upon his thigh. 32 Therefore the children of Israel eat not *of* the sinew which shrank, which *is* upon the hollow of the thigh, unto this day; because he touched the hollow of Jacob's thigh in the sinew that shrank.

Reconciliation with Esau

33 And Jacob lifted up his eyes, and looked, and, behold, Esau came, and with him four hundred men. And he divided the children unto Leah, and unto Rachel, and unto the two handmaids. 2 And he put the handmaids and their children foremost, and Leah and her children after, and Rachel and Joseph hindermost. 3 And he passed over before them, and bowed himself to the ground seven times, until he came near to his brother. 4 And Esau ran to meet him, and embraced him, and fell on his neck, and kissed him: and they wept. 5 And he lifted up his eyes, and saw the women and the children, and said, "Who *are* those with thee?" And he said, "The children which God hath graciously given thy servant." 6 Then the handmaidens came near, they and their children, and they bowed themselves.

---

52. NEB: "When I crossed the Jordan, I had nothing but the staff in my hand; now I have two companies."

53. (32:24-32) This enigmatic story explains a Jewish dietary taboo and tells how Peniel got its name. It probably derived from an ancient tradition wherein one fought with an evil spirit—here, perhaps a river demon—who had to vanish before sunrise.

7 And Leah also with her children came near, and bowed themselves: and after came Joseph near and Rachel, and they bowed themselves. 8 And he said, "What *meanest* thou by all this drove which I met?" And he said, "*These are* to find grace in the sight of my lord." 9 And Esau said, "I have enough, my brother; keep that thou hast unto thyself." 10 And Jacob said, "Nay, I pray thee, if now I have found grace in thy sight, then receive my present at my hand: for therefore I have seen thy face, as though I had seen the face of God, and thou wast pleased with me. 11 Take, I pray thee, my blessing that is brought to thee; because God hath dealt graciously with me, and because I have enough." And he urged him, and he took *it.* 12 And he said, "Let us take our journey, and let us go, and I will go before thee." 13 And he said unto him, "My lord knoweth that the children *are* tender, and the flocks and herds with young *are* with me; and if men should overdrive them one day, all the flock will die. 14 Let my lord, I pray thee, pass over before his servant; and I will lead on softly, according as the cattle that goeth before me and the children be able to endure, until I come unto my lord unto Seir." 15 And Esau said, "Let me now leave with thee *some* of the folk that *are* with me." And he said, "What needeth it? let me find grace in the sight of my lord." 16 So Esau returned that day on his way unto Seir. 17 And Jacob journeyed to Succoth, and built him a house, and made booths for his cattle: therefore the name of the place is called Succoth.

18 And Jacob came to Shalem, a city of Shechem,[54] which *is* in the land of Canaan, when he came from Padan-aram; and pitched his tent before the city. 19 And he bought a parcel of a field, where he had spread his tent, at the hand of the children of Hamor, Shechem's father, for a hundred pieces of money. 20 And he erected there an altar, and called it El-Elohe-Israel.

Dinah Is Ravished and Revenged

34 And Dinah the daughter of Leah, which she bare unto Jacob, went out to see the daughters of the land. 2 And when Shechem the son of Hamor the Hivite, prince of the country, saw her, he took her, and lay with her, and defiled her. 3 And his soul clave unto Dinah the daughter of Jacob, and he loved the damsel, and spake kindly unto the damsel. 4 And Shechem spake unto his father Hamor, saying, "Get me this damsel to wife." 5 And Jacob heard that he had defiled

54. (33:18-19) These verses show that the name *Shechem* applies both to Hamor's son and to the place he lives.

Dinah his daughter: now his sons were with his cattle in the field: and Jacob held his peace until they were come. 6 And Hamor the father of Shechem went out unto Jacob to commune with him. 7 And the sons of Jacob came out of the field when they heard *it:* and the men were grieved, and they were very wroth, because he had wrought folly in Israel in lying with Jacob's daughter; which thing ought not to be done. 8 And Hamor communed with them, saying, "The soul of my son Shechem longeth for your soul of my son Shechem longeth for your daughter: I pray you give her him to wife. 9 And make ye marriages with us, *and* give your daughters unto us, and take our daughters unto you. 10 And ye shall dwell with us: and the land shall be before you; dwell and trade ye therein, and get you possessions therein." 11 And Shechem said unto her father and unto her brethren, "Let me find grace in your eyes, and what ye shall say unto me I will give. 12 Ask me never so much dowry and gift, and I will give according as ye shall say unto me: but give me the damsel to wife." 13 And the sons of Jacob answered Shechem and Hamor his father deceitfully, and said, because he had defiled Dinah their sister: 14 And they say unto them, "We cannot do this thing, to give our sister to one that is uncircumcised; for that *were* a reproach unto us: 15 But in this will we consent unto you: If ye will be as we *be*, that every male of you be circumcised; 16 Then will we give our daughters unto you, and we will take your daughters to us, and we will dwell with you, and we will become one people. 17 But if ye will not hearken unto us, to be circumcised; then will we take our daughter, and we will be gone."

18 And their words pleased Hamor and Shechem Hamor's son. 19 And the young man deferred not to do the thing, because he had delight in Jacob's daughter: and he *was* more honorable than all the house of his father. 20 And Hamor and Shechem his son came unto the gate of their city, and communed with the men of their city, saying, 21 "These men *are* peaceable with us; therefore let them dwell in the land, and trade therein; for the land, behold, *it is* large enough for them; let us take their daughters to us for wives, and let us give them our daughters. 22 Only herein will the men consent unto us for to dwell with us, to be one people, if every male among us be circumcised, as they *are* circumcised. 23 *Shall* not their cattle and their substance and every beast of theirs *be* ours? only let us consent unto them, and they will dwell with us." 24 And unto Hamor and unto Shechem his son hearkened all that went out of the gate of his city; and every male was circumcised, all that went out of the

gate of his city.[55]   25 And it came to pass on the third day, when they were sore, that two of the sons of Jacob, Simeon and Levi, Dinah's brethren, took each man his sword, and came upon the city boldly, and slew all the males.   26 And they slew Hamor and Shechem his son with the edge of the sword, and took Dinah out of Shechem's house, and went out.   27 The sons of Jacob came upon the slain, and spoiled the city, because they had defiled their sister.   28 They took their sheep, and their oxen, and their asses, and that which *was* in the city, and that which *was* in the field, 29 And all their wealth, and all their little ones, and their wives took they captive, and spoiled even all that *was* in the house.

30 And Jacob said to Simeon and Levi, "Ye have troubled me to make me to stink among the inhabitants of the land, among the Canaanites and the Perizzites: and I *being* few in number, they shall gather themselves together against me, and slay me; and I shall be destroyed, I and my house."   31 And they said, "Should he deal with our sister as with a harlot?"

Jacob Returns to Bethel

35 And God said unto Jacob, "Arise, go up to Beth-el, and dwell there: and make there an altar unto God, that appeared unto thee when thou fleddest from the face of Esau thy brother." 2 Then Jacob said unto his household, and to all that *were* with him, "Put away the strange gods that *are* among you, and be clean, and change your garments: 3 And let us arise, and go up to Beth-el; and I will make there an altar unto God, who answered me in the day of my distress, and was with me in the way which I went."   4 And they gave unto Jacob all the strange gods which *were* in their hand, and *all their* earrings which *were* in their ears; and Jacob hid them under the oak which *was* by Shechem.   5 And they journeyed: and the terror of God was upon the cities that *were* round about them, and they did not pursue after the sons of Jacob.   6 So Jacob came to Luz which *is* in the land of Canaan, that *is,* Beth-el, he and all the people that *were* with him. 7 And he built there an altar, and called the place El-beth-el; because there God appeared unto him, when he fled from the face of his brother.[56] 8 But Deborah Rebekah's nurse died, and she

was buried beneath Beth-el under an oak: and the name of it was called Allon-bachuth.

9 And God appeared unto Jacob again, when he came out of Padan-aram, and blessed him. 10 And God said unto him, "Thy name *is* Jacob: thy name shall not be called any more Jacob, but Israel shall be thy name"; and he called his name Israel.   11 And God said unto him, "I *am* God Almighty: be fruitful and multiply; a nation and a company of nations shall be of thee, and kings shall come out of thy loins;   12 And the land which I gave Abraham and Isaac, to thee I will give it, and to thy seed after thee will I give the land."   13 And God went up from him in the place where he talked with him.   14 And Jacob set up a pillar in the place where he talked with him, *even* a pillar of stone: and he poured a drink offering thereon, and he poured oil thereon. 15 And Jacob called the name of the place where God spake with him, Beth-el.

16 And they journeyed from Beth-el; and there was but a little way to come to Ephrath: and Rachel travailed, and she had hard labor.   17 And it came to pass, when she was in hard labor, that the midwife said unto her, "Fear not; thou shalt have this son also."   18 And it came to pass, as her soul was in departing, (for she died,) that she called his name Ben-oni: but his father called him Benjamin.   19 And Rachel died, and was buried in the way to Ephrath, which *is* Bethlehem. 20 And Jacob set a pillar upon her grave: that *is* the pillar of Rachel's grave unto this day.

21 And Israel journeyed, and spread his tent beyond the tower of Edar.   22 And it came to pass, when Israel dwelt in that land, that Reuben went and lay with Bilhah his father's concubine: and Israel heard *it*.[57]

Now the sons of Jacob were twelve: 23 The sons of Leah; Reuben, Jacob's firstborn, and Simeon, and Levi, and Judah, and Issachar, and Zebulun: 24 The sons of Rachel; Joseph, and Benjamin: 25 And the sons of Bilhah, Rachel's handmaid; Dan, and Naphtali: 26 And the sons of Zilpah, Leah's handmaid; Gad, and Asher. These *are* the sons of Jacob, which were born to him in Padan-aram.

27 And Jacob came unto Isaac his father unto Mamre, unto the city of Arba, which *is* Hebron,

---

55. I.e., all the men capable of marching out to war. With these men disabled, the city is vulnerable to Simeon, Levi, and their followers.

56. (35:1-7) With these acts—the ritual purification, the rejection of false gods and the amulets of idolatry, and the building of the altar—Jacob is fulfilling the promise made in 28:20-22.

57. (35:21-22) This fragment explains Reuben's loss of prestige as the first-born son. Jacob recalls the event in his deathbed testament (49:3-4).

where Abraham and Isaac sojourned. 28 And the days of Isaac were a hundred and fourscore years. 29 And Isaac gave up the ghost, and died, and was gathered unto his people, *being* old and full of days: and his sons Esau and Jacob buried him.

The Descendants of Esau

36 Now these *are* the generations of Esau, who *is* Edom. 2 Esau took his wives of the daughters of Canaan; Adah the daughter of Elon the Hittite, and Aholibamah the daughter of Anah the daughter of Zibeon the Hivite; 3 And Bashemath Ishmael's daughter, sister of Nebajoth. 4 And Adah bare to Esau Eliphaz, and Bashemath bare Reuel; 5 And Aholibamah bare Jeush, and Jaalam, and Korah: these *are* the sons of Esau, which were born unto him in the land of Canaan. 6 And Esau took his wives, and his sons, and his daughters, and all the persons of his house, and his cattle, and all his beasts, and all his substance, which he had got in the land of Canaan; and went into the country from the face of his brother Jacob. 7 For their riches were more than that they might dwell together; and the land wherein they were strangers could not bear them because of their cattle. 8 Thus dwelt Esau in mount Seir: Esau *is* Edom.

9 And these *are* the generations of Esau the father of the Edomites in mount Seir: 10 These *are* the names of Esau's sons; Eliphaz the son of Adah the wife of Esau, Reuel the son of Bashemath the wife of Esau. 11 And the sons of Eliphaz were Teman, Omar, Zepho, and Gatam, and Kenaz. 12 And Timna was concubine to Eliphaz Esau's son; and she bare to Eliphaz Amalek: these *were* the sons of Adah Esau's wife. 13 And these *are* the sons of Reuel; Nahath, and Zerah, Shammah, and Mizzah: these were the sons of Bashemath Esau's wife. 14 And these were the sons of Aholibamah, the daughter of Anah the daughter of Zibeon, Esau's wife: and she bare to Esau Jeush, and Jaalam, and Korah.

15 These *were* dukes of the sons of Esau: the sons of Eliphaz the first born *son* of Esau; duke Teman, duke Omar, duke Zepho, duke Kenaz, 16 Duke Korah, duke Gatam, *and* duke Amalek: these *are* the dukes *that came* of Eliphaz in the land of Edom: these *were* the sons of Adah. 17 And these *are* the sons of Reuel Esau's son; duke Nahath, duke Zerah, duke Shammah, duke Mizzah: these *are* the dukes *that came* of Reuel in the land of Edom: these *are* the sons of Bashemath Esau's wife. 18 And these *are* the sons of Aholibamah Esau's wife; duke Jeush, duke Jaalam, duke Korah: these *were* the dukes

that came of Aholibamah the daughter of Anah, Esau's wife. 19 These *are* the sons of Esau, who *is* Edom, and these *are* their dukes.

20 These *are* the sons of Seir the Horite, who inhabited the land; Lotan, and Shobal, and Zibeon, and Anah, 21 And Dishon, and Ezer, and Dishan: these *are* the dukes of the Horites, the children of Seir in the land of Edom. 22 And the children of Lotan were Hori and Hemam; and Lotan's sister *was* Timna. 23 And the children of Shobal *were* these; Alvan, and Manahath, and Ebal, Shepho, and Onam. 24 And these *are* the children of Zibeon; both Ajah, and Anah: this *was that* Anah that found the mules in the wilderness, as he fed the asses of Zibeon his father. 25 And the children of Anah *were* these; Dishon, and Aholibamah the daughter of Anah. 26 And these *are* the children of Dishon; Hemdan, and Eshban, and Ithran, and Cheran. 27 The children of Ezer *are* these; Bilhan, and Zaavan, and Akan. 28 The children of Dishan *are* these; Uz, and Aran. 29 These *are* the dukes *that came* of the Horites; duke Lotan, duke Shobal, duke Zibeon, duke Anah, 30 Duke Dishon, duke Ezer, duke Dishan: these *are* the dukes *that came* of Hori, among their dukes in the land of Seir.

31 And these *are* the kings that reigned in the land of Edom, before there reigned any king over the children of Israel. 32 And Bela the son of Beor reigned in Edom: and the name of his city *was* Dinhabah. 33 And Bela died, and Jobab the son of Zerah of Bozrah reigned in his stead. 34 And Jobab died, and Husham of the land of Temani reigned in his stead. 35 And Husham died, and Hadad the son of Bedad, who smote Midian in the field of Moab, reigned in his stead: and the name of his city *was* Avith. 36 And Hadad died, and Samlah of Masrekah reigned in his stead. 37 And Samlah died, and Saul of Rehoboth *by* the river reigned in his stead. 38 And Saul died, and Baal-hanan the son of Achbor reigned in his stead. 39 And Baal-hanan the son of Achbor died, and Hadar reigned in his stead: and the name of his city *was* Pau; and his wife's name *was* Mehetabel, the daughter of Matred, the daughter of Mezahab. 40 And these *are* the names of the dukes *that came* of Esau, according to their families, after their places, by their names; duke Timnah, duke Alvah, duke Jetheth, 41 Duke Aholibamah, duke Elah, duke Pinon, 42 Duke Kenaz, duke Teman, duke Mibzar, 43 Duke Magdiel, duke Iram: these *be* the dukes of Edom, according to their habitations in the land of their possession: he *is* Esau the father of the Edomites.

JOSEPH

Joseph Sold into Egypt

37 And Jacob dwelt in the land wherein his father was a stranger, in the land of Canaan. 2 These *are* the generations of Jacob.

Joseph, *being* seventeen years old, was feeding the flock with his brethren; and the lad *was* with the sons of Bilhah, and with the sons of Zilpah, his father's wives: and Joseph brought unto his father their evil report. 3 Now Israel loved Joseph more than all his children, because he *was* the son of his old age: and he made him a coat of *many* colors. 4 And when his brethren saw that their father loved him more than all his brethren, they hated him, and could not speak peaceably unto him.

5 And Joseph dreamed a dream, and he told *it* his brethren: and they hated him yet the more. 6 And he said unto them, "Hear, I pray you, this dream which I have dreamed: 7 For, behold, we *were* binding sheaves in the field, and, lo, my sheaf arose, and also stood upright; and, behold, your sheaves stood round about, and made obeisance to my sheaf." 8 And his brethren said to him, "Shalt thou indeed reign over us? or shalt thou indeed have dominion over us?" And they hated him yet the more for his dreams, and for his words. 9 And he dreamed yet another dream, and told it his brethren, and said, "Behold, I have dreamed a dream more; and, behold, the sun and the moon and the eleven stars made obeisance to me." 10 And he told *it* to his father, and to his brethren: and his father rebuked him, and said unto him, "What *is* this dream that thou hast dreamed? Shall I and thy mother and thy brethren indeed come to bow down ourselves to thee to the earth?" 11 And his brethren envied him; but his father observed the saying.

12 And his brethren went to feed their father's flock in Shechem. 13 And Israel said unto Joseph, "Do not thy brethren feed *the flock* in Shechem? come, and I will send thee unto them." And he said to him, "Here *am I.*" 14 And he said to him, "Go, I pray thee, see whether it be well with thy brethren, and well with the flocks; and bring me word again." So he sent him out of the vale of Hebron, and he came to Shechem. 15 And a certain man found him, and, behold, *he was* wandering in the field: and the man asked him, saying, "What seekest thou?" 16 And he said, "I seek my brethren: tell me, I pray thee, where they feed *their flocks.*" 17 And the man said, "They are departed hence; for I heard them say, 'Let us go to Dothan.'" And Joseph went after his brethren, and found them in Dothan.

18 And when they saw him afar off, even before he came near unto them, they conspired against him to slay him. 19 And they said one to another, "Behold, this dreamer cometh. 20 Come now therefore, and let us slay him, and cast him into some pit, and we will say, 'Some evil beast hath devoured him'; and we shall see what will become of his dreams." 21 And Reuben heard *it,* and he delivered him out of their hands; and said, "Let us not kill him." 22 And Reuben said unto them, "Shed no blood, *but* cast him into this pit that *is* in the wilderness, and lay no hand upon him"; that he might rid him out of their hands, to deliver him to his father again.

23 And it came to pass, when Joseph was come unto his brethren, that they stripped Joseph out of his coat, *his* coat of *many* colors that *was* on him; 24 And they took him, and cast him into a pit: and the pit *was* empty, *there was* no water in it.[58] 25 And they sat down to eat bread: and they lifted up their eyes and looked, and, behold, a company of Ishmaelites came from Gilead, with their camels bearing spicery and balm and myrrh, going to carry *it* down to Egypt. 26 And Judah said unto his brethren, "What profit *is it* if we slay our brother, and conceal his blood? 27 Come, and let us sell him to the Ishmaelites, and let not our hand be upon him; for he *is* our brother *and* our flesh: and his brethren were content." 28 Then there passed by Midianites merchantmen; and they drew and lifted up Joseph out of the pit, and sold Joseph to the Ishmaelites for twenty *pieces* of silver: and they brought Joseph into Egypt.

29 And Reuben returned unto the pit; and, behold, Joseph *was* not in the pit; and he rent his clothes. 30 And he returned unto his brethren, and said, "The child *is* not; and I, whither shall I go?" 31 And they took Joseph's coat, and killed a kid of the goats, and dipped the coat in the blood; 32 And they sent the coat of *many* colors, and they brought *it* to their father; and said, "This have we found: know now whether it *be* thy son's coat or no." 33 And he knew it, and said, "*It is* my son's coat; an evil beast hath devoured him; Joseph is without doubt rent in pieces." 34 And Jacob rent his clothes, and put sackcloth upon his loins, and mourned for his son many days. 35 And all his sons and all his daughters rose up to comfort him; but he refused to be comforted; and he said, "For I will go down into the grave unto my son mourning." Thus his father wept for him. 36 And the Midianites sold him into Egypt unto Potiphar, an officer of Pharaoh's, *and* captain of the guard.

---

58. The pits were cisterns used to store rain water.

Judah and Tamar

38 And it came to pass at that time, that Judah went down from his brethren, and turned in to a certain Adullamite, whose name *was* Hirah. 2 And Judah saw there a daughter of a certain Canaanite, whose name *was* Shuah; and he took her, and went in unto her. 3 And she conceived, and bare a son; and he called his name Er. 4 And she conceived again, and bare a son; and she called his name Onan. 5 And she yet again conceived, and bare a son; and called his name Shelah: and he was at Chezib, when she bare him. 6 And Judah took a wife for Er his firstborn, whose name *was* Tamar. 7 And Er, Judah's firstborn, was wicked in the sight of the LORD; and the LORD slew him. 8 And Judah said unto Onan, "Go in unto thy brother's wife, and marry her, and raise up seed to thy brother." 9 And Onan knew that the seed should not be his; and it came to pass, when he went in unto his brother's wife, that he spilled *it* on the ground, lest that he should give seed to his brother. 10 And the thing which he did displeased the LORD: wherefore he slew him also. 11 Then said Judah to Tamar his daughter-in-law, "Remain a widow at thy father's house, till Shelah my son be grown":[59] for he said, "Lest peradventure he die also, as his brethren *did.*" And Tamar went and dwelt in her father's house.

12 And in process of time the daughter of Shuah Judah's wife died; and Judah was comforted, and went up unto his sheepshearers to Timnath, he and his friend Hirah the Adullamite. 13 And it was told Tamar, saying, "Behold, thy father-in-law goeth up to Timnath to shear his sheep." 14 And she put her widow's garments off from her, and covered her with a veil, and wrapped herself, and sat in an open place, which *is* by the way to Timnath; for she saw that Shelah was grown, and she was not given unto him to wife.[60] 15 When Judah saw her, he thought her *to be* a harlot; because she had covered her face. 16 And he turned unto her by the way, and said, "Go to, I pray thee, let me come in unto thee"; (for he knew not that she *was* his daughter-in-law:) and she said, "What wilt thou give me, that thou mayest come in unto me?" 17 And he said, "I will send *thee* a kid from the flock." And she said, "Wilt thou give *me* a pledge, till thou send *it?*" 18 And he said, "What pledge shall I give thee?" And she said, "Thy signet, and thy bracelets, and thy staff that *is* in thine hand." And he gave *it* her, and came in unto her, and she conceived by him. 19 And she arose, and went away, and laid by her veil from her, and put on the garments of her widowhood. 20 And Judah sent the kid by the hand of his friend the Adullamite, to receive *his* pledge from the woman's hand: but he found her not. 21 Then he asked the men of that place, saying, "Where *is* the harlot, that *was* openly by the wayside?" And they said, "There was no harlot in this *place.*" 22 And he returned to Judah, and said, "I cannot find her; and also the men of the place said, *that* there was no harlot in this *place.*" 23 And Judah said, "Let her take *it* to her, lest we be shamed: behold, I sent this kid, and thou hast not found her."

24 And it came to pass about three months after, that it was told Judah, saying, "Tamar thy daughter-in-law hath played the harlot; and also, behold, she *is* with child by whoredom." And Judah said, "Bring her forth, and let her be burnt." 25 When she *was* brought forth she sent to her father-in-law, saying, "By the man, whose these *are, am* I with child": and she said, "Discern, I pray thee, whose *are* these, the signet, and bracelets, and staff." 26 And Judah acknowledged *them,* and said, "She hath been more righteous than I; because that I gave her not to Shelah my son." And he knew her again no more. 27 And it came to pass in the time of her travail, that, behold, twins *were* in her womb. 28 And it came to pass, when she travailed, that *the one* put out *his* hand: and the midwife took and bound upon his hand a scarlet thread, saying, "This came out first." 29 And it came to pass, as he drew back his hand, that, behold, his brother came out: and she said, "How hast thou broken forth? *this* breach *be* upon thee": therefore his name was called Pharez. 30 And afterward came out his brother, that had the scarlet thread upon his hand: and his name was called Zarah.

Joseph and Potiphar's Wife

39 And Joseph was brought down to Egypt; and Potiphar, an officer[61] of Pharaoh, captain of the

---

59. (38:8-11) The levirate marriage obligation is codified in *Deuteronomy* 25:5-6: "If brethren dwell together, and one of them die, and have no child, the wife of the dead shall not marry without unto a stranger; her husband's brother shall go in unto her, and take her to him to wife and perform the duty of a husband's brother unto her. And it shall be, that the firstborn which she beareth shall succeed in the name of his brother which is dead, that his name be not put out of Israel." Both Onan and Judah fail this obligation. Onan refuses to sire a son to perpetuate his brother's name. Judah does not give Shelah to Tamar.

60. The suggestion is that Judah feels his sons died because of some sinister power related to Tamar. (See the demon-lover story in *Tobit* 3:7-8.)

61. The word translated "officer" literally means "eunuch." However, only NEB retains that reading.

guard, an Egyptian, bought him of the hands of the Ishmaelites, which had brought him down thither. 2 And the LORD was with Joseph, and he was a prosperous man; and he was in the house of his master the Egyptian. 3 And his master saw that the LORD *was* with him, and that the LORD made all that he did to prosper in his hand. 4 And Joseph found grace in his sight, and he served him: and he made him overseer over his house, and all *that* he had he put into his hand. 5 And it came to pass from the time *that* he had made him overseer in his house, and over all that he had, that the LORD blessed the Egyptian's house for Joseph's sake; and the blessing of the LORD was upon all that he had in the house, and in the field. 6 And he left all that he had in Joseph's hand; and he knew not aught he had, save the bread which he did eat. And Joseph was a goodly person, and well-favored.

7 And it came to pass after these things, that his master's wife cast her eyes upon Joseph; and she said, "Lie with me." 8 But he refused, and said unto his master's wife, "Behold, my master wotteth not what *is* with me in the house, and he hath committed all that he hath to my hand; 9 *There is* none greater in this house than I; neither hath he kept back any thing from me but thee, because thou *art* his wife: how then can I do this great wickedness, and sin against God?" 10 And it came to pass, as she spake to Joseph day by day, that he hearkened not unto her, to lie by her, *or* to be with her. 11 And it came to pass about this time, that *Joseph* went into the house to do his business; and *there was* none of the men of the house there within. 12 And she caught him by his garment, saying, "Lie with me": and he left his garment in her hand, and fled, and got him out. 13 And it came to pass, when she saw that he had left his garment in her hand, and was fled forth, 14 That she called unto the men of her house, and spake unto them, saying, "See, he hath brought in a Hebrew unto us to mock us; he came in unto me to lie with me, and I cried with a loud voice: 15 And it came to pass, when he heard that I lifted up my voice and cried, that he left his garment with me, and fled, and got him out." 16 And she laid up his garment by her, until his lord came home. 17 And she spake unto him according to these words, saying, "The Hebrew servant, which thou hast brought unto us, came in unto me to mock me. 18 And it came to pass, as I lifted up my voice and cried, that he left his garment with me, and fled out." 19 And it came to pass, when his master heard the words of his wife, which she spake unto him, saying, "After this manner did thy servant to me"; that his wrath was kindled. 20 And Joseph's master took him, and put him into the prison, a place where

the king's prisoners *were* bound: and he was there in the prison.

21 But the LORD was with Joseph, and showed him mercy, and gave him favor in the sight of the keeper of the prison. 22 And the keeper of the prison committed to Joseph's hand all the prisoners that *were* in the prison; and whatsoever they did there, he was the doer *of it.* 23 The keeper of the prison looked not to any thing *that was* under his hand; because the LORD was with him, and *that* which he did, the LORD made *it* to prosper.

Joseph Interprets Dreams

40 And it came to pass after these things, *that* the butler of the king of Egypt and *his* baker had offended their lord the king of Egypt. 2 And Pharaoh was wroth against two *of* his officers, against the chief of the butlers, and against the chief of the bakers. 3 And he put them in ward in the house of the captain of the guard, into the prison, the place where Joseph *was* bound. 4 And the captain of the guard charged Joseph with them, and he served them: and they continued a season in ward. 5 And they dreamed a dream both of them, each man his dream in one night, each man according to the interpretation of his dream, the butler and the baker of the king of Egypt, which *were* bound in the prison. 6 And Joseph came in unto them in the morning, and looked upon them, and, behold, they *were* sad. 7 And he asked Pharaoh's officers that *were* with him in the ward of his lord's house, saying, "Wherefore look ye *so* sadly to-day?" 8 And they said unto him, "We have dreamed a dream, and *there is* no interpreter of it." And Joseph said unto them, "*Do* not interpretations *belong* to God? tell me *them,* I pray you."

9 And the chief butler told his dream to Joseph, and said to him, "In my dream, behold, a vine *was* before me; 10 And in the vine *were* three branches: and it *was* as though it budded, *and* her blossoms shot forth; and the clusters thereof brought forth ripe grapes: 11 And Pharaoh's cup *was* in my hand: and I took the grapes, and pressed them into Pharaoh's cup, and I gave the cup into Pharaoh's hand." 12 And Joseph said unto him, "This *is* the interpretation of it: The three branches *are* three days: 13 Yet within three days shall Pharaoh lift up thine head,[62] and restore thee unto thy place; and thou shalt deliver Pharaoh's cup into his hand, after the former manner when thou wast his butler. 14 But think on me when it shall be well with thee, and show

---

62. The phrase involves a pun. Here it means to raise one from bondage and restore his pride and position. In verse 19, it means to hang a person.

kindness, I pray thee, unto me, and make mention of me unto Pharaoh, and bring me out of this house: 15 For indeed I was stolen away out of the land of the Hebrews: and here also have I done nothing that they should put me into the dungeon."

16 When the chief baker saw that the interpretation was good, he said unto Joseph, "I also *was* in my dream, and, behold, *I had* three white baskets on my head: 17 And in the uppermost basket *there was* of all manner of bakemeats for Pharaoh; and the birds did eat them out of the basket upon my head." 18 And Joseph answered and said, "This *is* the interpretation thereof: The three baskets *are* three days: 19 Yet within three days shall Pharaoh lift up thy head from off thee, and shall hang thee on a tree; and the birds shall eat thy flesh from off thee."

20 And it came to pass the third day, *which was* Pharaoh's birthday, that he made a feast unto all his servants: and he lifted up the head of the chief butler and of the chief baker among his servants. 21 And he restored the chief butler unto his butlership again; and he gave the cup into Pharaoh's hand: 22 But he hanged the chief baker: as Joseph had interpreted to them. 23 Yet did not the chief butler remember Joseph, but forgat him.

Pharaoh's Dreams

41 And it came to pass at the end of two full years, that Pharaoh dreamed: and, behold, he stood by the river. 2 And, behold, there came up out of the river seven well-favored kine and fatfleshed; and they fed in a meadow. 3 And, behold, seven other kine came up after them out of the river, ill-favored and lean-fleshed; and stood by the *other* kine upon the brink of the river. 4 And the ill-favored and lean-fleshed kine did eat up the seven well-favored and fat kine. So Pharaoh awoke. 5 And he slept and dreamed the second time: and, behold, seven ears of corn came up upon one stalk, rank and good. 6 And, behold, seven thin ears and blasted with the east wind sprung up after them. 7 And the seven thin ears devoured the seven rank and full ears. And Pharaoh awoke, and, behold, *it was* a dream. 8 And it came to pass in the morning that his spirit was troubled; and he sent and called for all the magicians of Egypt, and all the wise men thereof: and Pharaoh told them his dream; but *there was* none that could interpret them unto Pharaoh.

9 Then spake the chief butler unto Pharaoh, saying, "I do remember my faults this day: 10 Pharaoh was wroth with his servants, and put me in ward in the captain of the guard's house, *both* me and the chief baker: 11 And we

dreamed a dream in one night, I and he; we dreamed each man according to the interpretation of his dream. 12 And *there was* there with us a young man, a Hebrew, servant to the captain of the guard; and we told him, and he interpreted to us our dreams; to each man according to his dream he did interpret. 13 And it came to pass, as he interpreted to us, so it was; me he restored unto mine office, and him he hanged."

14 Then Pharaoh sent and called Joseph, and they brought him hastily out of the dungeon: and he shaved *himself,* and changed his raiment, and came in unto Pharaoh. 15 And Pharaoh said unto Joseph, "I have dreamed a dream, and *there is* none that can interpret it: and I have heard say of thee, *that* thou canst understand a dream to interpret it." 16 And Joseph answered Pharaoh, saying, "*It is* not in me: God shall give Pharaoh an answer of peace." 17 And Pharaoh said unto Joseph, "In my dream, behold, I stood upon the bank of the river: 18 And, behold, there came up out of the river seven kine, fat-fleshed and well-favored; and they fed in a meadow: 19 And, behold, seven other kine came up after them, poor and very ill-favored and lean-fleshed, such as I never saw in all the land of Egypt for badness: 20 And the lean and the ill-favored kine did eat up the first seven fat kine: 21 And when they had eaten them up, it could not be known that they had eaten them; but they *were* still ill-favored, as at the beginning. So I awoke. 22 And I saw in my dream, and, behold, seven ears came up in one stalk, full and good: 23 And, behold, seven ears, withered, thin, *and* blasted with the east wind, sprung up after them: 24 And the thin ears devoured the seven good ears: and I told *this* unto the magicians; but *there was* none that could declare *it* to me."

25 And Joseph said unto Pharaoh, "The dream of Pharaoh *is* one: God hath showed Pharaoh what he *is* about to do. 26 The seven good kine *are* seven years; and the seven good ears *are* seven years: the dream *is* one. 27 And the seven thin and ill-favored kine that came up after them *are* seven years; and the seven empty ears blasted with the east wind shall be seven years of famine. 28 This *is* the thing which I have spoken unto Pharaoh: What God *is* about to do he showeth unto Pharaoh. 29 Behold, there come seven years of great plenty throughout all the land of Egypt: 30 And there shall arise after them seven years of famine; and all the plenty shall be forgotten in the land of Egypt; and the famine shall consume the land; 31 And the plenty shall not be known in the land by reason of that famine following; for it *shall be* very grievous. 32 And for that the dream was doubled unto Pharaoh twice; *it is* because the thing *is* established by

God,[63] and God will shortly bring it to pass. 33 Now therefore let Pharaoh look out a man discreet and wise, and set him over the land of Egypt. 34 Let Pharaoh do *this,* and let him appoint officers over the land, and take up the fifth part of the land of Egypt in the seven plenteous years. 35 And let them gather all the food of those good years that come, and lay up corn under the hand of Pharaoh, and let them keep food in the cities. 36 And that food shall be for store to the land against the seven years of famine, which shall be in the land of Egypt; that the land perish not through the famine."

Joseph's Rise to Power

37 And the thing was good in the eyes of Pharaoh, and in the eyes of all his servants. 38 And Pharaoh said unto his servants, "Can we find *such a one* as this *is,* a man in whom the Spirit of God *is?*" 39 And Pharaoh said unto Joseph, "Forasmuch as God hath showed thee all this, *there is* none so discreet and wise as thou *art:* 40 Thou shalt be over my house, and according unto thy word shall all my people be ruled: only in the throne will I be greater than thou." 41 And Pharaoh said unto Joseph, "See, I have set thee over all the land of Egypt." 42 And Pharaoh took off his ring from his hand, and put it upon Joseph's hand, and arrayed him in vestures of fine linen, and put a gold chain about his neck; 43 And he made him to ride in the second chariot which he had; and they cried before him, "Bow the knee": and he made him *ruler* over all the land of Egypt. 44 And Pharaoh said unto Joseph, "I *am* Pharaoh, and without thee shall no man lift up his hand or foot in all the land of Egypt." 45 And Pharaoh called Joseph's name Zaphnath-paaneah; and he gave him to wife Asenath the daughter of Poti-pherah priest of On.[64] And Joseph went out over *all* the land of Egypt.

46 And Joseph *was* thirty years old when he stood before Pharaoh king of Egypt. And Joseph went out from the presence of Pharaoh, and went throughout all the land of Egypt. 47 And in the seven plenteous years the earth brought forth by handfuls. 48 And he gathered up all the food of the seven years, which were in the land of Egypt, and laid up the food in the cities: the food of the field, which *was* round about every city, laid he up in the same. 49 And Joseph gathered corn as the sand of the sea, very much, until he left numbering; for *it was* without number. 50 And unto Joseph were born two sons, before the years of famine came: which Asenath the daughter of Poti-pherah priest of On bare unto him. 51 And Joseph called the name of the firstborn Manasseh: "For God," *said he,* "hath made me forget all my toil, and all my father's house." 52 And the name of the second called he Ephraim: "For God hath caused me to be fruitful in the land of my affliction."

53 And the seven years of plenteousness, that was in the land of Egypt, were ended. 54 And the seven years of dearth began to come, according as Joseph had said: and the dearth was in all lands; but in all the land of Egypt there was bread. 55 And when all the land of Egypt was famished, the people cried to Pharaoh for bread: and Pharaoh said unto all the Egyptians, "Go unto Joseph; what he saith to you, do." 56 And the famine was over all the face of the earth: and Joseph opened all the storehouses, and sold unto the Egyptians; and the famine waxed sore in the land of Egypt. 57 And all countries came into Egypt to Joseph for to buy *corn;* because that the famine was *so* sore in all lands.

Joseph Meets His Brothers

42 Now when Jacob saw that there was corn in Egypt, Jacob said unto his sons, "Why do ye look one upon another?" 2 And he said, "Behold, I have heard that there is corn in Egypt: get you down thither, and buy for us from thence; that we may live, and not die." 3 And Joseph's ten brethren went down to buy corn in Egypt. 4 But Benjamin, Joseph's brother, Jacob sent not with his brethren; for he said, "Lest peradventure mischief befall him." 5 And the sons of Israel came to buy *corn* among those that came: for the famine was in the land of Canaan.

6 And Joseph *was* the governor over the land, *and* he *it was* that sold to all the people of the land: and Joseph's brethren came, and bowed down themselves before him *with* their faces to the earth.[65] 7 And Joseph saw his brethren, and he knew them, but made himself strange unto them, and spake roughly unto them; and he said unto them, "Whence come ye?" And they said, "From the land of Canaan to buy food." 8 And Joseph knew his brethren, but they knew not him. 9 And Joseph remembered the dreams which he dreamed of them, and said unto them, "Ye *are* spies; to see the nakedness of the land ye are come."[66] 10 And they said unto him, "Nay, my

---

63. NEB: "The doubling of Pharaoh's dream means that God is already resolved to do this."

64. (41:42-45) The rites of investiture culminate in the giving of an Egyptian name. Joseph's marriage to a lady of rank indicates his complete adoption into the Egyptian court.

65. As his brothers bow before him, they fulfill the prophecy of Joseph's dream (37:6-8).

66. I.e., spies from Canaan reconnoitering the military weakness of Egypt.

lord, but to buy food are thy servants come. 11 We *are* all one man's sons; we *are* true *men;* thy servants are no spies." 12 And he said unto them, "Nay, but to see the nakedness of the land ye are come." 13 And they said, "Thy servants *are* twelve brethren, the sons of one man in the land of Canaan; and, behold, the youngest *is* this day with our father, and one *is* not." 14 And Joseph said unto them, "That *is it* that I spake unto you, saying, 'Ye *are* spies': 15 Hereby ye shall be proved: By the life of Pharaoh ye shall not go forth hence, except your youngest brother come hither. 16 Send one of you, and let him fetch your brother, and ye shall be kept in prison, that your words may be proved, whether *there be any* truth in you: or else by the life of Pharaoh surely ye *are* spies." 17 And he put them all together into ward three days.

18 And Joseph said unto them the third day, "This do, and live; *for* I fear God: 19 If ye *be* true *men,* let one of your brethren be bound in the house of your prison: go ye, carry corn for the famine of your houses: 20 But bring your youngest brother unto me; so shall your words be verified, and ye shall not die." And they did so.[67] 21 And they said one to another, "We *are* verily guilty concerning our brother, in that we saw the anguish of his soul, when he besought us, and we would not hear; therefore is this distress come upon us." 22 And Reuben answered them, saying, "Spake I not unto you, saying, 'Do not sin against the child'; and ye would not hear? therefore, behold, also his blood is required." 23 And they knew not that Joseph understood *them;* for he spake unto them by an interpreter. 24 And he turned himself about from them, and wept; and returned to them again, and communed with them, and took from them Simeon, and bound him before their eyes.

Jacob's Sons Return to Canaan

25 Then Joseph commanded to fill their sacks with corn, and to restore every man's money into his sack, and to give them provision for the way: and thus did he unto them.

26 And they laded their asses with the corn, and departed thence. 27 And as one of them opened his sack to give his ass provender in the inn, he espied his money; for, behold, it *was* in his sack's mouth. 28 And he said unto his brethren, "My money is restored; and, lo, *it is* even in my sack": and their heart failed *them,* and they were afraid, saying one to another, "What *is* this *that* God hath done unto us?"

29 And they came unto Jacob their father unto the land of Canaan, and told him all that befell unto them; saying, 30 "The man, *who is* the lord of the land, spake roughly to us, and took us for spies of the country. 31 And we said unto him, '*We are* true *men;* we are no spies: 32 We *be* twelve brethren, sons of our father; one *is* not, and the youngest *is* this day with our father in the land of Canaan.' 33 And the man, the lord of the country, said unto us, 'Hereby shall I know that ye *are* true *men;* leave one of your brethren *here* with me, and take *food for* the famine of your households, and be gone: 34 And bring your youngest brother unto me: then shall I know that ye *are* no spies, but *that* ye *are* true *men:* so will I deliver you your brother, and ye shall traffic in the land.' "

35 And it came to pass as they emptied their sacks, that, behold, every man's bundle of money *was* in his sack: and when *both* they and their father saw the bundles of money, they were afraid. 36 And Jacob their father said unto them, "Me have ye bereaved *of my children:* Joseph *is* not, and Simeon *is* not, and ye will take Benjamin *away:* all these things are against me." 37 And Reuben spake unto his father, saying, "Slay my two sons, if I bring him not to thee: deliver him into my hand, and I will bring him to thee again." 38 And he said, "My son shall not go down with you; for his brother is dead, and he is left alone: if mischief befall him by the way in the which ye go, then shall ye bring down my gray hairs with sorrow to the grave." [68]

Benjamin Is Brought to Egypt

43 And the famine *was* sore in the land. 2 And it came to pass, when they had eaten up the corn which they had brought out of Egypt, their father said unto them, "Go again, buy us a little food." 3 And Judah spake unto him, saying, "The man did solemnly protest unto us, saying, 'Ye shall not see my face, except your brother *be* with you.' 4 If thou wilt send our brother with us, we will go down and buy thee food: 5 But if thou wilt not send *him,* we will not go down: for the man said unto us, 'Ye shall not see my face, except your brother *be* with you.' " 6 And Israel said, "Wherefore dealt ye so ill with me, *as* to tell the man whether ye had yet a brother?" 7 And they said, "The man asked us straitly of our state, and of our kindred, saying, '*Is* your father yet alive? have ye *another* brother?' and we told him according to the tenor of these words: Could we certainly know that he would say, 'Bring your brother down'?" 8 And Judah said unto Israel

---

67. NAB: "To this they agreed."

68. The family appears to forget imprisoned Simeon. They do not return to Egypt until their food runs out.

his father, "Send the lad with me, and we will arise and go; that we may live, and not die, both we, and thou, *and* also our little ones. 9 I will be surety for him; of my hand shalt thou require him: if I bring him not unto thee, and set him before thee, then let me bear the blame for ever: 10 For except we had lingered, surely now we had returned this second time." 11 And their father Israel said unto them, "If *it must be* so now, do this; take of the best fruits in the land in your vessels, and carry down the man a present, a little balm, and a little honey, spices and myrrh, nuts and almonds: 12 And take double money in your hand; and the money that was brought again in the mouth of your sacks, carry *it* again in your hand; peradventure it *was* an oversight. 13 Take also your brother, and arise, go again unto the man: 14 And God Almighty give you mercy before the man, that he may send away your other brother, and Benjamin. If I be bereaved *of my children,* I am bereaved."

15 And the men took that present, and they took double money in their hand, and Benjamin; and rose up, and went down to Egypt, and stood before Joseph. 16 And when Joseph saw Benjamin with them, he said to the ruler of his house, "Bring *these* men home, and slay, and make ready; for *these* men shall dine with me at noon." 17 And the man did as Joseph bade; and the man brought the men into Joseph's house. 18 And the men were afraid, because they were brought into Joseph's house; and they said, "Because of the money that was returned in our sacks at the first time are we brought in; that he may seek occasion against us, and fall upon us, and take us for bondmen, and our asses."

19 And they came near to the steward of Joseph's house, and they communed with him at the door of the house, 20 And said, "O sir, we came indeed down at the first time to buy food: 21 And it came to pass, when we came to the inn, that we opened our sacks, and, behold, *every* man's money *was* in the mouth of his sack, our money in full weight: and we have brought it again in our hand. 22 And other money have we brought down in our hands to buy food: we cannot tell who put our money in our sacks." 23 And he said, "Peace *be* to you, fear not: your God, and the God of your father, hath given you treasure in your sacks: I had your money." And he brought Simeon out unto them. 24 And the man brought the men into Joseph's house, and gave *them* water, and they washed their feet; and he gave their asses provender. 25 And they made ready the present against Joseph came at noon: for they heard that they should eat bread there.

26 And when Joseph came home, they brought him the present which *was* in their hand into the house, and bowed themselves to him to the earth. 27 And he asked them of *their* welfare, and said, "*Is* your father well, the old man of whom ye spake? *Is* he yet alive?" 28 And they answered, "Thy servant our father *is* in good health, he *is* yet alive." And they bowed down their heads, and made obeisance. 29 And he lifted up his eyes, and saw his brother Benjamin, his mother's son, and said, "*Is* this your younger brother, of whom ye spake unto me?" And he said, "God be gracious unto thee, my son." 30 And Joseph made haste; for his bowels did yearn upon his brother: and he sought *where* to weep; and he entered into *his* chamber, and wept there. 31 And he washed his face, and went out, and refrained himself, and said, "Set on bread." 32 And they set on for him by himself, and for them by themselves, and for the Egyptians, which did eat with them, by themselves: because the Egyptians might not eat bread with the Hebrews; for that *is* an abomination unto the Egyptians. 33 And they sat before him, the firstborn according to his birthright, and the youngest according to his youth: and the men marveled one at another. 34 And he took *and sent* messes unto them from before him: but Benjamin's mess was five times so much as any of theirs. And they drank, and were merry with him.

44 And he commanded the steward of his house, saying, "Fill the men's sacks *with* food, as much as they can carry, and put every man's money in his sack's mouth. 2 And put my cup, the silver cup, in the sack's mouth of the youngest, and his corn money." And he did according to the word that Joseph had spoken. 3 As soon as the morning was light, the men were sent away, they and their asses. 4 *And* when they were gone out of the city, *and* not *yet* far off, Joseph said unto his steward, "Up, follow after the men; and when thou dost overtake them, say unto them, 'Wherefore have ye rewarded evil for good? 5 *Is* not this *it* in which my lord drinketh, and whereby indeed he divineth?[69] ye have done evil in so doing.'" 6 And he overtook them, and he spake unto them these same words. 7 And they said unto him, "Wherefore saith my lord these words? God forbid that thy servants should do according to this thing: 8 Behold, the money, which we found in our sacks' mouths, we brought again unto thee out of the land of Canaan: how then should we steal out of thy lord's house silver or gold? 9 With whomsoever of thy servants it be found, both let him die, and we also will be my lord's bondmen." 10 And he said, "Now also *let* it *be*

---

69. Divination was based on the way water fell into a cup or on patterns which oil-drops formed in water.

according unto your words: he with whom it is found shall be my servant; and ye shall be blameless." 11 Then they speedily took down every man his sack to the ground, and opened every man his sack. 12 And he searched, *and* began at the eldest, and left at the youngest: and the cup was found in Benjamin's sack. 13 Then they rent their clothes, and laded every man his ass, and returned to the city.

14 And Judah and his brethren came to Joseph's house; for he *was* yet there: and they fell before him on the ground. 15 And Joseph said unto them, "What deed *is* this that ye have done? wot ye not that such a man as I can certainly divine?" 16 And Judah said, "What shall we say unto my lord? what shall we speak? or how shall we clear ourselves? God hath found out the iniquity of thy servants:[70] behold, we *are* my lord's servants, both we, and *he* also with whom the cup is found." 17 And he said, "God forbid that I should do so: *but* the man in whose hand the cup is found, he shall be my servant; and as for you, get you up in peace unto your father."

Judah's Plea for Benjamin [71]

18 Then Judah came near unto him, and said, "O my lord, let thy servant, I pray thee, speak a word in my lord's ears, and let not thine anger burn against thy servant: for thou *art* even as Pharaoh. 19 My lord asked his servants, saying, 'Have ye a father, or a brother?' 20 And we said unto my lord, 'We have a father, an old man, and a child of his old age, a little one; and his brother is dead, and he alone is left of his mother, and his father loveth him.' 21 And thou saidst unto thy servants, 'Bring him down unto me, that I may set mine eyes upon him.' 22 And we said unto my lord, 'The lad cannot leave his father: for *if* he should leave his father, *his father* would die.' 23 And thou saidst unto thy servants, 'Except your youngest brother come down with you, ye shall see my face no more.' 24 And it came to pass when we came up unto thy servant my father, we told him the words of my lord. 25 And our father said, 'Go again, *and* buy us a little food.' 26 And we said, 'We cannot go down: if our youngest brother be with us, then will we go down: for we may not see the man's face, except our youngest brother *be* with us.' 27 And thy servant my father said unto us, 'Ye know that my wife bare me two *sons:* 28 And the one went out

70. Judah recalls their treatment of Joseph years earlier.
71. (44:18-34) In IB, Cuthbert A. Simpson submits, "Judah's speech in these verses is one of the best pieces of writing found in J, and indeed in the Old Testament." It makes eloquent use of repetition and formal court style.

from me, and I said, "Surely he is torn in pieces"; and I saw him not since: 29 And if ye take this also from me, and mischief befall him, ye shall bring down my gray hairs with sorrow to the grave.' 30 Now therefore when I come to thy servant my father, and the lad *be* not with us; seeing that his life is bound up in the lad's life; 31 It shall come to pass, when he seeth that the lad *is* not *with us,* that he will die: and thy servants shall bring down the gray hairs of thy servant our father with sorrow to the grave. 32 For thy servant became surety for the lad unto my father, saying, 'If I bring him not unto thee, then I shall bear the blame to my father for ever.' 33 Now therefore, I pray thee, let thy servant abide instead of the lad a bondman to my lord; and let the lad go up with his brethren. 34 For how shall I go up to my father, and the lad *be* not with me? lest peradventure I see the evil that shall come on my father."

Joseph Reveals His Identity

45 Then Joseph could not refrain himself before all them that stood by him;[72] and he cried, "Cause every man to go out from me." And there stood no man with him, while Joseph made himself known unto his brethren. 2 And he wept aloud: and the Egyptians and the house of Pharaoh heard. 3 And Joseph said unto his brethren, "I *am* Joseph; doth my father yet live?" And his brethren could not answer him; for they were troubled at his presence. 4 And Joseph said unto his brethren, "Come near to me, I pray you." And they came near. And he said, "I *am* Joseph your brother, whom ye sold into Egypt. 5 Now therefore be not grieved, nor angry with yourselves, that ye sold me hither: for God did send me before you to preserve life. 6 For these two years *hath* the famine *been* in the land: and yet *there are* five years, in the which *there shall* neither *be* earing nor harvest. 7 And God sent me before you to preserve you a posterity in the earth, and to save your lives by a great deliverance. 8 So now *it was* not you *that* sent me hither, but God: and he hath made me a father to Pharaoh, and lord of all his house, and a ruler throughout all the land of Egypt. 9 Haste ye, and go up to my father, and say unto him, 'Thus saith thy son Joseph, "God hath made me lord of all Egypt: come down unto me, tarry not: 10 And thou shalt dwell in the land of Goshen, and thou shalt be near unto me, thou, and thy children, and thy children's children, and thy flocks, and thy herds, and all that thou hast: 11 And there will I nour-

72. NEB: "Joseph could no longer control his feelings in front of his attendants."

ish thee; for yet *there are* five years of famine; lest thou, and thy household, and all that thou hast, come to poverty." ' 12 And, behold, your eyes see, and the eyes of my brother Benjamin, that *it is* my mouth that speaketh unto you. 13 And ye shall tell my father of all my glory in Egypt, and of all that ye have seen; and ye shall haste and bring down my father hither." 14 And he fell upon his brother Benjamin's neck, and wept; and Benjamin wept upon his neck. 15 Moreover he kissed all his brethren, and wept upon them: and after that his brethren talked with him.

16 And the fame thereof was heard in Pharaoh's house, saying, "Joseph's brethren are come": and it pleased Pharaoh well, and his servants. 17 And Pharaoh said unto Joseph, "Say unto thy brethren, 'This do ye; lade your beasts, and go, get you unto the land of Canaan; 18 And take your father and your households, and come unto me: and I will give you the good of the land of Egypt, and ye shall eat the fat of the land. 19 Now thou art commanded, this do ye; take you wagons out of the land of Egypt for your little ones, and for your wives, and bring your father, and come. 20 Also regard not your stuff;[73] for the good of all the land of Egypt *is* yours.' " 21 And the children of Israel did so: and Joseph gave them wagons, according to the commandment of Pharaoh, and gave them provision for the way. 22 To all of them he gave each man changes of raiment; but to Benjamin he gave three hundred *pieces* of silver, and five changes of raiment. 23 And to his father he sent after this *manner;* ten asses laden with the good things of Egypt, and ten she asses laden with corn and bread and meat for his father by the way. 24 So he sent his brethren away, and they departed: and he said unto them, "See that ye fall not out by the way." 25 And they went up out of Egypt, and came into the land of Canaan unto Jacob their father, 26 And told him, saying, "Joseph *is* yet alive, and he *is* governor over all the land of Egypt." And Jacob's heart fainted, for he believed them not. 27 And they told him all the words of Joseph, which he had said unto them: and when he saw the wagons which Joseph had sent to carry him, the spirit of Jacob their father revived. 28 And Israel said, "*It is* enough; Joseph my son *is* yet alive: I will go and see him before I die."

Jacob Comes to Egypt

46 And Israel took his journey with all that he had, and came to Beer-sheba, and offered sacri-

73. JB: "Never mind about your property."

fices unto the God of his father Isaac. 2 And God spake unto Israel in the visions of the night, and said, "Jacob, Jacob." And he said, "Here *am* I." 3 And he said, "I *am* God, the God of thy father: fear not to go down into Egypt; for I will there make of thee a great nation. 4 I will go down with thee into Egypt; and I will also surely bring thee up *again:* and Joseph shall put his hand upon thine eyes." 5 And Jacob rose up from Beer-sheba: and the sons of Israel carried Jacob their father, and their little ones, and their wives, in the wagons which Pharaoh had sent to carry him. 6 And they took their cattle, and their goods, which they had gotten in the land of Canaan, and came into Egypt, Jacob, and all his seed with him: 7 His sons, and his sons' sons with him, his daughters, and his sons' daughters, and all his seed brought he with him into Egypt.

8 And these *are* the names of the children of Israel, which came into Egypt, Jacob and his sons: Reuben, Jacob's firstborn. 9 And the sons of Reuben; Hanoch, and Phallu, and Hezron, and Carmi. 10 And the sons of Simeon; Jemuel, and Jamin, and Ohad, and Jachin, and Zohar, and Shaul the son of a Canaanitish woman. 11 And the sons of Levi; Gershon, Kohath, and Merari. 12 And the sons of Judah; Er, and Onan, and Shelah, and Pharez, and Zarah: but Er and Onan died in the land of Canaan. And the sons of Pharez were Hezron and Hamul. 13 And the sons of Issachar; Tola, and Phuvah, and Job, and Shimron. 14 And the sons of Zebulun; Sered, and Elon, and Jahleel. 15 These *be* the sons of Leah, which she bare unto Jacob in Padan-aram, with his daughter Dinah: all the souls of his sons and his daughters *were* thirty and three. 16 And the sons of Gad; Ziphion, and Haggi, Shuni, and Ezbon, Eri, and Arodi, and Areli. 17 And the sons of Asher; Jimnah, and Ishuah, and Isui, and Beriah, and Serah their sister: and the sons of Beriah; Heber, and Malchiel. 18 These *are* the sons of Zilpah, whom Laban gave to Leah his daughter; and these she bare unto Jacob, *even* sixteen souls. 19 The sons of Rachel Jacob's wife; Joseph, and Benjamin. 20 And unto Joseph in the land of Egypt were born Manasseh and Ephraim, which Asenath the daughter of Potipherah priest of On bare unto him. 21 And the sons of Benjamin *were* Belah, and Becher, and Ashbel, Gera, and Naaman, Ehi, and Rosh, Muppim, and Huppim, and Ard. 22 These *are* the sons of Rachel, which were born to Jacob: all the souls *were* fourteen. 23 And the sons of Dan; Hushim. 24 And the sons of Naphtali; Jahzeel, and Guni, and Jezer, and Shillem. 25 These *are* the sons of Bilhah, which Laban gave unto Rachel his daughter, and she bare these unto Jacob:

all the souls *were* seven. 26 All the souls that came with Jacob into Egypt, which came out of his loins, besides Jacob's sons' wives, all the souls *were* threescore and six; 27 And the sons of Joseph, which were borne him in Egypt, *were* two souls: all the souls of the house of Jacob, which came into Egypt, *were* threescore and ten.[74]

28 And he sent Judah before him unto Joseph, to direct his face unto Goshen; and they came into the land of Goshen. 29 And Joseph made ready his chariot, and went up to meet Israel his father, to Goshen, and presented himself unto him; and he fell on his neck, and wept on his neck a good while. 30 And Israel said unto Joseph, "Now let me die, since I have seen thy face, because thou *art* yet alive." 31 And Joseph said unto his brethren, and unto his father's house, "I will go up, and show Pharaoh, and say unto him, 'My brethren, and my father's house, which *were* in the land of Canaan, are come unto me; 32 And the men *are* shepherds, for their trade hath been to feed cattle; and they have brought their flocks, and their herds, and all that they have.' 33 And it shall come to pass, when Pharaoh shall call you, and shall say, 'What *is* your occupation?' 34 That ye shall say, 'Thy servants' trade hath been about cattle from our youth even until now, both we, *and* also our fathers': that ye may dwell in the land of Goshen; for every shepherd *is* an abomination unto the Egyptians."

47 Then Joseph came and told Pharaoh, and said, "My father and my brethren, and their flocks, and their herds, and all that they have, are come out of the land of Canaan; and, behold, they *are* in the land of Goshen." 2 And he took some of his brethren, *even* five men, and presented them unto Pharaoh. 3 And Pharaoh said unto his brethren, "What *is* your occupation?" And they said unto Pharaoh, "Thy servants *are* shepherds, both we, *and* also our fathers." 4 They said moreover unto Pharaoh, "For to sojourn in the land are we come; for thy servants have no pasture for their flocks; for the famine *is* sore in the land of Canaan: now therefore, we pray thee, let thy servants dwell in the land of Goshen." 5 And Pharaoh spake unto Joseph, saying, "Thy father and thy brethren are come unto thee: 6 The land of Egypt *is* before thee; in the best of the land make thy father and brethren to dwell; in the land of Goshen let them dwell: and if thou knowest *any* men of activity among them, then make them rulers over my cattle." 7 And Joseph brought in Jacob his father, and set

him before Pharaoh: and Jacob blessed Pharaoh. 8 And Pharaoh said unto Jacob, "How old *art* thou?" 9 And Jacob said unto Pharaoh, "The days of the years of my pilgrimage *are* a hundred and thirty years: few and evil have the days of the years of my life been, and have not attained unto the days of the years of the life of my fathers in the days of their pilgrimage." 10 And Jacob blessed Pharaoh, and went out from before Pharaoh. 11 And Joseph placed his father and his brethren, and gave them a possession in the land of Egypt, in the best of the land, in the land of Rameses, as Pharaoh had commanded. 12 And Joseph nourished his father, and his brethren, and all his father's household, with bread, according to *their* families.

Joseph's Agrarian Policy

13 And *there was* no bread in all the land; for the famine *was* very sore, so that the land of Egypt and *all* the land of Canaan fainted by reason of the famine. 14 And Joseph gathered up all the money that was found in the land of Egypt, and in the land of Canaan, for the corn which they bought: and Joseph brought the money into Pharaoh's house. 15 And when money failed in the land of Egypt, and in the land of Canaan, all the Egyptians came unto Joseph, and said, "Give us bread: for why should we die in thy presence? for the money faileth." 16 And Joseph said, "Give your cattle; and I will give you for your cattle, if money fail." 17 And they brought their cattle unto Joseph: and Joseph gave them bread *in exchange* for horses, and for the flocks, and for the cattle of the herds, and for the asses: and he fed them with bread for all their cattle for that year. 18 When that year was ended, they came unto him the second year, and said unto him, "We will not hide *it* from my lord, how that our money is spent; my lord also hath our herds of cattle; there is not aught left in the sight of my lord, but our bodies, and our lands: 19 Wherefore shall we die before thine eyes, both we and our land? buy us and our land for bread, and we and our land will be servants unto Pharaoh: and give *us* seed, that we may live, and not die, that the land be not desolate." 20 And Joseph bought all the land of Egypt for Pharaoh; for the Egyptians sold every man his field, because the famine prevailed over them: so the land became Pharaoh's. 21 And as for the people, he removed them to cities from *one* end of the borders of Egypt even to the *other* end thereof. 22 Only the land of the priests bought he not; for the priests had a portion *assigned them* of Pharaoh, and did eat their portion which Pharaoh gave them: wherefore they sold not their lands.

---

74. (46:8-27) The members of the tribe of Israel are arranged to total the perfect number seventy. The computation is not easy to follow.

23 Then Joseph said unto the people, "Behold, I have bought you this day and your land for Pharaoh: lo, *here is* seed for you, and ye shall sow the land. 24 And it shall come to pass in the increase, that ye shall give the fifth *part* unto Pharaoh, and four parts shall be your own, for seed of the field, and for your food, and for them of your households, and for food for your little ones." 25 And they said, "Thou hast saved our lives: let us find grace in the sight of my lord, and we will be Pharaoh's servants." 26 And Joseph made it a law over the land of Egypt unto this day, *that* Pharaoh should have the fifth *part;* except the land of the priests only, *which* became not Pharaoh's.

Jacob Adopts Joseph's Sons

27 And Israel dwelt in the land of Egypt, in the country of Goshen; and they had possessions therein, and grew, and multiplied exceedingly.
28 And Jacob lived in the land of Egypt seventeen years: so the whole age of Jacob was a hundred forty and seven years. 29 And the time drew nigh that Israel must die: and he called his son Joseph, and said unto him, "If now I have found grace in thy sight, put, I pray thee, thy hand under my thigh, and deal kindly and truly with me; bury me not, I pray thee, in Egypt: 30 But I will lie with my fathers, and thou shalt carry me out of Egypt, and bury me in their buryingplace." And he said, "I will do as thou hast said." 31 And he said, "Swear unto me." And he sware unto him. And Israel bowed himself upon the bed's head.
48 And it came to pass after these things, that *one* told Joseph, "Behold, thy father *is* sick": and he took with him his two sons, Manasseh and Ephraim. 2 And *one* told Jacob, and said, "Behold, thy son Joseph cometh unto thee": and Israel strengthened himself, and sat upon the bed. 3 And Jacob said unto Joseph, "God Almighty appeared unto me at Luz in the land of Canaan, and blessed me, 4 And said unto me, 'Behold, I will make thee fruitful, and multiply thee, and I will make of thee a multitude of people; and will give this land to thy seed after thee *for* an everlasting possession.' 5 And now thy two sons, Ephraim and Manasseh, which were born unto thee in the land of Egypt, before I came unto thee into Egypt, *are* mine; as Reuben and Simeon, they shall be mine. 6 And thy issue, which thou begettest after them, shall be thine, *and* shall be called after the name of their brethren in their inheritance. 7 And as for me, when I came from Padan, Rachel died by me in the land of Canaan

in the way, when yet *there was* but a little way to come unto Ephrath: and I buried her there in the way of Ephrath; the same *is* Bethlehem."

8 And Israel beheld Joseph's sons, and said, "Who *are* these?" 9 And Joseph said unto his father, "They *are* my sons, whom God hath given me in this *place.*" And he said, "Bring them, I pray thee, unto me, and I will bless them." 10 Now the eyes of Israel were dim for age, *so that* he could not see. And he brought them near unto him; and he kissed them, and embraced them. 11 And Israel said unto Joseph, "I had not thought to see thy face: and, lo, God hath showed me also thy seed." 12 And Joseph brought them out from between his knees, and he bowed himself with his face to the earth. 13 And Joseph took them both, Ephraim in his right hand toward Israel's left hand, and Manasseh in his left hand toward Israel's right hand, and brought *them* near unto him. 14 And Israel stretched out his right hand, and laid *it* upon Ephraim's head, who *was* the younger, and his left hand upon Manasseh's head, guiding his hands wittingly; for Manasseh *was* the firstborn. 15 And he blessed Joseph, and said, "God, before whom my fathers Abraham and Isaac did walk, the God which fed me all my life long unto this day, 16 The Angel which redeemed me from all evil, bless the lads; and let my name be named on them, and the name of my fathers Abraham and Isaac; and let them grow into a multitude in the midst of the earth." 17 And when Joseph saw that his father laid his right hand upon the head of Ephraim, it displeased him: and he held up his father's hand, to remove it from Ephraim's head unto Manasseh's head. 18 And Joseph said unto his father, "Not so, my father: for this *is* the firstborn; put thy right hand upon his head." 19 And his father refused, and said, "I know *it,* my son, I know *it:* he also shall become a people, and he also shall be great: but truly his younger brother shall be greater than he, and his seed shall become a multitude of nations." 20 And he blessed them that day, saying, "In thee shall Israel bless, saying, 'God make thee as Ephraim and as Manasseh'": and he set Ephraim before Manasseh. 21 And Israel said unto Joseph, "Behold, I die; but God shall be with you, and bring you again unto the land of your fathers. 22 Moreover I have given to thee one portion above thy brethren, which I took out of the hand of the Amorite with my sword and with my bow." [75]

75. (48:1-22) This story explains why the house of Joseph divided into two parts, each with full tribal status, and why the tribe of Ephraim gained preeminence over that of Manasseh.

Jacob's Testament

49 And Jacob called unto his sons, and said, "Gather yourselves together, that I may tell you *that* which shall befall you in the last days.[76]

2 "Gather yourselves together, and hear, ye sons of Jacob;
   And hearken unto Israel your father.

3 "Reuben, thou *art* my firstborn,
   My might, and the beginning of my strength,
   The excellency of dignity, and the excellency of power:
4 Unstable as water, thou shalt not excel;
   Because thou wentest up to thy father's bed;
   Then defiledst thou *it:* he went up to my couch.

5 "Simeon and Levi *are* brethren;
   Instruments of cruelty *are in* their habitations.
6 O my soul, come not thou into their secret;
   Unto their assembly, mine honor, be not thou united:
   For in their anger they slew a man,
   And in their self-will they digged down a wall.[77]
7 Cursed *be* their anger, for *it was* fierce;
   And their wrath, for it was cruel:
   I will divide them in Jacob,
   And scatter them in Israel.

8 "Judah, thou *art he* whom thy brethren shall praise:
   Thy hand *shall be* in the neck of thine enemies;
   Thy father's children shall bow down before thee.
9 Judah *is* a lion's whelp:
   From the prey, my son, thou art gone up:

10 He stooped down, he couched as a lion,
    And as an old lion; who shall rouse him up? [78]
10 The sceptre shall not depart from Judah,
    Nor a lawgiver from between his feet,
    Until Shiloh come;
    And unto him *shall* the gathering of the people *be*.[79]
11 Binding his foal unto the vine,
    And his ass's colt unto the choice vine;
    He washed his garments in wine,
    And his clothes in the blood of grapes:
12 His eyes *shall be* red with wine,
    And his teeth white with milk.

13 "Zebulun shall dwell at the haven of the sea;
    And he *shall be* for a haven of ships;
    And his border *shall be* unto Zidon.

14 "Issachar *is* a strong ass
    Couching down between two burdens:
15 And he saw that rest *was* good,
    And the land that *it was* pleasant;
    And bowed his shoulder to bear,
    And became a servant unto tribute.

16 "Dan shall judge his people,
    As one of the tribes of Israel.
17 Dan shall be a serpent by the way,
    An adder in the path,
    That biteth the horse heels,
    So that his rider shall fall backward.

18 "I have waited for thy salvation, O Lord.[80]

19 "Gad, a troop shall overcome him:
    But he shall overcome at the last.

20 "Out of Asher his bread *shall be* fat,
    And he shall yield royal dainties.

21 "Naphtali *is* a hind let loose:
    He giveth goodly words.

---

76. (49:1-27) What were originally independent tribal oracles are here attributed to Jacob. Collected during the time of David, they represent the Nation of Israel's verdict on the tribes. Jacob says that *Reuben* will suffer because he defiled his father's bed; *Simeon* and *Levi* will fade because of their cruelty at Shechem; *Judah* will conquer and live in a fertile land; *Zebulun* will gain access to the Mediterranean; *Issachar* will choose to live as a comfortable slave; *Dan* will grow to power through guerilla attacks; *Gad* will prevail despite attacks of desert marauders; *Asher* will live in a fertile land; *Naphtali* will have the vitality to win new territory; *Joseph* will repel attacks and enjoy the choicest blessings; and *Benjamin* will have a zest for war.

77. RSV: "in their wantonness they hamstring oxen."

78. NEB:
   "Judah, you lion's whelp,
       you have returned from the kill, my son,
       and crouch and stretch like a lion;
       and, like a lion, who dare rouse you?"

79. In IB, Cuthbert A. Simpson calls this verse "cryptic in the extreme." Probably it is a veiled prophecy of David. RSV:
   "The scepter shall not depart from Judah,
       nor the ruler's staff from between his feet,
   until he comes to whom it belongs;
       and to him shall be the obedience of the peoples."

80. In IB, Cuthbert A. Simpson calls this an "ejaculatory gloss." It is unrelated to anything that precedes or follows it.

22   "Joseph *is* a fruitful bough,
        Even a fruitful bough by a well;
        Whose branches run over the wall:
23   The archers have sorely grieved him,
        And shot *at him,* and hated him:
24   But his bow abode in strength,
        And the arms of his hands were made
            strong
        By the hands of the mighty *God* of Jacob;
        (From thence *is* the shepherd, the stone of
            Israel;)
25   *Even* by the God of thy father, who shall
            help thee;
        And by the Almighty, who shall bless thee
        With blessings of heaven above,
        Blessings of the deep that lieth under,
        Blessings of the breasts, and of the womb:
26   The blessings of thy father have prevailed
        Above the blessings of my progenitors
        Unto the utmost bound of the everlasting
            hills:
        They shall be on the head of Joseph,
        And on the crown of the head of him that
            was separate from his brethren.

27   "Benjamin shall raven *as* a wolf:
        In the morning he shall devour the prey,
        And at night he shall divide the spoil."

The Death and Burial of Jacob

28 All these *are* the twelve tribes of Israel: and
this *is it* that their father spake unto them, and
blessed them; every one according to his blessing
he blessed them. 29 And he charged them, and
said unto them, "I am to be gathered unto my
people: bury me with my fathers in the cave that
is in the field of Ephron the Hittite, 30 In the
cave that *is* in the field of Machpelah, which *is* before Mamre, in the land of Canaan, which Abraham bought with the field of Ephron the Hittite
for a possession of a buryingplace. 31 There they
buried Abraham and Sarah his wife; there they
buried Isaac and Rebekah his wife; and there I
buried Leah. 32 The purchase of the field and of
the cave that *is* therein *was* from the children of
Heth." 33 And when Jacob had made an end of
commanding his sons, he gathered up his feet into
the bed, and yielded up the ghost, and was gathered unto his people.
50 And Joseph fell upon his father's face, and
wept upon him, and kissed him. 2 And Joseph
commanded his servants the physicians to em-
balm his father: and the physicians embalmed Israel. 3 And forty days were fulfilled for him; for
so are fulfilled the days of those which are embalmed: and the Egyptians mourned for him
threescore and ten days.

4 And when the days of his mourning were
past, Joseph spake unto the house of Pharaoh,
saying, "If now I have found grace in your eyes,
speak, I pray you, in the ears of Pharaoh,[81] saying,
5 My father made me swear, saying, 'Lo, I die: in
my grave which I have digged for me in the land
of Canaan, there shalt thou bury me.' Now
therefore let me go up, I pray thee, and bury my
father, and I will come again." 6 And Pharaoh
said, "Go up, and bury thy father, according as
he made thee swear." 7 And Joseph went up to
bury his father: and with him went up all the
servants of Pharaoh, the elders of his house, and
all the elders of the land of Egypt, 8 And all the
house of Joseph, and his brethren, and his father's
house: only their little ones, and their flocks, and
their herds, they left in the land of Goshen.
9 And there went up with him both chariots and
horsemen: and it was a very great company.
10 And they came to the threshingfloor of Atad,
which *is* beyond Jordan; and there they mourned
with a great and very sore lamentation: and he
made a mourning for his father seven days.
11 And when the inhabitants of the land, the Canaanites, saw the mourning in the floor of Atad,
they said, "This *is* a grievous mourning to the
Egyptians": wherefore the name of it was called
Abel-mizraim, which *is* beyond Jordan. 12 And
his sons did unto him according as he commanded them: 13 For his sons carried him into
the land of Canaan, and buried him in the cave of
the field of Machpelah, which Abraham bought
with the field for a possession of a buryingplace of
Ephron the Hittite, before Mamre. 14 And
Joseph returned into Egypt, he, and his brethren,
and all that went up with him to bury his father,
after he had buried his father.

The Last Days of Joseph

15 And when Joseph's brethren saw that their
father was dead, they said, "Joseph will peradventure hate us, and will certainly requite us all
the evil which we did unto him." 16 And they
sent a messenger unto Joseph, saying, "Thy father
did command before he died, saying, 17 'So shall
ye say unto Joseph, "Forgive, I pray thee now,
the trespass of thy brethren, and their sin; for
they did unto thee evil" ': and now, we pray thee,
forgive the trespass of the servants of the God of
thy father." And Joseph wept when they spake
unto him. 18 And his brethren also went and fell
down before his face; and they said, "Behold, we
be thy servants." 19 And Joseph said unto them,
"Fear not: for *am* I in the place of God? 20 But

---

81. JB: "If I may presume to enjoy your favour, please see that
    this message reaches Pharaoh's ears."

as for you, ye thought evil against me; *but* God meant it unto good, to bring to pass, as *it is* this day, to save much people alive. 21 Now therefore fear ye not: I will nourish you, and your little ones." And he comforted them, and spake kindly unto them.

22 And Joseph dwelt in Egypt, he, and his father's house: and Joseph lived a hundred and ten years. 23 And Joseph saw Ephraim's children of the third *generation:* the children also of Machir the son of Manasseh were brought up upon Joseph's knees. 24 And Joseph said unto his brethren, "I die; and God will surely visit you, and bring you out of this land unto the land which he sware to Abraham, to Isaac, and to Jacob." 25 And Joseph took an oath of the children of Israel, saying, "God will surely visit you, and ye shall carry up my bones from hence." 26 So Joseph died, *being* a hundred and ten years old: and they embalmed him, and he was put in a coffin in Egypt.

Introduction to
EXODUS

"Let my people go."

W. F. Thrall and A. Hibbard define an epic as "a long narrative poem in elevated style presenting characters of high position in a series of adventures which form an organic whole through their relation to a central figure of heroic proportions and through their development of episodes important to the history of a nation or race." * This describes *Exodus*.

Exodus is an epic adventure. It presents a powerful hero, a formidable antagonist, huge armies, a faithful god, and a miraculous victory. Specific events include murder, exile, confrontation, magic, plagues, flight, hardship, and mutiny. All the adventures implement the promise made by Yahweh to the patriarchs: "I will make of you a great nation." The Israelites move from slavery toward the formation of an important nation governed by a system of law.

The first chapter establishes the context of exploitation which calls forth the hero. It lists the twelve tribes in order to relate the book to the patriarchal narratives of *Genesis* and to assure all Israelites that they share in the deliverance. Some four hundred years after the death of Joseph, an insurgent Egyptian nationalism revokes the favored status enjoyed by the Jews. The Pharaoh imposes on them the *corvée,* the demand for unpaid labor on public construction. The action virtually enslaves them. To retain the Israelites as an economic boon without sacrificing Egyptian security, he orders the execution of all newborn sons. Thus the context for the birth of Moses is prepared.

Like later epic heroes, Moses is animated both by divine purpose and by his own nature. From his birth story—which reflects the legend of Sargon of Argade, an early Babylonian king who was placed in a basket on the water and later reared as a ruler—through all his adventures, Moses is a man directed by the Lord. Yahweh calls him to service and is ever present with his injunctions and his mighty works. Nevertheless, Moses is not simply an instrument of God. His humanity appears in his anger at the enslavement of his people and in his reluctance to answer God's call because of his lack of eloquence. (Tradition makes him a stammerer.) He is tenacious in negotiating with Pharaoh, frustrated and fearful before the murmuring Israelites, and confident in the face of Pharaoh's approaching army. Through these adventures, he is absolute in his fidelity to Yahweh.

While Yahweh's commitment to the Israelites is demonstrated throughout *Exodus*, three of the episodes—the Passover, the deliverance at the Sea of Reeds, and the Sinai Covenant—provide the heritage and bonds for the nation.

* In *A Handbook to Literature*, The Bobbs-Merrill Company, Inc., 1972.

Once the nation was established, the Israelites looked back on the Passover—the final disaster leveled on the Egyptians preceding the escape—as the event which inaugurated the rise from slavery to nationhood. The feast of the Unleavened Bread became one of three annual obligatory services. And the words used to explain the event to future generations emphasize Yahweh's fidelity: "It is the sacrifice of the Lord's passover, who passed over the houses of the children of Israel in Egypt, when he smote the Egyptians and delivered our houses" (12:27).

Even more important in Jewish belief was the miraculous passage through the Sea of Reeds. Early in the exodus, the children of Israel find themselves pursued by a mighty army and blocked by the sea. Yahweh delivers them. Though all attempts to explain exactly what happened are inadequate, the significance of the deliverance is clear and almost impossible to overstate. In IB, J. Coert Rylaarsdam declares, "It was the redemptive event which became the foundation of Israel's existence as the people of God. . . . The event is for the O.T. what Jesus as Christ is for the N.T.— the normative and revealing act of God."

By the time the Israelites encamp at Sinai, their shared experiences provide the bases for unity. At Sinai, the Decalogue and the Covenant Code establish the legal basis for nationhood. As J. A. Bewer notes in *The Literature of the Old Testament* (1962), the Ten Commandments emphasize "the fundamental obligation of 'monolatry,' that is, of worshipping Yahweh alone as its God, and of obedience to the will of God, which is principally social morality." The Book of the Covenant (20:23–23:19) is the oldest Hebrew legal code. In it there is a recognition of community without which there can be no nation.

The epic is attributed to J, E, and P (see Introduction to *Genesis*), and the multiple authorship is evident throughout the book. It accounts for the duplication of episodes: Moses' call is described twice, as is the injunction that the Israelites not approach Mount Sinai; similarly, the third and fourth plagues may relate to a single event. It leads to the juxtaposition of late passages with very early ones: the triumphal Song of Moses is followed by the ancient Song of Miriam. It causes confusion of names: Moses' father-in-law is called both Reuel and Jethro; the holy mountain is both Horeb and Sinai. And it accounts for vexing interpolations: lengthy instructions concerning religious rites intrude between the announcement and the execution of the tenth plague. However, such features do not impair the unified movement of *Exodus*.

The historicity of the book remains a complex question. Clearly the authors were recalling some event which contributed to national liberation. Evidence suggests that the event occurred during the 19th Dynasty in the reign of Rameses II (ca. 1301–1234 B.C.), but the earliest accounts used in the composition of *Exodus* were written hundreds of years after the experience, and the concern of the authors was religious, not historical. They emphasized that the Israelites were the people of God, and that there was a divine basis for their laws, their civil organization, and their religious rites. The result is a kind of idealized history which presents the exodus event as an act of national redemption.

The present selection (Chapters 1 through 22) relates the epic events which take the Israelites from bondage to the divine encounter at Mount Sinai. The remainder of the book, thought to be P material, is concerned with religious ordinances.

EXODUS

THE ISRAELITES IN EGYPT

Israel Enslaved

1 Now these *are* the names of the children of Israel, which came into Egypt; every man and his household came with Jacob. 2 Reuben, Simeon, Levi, and Judah, 3 Issachar, Zebulun, and Benjamin, 4 Dan, and Naphtali, Gad, and Asher. 5 And all the souls that came out of the loins of Jacob were seventy souls: for Joseph was in Egypt *already*. 6 And Joseph died, and all his brethren, and all that generation.

7 And the children of Israel were fruitful, and increased abundantly, and multiplied, and waxed exceeding mighty; and the land was filled with them. 8 Now there arose up a new king over Egypt, which knew not Joseph. 9 And he said unto his people, "Behold, the people of the children of Isarel *are* more and mightier than we: 10 Come on, let us deal wisely with them; lest they multiply, and it come to pass, that, when there falleth out any war, they join also unto our enemies, and fight against us, and *so* get them up out of the land." 11 Therefore they did set over them taskmasters to afflict them with their burdens. And they built for Pharaoh treasure cities, Pithom and Raamses. 12 But the more they afflicted them, the more they multiplied and grew. And they were grieved because of [1] the children of Israel. 13 And the Egyptians made the children of Israel to serve with rigor: 14 And they made their lives bitter with hard bondage, in mortar, and in brick, and in all manner of service in the field: all their service, wherein they made them serve, *was* with rigor.

15 And the king of Egypt spake to the Hebrew midwives, of which the name of the one *was* Shiphrah, and the name of the other Puah; 16 And he said, "When ye do the office of a midwife to the Hebrew women, and see *them* upon the stools, if it *be* a son, then ye shall kill him; but if it *be* a daughter, then she shall live." 17 But the midwives feared God, and did not as the king of Egypt commanded them, but saved the men children alive. 18 And the king of Egypt called for the midwives, and said unto them, "Why have ye done this thing, and have saved the men children alive?" 19 And the midwives said unto Pharaoh, "Because the Hebrew women *are* not as the Egyptian women; for they *are* lively, and are delivered ere the midwives come in unto them." 20 Therefore God dealt well with the midwives: and the people multiplied, and waxed very mighty. 21 And it came to pass, because the midwives feared God, that he made them houses. 22 And Pharaoh charged all his people, saying, "Every son that is born ye shall cast into the river, and every daughter ye shall save alive."

Moses

2 And there went a man of the house of Levi, and took *to wife* a daughter of Levi.

2 And the woman conceived, and bare a son: and when she saw him that he *was* a goodly *child*, she hid him three months. 3 And when she could not longer hide him, she took for him an ark of bulrushes, and daubed it with slime and with pitch, and put the child therein, and she laid *it* in the flags by the river's brink. 4 And his sister stood afar off, to wit what would be done to him. 5 And the daughter of Pharaoh came down to wash *herself* at the river; and her maidens walked along by the river's side: and when she saw the ark among the flags, she sent her maid to fetch it. 6 And when she had opened *it*, she saw the child: and, behold, the babe wept. And she had compassion on him, and said, "This *is one* of the Hebrews' children." 7 Then said his sister to Pharaoh's daughter, "Shall I go and call to thee a nurse of the Hebrew women, that she may nurse the child for thee?" 8 And Pharaoh's daughter said to her, "Go." And the maid went and called the child's mother. 9 And Pharaoh's daughter said unto her, "Take this child away, and nurse it for me, and I will give *thee* thy wages." And the woman took the child, and nursed it. 10 And the child grew, and she brought him unto Pharaoh's daughter, and he became her son. And she called his name Moses: and she said, "Because I drew him out of the water."

11 And it came to pass in those days, when Moses was grown, that he went out unto his brethren, and looked on their burdens: and he spied an Egyptian smiting a Hebrew,[2] one of his brethren. 12 And he looked this way and that way, and when he saw that *there was* no man, he slew the Egyptian, and hid him in the sand. 13 And when he went out the second day, behold, two men of the Hebrews strove together: and he said to him that did the wrong, "Wherefore smitest thou thy fellow?" 14 And he said,

---

1. RSV: "in dread of." In IB, J. Coert Rylaarsdam notes, "The Hebrew word conveys an element of awe; there was something eerie and unnerving about this people."

2. MEEK: "kill a Hebrew."

"Who made thee a prince and a judge over us? intendest thou to kill me, as thou killedst the Egyptian?" And Moses feared, and said, "Surely this thing is known."

15 Now when Pharaoh heard this thing, he sought to slay Moses. But Moses fled from the face of Pharaoh, and dwelt in the land of Midian: and he sat down by a well. 16 Now the priest of Midian had seven daughters: and they came and drew *water,* and filled the troughs to water their father's flock. 17 And the shepherds came and drove them away: but Moses stood up and helped them, and watered their flock. 18 And when they came to Reuel their father, he said, "How *is it that* ye are come so soon to-day?" 19 And they said, "An Egyptian delivered us out of the hand of the shepherds, and also drew *water* enough for us, and watered the flock." 20 And he said unto his daughters, "And where *is* he? why *is* it *that* ye have left the man? call him, that he may eat bread." 21 And Moses was content to dwell with the man: and he gave Moses Zipporah his daughter. 22 And she bare *him* a son, and he called his name Gershom: for he said, "I have been a stranger in a strange land."

Moses Is Called

23 And it came to pass in process of time, that the king of Egypt died: and the children of Israel sighed by reason of the bondage, and they cried, and their cry came up unto God by reason of the bondage. 24 And God heard their groaning, and God remembered his covenant with Abraham, with Isaac, and with Jacob. 25 And God looked upon the children of Israel, and God had respect unto *them.*
3 Now Moses kept the flock of Jethro his father-in-law, the priest of Midian: and he led the flock to the back side of the desert, and came to the mountain of God, *even* to Horeb. 2 And the Angel of the LORD appeared unto him in a flame of fire out of the midst of a bush: and he looked, and, behold, the bush burned with fire, and the bush *was* not consumed. 3 And Moses said, "I will now turn aside, and see this great sight, why the bush is not burnt." 4 And when the LORD saw that he turned aside to see, God called unto him out of the midst of the bush, and said, "Moses, Moses." And he said, "Here *am* I." 5 And he said, "Draw not nigh hither: put off thy shoes from off thy feet; for the place whereon thou standest *is* holy ground." 6 Moreover he said, "I *am* the God of thy father, the God of Abraham, the God of Isaac, and the God of Jacob." And Moses hid his face; for he was afraid to look upon God.

7 And the LORD said, "I have surely seen the affliction of my people which *are* in Egypt, and have heard their cry by reason of their taskmasters; for I know their sorrows; 8 And I am come down to deliver them out of the hand of the Egyptians, and to bring them up out of that land unto a good land and a large, unto a land flowing with milk and honey; unto the place of the Canaanites, and the Hittites, and the Amorites, and the Perizzites, and the Hivites, and the Jebusites. 9 Now therefore, behold, the cry of the children of Israel is come unto me: and I have also seen the oppression wherewith the Egyptians oppress them. 10 Come now therefore, and I will send thee unto Pharaoh, that thou mayest bring forth my people the children of Israel out of Egypt." 11 And Moses said unto God, "Who *am* I, that I should go unto Pharaoh, and that I should bring forth the children of Israel out of Egypt?" 12 And he said, "Certainly I will be with thee; and this *shall be* a token unto thee, that I have sent thee: When thou hast brought forth the people out of Egypt, ye shall serve God upon this mountain." [3]

13 And Moses said unto God, "Behold, *when* I come unto the children of Israel, and shall say unto them, 'The God of your fathers hath sent me unto you'; and they shall say to me, 'What *is* his name?' what shall I say unto them?" 14 And God said unto Moses, "I AM THAT I AM":[4] and he said, "Thus shalt thou say unto the children of Israel, 'I AM hath sent me unto you.'" 15 And God said moreover unto Moses, "Thus shalt thou say unto the children of Israel, 'The LORD God of your fathers, the God of Abraham, the God of Isaac, and the God of Jacob, hath sent me unto you': this *is* my name for ever, and this *is* my memorial unto all generations. 16 Go, and gather the elders of Israel together, and say unto them, 'The LORD God of your fathers, the God of Abraham, of Isaac, and of Jacob, appeared unto me, saying, "I have surely visited you, and *seen* that which is done to you in Egypt: 17 And I have said, I will bring you up out of the affliction of Egypt unto the land of the Canaanites, and the Hittites, and the Amorites, and the Perizzites, and the Hivites, and the Jebusites, unto a land flowing

---

3. It is hard to conceive how the token (RSV: "sign") would be to "serve God upon this mountain." JB suggests the sign is described in 4:1-9 and that the present text is incomplete: " 'I shall be with you,' was the answer 'and this is the sign by which you shall know that it is I who have sent you . . . After you have led the people out of Egypt, you are to offer worship to God on this mountain.' "
4. The etymology of the Hebrew name for God, "Yahweh," is related to the verb "to be." Thus, God's answer to Moses permits a variety of translations: RSV, MEEK, JB: "I am who I am"; KNOX: "I am the God who IS"; NAB: "I am who am"; NEB: "I AM: that is who I am"; MOFFATT: "I-will-be-what-I-will-be." The description seems intentionally obscure.

with milk and honey." ' 18 And they shall hearken to thy voice: and thou shalt come, thou and the elders of Israel, unto the king of Egypt, and ye shall say unto him, 'The LORD God of the Hebrews hath met with us: and now let us go, we beseech thee, three days' journey into the wilderness, that we may sacrifice to the LORD our God.'

19 "And I am sure that the king of Egypt will not let you go, no, not by a mighty hand. 20 And I will stretch out my hand, and smite Egypt with all my wonders which I will do in the midst thereof: and after that he will let you go. 21 And I will give this people favor in the sight of the Egyptians: and it shall come to pass, that, when ye go, ye shall not go empty: 22 But every woman shall borrow of her neighbor, and of her that sojourneth in her house, jewels of silver, and jewels of gold, and raiment: and ye shall put *them* upon your sons, and upon your daughters; and ye shall spoil the Egyptians."

4 And Moses answered and said, "But, behold, they will not believe me, nor hearken unto my voice: for they will say, 'The LORD hath not appeared unto thee.' " 2 And the LORD said unto him, "What *is* that in thine hand?" And he said, "A rod." 3 And he said, "Cast it on the ground." And he cast it on the ground, and it became a serpent; and Moses fled from before it. 4 And the LORD said unto Moses, "Put forth thine hand, and take it by the tail." And he put forth his hand, and caught it, and it became a rod in his hand: 5 "That they may believe that the LORD God of their fathers, the God of Abraham, the God of Isaac, and the God of Jacob, hath appeared unto thee." 6 And the LORD said furthermore unto him, "Put now thine hand into thy bosom." And he put his hand into his bosom: and when he took it out, behold, his hand *was* leprous as snow. 7 And he said, "Put thine hand into thy bosom again." And he put his hand into his bosom again; and plucked it out of his bosom, and, behold, it was turned again as his *other* flesh. 8 "And it shall come to pass, if they will not believe thee, neither hearken to the voice of the first sign, that they will believe the voice of the latter sign. 9 And it shall come to pass, if they will not believe also these two signs, neither hearken unto thy voice, that thou shalt take of the water of the river, and pour *it* upon the dry *land:* and the water which thou takest out of the river shall become blood upon the dry *land.*"

10 And Moses said unto the LORD, "O my Lord, I *am* not eloquent, neither heretofore, nor since thou hast spoken unto thy servant; but I *am* slow of speech, and of a slow tongue." 11 And the LORD said unto him, "Who hath made man's mouth? or who maketh the dumb, or deaf, or the seeing, or the blind? have not I the LORD? 12 Now therefore go, and I will be with thy mouth, and teach thee what thou salt say." 13 And he said, "O my Lord, send, I pray thee, by the hand *of him whom* thou wilt send." [5] 14 And the anger of the LORD was kindled against Moses, and he said, "*Is* not Aaron the Levite thy brother? I know that he can speak well. And also, behold, he cometh forth to meet thee: and when he seeth thee, he will be glad in his heart. 15 And thou shalt speak unto him, and put words in his mouth: and I will be with thy mouth, and with his mouth, and will teach you what ye shall do. 16 And he shall be thy spokesman unto the people: and he shall be, *even* he shall be to thee instead of a mouth, and thou shalt be to him instead of God. 17 And thou shalt take this rod in thine hand, wherewith thou shalt do signs."

The Return to Egypt

18 And Moses went and returned to Jethro his father-in-law, and said unto him, "Let me go, I pray thee, and return unto my brethren which *are* in Egypt, and see whether they be yet alive." And Jethro said to Moses, "Go in peace." 19 And the LORD said unto Moses in Midian, "Go, return into Egypt: for all the men are dead which sought thy life." 20 And Moses took his wife and his sons, and set them upon an ass, and he returned to the land of Egypt: and Moses took the rod of God in his hand. 21 And the LORD said unto Moses, "When thou goest to return into Egypt, see that thou do all those wonders before Pharaoh, which I have put in thine hand: but I will harden his heart, that he shall not let the people go. 22 And thou shalt say unto Pharaoh, 'Thus saith the LORD, "Israel *is* my son, *even* my firstborn: 23 And I say unto thee, Let my son go, that he may serve me: and if thou refuse to let him go, behold, I will slay thy son, *even* thy firstborn." ' "

24 And it came to pass by the way in the inn, that the LORD met him, and sought to kill him. 25 Then Zipporah took a sharp stone, and cut off the foreskin of her son, and cast *it* at his feet, and said, "Surely a bloody husband *art* thou to me." 26 So he let him go: then she said, "A bloody husband *thou art,*" because of the circumcision.[6]

27 And the LORD said to Aaron, "Go into the wilderness to meet Moses." And he went, and

---

5. RSV: "Oh, my Lord, send, I pray, some other person."
6. (4:24-26) The phrase "bridegroom of blood" recalls belief in demonic attacks (see *Tobit* 3:8) and circumcision performed on the wedding night to placate the demon. With reason, JB calls this "A mysterious narrative difficult to interpret."

met him in the mount of God, and kissed him. 28 And Moses told Aaron all the words of the LORD who had sent him, and all the signs which he had commanded him. 29 And Moses and Aaron went and gathered together all the elders of the children of Israel: 30 And Aaron spake all the words which the LORD had spoken unto Moses, and did the signs in the sight of the people. 31 And the people believed: and when they heard that the LORD had visited the children of Israel, and that he had looked upon their affliction, then they bowed their heads and worshipped.

Moses and Pharaoh

5 And afterward Moses and Aaron went in, and told Pharaoh, "Thus saith the LORD God of Israel, 'Let my people go, that they may hold a feast unto me in the wilderness.'" 2 And Pharaoh said, "Who *is* the LORD, that I should obey his voice to let Israel go? I know not the LORD,[7] neither will I let Israel go." 3 And they said, "The God of the Hebrews hath met with us: let us go, we pray thee, three days' journey into the desert, and sacrifice unto the LORD our God; lest he fall upon us with pestilence, or with the sword." 4 And the king of Egypt said unto them, "Wherefore do ye, Moses and Aaron, let the people from their works? get you unto your burdens." 5 And Pharaoh said, "Behold, the people of the land now *are* many, and ye make them rest from their burdens." 6 And Pharaoh commanded the same day the taskmasters of the people, and their officers, saying, 7 "Ye shall no more give the people straw to make brick, as heretofore: let them go and gather straw for themselves. 8 And the tale of the bricks, which they did make heretofore, ye shall lay upon them; ye shall not diminish *aught* thereof: for they *be* idle; therefore they cry, saying, 'Let us go *and* sacrifice to our God.' 9 Let there more work be laid upon the men, that they may labor therein; and let them not regard vain words."

10 And the taskmasters of the people went out, and their officers, and they spake to the people, saying, "Thus saith Pharaoh, 'I will not give you straw. 11 Go ye, get you straw where ye can find it: yet not aught of your work shall be diminished.'" 12 So the people were scattered abroad throughout all the land of Egypt to gather stubble instead of straw. 13 And the taskmasters hasted *them,* saying, "Fulfil your works, *your* daily tasks, as when there was straw." 14 And the officers of the children of Israel, which Pharaoh's taskmas-

ters had set over them, were beaten, *and* demanded, "Wherefore have ye not fulfilled your task in making brick both yesterday and to-day, as heretofore?"

15 Then the officers of the children of Israel came and cried unto Pharaoh, saying, "Wherefore dealest thou thus with thy servants? 16 There is no straw given unto thy servants, and they say to us, 'Make brick': and, behold, thy servants *are* beaten; but the fault *is* in thine own people." 17 But he said, "Ye *are* idle, *ye are* idle: therefore ye say, 'Let us go *and* do sacrifice to the LORD.' 18 Go therefore now, *and* work; for there shall no straw be given you, yet shall ye deliver the tale of bricks." 19 And the officers of the children of Israel did see *that* they *were* in evil *case,* after it was said, "Ye shall not minish *aught* from your bricks of your daily task."

20 And they met Moses and Aaron, who stood in the way, as they came forth from Pharaoh: 21 And they said unto them, "The LORD look upon you, and judge; because ye have made our savor to be abhorred in the eyes of Pharaoh, and in the eyes of his servants, to put a sword in their hand to slay us." 22 And Moses returned unto the LORD, and said, "Lord, wherefore hast thou *so* evil entreated this people? why *is it that* thou hast sent me? 23 For since I came to Pharaoh to speak in thy name, he hath done evil to this people; neither hast thou delivered thy people at all." **6** Then the LORD said unto Moses, "Now shalt thou see what I will do to Pharaoh: for with a strong hand shall he let them go, and with a strong hand shall he drive them out of his land." 2 And God spake unto Moses, and said unto him, "I *am* the LORD: 3 And I appeared unto Abraham, unto Isaac, and unto Jacob, by *the name of* God Almighty; but by my name JEHOVAH was I not known to them. 4 And I have also established my covenant with them, to give them the land of Canaan, the land of their pilgrimage, wherein they were strangers. 5 And I have also heard the groaning of the children of Israel, whom the Egyptians keep in bondage; and I have remembered my covenant. 6 Wherefore say unto the children of Israel, 'I *am* the LORD, and I will bring you out from under the burdens of the Egyptians, and I will rid you out of their bondage, and I will redeem you with a stretched out arm, and with great judgments: 7 And I will take you to me for a people, and I will be to you a God: and ye shall know that I *am* the LORD your God, which bringeth you out from under the burdens of the Egyptians. 8 And I will bring you in unto the land, concerning the which I did swear to give it to Abraham, to Isaac, and to Jacob; and I will give it you for a heritage: I *am* the LORD.'"

---

7. Pharaoh, a polytheist, does not think Israel's is a particularly important god. This attitude provokes much that follows. See 7:5, 11:9, 14:8, etc.

9 And Moses spake so unto the children of Israel: but they hearkened not unto Moses for anguish of spirit, and for cruel bondage.

10 And the LORD spake unto Moses, saying, 11 "Go in, speak unto Pharaoh king of Egypt, that he let the children of Israel go out of his land." 12 And Moses spake before the LORD, saying, "Behold, the children of Israel have not hearkened unto me; how then shall Pharaoh hear me, who *am* of uncircumcised lips?" [8] 13 And the LORD spake unto Moses and unto Aaron, and gave them a charge unto the children of Israel, and unto Pharaoh king of Egypt, to bring the children of Israel out of the land of Egypt.

14 These *be* the heads of their fathers' houses: The sons of Reuben the firstborn of Israel; Hanoch, and Pallu, Hezron, and Carmi: these *be* the families of Reuben. 15 And the sons of Simeon; Jemuel, and Jamin, and Ohad, and Jachin, and Zohar, and Shaul the son of a Canaanitish woman: these *are* the families of Simeon. 16 And these *are* the names of the sons of Levi according to their generations; Gershon, and Kohath, and Merari: and the years of the life of Levi *were* a hundred thirty and seven years. 17 The sons of Gershon; Libni, and Shimi, according to their families. 18 And the sons of Kohath; Amram, and Izhar, and Hebron, and Uzziel: and the years of the life of Kohath *were* a hundred thirty and three years. 19 And the sons of Merari; Mahali and Mushi: these *are* the families of Levi according to their generations. 20 And Amram took him Jochebed his father's sister to wife; and she bare him Aaron and Moses: and the years of the life of Amram *were* a hundred and thirty and seven years. 21 And the sons of Izhar; Korah, and Nepheg, and Zichri. 22 And the sons of Uzziel; Mishael, and Elzaphan, and Zithri. 23 And Aaron took him Elisheba, daughter of Amminadab, sister of Naashon, to wife; and she bare him Nadab and Abihu, Eleazar and Ithamar. 24 And the sons of Korah; Assir, and Elkanah, and Abiasaph: these *are* the families of the Korhites. 25 And Eleazar Aaron's son took him *one* of the daughters of Putiel to wife; and she bare him Phinehas: these *are* the heads of the fathers of the Levites according to their families. 26 These *are* that Aaron and Moses, to whom the LORD said, "Bring out the children of Israel from the land of Egypt according to their armies." 27 These *are* they which spake to Pharaoh king of Egypt, to bring out the children of Israel from Egypt: these *are* that Moses and Aaron.

28 And it came to pass on the day *when* the LORD spake unto Moses in the land of Egypt, 29 That the LORD spake unto Moses, saying, "I *am* the LORD: speak thou unto Pharaoh king of Egypt all that I say unto thee." 30 And Moses said before the LORD, "Behold, I *am* of uncircumcised lips, and how shall Pharaoh hearken unto me?"

7 And the LORD said unto Moses, "See, I have made thee a god to Pharaoh; and Aaron thy brother shall be thy prophet. 2 Thou shalt speak all that I command thee; and Aaron thy brother shall speak unto Pharaoh, that he send the children of Israel out of his land. 3 And I will harden Pharaoh's heart, and multiply my signs and my wonders in the land of Egypt. 4 But Pharaoh shall not hearken unto you, that I may lay my hand upon Egypt, and bring forth mine armies, *and* my people the children of Israel, out of the land of Egypt by great judgments. 5 And the Egyptians shall know that I *am* the LORD, when I stretch forth mine hand upon Egypt, and bring out the children of Israel from among them." 6 And Moses and Aaron did as the LORD commanded them, so did they. 7 And Moses *was* fourscore years old, and Aaron fourscore and three years old, when they spake unto Pharaoh. 8 And the LORD spake unto Moses and unto Aaron, saying, 9 "When Pharaoh shall speak unto you, saying, 'Show a miracle for you': then thou shalt say unto Aaron, 'Take thy rod, and cast *it* before Pharaoh,' *and* it shall become a serpent."

10 And Moses and Aaron went in unto Pharaoh, and they did so as the LORD commanded: and Aaron cast down his rod before Pharaoh, and before his servants, and it became a serpent. 11 Then Pharaoh also called the wise men and the sorcerers: now the magicians of Egypt, they also did in like manner with their enchantments. 12 For they cast down every man his rod, and they became serpents: but Aaron's rod swallowed up their rods. 13 And he hardened Pharaoh's heart, that he hearkened not unto them; as the LORD had said.

The Ten Plagues [9]
Water becomes Blood

14 And the LORD said unto Moses, "Pharaoh's heart *is* hardened, he refuseth to let the people go.

---

8. KNOX: "The Israelites will not listen to me; what hope is there that Pharao will listen to me? A man, moreover, so tongue-tied." The question is repeated in 6:30 and answered in 7:1-2.

9. (7:14–11:10) In Volume 10 ("*Exodus*") of the *Layman's Bible Commentary* (John Knox Press, 1963), B. Davie Napier writes: "There is no good reason to doubt that the essence of the major historical episodes is preserved. If the
(continued)

15 Get thee unto Pharaoh in the morning; lo, he goeth out unto the water; and thou shalt stand by the river's brink against he come; and the rod which was turned to a serpent shalt thou take in thine hand. 16 And thou shalt say unto him, 'The LORD God of the Hebrews hath sent me unto thee, saying, "Let my people go, that they may serve me in the wilderness: and, behold, hitherto thou wouldest not hear." 17 Thus saith the LORD, "In this thou shalt know that I *am* the LORD: behold, I will smite with the rod that *is* in mine hand upon the waters which *are* in the river, and they shall be turned to blood. 18 And the fish that *is* in the river shall die, and the river shall stink; and the Egyptians shall loathe to drink of the water of the river." ' " 19 And the LORD spake unto Moses, "Say unto Aaron, 'Take thy rod, and stretch out thine hand upon the waters of Egypt, upon their streams, upon their rivers, and upon their ponds, and upon all their pools of water, that they may become blood; and *that* there may be blood throughout all the land of Egypt, both in *vessels of* wood, and in *vessels of* stone.' "

20 And Moses and Aaron did so, as the LORD commanded; and he lifted up the rod, and smote the waters that *were* in the river, in the sight of Pharaoh, and in the sight of his servants; and all the waters that *were* in the river were turned to blood. 21 And the fish that *was* in the river died; and the river stank, and the Egyptians could not drink of the water of the river; and there was blood throughout all the land of Egypt. 22 And the magicians of Egypt did so with their enchantments: and Pharaoh's heart was hardened, neither did he hearken unto them; as the LORD had said. 23 And Pharaoh turned and went into his house, neither did he set his heart to this also. 24 And all the Egyptians digged round about the river for water to drink; for they could not drink of the water of the river. 25 And seven days were fulfilled, after that the LORD had smitten the river.

Frogs

8 And the LORD spake unto Moses, "Go unto Pharaoh, and say unto him, 'Thus saith the LORD, "Let my people go, that they may serve me. 2 And if thou refuse to let *them* go, behold, I will smite all thy borders with frogs: 3 And the river shall bring forth frogs abundantly, which shall go up and come into thine house, and into thy bedchamber, and upon thy bed, and into the house of thy servants, and upon thy people, and into thine ovens, and into thy kneadingtroughs: 4 And the frogs shall come up both on thee, and upon thy people, and upon all thy servants." ' " 5 And the LORD spake unto Moses, "Say unto Aaron, 'Stretch forth thine hand with thy rod over the streams, over the rivers, and over the ponds, and cause frogs to come up upon the land of Egypt.' " 6 And Aaron stretched out his hand over the waters of Egypt; and the frogs came up, and covered the land of Egypt. 7 And the magicians did so with their enchantments, and brought up frogs upon the land of Egypt.

8 Then Pharaoh called for Moses and Aaron, and said, "Entreat the LORD, that he may take away the frogs from me, and from my people; and I will let the people go, that they may do sacrifice unto the LORD." 9 And Moses said unto Pharaoh, "Glory over me: when shall I entreat for thee, and for thy servants, and for thy people, to destroy the frogs from thee and thy houses, *that* they may remain in the river only?" 10 And he said, "To-morrow." And he said, "*Be it* according to thy word; that thou mayest know that *there is* none like unto the LORD our God. 11 And the frogs shall depart from thee, and from thy houses, and from thy servants, and from thy people; they shall remain in the river only." 12 And Moses and Aaron went out from Pharaoh: and Moses cried unto the LORD because of the frogs which he had brought against Pharaoh. 13 And the LORD did according to the word of Moses; and the frogs died out of the houses, out of the villages, and out of the fields. 14 And they gathered them together upon heaps; and the land stank. 15 But when Pharaoh saw that there was respite, he hardened his heart, and hearkened not unto them; as the LORD had said.

Lice

16 And the LORD said unto Moses, "Say unto Aaron, 'Stretch out thy rod, and smite the dust of the land, that it may become lice[10] throughout all the land of Egypt.' " 17 And they did so; for Aaron stretched out his hand with his rod, and smote the dust of the earth, and it became lice in man, and in beast; all the dust of the land became lice throughout all the land of Egypt. 18 And the magicians did so with their enchantments to bring forth lice, but they could not: so there were lice upon man, and upon beast. 19 Then the magicians said unto Pharaoh, "This *is* the finger of God":[11] and Pharaoh's heart was hardened, and

---

occurrence in Egypt of hail and locusts in catastrophic severity is rare, plagues of frogs, insects, and always related diseases are a repeated phenomenon of Egypt's history. The waters turned to blood reminds us that when the Nile begins its annual rise, red dirt from the mountains of Abyssinia colors the water. And darkness over the land has for centuries periodically occurred as a result of violent sandstorms. But to pass this narrative off merely as accurate history is grossly to misinterpret it."

10. RSV, NAB, KNOX, MOFFATT: "gnats."
11. Presumably, this refers to Aaron's rod.

he hearkened not unto them; as the LORD had said.

Flies

20 And the LORD said unto Moses, "Rise up early in the morning, and stand before Pharaoh; lo, he cometh forth to the water; and say unto him, 'Thus saith the LORD, "Let my people go, that they may serve me. 21 Else, if thou wilt not let my people go, behold, I will send swarms of flies upon thee, and upon thy servants, and upon thy people, and into thy houses: and the houses of the Egyptians shall be full of swarms of flies, and also the ground whereon they *are*. 22 And I will sever in that day the land of Goshen, in which my people dwell, that no swarms of flies shall be there; to the end thou mayest know that I *am* the LORD in the midst of the earth. 23 And I will put a division between my people and thy people: to-morrow shall this sign be." ' " 24 And the LORD did so; and there came a grievous swarm of flies into the house of Pharaoh, and *into* his servants' houses, and into all the land of Egypt: the land was corrupted by reason of the swarm of flies.

25 And Pharaoh called for Moses and for Aaron, and said, "Go ye, sacrifice to your God in the land." 26 And Moses said, "It is not meet so to do; for we shall sacrifice the abomination of the Egyptians to the LORD our God: lo, shall we sacrifice the abomination of the Egyptians before their eyes, and will they not stone us? 27 We will go three days' journey into the wilderness, and sacrifice to the LORD our God, as he shall command us." 28 And Pharaoh said, "I will let you go, that ye may sacrifice to the LORD your God in the wilderness; only ye shall not go very far away: entreat for me." 29 And Moses said, "Behold, I go out from thee, and I will entreat the LORD that the swarms of flies may depart from Pharaoh, from his servants, and from his people, to-morrow: but let not Pharaoh deal deceitfully any more in not letting the people go to sacrifice to the LORD." 30 And Moses went out from Pharaoh, and entreated the LORD. 31 And the LORD did according to the word of Moses; and he removed the swarms of flies from Pharaoh, from his servants, and from his people; there remained not one. 32 And Pharaoh hardened his heart at this time also, neither would he let the people go.

Cattle Plague

9 Then the LORD said unto Moses, "Go in unto Pharaoh, and tell him, 'Thus saith the LORD God of the Hebrews, "Let my people go, that they may serve me. 2 For if thou refuse to let *them* go, and wilt hold them still, 3 Behold, the hand of the LORD is upon thy cattle which *is* in the field, upon the horses, upon the asses, upon the camels, upon the oxen, and upon the sheep: *there shall be* a very grievous murrain. 4 And the LORD shall sever between the cattle of Israel and the cattle of Egypt: and there shall nothing die of all *that is* the children's of Israel." ' " 5 And the LORD appointed a set time, saying, "To-morrow the LORD shall do this thing in the land." 6 And the LORD did that thing on the morrow, and all the cattle of Egypt died: but of the cattle of the children of Israel died not one. 7 And Pharaoh sent, and, behold, there was not one of the cattle of the Israelites dead. And the heart of Pharaoh was hardened, and he did not let the people go.

Boils

8 And the LORD said unto Moses and unto Aaron, "Take to you handfuls of ashes of the furnace, and let Moses sprinkle it toward the heaven in the sight of Pharaoh. 9 And it shall become small dust in all the land of Egypt, and shall be a boil breaking forth *with* blains upon man, and upon beast, throughout all the land of Egypt." 10 And they took ashes of the furnace, and stood before Pharaoh; and Moses sprinkled it up toward heaven; and it became a boil breaking forth *with* blains upon man, and upon beast. 11 And the magicians could not stand before Moses because of the boils; for the boil was upon the magicians, and upon all the Egyptians. 12 And the LORD hardened the heart of Pharaoh, and he hearkened not unto them; as the LORD had spoken unto Moses.

Hail

13 And the LORD said unto Moses, "Rise up early in the morning, and stand before Pharaoh, and say unto him, 'Thus saith the LORD God of the Hebrews, "Let my people go, that they may serve me. 14 For I will at this time send all my plagues upon thine heart, and upon thy servants, and upon thy people; that thou mayest know that *there is* none like me in all the earth. 15 For now I will stretch out my hand, that I may smite thee and thy people with pestilence; and thou shalt be cut off from the earth.[12] 16 And in very deed for this *cause* have I raised thee up, for to show *in* thee my power; and that my name may be declared throughout all the earth. 17 As yet exaltest thou thyself against my people, that thou wilt not let them go? 18 Behold, to-morrow about this time I will cause it to rain a very grievous hail, such as hath not been in Egypt since the foundation thereof even until now. 19 Send

---

12. RSV: "For by now I could have put forth my hand and struck you and your people with pestilence, and you would have been cut off from the earth."

therefore now, *and* gather thy cattle, and all that thou hast in the field; *for upon* every man and beast which shall be found in the field, and shall not be brought home, the hail shall come down upon them, and they shall die." ' " 20 He that feared the word of the Lord among the servants of Pharaoh made his servants and his cattle flee into the houses: 21 And he that regarded not the word of the Lord left his servants and his cattle in the field.

22 And the Lord said unto Moses, "Stretch forth thine hand toward heaven, that there may be hail in all the land of Egypt, upon man, and upon beast, and upon every herb of the field, throughout the land of Egypt." 23 And Moses stretched forth his rod toward heaven: and the Lord sent thunder and hail, and the fire ran along upon the ground; and the Lord rained hail upon the land of Egypt. 24 So there was hail, and fire mingled with the hail, very grievous, such as there was none like it in all the land of Egypt since it became a nation. 25 And the hail smote throughout all the land of Egypt all that *was* in the field, both man and beast; and the hail smote every herb of the field, and brake every tree of the field. 26 Only in the land of Goshen, where the children of Israel *were,* was there no hail.

27 And Pharaoh sent, and called for Moses and Aaron, and said unto them, "I have sinned this time: the Lord *is* righteous, and I and my people *are* wicked. 28 Entreat the Lord (for *it is* enough) that there be no *more* mighty thunderings and hail; and I will let you go, and ye shall stay no longer." 29 And Moses said unto him, "As soon as I am gone out of the city, I will spread abroad my hands unto the Lord; *and* the thunder shall cease, neither shall there be any more hail; that thou mayest know how that the earth *is* the Lord's. 30 But as for thee and thy servants, I know that ye will not yet fear the Lord God." 31 And the flax and the barley was smitten: for the barley *was* in the ear, and the flax *was* bolled. 32 But the wheat and the rye were not smitten: for they *were* not grown up.[13] 33 And Moses went out of the city from Pharaoh, and spread abroad his hands unto the Lord: and the thunders and hail ceased, and the rain was not poured upon the earth. 34 And when Pharaoh saw that the rain and the hail and the thunders were ceased, he sinned yet more, and hardened his heart, he and his servants. 35 And the heart of Pharaoh was hardened, neither would he let the children of Israel go; as the Lord had spoken by Moses.

Locusts

10 And the Lord said unto Moses, "Go in unto Pharaoh: for I have hardened his heart, and the heart of his servants, that I might show these my signs before him: 2 And that thou mayest tell in the ears of thy son, and of thy son's son, what things I have wrought in Egypt, and my signs which I have done among them; that ye may know how that I *am* the Lord." 3 And Moses and Aaron came in unto Pharaoh, and said unto him, "Thus saith the Lord God of the Hebrews, 'How long wilt thou refuse to humble thyself before me? let my people go, that they may serve me. 4 Else, if thou refuse to let my people go, behold, to-morrow will I bring the locusts into thy coast: 5 And they shall cover the face of the earth, that one cannot be able to see the earth: and they shall eat the residue of that which is escaped, which remaineth unto you from the hail, and shall eat every tree which groweth for you out of the field: 6 And they shall fill thy houses, and the houses of all thy servants, and the houses of all the Egyptians; which neither thy fathers, nor thy fathers' fathers have seen, since the day that they were upon the earth unto this day.' " And he turned himself, and went out from Pharaoh. 7 And Pharaoh's servants said unto him, "How long shall this man be a snare unto us? let the men go, that they may serve the Lord their God: knowest thou not yet that Egypt is destroyed?" 8 And Moses and Aaron were brought again unto Pharaoh: and he said unto them, "Go, serve the Lord your God: *but* who *are* they that shall go?" 9 And Moses said, "We will go with our young and with our old, with our sons and with our daughters, with our flocks and with our herds will we go; for we *must hold* a feast unto the Lord." 10 And he said unto them, "Let the Lord be so with you, as I will let you go, and your little ones:[14] look *to it;* for evil *is* before you. 11 Not so: go now ye *that are* men, and serve the Lord; for that ye did desire." And they were driven out from Pharaoh's presence.

12 And the Lord said unto Moses, "Stretch out thine hand over the land of Egypt for the locusts, that they may come up upon the land of Egypt, and eat every herb of the land, *even* all that the hail hath left." 13 And Moses stretched forth his rod over the land of Egypt, and the Lord brought an east wind upon the land all that day, and all *that* night; *and* when it was morning, the east wind brought the locusts. 14 And the locusts went up over all the land of Egypt, and rested in

---

13. (9:31-32) Moffatt, Knox, and NEB put these verses in parentheses. They show that after the hailstorm there is still grain for the locusts to destroy.

14. A sarcastic blessing. Meek: "May the Lord be with you . . . just as soon as I let you and your dependents go!" Pharaoh will let the Israelite men go out to worship, but he intends to keep their families in Egypt.

all the coasts of Egypt: very grievous *were they;* before them there were no such locusts as they, neither after them shall be such. 15 For they covered the face of the whole earth, so that the land was darkened; and they did eat every herb of the land, and all the fruit of the trees which the hail had left: and there remained not any green thing in the trees, or in the herbs of the field, through all the land of Egypt.

16 Then Pharaoh called for Moses and Aaron in haste; and he said, "I have sinned against the LORD your God, and against you. 17 Now therefore forgive, I pray thee, my sin only this once, and entreat the LORD your God, that he may take away from me this death only." 18 And he went out from Pharaoh, and entreated the LORD. 19 And the LORD turned a mighty strong west wind, which took away the locusts, and cast them into the Red sea; there remained not one locust in all the coasts of Egypt. 20 But the LORD hardened Pharaoh's heart, so that he would not let the children of Israel go.

Darkness

21 And the LORD said unto Moses, "Stretch out thine hand toward heaven, that there may be darkness over the land of Egypt, even darkness *which* may be felt." 22 And Moses stretched forth his hand toward heaven; and there was a thick darkness in all the land of Egypt three days: 23 They saw not one another, neither rose any from his place for three days: but all the children of Israel had light in their dwellings.

24 And Pharaoh called unto Moses, and said, "Go ye, serve the LORD; only let your flocks and your herds be stayed: let your little ones also go with you." 25 And Moses said, "Thou must give us also sacrifices and burnt offerings, that we may sacrifice unto the LORD our God. 26 Our cattle also shall go with us; there shall not a hoof be left behind; for thereof must we take to serve the LORD our God; and we know not with what we must serve the LORD, until we come thither." 27 But the LORD hardened Pharaoh's heart, and he would not let them go.

28 And Pharaoh said unto him, "Get thee from me, take heed to thyself, see my face no more; for in *that* day thou seest my face thou shalt die." 29 And Moses said, "Thou hast spoken well, I will see thy face again no more."

Death of the Firstborn

11 And the LORD said unto Moses, "Yet will I bring one plague *more* upon Pharaoh, and upon Egypt; afterward he will let you go hence: when he shall let *you* go, he shall surely thrust you out hence altogether. 2 Speak now in the ears of the people, and let every man borrow of his neighbor,

and every woman of her neighbor, jewels of silver, and jewels of gold." 3 And the LORD gave the people favor in the sight of the Egyptians. Moreover, the man Moses *was* very great in the land of Egypt, in the sight of Pharaoh's servants, and in the sight of the people.

4 And Moses said,[15] "Thus saith the LORD, 'About midnight will I go out into the midst of Egypt: 5 And all the firstborn in the land of Egypt shall die, from the firstborn of Pharaoh that sitteth upon his throne, even unto the firstborn of the maidservant that *is* behind the mill; and all the firstborn of beasts. 6 And there shall be a great cry throughout all the land of Egypt, such as there was none like it, nor shall be like it any more. 7 But against any of the children of Israel shall not a dog move his tongue, against man or beast: that ye may know how that the LORD doth put a difference between the Egyptians and Israel.' 8 And all these thy servants shall come down unto me, and bow down themselves unto me, saying, 'Get thee out, and all the people that follow thee': and after that I will go out." And he went out from Pharaoh in a great anger. 9 And the LORD said unto Moses, "Pharaoh shall not hearken unto you; that my wonders may be multiplied in the land of Egypt." 10 And Moses and Aaron did all these wonders before Pharaoh: and the LORD hardened Pharaoh's heart, so that he would not let the children of Israel go out of his land.

THE LIBERATION FROM EGYPT

The Passover [16]

12 And the LORD spake unto Moses and Aaron in the land of Egypt, saying, "This month *shall be* unto you the beginning of months: it *shall be* the first month of the year to you. 3 Speak ye unto all the congregation of Israel, saying, 'In the tenth *day* of this month they shall take to them every man a lamb, according to the house of *their* fathers, a lamb for a house: 4 And if the household be too little for the lamb, let him and his neighbor next unto his house take *it* according to the number of the souls; every man according to his eating shall make your count for the lamb. 5 Your lamb shall be without blemish, a male of the first year: ye shall take *it* out from the sheep, or from the goats: 6 And ye shall keep it up until the fourteenth day of the same month: and the

---

15. Moses is speaking to Pharaoh (see verse 8).
16. (12:1–13:16) These passages which separate the announcement and the execution of the tenth plague form a section in which three rites—Passover, Unleavened Bread, and the Dedication of the Firstborn—are reinterpreted as memorials of the Lord's deliverance of his people.

whole assembly of the congregation of Israel shall kill it in the evening. 7 And they shall take of the blood, and strike *it* on the two side posts and on the upper doorpost of the houses, wherein they shall eat it. 8 And they shall eat the flesh in that night, roast with fire, and unleavened bread; *and* with bitter *herbs* they shall eat it. 9 Eat not of it raw, nor sodden at all with water, but roast *with* fire; his head with his legs, and with the purtenance thereof. 10 And ye shall let nothing of it remain until the morning; and that which remaineth of it until the morning ye shall burn with fire. 11 And thus shall ye eat it; *with* your loins girded, your shoes on your feet, and your staff in your hand; and ye shall eat it in haste: it *is* the LORD's passover. 12 For I will pass through the land of Egypt this night, and will smite all the firstborn in the land of Egypt, both man and beast; and against all the gods of Egypt I will execute judgment: I *am* the LORD. 13 And the blood shall be to you for a token upon the houses where ye *are:* and when I see the blood, I will pass over you, and the plague shall not be upon you to destroy *you,* when I smite the land of Egypt. 14 And this day shall be unto you for a memorial; and ye shall keep it a feast to the LORD throughout your generations: ye shall keep it a feast by an ordinance for ever.

15 " 'Seven days shall ye eat unleavened bread; even the first day ye shall put away leaven out of your houses: for whosoever eateth leavened bread from the first day until the seventh day, that soul shall be cut off from Israel. 16 And in the first day *there shall be* a holy convocation, and in the seventh day there shall be a holy convocation to you; no manner of work shall be done in them, save *that* which every man must eat, that only may be done of you. 17 And ye shall observe *the feast of* unleavened bread; for in this selfsame day have I brought your armies out of the land of Egypt: therefore shall ye observe this day in your generations by an ordinance for ever. 18 In the first *month,* on the fourteenth day of the month at even, ye shall eat unleavened bread, until the one and twentieth day of the month at even. 19 Seven days shall there be no leaven found in your houses: for whosoever eateth that which is leavened, even that soul shall be cut off from the congregation of Israel, whether he be a stranger, or born in the land. 20 Ye shall eat nothing leavened; in all your habitations shall ye eat unleavened bread.' "

21 Then Moses called for all the elders of Israel, and said unto them, "Draw out and take you a lamb according to your families, and kill the passover. 22 And ye shall take a bunch of hyssop, and dip *it* in the blood that *is* in the basin, and strike the lintel and the two side posts with the blood that *is* in the basin; and none of you shall go out at the door of his house until the morning. 23 For the LORD will pass through to smite the Egyptians; and when he seeth the blood upon the lintel, and on the two side posts, the LORD will pass over the door, and will not suffer the destroyer to come in unto your houses to smite *you.* 24 And ye shall observe this thing for an ordinance to thee and to thy sons for ever. 25 And it shall come to pass, when ye be come to the land which the LORD will give you, according as he hath promised, that ye shall keep this service. 26 And it shall come to pass, when your children shall say unto you, 'What mean ye by this service?' 27 That ye shall say, 'It *is* the sacrifice of the LORD's passover, who passed over the houses of the children of Israel in Egypt, when he smote the Egyptians, and delivered our houses.' " And the people bowed the head and worshipped. 28 And the children of Israel went away, and did as the LORD had commanded Moses and Aaron, so did they.

29 And it came to pass, that at midnight the LORD smote all the firstborn in the land of Egypt, from the firstborn of Pharaoh that sat on his throne unto the firstborn of the captive that *was* in the dungeon; and all the firstborn of cattle. 30 And Pharaoh rose up in the night, he, and all his servants, and all the Egyptians; and there was a great cry in Egypt: for *there was* not a house where *there was* not one dead. 31 And he called for Moses and Aaron by night, and said, "Rise up, *and* get you forth from among my people, both ye and the children of Israel; and go, serve the LORD, as ye have said. 32 Also take your flocks and your herds, as ye have said, and be gone; and bless me also." 33 And the Egyptians were urgent upon the people, that they might send them out of the land in haste; for they said, "We *be* all dead *men.*" 34 And the people took their dough before it was leavened, their kneadingtroughs being bound up in their clothes upon their shoulders. 35 And the children of Israel did according to the word of Moses; and they borrowed of the Egyptians jewels of silver, and jewels of gold, and raiment: 36 And the LORD gave the people favor in the sight of the Egyptians, so that they lent unto them such things as they required: and they spoiled the Egyptians.

37 And the children of Israel journeyed from Rameses to Succoth, about six hundred thousand on foot *that were* men, beside children.[17] 38 And

---

17. The figure is incredibly large: 600,000 men with their families would amount to two and a half million people.

a mixed multitude went up also with them; and flocks, and herds, *even* very much cattle. 39 And they baked unleavened cakes of the dough which they brought forth out of Egypt, for it was not leavened; because they were thrust out of Egypt, and could not tarry, neither had they prepared for themselves any victuals.

40 Now the sojourning of the children of Israel, who dwelt in Egypt, *was* four hundred and thirty years. 41 And it came to pass at the end of the four hundred and thirty years, even the selfsame day it came to pass, that all the hosts of the LORD went out from the land of Egypt. 42 It *is* a night to be much observed unto the LORD for bringing them out from the land of Egypt: this *is* that night of the LORD to be observed of all the children of Israel in their generations.

43 And the LORD said unto Moses and Aaron, "This *is* the ordinance of the passover: There shall no stranger eat thereof: 44 But every man's servant that is bought for money, when thou hast circumcised him, then shall he eat thereof. 45 A foreigner and a hired servant shall not eat thereof. 46 In one house shall it be eaten; thou shalt not carry forth aught of the flesh abroad out of the house; neither shall ye break a bone thereof. 47 All the congregation of Israel shall keep it. 48 And when a stranger shall sojourn with thee, and will keep the passover to the LORD, let all his males be circumcised, and then let him come near and keep it; and he shall be as one that is born in the land: for no uncircumcised person shall eat thereof. 49 One law shall be to him that is homeborn, and unto the stranger that sojourneth among you." 50 Thus did all the children of Israel; as the LORD commanded Moses and Aaron, so did they. 51 And it came to pass the selfsame day, *that* the LORD did bring the children of Israel out of the land of Egypt by their armies.

13 And the LORD spake unto Moses, saying, 2 "Sanctify unto me all the firstborn, whatsoever openeth the womb among the children of Israel, *both* of man and of beast: it *is* mine."

3 And Moses said unto the people, "Remember this day, in which ye came out from Egypt, out of the house of bondage; for by strength of hand the LORD brought you out from this *place:* there shall no leavened bread be eaten. 4 This day came ye out in the month Abib. 5 And it shall be when the LORD shall bring thee into the land of the Canaanites, and the Hittites, and the Amorites, and the Hivites, and the Jebusites, which he sware unto thy fathers to give thee, a land flowing with milk and honey, that thou shalt keep this service in this month. 6 Seven days thou shalt eat un-

leavened bread, and in the seventh day *shall be* a feast to the LORD. 7 Unleavened bread shall be eaten seven days; and there shall no leavened bread be seen with thee, neither shall there be leaven seen with thee in all thy quarters. 8 And thou shalt show thy son in that day, saying, '*This is done* because of that *which* the LORD did unto me when I came forth out of Egypt.' 9 And it shall be for a sign unto thee upon thine hand, and for a memorial between thine eyes,[18] that the LORD's law may be in thy mouth: for with a strong hand hath the LORD brought thee out of Egypt. 10 Thou shalt therefore keep this ordinance in his season from year to year.

11 "And it shall be when the LORD shall bring thee into the land of the Canaanites, as he sware unto thee and to thy fathers, and shall give it thee, 12 That thou shalt set apart unto the LORD all that openeth the matrix, and every firstling that cometh of a beast which thou hast; the male *shall be* the LORD's. 13 And every firstling of an ass thou shalt redeem with a lamb; and if thou wilt not redeem it, then thou shalt break his neck: and all the firstborn of man among thy children shalt thou redeem. 14 And it shall be when thy son asketh thee in time to come, saying, 'What *is* this?' that thou shalt say unto him, 'By strength of hand the LORD brought us out from Egypt, from the house of bondage: 15 And it came to pass, when Pharaoh would hardly let us go, that the LORD slew all the firstborn in the land of Egypt, both the firstborn of man, and the firstborn of beast: therefore I sacrifice to the LORD all that openeth the matrix, being males; but all the firstborn of my children I redeem.' 16 And it shall be for a token upon thine hand, and for frontlets between thine eyes: for by strength of hand the LORD brought us forth out of Egypt."

Crossing the Red Sea

17 And it came to pass, when Pharaoh had let the people go, that God led them not *through* the way of the land of the Philistines, although that *was* near; for God said, "Lest peradventure the people repent when they see war, and they return to Egypt": 18 But God led the people about, *through* the way of the wilderness of the Red sea: and the children of Israel went up harnessed out of the land of Egypt. 19 And Moses took the bones of Joseph with him: for he had straitly sworn the children of Israel, saying, "God will surely visit you; and ye shall carry up my bones away hence with you." 20 And they took their

18. The reference is to the use of phylacteries—a small case fastened by straps to the forehead. Inside the case were four passages of Scripture—*Exodus* 13:1-10 and 13:11-16; *Deuteronomy* 6:4-9 and 11:13-21.

journey from Succoth, and encamped in Etham, in the edge of the wilderness. 21 And the LORD went before them by day in a pillar of a cloud, to lead them the way; and by night in a pillar of fire, to give them light; to go by day and night. 22 He took not away the pillar of the cloud by day, nor the pillar of fire by night, *from* before the people. **14** And the LORD spake unto Moses, saying, 2 "Speak unto the children of Israel, that they turn[19] and encamp before Pi-hahiroth, between Migdol and the sea, over against Baal-zephon: before it shall ye encamp by the sea. 3 For Pharaoh will say of the children of Israel, 'They *are* entangled in the land, the wilderness hath shut them in.' 4 And I will harden Pharaoh's heart, that he shall follow after them; and I will be honored upon Pharaoh, and upon all his host; that the Egyptians may know that I *am* the LORD." And they did so. 5 And it was told the king of Egypt that the people fled: and the heart of Pharaoh and of his servants was turned against the people, and they said, "Why have we done this, that we have let Israel go from serving us?" 6 And he made ready his chariot, and took his people with him: 7 And he took six hundred chosen chariots, and all the chariots of Egypt, and captains over every one of them. 8 And the LORD hardened the heart of Pharaoh king of Egypt, and he pursued after the children of Israel: and the children of Israel went out with a high hand. 9 But the Egyptians pursued after them, all the horses *and* chariots of Pharaoh, and his horsemen, and his army, and overtook them encamping by the sea, beside Pi-hahiroth, before Baal-zephon.

10 And when Pharaoh drew nigh, the children of Israel lifted up their eyes, and, behold, the Egyptians marched after them; and they were sore afraid: and the children of Israel cried out unto the LORD. 11 And they said unto Moses, "Because *there were* no graves in Egypt, hast thou taken us away to die in the wilderness? wherefore hast thou dealt thus with us, to carry us forth out of Egypt? 12 *Is* not this the word that we did tell thee in Egypt, saying, 'Let us alone, that we may serve the Egyptians?' For *it had been* better for us to serve the Egyptians, than that we should die in the wilderness." 13 And Moses said unto the people, "Fear ye not, stand still, and see the salvation of the LORD, which he will show to you to-day: for the Egyptians whom ye have seen to-day, ye shall see them again no more for ever. 14 The LORD shall fight for you, and ye shall hold your peace."

15 And the LORD said unto Moses, "Wherefore criest thou unto me? speak unto the children of Israel, that they go forward: 16 But lift thou up thy rod, and stretch out thine hand over the sea, and divide it: and the children of Israel shall go on dry *ground* through the midst of the sea. 17 And I, behold, I will harden the hearts of the Egyptians, and they shall follow them: and I will get me honor upon Pharaoh, and upon all his host, upon his chariots, and upon his horsemen. 18 And the Egyptians shall know that I *am* the LORD, when I have gotten me honor upon Pharaoh, upon his chariots, and upon his horsemen." 19 And the Angel of God, which went before the camp of Israel, removed and went behind them; and the pillar of the cloud went from before their face, and stood behind them: 20 And it came between the camp of the Egyptians and the camp of Israel; and it was a cloud and darkness *to them,* but it gave light by night *to these:* so that the one came not near the other all the night.

21 And Moses stretched out his hand over the sea; and the LORD caused the sea to go *back* by a strong east wind all that night, and made the sea dry *land,* and the waters were divided. 22 And the children of Israel went into the midst of the sea upon the dry *ground:* and the waters *were* a wall unto them on their right hand, and on their left. 23 And the Egyptians pursued, and went in after them to the midst of the sea, *even* all Pharaoh's horses, his chariots, and his horsemen. 24 And it came to pass, that in the morning watch the LORD looked unto the host of the Egyptians through the pillar of fire and of the cloud, and troubled the host of the Egyptians, 25 And took off [20] their chariot wheels, that they drave them heavily: so that the Egyptians said, "Let us flee from the face of Israel; for the LORD fighteth for them against the Egyptians."

26 And the LORD said unto Moses, "Stretch out thine hand over the sea, that the waters may come again upon the Egyptians, upon their chariots, and upon their horsemen." 27 And Moses stretched forth his hand over the sea, and the sea returned to his strength when the morning appeared; and the Egyptians fled against it; and the LORD overthrew the Egyptians in the midst of the sea.[21] 28 And the waters returned, and covered the chariots, and the horsemen, *and* all the host of Pharaoh that came into the sea after them; there remained not so much as one of them. 29 But the children of Israel walked upon dry *land* in the midst of the sea; and the waters *were* a wall unto

---

19. RSV: "turn back." This seems a calculated military strategy to draw the attack of Pharaoh's army. The sea is thought to be the "sea of reeds," a shallow body of water probably in the area of Lake Timsah.

20. (14:24-25) MOFFATT, JB: "clogged." One can read these verses to mean that a storm with lightning caused the chariot wheels to be stuck fast in mud.

21. BERKELEY: "The Lord tumbled the Egyptians into the middle of the sea." The image is that of shaking fruit from a tree.

them on their right hand, and on their left. 30 Thus the LORD saved Israel that day out of the hand of the Egyptians; and Israel saw the Egyptians dead upon the seashore. 31 And Israel saw that great work which the LORD did upon the Egyptians: and the people feared the LORD, and believed the LORD, and his servant Moses.

Song of Victory

15 Then sang Moses and the children of Israel this song unto the LORD, and spake, saying,
"I will sing unto the LORD, for he hath triumphed gloriously:
The horse and his rider hath he thrown into the sea.
2 The LORD *is* my strength and song,
And he is become my salvation:
He *is* my God, and I will prepare him a habitation;
My father's God, and I will exalt him.
3 The LORD *is* a man of war:
The LORD *is* his name.

4 "Pharaoh's chariots and his host hath he cast into the sea:
His chosen captains also are drowned in the Red sea.
5 The depths have covered them:
They sank into the bottom as a stone.
6 Thy right hand, O LORD, is become glorious in power:
Thy right hand, O LORD, hath dashed in pieces the enemy.
7 And in the greatness of thine excellency thou hast overthrown them that rose up against thee:
Thou sentest forth thy wrath, *which* consumed them as stubble.
8 And with the blast of thy nostrils the waters were gathered together,
The floods stood upright as a heap,
And the depths were congealed in the heart of the sea.
9 The enemy said,
'I will pursue, I will overtake,
I will divide the spoil; my lust shall be satisfied upon them;
I will draw my sword, my hand shall destroy them.'
10 Thou didst blow with thy wind, the sea covered them:
They sank as lead in the mighty waters.

11 "Who *is* like unto thee, O LORD, among the gods?
Who *is* like thee, glorious in holiness,
Fearful *in* praises, doing wonders?

12 Thou stretchedst out thy right hand,
The earth swallowed them.
13 Thou in thy mercy hast led forth the people *which* thou hast redeemed:
Thou hast guided *them* in thy strength unto thy holy habitation.

14 "The people shall hear, *and* be afraid:
Sorrow shall take hold on the inhabitants of Palestina.
15 Then the dukes of Edom shall be amazed;
The mighty men of Moab, trembling shall take hold upon them;
All the inhabitants of Canaan shall melt away.
16 Fear and dread shall fall upon them;
By the greatness of thine arm they shall be *as* still as a stone;
Till thy people pass over, O LORD,
Till the people pass over, *which* thou hast purchased.
17 Thou shalt bring them in, and plant them in the mountain of thine inheritance,
In the place, O LORD, *which* thou hast made for thee to dwell in;
In the sanctuary, O LORD, *which* thy hands have established.[22]
18 The LORD shall reign for ever and ever."

19 For the horse of Pharaoh went in with his chariots and with his horsemen into the sea, and the LORD brought again the waters of the sea upon them; but the children of Israel went on dry *land* in the midst of the sea. 20 And Miriam the prophetess, the sister of Aaron, took a timbrel in her hand; and all the women went out after her with timbrels and with dances. 21 And Miriam answered them,
"Sing ye to the LORD, for he hath triumphed gloriously:
The horse and his rider hath he thrown into the sea."

ISRAEL IN THE WILDERNESS
The Crises

22 So Moses brought Israel from the Red sea, and they went out into the wilderness of Shur; and they went three days in the wilderness, and found no water. 23 And when they came to Marah, they could not drink of the waters of Marah, for they *were* bitter: therefore the name of it was called Marah. 24 And the people murmured against Moses, saying, "What shall we

---

22. An anachronism. The song was written after the establishment of the Temple in Jerusalem.

drink?" 25 And he cried unto the Lord; and the Lord showed him a tree, *which* when he had cast into the waters, the waters were made sweet: there he made for them a statute and an ordinance, and there he proved them,[23] 26 And said, "If thou wilt diligently hearken to the voice of the Lord thy God, and wilt do that which is right in his sight, and wilt give ear to his commandments, and keep all his statutes, I will put none of these diseases upon thee, which I have brought upon the Egyptians: for I *am* the Lord that healeth thee." 27 And they came to Elim, where *were* twelve wells of water, and threescore and ten palm trees: and they encamped there by the waters.

16 And they took their journey from Elim, and all the congregation of the children of Israel came unto the wilderness of Sin, which *is* between Elim and Sinai, on the fifteenth day of the second month after their departing out of the land of Egypt. 2 And the whole congregation of the children of Israel murmured against Moses and Aaron in the wilderness: 3 And the children of Israel said unto them, "Would to God we had died by the hand of the Lord in the land of Egypt, when we sat by the fleshpots,[24] *and* when we did eat bread to the full; for ye have brought us forth into this wilderness, to kill this whole assembly with hunger."

4 Then said the Lord unto Moses, "Behold, I will rain bread from heaven for you; and the people shall go out and gather a certain rate every day, that I may prove them, whether they will walk in my law, or no. 5 And it shall come to pass, that on the sixth day they shall prepare *that* which they bring in; and it shall be twice as much as they gather daily." 6 And Moses and Aaron said unto all the children of Israel, "At even, then ye shall know that the Lord hath brought you out from the land of Egypt: 7 And in the morning, then ye shall see the glory of the Lord; for that he heareth your murmurings against the Lord: and what *are* we, that ye murmur against us?" 8 And Moses said, "*This shall be,* when the Lord shall give you in the evening flesh to eat, and in the morning bread to the full; for that the Lord heareth your murmurings which ye murmur against him: and what *are* we? your murmurings *are* not against us, but against the Lord." [25]

9 And Moses spake unto Aaron, "Say unto all the congregation of the children of Israel, 'Come near before the Lord: for he hath heard your murmurings.'" 10 And it came to pass, as Aaron spake unto the whole congregation of the children of Israel, that they looked toward the wilderness, and, behold, the glory of the Lord appeared in the cloud. 11 And the Lord spake unto Moses, saying, 12 "I have heard the murmurings of the children of Israel: speak unto them, saying, 'At even ye shall eat flesh, and in the morning ye shall be filled with bread; and ye shall know that I *am* the Lord your God.'"

13 And it came to pass, that at even the quails came up, and covered the camp: and in the morning the dew lay round about the host. 14 And when the dew that lay was gone up, behold, upon the face of the wilderness *there lay* a small round thing, *as* small as the hoar frost on the ground. 15 And when the children of Israel saw *it,* they said one to another, "It *is* manna": for they wist not what it *was.*[26] And Moses said unto them, "This *is* the bread which the Lord hath given you to eat. 16 This *is* the thing which the Lord hath commanded, 'Gather of it every man according to his eating, an omer for every man, *according to* the number of your persons; take ye every man for *them* which *are* in his tents.'" 17 And the children of Israel did so, and gathered, some more, some less. 18 And when they did mete *it* with an omer, he that gathered much had nothing over, and he that gathered little had no lack; they gathered every man according to his eating. 19 And Moses said, "Let no man leave of it till the morning." 20 Notwithstanding they hearkened not unto Moses; but some of them left of it until the morning, and it bred worms, and stank: and Moses was wroth with them. 21 And they gathered it every morning, every man according to his eating: and when the sun waxed hot, it melted. 22 And it came to pass, *that* on the sixth day they gathered twice as much bread, two omers for one *man:* and all the rulers of the congregation came and told Moses. 23 And he said unto them, "This *is that* which the Lord hath said, 'To-morrow *is* the rest of the holy sabbath unto the Lord: bake *that* which ye will bake *to-day,* and seethe that ye will seethe; and that which remaineth over lay up for you to be kept until the morning.'" 24 And they laid it up till the morning, as Moses bade: and it did not stink, neither was there any worm therein. 25 And Moses said, "Eat that to-day; for to-day *is* a sabbath unto the Lord: to-day ye shall not find it in the field. 26 Six days ye shall gather it; but on the seventh day, *which is* the sabbath, in it there shall be

---

23. NAB: "It was here that the Lord, in making rules and regulations for them, put them to the test." Verse 26 defines the test.

24. Knox: "where we sat down to bowls of meat."

25. (16:6-8) These verses seem to be out of order. Moffatt puts them after verse 12.

26. NEB: "When the Israelites saw it, they said to one another, 'What is that?', because they did not know what it was."

none." 27 And it came to pass, *that* there went out *some* of the people on the seventh day for to gather, and they found none. 28 And the LORD said unto Moses, "How long refuse ye to keep my commandments and my laws? 29 See, for that the LORD hath given you the sabbath, therefore he giveth you on the sixth day the bread of two days: abide ye every man in his place, let no man go out of his place on the seventh day." 30 So the people rested on the seventh day.

31 And the house of Israel called the name thereof Manna: and it *was* like coriander seed, white; and the taste of it *was* like wafers *made* with honey. 32 And Moses said, "This *is* the thing which the LORD commandeth, 'Fill an omer of it to be kept for your generations; that they may see the bread wherewith I have fed you in the wilderness, when I brought you forth from the land of Egypt.' " 33 And Moses said unto Aaron, "Take a pot, and put an omer full of manna therein, and lay it up before the LORD, to be kept for your generations." 34 As the LORD commanded Moses, so Aaron laid it up before the Testimony, to be kept. 35 And the children of Israel did eat manna forty years, until they came to a land inhabited: they did eat manna, until they came unto the borders of the land of Canaan. 36 Now an omer *is* the tenth *part* of an ephah.

17 And all the congregation of the children of Israel journeyed from the wilderness of Sin, after their journeys, according to the commandment of the LORD, and pitched in Rephidim: and *there was* no water for the people to drink. 2 Wherefore the people did chide with Moses, and said, "Give us water that we may drink." And Moses said unto them, "Why chide ye with me? wherefore do ye tempt the LORD?" 3 And the people thirsted there for water; and the people murmured against Moses, and said, "Wherefore *is* this *that* thou hast brought us up out of Egypt, to kill us and our children and our cattle with thirst?" 4 And Moses cried unto the LORD, saying, "What shall I do unto this people? they be almost ready to stone me." 5 And the LORD said unto Moses, "Go on before the people, and take with thee of the elders of Israel; and thy rod, wherewith thou smotest the river, take in thine hand, and go. 6 Behold, I will stand before thee there upon the rock in Horeb; and thou shalt smite the rock, and there shall come water out of it, that the people may drink." And Moses did so in the sight of the elders of Israel. 7 And he called the name of the place Massah, and Meribah, because of the chiding of the children of Israel, and because they tempted the LORD, saying, "Is the LORD among us, or not?"

8 Then came Amalek,[27] and fought with Israel in Rephidim. 9 And Moses said unto Joshua, "Choose us out men, and go out, fight with Amalek: to-morrow I will stand on the top of the hill with the rod of God in mine hand." 10 So Joshua did as Moses had said to him, and fought with Amalek: and Moses, Aaron, and Hur went up to the top of the hill. 11 And it came to pass, when Moses held up his hand, that Israel prevailed: and when he let down his hand, Amalek prevailed. 12 But Moses' hands *were* heavy; and they took a stone, and put *it* under him, and he sat thereon; and Aaron and Hur stayed up his hands, the one on the one side, and other on the other side; and his hands were steady until the going down of the sun. 13 And Joshua discomfited Amalek and his people with the edge of the sword.

14 And the LORD said unto Moses, "Write this *for* a memorial in a book, and rehearse *it* in the ears of Joshua: for I will utterly put out the remembrance of Amalek from under heaven." 15 And Moses built an altar, and called the name of it Jehovah-nissi:[28] 16 For he said, "Because the LORD hath sworn *that* the LORD *will have* war with Amalek from generation to generation."

Jethro Visits Moses

18 When Jethro, the priest of Midian, Moses' father-in-law, heard of all that God had done for Moses, and for Israel his people, *and* that the LORD had brought Israel out of Egypt; 2 Then Jethro, Moses' father-in-law, took Zipporah, Moses' wife, after he had sent her back, 3 And her two sons; of which the name of the one *was* Gershom; for he said, "I have been an alien in a strange land": 4 And the name of the other *was* Eliezer; "for the God of my father," *said he, "was* mine help, and delivered me from the sword of Pharaoh": 5 And Jethro, Moses' father-in-law, came with his sons and his wife unto Moses into the wilderness, where he encamped at the mount of God. 6 And he said unto Moses, "I thy father-in-law Jethro am come unto thee, and thy wife, and her two sons with her." 7 And Moses went out to meet his father-in-law, and did obeisance, and kissed him; and they asked each other of *their* welfare; and they came into the tent. 8 And Moses told his father-in-law all that the LORD had done unto Pharaoh and to the Egyptians for Israel's sake, *and* all the travail that had come upon them by the way, and *how* the LORD delivered them. 9 And Jethro rejoiced for all the goodness

27. The Amalekites, a fierce desert tribe, were thought to be descendents of Esau (see *Genesis* 36:12).
28. This means "the Lord is my banner."

which the LORD had done to Israel, whom he had delivered out of the hand of the Egyptians. 10 And Jethro said, "Blessed *be* the LORD, who hath delivered you out of the hand of the Egyptians, and out of the hand of Pharaoh, who hath delivered the people from under the hand of the Egyptians. 11 Now I know that the LORD *is* greater than all gods: for in the thing wherein they dealt proudly *he was* above them." 12 And Jethro, Moses' father-in-law, took a burnt offering and sacrifices for God: and Aaron came, and all the elders of Israel, to eat bread with Moses' father-in-law before God.

13 And it came to pass on the morrow, that Moses sat to judge the people: and the people stood by Moses from the morning unto the evening. 14 And when Moses' father-in-law saw all that he did to the people, he said, "What *is* this thing that thou doest to the people? Why sittest thou thyself alone, and all the people stand by thee from morning unto even?" 15 And Moses said unto his father-in-law, "Because the people come unto me to inquire of God: 16 When they have a matter, they come unto me; and I judge between one and another, and I do make *them* know the statutes of God, and his laws."

17 And Moses' father-in-law said unto him, "The thing that thou doest *is* not good. 18 Thou wilt surely wear away, both thou, and this people that *is* with thee: for this thing *is* too heavy for thee; thou art not able to perform it thyself alone. 19 Hearken now unto my voice, I will give thee counsel, and God shall be with thee: Be thou for the people to God-ward, that thou mayest bring the causes unto God: 20 And thou shalt teach them ordinances and laws, and shalt show them the way wherein they must walk, and the work that they must do. 21 Moreover thou shalt provide out of all the people able men, such as fear God, men of truth, hating covetousness; and place *such* over them, *to be* rulers of thousands, *and* rulers of hundreds, rulers of fifties, and rulers of tens: 22 And let them judge the people at all seasons: and it shall be, *that* every great matter they shall bring unto thee, but every small matter they shall judge: so shall it be easier for thyself, and they shall bear *the burden* with thee. 23 If thou shalt do this thing, and God command thee *so,* then thou shalt be able to endure, and all this people shall also go to their place in peace."

24 So Moses hearkened to the voice of his father-in-law, and did all that he had said. 25 And Moses chose able men out of all Israel, and made them heads over the people, rulers of thousands, rulers of hundreds, rulers of fifties, and rulers of tens. 26 And they judged the people at all seasons: the hard causes they brought unto Moses, but every small matter they judged themselves. 27 And Moses let his father-in-law depart; and he went his way into his own land.

THE COVENANT AT SINAI

19 In the third month, when the children of Israel were gone forth out of the land of Egypt, the same day came they *into* the wilderness of Sinai. 2 For they were departed from Rephidim, and were come *to* the desert of Sinai, and had pitched in the wilderness; and there Israel camped before the mount. 3 And Moses went up unto God, and the LORD called unto him out of the mountain, saying, "Thus shalt thou say to the house of Jacob, and tell the children of Israel; 4 'Ye have seen what I did unto the Egyptians, and *how* I bare you on eagles' wings, and brought you unto myself. 5 Now therefore, if ye will obey my voice indeed, and keep my covenant, then ye shall be a peculiar treasure unto me above all people: for all the earth *is* mine: 6 And ye shall be unto me a kingdom of priests, and a holy nation.' These *are* the words which thou shalt speak unto the children of Israel."

7 And Moses came and called for the elders of the people, and laid before their faces all these words which the LORD commanded him. 8 And all the people answered together, and said, "All that the LORD hath spoken we will do." And Moses returned the words of the people unto the LORD. 9 And the LORD said unto Moses, "Lo, I come unto thee in a thick cloud, that the people may hear when I speak with thee, and believe thee for ever." And Moses told the words of the people unto the LORD. 10 And the LORD said unto Moses, "Go unto the people, and sanctify them to-day and to-morrow, and let them wash their clothes, 11 And be ready against the third day: for the third day the LORD will come down in the sight of all the people upon mount Sinai. 12 And thou shalt set bounds unto the people round about, saying, 'Take heed to yourselves, *that ye* go *not* up into the mount, or touch the border of it: whosoever toucheth the mount shall be surely put to death: 13 There shall not a hand touch it,[29] but he shall surely be stoned, or shot through; whether *it be* beast or man, it shall not live': when the trumpet soundeth long, they shall come up to the mount." 14 And Moses went down from the mount unto the people, and sanc-

---

29. NAB: "No hand shall touch him." The transgressor is taboo. The inviolable sanctity of the mountain reflects later practice in the Temple, where only priests could enter the Holy of Holies.

tified the people; and they washed their clothes. 15 And he said unto the people, "Be ready against the third day: come not at *your* wives."

16 And it came to pass on the third day in the morning, that there were thunders and lightnings, and a thick cloud upon the mount, and the voice of the trumpet exceeding loud; so that all the people that *was* in the camp trembled. 17 And Moses brought forth the people out of the camp to meet with God; and they stood at the nether part of the mount. 18 And mount Sinai was altogether on a smoke, because the LORD descended upon it in fire: and the smoke thereof ascended as the smoke of a furnace, and the whole mount quaked greatly. 19 And when the voice of the trumpet sounded long, and waxed louder and louder, Moses spake, and God answered him by a voice. 20 And the LORD came down upon mount Sinai, on the top of the mount: and the LORD called Moses *up* to the top of the mount; and Moses went up. 21 And the LORD said unto Moses, "Go down, charge the people, lest they break through unto the LORD to gaze, and many of them perish. 22 And let the priests also, which come near to the LORD, sanctify themselves, lest the LORD break forth upon them." 23 And Moses said unto the LORD, "The people cannot come up to mount Sinai: for thou chargedst us, saying, 'Set bounds about the mount, and sanctify it.'" 24 And the LORD said unto him, "Away, get thee down, and thou shalt come up, thou, and Aaron with thee: but let not the priests and the people break through to come up unto the LORD, lest he break forth upon them." 25 So Moses went down unto the people, and spake unto them.

The Decalogue

20 And God spake all these words,[30] saying, 2 "I *am* the LORD thy God, which have brought thee out of the land of Egypt, out of the house of bondage. 3 Thou shalt have no other gods before me.

4 "Thou shalt not make unto thee any graven image, or any likeness *of any thing* that *is* in heaven above, or that *is* in the earth beneath, or that *is* in the water under the earth: 5 Thou shalt not bow down thyself to them, nor serve them: For I the LORD thy God *am* a jealous God, visiting the iniquity of the fathers upon the children unto the third and fourth *generation* of them that hate me; 6 And showing mercy unto thousands of them that love me, and keep my commandments.

7 "Thou shalt not take the name of the LORD thy God in vain: for the LORD will not hold him guiltless that taketh his name in vain.

8 "Remember the sabbath day, to keep it holy. 9 Six days shalt thou labor, and do all thy work: 10 But the seventh day *is* the sabbath of the LORD thy God: *in it* thou shalt not do any work, thou, nor thy son, nor thy daughter, thy manservant, nor thy maidservant, nor thy cattle, nor thy stranger that *is* within thy gates: 11 For *in* six days the LORD made heaven and earth, the sea, and all that in them *is,* and rested the seventh day: wherefore the LORD blessed the sabbath day, and hallowed it.

12 "Honor thy father and thy mother: that thy days may be long upon the land which the LORD thy God giveth thee.

13 "Thou shalt not kill.

14 "Thou shalt not commit adultery.

15 "Thou shalt not steal.

16 "Thou shalt not bear false witness against thy neighbor.

17 "Thou shalt not covet thy neighbor's house, thou shalt not covet thy neighbor's wife, nor his manservant, nor his maidservant, nor his ox, nor his ass, nor any thing that *is* thy neighbor's."

18 And all the people saw the thunderings, and the lightnings, and the noise of the trumpet, and the mountain smoking: and when the people saw *it,* they removed, and stood afar off. 19 And they said unto Moses, "Speak thou with us, and we will hear: but let not God speak with us, lest we die." 20 And Moses said unto the people, "Fear not: for God is come to prove you, and that his fear may be before your faces, that ye sin not." 21 And the people stood afar off, and Moses drew near unto the thick darkness where God *was.*

22 And the LORD said unto Moses, "Thus thou shalt say unto the children of Israel, 'Ye have seen that I have talked with you from heaven. 23 Ye shall not make with me gods of silver, neither shall ye make unto you gods of gold.

24 "'An altar of earth thou shalt make unto me, and shalt sacrifice thereon thy burnt offerings, and thy peace offerings, thy sheep, and thine oxen: in all places where I record my name I will come unto thee, and I will bless thee. 25 And if thou wilt make me an altar of stone, thou shalt not build it of hewn stone: for if thou lift up thy tool upon it, thou hast polluted it. 26 Neither shalt thou go up by steps unto mine altar, that thy nakedness be not discovered thereon.'

---

30. The transition is abrupt. This message is addressed to all the Israelites. See 20:19.

The Covenant Code [31]

21 "Now these *are* the judgments which thou shalt set before them.

2 " 'If thou buy a Hebrew servant, six years he shall serve: and in the seventh he shall go out free for nothing. 3 If he came in by himself, he shall go out by himself: if he were married, then his wife shall go out with him. 4 If his master have given him a wife, and she have borne him sons or daughters; the wife and her children shall be her master's, and he shall go out by himself. 5 And if the servant shall plainly say, "I love my master, my wife, and my children; I will not go out free": 6 Then his master shall bring him unto the judges; he shall also bring him to the door, or unto the doorpost; and his master shall bore his ear through with an awl; and he shall serve him for ever.

7 " 'And if a man sell his daughter to be a maidservant,[32] she shall not go out as the menservants do. 8 If she please not her master, who hath betrothed her to himself, then shall he let her be redeemed: to sell her unto a strange nation he shall have no power, seeing he hath dealt deceitfully with her. 9 And if he have betrothed her unto his son, he shall deal with her after the manner of daughters. 10 If he take him another *wife,* her food, her raiment, and her duty of marriage, shall he not diminish. 11 And if he do not these three unto her, then shall she go out free without money.

12 " 'He that smiteth a man, so that he die, shall be surely put to death. 13 And if a man lie not in wait, but God deliver *him* into his hand; then I will appoint thee a place whither he shall flee. 14 But if a man come presumptuously upon his neighbor, to slay him with guile; thou shalt take him from mine altar, that he may die.[33]

15 " 'And he that smiteth his father, or his mother, shall be surely put to death.

16 " 'And he that stealeth a man, and selleth him, or if he be found in his hand, he shall surely be put to death.

17 " 'And he that curseth his father, or his mother, shall surely be put to death.

18 " 'And if men strive together, and one smite another with a stone, or with *his* fist, and he die not, but keepeth *his* bed: 19 If he rise again, and walk abroad upon his staff, then shall he that smote *him* be quit: only he shall pay *for* the loss of his time, and shall cause *him* to be thoroughly healed.

20 " 'And if a man smite his servant, or his maid, with a rod, and he die under his hand; he shall be surely punished. 21 Notwithstanding, if he continue a day or two, he shall not be punished: for he *is* his money.

22 " 'If men strive, and hurt a woman with child, so that her fruit depart *from her,* and yet no mischief follow: he shall be surely punished, according as the woman's husband will lay upon him; and he shall pay as the judges *determine.* 23 And if *any* mischief follow, then thou shalt give life for life, 24 Eye for eye, tooth for tooth, hand for hand, foot for foot, 25 Burning for burning, wound for wound, stripe for stripe.[34]

26 " 'And if a man smite the eye of his servant, or the eye of his maid, that it perish; he shall let him go free for his eye's sake. 27 And if he smite out his manservant's tooth, or his maidservant's tooth; he shall let him go free for his tooth's sake.

28 " 'If an ox gore a man or a woman, that they die: then the ox shall be surely stoned, and his flesh shall not be eaten; but the owner of the ox *shall be* quit. 29 But if the ox were wont to push with his horn in time past, and it hath been testified to his owner, and he hath not kept him in, but that he hath killed a man or a woman; the ox shall be stoned, and his owner also shall be put to death. 30 If there be laid on him a sum of money, then he shall give for the ransom of his life whatsoever is laid upon him. 31 Whether he have gored a son, or have gored a daughter, according to this judgment shall it be done unto him. 32 If the ox shall push a manservant or a maidservant; he shall give unto their master thirty shekels of silver, and the ox shall be stoned.

33 " 'And if a man shall open a pit, or if a man shall dig a pit, and not cover it, and an ox or an ass fall therein; 34 The owner of the pit shall make *it* good, *and* give money unto the owner of them; and the dead *beast* shall be his. 35 " 'And if one man's ox hurt another's, that he die; then they shall sell the live ox, and divide the money of it; and the dead *ox* also they shall divide. 36 Or if it be known that the ox hath used to push in time past, and his owner hath not kept him in; he shall surely pay ox for ox; and the dead shall be his own.' "

---

31. (21:1-36) These laws, which relate to a stable agricultural economy, appear to have been written after the settlement of Canaan. Verses 2-11 concern Israelite slaves; 12-17, capital crimes; 18-32, noncapital offenses; and 33-36, property.
32. I.e., a concubine.
33. (21:13-14) If one man kills another accidentally, he can find asylum from an "avenger of blood" at the Lord's altar. One found guilty of murder is to be removed from the sacred area and executed.
34. (21:23-25) This statement is not so much a demand for vengeance as it is a limitation on excessive vengeance. Contrast the sentiment of Lamech (*Genesis* 4:23-24) and of Levi and Simeon (*Genesis* 34:25-31).

Introduction to
JUDGES

"Nevertheless the Lord raised up judges, which delivered them out of the hand of those that spoiled them."

Judges relates events from the death of Joshua to the emergence of Samuel. Though *Joshua* reports that the Israelites took Palestine in several brief campaigns, much of the country had not been conquered and was not to be won for generations. The stories in *Judges* show the slow and often chaotic progress toward final victory and the establishment of the kingdom. Many are folk tales and old legends preserved by individual tribes about their favorite heroes. Around 600 B.C., these stories were collected and merged into a continuous historical narrative that conveyed a religious message.

The author sought to explain why—despite God's covenant with Israel—the Canaanites retained possession of much of the promised land for centuries. (The events in *Judges* are dated from 1200 to 1000 B.C.) To do this, he put the old stories and legends into an artificial framework describing cycles of infidelity. In each cycle, the Israelites begin to worship false gods and, in punishment, are conquered by an enemy; later they are rescued by a judge (i.e., a hero or deliverer) and prosper until such time as the judge dies and a new generation becomes unfaithful to Yahweh. This framework offers an account of twelve judges: six are barely mentioned, and six have more elaborate narratives. The present selection contains the stories of Othniel, Ehud, Shamgar, Deborah, and Samson.

In the accounts, a judge is one seized by divine power. With sudden gifts of wisdom, strength, eloquence, or holiness, he rouses Israel against its oppressors. As Norman K. Gottwald (*A Light to the Nations*, Harper & Row, 1959) explains, "The charismatic does not reign by heredity or election; he is a 'bearer of the spirit' whose right to the support of his community is self-authenticating." The description of Othniel applies to each of the heroes: "the Spirit of the Lord came upon him, and he judged Israel."

Judges links a number of folk tales to form a loose historical narrative expressing a religious judgment. It insists that the fortunes of Israel depend entirely on the fidelity of the Jewish people to Yahweh. But one would miss much of the literary value of the book if he did not recognize that the richly detailed stories of tribal heroes—especially the left-handed Ehud, the eloquent Deborah, the wily Jael, and the slow-witted Samson—have a memorable vitality in their own right.

THE CHARISMATIC LEADERS

The Covenant Recalled

2 And an Angel of the LORD came up from Gilgal to Bochim, and said, "I made you to go up out of Egypt, and have brought you unto the land which I sware unto your fathers; and I said, 'I will never break my covenant with you. 2 And ye shall make no league with the inhabitants of this land; ye shall throw down their altars': but ye have not obeyed my voice; why have ye done this? 3 Wherefore I also said, 'I will not drive them out from before you; but they shall be *as thorns* in your sides, and their gods shall be a snare unto you.'" 4 And it came to pass, when the Angel of the LORD spake these words unto all the children of Israel, that the people lifted up their voice, and wept. 5 And they called the name of that place Bochim: and they sacrificed there unto the LORD.

The Cycle of Infidelity

6 And when Joshua had let the people go, the children of Israel went every man unto his inheritance to possess the land. 7 And the people served the LORD all the days of Joshua, and all the days of the elders that outlived Joshua, who had seen all the great works of the LORD, that he did for Israel. 8 And Joshua the son of Nun, the servant of the LORD, died, *being* a hundred and ten years old. 9 And they buried him in the border of his inheritance in Timnath-heres, in the mount of Ephraim, on the north side of the hill Gaash. 10 And also all that generation were gathered unto their fathers: and there arose another generation after them, which knew not the LORD, nor yet the works which he had done for Israel.

11 And the children of Israel did evil in the sight of the LORD, and served Baalim: 12 And they forsook the LORD God of their fathers, which brought them out of the land of Egypt, and followed other gods, of the gods of the people that *were* round about them, and bowed themselves unto them, and provoked the LORD to anger. 13 And they forsook the LORD, and served Baal and Ashtaroth.[1] 14 And the anger of the LORD was hot against Israel, and he delivered them into the hands of spoilers that spoiled them, and he sold them into the hands of their enemies round

about, so that they could not any longer stand before their enemies. 15 Whithersoever they went out, the hand of the LORD was against them for evil, as the LORD had said, and as the LORD had sworn unto them: and they were greatly distressed.

16 Nevertheless the LORD raised up judges, which delivered them out of the hand of those that spoiled them. 17 And yet they would not hearken unto their judges, but they went a whoring after other gods,[2] and bowed themselves unto them: they turned quickly out of the way which their fathers walked in, obeying the commandments of the LORD; *but* they did not so. 18 And when the LORD raised them up judges, then the LORD was with the judge, and delivered them out of the hand of their enemies all the days of the judge: for it repented the LORD because of their groanings by reason of them that oppressed them and vexed them. 19 And it came to pass, when the judge was dead, *that* they returned, and corrupted *themselves* more than their fathers, in following other gods to serve them, and to bow down unto them; they ceased not from their own doings, nor from their stubborn way. 20 And the anger of the LORD was hot against Israel; and he said, "Because that this people hath transgressed my covenant which I commanded their fathers, and have not hearkened unto my voice; 21 I also will not henceforth drive out any from before them of the nations which Joshua left when he died: 22 That through them I may prove Israel, whether they will keep the way of the LORD to walk therein, as their fathers did keep *it*, or not." 23 Therefore the LORD left those nations, without driving them out hastily; neither delivered he them into the hand of Joshua.

3 Now these *are* the nations which the LORD left, to prove Israel by them, *even* as many of *Israel* as had not known all the wars of Canaan; 2 Only that the generations of the children of Israel might know to teach them war, at the least such as before knew nothing thereof; 3 *Namely,* five lords of the Philistines, and all the Canaanites, and the Sidonians, and the Hivites that dwelt in mount Lebanon, from mount Baal-hermon unto the entering in of Hamath. 4 And they were to prove Israel by them, to know whether they would hearken unto the commandments of the

---

1. These are male and female gods of the Canaanites. The plural of Baal is "Baalim" (3:7).

2. Since Israel considered itself wed to Yahweh, idolatry was commonly referred to as adultery and fornication.

LORD, which he commanded their fathers by the hand of Moses. 5 And the children of Israel dwelt among the Canaanites, Hittites, and Amorites, and Perizzites, and Hivites, and Jebusites: 6 And they took their daughters to be their wives, and gave their daughters to their sons, and served their gods.

Othniel

7 And the children of Israel did evil in the sight of the LORD, and forgat the LORD their God, and served Baalim and the groves. 8 Therefore the anger of the LORD was hot against Israel, and he sold them into the hand of Chushan-rishathaim king of Mesopotamia: and the children of Israel served Chushan-rishathaim eight years. 9 And when the children of Israel cried unto the LORD, the LORD raised up a deliverer to the children of Israel, who delivered them, *even* Othniel the son of Kenaz, Caleb's younger brother. 10 And the Spirit of the LORD came upon him, and he judged Israel, and went out to war: and the LORD delivered Chushan-rishathaim king of Mesopotamia into his hand; and his hand prevailed against Chushan-rishathaim. 11 And the land had rest forty years:[3] and Othniel the son of Kenaz died.

Ehud

12 And the children of Israel did evil again in the sight of the LORD: and the LORD strengthened Eglon the king of Moab against Israel, because they had done evil in the sight of the LORD. 13 And he gathered unto him the children of Ammon and Amalek, and went and smote Israel, and possessed the city of palm trees. 14 So the children of Israel served Eglon the king of Moab eighteen years. 15 But when the children of Israel cried unto the LORD, the LORD raised them up a deliverer, Ehud the son of Gera, a Benjamite, a man left-handed: and by him the children of Israel sent a present unto Eglon the king of Moab. 16 But Ehud made him a dagger which had two edges, of a cubit length; and he did gird it under his raiment upon his right thigh. 17 And he brought the present unto Eglon king of Moab: and Eglon *was* a very fat man. 18 And when he had made an end to offer the present, he sent away the people that bare the present. 19 But he himself turned again from the quarries that *were* by Gilgal, and said, "I have a secret errand unto thee, O king": who said, "Keep silence." And all that stood by him went out from him. 20 And

Ehud came unto him; and he was sitting in a summer parlor, which he had for himself alone. And Ehud said, "I have a message from God unto thee." And he arose out of *his* seat. 21 And Ehud put forth his left hand, and took the dagger from his right thigh, and thrust it into his belly: 22 And the haft also went in after the blade; and the fat closed upon the blade, so that he could not draw the dagger out of his belly; and the dirt came out.[4] 23 Then Ehud went forth through the porch, and shut the doors of the parlor upon him, and locked them. 24 When he was gone out, his servants came; and when they saw that, behold, the doors of the parlor *were* locked, they said, "Surely he covereth his feet in his summer chamber." 25 And they tarried till they were ashamed: and, behold, he opened not the doors of the parlor; therefore they took a key, and opened *them:* and, behold, their lord *was* fallen down dead on the earth. 26 And Ehud escaped while they tarried, and passed beyond the quarries, and escaped unto Seirath. 27 And it came to pass, when he was come, that he blew a trumpet in the mountain of Ephraim, and the children of Israel went down with him from the mount, and he before them. 28 And he said unto them, "Follow after me: for the LORD hath delivered your enemies the Moabites into your hand." And they went down after him, and took the fords of Jordan toward Moab, and suffered not a man to pass over. 29 And they slew of Moab at that time about ten thousand men, all lusty, and all men of valor; and there escaped not a man. 30 So Moab was subdued that day under the hand of Israel. And the land had restfourscore years.

Shamgar

31 And after him was Shamgar the son of Anath, which slew of the Philistines six hundred men with an oxgoad: and he also delivered Israel.[5]

Deborah

4 And the children of Israel again did evil in the sight of the LORD, when Ehud was dead. 2 And the LORD sold them into the hand of Jabin king of Canaan, that reigned in Hazor; the captain of whose host *was* Sisera, which dwelt in Harosheth of the Gentiles. 3 And the children of Israel

---

3. Forty years was considered a generation. Generalized time periods in *Judges*—and elsewhere throughout Scripture—often take some form of the number forty.

4. KNOX: "thereupon the bowels discharged their load."
5. This verse contains the entire account of Shamgar as judge. However, he is mentioned in Deborah's song (5:6), and it is significant that he slays Philistines, who become a major threat in the time of Samson. Because Chapter 4 begins with a reference to Ehud, this passage seems out of place.

cried unto the LORD: for he had nine hundred chariots of iron; and twenty years he mightily oppressed the children of Israel.

4 And Deborah, a prophetess, the wife of Lapidoth, she judged Israel at that time. 5 And she dwelt under the palm tree of Deborah, between Ramah and Beth-el in mount Ephraim: and the children of Israel came up to her for judgment. 6 And she sent and called Barak the son of Abinoam out of Kedesh-naphtali, and said unto him, "Hath not the LORD God of Israel commanded, *saying,* 'Go and draw toward mount Tabor, and take with thee ten thousand men of the children of Naphtali and of the children of Zebulun? 7 And I will draw unto thee, to the river Kishon, Sisera the captain of Jabin's army, with his chariots and his multitude; and I will deliver him into thine hand.' " 8 And Barak said unto her, "If thou wilt go with me, then I will go: but if thou wilt not go with me, *then* I will not go."[6] 9 And she said, "I will surely go with thee: notwithstanding the journey that thou takest shall not be for thine honor; for the LORD shall sell Sisera into the hand of a woman." And Deborah arose and went with Barak to Kedesh. 10 And Barak called Zebulun and Naphtali to Kedesh; and he went up with ten thousand men at his feet: and Deborah went up with him.

11 Now Heber the Kenite, *which was* of the children of Hobab the father-in-law of Moses, had severed himself from the Kenites, and pitched his tent unto the plain of Zaanaim, which *is* by Kedesh.

12 And they showed Sisera that Barak the son of Abinoam was gone up to mount Tabor. 13 And Sisera gathered together all his chariots, *even* nine hundred chariots of iron, and all the people that *were* with him, from Harosheth of the Gentiles unto the river of Kishon. 14 And Deborah said unto Barak, "Up; for this *is* the day in which the LORD hath delivered Sisera into thine hand: is not the LORD gone out before thee?" So Barak went down from mount Tabor, and ten thousand men after him. 15 And the LORD discomfited Sisera, and all *his* chariots, and all *his* host, with the edge of the sword before Barak; so that Sisera lighted down off *his* chariot, and fled away on his feet. 16 But Barak pursued after the chariots, and after the host, unto Harosheth of the Gentiles: and all the host of Sisera fell upon the edge of the sword; *and* there was not a man left.

17 Howbeit Sisera fled away on his feet to the tent of Jael the wife of Heber the Kenite: for *there*

was peace between Jabin the king of Hazor and the house of Heber the Kenite. 18 And Jael went out to meet Sisera, and said unto him, "Turn in, my lord, turn in to me; fear not." And when he had turned in unto her into the tent, she covered him with a mantle. 19 And he said unto her, "Give me, I pray thee, a little water to drink; for I am thirsty." And she opened a bottle of milk, and gave him drink, and covered him. 20 Again he said unto her, "Stand in the door of the tent, and it shall be, when any man doth come and inquire of thee, and say, 'Is there any man here?' that thou shalt say, 'No.' " 21 Then Jael Heber's wife took a nail of the tent, and took a hammer in her hand, and went softly unto him, and smote the nail into his temples, and fastened it into the ground: for he was fast asleep and weary. So he died. 22 And, behold, as Barak pursued Sisera, Jael came out to meet him, and said unto him, "Come and I will show thee the man whom thou seekest." And when he came into her *tent,* behold, Sisera lay dead, and the nail *was* in his temples. 23 So God subdued on that day Jabin the king of Canaan before the children of Israel. 24 And the hand of the children of Israel prospered, and prevailed against Jabin the king of Canaan, until they had destroyed Jabin king of Canaan.

The Song of Deborah[7]

5 Then sang Deborah and Barak the son of Abinoam on that day, saying,

2   "Praise ye the LORD for the avenging of Israel,
When the people willingly offered themselves.

3   Hear, O ye kings; give ear, O ye princes;
I, *even* I, will sing unto the LORD;
I will sing *praise* to the LORD God of Israel.

4   "LORD, when thou wentest out of Seir,
When thou marchedst out of the field of Edom,
The earth trembled, and the heavens dropped,
The clouds also dropped water.

5   The mountains melted from before the LORD,
Even that Sinai from before the LORD God of Israel.

---

6. **Barak, the Israelite** commander, feels the company of the prophetess assures the presence of God.

7. (5:1-31) In IB, Jacob M. Myers divides the song as follows: 1, introductory note; 2-5, invocation; 6-9, conditions in Israel; 10-11, call to rejoice; 12-18, roll call of the tribes; 19-22, battle scene; 23-27, Meroz and Jael; 28-30, scene in palace of Sisera; 31, the refrain. The Hebrew text is very old and in some places almost unintelligible.

6   "In the days of Shamgar the son of
Anath,
In the days of Jael, the highways were
unoccupied,
And the travelers walked through byways.

7   *The inhabitants of* the villages ceased, they
ceased in Israel,
Until that I Deborah arose,
That I arose a mother in Israel.

8   They chose new gods;
Then *was* war in the gates:
Was there a shield or spear seen
Among forty thousand in Israel?

9   My heart *is* toward the governors of Israel,
That offered themselves willingly among
the people.
Bless ye the LORD.

10   "Speak, ye that ride on white asses,
Ye that sit in judgment,
And walk by the way.

11   *They that are delivered* from the noise of
archers in the places of drawing water,
There shall they rehearse the righteous
acts of the LORD,
Even the righteous acts *toward the inhabitants* of his villages in Israel:
Then shall the people of the LORD go
down to the gates.

12   "Awake, awake, Deborah:
Awake, awake, utter a song:
Arise, Barak, and lead thy captivity cap-
tive,
Thou son of Abinoam.

13   Then he made him that remaineth have
dominion over the nobles among the
people:
The LORD made me have dominion over
the mighty.

14   Out of Ephraim *was there* a root of them
against Amalek;
After thee, Benjamin, among thy people;
Out of Machir came down governors, and
out of Zebulun they that handle the pen
of the writer.

15   And the princes of Issachar *were* with
Deborah;
Even Issachar, and also Barak:
He was sent on foot into the valley.
For the divisions of Reuben
There were great thoughts of heart.

16   Why abodest thou among the sheepfolds,
To hear the bleatings of the flocks?
For the divisions of Reuben
There were great searchings of heart.

17   Gilead abode beyond Jordan:

And why did Dan remain in ships?
Asher continued on the seashore,
And abode in his breaches.

18   Zebulun and Naphtali *were* a people *that*
jeoparded their lives unto the death
In the high places of the field.

19   "The kings came *and* fought;
Then fought the kings of Canaan
In Taanach by the waters of Megiddo;
They took no gain of money.

20   They fought from heaven;
The stars in their courses fought against
Sisera.

21   The river of Kishon swept them away,
That ancient river, the river Kishon.[8]
O my soul, thou hast trodden down
strength.

22   Then were the horsehoofs broken
By the means of the prancings, the prancings of their mighty ones.

23   " 'Curse ye Meroz,' said the angel of the
LORD,
'Curse ye bitterly the inhabitants thereof;
Because they came not to the help of the
LORD,
To the help of the LORD against the
mighty.'

24   "Blessed above women shall Jael the wife
of Heber the Kenite be;
Blessed shall she be above women in the
tent.

25   He asked water, *and* she gave *him* milk;
She brought forth butter in a lordly
dish.

26   She put her hand to the nail,
And her right hand to the workmen's
hammer;
And with the hammer she smote Sisera,
she smote off his head,
When she had pierced and stricken
through his temples.

27   At her feet he bowed, he fell, he lay down:
At her feet he bowed, he fell:
Where he bowed, there he fell down dead.

28   "The mother of Sisera looked out at a
window,
And cried through the lattice,
'Why is his chariot *so* long in coming?
Why tarry the wheels of his chariots?'

29   Her wise ladies answered her,
Yea, she returned answer to herself,

---

8. These lines, taken with verses 4 and 5, suggest that a violent
storm aided the Israelites in battle.

30 'Have they not sped? have they *not* di-
        vided the prey;
    To every man a damsel *or* two;
    To Sisera a prey of divers colors,
    A prey of divers colors of needlework,
    Of divers colors of needlework on both
        sides,
    Meet for the necks of *them that take* the
        spoil?'

31 "So let all thine enemies perish, O LORD:
    But *let* them that love him *be* as the sun
        when he goeth forth in his might."
And the land had rest forty years.

*   *   *

Samson

13 And the children of Israel did evil again in
the sight of the LORD; and the LORD delivered
them into the hand of the Philistines forty years.[9]

2 And there was a certain man of Zorah, of the
family of the Danites, whose name *was* Manoah;
and his wife *was* barren, and bare not. 3 And the
angel of the LORD appeared unto the woman, and
said unto her, "Behold now, thou *art* barren, and
bearest not: but thou shalt conceive, and bear a
son. 4 Now therefore beware, I pray thee, and
drink not wine nor strong drink, and eat not any
unclean *thing:* 5 For, lo, thou shalt conceive, and
bear a son; and no razor shall come on his head:
for the child shall be a Nazarite unto God from
the womb:[10] and he shall begin to deliver Israel
out of the hand of the Philistines." 6 Then the
woman came and told her husband, saying, "A
man of God came unto me, and his countenance
was like the countenance of an angel of God, very
terrible: but I asked him not whence he *was,* neither told he me his name: 7 But he said unto me,
'Behold, thou shalt conceive, and bear a son; and
now drink no wine nor strong drink, neither eat
any unclean *thing:* for the child shall be a Nazarite to God from the womb to the day of his
death.' "

8 Then Manoah entreated the LORD, and said,
"O my Lord, let the man of God which thou didst
send come again unto us, and teach us what we
shall do unto the child that shall be born."
9 And God hearkened to the voice of Manoah;
and the angel of God came again unto the woman
as she sat in the field: but Manoah her husband
was not with her. 10 And the woman made

haste, and ran, and showed her husband, and said
unto him, "Behold, the man hath appeared unto
me, that came unto me the *other* day." 11 And
Manoah arose, and went after his wife, and came
to the man, and said unto him, "*Art* thou the man
that spakest unto the woman?" And he said, "I
am." 12 And Manoah said, "Now let thy words
come to pass. How shall we order the child, and
how shall we do unto him?" 13 And the angel of
the LORD said unto Manoah, "Of all that I said
unto the woman let her beware. 14 She may not
eat of any *thing* that cometh of the vine, neither
let her drink wine or strong drink, nor eat any unclean *thing:* all that I commanded her let her observe."

15 And Manoah said unto the angel of the
LORD, "I pray thee, let us detain thee, until we
shall have made ready a kid for thee." 16 And
the angel of the LORD said unto Manoah,
"Though thou detain me, I will not eat of thy
bread: and if thou wilt offer a burnt offering, thou
must offer it unto the LORD." For Manoah knew
not that he *was* an angel of the LORD. 17 And
Manoah said unto the angel of the LORD, "What
is thy name, that when thy sayings come to pass
we may do thee honor?" 18 And the angel of the
LORD said unto him, "Why askest thou thus after
my name, seeing it *is* secret?" 19 So Manoah
took a kid with a meat offering, and offered *it*
upon a rock unto the LORD: and *the angel* did
wondrously;[11] and Manoah and his wife looked
on. 20 For it came to pass, when the flame went
up toward heaven from off the altar, that the
angel of the LORD ascended in the flame of the
altar: and Manoah and his wife looked on *it,* and
fell on their faces to the ground. 21 But the angel
of the LORD did no more appear to Manoah and
to his wife. Then Manoah knew that he *was* an
angel of the LORD. 22 And Manoah said unto
his wife, "We shall surely die, because we have
seen God." 23 But his wife said unto him, "If the
LORD were pleased to kill us, he would not have
received a burnt offering and a meat offering at
our hands, neither would he have showed us all
these *things,* nor would as at this time have told us
such things as these."

24 And the woman bare a son, and called his
name Samson: and the child grew, and the LORD
blessed him. 25 And the Spirit of the LORD
began to move him at times in the camp of Dan
between Zorah and Eshtaol.

The Marriage of Samson

14 And Samson went down to Timnath, and saw
a woman in Timnath of the daughters of the Phil-

---

9. The Philistines, Peoples of the Sea, began a gradual infiltra-
tion into Palestine sometime after 1200 B.C.
10. A Nazarite was consecrated to God by special vows. *Numbers* 6:3 gives the Nazarite rule concerning hair. Samson's
strength lies in his fidelity to this rule.

11. NEB: "to him whose works are full of wonder."

istines. 2 And he came up, and told his father and his mother, and said, "I have seen a woman in Timnath of the daughters of the Philistines: now therefore get her for me to wife." 3 Then his father and his mother said unto him, "*Is there* never a woman among the daughters of thy brethren, or among all my people, that thou goest to take a wife of the uncircumcised Philistines?" And Samson said unto his father, "Get her for me; for she pleaseth me well." 4 But his father and his mother knew not that it *was* of the LORD, that he sought an occasion against the Philistines: for at that time the Philistines had dominion over Israel.

5 Then went Samson down, and his father and his mother, to Timnath, and came to the vineyards of Timnath: and, behold, a young lion roared against him. 6 And the Spirit of the LORD came mightily upon him, and he rent him as he would have rent a kid, and *he had* nothing in his hand: but he told not his father or his mother what he had done. 7 And he went down, and talked with the woman; and she pleased Samson well. 8 And after a time he returned to take her, and he turned aside to see the carcass of the lion: and, behold, *there was* a swarm of bees and honey in the carcass of the lion. 9 And he took thereof in his hands, and went on eating, and came to his father and mother, and he gave them, and they did eat: but he told not them that he had taken the honey out of the carcass of the lion.

10 So his father went down unto the woman: and Samson made there a feast; for so used the young men to do. 11 And it came to pass, when they saw him, that they brought thirty companions to be with him. 12 And Samson said unto them, "I will now put forth a riddle unto you: if ye can certainly declare it me within the seven days of the feast, and find *it* out, then I will give you thirty sheets and thirty change of garments: 13 But if ye cannot declare *it* me, then shall ye give me thirty sheets and thirty change of garments." And they said unto him, "Put forth thy riddle, that we may hear it."

14 And he said unto them,

"Out of the eater came forth meat,
And out of the strong came forth sweetness."

And they could not in three days expound the riddle.

15 And it came to pass on the seventh day, that they said unto Samson's wife, "Entice thy husband, that he may declare unto us the riddle, lest we burn thee and thy father's house with fire: have ye called us to take that we have? *is it* not *so?*" [12] 16 And Samson's wife wept before him,

and said, "Thou dost but hate me, and lovest me not: thou hast put forth a riddle unto the children of my people, and hast not told *it* me." And he said unto her, "Behold, I have not told *it* my father nor my mother, and shall I tell *it* thee?" 17 And she wept before him the seven days, while their feast lasted: and it came to pass on the seventh day, that he told her, because she lay sore upon him: and she told the riddle to the children of her people.

18 And the men of the city said unto him on the seventh day before the sun went down,

"What *is* sweeter than honey?
And what *is* stronger than a lion?"

And he said unto them,

"If ye had not plowed with my heifer,
Ye had not found out my riddle."

19 And the Spirit of the LORD came upon him, and he went down to Ashkelon, and slew thirty men of them, and took their spoil, and gave change of garments unto them which expounded the riddle. And his anger was kindled, and he went up to his father's house. 20 But Samson's wife was *given* to his companion, whom he had used as his friend.

15 But it came to pass within a while after, in the time of wheat harvest, that Samson visited his wife with a kid; and he said, "I will go in to my wife into the chamber." But her father would not suffer him to go in. 2 And her father said, "I verily thought that thou hadst utterly hated her; therefore I gave her to thy companion: *is* not her younger sister fairer than she? take her, I pray thee, instead of her." 3 And Samson said concerning them, "Now shall I be more blameless than the Philistines, though I do them a displeasure." 4 And Samson went and caught three hundred foxes, and took firebrands, and turned tail to tail, and put a firebrand in the midst between two tails. 5 And when he had set the brands on fire, he let *them* go into the standing corn of the Philistines, and burnt up both the shocks, and also the standing corn, with the vineyards *and* olives. 6 Then the Philistines said, "Who hath done this?" And they answered, "Samson, the son-in-law of the Timnite, because he had taken his wife, and given her to his companion." And the Philistines came up, and burnt her and her father with fire. 7 And Samson said unto them, "Though ye have done this, yet will I be avenged of you, and after that I will cease." 8 And he smote them hip and thigh with a great slaughter: and he went down and dwelt in the top of the rock Etam.

9 Then the Philistines went up, and pitched in Judah, and spread themselves in Lehi. 10 And

---

12. NAB: "Did you invite us here to reduce us to poverty?"

the men of Judah said, "Why are ye come up against us?" And they answered, "To bind Samson are we come up, to do to him as he hath done to us." 11 Then three thousand men of Judah went to the top of the rock Etam, and said to Samson, "Knowest thou not that the Philistines *are* rulers over us? what *is* this *that* thou hast done unto us?" And he said unto them, "As they did unto me, so have I done unto them." 12 And they said unto him, "We are come down to bind thee, that we may deliver thee into the hand of the Philistines." And Samson said unto them, "Swear unto me, that ye will not fall upon me yourselves." 13 And they spake unto him, saying, "No; but we will bind thee fast, and deliver thee into their hand: but surely we will not kill thee." And they bound him with two new cords, and brought him up from the rock.

14 *And* when he came unto Lehi, the Philistines shouted against him: and the Spirit of the LORD came mightily upon him, and the cords that *were* upon his arms became as flax that was burnt with fire, and his bands loosed from off his hands. 15 And he found a new jawbone of an ass, and put forth his hand, and took it, and slew a thousand men therewith. 16 And Samson said,

"With the jawbone of an ass, heaps upon
    heaps,[13]
With the jaw of an ass have I slain a thousand men."

17 And it came to pass, when he had made an end of speaking, that he cast away the jawbone out of his hand, and called that place Ramath-lehi.

18 And he was sore athirst, and called on the LORD, and said, "Thou hast given this great deliverance into the hand of thy servant: and now shall I die for thirst, and fall into the hand of the uncircumcised?" 19 But God clave a hollow place that *was* in the jaw, and there came water thereout;[14] and when he had drunk, his spirit came again, and he revived: wherefore he called the name thereof En-hakkore, which *is* in Lehi unto this day. 20 And he judged Israel in the days of the Philistines twenty years.

16 Then went Samson to Gaza, and saw there a harlot, and went in unto her. 2 *And it was told* the Gazites, saying, "Samson is come hither." And they compassed *him* in, and laid wait for him all night in the gate of the city, and were quiet all the night, saying, "In the morning, when it is day,

we shall kill him." 3 And Samson lay till midnight, and arose at midnight, and took the doors of the gate of the city, and the two posts, and went away with them, bar and all, and put *them* upon his shoulders, and carried them up to the top of a hill that *is* before Hebron.[15]

Samson and Delilah

4 And it came to pass afterward, that he loved a woman in the valley of Sorek, whose name *was* Delilah. 5 And the lords of the Philistines came up unto her, and said unto her, "Entice him, and see wherein his great strength *lieth*, and by what *means* we may prevail against him, that we may bind him to afflict him: and we will give thee every one of us eleven hundred *pieces* of silver." 6 And Delilah said to Samson, "Tell me, I pray thee, wherein thy great strength *lieth*, and wherewith thou mightest be bound to afflict thee." 7 And Samson said unto her, "If they bind me with seven green withes that were never dried, then shall I be weak, and be as another man." 8 Then the lords of the Philistines brought up to her seven green withes which had not been dried, and she bound him with them. 9 Now *there were* men lying in wait, abiding with her in the chamber. And she said unto him, "The Philistines *be* upon thee, Samson!" And he brake the withes, as a thread of tow is broken when it toucheth the fire. So his strength was not known.

10 And Delilah said unto Samson, "Behold, thou hast mocked me, and told me lies: now tell me, I pray thee, wherewith thou mightest be bound." 11 And he said unto her, "If they bind me fast with new ropes that never were occupied, then shall I be weak, and be as another man." 12 Delilah therefore took new ropes, and bound him therewith, and said unto him, "The Philistines *be* upon thee, Samson!" And *there were* liers in wait abiding in the chamber. And he brake them from off his arms like a thread.

13 And Delilah said unto Samson, "Hitherto thou hast mocked me, and told me lies: tell me wherewith thou mightest be bound." And he said unto her, "If thou weavest the seven locks of my head with the web." 14 And she fastened *it* with the pin, and said unto him, "The Philistines *be* upon thee, Samson!" And he awaked out of his sleep, and went away with the pin of the beam, and with the web.

15 And she said unto him, "How canst thou say, 'I love thee,' when thine heart *is* not with me? Thou hast mocked me these three times, and hast not told me wherein thy great strength *lieth*."

---

13. This verse involves a pun. In Hebrew, the words for "ass" and "heap[s]" are identical.
14. NEB: "God split open the Hollow of Lehi and water came out of it."

15. Samson's great strength is illustrated by the fact that Hebron is forty miles from Gaza.

16 And it came to pass, when she pressed him daily with her words, and urged him, *so* that his soul was vexed unto death; 17 That he told her all his heart, and said unto her, "There hath not come a razor upon mine head; for I *have been* a Nazarite unto God from my mother's womb: if I be shaven, then my strength will go from me, and I shall become weak, and be like any *other* man."

18 And when Delilah saw that he had told her all his heart, she sent and called for the lords of the Philistines, saying, "Come up this once, for he hath showed me all his heart." Then the lords of the Philistines came up unto her, and brought money in their hand. 19 And she made him sleep upon her knees; and she called for a man, and she caused him to shave off the seven locks of his head; and she began to afflict him, and his strength went from him. 20 And she said, "The Philistines *be* upon thee, Samson!" And he awoke out of his sleep, and said, "I will go out as at other times before, and shake myself." And he wist not that the LORD was departed from him. 21 But the Philistines took him, and put out his eyes, and brought him down to Gaza, and bound him with fetters of brass; and he did grind in the prison house. 22 Howbeit the hair of his head began to grow again after he was shaven.

23 Then the lords of the Philistines gathered them together for to offer a great sacrifice unto Dagon their god,[16] and to rejoice: for they said, "Our god hath delivered Samson our enemy into our hand." 24 And when the people saw him, they praised their god: for they said, "Our god hath delivered into our hands our enemy, and the destroyer of our country, which slew many of us." 25 And it came to pass, when their hearts were merry, that they said, "Call for Samson, that he may make us sport." And they called for Samson out of the prison house; and he made them sport: and they set him between the pillars. 26 And Samson said unto the lad that held him by the hand, "Suffer me that I may feel the pillars whereupon the house standeth, that I may lean upon them." 27 Now the house was full of men and women; and all the lords of the Philistines *were* there; and *there were* upon the roof about three thousand men and women, that beheld while Samson made sport.

28 And Samson called unto the LORD, and said, "O Lord GOD, remember me, I pray thee, and strengthen me, I pray thee, only this once, O God, that I may be at once avenged of the Philistines for my two eyes." [17] 29 And Samson took hold of the two middle pillars upon which the house stood, and on which it was borne up, of the one with his right hand, and of the other with his left. 30 And Samson said, "Let me die with the Philistines." And he bowed himself with *all his* might; and the house fell upon the lords, and upon all the people that *were* therein. So the dead which he slew at his death were more than *they* which he slew in his life. 31 Then his brethren and all the house of his father came down, and took him, and brought *him* up, and buried him between Zorah and Eshtaol in the buryingplace of Manoah his father. And he judged Israel twenty years.

16. In Canaanite belief, Dagon was the father of Baal.

17. Except for his charismatic gift, Samson does not resemble the other judges. All of his motives and battles are personal rather than religious or national.

Introduction to
RUTH

"Blessed be the Lord, which hath not left thee without a kinsman, that his name may be famous in Israel."

Composed between 450 and 250 B.C. and set in "the days when the judges ruled," *Ruth* is a religious narrative which comments on Israel's missionary role. It describes an ideal proselyte.

The book conforms to the criteria of a short story. *Ruth* offers a simple plot related through scenes which detail the action, delineate the characters, and develop the suspense. Realistic details—gleaning in the fields, carousing at harvest's completion, retaining property within the family, negotiating levirate marriage—add dramatic vigor to the story. While the main characters reveal notable courtesy, compassion, honor, and graciousness, the lesser figures—Orpah, the unnamed kinsman, the harvest laborers from whom Boaz seeks to protect Ruth—keep the tale from being simply an idyllic pastoral. Roughly two-thirds of the story is expressed through dialogue.

Following the exile (i.e., after 539 B.C.), one tendency of the Jewish people was to withdraw from the outer world and emphasize their exclusive role as the chosen of God. Characteristic of this concern were the stern decrees of Ezra and Nehemiah which required Hebrew men to divorce their foreign wives and marry only within the Jewish community. The book of *Ruth*, like *Jonah*, illustrates a more liberal attitude. There was great doctrinal impact in the story of a pious, self-sacrificing convert from the scorned Moabite people, who becomes the ancestress of King David.

In the Hebrew canon, *Ruth* belongs to the classification known as "The Writings." There it joins *Job, The Song of Songs, Ecclesiastes*, and seven more works described as "the other books" of Judaism. Its acceptance as canonical was assured by its popularity among the people and by its link to David. In the Greek and Latin canons, *Ruth* follows *Judges* because the story is set in that era.

RUTH

NAOMI'S MISFORTUNE

1 Now it came to pass in the days when the judges ruled, that there was a famine in the land. And a certain man of Bethlehemjudah went to sojourn in the country of Moab,[1] he, and his wife, and his two sons. 2 And the name of the man *was* Elimelech, and the name of his wife Naomi, and the name of his two sons Mahlon and Chilion, Ephrathites of Bethlehemjudah. And they came into the country of Moab, and continued there. 3 And Elimelech Naomi's husband died; and she was left, and her two sons. 4 And they took them wives of the women of Moab; the name of the one *was* Orpah, and the name of the other Ruth: and they dwelt there about ten years. 5 And Mahlon and Chilion died also both of them; and the woman was left of her two sons and her husband.

6 Then she arose with her daughters-in-law, that she might return from the country of Moab: for she had heard in the country of Moab how that the LORD had visited his people in giving them bread. 7 Wherefore she went forth out of the place where she was, and her two daughters-in-law with her; and they went on the way to return unto the land of Judah. 8 And Naomi said unto her two daughters-in-law, "Go, return each to her mother's house: the LORD deal kindly with you, as ye have dealt with the dead, and with me. 9 The LORD grant you that ye may find rest, each *of you* in the house of her husband." [2] Then she kissed them; and they lifted up their voice, and wept. 10 And they said unto her, "Surely we will return with thee unto thy people." 11 And Naomi said, "Turn again, my daughters: why will ye go with me? *are* there yet *any more* sons in my womb, that they may be your husbands?[3] 12 Turn again, my daughters, go *your way;* for I am too old to have a husband. If I should say, I have hope, *if* I should have a husband also to-night, and should also bear sons; 13 Would ye tarry for them till they were grown? would ye stay for them from having husbands? nay, my daughters; for it grieveth me much for your sakes that the hand of the LORD is gone out against

me." 14 And they lifted up their voice, and wept again: and Orpah kissed her mother-in-law; but Ruth clave unto her.

15 And she said, "Behold, thy sister-in-law is gone back unto her people, and unto her gods: return thou after thy sister-in-law." 16 And Ruth said, "Entreat me not to leave thee, *or* to return from following after thee: for whither thou goest, I will go; and where thou lodgest, I will lodge: thy people *shall be* my people, and thy God my God: 17 Where thou diest, will I die, and there will I be buried: the LORD do so to me, and more also, *if aught* but death part thee and me." 18 When she saw that she was steadfastly minded to go with her, then she left speaking unto her.

19 So they two went until they came to Bethlehem. And it came to pass, when they were come to Bethlehem, that all the city was moved about them, and they said, "*Is* this Naomi?" 20 And she said unto them, "Call me not Naomi, call me Mara: for the Almighty hath dealt very bitterly with me.[4] 21 I went out full, and the LORD hath brought me home again empty: why *then* call ye me Naomi, seeing the LORD hath testified against me, and the Almighty hath afflicted me?" 22 So Naomi returned, and Ruth the Moabitess, her daughter-in-law, with her, which returned out of the country of Moab: and they came to Bethlehem in the beginning of barley harvest.

RUTH MEETS BOAZ

2 And Naomi had a kinsman of her husband's, a mighty man of wealth, of the family of Elimelech; and his name *was* Boaz. 2 And Ruth the Moabitess said unto Naomi, "Let me now go to the field, and glean ears of corn after *him* in whose sight I shall find grace." [5] And she said unto her, "Go, my daughter." 3 And she went, and came, and gleaned in the field after the reapers: and her hap was to light on a part of the field *belonging* unto Boaz, who *was* of the kindred of Elimelech. 4 And, behold, Boaz came from Bethlehem, and said unto the reapers, "The LORD *be* with you." And they answered him, "The LORD bless thee." 5 Then said Boaz unto his servant that was set over the reapers, "Whose damsel *is* this?" 6 And the servant that was set over the reapers answered

---

1. A sojourner was a resident alien who forfeited all legal rights. The Moabites, whose incestuous origin is described in *Genesis* 19:30-38, were expressly prohibited from participation in Jewish affairs (*Deuteronomy* 23:3).
2. KNOX: "May you live at ease with new husbands."
3. (1:11-12) Naomi's speech assumes the levirate marriage obligation. (See footnote 59 to *Genesis* 38:8-11.) In 4:16, Boaz invokes the levirate tradition to claim Ruth.

4. Naomi means "pleasant one"; Mara, "bitter."
5. Under the Law, the poor have this right, but it does not extend to a foreigner. Ruth must depend on the good will of the property owner.

and said, "It *is* the Moabitish damsel that came back with Naomi out of the country of Moab: 7 And she said; 'I pray you, let me glean and gather after the reapers among the sheaves': so she came, and hath continued even from the morning until now, that she tarried a little in the house."

8 Then said Boaz unto Ruth, "Hearest thou not, my daughter? Go not to glean in another field, neither go from hence, but abide here fast by my maidens:[6] 9 *Let* thine eyes *be* on the field that they do reap, and go thou after them: have I not charged the young men that they shall not touch thee? and when thou art athirst, go unto the vessels, and drink of *that* which the young men have drawn." 10 Then she fell on her face, and bowed herself to the ground, and said unto him, "Why have I found grace in thine eyes, that thou shouldest take knowledge of me, seeing I *am* a stranger?" 11 And Boaz answered and said unto her, "It hath fully been showed me, all that thou hast done unto thy mother-in-law since the death of thine husband; and *how* thou hast left thy father and thy mother, and the land of thy nativity, and art come unto a people which thou knewest not heretofore. 12 The LORD recompense thy work, and a full reward be given thee of the LORD God of Israel, under whose wings thou art come to trust." 13 Then she said, "Let me find favor in thy sight, my lord; for that thou hast comforted me, and for that thou hast spoken friendly unto thine handmaid, though I be not like unto one of thine handmaidens." 14 And Boaz said unto her, "At mealtime come thou hither, and eat of the bread, and dip thy morsel in the vinegar." And she sat beside the reapers: and he reached her parched *corn,* and she did eat, and was sufficed, and left. 15 And when she was risen up to glean, Boaz commanded his young men, saying, "Let her glean even among the sheaves, and reproach her not: 16 And let fall also *some* of the handfuls of purpose for her, and leave *them,* that she may glean *them,* and rebuke her not."

17 So she gleaned in the field until even, and beat out that she had gleaned: and it was about an ephah of barley. 18 And she took *it* up, and went into the city; and her mother-in-law saw what she had gleaned: and she brought forth, and gave to her that she had reserved after she was sufficed. 19 And her mother-in-law said unto her, "Where hast thou gleaned to-day? and where wroughtest thou? blessed be he that did take knowledge of thee." And she showed her mother-in-law with whom she had wrought, and said, "The man's name with whom I wrought to-day *is* Boaz." 20 And Naomi said unto her daughter-in-law, "Blessed *be* he of the LORD, who hath not left off his kindness to the living and to the dead." And Naomi said unto her, "The man *is* near of kin unto us, one of our next kinsmen." 21 And Ruth the Moabitess said, "He said unto me also, 'Thou shalt keep fast by my young men, until they have ended all my harvest.'" 22 And Naomi said unto Ruth her daughter-in-law, "*It is* good, my daughter, that thou go out with his maidens, that they meet thee not in any other field." 23 So she kept fast by the maidens of Boaz to glean unto the end of barley harvest and of wheat harvest; and dwelt with her mother-in-law.

NAOMI'S PLAN

3 Then Naomi her mother-in-law said unto her, "My daughter, shall I not seek rest for thee, that it may be well with thee? 2 And now *is* not Boaz of our kindred, with whose maidens thou wast? Behold, he winnoweth barley to-night in the threshing floor. 3 Wash thyself therefore, and anoint thee, and put thy raiment upon thee, and get thee down to the floor: *but* make not thyself known unto the man, until he shall have done eating and drinking. 4 And it shall be, when he lieth down, that thou shalt mark the place where he shall lie, and thou shalt go in, and uncover his feet, and lay thee down; and he will tell thee what thou shalt do."[7] 5 And she said unto her, "All that thou sayest unto me I will do."

6 And she went down unto the floor, and did according to all that her mother-in-law bade her. 7 And when Boaz had eaten and drunk, and his heart was merry, he went to lie down at the end of the heap of corn: and she came softly, and uncovered his feet, and laid her down. 8 And it came to pass at midnight, that the man was afraid, and turned himself: and, behold, a woman lay at his feet. 9 And he said, "Who *art* thou?" And she answered, "I *am* Ruth thine handmaid: spread therefore thy skirt over thine handmaid; for thou *art* a near kinsman." 10 And he said, "Blessed *be* thou of the LORD, my daughter; *for* thou hast showed more kindness in the latter end than at the beginning, inasmuch as thou followedst not young men, whether poor or rich. 11 And now, my daughter, fear not; I will do to thee all that thou requirest: for all the city of my people doth

---

6. Boaz' concern for Ruth's safety indicates the danger an unprotected young woman might face among the laborers. The "maidens" are maidservants who bind the sheaves.

7. (3:1-4) Naomi's counsel may not be as blatant as it appears. Boaz is known to be a religious man, and under levirate tradition, he is an eligible husband. However, the counsel is certainly direct.

know that thou *art* a virtuous woman. 12 And now it is true that I *am thy* near kinsman: howbeit there is a kinsman nearer than I. 13 Tarry this night, and it shall be in the morning, *that* if he will perform unto thee the part of a kinsman, well; let him do the kinsman's part: but if he will not do the part of a kinsman to thee, then will I do the part of a kinsman to thee, *as* the LORD liveth: lie down until the morning."

14 And she lay at his feet until the morning: and she rose up before one could know another.[8] And he said, "Let it not be known that a woman came into the floor." 15 Also he said, "Bring the veil that *thou hast* upon thee, and hold it." And when she held it, he measured six *measures* of barley, and laid *it* on her: and she went into the city. 16 And when she came to her mother-in-law, she said; "Who *art* thou, my daughter?"[9] And she told her all that the man had done to her. 17 And she said, "These six *measures* of barley gave he me; for he said to me, 'Go not empty unto thy mother-in-law.'" 18 Then said she, "Sit still, my daughter, until thou know how the matter will fall: for the man will not be in rest, until he have finished the thing this day."

BOAZ' RESPONSE

4 Then went Boaz up to the gate, and sat him down there: and, behold, the kinsman of whom Boaz spake came by; unto whom he said, "Ho, such a one! turn aside, sit down here." And he turned aside, and sat down. 2 And he took ten men of the elders of the city, and said, "Sit ye down here." And they sat down. 3 And he said unto the kinsman, "Naomi, that is come again out of the country of Moab, selleth a parcel of land, which *was* our brother Elimelech's:[10] 4 And I thought to advertise thee, saying, 'Buy *it* before the inhabitants, and before the elders of my people.' If thou wilt redeem *it,* redeem *it:* but if thou wilt not redeem *it, then* tell me, that I may know: for *there is* none to redeem *it* besides thee; and I *am* after thee." And he said, "I will redeem *it.*" 5 Then said Boaz, "What day thou buyest the field of the hand of Naomi, thou must buy *it* also of Ruth the Moabitess, the wife of the dead, to raise up the name of the dead upon his inheritance."[11] 6 And the kinsman said, "I cannot re-

deem *it* for myself, lest I mar mine own inheritance: redeem thou my right to thyself; for I cannot redeem *it.*"

7 Now this *was the manner* in former time in Israel concerning redeeming and concerning changing, for to confirm all things; a man plucked off his shoe, and gave *it* to his neighbor: and this *was* a testimony in Israel. 8 Therefore the kinsman said unto Boaz, "Buy *it* for thee." So he drew off his shoe. 9 And Boaz said unto the elders, and *unto* all the people, "Ye *are* witnesses this day, that I have bought all that *was* Elimelech's, and all that *was* Chilion's and Mahlon's, of the hand of Naomi. 10 Moreover Ruth the Moabitess, the wife of Mahlon, have I purchased to be my wife, to raise up the name of the dead upon his inheritance, that the name of the dead be not cut off from among his brethren, and from the gate of his place: ye *are* witnesses this day." 11 And all the people that *were* in the gate, and the elders, said, "*We are* witnesses. The LORD make the woman that is come into thine house like Rachel and like Leah, which two did build the house of Israel: and do thou worthily in Ephratah, and be famous in Bethlehem: 12 And let thy house be like the house of Pharez, whom Tamar bare unto Judah, of the seed which the LORD shall give thee of this young woman."

13 So Boaz took Ruth, and she was his wife: and when he went in unto her, the LORD gave her conception, and she bare a son. 14 And the women said unto Naomi, "Blessed *be* the LORD, which hath not left thee this day without a kinsman, that his name may be famous in Israel. 15 And he shall be unto thee a restorer of *thy* life, and a nourisher of thine old age: for thy daughter-in-law, which loveth thee, which is better to thee than seven sons, hath borne him." 16 And Naomi took the child, and laid it in her bosom, and became nurse unto it. 17 And the women her neighbors gave it a name, saying, "There is a son born to Naomi"; and they called his name Obed: he *is* the father of Jesse, the father of David.

18 Now these are the generations of Pharez: Pharez begat Hezron, 19 And Hezron begat Ram, and Ram begat Amminadab, 20 And Amminadab begat Nahshon, and Nahshon begat Salmon, 21 And Salmon begat Boaz, and Boaz begat Obed, 22 And Obed begat Jesse, and Jesse begat David.[12]

---

8. KNOX: "he rose while it was still too early for men to recognize one another."

9. For "Who," all modern translations read "How."

10. In mentioning the "parcel of land," Boaz may be employing a legal fiction.

11. NEB: "Then Boaz said, 'On the day when you acquire the field from Naomi, you also acquire Ruth the Moabitess, the dead man's wife, so as to perpetuate the name of the dead man with his patrimony.'"

12. (4:18-22) The genealogy was added at a later date. The author wanted to emphasize David's Judean descent.

Introduction to
I and II SAMUEL

"And Samuel said to all the people, 'See ye him whom the Lord hath chosen, that there is none like him among all the people.' And all the people shouted, 'God save the king.'"

For almost a century (ca. 1030–961 B.C.), Israel's history was dominated by three men: Samuel, the last of the judges; Saul, the first monarch; and David, the king who unified the nation. The present selections from *I* and *II Samuel* traces that history by focusing on the biography of these national heroes.

W. F. Thrall and A. Hibbard specify that "biography as a literary form satisfies three inherent promptings of man: the commemorative instinct, the didactic or moralizing instinct, and, perhaps most important of all, the instinct of curiosity." * The accounts of Samuel, Saul, and David reveal the working of all three promptings, though only the first two require comment.

As the figure responsible for the transition of Israel from a loose tribal federation to a monarchy, Samuel deserved commemoration. The circumstances surrounding his birth link him to Isaac, Jacob, and Samson, each of whom had a mother who was thought barren until the Lord answered her prayers. As a child, he is dedicated to God; and, as he grows, "the Lord was with him, and did let none of his words fall to the ground." Emerging as an accepted prophet, he guides the thundering defeat of the Philistines at Ebenezer. The Israelite victory verifies Samuel's charismatic leadership, links him to the judges, and contributes to his fame. He judges Israel all the days of his life, and, prior to Saul's kingship, he is a unifying figure for all the tribes.

The story of Samuel's anointing Saul and of Saul's reign thereafter illustrates the didactic element in biography. The views of the authors and editors become pervasive. It is clear that two interwoven documents, traditionally called the Early Source and the Late Source, recount the experience of Saul and that these differ: one favors the monarchy; the other opposes it. Further, *Samuel* was edited by Judeans, men whose southern heritage and loyalties kept them from extolling Saul, the northerner. By praising the acts of David, they were justifying a southerner's right to be king.

The two accounts of the selection of Saul illustrate the moralizing instinct. The first account (8; 10:17-25) was compiled in the latter days of the monarchy when the tyrannical policies of Solomon had led many to dishonor the kingship. In this Late Source, the demand for a king originates with faithless Israelites. Samuel protests and spells out the perils of living under a monarchy. When the demand persists, the Lord tells Samuel to grant their wish. There is jealousy, irritation, and grudging assent in his injunction: "Hearken unto their voice, and make them a king."

*In *A Handbook to Literature*, The Bobbs-Merrill Company, Inc., 1936.

The second account (9:1–10:16) was written some sixty years earlier and reveals the national enthusiasm following a military victory. In the Early Source, the Lord initiates the monarchy. The elaborate details of Saul's meeting with Samuel emphasize the divine origin of kingship. Saul goes looking for his father's donkeys and finds a domain as Samuel, the famous seer, anoints him privately. The anointing is publicly acclaimed following Saul's charismatic rallying of the tribes to defend Jabesh-gilead from the Ammonites. And "they made Saul king before the Lord in Gilgal."

The use of divergent sources leads to repetition (the description of Saul's dancing among the prophets is repeated, as is the story of his hurling a javelin at David) and contradiction (first David serves Saul as a musician; then he kills Goliath; then Saul asks who he is). Routinely, however, the Late Source presents Samuel as a great ruler, suggests the monarchy is a mistake, and describes Saul as a sinner. The Early Source extols the kingdom, gives modest praise to Samuel, portrays Saul as a nobly tragic figure, and champions David as a great hero. (In the selection from *I Samuel*, Early Source materials seem evident in 9:1–10:16; 11:1-15; 16:14-23; 17:1-11, 32-40; 18:6-9, 20-29; 19:11-17; 26:1-25; 28:3-25; and 31:1-13. Late Source materials appear in 3:1–4:1; 7:3–8:22; 10:17-27; 15:1–16:3; 17:12-31, 55-58; 18:1-5; and 19:1-10.)

Though derived from mixed and often hostile sources, the story of Saul is a powerful tragedy. His downfall begins with his victory over the Amalekites. Though commanded to perform the rite of *chērem,* i.e., to kill every living creature, he spares King Agag along with the best livestock of the city. Whether motivated by humanity, weakness, or naïveté, Saul has disobeyed Yahweh. And Samuel's response is total: "Because thou hast rejected the word of the Lord, he hath also rejected thee from being king." There is nothing Saul can do to regain the favor of Samuel's stern and almost capricious God. Presently, after Samuel secretly anoints young David as king, "the Spirit of the Lord departed from Saul, and an evil spirit from the Lord troubled him." To neutralize Saul's occasional madness, David is introduced into the court as a musician.

As one anointed to succeed Saul, David conducts himself very prudently. He establishes a classic friendship with Saul's son, Jonathan; he fights the Philistines so effectively that the people extol him over the king; he marries Saul's daughter, Michal; he refuses to act against the divinely chosen monarch; and he "behaved himself wisely in all his ways." Though David displays many worthy qualities—most notably, the absolute confidence in the Lord which enables him to face Goliath—one is reminded of the experience of Jacob and of Joseph, i.e., of the wily young man who outwits his elder brother.

As David's popularity increases, Saul's declines rapidly. Alternating between passion and remorse, he moves from suspicion, to attempted murder, to outright persecution. Finally, as the Philistines mass against him and the Lord refuses to respond to his prayers, he is driven in desperation to visit the witch of Endor. She conjures Samuel's ghost, which pronounces Saul's doom: "Tomorrow shalt thou and thy sons be with me." After this gripping scene, the death of Saul in battle is almost anticlimactic. The noble figure who was taller than the sons of Israel, who was chosen by God to be their first king, has been reduced to a fearful leader who must disguise himself so he can seek the illegal counsel of "a woman that hath a familiar spirit."

The biography of Saul is a touching document. Though edited by Judeans committed to championing David, it does reveal Saul's fine qualities. He refuses to establish an opulent court; he does not exercise oppressive measures against his subjects; he fulfills the Law by banning necromancers from the state; in his despair he continues to call on the Lord; and he dies defending his land and people to the best of his ability. The evidence supports Norman K. Gottwald's summary judgment: "Biblical tradition, the synagogue, and the church have been too niggardly in giving credit to one of the noblest of their progenitors, great in his inception to the kingship and regal in his downfall, victim not alone or even primarily of Philistine arms but prey to a demented mind and an ambitious subordinate." *

The "ambitious subordinate" becomes the colossus of the nation's history. In the selection from *II Samuel*, the biography of David moves from his lament for the death of Saul to his grief at the death of his first son by Bath-sheba. Almost all of it is from the Early Source.

Following the deaths of Samuel and Jonathan, David's mastery of circumstances enables him to secure the throne of Israel and to unite the nation to a degree never before known. His public lamentation for Saul affirms his devotion to the king and increases his popularity among Saul's former subjects. He is anointed King of Judah and, after seven years, King of Israel. In two masterful strokes, he secures his position. He captures Jerusalem, a previously impregnable stronghold, and designates it as the nation's capital. Because the city has no ties to either north or south, both areas can accept it as the political center. Then David brings the ark of God to Jerusalem. The move enhances the city as a symbol of national unity, and the king begins his long reign on a secure political-religious base.

David's judiciousness as king contrasts with the impetuousness of his private life. The story of his affair with Bath-sheba makes no effort to conceal or vindicate his actions. The tale begins with sudden passion, as he calls the woman to him directly after seeing her in her bath. It becomes a comedy when she finds herself pregnant and David calls her husband Uriah home from battle and unsuccessfully tries to get him to visit his wife and thus legitimize the expected baby. And it moves to tragedy when David orders Uriah's death and brings upon himself the wrath of Nathan, who prophesies the death of Bath-sheba's child.

As the biography in *Samuel* continues, David pursues his forty-year reign, and Bath-sheba bears him a son, Solomon. The subsequent deaths of Amnon and Absalom open the way for Solomon to become king.

*In *A Light to the Nation*, Harper & Row, 1959.

I SAMUEL

SAMUEL

Samuel's Birth and Dedication

1 Now there was a certain man of Ramathaim-zophim, of mount Ephraim, and his name *was* Elkanah, the son of Jeroham, the son of Elihu, the son of Tohu, the son of Zuph, an Ephrathite: 2 And he had two wives; the name of the one *was* Hannah, and the name of the other Peninnah: and Peninnah had children, but Hannah had no children. 3 And this man went up out of his city yearly to worship and to sacrifice unto the LORD of hosts in Shiloh. And the two sons of Eli, Hophni and Phinehas, the priests of the LORD, *were* there. 4 And when the time was that Elkanah offered, he gave to Peninnah his wife, and to all her sons and her daughters, portions: 5 But unto Hannah he gave a worthy portion; for he loved Hannah: but the LORD had shut up her womb. 6 And her adversary also provoked her sore, for to make her fret, because the LORD had shut up her womb. 7 And *as* he did so year by year, when she went up to the house of the LORD, so she provoked her; therefore she wept, and did not eat. 8 Then said Elkanah her husband to her, "Hannah, why weepest thou? and why eatest thou not? and why is thy heart grieved? *am* not I better to thee than ten sons?"

9 So Hannah rose up after they had eaten in Shiloh, and after they had drunk. Now Eli the priest sat upon a seat by a post of the temple of the LORD. 10 And she *was* in bitterness of soul, and prayed unto the LORD, and wept sore. 11 And she vowed a vow, and said, "O LORD of hosts, if thou wilt indeed look on the affliction of thine handmaid, and remember me, and not forget thine handmaid, but wilt give unto thine handmaid a man child, then I will give him unto the LORD all the days of his life, and there shall no razor come upon his head." [1] 12 And it came to pass, as she continued praying before the LORD, that Eli marked her mouth. 13 Now Hannah, she spake in her heart; only her lips moved, but her voice was not heard: therefore Eli thought she had been drunken. 14 And Eli said unto her, "How long wilt thou be drunken? put away thy wine from thee." 15 And Hannah answered and said, "No, my lord, I *am* a woman of a sorrowful spirit: I have drunk neither wine nor strong drink, but have poured out my soul before the LORD. 16 Count not thine handmaid for a daughter of Belial: for out of the abundance

of my complaint and grief have I spoken hitherto." 17 Then Eli answered and said, "Go in peace: and the God of Israel grant *thee* thy petition that thou hast asked of him." 18 And she said, "Let thine handmaid find grace in thy sight." So the woman went her way, and did eat, and her countenance was no more *sad.* 19 And they rose up in the morning early, and worshipped before the LORD, and returned, and came to their house to Ramah: and Elkanah knew Hannah his wife; and the LORD remembered her. 20 Wherefore it came to pass, when the time was come about after Hannah had conceived, that she bare a son, and called his name Samuel, *saying,* "Because I have asked him of the LORD."

21 And the man Elkanah, and all his house, went up to offer unto the LORD the yearly sacrifice, and his vow. 22 But Hannah went not up; for she said unto her husband, "*I will not go up* until the child be weaned, and *then* I will bring him, that he may appear before the LORD, and there abide for ever." 23 And Elkanah her husband said unto her, "Do what seemeth thee good; tarry until thou have weaned him; only the LORD establish his word." So the woman abode, and gave her son suck until she weaned him. 24 And when she had weaned him, she took him up with her, with three bullocks, and one ephah of flour, and a bottle of wine, and brought him unto the house of the LORD in Shiloh: and the child *was* young. 25 And they slew a bullock, and brought the child to Eli. 26 And she said, "O my lord, *as* thy soul liveth, my lord, I *am* the woman that stood by thee here, praying unto the LORD. 27 For this child I prayed; and the LORD hath given me my petition which I asked of him: 28 Therefore also I have lent him to the LORD; as long as he liveth he shall be lent to the LORD." And he worshipped the LORD there.

Hannah's Song of Praise [2]

2 And Hannah prayed, and said,
> "My heart rejoiceth in the LORD,
> Mine horn is exalted in the LORD;
> My mouth is enlarged over mine enemies;[3]
> Because I rejoice in thy salvation.

2   "*There is* none holy as the LORD:

---

1. See footnote 10 to *Judges* 13:5.

2. (2:1-10) This is a psalm of national thanksgiving. It was attributed to Hannah because of verse 5c.
3. RSV: "my strength is exalted in the LORD. My mouth derides my enemies."

For *there is* none besides thee:
Neither *is there* any rock like our God.

3   "Talk no more so exceeding proudly;
Let *not* arrogancy come out of your mouth:
For the LORD *is* a God of knowledge,
And by him actions are weighed.

4   "The bows of the mighty men *are* broken,
And they that stumbled are girded with strength.

5   *They that were* full have hired out themselves for bread;
And *they that were* hungry ceased:
So that the barren hath borne seven;
And she that hath many children is waxed feeble.

6   "The LORD killeth, and maketh alive:
He bringeth down to the grave, and bringeth up.[4]

7   The LORD maketh poor, and maketh rich:
He bringeth low, and lifteth up.

8   He raiseth up the poor out of the dust,
And lifteth up the beggar from the dunghill,
To set *them* among princes,
And to make them inherit the throne of glory:

   "For the pillars of the earth *are* the LORD's,
And he hath set the world upon them.

9   He will keep the feet of his saints,
And the wicked shall be silent in darkness;
For by strength shall no man prevail.

10   The adversaries of the LORD shall be broken to pieces;
Out of heaven shall he thunder upon them:

   "The LORD shall judge the ends of the earth;
And he shall give strength unto his king,
And exalt the horn of his anointed."

11 And Elkanah went to Ramah to his house. And the child did minister unto the LORD before Eli the priest.

*   *   *

Samuel's Call

3 And the child Samuel ministered unto the LORD before Eli. And the word of the LORD was precious in those days; *there was* no open vision.[5] 2 And it came to pass at that time, when Eli *was* laid down in his place, and his eyes began to wax dim, *that* he could not see; 3 And ere the lamp of God went out in the temple of the LORD, where the ark of God *was,* and Samuel was laid down *to sleep;* 4 That the LORD called, "Samuel": and he answered, "Here *am* I." 5 And he ran unto Eli, and said, "Here *am* I; for thou calledst me." And he said, "I called not; lie down again." And he went and lay down. 6 And the LORD called yet again, "Samuel." And Samuel arose and went to Eli, and said, "Here *am* I; for thou didst call me." And he answered, "I called not, my son; lie down again." 7 Now Samuel did not yet know the LORD, neither was the word of the LORD yet revealed unto him. 8 And the LORD called Samuel again the third time. And he arose and went to Eli, and said, "Here *am* I; for thou didst call me." And Eli perceived that the LORD had called the child. 9 Therefore Eli said unto Samuel, "Go, lie down: and it shall be, if he call thee; that thou shalt say, 'Speak, LORD; for thy servant heareth.' " So Samuel went and lay down in his place.

10 And the LORD came, and stood, and called as at other times, "Samuel, Samuel." Then Samuel answered, "Speak; for thy servant heareth." 11 And the LORD said to Samuel, "Behold, I will do a thing in Israel, at which both the ears of every one that heareth it shall tingle. 12 In that day I will perform against Eli all *things* which I have spoken concerning his house: when I begin, I will also make an end. 13 For I have told him that I will judge his house for ever for the iniquity which he knoweth; because his sons made themselves vile, and he restrained them not. 14 And therefore I have sworn unto the house of Eli, that the iniquity of Eli's house shall not be purged with sacrifice nor offering for ever." 15 And Samuel lay until the morning, and opened the doors of the house of the LORD. And Samuel feared to show Eli the vision. 16 Then Eli called Samuel, and said, "Samuel, my son." And he answered, "Here *am* I." 17 And he said, "What *is* the thing that *the* LORD hath said unto thee? I pray thee hide *it* not from me: God do so to thee, and more also, if thou hide *any* thing from me of all the things that he said unto thee." 18 And Samuel told him every whit, and hid nothing from him. And he said, "It *is* the LORD: let him do what seemeth him good."

19 And Samuel grew, and the LORD was with him, and did let none of his words fall to the ground. 20 And all Israel from Dan even to

---

4. The lines refer to birth and to recovery from serious trouble or desperate illness.

5. MOFFATT: "A word from the Eternal was rare in those days; visions were not common."

Beer-sheba knew that Samuel *was* established *to be* a prophet of the LORD. 21 And the LORD appeared again in Shiloh: for the LORD revealed himself to Samuel in Shiloh by the word of the LORD.

4 And the word of Samuel came to all Israel.

*   *   *

Samuel the Judge

7

3 And Samuel spake unto all the house of Israel, saying, "If ye do return unto the LORD with all your hearts, *then* put away the strange god and Ashtaroth from among you, and prepare your hearts unto the LORD, and serve him only: and he will deliver you out of the hand of the Philistines." 4 Then the children of Israel did put away Baalim and Ashtaroth, and served the LORD only.

5 And Samuel said, "Gather all Israel to Mizpeh, and I will pray for you unto the LORD." 6 And they gathered together to Mizpeh, and drew water, and poured *it* out before the LORD, and fasted on that day, and said there, "We have sinned against the LORD." And Samuel judged the children of Israel in Mizpeh. 7 And when the Philistines heard that the children of Israel were gathered together to Mizpeh, the lords of the Philistines went up against Israel. And when the children of Israel heard *it,* they were afraid of the Philistines. 8 And the children of Israel said to Samuel, "Cease not to cry unto the LORD our God for us, that he will save us out of the hand of the Philistines." 9 And Samuel took a sucking lamb, and offered *it for* a burnt offering wholly unto the LORD: and Samuel cried unto the LORD for Israel; and the LORD heard him. 10 And as Samuel was offering up the burnt offering, the Philistines drew near to battle against Israel: but the LORD thundered with a great thunder on that day upon the Philistines, and discomfited them; and they were smitten before Israel. 11 And the men of Israel went out of Mizpeh, and pursued the Philistines, and smote them, until *they came* under Beth-car. 12 Then Samuel took a stone, and set *it* between Mizpeh and Shen, and called the name of it Eben-ezer, saying, "Hitherto hath the LORD helped us."

13 So the Philistines were subdued, and they came no more into the coast of Israel: and the hand of the LORD was against the Philistines all the days of Samuel. 14 And the cities which the Philistines had taken from Israel were restored to Israel, from Ekron even unto Gath; and the coasts thereof did Israel deliver out of the hands of the Philistines. And there was peace between Israel and the Amorites. 15 And Samuel judged Israel all the days of his life. 16 And he went from year to year in circuit to Beth-el, and Gilgal, and Mizpeh, and judged Israel in all those places. 17 And his return *was* to Ramah, for there *was* his house; and there he judged Israel; and there he built an altar unto the LORD.

The Demand for a King

8 And it came to pass, when Samuel was old, that he made his sons judges over Israel. 2 Now the name of his firstborn was Joel; and the name of his second, Abiah: *they were* judges in Beersheba. 3 And his sons walked not in his ways, but turned aside after lucre, and took bribes, and perverted judgment.

4 Then all the elders of Israel gathered themselves together, and came to Samuel unto Ramah, 5 And said unto him, "Behold, thou art old, and thy sons walk not in thy ways: now make us a king to judge us like all the nations." [6] 6 But the thing displeased Samuel, when they said, "Give us a king to judge us." And Samuel prayed unto the LORD. 7 And the LORD said unto Samuel, "Hearken unto the voice of the people in all that they say unto thee: for they have not rejected thee, but they have rejected me, that I should not reign over them. 8 According to all the works which they have done since the day that I brought them up out of Egypt even unto this day, wherewith they have forsaken me, and served other gods, so do they also unto thee. 9 Now therefore hearken unto their voice: howbeit yet protest solemnly unto them, and show them the manner of the king that shall reign over them."

10 And Samuel told all the words of the LORD unto the people that asked of him a king. 11 And he said, "This will be the manner of the king that shall reign over you:[7] He will take your sons, and appoint *them* for himself, for his chariots, and *to be* his horsemen; and *some* shall run before his chariots. 12 And he will appoint him captains over thousands, and captains over fifties; and *will set them* to ear his ground, and to reap his harvest, and to make his instruments of war, and instruments of his chariots. 13 And he will take your daughters *to be* confectionaries, and *to be* cooks, and *to be* bakers. 14 And he will take your fields, and your vineyards, and your oliveyards, *even* the best *of them,* and give *them* to his servants.

---

6. In IB, George B. Caird explains: "The crux of the elders' offense seems to have been that they wanted Israel to be *like all the nations.* The essential difference between Israel and the heathen nations lay just in this, that the Lord was their king who ruled over them through his representative the priest or judge."

7. (8:11-18) This Late Source description of monarchy probably reflects evils which occurred during the reign of Solomon.

15 And he will take the tenth of your seed, and of your vineyards, and give to his officers, and to his servants. 16 And he will take your menservants, and your maidservants, and your goodliest young men, and your asses, and put *them* to his work. 17 He will take the tenth of your sheep: and ye shall be his servants. 18 And ye shall cry out in that day because of your king which ye shall have chosen you; and the LORD will not hear you in that day." 19 Nevertheless the people refused to obey the voice of Samuel; and they said, "Nay; but we will have a king over us; 20 That we also may be like all the nations; and that our king may judge us, and go out before us, and fight our battles." 21 And Samuel heard all the words of the people, and he rehearsed them in the ears of the LORD. 22 And the LORD said to Samuel, "Hearken unto their voice, and make them a king." And Samuel said unto the men of Israel, "Go ye every man unto his city."

SAUL

The Anointing of Saul

9 Now there was a man of Benjamin, whose name *was* Kish, the son of Abiel, the son of Zeror, the son of Bechorath, the son of Aphiah, a Benjamite, a mighty man of power. 2 And he had a son, whose name *was* Saul, a choice young man,[8] and a goodly: and *there was* not among the children of Israel a goodlier person than he: from his shoulders and upward *he was* higher than any of the people. 3 And the asses of Kish Saul's father were lost. And Kish said to Saul his son, "Take now one of the servants with thee, and arise, go seek the asses." 4 And he passed through mount Ephraim, and passed through the land of Shalisha, but they found *them* not: then they passed through the land of Shalim, and *there they were* not: and he passed through the land of the Benjamites, but they found *them* not.

5 *And* when they were come to the land of Zuph, Saul said to his servant that *was* with him, "Come, and let us return; lest my father leave *caring* for the asses, and take thought for us." 6 And he said unto him, "Behold now, *there is* in this city a man of God, and *he is* an honorable man; all that he saith cometh surely to pass: now let us go thither; peradventure he can show us our way that we should go." 7 Then said Saul to his servant, "But, behold, *if* we go, what shall we bring the man? for the bread is spent in our vessels, and *there is* not a present to bring to the man of God: what have we?" 8 And the servant answered

Saul again, and said, "Behold, I have here at hand the fourth part of a shekel of silver: *that* will I give to the man of God, to tell us our way." 9 (Beforetime in Israel, when a man went to inquire of God, thus he spake, "Come, and let us go to the seer": for *he that is* now *called* a Prophet was beforetime called a Seer.) 10 Then said Saul to his servant, "Well said; come, let us go." So they went unto the city where the man of God *was*. 11 *And* as they went up the hill to the city, they found young maidens going out to draw water, and said unto them, "Is the seer here?" 12 And they answered them, and said, "He is; behold, *he is* before you: make haste now, for he came to-day to the city; for *there is* a sacrifice of the people to-day in the high place: 13 As soon as ye be come into the city, ye shall straightway find him, before he go up to the high place to eat: for the people will not eat until he come, because he doth bless the sacrifice; *and* afterward they eat that be bidden. Now therefore get you up; for about this time ye shall find him." 14 And they went up into the city: *and* when they were come into the city, behold, Samuel came out against them, for to go up to the high place.

15 Now the LORD had told Samuel in his ear a day before Saul came, saying, 16 "To-morrow about this time I will send thee a man out of the land of Benjamin, and thou shalt anoint him *to be* captain over my people Israel, that he may save my people out of the hand of the Philistines: for I have looked upon my people, because their cry is come unto me." 17 And when Samuel saw Saul, the LORD said unto him, "Behold the man whom I spake to thee of! this same shall reign over my people." 18 Then Saul drew near to Samuel in the gate, and said, "Tell me, I pray thee, where the seer's house *is*." 19 And Samuel answered Saul, and said, "I *am* the seer: go up before me unto the high place; for ye shall eat with me to-day, and to-morrow I will let thee go, and will tell thee all that *is* in thine heart. 20 And as for thine asses that were lost three days ago, set not thy mind on them; for they are found. And on whom *is* all the desire of Israel? *Is it* not on thee, and on all thy father's house?" 21 And Saul answered and said, "*Am* not I a Benjamite, of the smallest of the tribes of Israel? and my family the least of all the families of the tribe of Benjamin? wherefore then speakest thou so to me?"

22 And Samuel took Saul and his servant, and brought them into the parlor, and made them sit in the chiefest place among them that were bidden, which *were* about thirty persons. 23 And Samuel said unto the cook, "Bring the portion which I gave thee, of which I said unto thee, 'Set it by thee.'" 24 And the cook took up the shoul-

---

8. MOFFATT: "a man in the prime of life." Saul already has grown sons.

der, and *that* which *was* upon it, and set *it* before Saul. And *Samuel* said, "Behold that which is left! set *it* before thee, *and* eat: for unto this time hath it been kept for thee since I said, 'I have invited the people.'" So Saul did eat with Samuel that day. 25 And when they were come down from the high place into the city, *Samuel* communed with Saul upon the top of the house. 26 And they arose early: and it came to pass about the spring of the day, that Samuel called Saul to the top of the house, saying, "Up, that I may send thee away." And Saul arose, and they went out both of them, he and Samuel, abroad. 27 *And* as they were going down to the end of the city, Samuel said to Saul, "Bid the servant pass on before us, (and he passed on,) but stand thou still a while, that I may show thee the word of God."

10 Then Samuel took a vial of oil, and poured *it* upon his head, and kissed him, and said, "*Is it* not because the LORD hath anointed thee *to be* captain over his inheritance? 2 When thou art departed from me to-day, then thou shalt find two men by Rachel's sepulchre in the border of Benjamin at Zelzah; and they will say unto thee, 'The asses which thou wentest to seek are found: and, lo, thy father hath left the care of the asses, and sorroweth for you, saying, "What shall I do for my son?"' 3 Then shalt thou go on forward from thence, and thou shalt come to the plain of Tabor, and there shall meet thee three men going up to God to Beth-el, one carrying three kids, and another carrying three loaves of bread, and another carrying a bottle of wine: 4 And they will salute thee, and give thee two *loaves* of bread; which thou shalt receive of their hands. 5 After that thou shalt come to the hill of God, where *is* the garrison of the Philistines: and it shall come to pass, when thou art come thither to the city, that thou shalt meet a company of prophets coming down from the high place with a psaltery, and a tabret, and a pipe, and a harp, before them; and they shall prophesy:[9] 6 And the Spirit of the LORD will come upon thee, and thou shalt prophesy with them, and shalt be turned into another man. 7 And let it be, when these signs are come unto thee, *that* thou do as occasion serve thee; for God *is* with thee. 8 And thou shalt go down before me to Gilgal; and, behold, I will come down unto thee, to offer burnt offerings, *and* to sacrifice sacrifices of peace offerings: seven days shalt thou tarry, till I come to thee, and show thee what thou shalt do."

9 And it was *so,* that, when he had turned his back to go from Samuel, God gave him another

heart: and all those signs came to pass that day. 10 And when they came thither to the hill, behold, a company of prophets met him; and the Spirit of God came upon him, and he prophesied among them.[10] 11 And it came to pass, when all that knew him beforetime saw that, behold, he prophesied among the prophets, then the people said one to another, "What *is* this *that* is come unto the son of Kish? *Is* Saul also among the prophets?" 12 And one of the same place answered and said, "But who *is* their father?" Therefore it became a proverb, "*Is* Saul also among the prophets?" 13 And when he had made an end of prophesying, he came to the high place.

14 And Saul's uncle said unto him and to his servant, "Whither went ye?" And he said, "To seek the asses: and when we saw that *they were* no where, we came to Samuel." 15 And Saul's uncle said, "Tell me, I pray thee, what Samuel said unto you." 16 And Saul said unto his uncle, "He told us plainly that the asses were found." But of the matter of the kingdom, whereof Samuel spake, he told him not.

The Election of Saul

17 And Samuel called the people together unto the LORD to Mizpeh; 18 And said unto the children of Israel, "Thus saith the LORD God of Israel, 'I brought up Israel out of Egypt, and delivered you out of the hand of the Egyptians, and out of the hand of all kingdoms, *and* of them that oppressed you': 19 And ye have this day rejected your God, who himself saved you out of all your adversities and your tribulations; and ye have said unto him, '*Nay,* but set a king over us.' Now therefore present yourselves before the LORD by your tribes, and by your thousands." 20 And when Samuel had caused all the tribes of Israel to come near, the tribe of Benjamin was taken.[11] 21 When he had caused the tribe of Benjamin to come near by their families, the family of Matri was taken, and Saul the son of Kish was taken: and when they sought him, he could not be found. 22 Therefore they inquired of the LORD further, if the man should yet come thither. And the LORD answered, "Behold, he hath hid himself among the stuff." [12] 23 And they ran and fetched him thence: and when he stood among the people, he was higher than any of the people from

---

9. Groups of wandering professional prophets were not uncommon. They relied on music to produce ecstatic trances.

10. (10:10-12) I.e., he dances ecstatically in the spirit of religious frenzy. "Is Saul also among the prophets?" can be an expression of cynicism or of awe. In IB, George B. Caird says that verse 12 is "usually dismissed as an unintelligible gloss."

11. NEB: "was picked by lot."

12. RSV, NAB, NEB: "among the baggage." Though it is clear the Late Source is scorning Saul, one can only speculate why he hides himself.

his shoulders and upward. 24 And Samuel said to all the people, "See ye him whom the LORD hath chosen, that *there is* none like him among all the people?" And all the people shouted, and said, "God save the king."

25 Then Samuel told the people the manner of the kingdom, and wrote *it* in a book, and laid *it* up before the LORD. And Samuel sent all the people away, every man to his house. 26 And Saul also went home to Gibeah; and there went with him a band of men, whose hearts God had touched. 27 But the children of Belial said, "How shall this man save us?" And they despised him, and brought him no presents. But he held his peace.

11 Then Nahash the Ammonite came up, and encamped against Jabesh-gilead: and all the men of Jabesh said unto Nahash, "Make a covenant with us, and we will serve thee." 2 And Nahash the Ammonite answered them, "On this condition will I make a covenant with you, that I may thrust out all your right eyes, and lay it for a reproach upon all Israel." [13] 3 And the elders of Jabesh said unto him, "Give us seven days' respite, that we may send messengers unto all the coasts of Israel: and then, if *there be* no man to save us, we will come out to thee." 4 Then came the messengers to Gibeah of Saul, and told the tidings in the ears of the people: and all the people lifted up their voices, and wept. 5 And, behold, Saul came after the herd out of the field; and Saul said, "What *aileth* the people that they weep?" And they told him the tidings of the men of Jabesh. 6 And the Spirit of God came upon Saul when he heard those tidings, and his anger was kindled greatly. 7 And he took a yoke of oxen, and hewed them in pieces, and sent *them* throughout all the coasts of Israel by the hands of messengers, saying, "Whosoever cometh not forth after Saul and after Samuel, so shall it be done unto his oxen." And the fear of the LORD fell on the people, and they came out with one consent. 8 And when he numbered them in Bezek, the children of Israel were three hundred thousand, and the men of Judah thirty thousand. 9 And they said unto the messengers that came, "Thus shall ye say unto the men of Jabesh-gilead, 'To-morrow, by *that time* the sun be hot, ye shall have help.' " And the messengers came and showed *it* to the men of Jabesh; and they were glad. 10 Therefore the men of Jabesh said, "To-morrow we will come out

unto you, and ye shall do with us all that seemeth good unto you."

11 And it was *so* on the morrow, that Saul put the people in three companies; and they came into the midst of the host in the morning watch, and slew the Ammonites until the heat of the day: and it came to pass, that they which remained were scattered, so that two of them were not left together. 12 And the people said unto Samuel, "Who *is* he that said, 'Shall Saul reign over us?' bring the men, that we may put them to death." 13 And Saul said, "There shall not a man be put to death this day: for to-day the LORD hath wrought salvation in Israel." 14 Then said Samuel to the people, "Come, and let us go to Gilgal, and renew the kingdom there." 15 And all the people went to Gilgal, and there they made Saul king before the LORD in Gilgal; and there they sacrificed sacrifices of peace offerings before the LORD; and there Saul and all the men of Israel rejoiced greatly.

*   *   *

THE DECLINE OF SAUL AND THE EMERGENCE OF DAVID
Saul's Offense

15 Samuel also said unto Saul, "The LORD sent me to anoint thee *to be* king over his people, over Israel: now therefore hearken thou unto the voice of the words of the LORD. 2 Thus saith the LORD of hosts, 'I remember *that* which Amalek did to Israel, how he laid *wait* for him in the way, when he came up from Egypt. 3 Now go and smite Amalek, and utterly destroy all that they have, and spare them not; but slay both man and woman, infant and suckling, ox and sheep, camel and ass.' " [14]

4 And Saul gathered the people together, and numbered them in Telaim, two hundred thousand footmen, and ten thousand men of Judah. 5 And Saul came to a city of Amalek, and laid wait in the valley. 6 And Saul said unto the Kenites, "Go, depart, get you down from among the Amalekites, lest I destroy you with them: for ye showed kindness to all the children of Israel, when they came up out of Egypt." So the Kenites departed from among the Amalekites. 7 And Saul smote the Amalekites from Havilah *until* thou comest to Shur, that *is* over against Egypt. 8 And he took Agag the king of the Amalekites alive, and utterly destroyed all the people with the edge of the sword. 9 But Saul and the people

---

13. (11:2-3) A warrior usually carried his shield in his left hand and his sword in his right. If blinded in the right eye, he would have to expose himself to attack in order to see. The seven days of grace add to the insult; Nahash is confident no one will come to aid Jabesh-gilead.

14. The command reflects a religious practice called *chērem*. This required that *everything* in the city be sacrificed to the Lord. To spare any person or to retain any of the spoil was sacrilege.

spared Agag, and the best of the sheep, and of the oxen, and of the fatlings, and the lambs, and all *that was* good, and would not utterly destroy them: but every thing *that was* vile and refuse, that they destroyed utterly.

10 Then came the word of the LORD unto Samuel, saying, 11 "It repenteth me that I have set up Saul *to be* king: for he is turned back from following me, and hath not performed my commandments." And it grieved Samuel; and he cried unto the LORD all night.[15] 12 And when Samuel rose early to meet Saul in the morning, it was told Samuel, saying, "Saul came to Carmel, and, behold, he set him up a place, and is gone about, and passed on, and gone down to Gilgal." 13 And Samuel came to Saul: and Saul said unto him, "Blessed *be* thou of the LORD: I have performed the commandment of the LORD." 14 And Samuel said, "What *meaneth* then this bleating of the sheep in mine ears, and the lowing of the oxen which I hear?" 15 And Saul said, "They have brought them from the Amalekites: for the people spared the best of the sheep and of the oxen, to sacrifice unto the LORD thy God; and the rest we have utterly destroyed." 16 Then Samuel said unto Saul, "Stay, and I will tell thee what the LORD hath said to me this night." And he said unto him, "Say on."

17 And Samuel said, "When thou *wast* little in thine own sight, *wast* thou not *made* the head of the tribes of Israel, and the LORD anointed thee king over Israel? 18 And the LORD sent thee on a journey, and said, 'Go and utterly destroy the sinners the Amalekites, and fight against them until they be consumed.' 19 Wherefore then didst thou not obey the voice of the LORD, but didst fly upon the spoil, and didst evil in the sight of the LORD?" 20 And Saul said unto Samuel, "Yea, I have obeyed the voice of the LORD, and have gone the way which the LORD sent me, and have brought Agag the king of Amalek, and have utterly destroyed the Amalekites. 21 But the people took of the spoil, sheep and oxen, the chief of the things which should have been utterly destroyed, to sacrifice unto the LORD thy God in Gilgal."

22 And Samuel said,
> "Hath the LORD *as great* delight in burnt
>   offerings and sacrifices,
> •As in obeying the voice of the LORD?
> Behold, to obey *is* better than sacrifice,
> *And* to hearken than the fat of rams.

23
> For rebellion *is as* the sin of witchcraft,
> And stubbornness *is as* iniquity and idolatry.

Because thou hast rejected the word of the LORD, he hath also rejected thee from *being* king."

24 And Saul said unto Samuel, "I have sinned: for I have transgressed the commandment of the LORD, and thy words: because I feared the people, and obeyed their voice. 25 Now therefore, I pray thee, pardon my sin, and turn again with me, that I may worship the LORD." 26 And Samuel said unto Saul, "I will not return with thee: for thou hast rejected the word of the LORD, and the LORD hath rejected thee from being king over Israel." 27 And as Samuel turned about to go away, he laid hold upon the skirt of his mantle, and it rent. 28 And Samuel said unto him, "The LORD hath rent the kingdom of Israel from thee this day, and hath given it to a neighbor of thine, *that is* better than thou. 29 And also the Strength of Israel will not lie nor repent: for he *is* not a man, that he should repent." 30 Then he said, "I have sinned: *yet* honor me now, I pray thee, before the elders of my people, and before Israel, and turn again with me, that I may worship the LORD thy God." 31 So Samuel turned again after Saul; and Saul worshipped the LORD.

32 Then said Samuel, "Bring ye hither to me Agag the king of the Amalekites." And Agag came unto him delicately. And Agag said, "Surely the bitterness of death is past." [16] 33 And Samuel said,
> "As thy sword hath made women childless,
>   So shall thy mother be childless among
>   women."

And Samuel hewed Agag in pieces before the LORD in Gilgal.

34 Then Samuel went to Ramah; and Saul went up to his house to Gibeah of Saul. 35 And Samuel came no more to see Saul until the day of his death: nevertheless Samuel mourned for Saul: and the LORD repented that he had made Saul king over Israel.

The Anointing of David

16 And the LORD said unto Samuel, "How long wilt thou mourn for Saul, seeing I have rejected him from reigning over Israel? fill thine horn with oil, and go, I will send thee to Jesse the Bethlehemite: for I have provided me a king among his sons." 2 And Samuel said, "How can I go? if Saul hear *it,* he will kill me." And the LORD said, "Take a heifer with thee, and say, 'I am come to

---

15. MOFFATT: "Samuel was angry with the Eternal and protested to him all night."

16. Translations of this passage differ. Following the Hebrew text, RSV writes, "And Agag came to him cheerfully. Agag said, 'Surely the bitterness of death is past.'" Following the Greek, WATERMAN writes, "Agag came to him with tottering steps; 'Death is a bitter thing,' said Agag."

sacrifice to the LORD.' 3 And call Jesse to the sacrifice, and I will show thee what thou shalt do: and thou shalt anoint unto me *him* whom I name unto thee." 4 And Samuel did that which the LORD spake, and came to Bethlehem. And the elders of the town trembled at his coming, and said, "Comest thou peaceably?" 5 And he said, "Peaceably: I am come to sacrifice unto the LORD: sanctify yourselves, and come with me to the sacrifice." And he sanctified Jesse and his sons, and called them to the sacrifice. 6 And it came to pass, when they were come, that he looked on Eliab, and said, "Surely the LORD's anointed *is* before him." 7 But the LORD said unto Samuel, "Look not on his countenance, or on the height of his stature; because I have refused him: for *the Lord seeth* not as man seeth; for man looketh on the outward appearance, but the LORD looketh on the heart." 8 Then Jesse called Abinadab, and made him pass before Samuel. And he said, "Neither hath the LORD chosen this." 9 Then Jesse made Shammah to pass by. And he said, "Neither hath the LORD chosen this." 10 Again, Jesse made seven of his sons to pass before Samuel. And Samuel said unto Jesse, "The LORD hath not chosen these." 11 And Samuel said unto Jesse, "Are here all *thy* children?" And he said, "There remaineth yet the youngest, and, behold, he keepeth the sheep." And Samuel said unto Jesse, "Send and fetch him: for we will not sit down till he come hither." 12 And he sent, and brought him in. Now he *was* ruddy, *and* withal of a beautiful countenance, and goodly to look to. And the LORD said, "Arise, anoint him: for this *is* he." 13 Then Samuel took the horn of oil, and anointed him in the midst of his brethren: and the Spirit of the LORD came upon David from that day forward. So Samuel rose up, and went to Ramah.

14 But the Spirit of the LORD departed from Saul, and an evil spirit from the LORD troubled him. 15 And Saul's servants said unto him, "Behold now, an evil spirit from God troubleth thee. 16 Let our lord now command thy servants, *which are* before thee, to seek out a man, *who is* a cunning player on a harp: and it shall come to pass, when the evil spirit from God is upon thee, that he shall play with his hand, and thou shalt be well." 17 And Saul said unto his servants, "Provide me now a man that can play well, and bring *him* to me." 18 Then answered one of the servants, and said, "Behold, I have seen a son of Jesse the Bethlehemite, *that is* cunning in playing, and a mighty valiant man, and a man of war, and prudent in matters, and a comely person, and the LORD *is* with him." 19 Wherefore Saul sent messengers unto Jesse, and said, "Send me David thy son, which *is* with the sheep." 20 And Jesse took an ass *laden* with bread, and a bottle of wine, and a kid, and sent *them* by David his son unto Saul. 21 And David came to Saul, and stood before him: and he loved him greatly; and he became his armor-bearer. 22 And Saul sent to Jesse, saying, "Let David, I pray thee, stand before me; for he hath found favor in my sight." 23 And it came to pass, when the *evil* spirit from God was upon Saul, that David took a harp, and played with his hand: so Saul was refreshed, and was well, and the evil spirit departed from him.

David and Goliath

17 Now the Philistines gathered together their armies to battle, and were gathered together at Shochoh, which *belongeth* to Judah, and pitched between Shochoh and Azekah, in Ephes-dammim. 2 And Saul and the men of Israel were gathered together, and pitched by the valley of Elah, and set the battle in array against the Philistines. 3 And the Philistines stood on a mountain on the one side, and Israel stood on a mountain on the other side: and *there was* a valley between them. 4 And there went out a champion out of the camp of the Philistines, named Goliath, of Gath, whose height *was* six cubits and a span. 5 And *he had* a helmet of brass upon his head, and he *was* armed with a coat of mail; and the weight of the coat *was* five thousand shekels of brass. 6 And *he had* greaves of brass upon his legs, and a target of brass between his shoulders. 7 And the staff of his spear *was* like a weaver's beam; and his spear's head *weighed* six hundred shekels of iron:[17] and one bearing a shield went before him. 8 And he stood and cried unto the armies of Israel, and said unto them, "Why are ye come out to set *your* battle in array? *am* not I a Philistine, and ye servants to Saul? choose you a man for you, and let him come down to me. 9 If he be able to fight with me, and to kill me, then will we be your servants: but if I prevail against him, and kill him, then shall ye be our servants, and serve us." 10 And the Philistine said, "I defy the armies of Israel this day; give me a man, that we may fight together." 11 When Saul and all Israel heard those words of the Philistine, they were dismayed, and greatly afraid.

12 Now David *was* the son of that Ephrathite of Bethlehemjudah, whose name *was* Jesse; and he had eight sons: and the man went among men *for* an old man in the days of Saul. 13 And the

---

17. (17:4-7) A shekel is half an ounce; a span is nine inches; a cubit, about eighteen inches. Thus Goliath's coat weighs a hundred fifty pounds; his spear head, nineteen pounds; and he stands nearly ten feet tall.

three eldest sons of Jesse went *and* followed Saul to the battle: and the names of his three sons that went to the battle *were* Eliab the firstborn, and next unto him Abinadab, and the third Shammah. 14 And David *was* the youngest: and the three eldest followed Saul. 15 But David went and returned from Saul to feed his father's sheep at Bethlehem. 16 And the Philistine drew near morning and evening, and presented himself forty days.

17 And Jesse said unto David his son, "Take now for thy brethren an ephah of this parched *corn,* and these ten loaves, and run to the camp to thy brethren; 18 And carry these ten cheeses unto the captain of *their* thousand, and look how thy brethren fare, and take their pledge." 19 Now Saul, and they, and all the men of Israel, *were* in the valley of Elah, fighting with the Philistines. 20 And David rose up early in the morning, and left the sheep with a keeper, and took, and went, as Jesse had commanded him; and he came to the trench, as the host was going forth to the fight, and shouted for the battle. 21 For Israel and the Philistines had put the battle in array, army against army. 22 And David left his carriage in the hand of the keeper of the carriage, and ran into the army, and came and saluted his brethren. 23 And as he talked with them, behold, there came up the champion, the Philistine of Gath, Goliath by name, out of the armies of the Philistines, and spake according to the same words: and David heard *them.* 24 And all the men of Israel, when they saw the man, fled from him, and were sore afraid. 25 And the men of Israel said, "Have ye seen this man that is come up? surely to defy Israel is he come up: and it shall be, *that* the man who killeth him, the king will enrich him with great riches, and will give him his daughter, and make his father's house free in Israel." [18]
26 And David spake to the men that stood by him, saying, "What shall be done to the man that killeth this Philistine, and taketh away the reproach from Israel? for who *is* this uncircumcised Philistine, that he should defy the armies of the living God?" 27 And the people answered him after this manner, saying, "So shall it be done to the man that killeth him." 28 And Eliab his eldest brother heard when he spake unto the men; and Eliab's anger was kindled against David, and he said, "Why camest thou down hither? and with whom hast thou left those few sheep in the wilder-

ness? I know thy pride, and the naughtiness of thine heart; for thou art come down that thou mightest see the battle." 29 And David said, "What have I now done? *Is there* not a cause?" 30 And he turned from him toward another, and spake after the same manner: and the people answered him again after the former manner. 31 And when the words were heard which David spake, they rehearsed *them* before Saul: and he sent for him.

32 And David said to Saul, "Let no man's heart fail because of him; thy servant will go and fight with this Philistine." 33 And Saul said to David, "Thou art not able to go against this Philistine to fight with him: for thou *art but* a youth, and he a man of war from his youth." 34 And David said unto Saul, "Thy servant kept his father's sheep, and there came a lion, and a bear, and took a lamb out of the flock: 35 And I went out after him, and smote him, and delivered *it* out of his mouth: and when he arose against me, I caught *him* by his beard, and smote him, and slew him. 36 Thy servant slew both the lion and the bear: and this uncircumcised Philistine shall be as one of them, seeing he hath defied the armies of the living God." 37 David said moreover, "The LORD that delivered me out of the paw of the lion, and out of the paw of the bear, he will deliver me out of the hand of this Philistine." And Saul said unto David, "Go, and the LORD be with thee." 38 And Saul armed David with his armor, and he put a helmet of brass upon his head; also he armed him with a coat of mail. 39 And David girded his sword upon his armor, and he assayed to go; for he had not proved *it.* [19] And David said unto Saul, "I cannot go with these; for I have not proved *them.*" And David put them off him. 40 And he took his staff in his hand, and chose him five smooth stones out of the brook, and put them in a shepherd's bag which he had, even in a scrip; and his sling *was* in his hand: and he drew near to the Philistine.

41 And the Philistine came on and drew near unto David; and the man that bare the shield *went* before him. 42 And when the Philistine looked about, and saw David, he disdained him: for he was *but* a youth, and ruddy, and of a fair countenance. 43 And the Philistine said unto David, "*Am* I a dog, that thou comest to me with staves?" [20] And the Philistine cursed David by his gods. 44 And the Philistine said to David, "Come to me, and I will give thy flesh unto the

---

18. NEB: "exempt his family from service due to Israel." The Late Source here refers to taxes and forced labor imposed during Solomon's reign.

19. NAB: "He walked with difficulty, however, since he had never tried armor before."
20. David is carrying his shepherd's staff.

fowls of the air, and to the beasts of the field." 45 Then said David to the Philistine, "Thou comest to me with a sword, and with a spear, and with a shield: but I come to thee in the name of the LORD of hosts, the God of the armies of Israel, whom thou hast defied. 46 This day will the LORD deliver thee into mine hand; and I will smite thee, and take thine head from thee; and I will give the carcasses of the host of the Philistines this day unto the fowls of the air, and to the wild beasts of the earth; that all the earth may know that there is a God in Israel. 47 And all this assembly shall know that the LORD saveth not with sword and spear: for the battle *is* the LORD's, and he will give you into our hands." 48 And it came to pass, when the Philistine arose, and came and drew nigh to meet David, that David hasted, and ran toward the army to meet the Philistine. 49 And David put his hand in his bag, and took thence a stone, and slang *it,* and smote the Philistine in his forehead, that the stone sunk into his forehead; and he fell upon his face to the earth. 50 So David prevailed over the Philistine with a sling and with a stone, and smote the Philistine, and slew him; but *there was* no sword in the hand of David. 51 Therefore David ran, and stood upon the Philistine, and took his sword, and drew it out of the sheath thereof, and slew him, and cut off his head therewith. And when the Philistines saw their champion was dead, they fled. 52 And the men of Israel and of Judah arose, and shouted, and pursued the Philistines, until thou come to the valley, and to the gates of Ekron. And the wounded of the Philistines fell down by the way to Shaaraim, even unto Gath, and unto Ekron. 53 And the children of Israel returned from chasing after the Philistines, and they spoiled their tents. 54 And David took the head of the Philistine, and brought it to Jerusalem;[21] but he put his armor in his tent.

55 And when Saul saw David go forth against the Philistine, he said unto Abner, the captain of the host, "Abner, whose son *is* this youth?" and Abner said, "*As* thy soul liveth, O king, I cannot tell." 56 And the king said, "Inquire thou whose son the stripling *is.*" 57 And as David returned from the slaughter of the Philistine, Abner took him, and brought him before Saul with the head of the Philistine in his hand. 58 And Saul said to him, "Whose son *art* thou, *thou* young man?" And David answered, "*I am* the son of thy servant Jesse the Bethlehemite."

Jonathan's Friendship; Saul's Jealousy

18 And it came to pass, when he had made an end of speaking unto Saul, that the soul of Jonathan was knit with the soul of David, and Jonathan loved him as his own soul. 2 And Saul took him that day, and would let him go no more home to his father's house. 3 Then Jonathan and David made a covenant, because he loved him as his own soul. 4 And Jonathan stripped himself of the robe that *was* upon him, and gave it to David, and his garments, even to his sword, and to his bow, and to his girdle. 5 And David went out whithersoever Saul sent him, *and* behaved himself wisely: and Saul set him over the men of war, and he was accepted in the sight of all the people, and also in the sight of Saul's servants.

6 And it came to pass as they came, when David was returned from the slaughter of the Philistine, that the women came out of all cities of Israel, singing and dancing, to meet king Saul, with tabrets, with joy, and with instruments of music. 7 And the women answered *one another* as they played, and said,

"Saul hath slain his thousands,
And David his ten thousands."

8 And Saul was very wroth, and the saying displeased him; and he said, "They have ascribed unto David ten thousands, and to me they have ascribed *but* thousands: and *what* can he have more but the kingdom?" 9 And Saul eyed David from that day and forward.

10 And it came to pass on the morrow, that the evil spirit from God came upon Saul, and he prophesied in the midst of the house: and David played with his hand, as at other times: and *there was* a javelin in Saul's hand. 11 And Saul cast the javelin; for he said, "I will smite David even to the wall *with it.*" And David avoided out of his presence twice.[22] 12 And Saul was afraid of David, because the LORD was with him, and was departed from Saul. 13 Therefore Saul removed him from him, and made him his captain over a thousand; and he went out and came in before the people. 14 And David behaved himself wisely in all his ways; and the LORD *was* with him. 15 Wherefore when Saul saw that he behaved himself very wisely, he was afraid of him. 16 But all Israel and Judah loved David, because he went out and came in before them.

17 And Saul said to David, "Behold my elder daughter Merab, her will I give thee to wife: only

---

21. In IB, George B. Caird suggests the emendation: "and brought it to Saul." David cannot carry the head to Jerusalem; the city is still held by the Jebusites.

22. (18:10-11) The episode is out of place here. It is reported again in 19:8-10.

be thou valiant for me, and fight the LORD's battles." For Saul said, "Let not mine hand be upon him, but let the hand of the Philistines be upon him." 18 And David said unto Saul, "Who *am* I? and what *is* my life, *or* my father's family in Israel, that I should be son-in-law to the king?" 19 But it came to pass at the time when Merab Saul's daughter should have been given to David, that she was given unto Adriel the Meholathite to wife. 20 And Michal Saul's daughter loved David: and they told Saul, and the thing pleased him. 21 And Saul said, "I will give him her, that she may be a snare to him, and that the hand of the Philistines may be against him." Wherefore Saul said to David, "Thou shalt this day be my son-in-law in *the one of* the twain." 22 And Saul commanded his servants, *saying,* "Commune with David secretly, and say, 'Behold, the king hath delight in thee, and all his servants love thee: now therefore be the king's son-in-law.'" 23 And Saul's servants spake those words in the ears of David. And David said, "Seemeth it to you a light thing to be a king's son-in-law, seeing that I *am* a poor man, and lightly esteemed?" 24 And the servants of Saul told him, saying, "On this manner spake David." 25 And Saul said, "Thus shall ye say to David, 'The king desireth not any dowry, but a hundred foreskins of the Philistines, to be avenged of the king's enemies.'" But Saul thought to make David fall by the hand of the Philistines. 26 And when his servants told David these words, it pleased David well to be the king's son-in-law: and the days were not expired. 27 Wherefore David arose and went, he and his men, and slew of the Philistines two hundred men; and David brought their foreskins, and they gave them in full tale to the king, that he might be the king's son-in-law. And Saul gave him Michal his daughter to wife. 28 And Saul saw and knew that the LORD *was* with David, and *that* Michal Saul's daughter loved him. 29 And Saul was yet the more afraid of David; and Saul became David's enemy continually.

30 Then the princes of the Philistines went forth: and it came to pass, after they went forth, *that* David behaved himself more wisely than all the servants of Saul; so that his name was much set by.

The Flight of David

19 And Saul spake to Jonathan his son, and to all his servants, that they should kill David. 2 But Jonathan Saul's son delighted much in David: and Jonathan told David, saying, "Saul my father seeketh to kill thee: now therefore, I pray thee, take heed to thyself until the morning, and abide in a secret place, and hide thyself:

3 And I will go out and stand beside my father in the field where thou *art,* and I will commune with my father of thee; and what I see, that I will tell thee."

4 And Jonathan spake good of David unto Saul his father, and said unto him, "Let not the king sin against his servant, against David; because he hath not sinned against thee, and because his works *have been* to thee-ward very good: 5 For he did put his life in his hand, and slew the Philistine, and the LORD wrought a great salvation for all Israel: thou sawest *it,* and didst rejoice: wherefore then wilt thou sin against innocent blood, to slay David without a cause?" 6 And Saul hearkened unto the voice of Jonathan: and Saul sware, "*As* the LORD liveth, he shall not be slain." 7 And Jonathan called David, and Jonathan showed him all those things. And Jonathan brought David to Saul, and he was in his presence, as in times past.

8 And there was war again: and David went out, and fought with the Philistines, and slew them with a great slaughter; and they fled from him. 9 And the evil spirit from the LORD was upon Saul, as he sat in his house with his javelin in his hand: and David played with *his* hand. 10 And Saul sought to smite David even to the wall with the javelin; but he slipped away out of Saul's presence, and he smote the javelin into the wall: and David fled, and escaped that night. 11 Saul also sent messengers unto David's house, to watch him, and to slay him in the morning: and Michal David's wife told him, saying, "If thou save not thy life to-night, to-morrow thou shalt be slain." 12 So Michal let David down through a window: and he went, and fled, and escaped. 13 And Michal took an image, and laid *it* in the bed, and put a pillow of goats' *hair* for his bolster, and covered *it* with a cloth. 14 And when Saul sent messengers to take David, she said, "He *is* sick." 15 And Saul sent the messengers *again* to see David, saying, "Bring him up to me in the bed, that I may slay him." 16 And when the messengers were come in, behold, *there was* an image in the bed, with a pillow of goats' *hair* for his bolster. 17 And Saul said unto Michal, "Why hast thou deceived me so, and sent away mine enemy, that he is escaped?" And Michal answered Saul, "He said unto me, 'Let me go; why should I kill thee?'" [23]

18 So David fled, and escaped, and came to Samuel to Ramah, and told him all that Saul had done to him. And he and Samuel went and dwelt in Naioth. 19 And it was told Saul, saying, "Be-

---

23. NEB: "Help me escape or I will kill you."

hold, David *is* at Naioth in Ramah." 20 And Saul sent messengers to take David: and when they saw the company of the prophets prophesying, and Samuel standing *as* appointed over them, the Spirit of God was upon the messengers of Saul, and they also prophesied. 21 And when it was told Saul, he sent other messengers, and they prophesied likewise. And Saul sent messengers again the third time, and they prophesied also. 22 Then went he also to Ramah, and came to a great well that *is* in Sechu: and he asked and said, "Where *are* Samuel and David?" And *one* said, "Behold, *they be* at Naioth in Ramah." 23 And he went thither to Naioth in Ramah: and the Spirit of God was upon him also, and he went on, and prophesied, until he came to Naioth in Ramah. 24 And he stripped off his clothes also, and prophesied before Samuel in like manner, and lay down naked all that day and all that night. Wherefore they say, "*Is* Saul also among the prophets?"

*   *   *

David Spares Saul's Life

26 And the Ziphites came unto Saul to Gibeah, saying, "Doth not David hide himself in the hill of Hachilah, *which is* before Jeshimon?" 2 Then Saul arose, and went down to the wilderness of Ziph, having three thousand chosen men of Israel with him, to seek David in the wilderness of Ziph. 3 And Saul pitched in the hill of Hachilah, which *is* before Jeshimon, by the way. But David abode in the wilderness, and he saw that Saul came after him into the wilderness. 4 David therefore sent out spies, and understood that Saul was come in very deed. 5 And David arose, and came to the place where Saul had pitched: and David beheld the place where Saul lay, and Abner the son of Ner, the captain of his host: and Saul lay in the trench, and the people pitched round about him. 6 Then answered David and said to Ahimelech the Hittite, and to Abishai the son of Zeruiah, brother to Joab, saying, "Who will go down with me to Saul to the camp?" And Abishai said, "I will go down with thee." 7 So David and Abishai came to the people by night: and, behold, Saul lay sleeping within the trench, and his spear stuck in the ground at his bolster: but Abner and the people lay round about him. 8 Then said Abishai to David, "God hath delivered thine enemy into thine hand this day: now therefore let me smite him, I pray thee, with the spear even to the earth at once, and I will not *smite* him the second time." 9 And David said to Abishai, "Destroy him not: for who can stretch forth his hand against the LORD's anointed, and be guiltless?" 10 David said furthermore, "*As* the LORD liveth,

the LORD shall smite him; or his day shall come to die; or he shall descend into battle, and perish. 11 The LORD forbid that I should stretch forth mine hand against the LORD's anointed: but, I pray thee, take thou now the spear that *is* at his bolster, and the cruse of water, and let us go." 12 So David took the spear and the cruse of water from Saul's bolster; and they gat them away, and no man saw *it*, nor knew *it*, neither awaked: for they *were* all asleep; because a deep sleep from the LORD was fallen upon them.

13 Then David went over to the other side, and stood on the top of a hill afar off; a great space *being* between them: 14 And David cried to the people, and to Abner the son of Ner, saying, "Answerest thou not, Abner?" Then Abner answered and said, "Who *art* thou *that* criest to the king?" 15 And David said to Abner, "*Art* not thou a *valiant* man? and who *is* like to thee in Israel? wherefore then hast thou not kept thy lord the king? for there came one of the people in to destroy the king thy lord. 16 This thing *is* not good that thou hast done. *As* the LORD liveth, ye *are* worthy to die, because ye have not kept your master, the LORD's anointed. And now see where the king's spear *is*, and the cruse of water that *was* at his bolster."

17 And Saul knew David's voice, and said, "*Is* this thy voice, my son David?" And David said, "*It is* my voice, my lord, O king." 18 And he said, "Wherefore doth my lord thus pursue after his servant? for what have I done? or what evil *is* in mine hand? 19 Now therefore, I pray thee, let my lord the king hear the words of his servant. If the LORD have stirred thee up against me, let him accept an offering: but if *they be* the children of men, cursed *be* they before the LORD; for they have driven me out this day from abiding in the inheritance of the LORD, saying, 'Go, serve other gods.' 20 Now therefore, let not my blood fall to the earth before the face of the LORD: for the king of Israel is come out to seek a flea, as when one doth hunt a partridge in the mountains." [24]

21 Then said Saul, "I have sinned: return, my son David; for I will no more do thee harm, because my soul was precious in thine eyes this day: behold, I have played the fool, and have erred exceedingly." 22 And David answered and said, "Behold the king's spear! and let one of the young men come over and fetch it. 23 The LORD render to every man his righteousness and his faithfulness: for the LORD delivered thee into *my* hand to-day, but I would not stretch forth mine

---

24. KNOX: "Why must the earth be stained with my blood, under the Lord's eye? A fine quarry for the king of Israel! A flea, a partridge on the hills, were as well worth his chase."

hand against the LORD's anointed. 24 And, behold, as thy life was much set by this day in mine eyes, so let my life be much set by in the eyes of the LORD, and let him deliver me out of all tribulation." 25 Then Saul said to David, "Blessed *be* thou, my son David: thou shalt both do great *things,* and also shalt still prevail." So David went on his way, and Saul returned to his place.

*   *   *

Saul and the Witch of Endor

28

3 Now Samuel was dead, and all Israel had lamented him, and buried him in Ramah, even in his own city. And Saul had put away those that had familiar spirits, and the wizards, out of the land. 4 And the Philistines gathered themselves together, and came and pitched in Shunem: and Saul gathered all Israel together, and they pitched in Gilboa. 5 And when Saul saw the host of the Philistines, he was afraid, and his heart greatly trembled. 6 And when Saul inquired of the LORD, the LORD answered him not, neither by dreams, nor by Urim, nor by prophets.[25]

7 Then said Saul unto his servants, "Seek me a woman that hath a familiar spirit, that I may go to her, and inquire of her." And his servants said to him, "Behold, *there is* a woman that hath a familiar spirit at En-dor." 8 And Saul disguised himself, and put on other raiment, and he went, and two men with him, and they came to the woman by night: and he said, "I pray thee, divine unto me by the familiar spirit, and bring me *him* up, whom I shall name unto thee." 9 And the woman said unto him, "Behold, thou knowest what Saul hath done, how he hath cut off those that have familiar spirits, and the wizards, out of the land: wherefore then layest thou a snare for my life, to cause me to die?" 10 And Saul sware to her by the LORD, saying, "*As* the LORD liveth, there shall no punishment happen to thee for this thing." 11 Then said the woman, "Whom shall I bring up unto thee?" And he said, "Bring me up Samuel." 12 And when the woman saw Samuel, she cried with a loud voice: and the woman spake to Saul, saying, "Why hast thou deceived me? for thou *art* Saul." 13 And the king said unto her, "Be not afraid: for what sawest thou?" And the woman said unto Saul, "I saw gods ascending out of the earth." 14 And he said unto her, "What form *is* he of?" And she said, "An old man cometh up; and he *is* covered with a mantle." And Saul perceived that it *was* Samuel, and he stooped

with *his* face to the ground, and bowed himself.

15 And Samuel said to Saul, "Why hast thou disquieted me, to bring me up?" And Saul answered, "I am sore distressed; for the Philistines make war against me, and God is departed from me, and answereth me no more, neither by prophets, nor by dreams: therefore I have called thee, that thou mayest make known unto me what I shall do." 16 Then said Samuel, "Wherefore then dost thou ask of me, seeing the LORD is departed from thee, and is become thine enemy? 17 And the LORD hath done to him, as he spake by me: for the LORD hath rent the kingdom out of thine hand, and given it to thy neighbor, *even* to David: 18 Because thou obeyedst not the voice of the LORD, nor executedst his fierce wrath upon Amalek, therefore hath the LORD done this thing unto thee this day. 19 Moreover the LORD will also deliver Israel with thee into the hand of the Philistines: and to-morrow *shalt* thou and thy sons *be* with me: the LORD also shall deliver the host of Israel into the hand of the Philistines."

20 Then Saul fell straightway all along on the earth, and was sore afraid, because of the words of Samuel; and there was no strength in him; for he had eaten no bread all the day, nor all the night. 21 And the woman came unto Saul, and saw that he was sore troubled, and said unto him, "Behold, thine handmaid hath obeyed thy voice, and I have put my life in my hand, and have hearkened unto thy words which thou spakest unto me. 22 Now therefore, I pray thee, hearken thou also unto the voice of thine handmaid, and let me set a morsel of bread before thee; and eat, that thou mayest have strength, when thou goest on thy way." 23 But he refused, and said, "I will not eat." But his servants, together with the woman, compelled him; and he hearkened unto their voice. So he arose from the earth, and sat upon the bed. 24 And the woman had a fat calf in the house; and she hasted, and killed it, and took flour, and kneaded *it,* and did bake unleavened bread thereof: 25 And she brought *it* before Saul, and before his servants; and they did eat. Then they rose up, and went away that night.

*   *   *

The Death of Saul

31 Now the Philistines fought against Israel: and the men of Israel fled from before the Philistines, and fell down slain in mount Gilboa. 2 And the Philistines followed hard upon Saul and upon his sons; and the Philistines slew Jonathan, and Abinadab, and Melchi-shua, Saul's sons. 3 And the battle went sore against Saul, and the archers hit him; and he was sore wounded of the archers.

---

25. The usual conventions for determining divine guidance—dreams, sacred lots, prophecy—are closed to Saul. *Urim* probably refers to a small flat stone, one of a pair cast by a priest seeking God's answer to a specific question.

4 Then said Saul unto his armor-bearer, "Draw thy sword, and thrust me through therewith; lest these uncircumcised come and thrust me through, and abuse me." But his armor-bearer would not; for he was sore afraid. Therefore Saul took a sword, and fell upon it. 5 And when his armor-bearer saw that Saul was dead, he fell likewise upon his sword, and died with him. 6 So Saul died, and his three sons, and his armor-bearer, and all his men, that same day together. 7 And when the men of Israel that *were* on the other side of the valley, and *they* that *were* on the other side Jordan, saw that the men of Israel fled, and that Saul and his sons were dead, they forsook the cities, and fled; and the Philistines came and dwelt in them.

8 And it came to pass on the morrow, when the Philistines came to strip the slain, that they found Saul and his three sons fallen in mount Gilboa. 9 And they cut off his head, and stripped off his armor, and sent into the land of the Philistines round about, to publish *it in* the house of their idols, and among the people. 10 And they put his armor in the house of Ashtaroth: and they fastened his body to the wall of Beth-shan. 11 And when the inhabitants of Jabesh-gilead heard of that which the Philistines had done to Saul, 12 All the valiant men arose, and went all night, and took the body of Saul and the bodies of his sons from the wall of Beth-shan, and came to Jabesh, and burnt them there. 13 And they took their bones, and buried *them* under a tree at Jabesh, and fasted seven days.[26]

26. (31:11-13) This recalls the events of Chapter 11, where Saul saved the inhabitants of Jabesh-gilead.

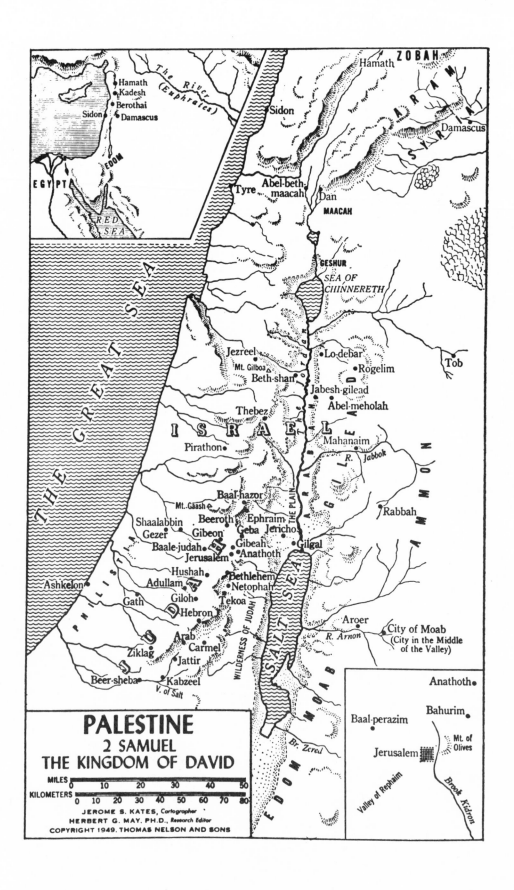

PALESTINE
2 SAMUEL
THE KINGDOM OF DAVID

MILES
0   10   20   30   40   50
KILOMETERS
0 10 20 30 40 50 60 70 80

JEROME S. KATES, Cartographer
HERBERT G. MAY, PH.D., Research Editor
COPYRIGHT 1949, THOMAS NELSON AND SONS

II SAMUEL

DAVID

1 Now it came to pass after the death of Saul, when David was returned from the slaughter of the Amalekites, and David had abode two days in Ziklag; 2 It came even to pass on the third day, that, behold, a man came out of the camp from Saul with his clothes rent, and earth upon his head: and *so* it was, when he came to David, that he fell to the earth, and did obeisance. 3 And David said unto him, "From whence comest thou?" And he said unto him, "Out of the camp of Israel am I escaped." 4 And David said unto him, "How went the matter? I pray thee, tell me." And he answered, "That the people are fled from the battle, and many of the people also are fallen and dead; and Saul and Jonathan his son are dead also." 5 And David said unto the young man that told him, "How knowest thou that Saul and Jonathan his son be dead?" 6 And the young man that told him said, "As I happened by chance upon mount Gilboa, behold, Saul leaned upon his spear; and, lo, the chariots and horsemen followed hard after him. 7 And when he looked behind him, he saw me, and called unto me. And I answered, 'Here *am* I.' 8 And he said unto me, 'Who *art* thou?' And I answered him, 'I *am* an Amalekite.' 9 He said unto me again, 'Stand, I pray thee, upon me, and slay me: for anguish is come upon me, because my life *is* yet whole in me.' 10 So I stood upon him, and slew him, because I was sure that he could not live after that he was fallen: and I took the crown that *was* upon his head, and the bracelet that *was* on his arm, and have brought them hither unto my lord." [1]

11 Then David took hold on his clothes, and rent them; and likewise all the men that *were* with him: 12 And they mourned, and wept, and fasted until even, for Saul, and for Jonathan his son, and for the people of the LORD, and for the house of Israel; because they were fallen by the sword. 13 And David said unto the young man that told him, "Whence *art* thou?" And he answered, "I *am* the son of a stranger, an Amalekite." 14 And David said unto him, "How wast thou not afraid to stretch forth thine hand to destroy the LORD's anointed?" 15 And David called one of the young men, and said, "Go near, *and* fall upon him." And he smote him that he died. 16 And David said unto him, "Thy blood *be* upon thy head; for thy mouth hath testified against thee, saying, 'I have slain the LORD's anointed.' "

David's Elegy over Saul and Jonathan [2]

17 And David lamented with this lamentation over Saul and over Jonathan his son: 18 (Also he bade them teach the children of Judah *the use of* the bow: behold, *it is* written in the book of Jasher:)[3]

19   The beauty of Israel is slain upon thy high places:
    How are the mighty fallen!

20   Tell *it* not in Gath,
    Publish *it* not in the streets of Askelon;
    Lest the daughters of the Philistines rejoice,
    Lest the daughters of the uncircumcised triumph.

21   Ye mountains of Gilboa,
    Let there be no dew, neither *let there be* rain, upon you,
    Nor fields of offerings:
    For there the shield of the mighty is vilely cast away,
    The shield of Saul, *as though he had* not *been* anointed with oil.

22   From the blood of the slain,
    From the fat of the mighty,[4]
    The bow of Jonathan turned not back,
    And the sword of Saul returned not empty.

23   Saul and Jonathan *were* lovely and pleasant in their lives,
    And in their death they were not divided:
    They were swifter than eagles,
    They were stronger than lions.

---

1. (1:1-10) Because the description of Saul's death differs from that given in both *I Samuel* 31 and *II Samuel* 4:10, some commentators suggest the young Amalekite is lying to win David's favor.

2. (1:17-27) In IB, George B. Caird writes: "There is general agreement that this poem can safely be attributed to David, and that it is therefore one of the earliest extant pieces of Hebrew literature."

3. JB: "It is written in the Book of the Just, so that it may be taught to the sons of Judah." Since the text of the poem is notably corrupt, IB suggests the confusing line about "the use of the bow" was originally part of the first line of the elegy.

4. NEB: "from the breast of the foeman."

24   Ye daughters of Israel, weep over Saul,
      Who clothed you in scarlet, with *other* de-
         lights;
      Who put on ornaments of gold upon your
         apparel.

25   How are the mighty fallen in the midst of
         the battle!
      O Jonathan, *thou wast* slain in thine high
         places.

26   I am distressed for thee, my brother Jona-
         than:
      Very pleasant hast thou been unto me:
      Thy love to me was wonderful,
      Passing the love of women.

27   How are the mighty fallen,
      And the weapons of war perished!

David, King of Judah and Israel

2 And it came to pass after this, that David inquired of the LORD, saying, "Shall I go up into
any of the cities of Judah?" And the LORD said
unto him, "Go up." And David said, "Whither
shall I go up?" And he said, "Unto Hebron."
2 So David went up thither, and his two wives
also, Ahinoam the Jezreelitess, and Abigail Na-
bal's wife the Carmelite. 3 And his men that
were with him did David bring up, every man
with his household: and they dwelt in the cities of
Hebron. 4 And the men of Judah came, and
there they anointed David king over the house of
Judah.

And they told David, saying, *That* the men of
Jabesh-gilead *were they* that buried Saul. 5 And
David sent messengers unto the men of Jabesh-
gilead, and said unto them, "Blessed *be* ye of the
LORD, that ye have showed this kindness unto
your lord, *even* unto Saul, and have buried him.
6 And now the LORD show kindness and truth
unto you: and I also will requite you this kindness, because ye have done this thing. 7 Therefore now let your hands be strengthened, and be
ye valiant: for your master Saul is dead, and also
the house of Judah have anointed me king over
them." [5]

8 But Abner the son of Ner, captain of Saul's
host, took Ish-bosheth the son of Saul, and
brought him over to Mahanaim; 9 And made
him king over Gilead, and over the Ashurites, and

over Jezreel, and over Ephraim, and over Benjamin, and over all Israel. 10 Ish-bosheth Saul's
son *was* forty years old when he began to reign
over Israel, and reigned two years. But the house
of Judah followed David. 11 And the time that
David was king in Hebron over the house of
Judah was seven years and six months.

*   *   *

5 Then[6] came all the tribes of Israel to David
unto Hebron, and spake, saying, "Behold, we *are*
thy bone and thy flesh. 2 Also in time past, when
Saul was king over us, thou wast he that leddest
out and broughtest in Israel: and the LORD said
to thee, 'Thou shalt feed my people Israel, and
thou shalt be a captain over Israel.' " 3 So all the
elders of Israel came to the king to Hebron; and
king David made a league with them in Hebron
before the LORD: and they anointed David king
over Israel.

4 David *was* thirty years old when he began to
reign, *and* he reigned forty years. 5 In Hebron he
reigned over Judah seven years and six months:
and in Jerusalem he reigned thirty and three years
over all Israel and Judah.

Military and Diplomatic Successes

6 And the king and his men went to Jerusalem
unto the Jebusites, the inhabitants of the land:
which spake unto David, saying, "Except thou
take away the blind and the lame, thou shalt not
come in hither." [7] thinking, "David cannot come
in hither." 7 Nevertheless, David took the
stronghold of Zion: the same *is* the city of David.
8 And David said on that day, "Whosoever get-
teth up to the gutter, and smiteth the Jebusites,
and the lame and the blind, *that are* hated of David's soul, *he shall be chief and captain.*" Wherefore they said, "The blind and the lame shall not
come into the house." 9 So David dwelt in the
fort, and called it the city of David. And David
built round about from Millo and inward.
10 And David went on, and grew great, and the
LORD God of hosts *was* with him.

11 And Hiram king of Tyre sent messengers to
David, and cedar trees, and carpenters, and ma-
sons: and they built David a house. 12 And

---

5. In this politically indirect line, David is asking the men of
Jabesh-gilead to acknowledge him as Saul's successor.

6. I.e., following the death of King Ish-bosheth, reported in
4:5-7.
7. NAB: "You cannot enter here: the blind and the lame will
drive you away!" The Jebusites believe city fortifications
are so strong that a garrison of blind and lame men could
repel an attack.

David perceived that the LORD had established him king over Israel, and that he had exalted his kingdom for his people Israel's sake.

13 And David took *him* more concubines and wives out of Jerusalem, after he was come from Hebron: and there were yet sons and daughters born to David. 14 And these *be* the names of those that were born unto him in Jerusalem; Shammuah, and Shobab, and Nathan, and Solomon, 15 Ibhar also, and Elishua, and Nepheg, and Japhia, 16 And Elishama, and Eliada, and Eliphalet.

17 But when the Philistines heard that they had anointed David king over Israel, all the Philistines came up to seek David; and David heard *of it,* and went down to the hold. 18 The Philistines also came and spread themselves in the valley of Rephaim. 19 And David inquired of the LORD, saying, "Shall I go up to the Philistines? wilt thou deliver them into mine hand?" And the LORD said unto David, "Go up: for I will doubtless deliver the Philistines into thine hand." 20 And David came to Baal-perazim, and David smote them there, and said, "The LORD hath broken forth upon mine enemies before me, as the breach of waters." Therefore he called the name of that place Baal-perazim. 21 And there they left their images, and David and his men burned them. 22 And the Philistines came up yet again, and spread themselves in the valley of Rephaim. 23 And when David inquired of the LORD, he said, "Thou shalt not go up; *but* fetch a compass behind them, and come upon them over against the mulberry trees. 24 And let it be, when thou hearest the sound of a going in the tops of the mulberry trees, that then thou shalt bestir thyself: for then shall the LORD go out before thee, to smite the host of the Philistines." 25 And David did so, as the LORD had commanded him; and smote the Philistines from Geba until thou come to Gazer.

The Ark in Jerusalem

6 Again, David gathered together all the chosen *men* of Israel, thirty thousand. 2 And David arose, and went with all the people that *were* with him from Baale of Judah, to bring up from thence the ark of God, whose name is called by the name of the LORD of hosts that dwelleth *between* the cherubim. 3 And they set the ark of God upon a new cart, and brought it out of the house of Abinadab that *was* in Gibeah: and Uzzah and Ahio, the sons of Abinadab, drave the new cart. 4 And they brought it out of the house of Abinadab which *was* at Gibeah, accompanying the ark of God: and Ahio went before the ark. 5 And David and all the house of Israel played before the LORD on all manner of *instruments made of* fir wood, even on harps, and on psalteries, and on timbrels, and on cornets, and on cymbals.

6 And when they came to Nachon's threshing-floor, Uzzah put forth *his hand* to the ark of God, and took hold of it; for the oxen shook *it.* 7 And the anger of the LORD was kindled against Uzzah, and God smote him there for *his* error; and there he died by the ark of God. 8 And David was displeased, because the LORD had made a breach upon Uzzah: and he called the name of the place Perez-uzzah to this day. 9 And David was afraid of the LORD that day, and said, "How shall the ark of the LORD come to me?" 10 So David would not remove the ark of the LORD unto him into the city of David: but David carried it aside into the house of Obed-edom the Gittite. 11 And the ark of the LORD continued in the house of Obed-edom the Gittite three months: and the LORD blessed Obed-edom, and all his household.

12 And it was told king David, saying, "The LORD hath blessed the house of Obed-edom, and all that *pertaineth* unto him, because of the ark of God." So David went and brought up the ark of God from the house of Obed-edom into the city of David with gladness. 13 And it was *so,* that when they that bare the ark of the LORD had gone six paces, he sacrificed oxen and fatlings. 14 And David danced before the LORD with all *his* might; and David *was* girded with a linen ephod. 15 So David and all the house of Israel brought up the ark of the LORD with shouting, and with the sound of the trumpet.

16 And as the ark of the LORD came into the city of David, Michal Saul's daughter looked through a window, and saw king David leaping and dancing before the LORD; and she despised him in her heart. 17 And they brought in the ark of the LORD, and set it in his place, in the midst of the tabernacle that David had pitched for it: and David offered burnt offerings and peace offerings before the LORD. 18 And as soon as David had made an end of offering burnt offerings and peace offerings, he blessed the people in the name of the LORD of hosts. 19 And he dealt among all the people, *even* among the whole multitude of Israel, as well to the women as men, to every one a cake of bread, and a good piece *of flesh,* and a flagon *of wine.* So all the people departed every one to his house.

20 Then David returned to bless his household.

And Michal the daughter of Saul came out to meet David, and said, "How glorious was the king of Israel to-day, who uncovered himself to-day in the eyes of the handmaids of his servants, as one of the vain fellows shamelessly uncovereth himself!" [8] 21 And David said unto Michal, "*It was* before the LORD, which chose me before my father, and before all his house, to appoint me ruler over the people of the LORD, over Israel: therefore will I play before the LORD. 22 And I will yet be more vile than thus, and will be base in mine own sight:[9] and of the maidservants which thou hast spoken of, of them shall I be had in honor."   23 Therefore Michal the daughter of Saul had no child unto the day of her death.

*   *   *

David and Bath-sheba

11 And it came to pass, after the year was expired, at the time when kings go forth *to battle,* that David sent Joab, and his servants with him, and all Israel; and they destroyed the children of Ammon, and besieged Rabbah. But David tarried still at Jerusalem.

2 And it came to pass in an eveningtide, that David arose from off his bed, and walked upon the roof of the king's house: and from the roof he saw a woman washing herself; and the woman *was* very beautiful to look upon. 3 And David sent and inquired after the woman. And *one* said, "*Is* not this Bath-sheba, the daughter of Eliam, the wife of Uriah the Hittite?"   4 And David sent messengers, and took her; and she came in unto him, and he lay with her; for she was purified from her uncleanness: and she returned unto her house. 5 And the woman conceived, and sent and told David, and said, "I *am* with child."

6 And David sent to Joab, *saying,* "Send me Uriah the Hittite." And Joab sent Uriah to David. 7 And when Uriah was come unto him, David demanded *of him* how Joab did, and how the people did, and how the war prospered. 8 And David said to Uriah, "Go down to thy house, and wash thy feet." And Uriah departed out of the king's house, and there followed him a mess *of meat* from the king. 9 But Uriah slept at the door of the king's house with all the servants of his lord, and went not down to his house. 10 And when they had told David, saying, "Uriah went not down unto his house," David said unto Uriah, "Camest thou not from *thy* journey? why *then* didst thou not go down unto thine house?"

11 And Uriah said unto David, "The ark, and Israel, and Judah, abide in tents; and my lord Joab, and the servants of my lord, are encamped in the open fields; shall I then go into mine house, to eat and to drink, and to lie with my wife? *as* thou livest, and *as* thy soul liveth, I will not do this thing." 12 And David said to Uriah, "Tarry here to-day also, and to-morrow I will let thee depart." So Uriah abode in Jerusalem that day, and the morrow. 13 And when David had called him, he did eat and drink before him; and he made him drunk: and at even he went out to lie on his bed with the servants of his lord, but went not down to his house.

14 And it came to pass in the morning, that David wrote a letter to Joab, and sent *it* by the hand of Uriah. 15 And he wrote in the letter, saying, "Set ye Uriah in the forefront of the hottest battle, and retire ye from him, that he may be smitten, and die." 16 And it came to pass, when Joab observed the city, that he assigned Uriah unto a place where he knew that valiant men were.[10] 17 And the men of the city went out, and fought with Joab: and there fell *some* of the people of the servants of David; and Uriah the Hittite died also. 18 Then Joab sent and told David all the things concerning the war; 19 And charged the messenger, saying, "When thou hast made an end of telling the matters of the war unto the king, 20 And if so be that the king's wrath arise, and he say unto thee, 'Wherefore approached ye so nigh unto the city when ye did fight? knew ye not that they would shoot from the wall? 21 Who smote Abimelech the son of Jerubbesheth? did not a woman cast a piece of a millstone upon him from the wall, that he died in Thebez? why went ye nigh the wall?' then say thou, 'Thy servant Uriah the Hittite is dead also.' "

22 So the messenger went, and came and showed David all that Joab had sent him for. 23 And the messenger said unto David, "Surely the men prevailed against us, and came out unto us into the field, and we were upon them even unto the entering of the gate. 24 And the shooters shot from off the wall upon thy servants; and *some* of the king's servants be dead, and thy servant Uriah the Hittite is dead also."   25 Then David said unto the messenger, "Thus shalt thou say unto Joab, 'Let not this thing displease thee, for the sword devoureth one as well as another: make thy battle more strong against the city, and overthrow it': and encourage thou him."

26 And when the wife of Uriah heard that Uriah her husband was dead, she mourned for

---

8. In *I Samuel* 19:23-24, Saul, possessed by the same kind of prophetic frenzy, danced naked before Samuel.

9. Modern translations follow the Greek text. WATERMAN: "I will be still more abandoned than that, and I will be vile in your eyes."

10. WATERMAN: "where he knew the best opposing troops were."

her husband. 27 And when the mourning was past, David sent and fetched her to his house, and she became his wife, and bare him a son. But the thing that David had done displeased the LORD.

12 And the LORD sent Nathan unto David. And he came unto him, and said unto him, "There were two men in one city; the one rich, and the other poor. 2 The rich *man* had exceeding many flocks and herds: 3 But the poor *man* had nothing, save one little ewe lamb, which he had bought and nourished up: and it grew up together with him, and with his children; it did eat of his own meat, and drank of his own cup, and lay in his bosom, and was unto him as a daughter. 4 And there came a traveler unto the rich man, and he spared to take of his own flock and of his own herd, to dress for the wayfaring man that was come unto him; but took the poor man's lamb, and dressed it for the man that was come to him." 5 And David's anger was greatly kindled against the man; and he said to Nathan, "*As* the LORD liveth, the man that hath done this *thing* shall surely die: 6 And he shall restore the lamb fourfold, because he did this thing, and because he had no pity."

7 And Nathan said to David, "Thou *art* the man. Thus saith the LORD God of Israel, 'I anointed thee king over Israel, and I delivered thee out of the hand of Saul; 8 And I gave thee thy master's house, and thy master's wives into thy bosom, and gave thee the house of Israel and of Judah; and if *that had been* too little, I would moreover have given unto thee such and such things. 9 Wherefore hast thou despised the commandment of the LORD, to do evil in his sight? thou hast killed Uriah the Hittite with the sword, and hast taken his wife *to be* thy wife, and hast slain him with the sword of the children of Ammon. 10 Now therefore the sword shall never depart from thine house; because thou hast despised me, and hast taken the wife of Uriah the Hittite to be thy wife.' 11 Thus saith the LORD, 'Behold, I will raise up evil against thee out of thine own house, and I will take thy wives before thine eyes, and give *them* unto thy neighbor, and he shall lie with thy wives in the sight of this sun. 12 For thou didst *it* secretly: but I will do this thing before all Israel, and before the sun.'" 13 And David said unto Nathan, "I have sinned against the LORD." And Nathan said unto David, "The LORD also hath put away thy sin; thou shalt not die.[11] 14 Howbeit, because by this deed thou hast given great occasion to the enemies of the LORD to blaspheme, the child also *that is* born unto thee shall surely die." 15 And Nathan departed unto his house.

And the LORD struck the child that Uriah's wife bare unto David, and it was very sick. 16 David therefore besought God for the child; and David fasted, and went in, and lay all night upon the earth. 17 And the elders of his house arose, *and went* to him, to raise him up from the earth: but he would not, neither did he eat bread with them. 18 And it came to pass on the seventh day, that the child died. And the servants of David feared to tell him that the child was dead: for they said, "Behold, while the child was yet alive, we spake unto him, and he would not hearken unto our voice: how will he then vex himself, if we tell him that the child is dead?" 19 But when David saw that his servants whispered, David perceived that the child was dead: therefore David said unto his servants, "Is the child dead?" And they said, "He is dead." 20 Then David arose from the earth, and washed, and anointed *himself,* and changed his apparel, and came into the house of the LORD, and worshipped: then he came to his own house; and when he required, they set bread before him, and he did eat. 21 Then said his servants unto him, "What thing *is* this that thou hast done? thou didst fast and weep for the child, *while it was* alive; but when the child was dead, thou didst rise and eat bread." 22 And he said, "While the child was yet alive, I fasted and wept: for I said, 'Who can tell *whether* GOD will be gracious to me, that the child may live?' 23 But now he is dead, wherefore should I fast? can I bring him back again? I shall go to him, but he shall not return to me."

24 And David comforted Bath-sheba his wife, and went in unto her, and lay with her: and she bare a son, and he called his name Solomon: and the LORD loved him.

11. (12:13-14) Contrast the total and irrevocable condemnation which follows Saul's confession of sin (*I Samuel* 15:24-29).

Introduction to
JOB

"And I desire to reason with God."

The anonymous author of *Job* has produced a universally admired work which defies literary classification. Attempts to define it as drama fail; though the book contains elements of a play, it cannot be staged. It cannot be called didactic poetry; the lessons taught are implicit rather than explicit. It does not conform to the criteria of an epic; no matter how heroic and cosmic Job's struggles are, the results of the conflict are personally, rather than racially or nationally, appropriated. There are many passages of lyric poetry, but these are always subordinated to the book's theme.

The theme is Job's integrity before God:

> Though he slay me, yet will I trust in him:
> but I will maintain mine own ways before him.

Regrettably, the KJV translators followed a marginal note to 13:15 rather than the text. Modern translations focus the theme more clearly:

> Let him kill me if he will; I have no other hope
> than to justify my conduct in his eyes. [JB]

> Behold, he will slay me; I have no hope;
> yet I will defend my ways to his face. [RSV]

To praise the patience and passivity of Job is to diminish the hero and reduce the book to a flat restatement of the righteousness-rewarded ethic. The main characteristics of Job are courage and honesty.

Scholarly problems relating to *Job* need not perplex the general reader. The Joban author has been identified, in the words of A. B. Davidson (*The Book of Job*, 1889), as "Job himself, Elihu, Moses, Solomon, Heman the Ezrahite, author of Ps. lxxxviii., Isaiah, Hezekiah, author of the hymn Is. xxxviii., Baruch the friend of Jeremiah, and who not?" His date has been established anywhere from the ninth to the second century B.C., and his locale from Edom to Israel to Egypt. The best modern opinion is that the author was a Jew writing in the fifth or fourth century B.C. Such speculation is not crucial, however, for the poet writes of human existence, not of history. *Job*, as it comes to us, has undergone reordering and smaller and larger interpolations by later hands; but this is not a disturbing factor. The book remains a powerful literary statement.

The poet's technique is simple yet provocative. He takes a popular folk tale and uses it as a frame for his poetic meditation. Divided in half, the tale appears as prologue and epilogue. The descriptions of the heavenly court, of the calamities befalling Job, and of great wealth he finally gains illustrate the primitive hyperbole of folk literature.

The prologue describes Job as "perfect and upright." His virtue is rewarded with "seven sons and three daughters," a perfect family, and with massive wealth. His fall derives from a wager between God and Satan. In an anthropomorphic scene picturing heaven as a kind of oriental court, Satan—i.e., the Adversary—proposes to test Job's fidelity, and God agrees. When Job bears up under the loss of his family and possessions, he is afflicted with "sore boils" (all attempts to identify the malady have been unsuccessful) and sits suffering in an ash heap. In two chapters, Job is reduced from a figure of perfection to an afflicted pauper. After a period of time, three friends approach him to offer comfort.

Now the Joban poet leaves the folk tale to begin his meditation on suffering. It starts with Job's cursing the day of his birth and continues through three cycles of speeches. In each cycle, Job's friends speak in turn and he responds to each. (The present text contains only the first cycle.) After the three cycles, Job offers summary comment. (Here only his Oath of Clearance—Chapter 31—is included.) Following a discourse by a new character, Elihu (Chapters 32–37, here omitted), the Lord answers Job in a whirlwind, and Job is humbled.

For the epilogue, the Joban poet returns to the folk tale. Eliphaz, Bildad, and Zophar are chided for their false counsel; Job's wealth is exactly doubled; he sires another perfect family and lives a long patriarchal life. The poet seems not to notice that the epilogue contradicts his previous conclusions. Though the views of the three counselors were often identical to those expressed by the Lord, God condemns them for their statements. After heroically challenging the proposition that God always rewards righteousness, Job is hugely rewarded for his virtue.

The frame tale is of minor importance, however; it is in the poetic meditation that the Joban poet reveals his psychological and theological insights. After describing Job's hapless condition, he traces his hero's mounting sense of divine injustice. The malediction of Chapter 3 shows the total despair of a man who rues his birth and would gladly embrace death. It is from this depth that Job begins his agonizing quest toward understanding and dignity.

The superficial counsel of his three friends contributes to this growth. While never actually accusing Job of sin, Eliphaz argues that all men—and, indeed, all angels—are imperfect in comparison with God and that Job should be grateful for "the chastening of the Almighty." Responding, Job complains directly to God and insists he is being deliberately and causelessly tortured. Bildad suggests that Job is suffering for the sins of his sons, who, by implication, have already been destroyed for their misdeeds. He urges him to "make supplication to the Almighty," confident that "God will not cast away a perfect man." Job answers that divine dealings reveal a God who lacks basic human decency. Warming to his defense, he longs for a "daysman" (an umpire, a legal arbitrator) who, he is certain, would rule against God. Again he calls directly to the Lord: "Show me wherefore thou contendest with me." Zophar, the least tolerant counselor, says what the other friends have only implied. He calls Job a liar and insists he is suffering deserved punishment for his sins: "Know therefore that God exacteth of thee less than thine iniquity deserveth." He tells him to repent. But Job will not repent for sins he has not committed. Again he seeks an audience with God: "Then call thou, and I will answer: or let me speak, and answer thou me." He is ready to stand before God and speak the truth: "a hypocrite shall not come before him." Job ends his speech with a long poem on human destiny (Chapter 14), in which he comments on the mortality of man, the finality of death, the illusion of an afterlife, and the certainty of annihilation. His tone is mature and resigned, that of a man who has learned from his suffering.

In his Oath of Clearance, Job catalogues sixteen possible sins (adultery, vanity, idolatry, and hypocrisy, among others) and declares his innocence of any of them. In climactic lines, he insists he could appear proudly before God bearing an indictment written by his worst enemy:

> Oh that one would hear me! behold, my desire is, that the Almighty would answer me, and that mine adversary had written a book.
> Surely I would take it upon my shoulder, and bind it as a crown to me.
> I would declare unto him the number of my steps; as a prince would I go near unto him.   [31:35-37]

Such an audacious metaphor appears nowhere else in the Bible. Job has risen from hopelessness to confidence. He is once again the oriental prince of the prologue.

Finally, Job's repeated demands for an audience evoke a response. Answering from the whirlwind, the Lord refuses to debate. He does not accuse Job of evil, but insists that Job has no capacity to judge divinity. In a tone of not unkind scorn, God contrasts mere human capabilities with his own creation of the world, his control of the forces of nature, and his care for animal life. In rhetorical question after rhetorical question, he demonstrates the infinite gap between man and God. Before this display of cosmic power, Job is moved to humility and silence.

As the book ends, Job's initial complaint about unmerited suffering remains unanswered. But the complaint is replaced by a sense of relationship: "I have heard of thee by the hearing of the ear; but now mine eye seeth thee." Job has not discovered why men suffer. But he knows that fidelity to God supersedes the good life.

JOB

PROLOGUE

1 There was a man in the land of Uz, whose name *was* Job; and that man was perfect and upright, and one that feared God, and eschewed evil. 2 And there were born unto him seven sons and three daughters. 3 His substance also was seven thousand sheep, and three thousand camels, and five hundred yoke of oxen, and five hundred she asses, and a very great household; so that this man was the greatest of all the men of the east. 4 And his sons went and feasted *in their* houses, every one his day; and sent and called for their three sisters to eat and to drink with them. 5 And it was so, when the days of *their* feasting were gone about, that Job sent and sanctified them, and rose up early in the morning, and offered burnt offerings *according* to the number of them all: for Job said, "It may be that my sons have sinned, and cursed God in their hearts." Thus did Job continually.

6 Now there was a day when the sons of God came to present themselves before the LORD, and Satan[1] came also among them. 7 And the LORD said unto Satan, "Whence comest thou?" Then Satan answered the LORD, and said, "From going to and fro in the earth, and from walking up and down in it." 8 And the LORD said unto Satan, "Hast thou considered my servant Job, that *there is* none like him in the earth, a perfect and an upright man, one that feareth God, and escheweth evil?" 9 Then Satan answered the LORD, and said, "Doth Job fear God for nought? 10 Hast not thou made a hedge about him, and about his house, and about all that he hath on every side? thou hast blessed the work of his hands, and his substance is increased in the land. 11 But put forth thine hand now, and touch all that he hath, and he will curse thee to thy face." 12 And the LORD said unto Satan, "Behold, all that he hath *is* in thy power; only upon himself put not forth thine hand." So Satan went forth from the presence of the LORD.

13 And there was a day when his sons and his daughters *were* eating and drinking wine in their eldest brother's house: 14 And there came a messenger unto Job, and said, "The oxen were plowing, and the asses feeding beside them: 15 And the Sabeans fell *upon them,* and took them away; yea, they have slain the servants with the edge of the sword; and I only am escaped alone to tell thee." 16 While he was yet speaking, there came also another, and said, "The fire of God is fallen from heaven, and hath burned up the sheep, and the servants, and consumed them; and I only am escaped alone to tell thee." 17 While he was yet speaking, there came also another, and said, "The Chaldeans made out three bands, and fell upon the camels, and have carried them away, yea, and slain the servants with the edge of the sword; and I only am escaped alone to tell thee." 18 While he was yet speaking, there came also another, and said, "Thy sons and thy daughters *were* eating and drinking wine in their eldest brother's house: 19 And, behold, there came a great wind from the wilderness, and smote the four corners of the house, and it fell upon the young men, and they are dead; and I only am escaped alone to tell thee." 20 Then Job arose, and rent his mantle, and shaved his head, and fell down upon the ground, and worshipped, 21 And said,

"Naked came I out of my mother's womb,
And naked shall I return thither:
The LORD gave, and the LORD hath taken away;
Blessed be the name of the LORD."

22 In all this Job sinned not, nor charged God foolishly.

2 Again there was a day when the sons of God came to present themselves before the LORD, and Satan came also among them to present himself before the LORD. 2 And the LORD said unto Satan, "From whence comest thou?" And Satan answered the LORD, and said, "From going to and fro in the earth, and from walking up and down in it." 3 And the LORD said unto Satan, "Hast thou considered my servant Job, that *there is* none like him in the earth, a perfect and an upright man, one that feareth God, and escheweth evil? and still he holdeth fast his integrity, although thou movedst me against him, to destroy him without cause." 4 And Satan answered the LORD, and said, "Skin for skin,[2] yea, all that a man hath will he give for his life. 5 But put forth thine hand now, and touch his bone and his flesh, and he will curse thee to thy face." 6 And the

---

1. MOFFATT: "the Adversary." Satan is not yet the demonic personification he becomes in later Judaism and in Christianity.

2. This phrase from bargaining—like "a hide for a hide"—means Job must suffer personal pain before he will turn against God.

LORD said unto Satan, "Behold, he *is* in thine hand; but save his life."

7 So went Satan forth from the presence of the LORD, and smote Job with sore boils from the sole of his foot unto his crown. 8 And he took him a potsherd to scrape himself withal; and he sat down among the ashes. 9 Then said his wife unto him, "Dost thou still retain thine integrity? curse God, and die." [3] 10 But he said unto her, "Thou speakest as one of the foolish women speaketh. What? shall we receive good at the hand of God, and shall we not receive evil?" In all this did not Job sin with his lips.

11 Now when Job's three friends heard of all this evil that was come upon him, they came every one from his own place; Eliphaz the Temanite, and Bildad the Shuhite, and Zophar the Naamathite: for they had made an appointment together to come to mourn with him, and to comfort him. 12 And when they lifted up their eyes afar off, and knew him not, they lifted up their voice, and wept; and they rent every one his mantle, and sprinkled dust upon their heads toward heaven. 13 So they sat down with him upon the ground seven days and seven nights, and none spake a word unto him: for they saw that *his* grief was very great.

JOB'S LAMENT [4]

3 After this opened Job his mouth, and cursed his day. 2 And Job spake, and said

3 "Let the day perish wherein I was born,
And the night *in which* it was said,
'There is a man child conceived.'

4 Let that day be darkness;
Let not God regard it from above,
Neither let the light shine upon it.

5 Let darkness and the shadow of death stain it;
Let a cloud dwell upon it;
Let the blackness of the day terrify it.

6 *As for* that night, let darkness seize upon it;
Let it not be joined unto the days of the year;
Let it not come into the number of the months.

7 Lo, let that night be solitary;
Let no joyful voice come therein.

8 Let them curse it that curse the day,

Who are ready to raise up their mourning.[5]

9 Let the stars of the twilight thereof be dark;
Let it look for light, but *have* none;
Neither let it see the dawning of the day:

10 Because it shut not up the doors of my *mother's* womb,
Nor hid sorrow from mine eyes.

11 "Why died I not from the womb?
Why did I *not* give up the ghost when I came out of the belly?

12 Why did the knees prevent me?
Or why the breasts that I should suck?

13 For now should I have lain still and been quiet,
I should have slept: then had I been at rest,

14 With kings and counselors of the earth,
Which built desolate places for themselves;

15 Or with princes that had gold,
Who filled their houses with silver:

16 Or as a hidden untimely birth I had not been;
As infants which never saw light.

17 There the wicked cease from troubling;
And there the weary be at rest.

18 There the prisoners rest together;
They hear not the voice of the oppressor.

19 The small and great are there;
And the servant is free from his master.

20 "Wherefore is light given to him that is in misery,
And life unto the bitter *in* soul;

21 Which long for death, but it *cometh* not;
And dig for it more than for hid treasures;

22 Which rejoice exceedingly,
And are glad, when they can find the grave?

23 *Why is light given* to a man whose way is hid,
And whom God hath hedged in?

24 For my sighing cometh before I eat,
And my roarings are poured out like the waters.

25 For the thing which I greatly feared is come upon me,
And that which I was afraid of is come unto me.

26 I was not in safety, neither had I rest,
Neither was I quiet; yet trouble came."

---

3. St. John Chrysostom and other commentators have argued that Job's wife was spared in order to increase his torment.

4. (3:1-26) Job curses his existence, wishing that he had never been born (2-10), that he had died at birth (11-19), and that he might die now (20-26).

5. RSV: "who are skilled to rouse up Leviathan." MOFFATT: "enchanters who can rouse the Dragon!" Had the monster been roused, chaos would have overcome created order, and Job would not have been born.

FIRST CYCLE OF SPEECHES

Eliphaz' Speech

4 Then Eliphaz the Temanite answered and said,

2 "*If* we assay to commune with thee, wilt thou be grieved?
But who can withhold himself from speaking?

3 Behold, thou hast instructed many,
And thou hast strengthened the weak hands.

4 Thy words have upholden him that was falling,
And thou hast strengthened the feeble knees.

5 But now it is come upon thee, and thou faintest;
It toucheth thee, and thou art troubled.

6 *Is* not *this* thy fear, thy confidence,
Thy hope, and the uprightness of thy ways?

7 Remember, I pray thee, who *ever* perished, being innocent?
Or where were the righteous cut off?

8 Even as I have seen, they that plow iniquity,
And sow wickedness, reap the same.

9 By the blast of God they perish,
And by the breath of his nostrils are they consumed.

10 The roaring of the lion, and the voice of the fierce lion,
And the teeth of the young lions, are broken.

11 The old lion perisheth for lack of prey,
And the stout lion's whelps are scattered abroad.

12 Now a thing was secretly brought to me,[6]
And mine ear received a little thereof.

13 "In thoughts from the visions of the night,
When deep sleep falleth on men,

14 Fear came upon me, and trembling,
Which made all my bones to shake.

15 Then a spirit passed before my face;
The hair of my flesh stood up:

16 It stood still, but I could not discern the form thereof:
An image *was* before mine eyes,
There was silence, and I heard a voice, *saying,*

17 'Shall mortal man be more just than God?
Shall a man be more pure than his Maker?

18 Behold, he put no trust in his servants;
And his angels he charged with folly:

19 How much less *in* them that dwell in houses of clay,
Whose foundation *is* in the dust,
Which are crushed before the moth?

20 They are destroyed from morning to evening:
They perish for ever without any regarding *it.*

21 Doth not their excellency *which is in* them go away?
They die, even without wisdom.'

5 "Call now, if there be any that will answer thee;
And to which of the saints[7] wilt thou turn?

2 For wrath killeth the foolish man,
And envy slayeth the silly one.

3 I have seen the foolish taking root:
But suddenly I cursed his habitation.

4 His children are far from safety,
And they are crushed in the gate, neither *is there* any to deliver *them.*[8]

5 Whose harvest the hungry eateth up,
And taketh it even out of the thorns,
And the robber swalloweth up their substance.

6 Although affliction cometh not forth of the dust,
Neither doth trouble spring out of the ground;

7 Yet man is born unto trouble,
As the sparks fly upward.

8 "I would seek unto God,
And unto God would I commit my cause:

9 Which doeth great things and unsearchable;
Marvelous things without number:

10 Who giveth rain upon the earth,
And sendeth waters upon the fields:

11 To set up on high those that be low;
That those which mourn may be exalted to safety.

12 He disappointeth the devices of the crafty,
So that their hands cannot perform *their* enterprise.

---

6. (4:12-16) Though his counsel is perfectly traditional, Eliphaz says it came to him by special revelation.

7. RSV: "the holy ones." Eliphaz, expressing a doctrine of retribution, rules out the hope that any divine being other than God can help Job.

8. This refers to the gate of the city, where justice is administered. NEB: "his children past help, / browbeaten in court with none to save them."

13 He taketh the wise in their own craftiness:
And the counsel of the froward is carried headlong.

14 They meet with darkness in the daytime,
And grope in the noonday as in the night.

15 But he saveth the poor from the sword,
From their mouth, and from the hand of the mighty.

16 So the poor hath hope,
And iniquity stoppeth her mouth.

17 "Behold, happy *is* the man whom God correcteth:
Therefore despise not thou the chastening of the Almighty:[9]

18 For he maketh sore, and bindeth up:
He woundeth, and his hands make whole.

19 He shall deliver thee in six troubles:
Yea, in seven there shall no evil touch thee.

20 In famine he shall redeem thee from death:
And in war from the power of the sword.

21 Thou shalt be hid from the scourge of the tongue:
Neither shalt thou be afraid of destruction when it cometh.

22 At destruction and famine thou shalt laugh:
Neither shalt thou be afraid of the beasts of the earth.

23 For thou shalt be in league with the stones of the field:
And the beasts of the field shall be at peace with thee.

24 And thou shalt know that thy tabernacle *shall be* in peace;
And thou shalt visit thy habitation, and shalt not sin.

25 Thou shalt know also that thy seed *shall be* great,
And thine offspring as the grass of the earth.

26 Thou shalt come to *thy* grave in a full age,
Like as a shock of corn cometh in in his season.

27 "Lo this, we have searched it, so it *is;*
Hear it, and know thou *it* for thy good."

Job's Reply to Eliphaz

6 But Job answered and said,

2 "Oh that my grief were thoroughly weighed,

And my calamity laid in the balances together!

3 For now it would be heavier than the sand of the sea:
Therefore my words are swallowed up.

4 For the arrows of the Almighty *are* within me,
The poison whereof drinketh up my spirit:
The terrors of God do set themselves in array against me.

5 Doth the wild ass bray when he hath grass?
Or loweth the ox over his fodder?

6 Can that which is unsavory be eaten without salt?
Or is there *any* taste in the white of an egg?

7 The things *that* my soul refused to touch
Are as my sorrowful meat.

8 "Oh that I might have my request;
And that God would grant *me* the thing that I long for!

9 Even that it would please God to destroy me;
That he would let loose his hand, and cut me off!

10 Then should I yet have comfort;
Yea, I would harden myself in sorrow: let him not spare;
For I have not concealed the words of the Holy One.[10]

11 What *is* my strength, that I should hope?
And what *is* mine end, that I should prolong my life?

12 *Is* my strength the strength of stones?
Or *is* my flesh of brass?

13 *Is* not my help in me?
And is wisdom driven quite from me?

14 "To him that is afflicted pity *should be showed* from his friend;
But he forsaketh the fear of the Almighty.[11]

15 My brethren have dealt deceitfully as a brook,
And as the stream of brooks they pass away;

16 Which are blackish by reason of the ice,
And wherein the snow is hid:

---

9. To catch the dramatic quality of the scene, one must imagine how this advice would be received by a man covered "with sore boils from the sole of his foot unto his crown."

10. NAB: "because I have not transgressed the commands of the Holy One."

11. These lines have received many interpretations. NEB: "Devotion is due from his friends / to one who despairs and loses faith in the Almighty." The following lines (15-20), though difficult, offer a clear general meaning: Job says his friends have failed him precisely when he needs them.

17   What time they wax warm, they vanish:
      When it is hot, they are consumed out of
          their place.
18   The paths of their way are turned aside;
      They go to nothing, and perish.
19   The troops of Tema looked,
      The companies of Sheba waited for
          them.
20   They were confounded because they had
          hoped;
      They came thither, and were ashamed.

21   For now ye are nothing;
      Ye see *my* casting down, and are afraid.
22   Did I say, 'Bring unto me'?
      Or, 'Give a reward for me of your sub-
          stance'?
23   Or, 'Deliver me from the enemy's hand'?
      Or, 'Redeem me from the hand of the
          mighty'?
24   Teach me, and I will hold my tongue:
      And cause me to understand wherein I
          have erred.
25   How forcible are right words!
      But what doth your arguing reprove?
26   Do ye imagine to reprove words,
      And the speeches of one that is desperate,
          which are as wind?
27   Yea, ye overwhelm the fatherless,
      And ye dig *a pit* for your friend.
28   Now therefore be content, look upon me;
      For *it is* evident unto you if I lie.

29   Return, I pray you, let it not be iniquity;
      Yea, return again, my righteousness *is* in
          it.
30   Is there iniquity in my tongue?
      Cannot my taste discern perverse things?

7   "*Is there* not an appointed time to man
          upon earth?
      Are not his days also like the days of a
          hireling?
2   As a servant earnestly desireth the
          shadow,
      And as a hireling looketh for *the reward of*
          his work;
3   So am I made to possess months of
          vanity,
      And wearisome nights are appointed to
          me.
4   When I lie down, I say,
      'When shall I arise, and the night be
          gone?'
      And I am full of tossings to and fro unto
          the dawning of the day.
5   My flesh is clothed with worms and clods
          of dust;

      My skin is broken, and become loath-
          some.
6   My days are swifter than a weaver's
          shuttle,
      And are spent without hope.

7   "O remember that my life *is* wind:[12]
      Mine eye shall no more see good.
8   The eye of him that hath seen me shall see
          me no *more:*
      Thine eyes *are* upon me, and I *am* not.
9   *As* the cloud is consumed and vanisheth
          away;
      So he that goeth down to the grave shall
          come up no *more.*
10   He shall return no more to his house,
      Neither shall his place know him any
          more.
11   Therefore I will not refrain my mouth;
      I will speak in the anguish of my spirit;
      I will complain in the bitterness of my
          soul.
12   *Am* I a sea, or a whale,
      That thou settest a watch over me?
13   When I say, 'My bed shall comfort me,
      My couch shall ease my complaint;'
14   Then thou scarest me with dreams,
      And terrifiest me through visions:
15   So that my soul chooseth strangling,
      And death rather than my life.
16   I loathe *it;* I would not live alway:
      Let me alone; for my days *are* vanity.
17   What *is* man, that thou shouldest magnify
          him?[13]
      And that thou shouldest set thine heart
          upon him?
18   And *that* thou shouldest visit him every
          morning,
      And try him every moment?
19   How long wilt thou not depart from
          me,
      Nor let me alone till I swallow down my
          spittle?
20   I have sinned; what shall I do unto thee,
      O thou preserver of men? [14]
      Why hast thou set me as a mark against
          thee,
      So that I am a burden to myself?
21   And why dost thou not pardon my trans-
          gression,
      And take away mine iniquity?

---

12. (7:7-21) This prayer of plaintive longing contains elements
    of irony and cynicism.
13. This seems an obvious parody of *Psalms* 8:4.
14. MOFFATT: "If I sin, what harm is that to thee, / O thou Spy
    upon mankind?" Even if he had sinned, Job submits, he
    would not deserve such punishment.

For now shall I sleep in the dust;
And thou shalt seek me in the morning,
but I shall not be."

Bildad's Speech

8 Then answered Bildad the Shuhite, and said,
2 "How long wilt thou speak these *things?*
And *how long shall* the words of thy
mouth *be like* a strong wind?
3 Doth God pervert judgment?
Or doth the Almighty pervert justice?
4 If thy children have sinned against him,
And he have cast them away for their
transgression;
5 If thou wouldest seek unto God betimes,
And make thy supplication to the Almighty;
6 If thou *wert* pure and upright;
Surely now he would awake for thee,
And make the habitation of thy righteousness prosperous.
7 Though thy beginning was small,
Yet thy latter end should greatly increase.

8 "For inquire, I pray thee, of the former
age,
And prepare thyself to the search of their
fathers:
9 (For we *are but of* yesterday, and know
nothing,
Because our days upon earth *are* a
shadow:)
10 Shall not they teach thee, *and* tell thee,
And utter words out of their heart?
11 Can the rush grow up without mire?
Can the flag grow without water?
12 Whilst it *is* yet in his greenness, *and* not
cut down,
It withereth before any *other* herb.
13 So *are* the paths of all that forget God;
And the hypocrite's hope shall perish:
14 Whose hope shall be cut off,
And whose trust *shall be* a spider's web.
15 He shall lean upon his house, but it shall
not stand:
He shall hold it fast, but it shall not
endure.
16 He *is* green before the sun,
And his branch shooteth forth in his
garden.
17 His roots are wrapped about the heap,
And seeth the place of stones.
18 If he destroy him from his place,
Then *it* shall deny him, *saying,* 'I have not
seen thee.'
19 Behold, this *is* the joy of his way,
And out of the earth shall others grow.

20 "Behold, God will not cast away a perfect
man,
Neither will he help the evildoers:
21 Till he fill thy mouth with laughing,
And thy lips with rejoicing.
22 They that hate thee shall be clothed with
shame;
And the dwelling place of the wicked shall
come to nought."

Job's Reply to Bildad

9 Then Job answered [15] and said,
2 "I know *it is* so of a truth:
But how should man be just with God?
3 If he will contend with him,
He cannot answer him one of a thousand.
4 *He is* wise in heart, and mighty in
strength:
Who hath hardened *himself* against him,
and hath prospered?
5 Which removeth the mountains, and they
know not;
Which overturneth them in his anger;
6 Which shaketh the earth out of her place,
And the pillars thereof tremble;
7 Which commandeth the sun, and it riseth
not;
And sealeth up the stars;
8 Which alone spreadeth out the heavens,
And treadeth upon the waves of the sea;
9 Which maketh Arcturus, Orion,
And Pleiades, and the chambers of the
south;
10 Which doeth great things past finding
out;
Yea, and wonders without number.
11 Lo, he goeth by me, and I see *him* not:
He passeth on also, but I perceive him
not.

12 "Behold, he taketh away, who can hinder
him?
Who will say unto him, 'What doest
thou?'
13 *If* God will not withdraw his anger,
The proud helpers do stoop under him.[16]
14 How much less shall I answer him,
And choose out my words *to reason* with
him?

15. (9:1-35) This answer suggests Job heard little from Bildad.
He is responding to Eliphaz' argument: "Shall mortal man
be more just than God? shall a man be more pure than his
Maker?" (4:17) Job comments on God's arbitrary omnipotence.
16. RSV: "beneath him bowed the helpers of Rahab." NEB:
"the partisans of Rahab lie prostrate at his feet." These are
monsters of the deep tamed by the creator God.

15   Whom, though I were righteous, *yet*
         would I not answer,
         But I would make supplication to my
         judge.[17]

16   If I had called, and he had answered me;
         Yet would I not believe that he had
         hearkened unto my voice.

17   For he breaketh me with a tempest,
         And multiplieth my wounds without
         cause.

18   He will not suffer me to take my breath,
         But filleth me with bitterness.

19   If *I speak* of strength, lo, *he is* strong:
         And if of judgment, who shall set me a
         time *to plead?*

20   If I justify myself, mine own mouth shall
         condemn me:
         If I say, 'I *am* perfect,' it shall also prove
         me perverse.

21   *Though* I *were* perfect, *yet* would I not
         know my soul:
         I would despise my life.

22   This *is* one *thing,* therefore I said *it,*
         He destroyeth the perfect and the wicked.

23   If the scourge slay suddenly,
         He will laugh at the trial of the innocent.

24   The earth is given into the hand of the
         wicked:
         He covereth the faces of the judges
         thereof;
         If not, where, *and* who *is* he? [18]

25   "Now my days are swifter than a post:
         They flee away, they see no good.

26   They are passed away as the swift ships:
         As the eagle *that* hasteth to the prey.

27   If I say, 'I will forget my complaint,
         I will leave off my heaviness, and comfort
         myself';

28   I am afraid of all my sorrows,
         I know that thou wilt not hold me inno-
         cent.

29   *If* I be wicked,
         Why then labor I in vain?

30   If I wash myself with snow water,
         And make my hands never so clean;

31   Yet shalt thou plunge me in the ditch,
         And mine own clothes shall abhor me.

32   "For *he is* not a man, as I *am, that* I
         should answer him,
         And we should come together in judg-
         ment.

33   Neither is there any daysman[19] betwixt us,
         That might lay his hand upon us both.

34   Let him take his rod away from me,
         And let not his fear terrify me:

35   *Then* would I speak, and not fear him;
         But *it is* not so with me.

10   "My soul is weary of my life;
         I will leave my complaint upon myself;
         I will speak in the bitterness of my soul.

2   I will say unto God, 'Do not condemn me;
         Show me wherefore thou contendest with
         me.

3   *Is it* good unto thee that thou shouldest
         oppress,
         That thou shouldest despise the work of
         thine hands,
         And shine upon the counsel of the wicked?

4   Hast thou eyes of flesh?
         Or seest thou as man seeth?

5   *Are* thy days as the days of man?
         Are thy years as man's days,[20]

6   That thou inquirest after mine iniquity,
         And searchest after my sin?

7   Thou knowest that I am not wicked;
         And *there is* none that can deliver out of
         thine hand.

8   Thine hands have made me and fashioned
         me
         Together round about; yet thou dost de-
         stroy me.

9   Remember, I beseech thee, that thou hast
         made me as the clay;
         And wilt thou bring me into dust again?

10   Hast thou not poured me out as milk,
         And curdled me like cheese?

11   Thou hast clothed me with skin and flesh,
         And hast fenced me with bones and sin-
         ews.

12   Thou hast granted me life and favor,
         And thy visitation hath preserved my
         spirit.

13   And these *things* hast thou hid in thine
         heart:
         I know that this *is* with thee.

14   If I sin, then thou markest me,
         And thou wilt not acquit me from mine
         iniquity.

15   If I be wicked, woe unto me;
         And *if* I be righteous, *yet* will I not lift up
         my head.

---

17. NAB: "Even though I were right, I could not answer him,
but should rather beg for what was due me."

18. KNOX: "So the whole world is given up into the power of
wrong-doers; he blinds the eyes of justice. He is answerable
for it; who else?" MOFFATT and NEB omit the final phrase.

19. RSV: "umpire." Job seeks a neutral party to judge his case.
The "him" in verse 34 refers to this desired arbitrator.

20. (10:4-5) Job speculates that God's judgments may be as
erroneous as man's and that his time—i.e., time in which to
inflict punishment—may be as limited.

I am full of confusion; therefore see thou mine affliction;

16 For it increaseth. Thou huntest me as a fierce lion:
And again thou showest thyself marvelous upon me.

17 Thou renewest thy witnesses against me,
And increasest thine indignation upon me;
Changes and war *are* against me.

18 Wherefore then hast thou brought me forth out of the womb?
Oh that I had given up the ghost, and no eye had seen me!

19 I should have been as though I had not been;
I should have been carried from the womb to the grave.

20 *Are* not my days few? cease *then,*
And let me alone, that I may take comfort a little,

21 Before I go *whence* I shall not return,
Even to the land of darkness and the shadow of death;

22 A land of darkness, as darkness *itself;*
And of the shadow of death, without any order,
And *where* the light *is* as darkness.' "

Zophar's Speech

11 Then answered Zophar the Naamathite, and said,

2 "Should not the multitude of words be answered?
And should a man full of talk be justified? [21]

3 Should thy lies make men hold their peace?
And when thou mockest, shall no man make thee ashamed?

4 For thou hast said, 'My doctrine *is* pure,
And I am clean in thine eyes.'

5 But oh that God would speak,
And open his lips against thee;

6 And that he would show thee the secrets of wisdom,
That *they are* double to that which is!
Know therefore that God exacteth of thee *less* than thine iniquity deserveth.

7 Canst thou by searching find out God?
Canst thou find out the Almighty unto perfection?

8 *It is* as high as heaven; what canst thou do?
Deeper than hell; what canst thou know?

9 The measure thereof *is* longer than the earth,
And broader than the sea.

10 If he cut off, and shut up,
Or gather together, then who can hinder him?

11 For he knoweth vain men:
He seeth wickedness also; will he not then consider *it?*

12 For vain man would be wise,
Though man be born *like* a wild ass's colt.[22]

13 "If thou prepare thine heart,
And stretch out thine hands toward him;

14 If iniquity *be* in thine hand, put it far away,
And let not wickedness dwell in thy tabernacles.

15 For then shalt thou lift up thy face without spot;
Yea, thou shalt be steadfast, and shalt not fear:

16 Because thou shalt forget *thy* misery,
And remember *it* as waters *that* pass away:

17 And *thine* age shall be clearer than the noonday;
Thou shalt shine forth, thou shalt be as the morning.

18 And thou shalt be secure, because there is hope;
Yea, thou shalt dig *about thee, and* thou shalt take thy rest in safety.

19 Also thou shalt lie down, and none shall make *thee* afraid;
Yea, many shall make suit unto thee.

20 But the eyes of the wicked shall fail,
And they shall not escape,
And their hope *shall be as* the giving up of the ghost."

Job's Reply to Zophar

12 And Job answered and said,

2 "No doubt but ye *are* the people,
And wisdom shall die with you.

3 But I have understanding as well as you;
I *am* not inferior to you:
Yea, who knoweth not such things as these?

---

21. MOFFATT: "Is a glib talker to carry the day?"

22. RSV: "But a stupid man will get understanding, when a wild ass's colt is born a man."

4   "I am *as* one mocked of his neighbor,[23]
     Who calleth upon God, and he answereth
     him:
     The just upright *man is* laughed to scorn.
5   He that is ready to slip with *his* feet
     Is as a lamp despised in the thought of
     him that is at ease.
6   The tabernacles of robbers prosper,
     And they that provoke God are secure;
     Into whose hand God bringeth *abun-
     dantly.*

7   "But ask now the beasts, and they shall
     teach thee;
     And the fowls of the air, and they shall
     tell thee:
8   Or speak to the earth, and it shall teach
     thee;
     And the fishes of the sea shall declare
     unto thee.
9   Who knoweth not in all these
     That the hand of the LORD hath wrought
     this?
10   In whose hand *is* the soul of every living
     thing,
     And the breath of all mankind.
11   Doth not the ear try words?
     And the mouth taste his meat?
12   With the ancient *is* wisdom;
     And in length of days understanding.
13   With him *is* wisdom and strength,
     He hath counsel and understanding.[24]
14   Behold, he breaketh down, and it cannot
     be built again:
     He shutteth up a man, and there can be
     no opening.
15   Behold, he withholdeth the waters, and
     they dry up:
     Also he sendeth them out, and they
     overturn the earth.
16   With him *is* strength and wisdom:
     The deceived and the deceiver *are* his.
17   He leadeth counselors away spoiled,
     And maketh the judges fools.
18   He looseth the bond of kings,
     And girdeth their loins with a girdle.
19   He leadeth princes away spoiled,
     And overthroweth the mighty.
20   He removeth away the speech of the
     trusty,

     And taketh away the understanding of the
     aged.
21   He poureth contempt upon princes,
     And weakeneth the strength of the
     mighty.
22   He discovereth deep things out of dark-
     ness,
     And bringeth out to light the shadow of
     death.[25]
23   He increaseth the nations, and destroyeth
     them:
     He enlargeth the nations, and straiteneth
     them *again.*
24   He taketh away the heart of the chief of
     the people of the earth,
     And causeth them to wander in a wilder-
     ness *where there is* no way.
25   They grope in the dark without light,
     And he maketh them to stagger like a
     drunken man.

13   "Lo, mine eye hath seen all *this,*
     Mine ear hath heard and understood it.
2   What ye know, *the same* do I know also:
     I *am* not inferior unto you.
3   Surely I would speak to the Almighty,
     And I desire to reason with God.
4   But ye *are* forgers of lies,
     Ye *are* all physicians of no value.
5   Oh that ye would altogether hold your
     peace!
     And it should be your wisdom.

6   Hear now my reasoning,
     And hearken to the pleadings of my lips.
7   Will ye speak wickedly for God?
     And talk deceitfully for him?
8   Will ye accept his person?
     Will ye contend for God?
9   Is it good that he should search you out?
     Or as one man mocketh another, do ye *so*
     mock him?
10   He will surely reprove you,
     If ye do secretly accept persons.
11   Shall not his excellency make you afraid?
     And his dread fall upon you?
12   Your remembrances *are* like unto ashes,
     Your bodies to bodies of clay.

13   "Hold your peace, let me alone, that I
     may speak,
     And let come on me what *will.*
14   Wherefore do I take my flesh in my teeth,
     And put my life in mine hand?

---

23. (12:4-6) These lines, interrupting the continuity of Job's
speech, seem an obvious interpolation. MOFFATT puts them
in double brackets.
24. (12:12-13) These are difficult lines. If they express Job, they
have to be taken as irony. MOFFATT's free translation is
perhaps best: "Wisdom, you argue, lies with aged men, a
long life means intelligence? / Nay, wisdom and authority
belong to God; strength and knowledge are his own."

25. NEB: "He uncovers mysteries deep in obscurity /
and into thick darkness he brings light." (In NEB, the passage
appears after v. 25, ending the chapter.)

15 Though he slay me, yet will I trust in him:
But I will maintain mine own ways before him.

16 He also *shall be* my salvation:
For a hypocrite shall not come before him.

17 Hear diligently my speech,
And my declaration with your ears.

18 Behold now, I have ordered *my* cause;
I know that I shall be justified.

19 Who *is* he *that* will plead with me?
For now, if I hold my tongue, I shall give up the ghost.

20 "Only do not two *things* unto me;[26]
Then will I not hide myself from thee.

21 Withdraw thine hand far from me:
And let not thy dread make me afraid.

22 Then call thou, and I will answer:
Or let me speak, and answer thou me.

23 How many *are* mine iniquities and sins?
Make me to know my transgression and my sin.

24 Wherefore hidest thou thy face,
And holdest me for thine enemy?

25 Wilt thou break a leaf driven to and fro?
And wilt thou pursue the dry stubble?

26 For thou writest bitter things against me,
And makest me to possess the iniquities of my youth.

27 Thou puttest my feet also in the stocks,
And lookest narrowly unto all my paths;
Thou settest a print[27] upon the heels of my feet.

28 And he, as a rotten thing, consumeth,
As a garment that is moth-eaten.[28]

14 "Man *that is* born of a woman
Is of few days, and full of trouble.

2 He cometh forth like a flower, and is cut down:
He fleeth also as a shadow, and continueth not.

3 And dost thou open thine eyes upon such a one,
And bringest me into judgment with thee?

4 Who can bring a clean *thing* out of an unclean?
Not one.

5 Seeing his days *are* determined,
The number of his months *are* with thee,
Thou hast appointed his bounds that he cannot pass;

6 Turn from him, that he may rest,
Till he shall accomplish, as a hireling, his day.

7 For there is hope of a tree,
If it be cut down, that it will sprout again,
And that the tender branch thereof will not cease.

8 Though the root thereof wax old in the earth,
And the stock thereof die in the ground;

9 *Yet* through the scent of water it will bud,
And bring forth boughs like a plant.

10 "But man dieth, and wasteth away:
Yea, man giveth up the ghost, and where *is* he?

11 *As* the waters fail from the sea,
And the flood decayeth and drieth up;

12 So man lieth down, and riseth not:
Till the heavens *be* no more, they shall not awake,
Nor be raised out of their sleep.

13 Oh that thou wouldest hide me in the grave,[29]
That thou wouldest keep me secret, until thy wrath be past,
That thou wouldest appoint me a set time, and remember me!

14 If a man die, shall he live *again?*
All the days of my appointed time will I wait,
Till my change come.

15 Thou shalt call, and I will answer thee:
Thou wilt have a desire to the work of thine hands.

16 For now thou numberest my steps:
Dost thou not watch over my sin?

17 My transgression *is* sealed up in a bag,
And thou sewest up mine iniquity.

18 "And surely the mountain falling cometh to nought,

---

26. Here, Job turns from his three friends and addresses God.
27. NEB: "a slave mark."
28. The lack of an antecedent for "he" shows this line is misplaced. NEB puts it after 14:2; MOFFATT and NAB, after 14:3.

29. (14:13-18) This momentary hope for immortality is expressed with clarity and eloquence in JB:

If only you would hide me in Sheol,
  and shelter me there until your anger is past,
fixing a certain day for calling me to mind—
  for once a man is dead can he come back to life?—
  day after day of my service I would wait
  for my relief to come.
Then you would call, and I should answer,
  you would want to see the work of your hands once more.
Now you count every step I take,
  but then you would cease to spy on my sins;
you would seal up my crime in a bag,
  and whiten my fault over.
But no! Soon or late the mountain falls,
  the rock moves from its place . . .

And the rock is removed out of his place.
19   The waters wear the stones:
     Thou washest away the things which grow
       out of the dust of the earth;
     And thou destroyest the hope of man.
20   Thou prevailest for ever against him, and
       he passeth:
     Thou changest his countenance, and
       sendest him away.
21   His sons come to honor, and he knoweth
       it not;
     And they are brought low, but he perceiv-
       eth *it* not of them.
22   But his flesh upon him shall have pain,
     And his soul within him shall mourn.”

*   *   *

Job's Oath of Innocence

31   “I made a covenant with mine eyes;
     Why then should I think upon a maid?
2   For what portion of God *is there* from
       above?
     And *what* inheritance of the Almighty
       from on high?
3   *Is* not destruction to the wicked?
     And a strange *punishment* to the workers
       of iniquity?
4   Doth not he see my ways,
     And count all my steps?

5   “If I have walked with vanity,
     Or if my foot hath hasted to deceit;
6   Let me be weighed in an even balance,
     That God may know mine integrity.

7   If my step hath turned out of the way,
     And mine heart walked after mine eyes,
     And if any blot hath cleaved to mine
       hands;
8   *Then* let me sow, and let another eat;
     Yea, let my offspring be rooted out.

9   If mine heart have been deceived by a
       woman,
     Or *if* I have laid wait at my neighbor's
       door;
10   *Then* let my wife grind unto another,
     And let others bow down upon her.
11   For this *is* a heinous crime;
     Yea, it *is* an iniquity *to be punished by* the
       judges.
12   For it *is* a fire *that* consumeth to destruc-
       tion,
     And would root out all mine increase.

13   If I did despise the cause of my manser-
       vant or of my maidservant,
     When they contended with me;

14   What then shall I do when God riseth up?
     And when he visiteth, what shall I answer
       him?
15   Did not he that made me in the womb
       make him?
     And did not one fashion us in the womb?

16   “If I have withheld the poor from *their*
       desire,
     Or have caused the eyes of the widow to
       fail;
17   Or have eaten my morsel myself alone,
     And the fatherless hath not eaten thereof;
18   (For from my youth he was brought up
       with me, as *with* a father,
     And I have guided her from my mother's
       womb;) [30]
19   If I have seen any perish for want of
       clothing,
     Or any poor without covering;
20   If his loins have not blessed me,
     And *if* he were *not* warmed with the fleece
       of my sheep;
21   If I have lifted up my hand against the
       fatherless,
     When I saw my help in the gate:
22   *Then* let mine arm fall from my shoulder
       blade,
     And mine arm be broken from the bone.
23   For destruction *from* God *was* a terror to
       me,
     And by reason of his highness I could not
       endure.

24   If I have made gold my hope,
     Or have said to the fine gold, 'Thou art' my
       confidence';
25   If I rejoiced because my wealth *was*
       great,
     And because mine hand had gotten
       much;
26   If I beheld the sun when it shined,[31]
     Or the moon walking *in* brightness;
27   And my heart hath been secretly enticed,
     Or my mouth hath kissed my hand:
28   This also *were* an iniquity *to be punished
       by* the judge:
     For I should have denied the God *that is*
       above.

29   “If I rejoiced at the destruction of him
       that hated me,
     Or lifted up myself when evil found him;

---

30. JB: “I, whom God has fostered father-like, since childhood,/
and guided since I left my mother's womb.”
31. (31:26-28) Job denies affiliation with any natural or astral
religion, affirming “the God that is above.”

30   (Neither have I suffered my mouth to sin
      By wishing a curse to his soul.)
31   If the men of my tabernacle said not,
      'Oh that we had of his flesh! we cannot be
      satisfied.'
32   The stranger did not lodge in the street:
      But I opened my doors to the traveler.
33   If I covered my transgressions as Adam,
      By hiding mine iniquity in my bosom:
34   Did I fear a great multitude,
      Or did the contempt of families terrify
      me,
      That I kept silence, *and* went not out of
      the door?

35   Oh that one would hear me!
      Behold, my desire *is, that* the Almighty
      would answer me,
      And *that* mine adversary had written a
      book.
36   Surely I would take it upon my shoulder,
      And bind it *as* a crown to me.
37   I would declare unto him the number of
      my steps;
      As a prince would I go near unto him.

38   "If my land cry against me,[32]
      Or that the furrows likewise thereof com-
      plain;
39   If I have eaten the fruits thereof without
      money,
      Or have caused the owners thereof to lose
      their life:
40   Let thistles grow instead of wheat,
      And cockle instead of barley."
The words of Job are ended.

*   *   *

The Answer from the Whirlwind

38 Then the LORD answered Job out of the
whirlwind, and said,
2   "Who *is* this that darkeneth counsel
      By words without knowledge?
3   Gird up now thy loins like a man;
      For I will demand of thee, and answer
      thou me.

4   "Where wast thou when I laid the founda-
      tions of the earth?
      Declare, if thou hast understanding.
5   Who hath laid the measures thereof, if
      thou knowest?
      Or who hath stretched the line upon it?

6   Whereupon are the foundations thereof
      fastened?
      Or who laid the corner stone thereof;
7   When the morning stars sang together,
      And all the sons of God shouted for
      joy?

8   "Or *who* shut up the sea with doors,
      When it brake forth, *as if* it had issued out
      of the womb?
9   When I made the cloud the garment
      thereof,
      And thick darkness a swaddling band for
      it,
10   And brake up for it my decreed *place,*
      And set bars and doors,
11   And said, 'Hitherto shalt thou come, but
      no further:
      And here shall thy proud waves be
      stayed'?

12   "Hast thou commanded the morning
      since thy days;
      And caused the dayspring to know his
      place;
13   That it might take hold of the ends of the
      earth,
      That the wicked might be shaken out of
      it? [33]
14   It is turned as clay *to* the seal;
      And they stand as a garment.
15   And from the wicked their light is with-
      holden,
      And the high arm shall be broken.

16   "Hast thou entered into the springs of the
      sea?
      Or hast thou walked in the search of the
      depth?
17   Have the gates of death been opened unto
      thee?
      Or hast thou seen the doors of the shadow
      of death?
18   Hast thou perceived the breadth of the
      earth?
      Declare if thou knowest it all.

19   "Where *is* the way *where* light dwelleth?
      And *as for* darkness, where *is* the place
      thereof,
20   That thou shouldest take it to the bound
      thereof,
      And that thou shouldest know the paths
      to the house thereof?

32. (31:38-40a) Because v. 37 is clearly the climax of Job's
    speech, most commentators believe these following verses
    are out of place. NAB puts them after v. 8; JB, after v. 15;
    MOFFATT, after v. 22; and NEB, after v. 28.

33. Dawn is pictured as a person lifting the darkness like a veil
    under which the earth has been sleeping. She shakes the
    wicked out of it like parasites.

21   Knowest thou *it,* because thou wast then born?
      Or *because* the number of thy days *is* great?

22   "Hast thou entered into the treasures of the snow?
      Or hast thou seen the treasures of the hail,
23   Which I have reserved against the time of trouble,
      Against the day of battle and war?

24   By what way is the light parted,
      Which scattereth the east wind upon the earth?

25   "Who hath divided a watercourse for the overflowing of waters,
      Or a way for the lightning of thunder;
26   To cause it to rain on the earth, *where* no man *is;*
      On the wilderness, wherein *there is* no man;
27   To satisfy the desolate and waste *ground;*
      And to cause the bud of the tender herb to spring forth?

28   "Hath the rain a father?
      Or who hath begotten the drops of dew?
29   Out of whose womb came the ice?
      And the hoary frost of heaven, who hath gendered it?
30   The waters are hid as *with* a stone,
      And the face of the deep is frozen.

31   "Canst thou bind the sweet influences of Pleiades,
      Or loose the bands of Orion?
32   Canst thou bring forth Mazzaroth in his season?
      Or canst thou guide Arcturus with his sons?
33   Knowest thou the ordinances of heaven?
      Canst thou set the dominion thereof in the earth?

34   "Canst thou lift up thy voice to the clouds,
      That abundance of waters may cover thee?
35   Canst thou send lightnings, that they may go,
      And say unto thee, 'Here we *are*'?
36   Who hath put wisdom in the inward parts?
      Or who hath given understanding to the heart?
37   Who can number the clouds in wisdom?
      Or who can stay the bottles of heaven,

38   When the dust groweth into hardness,
      And the clods cleave fast together?

39   "Wilt thou hunt the prey for the lion?
      Or fill the appetite of the young lions,
40   When they couch in *their* dens,
      And abide in the covert to lie in wait?
41   Who provideth for the raven his food?
      When his young ones cry unto God,
      They wander for lack of meat.

39   "Knowest thou the time when the wild goats of the rock bring forth?
      Or canst thou mark when the hinds do calve?
2   Canst thou number the months *that* they fulfil?
      Or knowest thou the time when they bring forth?
3   They bow themselves, they bring forth their young ones,
      They cast out their sorrows.
4   Their young ones are in good liking, they grow up with corn;
      They go forth, and return not unto them.

5   "Who hath sent out the wild ass free?
      Or who hath loosed the bands of the wild ass?
6   Whose house I have made the wilderness,
      And the barren land his dwellings.
7   He scorneth the multitude of the city,
      Neither regardeth he the crying of the driver.
8   The range of the mountains *is* his pasture,
      And he searcheth after every green thing.

9   "Will the unicorn[34] be willing to serve thee,
      Or abide by thy crib?
10   Canst thou bind the unicorn with his band in the furrow?
      Or will he harrow the valleys after thee?
11   Wilt thou trust him, because his strength *is* great?
      Or wilt thou leave thy labor to him?
12   Wilt thou believe him, that he will bring home thy seed,
      And gather *it into* thy barn?

13   "*Gavest thou* the goodly wings unto the peacocks?
      Or wings and feathers unto the ostrich? [35]

34. Regrettably, all modern translations read "the wild ox."
35. (39:13-18) While God in his providence withheld beauty and wisdom from the ostrich, he gave it great speed to fulfil its purposes.

14   Which leaveth her eggs in the earth,
      And warmeth them in the dust,
15   And forgetteth that the foot may crush
      them,
      Or that the wild beast may break them.
16   She is hardened against her young ones,
      as though *they were* not hers:
      Her labor is in vain without fear;
17   Because God hath deprived her of wis-
      dom,
      Neither hath he imparted to her under-
      standing.
18   What time she lifteth up herself on high,
      She scorneth the horse and his rider.

19   "Hast thou given the horse strength?
      Hast thou clothed his neck with thunder?
20   Canst thou make him afraid as a grass-
      hopper?
      The glory of his nostrils *is* terrible.
21   He paweth in the valley, and rejoiceth in
      his strength:
      He goeth on to meet the armed men.
22   He mocketh at fear, and is not affrighted;
      Neither turneth he back from the sword.
23   The quiver rattleth against him,
      The glittering spear and the shield.
24   He swalloweth the ground with fierceness
      and rage:
      Neither believeth he that *it is* the sound of
      the trumpet.[36]
25   He saith among the trumpets, 'Ha, ha!'
      And he smelleth the battle afar off,
      The thunder of the captains, and the
      shouting.

26   "Doth the hawk fly by thy wisdom,
      And stretch her wings toward the south?
27   Doth the eagle mount up at thy com-
      mand,
      And make her nest on high?
28   She dwelleth and abideth on the rock,
      Upon the crag of the rock, and the strong
      place.
29   From thence she seeketh the prey,
      And her eyes behold afar off.
30   Her young ones also suck up blood:
      And where the slain *are,* there *is* she."

40 Moreover the LORD answered Job, and said,
2   "Shall he that contendeth with the Al-
      mighty instruct *him?*
      He that reproveth God, let him answer
      it."

3 Then Job answered the LORD, and said,
4   "Behold, I am vile; what shall I answer
      thee?
      I will lay mine hand upon my mouth.
5   Once have I spoken; but I will not an-
      swer:
      Yea, twice; but I will proceed no further."

6 Then answered the LORD unto Job out of the
      whirlwind, and said,

7   "Gird up thy loins now like a man:
      I will demand of thee, and declare thou
      unto me.
8   Wilt thou also disannul my judgment?
      Wilt thou condemn me, that thou mayest
      be righteous?
9   Hast thou an arm like God?
      Or canst thou thunder with a voice like
      him?
10   Deck thyself now *with* majesty and excel-
      lency;
      And array thyself with glory and beauty.
11   Cast abroad the rage of thy wrath:
      And behold every one *that is* proud, and
      abase him.
12   Look on every one *that is* proud, *and*
      bring him low;
      And tread down the wicked in their place.
13   Hide them in the dust together;
      And bind their faces in secret.
14   Then will I also confess unto thee
      That thine own right hand can save
      thee.

15   "Behold now behemoth,[37]
      Which I made with thee;
      He eateth grass as an ox.
16   Lo now, his strength *is* in his loins,
      And his force *is* in the navel of his belly.
17   He moveth his tail like a cedar:
      The sinews of his stones are wrapped
      together.
18   His bones *are as* strong pieces of brass;
      His bones *are* like bars of iron.
19   He *is* the chief of the ways of God:
      He that made him can make his sword to
      approach *unto him.*
20   Surely the mountains bring him forth
      food,
      Where all the beasts of the field play.

---

36. NEB: "Trembling with eagerness, he devours the ground /
and cannot be held in when he hears the horn."

37. (40:15–41:34) Behemoth and Leviathan resemble the hippo-
potamus and the crocodile, but they are described as
primeval monsters who are subject to the power of God.
The discourse on these creatures is thought to be a later
addition by another poet. The descriptions are anticlimactic
here and seem to belong—if anywhere—in Chapter 39 on
animal life.

21   He lieth under the shady trees,
      In the covert of the reed, and fens.
22   The shady trees cover him *with* their
      shadow;
      The willows of the brook compass him
      about.
23   Behold, he drinketh up a river, *and* hast-
      eth not:
      He trusteth that he can draw up Jordan
      into his mouth.
24   He taketh it with his eyes:
      His nose pierceth through snares.[38]

41   "Canst thou draw out leviathan with a
      hook?
      Or his tongue with a cord *which* thou let-
      test down?
2   Canst thou put a hook into his nose?
      Or bore his jaw through with a thorn?
3   Will he make many supplications unto
      thee?
      Will he speak soft *words* unto thee?
4   Will he make a covenant with thee?
      Wilt thou take him for a servant for ever?
5   Wilt thou play with him as *with* a bird?
      Or wilt thou bind him for thy maidens?
6   Shall the companions make a banquet of
      him?
      Shall they part him among the mer-
      chants? [39]
7   Canst thou fill his skin with barbed irons?
      Or his head with fish spears?
8   Lay thine hand upon him,
      Remember the battle, do no more.
9   Behold, the hope of him is in vain:
      Shall not *one* be cast down even at the
      sight of him?
10   None *is so* fierce that dare stir him up:
      Who then is able to stand before me?
11   Who hath prevented me, that I should
      repay *him?*
      Whatsoever is under the whole heaven is
      mine.[40]
12   I will not conceal his parts,
      Nor his power, nor his comely proportion.

38. (40:23-24) NAB:
    "If the river grows violent, he is not disturbed;
      he is tranquil though the torrent surges about his
      mouth.
    Who can capture him by his eyes,
      or pierce his nose with a trap?"
    The eyes and nose are the only exposed parts of a submerged
    hippopotamus.
39. KNOX: "Is he to be divided up among fellow fishermen, sold
    piece-meal to the merchants?"
40. (41:10-11) JB: "Who can attack him with impunity? / No
    one beneath all heaven." MOFFATT, NEB, and NAB concur
    in making these verses describe, not God, but the Levia-
    than.

13   Who can discover the face of his gar-
      ment?
      Or who can come *to him* with his double
      bridle?
14   Who can open the doors of his face?
      His teeth *are* terrible round about.
15   *His* scales *are his* pride,
      Shut up together *as with* a close seal.
16   One is so near to another,
      That no air can come between them.
17   They are joined one to another,
      They stick together, that they cannot be
      sundered.
18   By his sneezings a light doth shine,
      And his eyes *are* like the eyelids of the
      morning.
19   Out of his mouth go burning lamps,
      And sparks of fire leap out.
20   Out of his nostrils goeth smoke,
      As *out* of a seething pot or caldron.
21   His breath kindleth coals,
      And a flame goeth out of his mouth.
22   In his neck remaineth strength,
      And sorrow is turned into joy before
      him.[41]
23   The flakes of his flesh are joined together:
      They are firm in themselves; they cannot
      be moved.
24   His heart is as firm as a stone;
      Yea, as hard as a piece of the nether *mill-
      stone.*
25   When he raiseth up himself, the mighty
      are afraid:
      By reason of breakings they purify them-
      selves.
26   The sword of him that layeth at him can-
      not hold:
      The spear, the dart, nor the habergeon.
27   He esteemeth iron as straw,
      And brass as rotten wood.
28   The arrow cannot make him flee:
      Sling stones are turned with him into
      stubble.
29   Darts are counted as stubble:
      He laugheth at the shaking of a spear.
30   Sharp stones *are* under him:
      He spreadeth sharp pointed things upon
      the mire.
31   He maketh the deep to boil like a pot:
      He maketh the sea like a pot of oint-
      ment.
32   He maketh a path to shine after him;
      One would think the deep *to be* hoary.
33   Upon earth there is not his like,
      Who is made without fear.

41. NEB: "and untiring energy dances ahead of him."

34   He beholdeth all high *things:*
       He *is* a king over all the children of
       pride." [42]

42 Then Job answered the LORD, and said,
2   "I know that thou canst do every *thing,*
       And *that* no thought can be withholden
       from thee.
3   'Who *is* he that hideth counsel without
       knowledge?'
       Therefore have I uttered that I under-
       stood not;
       Things too wonderful for me, which I
       knew not.
4   'Hear, I beseech thee, and I will speak:
       I will demand of thee, and declare thou
       unto me.' [43]
5   I have heard of thee by the hearing of the
       ear;
       But now mine eye seeth thee:
6   Wherefore I abhor *myself,* and repent
       In dust and ashes."

EPILOGUE

7 And it was *so,* that after the LORD had spoken these words unto Job, the LORD said to Eliphaz the Temanite, "My wrath is kindled against thee, and against thy two friends: for ye have not spoken of me *the thing that is* right, as my servant Job *hath.* 8 Therefore take unto you now seven bullocks and seven rams, and go to my servant Job, and offer up for yourselves a burnt offering; and my servant Job shall pray for you: for him will I accept: lest I deal with you *after your* folly, in that ye have not spoken of me *the thing which is* right, like my servant Job." 9 So Eliphaz the Temanite and Bildad the Shuhite *and* Zophar the Naamathite went, and did according as the LORD commanded them: the LORD also accepted Job. 10 And the LORD turned the captivity of Job, when he prayed for his friends: also the LORD gave Job twice as much as he had before. 11 Then came there unto him all his brethren, and all his sisters, and all they that had been of his acquaintance before, and did eat bread with him in his house: and they bemoaned him, and comforted him over all the evil that the LORD had brought upon him: every man also gave him a piece of money, and every one an earring of gold. 12 So the LORD blessed the latter end of Job more than his beginning: for he had fourteen thousand sheep, and six thousand camels, and a thousand yoke of oxen, and a thousand she asses. 13 He had also seven sons and three daughters. 14 And he called the name of the first, Jemima; and the name of the second, Kezia; and the name of the third, Keren-happuch. 15 And in all the land were no women found *so* fair as the daughters of Job: and their father gave them inheritance among their brethren. 16 After this lived Job a hundred and forty years,[44] and saw his sons, and his sons' sons, *even* four generations. 17 So Job died, *being* old and full of days.

---

42. NEB: "He looks down on all creatures, even the highest; / he is king over all proud beasts."

43. (42:3a and 4) These lines make sense only if one imagines Job reminiscing on God's earlier statements (38:2 and 3).

44. Just as Job's goods are exactly doubled, so he now lives 140 years, twice the usual lifetime of man.

Introduction to
PSALMS

"For the Lord is great, and greatly to be praised:
He is to be feared above all gods.
For all the gods of the nations are idols:
But the Lord made the heavens."

The psalms are the religious poetry of Israel. The Psalter consists of a hundred and fifty songs compiled from earlier collections. Shaped by different editors over a period of years, it took its present form between 400 and 200 B.C.

About half the poems are ascribed to King David; others are credited to Asaph, Heman, Ethan, Moses, Solomon, and the sons of Korah. The ascriptions are unreliable. While it is possible that David wrote certain of the psalms, it is more likely that editors recalled his reputation as a poet and musician and sought to add prestige to the collection by invoking his name.

The *Psalms* illustrate the repetitive quality of Hebrew poetry. Regularly, one line will repeat the thought of the preceding one:

> Blessed is the man that walketh not in the counsel
> of the ungodly,
> Nor standeth in the way of sinners.   [1:1]

Or a second line will contrast with the first:

> For the Lord knoweth the way of the righteous:
> But the way of the ungodly shall perish.   [1:6]

Or it will complete an idea or image:

> And he shall be like a tree planted by the rivers
> of water,
> That bringeth forth his fruit in his season.   [1:3]

In balanced lines, the psalmists compare their present misery to their future hopes; God's omnipotence to man's vulnerability; and the fate of the Jews with that of their enemies.

The poems in the Psalter have no identifiable order. Some psalms seem ancient and others may have been written as late as 200 B.C., but there is no chronological organization. The poems express a variety of thoughts and feelings—trust in God, love of the Law, an almost pagan appreciation of nature, a yearning for the Temple, a desire for vengeance on Israel's enemies, thanksgiving for blessings, and an awed sense of God's power and eternal command—but there is no arrangement or development of ideas.

There are recognizable kinds of psalms in the Psalter, but no one has devised a

satisfactory system for classifying them. The commentator who defines eight kinds
of psalms invariably finds that one poem falls into three categories and another fits
into none. However, most classification systems recognize individual and collective
petitions; individual and collective thanksgivings; liturgical psalms; hymns glorifying God as creator and king; pilgrim psalms, relating to the ascent to Jerusalem;
songs of Zion, expressing devotion to the holy city; wisdom psalms, meditating on
life and on the ways of God; and songs of trust.

In the following selection, each psalm is identified by type, and all these types are
represented.

PSALMS

PSALM 1

[A wisdom psalm. It introduces the Psalter by contrasting the fate of the righteous with that of the wicked, i.e., of those who reverence the words of the psalms with those who follow "the counsel of the ungodly."]

1 Blessed [1] *is* the man that walketh not in the
   counsel of the ungodly,
   Nor standeth in the way of sinners,
   Nor sitteth in the seat of the scornful.
2 But his delight *is* in the law of the LORD;
   And in his law doth he meditate day and
   night.
3 And he shall be like a tree planted by the
   rivers of water,
   That bringeth forth his fruit in his season;
   His leaf also shall not wither;
   And whatsoever he doeth shall prosper.

4 The ungodly *are* not so:
   But *are* like the chaff which the wind driveth
   away.
5 Therefore the ungodly shall not stand in the
   judgment,
   Nor sinners in the congregation of the righteous.
6 For the LORD knoweth the way of the righteous:
   But the way of the ungodly shall perish.[2]

PSALM 8

[A creation hymn, celebrating the glory of God and the God-given dignity of man. The allusions to Eden make no reference to man's fall.]

1 O LORD our Lord,
   How excellent *is* thy name in all the earth!
   Who hast set thy glory above the heavens.
2 Out of the mouth of babes and sucklings hast
   thou ordained strength
   Because of thine enemies,
   That thou mightest still the enemy and the
   avenger.[3]

3 When I consider thy heavens, the work of
   thy fingers,
   The moon and the stars, which thou hast ordained;
4 What is man, that thou art mindful of him?
   And the son of man,[4] that thou visitest him?
5 For thou hast made him a little lower than
   the angels,
   And hast crowned him with glory and honor.
6 Thou madest him to have dominion over the
   works of thy hands;
   Thou hast put all *things* under his feet:
7 All sheep and oxen,
   Yea, and the beasts of the field;
8 The fowl of the air, and the fish of the sea,
   And whatsoever passeth through the paths of
   the seas.

9 O LORD our Lord,
   How excellent *is* thy name in all the earth!

PSALM 19

[A creation hymn, praising God as the author of nature and of the Law. Probably there are two separate psalms here (1-6 and 7-14), with the second added to modify the pagan tendencies of the first.]

1 The heavens declare the glory of God;
   And the firmament showeth his handiwork.
2 Day unto day uttereth speech,
   And night unto night showeth knowledge.[5]
3 *There is* no speech nor language,
   Where their voice is not heard.
4 Their line[6] is gone out through all the earth,
   And their words to the end of the world.
   In them hath he set a tabernacle for the sun,
5 Which *is* as a bridegroom coming out of his
   chamber,
   And rejoiceth as a strong man to run a race.
6 His going forth *is* from the end of the
   heaven,
   And his circuit unto the ends of it:

---

1. MOFFATT, JB: "Happy."
2. KNOX: "They walk, the just, under the Lord's protection; the path of the wicked, how soon is it lost to sight!"
3. The text of v. 2 is corrupt, and translations differ consider-
   ably:
   TEV: "Your praise reaches up to the heavens;
         it is sung by children and babies.
         You have built a fortress against your foes
         to stop your enemies and adversaries."

NEB: "Thy majesty is praised high as the heavens!
      Out of the mouths of babes, of infants at the
         breast,
         thou hast rebuked the mighty,
      silencing enmity and vengeance to teach thy foes
         a lesson."
4. I.e., individual man. MOFFATT: "a mortal man."
5. TEV: "Each day announces it to the following day; each night repeats it to the next."
6. RSV: "yet their voice."

And there is nothing hid from the heat thereof.

7 The law of the LORD *is* perfect, converting the soul:
The testimony of the LORD *is* sure, making wise the simple.

8 The statutes of the LORD *are* right, rejoicing the heart:
The commandment of the LORD *is* pure, enlightening the eyes.

9 The fear of the LORD *is* clean, enduring for ever:
The judgments of the LORD *are* true *and* righteous altogether.

10 More to be desired *are they* than gold, yea, than much fine gold:
Sweeter also than honey and the honeycomb.

11 Moreover by them is thy servant warned:
And in keeping of them *there is* great reward.

12 Who can understand *his* errors?
Cleanse thou me from secret *faults.*

13 Keep back thy servant also from presumptuous *sins;*
Let them not have dominion over me:
Then shall I be upright,
And I shall be innocent from the great transgression.[7]

14 Let the words of my mouth, and the meditation of my heart,
Be acceptable in thy sight,
O LORD, my strength, and my redeemer.

PSALM 23

[A psalm of trust. God's care for his people is described through two images: a shepherd with his flock (1-4) and a host with his guest (5-6).]

1 The LORD *is* my shepherd; I shall not want.
2 He maketh me to lie down in green pastures:
He leadeth me beside the still waters.
3 He restoreth my soul:
He leadeth me in the paths of righteousness for his name's sake.[8]
4 Yea, though I walk through the valley of the shadow of death,
I will fear no evil: for thou *art* with me;
Thy rod and thy staff they comfort me.

---

7. NEB: "any great transgression."
8. KNOX: "as in honor pledged." MOFFATT: "as he himself is true." The assurance is that God will keep his promises.

5 Thou preparest a table before me in the presence of mine enemies:[9]
Thou anointest my head with oil; my cup runneth over.

6 Surely goodness and mercy shall follow me all the days of my life:
And I will dwell in the house of the LORD for ever.[10]

PSALM 42–43

[An individual petition. The psalmist is in the north of Palestine and yearns to make another pilgrimage to the Temple at Jerusalem, but he cannot. In one reading, he is too sick to travel. In another, he is in exile, perhaps as a slave or a prisoner of war. Either interpretation can be persuasive.]

[42]

1 As the hart panteth after the water brooks,
So panteth my soul after thee, O God.
2 My soul thirsteth for God, for the living God:
When shall I come and appear before God?
3 My tears have been my meat day and night,
While they continually say unto me, "Where *is* thy God?" [11]
4 When I remember these *things,* I pour out my soul in me:
For I had gone with the multitude, I went with them to the house of God,
With the voice of joy and praise, with a multitude that kept holyday.
5 Why art thou cast down, O my soul?
And *why* art thou disquieted in me?
Hope thou in God: for I shall yet praise him
For the help of his countenance.[12]

6 O my God, my soul is cast down within me:
Therefore will I remember thee from the land of Jordan,
And of the Hermonites, from the hill Mizar.
7 Deep calleth unto deep at the noise of thy waterspouts:
All thy waves and thy billows are gone over me.

---

9. (23:5-6) G. Ernest Wright and Reginald H. Fuller (*The Book of the Acts of God,* Doubleday, 1957) clarify the scene: "In the second part of the psalm the picture changes to a bedouin encampment in the desert. Arab hospitality is proverbial, and protection that it affords is here used as a symbol of the goodness of God. The 'I' of the psalm is now a lone fugitive in the desert."
10. NAB: "for years to come." JB: "as long as I live."
11. I.e., "Why does he fail to answer your prayers?"
12. This obscure line is reconstructed in most modern translations. NEB: "my deliverer, my God." TEV: "my Savior and my God." The KJV translation is acceptable, however: the psalmist praises God for having attended to his prayer, for turning his face toward him.

8   *Yet* the LORD will command his loving-kind-
     ness in the daytime,
     And in the night his song *shall be* with me,
     And my prayer unto the God of my life.
9   I will say unto God my rock, "Why hast thou
     forgotten me?
     Why go I mourning because of the oppres-
     sion of the enemy?"
10   *As* with a sword in my bones, mine enemies
     reproach me;
     While they say daily unto me, "Where *is* thy
     God?"
11   Why art thou cast down, O my soul?
     And why art thou disquieted within me?
     Hope thou in God: for I shall yet praise him,
     Who is the health of my countenance, and
     my God.

[43]

1   Judge me, O God, and plead my cause
     against an ungodly nation:
     O deliver me from the deceitful and unjust
     man.
2   For thou *art* the God of my strength: why
     dost thou cast me off? [13]
     Why go I mourning because of the oppres-
     sion of the enemy?
3   O send out thy light and thy truth: let them
     lead me;
     Let them bring me unto thy holy hill, and to
     thy tabernacles.
4   Then will I go unto the altar of God,
     Unto God my exceeding joy:
     Yea, upon the harp will I praise thee, O God
     my God.
5   Why art thou cast down, O my soul?
     And why art thou disquieted within me?
     Hope in God: for I shall yet praise him,
     Who is the health of my countenance, and
     my God.

PSALM 46

[A song of Zion, affirming that God's presence in the Temple
safeguards Jerusalem. The threatening elements, while they
could refer to any physical or social upheaval, seem to relate
more specifically to the apocalyptic turbulence expected in the
last days.]

1   God *is* our refuge and strength,
     A very present help in trouble.
2   Therefore will not we fear, though the earth
     be removed,
     And though the mountains be carried into
     the midst of the sea;

3   *Though* the waters thereof roar *and* be trou-
     bled,
     Though the mountains shake with the swell-
     ing thereof.

4   *There is* a river, the streams whereof shall
     make glad the city of God,
     The holy *place* of the tabernacles of the Most
     High.
5   God *is* in the midst of her; she shall not be
     moved:
     God shall help her, *and that* right early.
6   The heathen raged, the kingdoms were
     moved:
     He uttered his voice, the earth melted.
7   The LORD of hosts *is* with us;
     The God of Jacob *is* our refuge.[14]

8   Come, behold the works of the LORD,
     What desolations he hath made in the earth.
9   He maketh wars to cease unto the end of the
     earth;
     He breaketh the bow, and cutteth the spear
     in sunder;
     He burneth the chariot in the fire.
10   "Be still, and know that I *am* God:
     I will be exalted among the heathen, I will be
     exalted in the earth."
11   The LORD of hosts *is* with us;
     The God of Jacob *is* our refuge.

PSALM 69

[An individual petition. This psalm has received a variety of
interpretations. In one reading, the psalmist is a leader whose
desire for religious reforms has created antagonism. His enemies
falsely accuse him of stealing (probably from the Temple) and
claim the sickness which has fallen on him is God's punishment
for his sins.]

1   Save me, O God;
     For the waters are come in unto *my* soul.
2   I sink in deep mire, where *there is* no
     standing:
     I am come into deep waters, where the floods
     overflow me.
3   I am weary of my crying: my throat is dried:
     Mine eyes fail while I wait for my God.[15]
4   They that hate me without a cause are more
     than the hairs of mine head:
     They that would destroy me, *being* mine
     enemies wrongfully, are mighty:
     Then I restored *that* which I took not away.

---

13. NAB: "For you, O God, are my strength. / Why do you
keep me so far away?"

14. NEB: "our high stronghold." MOFFATT: "our fortress."
15. TEV: "I am worn out from calling for help, and my throat
is aching; / my eyes are strained from looking for your
help."

5   O God, thou knowest my foolishness;
    And my sins are not hid from thee.

6   Let not them that wait on thee, O Lord God
    of hosts, be ashamed for my sake:
    Let not those that seek thee be confounded
    for my sake, O God of Israel.

7   Because for thy sake I have borne reproach;
    Shame hath covered my face.

8   I am become a stranger unto my brethren,
    And an alien unto my mother's children.

9   For the zeal of thine house hath eaten me up;
    And the reproaches of them that reproached
    thee are fallen upon me.

10 When I wept, *and chastened* my soul with
    fasting,
    That was to my reproach.

11 I made sackcloth also my garment;
    And I became a proverb to them.

12 They that sit in the gate speak against me;
    And I *was* the song of the drunkards.

13 But as for me, my prayer *is* unto thee, O
    Lord, *in* an acceptable time:[16]
    O God, in the multitude of thy mercy hear
    me, in the truth of thy salvation.

14 Deliver me out of the mire, and let me not
    sink:
    Let me be delivered from them that hate me,
    and out of the deep waters.

15 Let not the waterflood overflow me,
    Neither let the deep swallow me up,
    And let not the pit shut her mouth upon
    me.

16 Hear me, O Lord; for thy loving-kindness *is*
    good:
    Turn unto me according to the multitude of
    thy tender mercies.

17 And hide not thy face from thy servant;
    For I am in trouble: hear me speedily.

18 Draw nigh unto my soul, *and* redeem it:
    Deliver me because of mine enemies.

19 Thou hast known my reproach, and my
    shame, and my dishonor:
    Mine adversaries *are* all before thee.

20 Reproach hath broken my heart; and I am
    full of heaviness:
    And I looked *for some* to take pity, but *there
    was* none;
    And for comforters, but I found none.

21 They gave me also gall for my meat;
    And in my thirst they gave me vinegar to
    drink.[17]

22 Let their table become a snare before them:

And *that which should have been* for *their*
welfare,[18] *let it become* a trap.

23 Let their eyes be darkened, that they see not;
    And make their loins continually to shake.

24 Pour out thine indignation upon them,
    And let thy wrathful anger take hold of
    them.

25 Let their habitation be desolate;
    And let none dwell in their tents.

26 For they persecute *him* whom thou hast
    smitten;
    And they talk to the grief of those whom
    thou hast wounded.

27 Add iniquity unto their iniquity:
    And let them not come into thy righteous-
    ness.

28 Let them be blotted out of the book of the
    living,
    And not be written with the righteous.

29 But I *am* poor and sorrowful:
    Let thy salvation, O God, set me up on high.

30 I will praise the name of God with a song,
    And will magnify him with thanksgiving.

31 *This* also shall please the Lord better than
    an ox
    Or bullock that hath horns and hoofs.

32 The humble shall see *this, and* be glad:
    And your heart shall live that seek God.

33 For the Lord heareth the poor,
    And despiseth not his prisoners.

34 Let the heaven and earth praise him,
    The seas, and every thing that moveth
    therein.

35 For God will save Zion,
    And will build the cities of Judah:
    That they may dwell there, and have it in
    possession.

36 The seed also of his servants shall inherit it:
    And they that love his name shall dwell
    therein.

PSALM 90

[A collective petition. It compares the brevity and frustration of
human life with the eternal grandeur of God, then prays for the
deliverance of Israel.]

1   Lord, thou has been our dwelling place in all
    generations.

2   Before the mountains were brought forth,
    Or ever thou hadst formed the earth and the
    world,

---

16. NAB: "for the time of your favor."
17. This verse is recalled in the crucifixion scene in all four gos-
    pels. See *Mark* 15:36.
18. This ambiguous phrase has received varying translations.
    RSV: "their sacrificial feasts." JB: "their plentiful supplies."
    TEV: "their celebrations." Smith: "their peace offerings."

Even from everlasting to everlasting, thou *art*
God.

3 Thou turnest man to destruction;
And sayest, "Return, ye children of men." [19]
4 For a thousand years in thy sight
Are but as yesterday when it is past,
And *as* a watch in the night.
5 Thou carriest them away as with a flood;
they are *as* a sleep:[20]
In the morning *they are* like grass *which*
groweth up.
6 In the morning it flourisheth, and groweth
up;
In the evening it is cut down, and withereth.
7 For we are consumed by thine anger,
And by thy wrath are we troubled.

8 Thou hast set our iniquities before thee,
Our secret *sins* in the light of thy countenance.
9 For all our days are passed away in thy
wrath:
We spend our years as a tale *that is told.*
10 The days of our years *are* threescore years
and ten;
And if by reason of strength *they be* fourscore years,
Yet *is* their strength labor and sorrow;
For it is soon cut off, and we fly away.
11 Who knoweth the power of thine anger?
Even according to thy fear, *so is* thy wrath.[21]
12 So teach *us* to number our days,
That we may apply *our* hearts unto wisdom.

13 Return, O LORD, how long?
And let it repent thee concerning thy servants.
14 O satisfy us early with thy mercy;
That we may rejoice and be glad all our
days.
15 Make us glad according to the days *wherein*
thou hast afflicted us,
And the years *wherein* we have seen evil.
16 Let thy work appear unto thy servants,
And thy glory unto their children.
17 And let the beauty of the LORD our God be
upon us:
And establish thou the work of our hands
upon us;

Yea, the work of our hands establish thou
it.[22]

PSALM 91

[A wisdom psalm, describing the protection and kindness which
the Lord gives to the faithful. The final verses (14-16), God's response to the prayer, were probably recited by a temple priest.]

1 He that dwelleth in the secret place of the
Most High
Shall abide under the shadow of the Almighty.
2 I [23] will say of the LORD, "*He is* my refuge
and my fortress:
My God; in him will I trust."
3 Surely he shall deliver thee from the snare of
the fowler,
And from the noisome pestilence.[24]
4 He shall cover thee with his feathers,
And under his wings shalt thou trust:
His truth *shall be thy* shield and buckler.
5 Thou shalt not be afraid for the terror by
night;
Nor for the arrow *that* flieth by day;
6 *Nor* for the pestilence *that* walketh in darkness;
Nor for the destruction *that* wasteth at noonday.
7 A thousand shall fall at thy side,
And ten thousand at thy right hand;
But it shall not come nigh thee.
8 Only with thine eyes shalt thou behold
And see the reward of the wicked.[25]
9 Because thou hast made the LORD, *which is*
my refuge,
Even the Most High, thy habitation;
10 There shall no evil befall thee,
Neither shall any plague come nigh thy
dwelling.
11 For he shall give his angels charge over thee,
To keep thee in all thy ways.
12 They shall bear thee up in *their* hands,
Lest thou dash thy foot against a stone.
13 Thou shalt tread upon the lion and adder:
The young lion and the dragon shalt thou
trample under feet.

---

19. TEV: "You tell men to return to what they were; / you
change them back to soil."
20. The Hebrew text is obscure. JB: "You brush men away like
waking dreams." NAB: "You make an end of them in their
sleep."
21. The text is probably corrupt. TEV: "Who knows what fear
your fury can bring?" NEB: "who feels thy wrath like those
that fear thee?"

22. NAB speculates that the last line is "an accidental repetition." But other sources note its rhetorical effectiveness.
KNOX: "Prosper our doings, Lord, prosper our doings yet."
23. To avoid pronoun confusion, most translations make the
"He" of v. 1 the subject of this sentence. Similarly, in v. 9,
"my" refuge is changed to "thy" or "your" refuge.
24. This passage, taken with vv. 6 and 7, suggest the psalmist is
referring to some current epidemic.
25. NEB: "With your own eyes you shall see all this; / you
shall watch the punishment of the wicked."

14 "Because he hath set his love upon me,
       therefore will I deliver him:
    I will set him on high, because he hath
       known my name.
15 He shall call upon me, and I will answer
       him:
    I *will be* with him in trouble;
    I will deliver him, and honor him.
16 With long life will I satisfy him,
    And show him my salvation."

PSALM 96

[A hymn celebrating God's kingship. The faithful proclaim the
coming of the Lord to rule the world; they invite pagan nations
and all created things to join in a song of praise.]

1   O sing unto the LORD a new song:
    Sing unto the LORD, all the earth.
2   Sing unto the LORD, bless his name;
    Show forth his salvation from day to day.
3   Declare his glory among the heathen,
    His wonders among all people.
4   For the LORD *is* great, and greatly to be
       praised:
    He *is* to be feared above all gods.
5   For all the gods of the nations *are* idols:
    But the LORD made the heavens.
6   Honor and majesty *are* before him:
    Strength and beauty *are* in his sanctuary.

7   Give unto the LORD, O ye kindreds of the
       people,
    Give unto the LORD glory and strength.
8   Give unto the LORD the glory *due unto* his
       name:
    Bring an offering, and come into his courts.
9   O worship the LORD in the beauty of holi-
       ness:[26]
    Fear before him, all the earth.
10 Say among the heathen *that* the LORD reign-
       eth:
    The world also shall be established that it
       shall not be moved:
    He shall judge the people righteously.

11 Let the heavens rejoice, and let the earth be
       glad;
    Let the sea roar, and the fulness thereof.
12 Let the field be joyful, and all that *is* therein:
    Then shall all the trees of the wood rejoice
13 Before the LORD: for he cometh,
    For he cometh to judge the earth:

He shall judge the world with righteousness,
And the people with his truth.

PSALM 115

[A liturgical hymn of praise. RSV suggests vv. 1-2 and 9-11 were
sung by a choir; 3-8, by a soloist; 12-13, by the congregation;
14-15, by a priest; and 16-18, by everyone present.]

1   Not unto us, O LORD, not unto us,
    But unto thy name give glory,
    For thy mercy, *and* for thy truth's sake.
2   Wherefore should the heathen say,
    "Where *is* now their God?" [27]

3   But our God *is* in the heavens:
    He hath done whatsoever he hath pleased.
4   Their idols *are* silver and gold,
    The work of men's hands.
5   They have mouths, but they speak not:
    Eyes have they, but they see not:
6   They have ears, but they hear not:
    Noses have they, but they smell not:
7   They have hands, but they handle not:
    Feet have they, but they walk not:
    Neither speak they through their throat.
8   They that make them are like unto them;
    So is every one that trusteth in them.

9   O Israel,[28] trust thou in the LORD:
    He *is* their help and their shield.
10 O house of Aaron, trust in the LORD:
    He *is* their help and their shield.
11 Ye that fear the LORD, trust in the LORD:
    He *is* their help and their shield.

12 The LORD hath been mindful of us: he will
       bless *us;*
    He will bless the house of Israel;
    He will bless the house of Aaron.
13 He will bless them that fear the LORD,
    Both small and great.

14 The LORD shall increase you more and more,
    You and your children.
15 Ye *are* blessed of the LORD
    Which made heaven and earth.

16 The heaven, *even* the heavens, *are* the
       LORD's:
    But the earth hath he given to the children of
       men.

---

26. The reference can be either to a general attitude of
    reverence or to garments befitting the ceremony. TEV:
    "Bow down before the Holy One when he appears."
    MOFFATT: "Kneel before God in sacred vestments."

27. MOFFATT: "Why should pagans sneer / 'Where is that God
    of theirs?' "
28. (115:9-11) "Israel," "house of Aaron," and "Ye that fear the
    Lord" refer, respectively, to the laity of Israelite birth, the
    priests, and converts to Judaism.

17 The dead praise not the LORD,
    Neither any that go down into silence.
18 But we[29] will bless the LORD
    From this time forth and for evermore.
    Praise the LORD.

PSALM 118

[A collective thanksgiving. Though the psalmist speaks as an individual (vv. 5-18), he seems to be describing the plight and deliverance of the Jewish nation.]

1   O give thanks unto the LORD; for *he is* good:
    Because his mercy *endureth* for ever.
2   Let Israel now say,
    That his mercy *endureth* for ever.
3   Let the house of Aaron now say,
    That his mercy *endureth* for ever.
4   Let them now that fear the LORD say,
    That his mercy *endureth* for ever.

5   I called upon the LORD in distress:
    The LORD answered me, *and set me* in a large place.[30]
6   The LORD *is* on my side; I will not fear:
    What can man do unto me?
7   The LORD taketh my part with them that help me:
    Therefore shall I see *my desire* upon them that hate me.
8   *It is* better to trust in the LORD
    Than to put confidence in man.
9   *It is* better to trust in the LORD
    Than to put confidence in princes.

10 All nations compassed me about:
    But in the name of the LORD will I destroy them.
11 They compassed me about; yea, they compassed me about:
    But in the name of the LORD I will destroy them.
12 They compassed me about like bees;
    They are quenched as the fire of thorns:
    For in the name of the LORD I will destroy them.
13 Thou hast thrust sore at me that I might fall:[31]
    But the LORD helped me.
14 The LORD *is* my strength and song,
    And is become my salvation.

15 The voice of rejoicing and salvation *is* in the tabernacles of the righteous:
    The right hand of the LORD doeth valiantly.
16 The right hand of the LORD is exalted:
    The right hand of the LORD doeth valiantly.
17 I shall not die, but live,
    And declare the works of the LORD.
18 The LORD hath chastened me sore:
    But he hath not given me over unto death.

19 Open to me the gates of righteousness:[32]
    I will go into them, *and* I will praise the LORD:
20 This gate of the LORD,
    Into which the righteous shall enter.

21 I will praise thee: for thou hast heard me,
    And art become my salvation.
22 The stone *which* the builders refused
    Is become the head *stone* of the corner.[33]
23 This is the LORD's doing;
    It *is* marvelous in our eyes.

24 This *is* the day *which* the LORD hath made;
    We will rejoice and be glad in it.
25 Save now, I beseech thee, O LORD:
    O LORD, I beseech thee, send now prosperity.
26 Blessed *be* he that cometh in the name of the LORD:
    We have blessed you out of the house of the LORD.
27 God *is* the LORD, which hath showed us light:
    Bind the sacrifice with cords,
    Even unto the horns of the altar.

28 Thou *art* my God, and I will praise thee:
    Thou art my God, I will exalt thee.
29 O give thanks unto the LORD; for *he is* good:
    For his mercy *endureth* for ever.

PSALM 121

[A pilgrim psalm. Probably recited by Jews pilgrimaging to Jerusalem, the poem refers to the many dangers and difficulties of the journey: the steep hills which contained bandits, the dangerous precipices where a foot might slip, the heat of the sun, and the contamination which spread itself at night.]

---

29. NEB, TEV: "we, the living."
30. RSV, TEV, NEB: "set me free."
31. The confusing "Thou" is omitted in all modern translations. NEB: "They thrust hard against me so that I nearly fall." JB: "I was pressed, pressed, about to fall."

32. (118:19-29) This seems to be a dramatic dialogue between the psalmist who wishes to enter the temple and the priests within. It is difficult to establish which lines are said by whom, but vv. 20 and 24-27 seem to come from the priests.
33. The stone rejected for building purposes which later becomes a cornerstone is Israel. In the New Testament, the verse is applied to Christ. See *Mark* 12:10.

1 I will lift up mine eyes unto the hills,
From whence cometh my help.[34]

2 My help *cometh* from the LORD,
Which made heaven and earth.

3 He will not suffer thy foot to be moved:
He that keepeth thee will not slumber.

4 Behold, he that keepeth Israel
Shall neither slumber nor sleep.

5 The LORD *is* thy keeper:
The LORD *is* thy shade upon thy right hand.

6 The sun shall not smite thee by day,
Nor the moon by night.

7 The LORD shall preserve thee from all evil:
He shall preserve thy soul.

8 The LORD shall preserve thy going out and
thy coming in
From this time forth, and even for evermore.

PSALM 128

[A wisdom psalm celebrating the domestic happiness which God gives those who serve him.]

1 Blessed *is* every one that feareth the LORD;
That walketh in his ways.

2 For thou shalt eat the labor of thine hands:
Happy *shalt* thou *be, and it shall be* well with thee.

3 Thy wife *shall be* as a fruitful vine
By the sides of thine house:
Thy children like olive plants
Round about thy table.

4 Behold, that thus shall the man be blessed
That feareth the LORD.

5 The LORD shall bless thee out of Zion:
And thou shalt see the good of Jerusalem
All the days of thy life.

6 Yea, thou shalt see thy children's children,
And peace upon Israel.

PSALM 130

[An individual petition. The psalmist admits his sins, yet trusts in the Lord. He suggests that Israel should adopt the same attitude.]

1 Out of the depths have I cried unto thee, O LORD.

2 Lord, hear my voice:
Let thine ears be attentive
To the voice of my supplications.

3 If thou, LORD, shouldest mark iniquities,
O Lord, who shall stand?

4 But *there is* forgiveness with thee,
That thou mayest be feared.[35]

5 I wait for the LORD, my soul doth wait,
And in his word do I hope.

6 My soul *waiteth* for the Lord
More than they that watch for the morning:
I say, more than they that watch for the morning.

7 Let Israel hope in the LORD:
For with the LORD *there is* mercy,
And with him *is* plenteous redemption.

8 And he shall redeem Israel
From all his iniquities.

PSALM 137

[A collective petition recalling the fall of Jerusalem and the Babylonian exile and invoking God's vengeance on the enemies of Israel.]

1 By the rivers of Babylon,
There we sat down, yea, we wept,
When we remembered Zion.

2 We hanged our harps
Upon the willows in the midst thereof.

3 For there[36] they that carried us away captive
required of us a song;
And they that wasted us *required of us* mirth,
saying,
"Sing us *one* of the songs of Zion."

4 How shall we sing the LORD's song
In a strange land?

5 If I forget thee, O Jerusalem,
Let my right hand forget *her cunning.*

6 If I do not remember thee,
Let my tongue cleave to the roof of my
mouth;
If I prefer not Jerusalem
Above my chief joy.

7 Remember, O LORD, the children of Edom
In the day of Jerusalem;
Who said, "Rase *it,* rase *it,*

---

34. Excepting KNOX, all modern translations read this line as a rhetorical question. JB: "Where is help to come from?" The rest of the psalm answers the question.

35. (130:3-4) MOFFATT:
> "If thou didst keep strict tally of sins,
> O Lord, who could live on?
> But thou hast pardon,
> that thou mayest be worshipped."

36. (137:2-3) The words "in the midst thereof" and "there" refer to Babylon. The psalmist, though no longer in Babylon, has not yet returned to his homeland.

Even to the foundation thereof." [37]

8 O daughter of Babylon, who art to be destroyed;
Happy *shall he be,* that rewardeth thee
As thou hast served us.

9 Happy *shall he be,* that taketh and dasheth
Thy little ones against the stones.[38]

PSALM 139

[An individual petition. After acknowledging God's omniscience, the psalmist pleads to be delivered from his enemies.]

1 O Lord, thou hast searched me, and known *me.*

2 Thou knowest my downsitting and mine uprising;
Thou understandest my thought afar off.

3 Thou compassest my path and my lying down,
And art acquainted *with* all my ways.

4 For *there is* not a word in my tongue,
But, lo, O Lord, thou knowest it altogether.

5 Thou hast beset me behind and before,
And laid thine hand upon me.

6 *Such* knowledge *is* too wonderful for me;
It is high, I cannot *attain* unto it.

7 Whither shall I go from thy Spirit?
Or whither shall I flee from thy presence?

8 If I ascend up into heaven, thou *art* there:
If I make my bed in hell, behold, thou *art* there.

9 *If* I take the wings of the morning,
And dwell in the uttermost parts of the sea;[39]

10 Even there shall thy hand lead me,
And thy right hand shall hold me.

11 If I say, "Surely the darkness shall cover me";
Even the night shall be light about me.

12 Yea, the darkness hideth not from thee;
But the night shineth as the day:
The darkness and the light *are* both alike *to thee.*

13 For thou hast possessed my reins:

Thou hast covered me in my mother's womb.[40]

14 I will praise thee; for I am fearfully *and* wonderfully made:
Marvelous *are* thy works;
And *that* my soul knoweth right well.

15 My substance was not hid from thee
When I was made in secret,
And curiously wrought in the lowest parts of the earth.[41]

16 Thine eyes did see my substance, yet being unperfect;
And in thy book all *my members* were written,
Which in continuance were fashioned,
When *as yet there was* none of them.

17 How precious also are thy thoughts unto me, O God!
How great is the sum of them!

18 *If* I should count them, they are more in number than the sand:
When I awake, I am still with thee.[42]

19 Surely thou wilt slay the wicked, O God:
Depart from me therefore, ye bloody men.

20 For they speak against thee wickedly,
And thine enemies take *thy name* in vain.

21 Do not I hate them, O Lord, that hate thee?
And am not I grieved with those that rise up against thee?

22 I hate them with perfect hatred:
I count them mine enemies.

23 Search me, O God, and know my heart:
Try me, and know my thoughts:

24 And see if *there be any* wicked way in me,
And lead me in the way everlasting.[43]

PSALM 150

[A hymn of praise. Every living being is called to join in a symphony of praise to the accompaniment of temple instruments of music.]

1 Praise ye the Lord.
Praise God in his sanctuary:
Praise him in the firmament of his power.[44]

37. NEB:
"Remember, O Lord, against the people of Edom
the day of Jerusalem's fall,
when they said, 'Down with it, down with it,
down to its very foundations!' "
The Edomites helped the Babylonians sack Jerusalem in 587 B.C.

38. JB: "A blessing on him who takes and dashes / your babies against the rock!"

39. The reference is to distant extremes: to the sun rising in the east and to the Mediterranean Sea extending to the west.

40. NEB: "Thou it was who didst fashion my inward parts; / thou didst knit me together in my mother's womb."

41. This figurative language relates the womb to the soil where seeds are brought to life. Knox: "in the dark recesses of the earth." JB: "in the limbo of the womb."

42. NAB: "did I reach the end of them, I should still be with you." Completing a preliminary survey of God's thoughts, the psalmist would find an infinitude of divine attributes still before him.

43. Knox: "lead me in the ways of old." NEB: "guide me in the ancient ways."

2 Praise him for his mighty acts:
   Praise him according to his excellent greatness.

3 Praise him with the sound of the trumpet:
   Praise him with the psaltery and harp.

44. TEV: "Praise God in his temple! / Praise his strength in
    heaven!"

4 Praise him with the timbrel and dance:
   Praise him with stringed instruments and
   organs.
5 Praise him upon the loud cymbals:
   Praise him upon the high sounding cymbals.

6 Let every thing that hath breath praise the
   LORD.
   Praise ye the LORD.

Introduction to
ECCLESIASTES

"That which is far off, and exceeding deep, who can find it out?"

Ecclesiastes is a Greek translation of the Hebrew *Koheleth*, meaning "the preacher." Writing about 200 B.C., the Preacher recalled the ideals and frustrations of his full life and spoke with qualified cynicism on the meaning of human experience. For him, life is sad, determined, absurd, and even enjoyable.

In the opening lines, Koheleth identifies himself with King Solomon, who had a reputation for wisdom. This identification gave immediate status to the book, but Solomon's authorship is seldom seriously defended. After the second chapter, the Preacher makes no reference to this literary role.

From the text itself, the author emerges as an aging cosmopolitan Jew, a man of wide experience. His world-weariness pervades the book: "Vanity of vanities . . . vanity of vanities; all is vanity." He finds all human activities aimless, fruitless, and transitory: "I have seen all the works that are done under the sun; and, behold, all is vanity and vexation of spirit." For "vexation of spirit," RSV reads "a striving after wind."

Such sentiments are expressed in poetry, aphorisms, and maxims. The poem which begins the book (1:1-11) shows the futility of life, both through its imagery and by the repetitious movement of the lines. The same pattern reinforces the determinism of the famous passage "a time to be born and a time to die" (3:1-8). And the poem on old age (11:7–12:8) captures the *carpe diem* spirit in original imagery and moving cadence.

The Preacher offers many aphorisms—i.e., succinct generalizations based on personal experience. Some seem trite:

> If the iron be blunt
> And he do not whet the edge,
> Then must he put to more strength:
> But wisdom is profitable to direct.   [10:10]

Some are poignant:

> For in much wisdom is much grief:
> And he that increaseth knowledge increaseth sorrow.   [1:18]

And some express a tragic finality:

> That which is crooked cannot be made straight:
> And that which is wanting cannot be numbered.   [1:15]

143

Koheleth's maxims—i.e., direct injunctions governing moral conduct—are usually straightforward:

> Be not hasty in thy spirit to be angry:
> For anger resteth in the bosom of fools.   [7:9]

A few seem ironic:

> Cast thy bread upon the waters:
> For thou shalt find it after many days.   [11:1]

But all advise the audience how to make the most of this precarious, futile life. The Preacher urges them to enjoy their work, to eat and drink with gladness, to seek good companionship, and to refrain from extremes in anything. Above all, he advises young people to rejoice in their youth. Koheleth's maxims are appropriate from one who recognizes the "vanity" of things:

> Go thy way, eat thy bread with joy,
> And drink thy wine with a merry heart;
> For God now accepteth thy works.
> Let thy garments be always white;
> And let thy head lack no ointment.
> Live joyfully with the wife whom thou lovest all
> the days of the life of thy vanity, which he hath
> given thee under the sun, all the days of thy vanity.   [9:7-9]

Though the central message of *Ecclesiastes* is clear, the ideas lack orderly arrangement. The observations seem flawed by repetition, discontinuity, and contradiction. The lack of unity and of consistent development led Gustav Bickell (*Der Prediger über den Wert des Deseins*, 1884) to speculate that Koheleth's pages were first altered by an editor, then put in confused order through an accident, and finally subjected to further retouching. More likely, other factors contributed to the disorder. It seems evident that the Preacher included in his work proverbs and quotations from other sources. Moreover, he sometimes differed from himself. On this, Robert Gordis (*Koheleth—The Man and His World*, 1955) makes an important judgment: "The contradictions that troubled earlier readers are, in part, normal variations in temper and mood and, in part, the consequence of his clear-sighted recognition that no one, not even he, has a monopoly on truth. These contrasting passages are not among the least of Koheleth's charms."

Many of the contradictions in *Ecclesiastes*, however, derive from editorial additions to the original text. Koheleth's observations concerning man's determined and fruitless life deviated too much from the tenets of Judaism to escape orthodox attention. For example, between 3:16 (which says that the wicked prosper in this world) and 3:18 (which declares that man and beast have the same fatal destiny), an editor inserted a verse promising that "God shall judge the righteous and the wicked." (Other interpolations are indicated in footnotes to the text.) The most disturbing addition occurs at the end of the book, where the editors added six verses, blunting the Preacher's indictment with the sardonic reflection that "of making many books there is no end" [12:12] and with a devout summary: "Let us hear the conclusion of the whole matter: Fear God, and keep his commandments: for this is the whole duty of man" [12:13].

It is wrong to interpret *Ecclesiastes* as an orthodox statement of religious views, and it is equally wrong to read it as a totally cynical and pessimistic book. Koheleth does recognize a God, though one beyond man's reach and comprehension ("God is in heaven, and thou upon earth; therefore let thy words be few" [5:2]). And amid his more somber observations, he reminds his audience that there is a time to plant, a time to heal, a time to build, a time to dance, and a time to love. No nihilist, he knows that "a living dog is better than a dead lion" [9:4].

ECCLESIASTES

1 The words of the Preacher, the son of David, king in Jerusalem.

2   Vanity of vanities, saith the Preacher,
       Vanity of vanities; all *is* vanity.

PROLOGUE

3   What profit hath a man of all his labor
       Which he taketh under the sun?
4   *One* generation passeth away, and *another*
       generation cometh:
       But the earth abideth for ever.
5   The sun also ariseth, and the sun goeth
       down,
       And hasteth to his place where he arose.
6   The wind goeth toward the south,
       And turneth about unto the north;
       It whirleth about continually,
       And the wind returneth again according
       to his circuits.
7   All the rivers run into the sea;
       Yet the sea *is* not full:
       Unto the place from whence the rivers
       come,
       Thither they return again.
8   All things *are* full of labor;
       Man cannot utter *it:*[1]
       The eye is not satisfied with seeing,
       Nor the ear filled with hearing.
9   The thing that hath been,
       It *is that* which shall be;
       And that which is done *is* that which shall
       be done:
       And *there is* no new *thing* under the
       sun.
10   Is there *any* thing whereof it may be
       said,
       "See, this *is* new"?
       It hath been already of old time,
       Which was before us.
11   *There is* no remembrance of former
       things;
       Neither shall there be *any* remembrance
       of *things* that are to come
       With *those* that shall come after.

KOHELETH'S INVESTIGATION OF LIFE

12 I the Preacher was king over Israel in Jerusalem. 13 And I gave my heart to seek and search out by wisdom concerning all *things* that are done under heaven: this sore travail hath God given to the sons of man to be exercised therewith. 14 I have seen all the works that are done under the sun; and, behold, all *is* vanity and vexation of spirit.

15   *That which is* crooked cannot be made
       straight:
       And that which is wanting cannot be
       numbered.

16 I communed with mine own heart, saying, "Lo, I am come to great estate, and have gotten more wisdom than all *they* that have been before me in Jerusalem: yea, my heart had great experience of wisdom and knowledge." 17 And I gave my heart to know wisdom, and to know madness and folly: I perceived that this also is vexation of spirit.

18   For in much wisdom *is* much grief:
       And he that increaseth knowledge increaseth sorrow.

The Pleasures of a King

2 I said in mine heart, "Go to now, I will prove thee with mirth; therefore enjoy pleasure": and, behold, this also *is* vanity. 2 I said of laughter, "*It is* mad": and of mirth, "What doeth it?" 3 I sought in mine heart to give myself unto wine, yet acquainting mine heart with wisdom; and to lay hold on folly, till I might see what *was* that good for the sons of men, which they should do under the heaven all the days of their life. 4 I made me great works; I builded me houses; I planted me vineyards: 5 I made me gardens and orchards, and I planted trees in them of all *kind of* fruits: 6 I made me pools of water, to water therewith the wood that bringeth forth trees: 7 I got *me* servants and maidens, and had servants born in my house; also I had great possessions of great and small cattle above all that were in Jerusalem before me: 8 I gathered me also silver and gold, and the peculiar treasure of kings and of the provinces: I gat me men singers and women singers, and the delights of the sons of men, *as* musical instruments, and that of all sorts.[2] 9 So I was great, and increased more than all that were before me in Jerusalem: also my wisdom remained with me. 10 And whatsoever mine eyes desired I kept not from them, I withheld not my

---

1. MOFFATT: "All things are aweary, weary beyond words."

2. RSV: "I got singers, both men and women, and many concubines, man's delight." The passage (4-9) describes Solomon.

heart from any joy; for my heart rejoiced in all my labor: and this was my portion of all my labor. 11 Then I looked on all the works that my hands had wrought, and on the labor that I had labored to do: and, behold, all *was* vanity and vexation of spirit, and *there was* no profit under the sun.

The Labors of a Man

12 And I turned myself to behold wisdom, and madness, and folly: for what *can* the man *do* that cometh after the king? *even* that which hath been already done. 13 Then I saw that wisdom excelleth folly, as far as light excelleth darkness. 14   The wise man's eyes *are* in his head;
But the fool walketh in darkness:
and I myself perceived also that one event happeneth to them all. 15 Then said I in my heart, "As it happeneth to the fool, so it happeneth even to me; and why was I then more wise?" Then I said in my heart, that this also *is* vanity. 16 For *there is* no remembrance of the wise more than of the fool for ever; seeing that which now *is* in the days to come shall all be forgotten. And how dieth the wise *man?* as the fool. 17 Therefore I hated life; because the work that is wrought under the sun *is* grievous unto me: for all *is* vanity and vexation of spirit.

18 Yea, I hated all my labor which I had taken under the sun: because I should leave it unto the man that shall be after me. 19 And who knoweth whether he shall be a wise *man* or a fool? yet shall he have rule over all my labor wherein I have labored, and wherein I have showed myself wise under the sun. This *is* also vanity. 20 Therefore I went about to cause my heart to despair of all the labor which I took under the sun. 21 For there is a man whose labor *is* in wisdom, and in knowledge, and in equity; yet to a man that hath not labored therein shall he leave it *for* his portion. This also *is* vanity and a great evil. 22 For what hath man of all his labor, and of the vexation of his heart, wherein he hath labored under the sun? 23 For all his days *are* sorrows, and his travail grief; yea, his heart taketh not rest in the night. This is also vanity.

24 *There is* nothing better for a man, *than* that he should eat and drink, and *that* he should make his soul enjoy good in his labor. This also I saw, that it *was* from the hand of God. 25 For who can eat, or who else can hasten *hereunto,* more than I? 26 For *God* giveth to a man that *is* good in his sight, wisdom, and knowledge, and joy: but to the sinner he giveth travail, to gather and to heap up, that he may give to *him that is* good

before God.[3] This also *is* vanity and vexation of spirit.

A Season for Everything

3   To every *thing there is* a season,
And a time to every purpose under the heaven:

2   A time to be born, and a time to die;
A time to plant, and a time to pluck up *that which is* planted;

3   A time to kill; and a time to heal;
A time to break down, and a time to build up;

4   A time to weep, and a time to laugh;
A time to mourn, and a time to dance;

5   A time to cast away stones, and a time to gather stones together;[4]
A time to embrace, and a time to refrain from embracing;

6   A time to get, and a time to lose;
A time to keep, and a time to cast away;

7   A time to rend, and a time to sew;
A time to keep silence, and a time to speak;

8   A time to love, and a time to hate;
A time of war, and a time of peace.

OBSERVATIONS

On Time

9 What profit hath he that worketh in that wherein he laboreth? 10 I have seen the travail, which God hath given to the sons of men to be exercised in it. 11 He hath made every *thing* beautiful in his time: also he hath set the world in their heart, so that no man can find out the work that God maketh from the beginning to the end.[5] 12 I know that *there is* no good in them, but for *a man* to rejoice, and to do good in his life. 13 And also that every man should eat and drink, and enjoy the good of all his labor, it *is* the gift of God. 14 I know that, whatsoever God doeth, it shall be for ever: nothing can be put to it, nor any

---

3. A pious interpolation, affirming the doctrine of divine retribution.
4. The Midrash Qoheleth Rabbah explains casting away and gathering stones as a metaphor for sexual indulgence and abstinence. More likely this is a general reference to occasions for exuberance and for restraint.
5. This means that God has given men capacity to contemplate time and space, but that the gift is not sufficient to provide meaningful answers. Translations differ. RSV: "he has put eternity into man's mind"; RSV (alternative reading): "he has put obscurity in man's mind"; MOFFATT: "for the mind of man he has appointed mystery"; NAB: ". . . has put the timeless into their hearts."

thing taken from it: and God doeth *it*, that *men* should fear before him. 15 That which hath been is now; and that which is to be hath already been; and God requireth that which is past.[6]

On Death

16 And moreover I saw under the sun the place of judgment, *that* wickedness *was* there; and the place of righteousness, *that* iniquity *was* there. 17 I said in mine heart, "God shall judge the righteous and the wicked: for *there is* a time there for every purpose and for every work." 18 I said in mine heart concerning the estate of the sons of men, that God might manifest them, and that they might see that they themselves are beasts. 19 For that which befalleth the sons of men befalleth beasts; even one thing befalleth them: as the one dieth, so dieth the other; yea, they have all one breath; so that a man hath no preeminence above a beast: for all *is* vanity. 20 All go unto one place; all are of the dust, and all turn to dust again. 21 Who knoweth the spirit of man that goeth upward, and the spirit of the beast that goeth downward to the earth?[7] 22 Wherefore I perceive that *there is* nothing better, than that a man should rejoice in his own works; for that *is* his portion: for who shall bring him to see what shall be after him?

On Position and Companionship

4 So I returned, and considered all the oppressions that are done under the sun: and behold the tears of *such as were* oppressed, and they had no comforter; and on the side of their oppressors *there was* power; but they had no comforter. 2 Wherefore I praised the dead which are already dead, more than the living which are yet alive. 3 Yea, better *is he* than both they, which hath not yet been, who hath not seen the evil work that is done under the sun.

4 Again, I considered all travail, and every right work, that for this a man is envied of his neighbor. This *is* also vanity and vexation of spirit.
5   The fool foldeth his hands together,
        And eateth his own flesh.[8]
6   Better *is* a handful *with* quietness,
        Than both the hands full *with* travail and
        vexation of spirit.

7 Then I returned, and I saw vanity under the sun.

8 There is one *alone*, and *there is* not a second; yea, he hath neither child nor brother: yet *is there* no end of all his labor; neither is his eye satisfied with riches; neither *saith he*, "For whom do I labor, and bereave my soul of good?" This *is* also vanity, yea, it *is* a sore travail. 9 Two *are* better than one; because they have a good reward for their labor. 10 For if they fall, the one will lift up his fellow: but woe to him *that is* alone when he falleth; for *he hath* not another to help him up. 11 Again, if two lie together, then they have heat: but how can one be warm *alone?* 12 And if one prevail against him, two shall withstand him; and a threefold cord is not quickly broken.

13 Better *is* a poor and a wise child, than an old and foolish king, who will no more be admonished. 14 For out of prison he cometh to reign; whereas also *he that is* born in his kingdom becometh poor. 15 I considered all the living which walk under the sun, with the second child that shall stand up in his stead. 16 *There is* no end of all the people, *even* of all that have been before them: they also that come after shall not rejoice in him.[9] Surely this also *is* vanity and vexation of spirit.

On Worship

5 Keep thy foot when thou goest to the house of God, and be more ready to hear, than to give the sacrifice of fools: for they consider not that they do evil. 2 Be not rash with thy mouth, and let not thine heart be hasty to utter *any* thing before God: for God *is* in heaven, and thou upon earth: therefore let thy words be few.
3   For a dream cometh through the multi-
        tude of business;
        And a fool's voice *is known* by multitude
        of words.
4 When thou vowest a vow unto God, defer not to pay it; for *he hath* no pleasure in fools: pay that which thou hast vowed. 5 Better *is it* that thou shouldest not vow, than that thou shouldest vow and not pay. 6 Suffer not thy mouth to cause thy flesh to sin; neither say thou before the angel, that it *was* an error: wherefore should God be angry at thy voice, and destroy the work of thine hands? 7 For in the multitude of dreams and many words *there are* also *divers* vanities: but fear thou God.

---

6. NEB: "and God summons each event back in its turn."
7. Koheleth's attitude toward death is agnostic. See 9:3 and 12:7.
8. This appears to be an interpolation. Verses 4 and 6 both reject the busy, industrious life.

9. (4:13-16) A difficult passage, again stressing the uselessness of seeking after fame. The king who rose from childhood obscurity will be replaced by a "second child" (i.e., a youth from a similar background), and the glory of the new king will also pass.

8 If thou seest the oppression of the poor, and violent perverting of judgment and justice in a province, marvel not at the matter: for *he that is* higher than the highest regardeth; and *there be* higher than they. 9 Moreover the profit of the earth is for all: the king *himself* is served by the field.[10]

On Wealth

10 He that loveth silver shall not be satisfied with silver; nor he that loveth abundance with increase: this *is* also vanity. 11 When goods increase, they are increased that eat them: and what good *is there* to the owners thereof, saving the beholding *of them* with their eyes? 12 The sleep of a laboring man *is* sweet, whether he eat little or much: but the abundance of the rich will not suffer him to sleep.

13 There is a sore evil *which* I have seen under the sun, *namely,* riches kept for the owners thereof to their hurt. 14 But those riches perish by evil travail: and he begetteth a son, and *there is* nothing in his hand. 15 As he came forth of his mother's womb, naked shall he return to go as he came, and shall take nothing of his labor, which he may carry away in his hand. 16 And this also *is* a sore evil, *that* in all points as he came, so shall he go: and what profit hath he that hath labored for the wind? 17 All his days also he eateth in darkness, and *he hath* much sorrow and wrath with his sickness.

18 Behold *that* which I have seen: *it is* good and comely *for one* to eat and to drink, and to enjoy the good of all his labor that he taketh under the sun all the days of his life, which God giveth him: for it *is* his portion. 19 Every man also to whom God hath given riches and wealth, and hath given him power to eat thereof, and to take his portion, and to rejoice in his labor; this *is* the gift of God. 20 For he shall not much remember the days of his life;[11] because God answereth *him* in the joy of his heart.

6 There is an evil which I have seen under the sun, and it *is* common among men: 2 A man to whom God hath given riches, wealth, and honor, so that he wanteth nothing for his soul of all that he desireth, yet God giveth him not power to eat thereof, but a stranger eateth it: this *is* vanity, and it *is* an evil disease. 3 If a man beget a hundred *children,* and live many years, so that the days of his years be many, and his soul be not filled with good, and also *that* he have no burial; I say, *that* an untimely birth *is* better than he.[12] 4 For he cometh in with vanity, and departeth in darkness, and his name shall be covered with darkness. 5 Moreover he hath not seen the sun, ŋor known *any thing:* this hath more rest than the other. 6 Yea, though he live a thousand years twice *told,* yet hath he seen no good: do not all go to one place?

7   All the labor of man *is* for his mouth,
     And yet the appetite is not filled.[13]

8 For what hath the wise more than the fool? what hath the poor, that knoweth to walk before the living? 9 Better *is* the sight of the eyes than the wandering of the desire: this *is* also vanity and vexation of spirit.

10 That which hath been is named already, and it is known that it *is* man: neither may he contend with him that is mightier than he. 11 Seeing there be many things that increase vanity, what *is* man the better? 12 For who knoweth what *is* good for man in *this* life, all the days of his vain life which he spendeth as a shadow? for who can tell a man what shall be after him under the sun?

On Wisdom and Folly

7   A good name *is* better than precious oint-
     ment;
     And the day of death than the day of
     one's birth.
2   *It is* better to go to the house of mourning,
     Than to go to the house of feasting:
     For that *is* the end of all men;
     And the living will lay *it* to his heart.
3   Sorrow *is* better than laughter:
     For by the sadness of the countenance the
     heart is made better.
4   The heart of the wise *is* in the house of
     mourning;
     But the heart of fools *is* in the house of
     mirth.
5   *It is* better to hear the rebuke of the wise,
     Than for a man to hear the song of
     fools.
6   For as the crackling of thorns under a pot,
     So *is* the laughter of the fool:
     This also *is* vanity.
7   Surely oppression maketh a wise man
     mad;

10. MOFFATT: "after all, a country prospers with a king who has control."
11. NAB: "For he will hardly dwell on the shortness of his life."
12. NAB: "the child born dead is more fortunate than he." The comparison is with the man of riches who lacks the capacity to enjoy them. Koheleth urges men to use and relish the transitory goods which earth provides.
13. Another interpolation, suggesting that man is created for higher purposes.

And a gift destroyeth the heart.[14]

8   Better *is* the end of a thing than the begin-
     ning thereof:
     And the patient in spirit *is* better than the
     proud in spirit.
9   Be not hasty in thy spirit to be angry:
     For anger resteth in the bosom of fools.

10 Say not thou, "What is *the cause* that the
former days were better than these?" for thou
dost not inquire wisely concerning this.
11   Wisdom *is* good with an inheritance:[15]
      And *by it there is* profit to them that see
      the sun.
12 For wisdom *is* a defense, *and* money *is* a
defense: but the excellency of knowledge *is, that*
wisdom giveth life to them that have it. 13 Consider the work of God: for who can make *that*
straight, which he hath made crooked? 14 In the
day of prosperity be joyful, but in the day of ad-
versity consider: God also hath set the one over
against the other, to the end that man should find
nothing after him.

15 All *things* have I seen in the days of my
vanity: there is a just *man* that perisheth in his
righteousness, and there is a wicked *man* that
prolongeth *his life* in his wickedness. 16 Be not
righteous over much, neither make thyself over
wise: why shouldest thou destroy thyself? 17 Be
not over much wicked, neither be thou foolish:
why shouldest thou die before thy time? 18 *It is*
good that thou shouldest take hold of this; yea,
also from this withdraw not thine hand: for he
that feareth God shall come forth of them all.
19 Wisdom strengtheneth the wise more than
ten mighty *men* which are in the city. 20 For
there is not a just man upon earth, that doeth
good, and sinneth not. 21 Also take no heed
unto all words that are spoken; lest thou hear thy
servant curse thee: 22 For oftentimes also thine
own heart knoweth that thou thyself likewise hast
cursed others.

23 All this have I proved by wisdom: I said, "I
will be wise"; but it *was* far from me. 24 That
which is far off, and exceeding deep, who can find
it out? 25 I applied mine heart to know, and to
search, and to seek out wisdom, and the reason *of
things,* and to know the wickedness of folly, even
of foolishness *and* madness: 26 And I find more

bitter than death the woman, whose heart *is*
snares and nets, *and* her hands *as* bands: whoso
pleaseth God shall escape from her; but the
sinner shall be taken by her. 27 "Behold, this
have I found," saith the Preacher, "*counting* one
by one, to find out the account; 28 Which yet
my soul seeketh, but I find not: one man among a
thousand have I found; but a woman among all
those have I not found. 29 Lo, this only have I
found, that God hath made man upright; but
they have sought out many inventions." [16]

8 Who *is* as the wise *man?* and who knoweth the
interpretation of a thing?
      A man's wisdom maketh his face to shine,
      And the boldness of his face shall be
      changed.
2 I *counsel thee* to keep the king's commandment,
and *that* in regard of the oath of God. 3 Be not
hasty to go out of his sight: stand not in an evil
thing; for he doeth whatsoever pleaseth him.
4 Where the word of a king *is, there is* power: and
who may say unto him, "What doest thou?"
5 Whoso keepeth the commandment shall feel no
evil thing: and a wise man's heart discerneth both
time and judgment. 6 Because to every purpose
there is time and judgment, therefore the misery
of man *is* great upon him. 7 For he knoweth not
that which shall be: for who can tell him when it
shall be? 8 *There is* no man that hath power over
the spirit to retain the spirit; neither *hath he*
power in the day of death: and *there is* no dis-
charge in *that* war; neither shall wickedness deliver those that are given to it. 9 All this have I
seen, and applied my heart unto every work that
is done under the sun: *there is* a time wherein one
man ruleth over another to his own hurt.

On Retribution and Reward

10 And so I saw the wicked buried, who had
come and gone from the place of the holy, and
they were forgotten in the city where they had so
done: this *is* also vanity. 11 Because sentence
against an evil work is not executed speedily,
therefore the heart of the sons of men is fully set
in them to do evil. 12 Though a sinner do evil a
hundred times, and his *days* be prolonged, yet
surely I know that it shall be well with them that
fear God, which fear before him: 13 But it shall
not be well with the wicked, neither shall he

---

14. Translations of this passage differ. RSV: "Surely oppression
makes the wise man foolish, and a bribe corrupts the mind."
NEB: "Slander drives a wise man crazy and breaks a strong
man's spirit." JB: "For laughter makes a fool of the wise
man and merriment corrupts his heart."

15. Moffatt: "Wisdom is as good as an inheritance."

16. NEB: "God, when he made man, made him straightforward, but man invents endless subtleties of his own."
Probably this is an editorial interpolation protesting vv.
16-18 and 20, where Koheleth urges moral compromise.
The succeeding verses (8:1-9) also recommend compromise.

prolong *his* days, *which are* as a shadow; because he feareth not before God.[17]

14 There is a vanity which is done upon the earth; that there be just *men,* unto whom it happeneth according to the work of the wicked; again, there be wicked *men,* to whom it happeneth according to the work of the righteous: I said that this also *is* vanity. 15 Then I commended mirth, because a man hath no better thing under the sun, than to eat, and to drink, and to be merry: for that shall abide with him of his labor the days of his life, which God giveth him under the sun.

16 When I applied mine heart to know wisdom, and to see the business that is done upon the earth:[18] (for also *there is that* neither day nor night seeth sleep with his eyes:) 17 Then I beheld all the work of God, that a man cannot find out the work that is done under the sun: because though a man labor to seek *it* out, yet he shall not find *it;* yea further; though a wise *man* think to know *it,* yet shall he not be able to find *it.*

9 For all this I considered in my heart even to declare all this, that the righteous, and the wise, and their works, *are* in the hand of God: no man knoweth either love or hatred *by* all *that is* before them. 2 All *things come* alike to all: *there is* one event to the righteous, and to the wicked; to the good and to the clean, and to the unclean; to him that sacrificeth, and to him that sacrificeth not: as *is* the good, so *is* the sinner; *and* he that sweareth, as *he* that feareth an oath. 3 This *is* an evil among all *things* that are done under the sun, that *there is* one event unto all: yea, also the heart of the sons of men is full of evil, and madness *is* in their heart while they live, and after that *they go* to the dead.

4 For to him that is joined to all the living there is hope: for a living dog is better than a dead lion. 5 For the living know that they shall die: but the dead know not any thing, neither have they any more a reward; for the memory of them is forgotten. 6 Also their love, and their hatred, and their envy, is now perished; neither have they any more a portion for ever in any *thing* that is done under the sun.

7 Go thy way, eat thy bread with joy,
And drink thy wine with a merry heart;
For God now accepteth thy works.

8 Let thy garments be always white;

And let thy head lack no ointment.
9 Live joyfully with the wife whom thou lovest all the days of the life of thy vanity, which he hath given thee under the sun, all the days of thy vanity: for that *is* thy portion in *this* life, and in thy labor which thou takest under the sun. 10 Whatsoever thy hand findeth to do, do *it* with thy might; for *there is* no work, nor device, nor knowledge, nor wisdom, in the grave, whither thou goest.

11 I returned, and saw under the sun, that the race *is* not to the swift, nor the battle to the strong, neither yet bread to the wise, nor yet riches to men of understanding, nor yet favor to men of skill; but time and chance happeneth to them all. 12 For man also knoweth not his time: as the fishes that are taken in an evil net, and as the birds that are caught in the snare; so *are* the sons of men snared in an evil time, when it falleth suddenly upon them.

13 This wisdom have I seen also under the sun, and it *seemed* great unto me: 14 *There was* a little city, and few men within it; and there came a great king against it, and besieged it, and built great bulwarks against it. 15 Now there was found in it a poor wise man, and he by his wisdom delivered the city; yet no man remembered that same poor man. 16 Then said I, "Wisdom *is* better than strength": nevertheless the poor man's wisdom *is* despised, and his words are not heard.[19]

17 The words of wise *men are* heard in quiet more than the cry of him that ruleth among fools. 18 Wisdom *is* better than weapons of war: but one sinner destroyeth much good.

10 Dead flies cause the ointment of the apothecary to send forth a stinking savor: *so doth* a little folly him that is in reputation for wisdom *and* honor. 2 A wise man's heart *is* at his right hand; but a fool's heart at his left. 3 Yea also, when he that is a fool walketh by the way, his wisdom faileth *him,* and he saith to every one *that* he *is* a fool.

On Prudence

4 If the spirit of the ruler rise up against thee,

---

17. (8:11-13) Between vv. 10 and 14, which say that just men suffer and evil men prosper, the editor inserts an orthodox statement of rewards and retribution.

18. Knox: "Should I cudgel my wits to grow wise, and know the meaning of all earth's tasks."

19. (9:13-16) The story illustrates that a poor man gains no fame, however wise he is. But the details of the story can be read in two different ways. RSV: "he by his wisdom delivered the city. Yet no one remembered that poor man." NEB: "he alone might have saved the town by his wisdom, but no one remembered that poor wise man."

Leave not thy place;
For yielding pacifieth great offenses.

5   There is an evil *which* I have seen under
the sun,
As an error *which* proceedeth from the
ruler:

6   Folly is set in great dignity,
And the rich sit in low place.

7   I have seen servants upon horses,
And princes walking as servants upon the
earth.

8   He that diggeth a pit shall fall into it;
And whoso breaketh a hedge, a serpent
shall bite him.

9   Whoso removeth stones shall be hurt
therewith;
And he that cleaveth wood shall be endangered thereby.[20]

10 If the iron be blunt,
And he do not whet the edge,
Then must he put to more strength:
But wisdom *is* profitable to direct.

11 Surely the serpent will bite without enchantment;
And a babbler is no better.

12 The words of a wise man's mouth *are* gracious;
But the lips of a fool will swallow up himself.

13 The beginning of the words of his mouth
is foolishness:
And the end of his talk *is* mischievous
madness.

14 A fool also is full of words:
A man cannot tell what shall be;
And what shall be after him, who can tell
him?

15 The labor of the foolish wearieth every
one of them,
Because he knoweth not how to go to the
city.[21]

16 Woe to thee, O land, when thy king *is* a
child,

And thy princes eat in the morning!

17 Blessed *art* thou, O land, when thy king *is*
the son of nobles,
And thy princes eat in due season,
For strength, and not for drunkenness!

18 By much slothfulness the building decayeth;
And through idleness of the hands the
house droppeth through.

19 A feast is made for laughter,
And wine maketh merry:

But money answereth all *things*.

20 Curse not the king, no not in thy thought;
And curse not the rich in thy bedchamber:
For a bird of the air shall carry the
voice,
And that which hath wings shall tell the
matter.

11 Cast thy bread upon the waters:
For thou shalt find it after many days.

2   Give a portion to seven, and also to eight;
For thou knowest not what evil shall be
upon the earth.[22]

3   If the clouds be full of rain,
They empty *themselves* upon the earth:
And if the tree fall toward the south, or
toward the north,
In the place where the tree falleth, there it
shall be.

4   He that observeth the wind shall not sow;
And he that regardeth the clouds shall not
reap.

5   As thou knowest not what *is* the way of
the spirit,
Nor how the bones *do grow* in the womb
of her that is with child:
Even so thou knowest not the works of
God
Who maketh all.

6   In the morning sow thy seed,
And in the evening withhold not thine
hand:
For thou knowest not whether shall prosper, either this or that,
Or whether they both *shall be* alike good.

On Youth and Age

7   Truly the light *is* sweet,
And a pleasant *thing it is* for the eyes to
behold the sun:

8   But if a man live many years,
And rejoice in them all;
Yet let him remember the days of darkness;
For they shall be many.
All that cometh *is* vanity.

9   Rejoice, O young man, in thy youth;
And let thy heart cheer thee in the days of
thy youth,
And walk in the ways of thine heart,
And in the sight of thine eyes:
But know thou, that for all these *things*

---

20. (10:7-9) Every occupation has its attendant danger.
21. NEB: "The fool wearies himself to death with all his labour,
for he does not know the way to town."

22. I.e., invest your money in several concerns so that, if one
fails, you will not lose everything. The point of vv. 1-6 is
that, even in a determined universe, man must act with
prudence.

God will bring thee into judgment.[23]

10   Therefore remove sorrow from thy heart,
And put away evil from thy flesh:
For childhood and youth *are* vanity.

12   Remember now thy Creator in the days of
thy youth,
While the evil days come not,
Nor the years draw nigh, when thou shalt
say,
"I have no pleasure in them";

2   While the sun, or the light, or the moon,
Or the stars, be not darkened,
Nor the clouds return after the rain:

3   In the day when the keepers of the house
shall tremble,
And the strong men shall bow themselves,
And the grinders cease because they are
few,
And those that look out of the windows
be darkened,

4   And the doors shall be shut in the streets,
When the sound of the grinding is low,
And he shall rise up at the voice of the
bird,
And all the daughters of music shall be
brought low;[24]

5   Also *when* they shall be afraid of *that
which is* high,
And fears *shall be* in the way,
And the almond tree shall flourish,
And the grasshopper shall be a burden,
And desire shall fail:
Because man goeth to his long home,

And the mourners go about the streets:

6   Or ever the silver cord be loosed,
Or the golden bowl be broken,
Or the pitcher be broken at the fountain,
Or the wheel broken at the cistern.

7   Then shall the dust return to the earth as
it was:
And the spirit shall return unto God who
gave it.[25]

8   Vanity of vanities, saith the Preacher;
All *is* vanity.

EPILOGUE

9 And moreover, because the Preacher was
wise, he still taught the people knowledge; yea, he
gave good heed, and sought out, *and* set in order
many proverbs. 10 The Preacher sought to find
out acceptable words: and *that which was* written
was upright, *even* words of truth. 11 The words
of the wise *are* as goads, and as nails fastened *by*
the masters of assemblies, *which* are given from
one shepherd.

12 And further, by these, my son, be admonished: of making many books *there is* no end; and
much study *is* a weariness of the flesh. 13 Let us
hear the conclusion of the whole matter: Fear
God, and keep his commandments: for this *is* the
whole *duty* of man. 14 For God shall bring every
work into judgment, with every secret thing,
whether *it be* good, or whether *it be* evil.[26]

---

23. Clearly, these two lines are a pious interpolation.
24. The reference is to musical notes, which the aging man can
no longer hear distinctly. KNOX: "and all the echoes of
music faint."

25. In IB, O. S. Rankin explains: "The *spirit* is the breath of life
which goes back to the source from which it came. Koheleth
does not mean that man's personality continues to exist."
26. (12:9-14) It seems clear that two editors are commenting on
the observations of Koheleth. The first (9-11) expresses
praise; the second (12-14), orthodox reserve.

Introduction to
THE SONG OF SONGS

"How fair and how pleasant art thou, O love, for delights!"

In *Of Education*, John Milton specified that poetry is "simple, sensuous, and passionate." No poem satisfies this definition better than *The Song of Songs*.

The work is an anthology of love lyrics composed over the centuries and collected by an unknown editor in the third century B.C. It has been attributed to King Solomon because *I Kings* 4:32 boasts that he wrote 1005 songs. This attribution led to the book's admission to the Hebrew canon, but scholars no longer credit Solomon's authorship. Actually "The Song of Songs, which is Solomon's" is better read to mean "the greatest of all songs, which is about Solomon."

The book seems out of place in a collection of sacred writings. It appears to have no religious or moral dimension: God is never mentioned in it. In extravagant imagery, it presents attitudes toward nature which seem more appropriate to a fertility deity than to Yahweh. The young man is described as a roe, a young hart, gold, ivory, pillars, an apple tree. The maiden's charms are honey, lilies, fruit, spices, wine. Acts of love are presented in terms of drinking, eating, and gathering flowers. ("My beloved is gone down into his garden, to the bed of spices, / To feed in the gardens, and to gather lilies" [6:2].) The season is spring. With sensuous metaphor, *The Song of Songs* celebrates physical love in a manner foreign to Scripture.

It is possible to read the poem as an allegory. It found a place in the canon, largely because Jews could identify the youth with Yahweh and the maiden with the nation Israel. This interpretation followed the lead of the prophet Hosea, who described the relationship between Yahweh and Israel as a marriage. Christians have read the book as a depiction of Christ and the church. Bernard of Clairvaux and other mystics felt the work defined the rapport between Christ and the individual believer. (The dream passages, 3:1-4 and 5:2-7, are favorites of all such allegorists.)

Modern readers tend to agree with Norman K. Gottwald (*A Light to the Nations*, Harper & Row, 1959), who scorns any allegorical interpretation: "The result of such mitigation of the plain meaning of the poems is a sickly religious eroticism far more objectionable than the healthy emotions expressed by the poet." And many who reject allegory still draw a religious meaning from the work. J. Coert Rylaarsdam observes: "What impresses the thoughtful reader of the Song of Solomon is that its composers respected nature, notably as expressed in human beings. . . . Its respect for life is expressed in the savoring of it; and it is this that makes it a very important commentary on the meaning of the confession that God is the Creator of all things." *

* In Volume 10 of the *Layman's Bible Commentary* (*Proverbs, Ecclesiastes, Song of Solomon*), John Knox Press, 1964.

Though *The Song of Songs* appears to be twenty-five or thirty independent poems unified solely by their theme, some commentators have sought a further unity. They note the frequent repetition of words and phrases which suggest that the same person is speaking at different points in the book. Observing the number and gender of pronouns, they infer that certain passages are directed to particular persons and that some of the passages seem to respond to others. On such evidence, they have been able to find a dramatic movement in the poem.

The dramatic framework, though subject to many variations, takes two main forms. In one reading, King Solomon has brought a Shulamite maiden from her rustic home to become his bride at Jerusalem; the lovers praise each other at length. In the other reading, Solomon has brought the maiden to Jerusalem, but she remains faithful to the shepherd she loves; in the end the King returns her to the shepherd, and true love prevails. Neither form is finally satisfying.

In the text which follows, passages are arranged to support the first reading. Following the pattern of the *Interpreter's Bible*, individual speeches are assigned to the Maiden, the Youth, and the Citizens of Jerusalem—sometimes specifically, the Daughters of Jerusalem. Following the divisions of the *Jerusalem Bible*, the book is presented as six poems, each poem recording a completed love experience. Headnotes explain the dramatic movement. This arrangement—intended to make the lyrics more intelligible and enjoyable—is, of course, but one of many ways to read *The Song of Songs*.

THE SONG OF SONGS

FIRST POEM

[Having been brought to Solomon's court, the village maiden speaks to the court ladies and awaits the king's arrival. When he enters, the two praise each other and express their love.]

1 The Song of songs, which *is* Solomon's.

THE MAIDEN

2 Let him kiss me with the kisses of his mouth:
For thy love *is* better than wine.

3 Because of the savor of thy good ointments
Thy name *is as* ointment poured forth,
Therefore do the virgins love thee.

4 Draw me, we will run after thee:
The King hath brought me into his chambers:

THE DAUGHTERS OF JERUSALEM
We will be glad and rejoice in thee,
We will remember thy love more than wine:
The upright love thee.

THE MAIDEN

5 I *am* black, but comely, O ye daughters of Jerusalem,
As the tents of Kedar,
As the curtains of Solomon.

6 Look not upon me, because I *am* black,
Because the sun hath looked upon me:
My mother's children were angry with me;
They made me the keeper of the vineyards;
But mine own vineyard have I not kept.

7 Tell me, O thou whom my soul loveth,
Where thou feedest, where thou makest *thy flock* to rest at noon:
For why should I be as one that turneth aside[1]
By the flocks of thy companions?

THE DAUGHTERS OF JERUSALEM

8 If thou know not, O thou fairest among women,
Go thy way forth by the footsteps of the flock,
And feed thy kids beside the shepherds' tents.

THE YOUTH

9 I have compared thee, O my love,
To a company of horses in Pharaoh's chariots.

10 Thy cheeks are comely with rows *of jewels,*
Thy neck with chains *of gold.*[2]

THE DAUGHTERS OF JERUSALEM

11 We will make thee borders of gold
With studs of silver.

THE MAIDEN

12 While the King *sitteth* at his table,
My spikenard sendeth forth the smell thereof.[3]

13 A bundle of myrrh *is* my well-beloved unto me;
He shall lie all night betwixt my breasts.

14 My beloved *is* unto me *as* a cluster of camphire
In the vineyards of En-gedi.

THE YOUTH

15 Behold, thou *art* fair, my love; behold, thou *art* fair;
Thou *hast* doves' eyes.

THE MAIDEN

16 Behold, thou *art* fair, my beloved, yea, pleasant:
Also our bed *is* green.

17 The beams of our house *are* cedar,
And our rafters of fir.[4]

2 I *am* the rose of Sharon,[5]
And the lily of the valleys.

THE YOUTH

2 As the lily among thorns,
So *is* my love among the daughters.

THE MAIDEN

3 As the apple tree among the trees of the wood,
So *is* my beloved among the sons.
I sat down under his shadow with great delight,

---

1. Because many of the words used are rare in Biblical Hebrew, the poems are sometimes hard to translate. Compare readings of this passage. KJV: "For why should I be as one that turneth aside"; RSV: "for why should I be like one who wanders"; MEEK: "for why should I be like one veiled"; JB: "That I may no more wander like a vagabond"; NEB: "that I may not be left picking lice."

2. (1:9-10) NAB footnotes, "The bridegroom compares the girl's beauty to the rich adornment of the royal chariot of Pharoah."

3. Spikenard is a precious perfume. MOFFATT: "When my king lies on his diwan, my charms breathe out their fragrance."

4. (1:16-17) These lines could refer to a site in the open woods. More probably they refer to a structure especially made for the consummation of a marriage.

5. NEB: "I am an asphodel in Sharon."

And his fruit *was* sweet to my taste.
4 He brought me to the banqueting house,
And his banner over me *was* love.
5 Stay me with flagons, comfort me with apples:
For I *am* sick of love.[6]
6 His left hand *is* under my head,
And his right hand doth embrace me.

7 I charge you, O ye daughters of Jerusalem,
By the roes, and by the hinds of the field,
That ye stir not up, nor awake *my* love,
Till he please.[7]

SECOND POEM

[Still in court, the maiden recalls when the king visited her home in the spring and they walked abroad. As he left, she urged him to return soon. In his absence, her vivid dreams reflected her yearning for him.]

THE MAIDEN
8 The voice of my beloved! behold, he cometh
Leaping upon the mountains, skipping upon the hills.
9 My beloved is like a roe or a young hart:
Behold, he standeth behind our wall,
He looketh forth at the windows,
Showing himself through the lattice.
10 My beloved spake, and said unto me,
"Rise up, my love, my fair one, and come away.
11 For, lo, the winter is past,
The rain is over *and* gone;
12 The flowers appear on the earth;
The time of the singing *of birds* is come,
And the voice of the turtle is heard in our land;
13 The fig tree putteth forth her green figs,
And the vines *with* the tender grape give a *good* smell.
Arise, my love, my fair one, and come away.
14 O my dove, *that art* in the clefts of the rock, in the secret *places* of the stairs,
Let me see thy countenance, let me hear thy voice;
For sweet *is* thy voice, and thy countenance *is* comely.
15 Take us the foxes,
The little foxes, that spoil the vines:
For our vines *have* tender grapes." [8]

16 My beloved *is* mine, and I *am* his:
He feedeth among the lilies.
17 Until the day break, and the shadows flee away,
Turn, my beloved,
And be thou like a roe or a young hart
Upon the mountains of Bether.

3 By night on my bed I sought him whom my soul loveth:
I sought him, but I found him not.
2 I will rise now, and go about the city
In the streets, and in the broad ways
I will seek him whom my soul loveth:
I sought him, but I found him not.
3 The watchmen that go about the city found me:
To whom I said, "Saw ye him whom my soul loveth?"
4 *It was* but a little that I passed from them,
But I found him whom my soul loveth:
I held him, and would not let him go,
Until I had brought him into my mother's house,
And into the chamber of her that conceived me.

5 I charge you, O ye daughters of Jerusalem,
By the roes, and by the hinds of the field,
That ye stir not up, nor awake *my* love,
Till he please.

THIRD POEM

[Citizens of Jerusalem comment on the royal procession which brings the king to his bride. Thereafter he praises the charms of the maiden, and she invites him to love. He greets her at a wedding feast the following morning.]

THE CITIZENS OF JERUSALEM
6 Who *is* this that cometh out of the wilderness like pillars of smoke,
Perfumed with myrrh and frankincense,
With all powders of the merchant?

7 Behold his bed, which *is* Solomon's;[9]
Threescore valiant men *are* about it,
Of the valiant of Israel.
8 They all hold swords, *being* expert in war:
Every man *hath* his sword upon his thigh
Because of fear in the night.

---

6. MOFFATT: "Sustain me with raisins,/revive me with apples,/for I swoon with love!"
7. This passage, which occurs following the act of love, is repeated exactly in 3:5 and substantially in 8:4.
8. RSV calls this an isolated fragment: "Apparently an allusion to what would spoil the luxuriance of love."

J. Coert Rylaarsdam (*The Proverbs, Ecclesiastes, The Song of Solomon,* 1964) concludes, "No really satisfactory interpretation of verse 15 seems to exist."
9. NEB: "Look; it is Solomon carried in his litter."

9 King Solomon made himself a chariot
    Of the wood of Lebanon.
10 He made the pillars thereof *of* silver,
    The bottom thereof *of* gold,
    The covering of it *of* purple,
    The midst thereof being paved *with* love,[10]
    For the daughters of Jerusalem.
11 Go forth, O ye daughters of Zion, and
    behold king Solomon
    With the crown wherewith his mother
    crowned him
    In the day of his espousals,
    And in the day of the gladness of his heart.

THE YOUTH

4 Behold, thou *art* fair, my love; behold, thou
    art fair;
    Thou *hast* doves' eyes within thy locks:
    Thy hair *is* as a flock of goats, that appear
    from mount Gilead.
2 Thy teeth *are* like a flock *of sheep that are
    even* shorn, which came up from the wash-
    ing;
    Whereof every one bear twins, and none *is*
    barren among them.
3 Thy lips *are* like a thread of scarlet, and thy
    speech *is* comely:
    Thy temples *are* like a piece of a pomegran-
    ate within thy locks.
4 Thy neck *is* like the tower of David
    Builded for an armory,
    Whereon there hang a thousand bucklers, all
    shields of mighty men.
5 Thy two breasts *are* like two young roes that
    are twins,
    Which feed among the lilies.
6 Until the day break, and the shadows flee
    away,
    I will get me to the mountain of myrrh, and
    to the hill of frankincense.
7 Thou *art* all fair, my love; *there is* no spot in
    thee.

8 Come with me from Lebanon; *my* spouse,
    with me from Lebanon:
    Look from the top of Amana, from the top of
    Shenir and Hermon,
    From the lions' dens, from the mountains of
    the leopards.

9 Thou hast ravished my heart, my sister,[11] *my*
    spouse;

10. RSV: "it was lovingly wrought within by the daughters of
Jerusalem." NEB: "and its lining was of leather." JB: "the
back was inlaid with ebony."
11. In Egyptian love poetry, the maiden was often called
"sister."

    Thou hast ravished my heart with one of
    thine eyes,
    With one chain of thy neck.
10 How fair is thy love, my sister, *my* spouse!
    How much better is thy love than, wine!
    And the smell of thine ointments than all
    spices!
11 Thy lips, O *my* spouse, drop *as* the honey-
    comb:
    Honey and milk *are* under thy tongue;
    And the smell of thy garments *is* like the
    smell of Lebanon.

12 A garden inclosed *is* my sister, *my* spouse;
    A spring shut up, a fountain sealed.
13 Thy plants *are* an orchard of pomegranates,
    with pleasant fruits;
    Camphire, with spikenard,
14 Spikenard and saffron;
    Calamus and cinnamon, with all trees of
    frankincense;
    Myrrh and aloes, with all the chief spices:
15 A fountain of gardens, a well of living
    waters,
    And streams from Lebanon.

THE MAIDEN

16 Awake, O north wind; and come, thou
    south;
    Blow upon my garden, *that* the spices thereof
    may flow out.
    Let my beloved come into his garden,
    And eat his pleasant fruits.

THE YOUTH

5 I am come into my garden, my sister, *my*
    spouse:
    I have gathered my myrrh with my spice;
    I have eaten my honeycomb with my honey;
    I have drunk my wine with my milk:
    Eat, O friends; drink, yea, drink abundantly,
    O beloved.

FOURTH POEM

[In court, the maiden comments on her lover's absence and
describes her yearning dreams. Her description of him is so
glowing that the court ladies offer to help her seek him.
Thereafter, the lovers are reunited, and he praises her beauty.]

THE MAIDEN

2 I sleep, but my heart waketh:
    It is the voice of my beloved that knocketh,
    saying,
    "Open to me, my sister, my love, my dove,
    my undefiled:
    For my head is filled with dew,
    And my locks with the drops of the night."

3 I have put off my coat; how shall I put it
   on?
   I have washed my feet; how shall I defile
   them?
4 My beloved put in his hand by the hole *of the
   door,*
   And my bowels were moved for him.[12]
5 I rose up to open to my beloved;
   And my hands dropped *with* myrrh,
   And my fingers *with* sweet smelling myrrh,
   Upon the handles of the lock.
6 I opened to my beloved;
   But my beloved had withdrawn himself, *and*
   was gone:
   My soul failed when he spake:
   I sought him, but I could not find him;
   I called him, but he gave me no answer.
7 The watchmen that went about the city
   found me,
   They smote me, they wounded me;
   The keepers of the walls took away my veil
   from me.

8 I charge you, O daughters of Jerusalem,
   If ye find my beloved, that ye tell him,
   That I *am* sick of love.

THE DAUGHTERS OF JERUSALEM
9 What *is* thy beloved more than *another*
   beloved, O thou fairest among women?
   What *is* thy beloved more than *another*
   beloved, that thou dost so charge us?

THE MAIDEN
10 My beloved *is* white and ruddy,
    The chiefest among ten thousand.
11 His head *is as* the most fine gold;
    His locks *are* bushy, *and* black as a raven:
12 His eyes *are as the eyes* of doves by the rivers
    of waters,
    Washed with milk, *and* fitly set:
13 His cheeks *are as* a bed of spices, *as* sweet
    flowers:
    His lips *like* lilies, dropping sweet smelling
    myrrh:
14 His hands *are as* gold rings set with the
    beryl:
    His belly *is as* bright ivory overlaid *with*
    sapphires:
15 His legs *are as* pillars of marble, set upon
    sockets of fine gold:
    His countenance *is* as Lebanon, excellent as
    the cedars:
16 His mouth *is* most sweet: yea, he *is* alto-
    gether lovely.

12. RSV: "My beloved put his hand to the latch, and my heart
    was thrilled within me."

This *is* my beloved, and this *is* my friend, O
daughters of Jerusalem.

THE DAUGHTERS OF JERUSALEM
6 Whither is thy beloved gone, O thou fairest
   among women?
   Whither is thy beloved turned aside? that we
   may seek him with thee.

THE MAIDEN
2 My beloved is gone down into his garden, to
   the beds of spices,
   To feed in the gardens, and to gather
   lilies.
3 I *am* my beloved's, and my beloved *is* mine:
   He feedeth among the lilies.

THE YOUTH
4 Thou *art* beautiful, O my love, as Tirzah,
   Comely as Jerusalem,
   Terrible as *an army* with banners.
5 Turn away thine eyes from me, for they have
   overcome me:
   Thy hair *is* as a flock of goats that appear
   from Gilead:
6 Thy teeth *are* as a flock of sheep which go up
   from the washing,
   Whereof every one beareth twins, and *there
   is* not one barren among them.
7 As a piece of a pomegranate *are* thy temples
   within thy locks.
8 There are threescore queens, and fourscore
   concubines,
   And virgins without number.
9 My dove, my undefiled is *but* one;
   She *is* the *only* one of her mother,
   She *is* the choice *one* of her that bare her.
   The daughters saw her, and blessed her;
   Yea, the queens and the concubines, and
   they praised her.
10 "Who *is* she *that* looketh forth as the morn-
    ing,
    Fair as the moon, clear as the sun,
    And terrible as *an army* with banners?"

FIFTH POEM

[As the maiden walks in Solomon's gardens, the court ladies ask
her to dance before them. As she does, the king praises her
exposed beauty. At her invitation, they go forth into the fields.]

THE MAIDEN
11 I went down into the garden of nuts
    To see the fruits of the valley,
    And to see whether the vine flourished, *and*
    the pomegranates budded.
12 Or ever I was aware,

My soul made me *like* the chariots of Ammi-nadib.[13]

THE DAUGHTERS OF JERUSALEM

13 Return, return, O Shulamite;
Return, return, that we may look upon thee.

THE YOUTH

What will ye see in the Shulamite?
As it were the company of two armies.[14]

7 How beautiful are thy feet with shoes, O prince's daughter!
The joints of thy thighs *are* like jewels,
The work of the hands of a cunning work-man.

2 Thy navel *is like* a round goblet, *which* want-eth not liquor:
Thy belly *is like* a heap of wheat set about with lilies.

3 Thy two breasts *are* like two young roes *that are* twins.

4 Thy neck *is* as a tower of ivory;
Thine eyes *like* the fishpools in Heshbon, by the gate of Bath-rabbim:
Thy nose *is* as the tower of Lebanon which looketh toward Damascus.

5 Thine head upon thee *is* like Carmel,
And the hair of thine head like purple;
The King *is* held in the galleries.[15]

6 How fair and how pleasant art thou, O love, for delights!

7 This thy stature is like to a palm tree,
And thy breasts to clusters *of grapes.*

8 I said, "I will go up to the palm tree,
I will take hold of the boughs thereof":
Now also thy breasts shall be as clusters of the vine,
And the smell of thy nose like apples;

9 And the roof of thy mouth like the best wine[16]
For my beloved, that goeth *down* sweetly,
Causing the lips of those that are asleep to speak.

THE MAIDEN

10 I *am* my beloved's, and his desire *is* toward me.

11 Come, my beloved, let us go forth into the field;
Let us lodge in the villages.

12 Let us get up early to the vineyards;
Let us see if the vine flourish, *whether* the tender grape appear,
And the pomegranates bud forth:
There will I give thee my loves.

13 The mandrakes give a smell,[17]
And at our gates *are* all manner of pleasant *fruits,*
New and old,
Which I have laid up for thee, O my beloved.

8 O that thou *wert* as my brother,
That sucked the breasts of my mother!
When I should find thee without,[18] *I* would kiss thee;
Yea, I should not be despised.

2 I would lead thee, *and* bring thee into my mother's house,
Who would instruct me:
I would cause thee to drink of spiced wine of the juice of my pomegranate.

3 His left hand *should be* under my head,
And his right hand should embrace me.

4 I charge you, O daughters of Jerusalem,
That ye stir not up, nor awake *my* love,
Until he please.

SIXTH POEM

[The lovers are seen returning from the fields. He recalls his first meeting with her, and she implores him to be faithful. She speaks of her chaste upbringing and sees her present bliss as a reward for her virtue. At the end, the lover calls to her, and she responds.]

THE DAUGHTERS OF JERUSALEM

5 Who *is* this that cometh up from the wilder-ness,
Leaning upon her beloved?

THE YOUTH

I raised thee up under the apple tree:
There thy mother brought thee forth;
There she brought thee forth *that* bare thee.

THE MAIDEN

6 Set me as a seal upon thine heart,
As a seal upon thine arm:
For love *is* strong as death;
Jealousy *is* cruel as the grave:
The coals thereof *are* coals of fire,

---

13. In IB, Theophile J. Meek calls this the one hopelessly cor-rupt verse in the poem: "Any restoration is a guess, and . . . there is none that is satisfactory." RSV and NAB as-sign the speech to the maiden; JB and NEB give it to the youth. MOFFATT, perhaps wisely, omits the passage.

14. NEB catches the spirit of the passage: "How you love to gaze on the Shulammite maiden, as she moves between the lines of dancers!"

15. JB, NAB: "a king is held captive in its tresses."

16. NEB: "and your whispers like spiced wine."

17. Mandrakes were prized for their aphrodisiac properties. (See *Genesis* 30:14-16.)

18. MOFFATT: "wherever I met you."

Which hath a most vehement flame.

7   Many waters cannot quench love,
    Neither can the floods drown it:
    If a man would give all the substance of his
    house for love,
    It would utterly be contemned.

8   "We have a little sister, and she hath no
    breasts:
    What shall we do for our sister in the day
    when she shall be spoken for?

9   If she *be* a wall, we will build upon her a pal-
    ace of silver:
    And if she *be* a door, we will inclose her with
    boards of cedar." [19]

10 I *am* a wall, and my breasts like towers:

---

19. (8:8-9) From her earliest youth, her brothers protected her
virtue. They said if she were a wall (i.e., virtuous, inaccessi-
ble), she would be rewarded; if she were a door, she would
be guarded.

Then was I in his eyes as one that found
    favor.

11 Solomon had a vineyard at Baal-hamon;
    He let out the vineyard unto keepers;
    Every one for the fruit thereof was to bring a
    thousand *pieces* of silver.

12 My vineyard, which *is* mine, *is* before me:
    Thou, O Solomon, *must have* a thousand,
    And those that keep the fruit thereof two
    hundred.

THE YOUTH

13 Thou that dwellest in the gardens,
    The companions hearken to thy voice:
    Cause me to hear *it*.

THE MAIDEN

14 Make-haste, my beloved,
    And be thou like to a roe or to a young
    hart
    Upon the mountains of spices.

Introduction to
AMOS

"For three transgressions of Israel, And for four, I will not turn away the punishment thereof."

During the reign of Jeroboam II (786–746 B.C.), Israel reached a level of national prosperity and prominence which many interpreted as a sign of divine favor. Then Amos, a Judean sheep-farmer, appeared, saying he had been called by the Lord to pronounce doom on the sinful nation.

Amos' message is that Israelites, through luxury and indulgence, have lost their special relationship with Yahweh. Though they maintain elaborate religious rituals, they are guilty of perverting justice, trading slaves, neglecting the poor, and ignoring clear signs of God's displeasure. The prophet delivers the words of the Lord: "For three transgressions of Israel, / And for four, I will not turn away the punishment thereof." A time of destruction and devastation is at hand.

With Amos begins the age of great prophecy. Initially in the Old Testament, men such as Abraham and Moses are called prophets because of their special rapport with God. Later, prophets are members of ecstatic groups—such as Saul meets in *I Samuel* 10:5-13—whose musically induced behavior distinguishes them as men seized by the spirit of the Lord. With the establishment of the kingdom appear prophet-counselors, men like Samuel, Nathan, and Elijah, who interpret covenant demands to the ruler. By the time of Amos—and, after him, Isaiah, Jeremiah, Ezekiel, and Daniel—prophets are recognized as "spokesmen" for Yahweh, mystic realists who proclaim their visions and insights to the nation and preach retribution and repentance. Such prophets need not be unworldly men. Amos says that a divine vision led him to prophesy, but his warnings reflect a realistic judgment that the Assyrian rulers would soon move to conquer Israel.

As T. R. Henn specifies, "Prophecy is in fact a complex and varied literary genre." * Typically, it consists of two elements. It offers autobiography as the author describes his encounter with God, his commission to preach, and the reception his preaching has received. And it offers oracular predictions of future events. These can be visions of a coming golden age (like the comforting passage, 9:11-15, which an editor appended to *Amos*); but more often they are proclamations of doom. In Old Testament prophecy, these begin with some form of the line: "Woe to them that are at ease in Zion."

The autobiography in *Amos* appears in one section (7:1–8:3) and in the brief superscription (1:1). From these, commentators have constructed a plausible narrative which provides a setting for the oracles. It appears that Amos, traveling from the barren Tekoan wilderness to seek the best price for his sheep, visited the

---

*In *The Bible as Literature*, Oxford University Press, 1970.

principal cities of Israel—Bethel, Gilgal, and Samaria—and was disheartened by the lavish displays of the wealthy and their indifference to the plight of the poor. In the solitude of his rugged homeland, he reflected on the corruption of Israel: its oppression of the weak, its carnal indulgence, and its perversion of justice. From this reflection came visions of God's plan to destroy the nation (7:1-9) and his own ministry to warn the Israelites. Thereafter, at a religious festival in King Jeroboam's royal chapel, Amos disrupted the proceedings by announcing the coming destruction of Damascus, Gaza, Tyrus, Edom, Ammon, and Moab. The worshipers probably shouted their approval as Amos used the rhetorical regularity of the oracles to enlist the people's enthusiasm for the punishment of Israel's enemies. They had less enthusiasm at the mention of Judah's punishment, and they responded in stunned silence as Amos announced Yahweh's punishment of Israel. At this, Amaziah, the royal chaplain, confronted Amos and told him to return to Judah and take his wild prophecies with him. It is after this event, some scholars suggest, that Amos began writing his message. While such a biographical narrative does accord with the facts in *Amos*, one should remember it is based on sketchy evidence and may well be more useful than true.

The oracular feature in prophecy usually takes two forms. The prophet interprets past events as manifestations of Yahweh's desires and intentions. And he announces events which will come to pass. In *Amos*, past occurrences are described in 4:6-11: the Lord says he sent famine, earthquakes, blight, war, pestilence, and fiery destruction on the Israelites, adding "Yet have ye not returned to me." Because the Israelites have failed him, the Lord will inflict on them the many acts of devastations which Amos describes.

It seems clear that *Amos* is not the product of sustained writing. Rather, a number of separate writings, dating from different periods in the prophet's life, were gathered and arranged, probably by a later editor. Though the book is a kind of anthology, the unique emphases of Amos' ministry are clear. He declares that Yahweh is the God of all nations. He insists that religious rites separate from moral righteousness are meaningless.

AMOS

1 The words of Amos, who was among the herdmen of Tekoa, which he saw concerning Israel in the days of Uzziah king of Judah, and in the days of Jeroboam the son of Joash king of Israel, two years before the earthquake. **2** And he said,

"The LORD will roar from Zion,
And utter his voice from Jerusalem;
And the habitations of the shepherds shall mourn,
And the top of Carmel shall wither."

JUDGMENTS AGAINST ISRAEL AND HER NEIGHBORS
Damascus

3 Thus saith the LORD;
"For three transgressions of Damascus,[1]
And for four,[2] I will not turn away *the punishment* thereof;
Because they have threshed Gilead with threshing instruments of iron:
4 But I will send a fire into the house of Hazael,
Which shall devour the palaces of Ben-hadad.
5 I will break also the bar of Damascus,
And cut off the inhabitant from the plain of Aven,
And him that holdeth the sceptre from the house of Eden:
And the people of Syria shall go into captivity unto Kir,"
Saith the LORD.

Gaza

6 Thus saith the LORD;
"For three transgressions of Gaza,[3]
And for four, I will not turn away *the punishment* thereof;
Because they carried away captive the whole captivity,
To deliver *them* up to Edom:
7 But I will send a fire on the wall of Gaza,
Which shall devour the palaces thereof:
8 And I will cut off the inhabitant from Ashdod,
And him that holdeth the sceptre from Ashkelon,
And I will turn mine hand against Ekron:
And the remnant of the Philistines shall perish,"
Saith the Lord GOD.

Tyrus

9 Thus saith the LORD;
"For three transgressions of Tyrus,[4]
And for four, I will not turn away *the punishment* thereof;
Because they delivered up the whole captivity to Edom,
And remembered not the brotherly covenant:
10 But I will send a fire on the wall of Tyrus,
Which shall devour the palaces thereof."

Edom

11 Thus saith the LORD;
"For three transgressions of Edom,[5]
And for four, I will not turn away *the punishment* thereof;
Because he did pursue his brother with the sword,
And did cast off all pity,
And his anger did tear perpetually,
And he kept his wrath for ever:
12 But I will send a fire upon Teman,
Which shall devour the palaces of Bozrah."

Ammon

13 Thus saith the LORD;
"For three transgressions of the children of Ammon,[6]
And for four, I will not turn away *the punishment* thereof;

---

1. (1:4-5) Damascus and Beth-eden ("Eden") were important cities in the Aramaean kingdom. Hazael founded the ruling dynasty, and Ben-hadad was his son. The conquest of Gilead is described in *II Kings* 10:32-33.
2. I.e., for enough and more than enough.
3. (1:6-8) Gaza, Ashdod, Ashkelon, and Ekron were important Philistine cities. The Philistines will suffer for capturing the whole population of villages and selling them into slavery at Edom.
4. (1:9-10) Tyre was a center for slave trading. The "brotherly covenant" may refer to kindred Phoenicians who had suffered oppression.
5. (1:11-12) Though the Edomites were akin to Israel (by descent from Esau), they had shown bitter hostility. Teman is probably a district in Edomite territory, and Bozrah a principal city.
6. (1:13-15) The Ammonites had brutalized Gilead solely to enlarge their territory. Rabbah was the capital of Ammon.

Because they have ripped up the women
with child, of Gilead,
That they might enlarge their border:

14 But I will kindle a fire in the wall of
Rabbah,
And it shall devour the palaces thereof,
With shouting in the day of battle,
With a tempest in the day of the whirl-
wind:

15 And their king shall go into captivity,
He and his princes together,"
Saith the LORD.

Moab

2 Thus saith the LORD;
"For three transgressions of Moab,[7]
And for four, I will not turn away *the
punishment* thereof;
Because he burned the bones of the king
of Edom into lime:

2 But I will send a fire upon Moab,
And it shall devour the palaces of Kir-
ioth:
And Moab shall die with tumult,
With shouting, *and* with the sound of the
trumpet:

3 And I will cut off the judge from the midst
thereof,
And will slay all the princes thereof with
him,"
Saith the LORD.

Judah

4 Thus saith the LORD;
"For three transgressions of Judah,
And for four, I will not turn away *the pun-
ishment* thereof;
Because they have despised the law of the
LORD,
And have not kept his command-
ments,
And their lies caused them to err,
After the which their fathers have walked:

5 But I will send a fire upon Judah,
And it shall devour the palaces of Jerusalem."

Israel

6 Thus saith the LORD;
"For three transgressions of Israel,
And for four, I will not turn away *the pun-
ishment* thereof;

Because they sold the righteous for silver,
And the poor for a pair of shoes;[8]

7 That pant after the dust of the earth on
the head of the poor,
And turn aside the way of the meek:[9]
And a man and his father will go in unto
the *same* maid,
To profane my holy name:[10]

8 And they lay *themselves* down upon
clothes laid to pledge
By every altar,
And they drink the wine of the con-
demned
In the house of their god.

9 Yet destroyed I the Amorite before them,
Whose height *was* like the height of the
cedars,
And he *was* strong as the oaks;
Yet I destroyed his fruit from above,
And his roots from beneath.

10 Also I brought you up from the land of
Egypt,
And led you forty years through the wil-
derness,
To possess the land of the Amorite.

11 And I raised up of your sons for prophets,
And of your young men for Nazarites.
Is it not even thus, O ye children of Is-
rael?"
Saith the LORD.

12 "But ye gave the Nazarites wine to drink;
And commanded the prophets, saying,
'Prophesy not.'

13 Behold, I am pressed under you,
As a cart is pressed *that is* full of
sheaves.[11]

14 Therefore the flight shall perish from the
swift,
And the strong shall not strengthen his
force,
Neither shall the mighty deliver himself:

15 Neither shall he stand that handleth the
bow;
And *he that is* swift of foot shall not
deliver *himself:*
Neither shall he that rideth the horse
deliver himself.

16 And *he that is* courageous among the
mighty

---

7. (2:1-2) Moab's main crime seems to have been the desecration of a corpse. Kirioth was a chief city of Moab.

8. A creditor would sell his debtor into slavery over a very
small sum of money.
9. NAB: "They trample the heads of the weak into the dust of
the earth, and force the lowly out of the way."
10. The reference is to temple prostitution, a feature of Canaanite nature worship.
11. RSV: "Behold, I will press you down in your place, as a cart
full of sheaves presses down."

Shall flee away naked in that day,"
Saith the LORD.

THREATS AGAINST ISRAEL
FOR HER SINS

3 Hear this word that the LORD hath spoken against you, O children of Israel, against the whole family which I brought up from the land of Egypt, saying,

2   "You only have I known of all the families of the earth:
Therefore I will punish you for all your iniquities.

3   "Can two walk together, except they be agreed?

4   Will a lion roar in the forest, when he hath no prey?
Will a young lion cry out of his den, if he have taken nothing?

5   Can a bird fall in a snare upon the earth, where no gin *is* for him?
Shall *one* take up a snare from the earth, and have taken nothing at all?

6   Shall a trumpet be blown in the city, and the people not be afraid?
Shall there be evil in a city, and the LORD hath not done *it?*

7   Surely the Lord GOD will do nothing,
But he revealeth his secret unto his servants the prophets.

8   The lion hath roared, who will not fear?
The Lord GOD hath spoken, who can but prophesy? [12]

The Fate of Samaria

9   "Publish in the palaces at Ashdod,
And in the palaces in the land of Egypt,
And say, 'Assemble yourselves upon the mountains of Samaria,
And behold the great tumults in the midst thereof,
And the oppressed in the midst thereof.'

10   For they know not to do right," saith the LORD,
"Who store up violence and robbery in their palaces."

11   Therefore thus saith the Lord GOD;
"An adversary *there shall be* even round about the land;
And he shall bring down thy strength from thee,

And thy palaces shall be spoiled."

12   Thus saith the LORD;
"As the shepherd taketh out of the mouth of the lion
Two legs, or a piece of an ear;
So shall the children of Israel be taken out
That dwell in Samaria in the corner of a bed,
And in Damascus *in* a couch." [13]

13   "Hear ye, and testify in the house of Jacob,"
Saith the Lord GOD, the God of hosts,

14   "That, in the day that I shall visit the transgressions of Israel upon him,
I will also visit the altars of Beth-el:[14]
And the horns of the altar shall be cut off,
And fall to the ground.

15   And I will smite the winter house with the summer house;
And the houses of ivory shall perish,
And the great houses shall have an end,"
Saith the LORD.

4   "Hear this word, ye kine of Bashan,
That *are* in the mountain of Samaria,
Which oppress the poor, which crush the needy,
Which say to their masters, 'Bring, and let us drink.'

2   The Lord GOD hath sworn by his holiness,
That, lo, the days shall come upon you,
That he will take you away with hooks,
And your posterity with fishhooks.

3   And ye shall go out at the breaches,
Every *cow at that which is* before her;
And ye shall cast *them* into the palace,"
Saith the LORD.[15]

Divine Warnings

4   "Come to Beth-el, and transgress;
At Gilgal multiply transgression;
And bring your sacrifices every morning,
And your tithes after three years:

5   And offer a sacrifice of thanksgiving with leaven,

---

12. (3:3-8) Every event has a cause; a prophet speaks because God directs him to.

13. The analogy is clearer in RSV: ". . . so shall the people of Israel who dwell in Samaria be rescued, with the corner of a couch and parts of a bed."

14. Bethel was the site of the court of King Jeroboam where Amos was silenced by Amaziah. Its destruction is described in 9:1.

15. (4:2-3) The pampered women of Samaria will lie dead in the streets, and their carcasses carried through breaches in the city walls and cast upon refuse heaps. NAB: "you shall be cast into the mire." NEB: "You shall each be . . . pitched on a dunghill."

And proclaim *and* publish the free offer-
ings:
For this liketh you, O ye children of
Israel,"
Saith the Lord GOD.[16]

6   "And I also have given you cleanness of
teeth in all your cities,
And want of bread in all your places:
Yet have ye not returned unto me,"
Saith the LORD.

7   "And also I have withholden the rain
from you,
When *there were* yet three months to the
harvest:
And I caused it to rain upon one city,
And caused it not to rain upon another
city:
One piece was rained upon,
And the piece whereupon it rained not
withered.
8   So two *or* three cities wandered unto one
city,
To drink water; but they were not sat-
isfied:
Yet have ye not returned unto me,"
Saith the LORD.

9   "I have smitten you with blasting and
mildew:
When your gardens and your vineyards
And your fig trees and your olive trees
increased,
The palmerworm devoured *them:*
Yet have ye not returned unto me,"
Saith the LORD.

10   "I have sent among you the pestilence
after the manner of Egypt:
Your young men have I slain with the
sword,
And have taken away your horses;
And I have made the stink of your camps
to come up unto your nostrils:
Yet have ye not returned unto me,"
Saith the LORD.

11   "I have overthrown *some* of you,
As God overthrew Sodom and Gomorrah,
And ye were as a firebrand plucked out of
the burning:
Yet have ye not returned unto me,"
Saith the LORD.

12   "Therefore thus will I do unto thee, O
Israel:
And because I will do this unto thee,
Prepare to meet thy God, O Israel."

13   For, lo, he that formeth the mountains,
and createth the wind,
And declareth unto man what *is* his
thought,
That maketh the morning darkness,
And treadeth upon the high places of the
earth,
The LORD, The God of hosts, *is* his
name.[17]

Exhortation and Denunciation

5   Hear ye this word which I take up against you,
even a lamentation, O house of Israel.
2   "The virgin of Israel is fallen; she shall no
more rise:
She is forsaken upon her land; *there is*
none to raise her up."
3 For thus saith the Lord GOD; "The city that
went out *by* a thousand shall leave a hundred,[18]
and that which went forth *by* a hundred shall
leave ten, to the house of Israel." 4 For thus saith
the LORD unto the house of Israel,
"Seek ye me, and ye shall live:
5   But seek not Beth-el,
Nor enter into Gilgal,
And pass not to Beer-sheba:
For Gilgal shall surely go into captivity,
And Beth-el shall come to nought."

6   Seek the LORD, and ye shall live;
Lest he break out like fire in the house of
Joseph,
And devour *it,* and *there be* none to
quench *it* in Beth-el.
7   Ye who turn judgment to wormwood,
And leave off righteousness in the earth,

8   *Seek him* that maketh the seven stars and
Orion,
And turneth the shadow of death into the
morning,
And maketh the day dark with night:
That calleth for the waters of the sea,
And poureth them out upon the face of
the earth:
The LORD *is* his name:
9   That strengtheneth the spoiled against the
strong,

16. (4:4-5) This ironical summons scorns Israel's love of public
rites. "Come to Beth-el, and transgress" is a strong paradox.

17. This doxology, like those in 5:8-9 and 9:5-6, is an interpolation added to Amos' text.
18. NEB: "The city that marched out to war a thousand strong
shall have but a hundred left."

So that the spoiled shall come against the fortress.[19]

10 They hate him that rebuketh in the gate,
    And they abhor him that speaketh up-
    rightly.
11 Forasmuch therefore as your treading *is*
    upon the poor,
    And ye take from him burdens of
    wheat:
    Ye have built houses of hewn stone,
    But ye shall not dwell in them;
    Ye have planted pleasant vineyards,
    But ye shall not drink wine of them.
12 For I know your manifold transgressions
    And your mighty sins:
    They afflict the just, they take a bribe,
    And they turn aside the poor in the gate
    from their right.
13 Therefore the prudent shall keep silence
    in that time;
    For it *is* an evil time.[20]

14 Seek good, and not evil, that ye may live:
    And so the LORD, the God of hosts, shall
    be with you, as ye have spoken.
15 Hate the evil, and love the good,
    And establish judgment in the gate:
    It may be that the LORD God of hosts
    Will be gracious unto the remnant of
    Joseph.[21]

"The Day of the Lord"

16 Therefore the LORD, the God of hosts,
    The Lord, saith thus;
    "Wailing *shall be* in all streets;
    And they shall say in all the highways,
    'Alas! alas!'
    And they shall call the husbandman to
    mourning,
    And such as are skilful of lamentation to
    wailing.
17 And in all vineyards *shall be* wailing:
    For I will pass through thee,"
    Saith the LORD.

18 Woe unto you that desire the day of the
    LORD!
    To what end *is* it for you?

The day of the LORD *is* darkness, and not light.
19 As if a man did flee from a lion,
    And a bear met him;
    Or went into the house, and leaned his
    hand on the wall,
    And a serpent bit him.[22]
20 *Shall* not the day of the LORD *be* dark-
    ness, and not light?
    Even very dark, and no brightness in it?

21 "I hate, I despise your feast days,
    And I will not smell in your solemn
    assemblies.
22 Though ye offer me burnt offerings and
    your meat offerings,
    I will not accept *them;*
    Neither will I regard the peace offerings of
    your fat beasts.
23 Take thou away from me the noise of thy
    songs;
    For I will not hear the melody of thy
    viols.
24 But let judgment run down as waters,
    And righteousness as a mighty stream.

25 "Have ye offered unto me sacrifices and offerings in the wilderness forty years, O house of
Israel? 26 But ye have borne the tabernacle of
your Moloch and Chiun your images, the star
of your god, which ye made to yourselves.
27 Therefore will I cause you to go into captivity
beyond Damascus," saith the LORD, whose name
is The God of hosts.

Invasion and Exile

6   "Woe to them *that are* at ease in Zion,
    And trust in the mountain of Samaria,
    Which are named chief of the nations,
    To whom the house of Israel came!
2   Pass ye unto Calneh, and see;
    And from thence go ye to Hamath the
    great:
    Then go down to Gath of the Philistines:
    Be they better than these kingdoms?
    Or their border greater than your bor-
    der?
3   Ye that put far away the evil day,
    And cause the seat of violence to come
    near;
4   That lie upon beds of ivory,
    And stretch themselves upon their
    couches,

19. (5:8-9) Because these lines break the continuity of thought,
JB, NAB, and NEB put them before v. 7. MOFFATT puts
them before v. 1.
20. This verse, which does not conform to Amos' usual opin-
ions, can mean either of two things: (a) because God's judgment is imminent, man need not cry out; or (b) a prophet is
not a prudent man. The first reading seems preferable.
21. I.e., gracious to the Northern Kingdom already devastated
by the punishments described in 4:6-11.

22. (5:18-19) This is a paradox. The Jews had been awaiting
"the day of the Lord" as a time which would establish
Israel's pre-eminence. Amos describes it as a fearful event
from which there can be no escape.

And eat the lambs out of the flock,
And the calves out of the midst of the stall;

5 That chant to the sound of the viol,
And invent to themselves instruments of music, like David;

6 That drink wine in bowls,[23]
And anoint themselves with the chief ointments:
But they are not grieved for the affliction of Joseph.[24]

7 Therefore now shall they go captive with the first that go captive, and the banquet of them that stretched themselves shall be removed."

8 The Lord GOD hath sworn by himself, saith the LORD the God of hosts, "I abhor the excellency of Jacob, and hate his palaces: therefore will I deliver up the city with all that is therein." 9 And it shall come to pass, if there remain ten men in one house, that they shall die. 10 And a man's uncle shall take him up, and he that burneth him, to bring out the bones out of the house, and shall say unto him that *is* by the sides of the house, "*Is there* yet *any* with thee?" and he shall say, "No." Then shall he say, "Hold thy tongue: for we may not make mention of the name of the LORD."

11 For, behold, the LORD commandeth,
And he will smite the great house with breaches,
And the little house with clefts.

12 Shall horses run upon the rock?
Will *one* plow *there* with oxen? [25]
For ye have turned judgment into gall,
And the fruit of righteousness into hemlock:

13 Ye which rejoice in a thing of nought,
Which say, "Have we not taken to us horns by our own strength?"

14 "But, behold, I will raise up against you a nation, O house of Israel," saith the LORD the God of hosts; "and they shall afflict you from the entering in of Hamath unto the river of the wilderness."

VISIONS OF ISRAEL'S DOOM

7 Thus hath the Lord GOD showed unto me; and, behold, he formed grasshoppers in the beginning of the shooting up of the latter growth;

and, lo, *it was* the latter growth after the king's mowings. 2 And it came to pass, *that* when they had made an end of eating the grass of the land, then I said,

"O Lord GOD, forgive, I beseech thee:
By whom shall Jacob arise? for he *is* small." [26]

3 The LORD repented for this: "It shall not be," saith the LORD.

4 Thus hath the Lord GOD showed unto me: and, behold, the Lord GOD called to contend by fire, and it devoured the great deep, and did eat up a part. 5 Then said I,

"O Lord GOD, cease, I beseech thee:
By whom shall Jacob arise? for he *is* small."

6 The LORD repented for this: "This also shall not be," saith the Lord GOD.

7 Thus he showed me: and, behold, the Lord stood upon a wall *made* by a plumbline, with a plumbline in his hand. 8 And the LORD said unto me, "Amos, what seest thou?" And I said, "A plumbline." Then said the Lord,

"Behold, I will set a plumbline in the midst of my people Israel:
I will not again pass by them any more:

9 And the high places of Isaac ˙shall be desolate,
And the sanctuaries of Israel shall be laid waste;
And I will rise against the house of Jeroboam with the sword." [27]

Amos and Amaziah

10 Then Amaziah the priest of Beth-el sent to Jeroboam king of Israel, saying, "Amos hath conspired against thee in the midst of the house of Israel: the land is not able to bear all his words. 11 For thus Amos saith, 'Jeroboam shall die by the sword, and Israel shall surely be led away captive out of their own land.'" 12 Also Amaziah said unto Amos, "O thou seer, go, flee thee away into the land of Judah, and there eat bread, and prophesy there: 13 But prophesy not again any more at Beth-el: for it *is* the king's chapel, and it *is* the king's court." 14 Then answered Amos, and said to Amaziah, "I *was* no prophet, neither *was* I a prophet's son; but I *was* a herd-

---

23. NEB: "by the bowlful."
24. I.e., they do not heed the clear signs of a coming day of disaster.
25. PHILLIPS: "Can horses race over rocks? / Can you plough the sea with oxen?" The examples parallel Israel's unnatural corrupton of justice.

26. In pleading for the Israelites, Amos describes them as they must appear to God. This contrasts with their proud evaluation of themselves.
27. (7:8-9) Because Israel is measured by the plumb line and found wanting, God disowns them. The declaration of doom is so final that Amos does not plead against it; instead, he begins his prophetic ministry. Apparently a period of preaching occurs between 7:9 and the exchange with Amaziah (7:10-17).

man, and a gatherer of sycamore fruit: 15 And the LORD took me as I followed the flock, and the LORD said unto me, 'Go, prophesy unto my people Israel.' 16 Now therefore hear thou the word of the LORD:

Thou sayest, 'Prophesy not against Israel,
And drop not *thy word* against the house of Isaac.'

17 Therefore thus saith the LORD;
'Thy wife shall be a harlot in the city,
And thy sons and thy daughters shall fall by the sword,
And thy land shall be divided by line;
And thou shalt die in a polluted land:
And Israel shall surely go into captivity forth of his land.' "

8 Thus hath the Lord GOD showed unto me: and behold a basket of summer fruit.

2 And he said, "Amos, what seest thou?" And I said, "A basket of summer fruit." [28] Then said the LORD unto me,

"The end is come upon my people of Israel;
I will not again pass by them any more.
3 And the songs of the temple shall be howlings in that day,"
Saith the Lord GOD:
"*There shall be* many dead bodies in every place;
They shall cast *them* forth with silence."

Punishment for Greed

4 Hear this, O ye that swallow up the needy,
Even to make the poor of the land to fail,
5 Saying, "When will the new moon be gone, that we may sell corn?
And the sabbath, that we may set forth wheat,
Making the ephah small, and the shekel great,
And falsifying the balances by deceit?
6 That we may buy the poor for silver,
And the needy for a pair of shoes;
Yea, and sell the refuse of the wheat?"
7 The LORD hath sworn by the excellency of Jacob,
"Surely I will never forget any of their works."
8 Shall not the land tremble for this,
And every one mourn that dwelleth therein?
And it shall rise up wholly as a flood;

And it shall be cast out and drowned, as *by* the flood of Egypt.

9 "And it shall come to pass in that day,"
Saith the Lord GOD,
"That I will cause the sun to go down at noon,
And I will darken the earth in the clear day:
10 And I will turn your feasts into mourning,
And all your songs into lamentation;
And I will bring up sackcloth upon all loins,
And baldness upon every head;
And I will make it as the mourning of an only *son,*
And the end thereof as a bitter day."

11 "Behold, the days come,"
Saith the Lord GOD,
"That I will send a famine in the land,
Not a famine of bread,
Nor a thirst for water,
But of hearing the words of the LORD:[29]
12 And they shall wander from sea to sea,
And from the north even to the east,
They shall run to and fro to seek the word of the LORD,
And shall not find *it.*
13 In that day shall the fair virgins
And young men faint for thirst.
14 They that swear by the sin of Samaria,
And say, 'Thy god, O Dan, liveth';
And, 'The manner of Beer-sheba liveth';
Even they shall fall, and never rise up again."

Fall of the Sanctuary

9 I saw the Lord standing upon the altar: and he said,

"Smite the lintel of the door, that the posts may shake:
And cut them in the head, all of them;[30]
And I will slay the last of them with the sword:
He that fleeth of them shall not flee away,
And he that escapeth of them shall not be delivered.
2 Though they dig into hell,
Thence shall mine hand take them;

---

28. (8:1-2) The image is ominous: summer fruit will quickly be consumed.

29. These lines are certainly an interpolation. The pious statement qualifies the powerful threat describing days of famine and thirst.

30. (9:1-4) This describes the sudden destruction of the sanctuary at Bethel. MOFFATT: " 'Strike the pillars on the top,' said he, 'that the ceiling may be shaken, break them on the heads of all the worshippers.' "

Though they climb up to heaven,
Thence will I bring them down:
3   And though they hide themselves in the
       top of Carmel,
   I will search and take them out thence;
   And though they be hid from my sight in
       the bottom of the sea,
   Thence will I command the serpent, and
       he shall bite them:
4   And though they go into captivity before
       their enemies,
   Thence will I command the sword, and it
       shall slay them:
   And I will set mine eyes upon them
   For evil, and not for good."

5   And the Lord GOD of hosts
   Is he that toucheth the land, and it shall
       melt,
   And all that dwell therein shall mourn:
   And it shall rise up wholly like a flood;
   And shall be drowned, as *by* the flood of
       Egypt.
6   *It is* he that buildeth his stories in the
       heaven,
   And hath founded his troop in the
       earth; [31]
   He that calleth for the waters of the
       sea,
   And poureth them out upon the face of
       the earth:
   The LORD *is* his name.

7   "*Are* ye not as children of the Ethopians
       unto me,
   O children of Israel?" saith the LORD.
   "Have not I brought up Israel out of the
       land of Egypt?
   And the Philistines from Caphtor, and the
       Syrians from Kir?"

A REMNANT SPARED

8   "Behold, the eyes of the Lord GOD *are*
       upon the sinful kingdom,
   And I will destroy it from off the face of
       the earth;

Saving that I will not utterly destroy the
   house of Jacob,"
Saith the LORD.

9   "For, lo, I will command,
   And I will sift the house of Israel among
       all nations,
   Like as *corn* is sifted in a sieve,
   Yet shall not the least grain fall upon the
       earth.
10   All the sinners of my people shall die by
       the sword,
   Which say, 'The evil shall not overtake
       nor prevent us.'

Restoration of the Kingdom

11   "In that day will I raise up the tabernacle
       of David that is fallen,[32]
   And close up the breaches thereof;
   And I will raise up his ruins,
   And I will build it as in the days of old:
12   That they may possess the remnant of
       Edom,
   And of all the heathen, which are called
       by my name,"
   Saith the LORD that doeth this.

13   "Behold, the days come," saith the LORD,
   "That the plowman shall overtake the
       reaper,
   And the treader of grapes him that soweth
       seed;
   And the mountains shall drop sweet wine,
   And all the hills shall melt.
14   And I will bring again the captivity[33] of
       my people of Israel,
   And they shall build the waste cities, and
       inhabit *them;*
   And they shall plant vineyards, and drink
       the wine thereof;
   They shall also make gardens, and eat the
       fruit of them.
15   And I will plant them upon their land,
   And they shall no more be pulled up
   Out of their land which I have given
       them,"
   Saith the LORD thy God.

---

31. PHILLIPS: "He is the One who builds his palaces in the
heavens / And makes his arch rest firmly upon the earth.
See illustration, p. 6.

32. (9:11-15) A later editor added this hopeful epilogue to
temper Amos' bitter prophecy.
33. JB, NEB: "restore the fortunes."

Introduction to
JONAH

"Therefore I fled before unto Tarshish: for I knew that thou art a gracious God, and merciful."

Written during a period of narrow Jewish nationalism (400–200 B.C.), the story of Jonah is a parable ridiculing prevalent attitudes of pride and vindictiveness.

The anonymous author chose as his model of intolerance the prophet Jonah, who, in the eighth century B.C., had made nationalistic predictions about the expansion of Israel's territory. But while most prophetic books consist of oracular predictions, the primary interest in *Jonah* is not in the eight-word prophecy: "Yet forty days and Nineveh shall be overthrown" (3:4). Instead, attention is focused on the childish stubbornness of the prophet himself.

A parable is a story illustrating a moral or religious truth. (See examples in *Luke*, pp. 250f.) Sometimes a parable leads men to pronounce judgment on themselves. Examples include Nathan's telling David of the rich man who stole the ewe lamb (*II Samuel* 12:1-7) and Jesus' telling a lawyer of the good Samaritan (*Luke* 10:25-37). *Jonah* is a parable of this kind. The story was directed toward Jews who, having endured much suffering under foreign oppressors, were bitter and vengeful toward other nations. Had they been asked to preach salvation to the Gentiles, many, like Jonah, would have opposed the idea. Yet, as the narrative progresses, even the most hostile Jews would commend the Gentile sailors who are reluctant to cast Jonah overboard and who acknowledge the power of his god. They would be moved by the sincere repentance of the king and citizens of Nineveh. And they would be irritated by the petulance of Jonah who wants to die because the Ninevite people were saved and his gourd plant was not. Finally, the parable would remind bigoted Jews that their own narrow attitudes parallel those of Jonah.

Some commentators believe that this message is reinforced by the symbolism of the "great fish." Jonah's three days in the belly of the fish are said to represent the period of the Babylonian captivity. The reading is supported by passages in *Jeremiah*: "Nebuchadrezzar the king of Babylon hath devoured me . . . he hath swallowed me up like a dragon" (51:34). "I will punish Bel in Babylon, and I will bring forth out of his mouth that which he hath swallowed up" (51:44). Thus *Jonah* can be read to describe pre-exilic Israel which did not pursue its missionary calling, and post-exilic Israel which somewhat grudgingly takes up its commission.

The psalm (2:2-9) is clearly an interpolation. Since Jonah is in the belly of the fish, the context requires a prayer for deliverance; instead, he voices a prayer of thanksgiving. The intrusion slows the rapid pace of the narrative, and its omission would leave no gap in the story.

Jonah is a parable designed to remind Israel of its missionary destiny. It ends abruptly during an interchange between the Lord and his reluctant prophet. One might wish to hear Jonah's answer to the Lord's final question, but there is no doubt what it has to be.

JONAH

A STUDY IN OBSTINACY
The Flight from God

1 Now the word of the LORD came unto Jonah the son of Amittai, saying, 2 "Arise, go to Nineveh, that great city, and cry against it; for their wickedness is come up before me." 3 But Jonah rose up to flee unto Tarshish from the presence of the LORD, and went down to Joppa; and he found a ship going to Tarshish: so he paid the fare thereof, and went down into it, to go with them unto Tarshish from the presence of the LORD.[1]

4 But the LORD sent out a great wind into the sea, and there was a mighty tempest in the sea, so that the ship was like to be broken. 5 Then the mariners were afraid, and cried every man unto his god, and cast forth the wares that *were* in the ship into the sea, to lighten *it* of them. But Jonah was gone down into the sides of the ship; and he lay, and was fast asleep. 6 So the shipmaster came to him, and said unto him, "What meanest thou, O sleeper? arise, call upon thy God, if so be that God[2] will think upon us, that we perish not." 7 And they said every one to his fellow, "Come, and let us cast lots, that we may know for whose cause this evil *is* upon us." So they cast lots, and the lot fell upon Jonah. 8 Then said they unto him, "Tell us, we pray thee, for whose cause this evil *is* upon us;[3] What *is* thine occupation? and whence comest thou? what *is* thy country? and of what people *art* thou?" 9 And he said unto them, "I *am* a Hebrew; and I fear the LORD, the God of heaven, which hath made the sea and the dry *land.*" 10 Then were the men exceedingly afraid, and said unto him, "Why hast thou done this?" For the men knew that he had fled from the presence of the LORD, because he had told them.

11 Then said they unto him, "What shall we do unto thee, that the sea may be calm unto us?" for the sea wrought, and was tempestuous. 12 And he said unto them, "Take me up, and cast me forth into the sea; so shall the sea be calm unto you: for I know that for my sake this great tempest *is* upon you." 13 Nevertheless the men rowed hard to bring *it* to the land; but they could not: for the sea wrought, and was tempestuous against them. 14 Wherefore they cried unto the LORD, and said, "We beseech thee, O LORD, we beseech thee, let us not perish for this man's life, and lay not upon us innocent blood: for thou, O LORD, hast done as it pleased thee." 15 So they took up Jonah, and cast him forth into the sea: and the sea ceased from her raging. 16 Then the men feared the LORD exceedingly, and offered a sacrifice unto the LORD, and made vows.

17 Now the LORD had prepared a great fish to swallow up Jonah. And Jonah was in the belly of the fish three days and three nights.

Jonah's Psalm

2 Then Jonah prayed unto the LORD his God out of the fish's belly, 2 And said,

"I cried by reason of mine affliction
Unto the LORD, and he heard me;
Out of the belly of hell cried I,
And thou heardest my voice.

3 For thou hadst cast me into the deep,
In the midst of the seas;
And the floods compassed me about:
All thy billows and thy waves passed over me.

4 Then I said, 'I am cast out of thy sight;
Yet I will look again toward thy holy temple.'

5 The waters compassed me about, *even* to the soul:
The depth closed me round about,
The weeds were wrapped about my head.

6 I went down to the bottoms of the mountains;
The earth with her bars *was* about me for ever:[4]
Yet hast thou brought up my life from corruption,
O LORD my God.

7 When my soul fainted within me
I remembered the LORD:
And my prayer came in unto thee,
Into thine holy temple.

---

1. Jonah is fleeing in earnest. Tarshish has been identified as a colony in southwest Spain, as far west as one could sail from Palestine.
2. RSV, JB, MOFFATT, NEB: "your god." The captain does not value Jonah's god over the gods of the other men. Believing that some god is causing the tempest, he wants to placate as many as possible.
3. It is unreasonable for the sailors to inquire "for whose cause this evil *is* upon us" since, through casting of lots, they already know the answer. The line, which does not appear in several Hebrew manuscripts, is omitted in NEB, MOFFATT, NAB, and JB.
4. The ocean bed was thought to be the foundation on which the earth rested. See illustration on p. 6.

8   They that observe lying vanities[5]
      Forsake their own mercy.
9   But I will sacrifice unto thee
      With the voice of thanksgiving;
      I will pay *that* that I have vowed.
      Salvation *is* of the LORD."
10 And the LORD spake unto the fish, and it
vomited out Jonah upon the dry *land.*

The Conversion of Nineveh

3 And the word of the LORD came unto Jonah
the second time, saying, 2 "Arise, go unto
Nineveh, that great city, and preach unto it the
preaching that I bid thee." 3 So Jonah arose, and
went unto Nineveh, according to the word of the
LORD. Now Nineveh was an exceeding great city
of three days' journey.[6] 4 And Jonah began to
enter into the city a day's journey, and he cried,
and said, "Yet forty days, and Nineveh shall be
overthrown."

5 So the people of Nineveh believed God, and
proclaimed a fast, and put on sackcloth, from the
greatest of them even to the least of them. 6 For
word came unto the king of Nineveh, and he
arose from his throne, and he laid his robe from
him, and covered *him* with sackcloth, and sat in
ashes. 7 And he caused *it* to be proclaimed and
published through Nineveh by the decree of the
king and his nobles, saying, "Let neither man nor
beast, herd nor flock, taste any thing: let them not
feed, nor drink water: 8 But let man and beast
be covered with sackcloth, and cry mightily unto
God: yea, let them turn every one from his evil
way, and from the violence that *is* in their hands.
9 Who can tell *if* God will turn and repent, and
turn away from his fierce anger, that we perish
not?"

10 And God saw their works, that they turned
from their evil way; and God repented of the evil,

---

5. NAB: "worship vain idols."
6. MOFFATT: "a great, great city, three days' journey across,
   from one side to another."

---

that he had said that he would do unto them; and
he did *it* not.

Jonah's Anger; God's Response

4 But it displeased Jonah exceedingly, and he
was very angry. 2 And he prayed unto the LORD,
and said, "I pray thee, O LORD, *was* not this my
saying, when I was yet in my country? Therefore
I fled before unto Tarshish: for I knew that thou
art a gracious God, and merciful, slow to anger,
and of great kindness, and repentest thee of the
evil. 3 Therefore now, O LORD, take, I beseech
thee, my life from me; for *it is* better for me to die
than to live." 4 Then said the LORD, "Doest thou
well to be angry?"

5 So Jonah went out of the city, and sat on the
east side of the city, and there made him a booth,
and sat under it in the shadow, till he might see
what would become of the city.[7] 6 And the LORD
God prepared a gourd, and made *it* to come up
over Jonah, that it might be a shadow over his
head, to deliver him from his grief. So Jonah was
exceeding glad of the gourd. 7 But God prepared
a worm when the morning rose the next day, and
it smote the gourd that it withered. 8 And it
came to pass, when the sun did arise, that God
prepared a vehement east wind; and the sun beat
upon the head of Jonah, that he fainted, and
wished in himself to die, and said, "*It is* better for
me to die than to live." 9 And God said to
Jonah, "Doest thou well to be angry for the
gourd?" And he said, "I do well to be angry, *even*
unto death." 10 Then said the LORD, "Thou hast
had pity on the gourd, for the which thou hast not
labored, neither madest it grow; which came up
in a night, and perished in a night: 11 And
should not I spare Nineveh, that great city,
wherein are more than sixscore thousand persons
that cannot discern between their right hand and
their left hand; and *also* much cattle?" [8]

---

7. Jonah still hopes to see Nineveh destroyed.
8. The suggestion is that the Ninevites had no opportunity to
   know Israel's god and that—like children (who do not know
   their right hand from their left) or like cattle—they were not
   responsible for their sinful acts.

THE APOCRYPHA

Tobias and the Angel. The School of Verocchio, 1435–88. Reproduced by permission of Trustees, The National Gallery, London.

Introduction to
THE APOCRYPHA

The fourteen books of the Apocrypha contain masterful short stories, profound meditations, reliable history, legendary history, choice poetry, and vivid apocalypse. They provide valuable information concerning the conditions of Jewish life and the development of religious thought in the decades separating the Old Testament from the New Testament.

These books have a strange relationship to other Biblical writings.

By the third century B.C., an estimated one million Jews lived in Alexandria, Egypt. Because many no longer remembered Hebrew, the language of their religious heritage, the Law was translated into *koiné,* the vernacular Greek, in about 250 B.C. The Prophets and the Writings—the other divisions of Hebrew Scripture—were translated in succeeding years, so that by 75 B.C. a Greek translation of the canon was available. This translation is called the *Septuagint,* a Latin word for "seventy," and is regularly designated by *LXX.*

In A.D. 382, Jerome was commissioned by Pope Damasus to translate the Bible into Latin. He worked initially from the *LXX,* but soon realized the importance of the Old Testament in Hebrew. When Jerome compared the *LXX* with the Hebrew documents, he discovered a discrepency. There were books and parts of books in the *LXX* which did not appear in the Hebrew. Jerome called these works the *Apocrypha* and suggested they were of secondary importance.

Apocrypha means "hidden" or "concealed things." Technically, it refers to writings which, having recorded revelations of the future, are then hidden away. In fact, it refers to writings produced and used by Alexandrian Jews.

The works have met varying religious responses. Palestinian Jews, like the Calvinist tradition centuries later, rejected them altogether. The Roman Catholic Church accepted the books as fully canonical. (Roman Catholic Bibles have no section designated as The Apocrypha.) And Lutheran and Anglican traditions find secondary value in the works. Martin Luther said they "are useful and good for reading"; Article Six of the Thirty-nine Articles declared, "And the other Books the Church doth read for example of life and instruction of manners."

Despite these rejections and reservations, the Apocryphal books have been translated and printed as part of the Bible through the centuries. In the King James Version, they were put immediately after the Old Testament.

Introduction to
TOBIT

*"For the good angel will keep him company and his journey shall be prosperous,
and he shall return safe."*

Piety, magic, dead bodies, a nagging wife, a faithful dog, a demon lover, and a
happy ending—there is something for everyone in *Tobit*. The genius of the
anonymous author lay in his ability to unite history, autobiography, prayers,
maxims, and pagan folklore into a didactic short story.

Written between 180–170 B.C., *Tobit* reflects Jewish life during the Diaspora.
Separated from the Temple in Jerusalem, faithful emigrants continue to follow the
ordinances of the Law. Tobit, an ideal Jew throughout, observes the dietary
prohibitions, exhorts his son to "take a wife of the seed of thy fathers," and performs
many acts of personal piety: he gives alms, he fasts and prays, he buries the dead.
He practices and teaches a form of the Golden Rule: "Do that to no man which
thou hatest" (4:15).

The story embodies a variety of literary forms. The historical setting (1:2) is given
in the formal style of official records. Like *Ruth*, *Jonah*, and *Judith*, the tale is set in
the remote past, the author seeking literary effect by calling up famous names from
former times. Tobit's affliction and his plea for death take the form of autobiography (1:2–3:6). His "deathbed" counsel to his son (4:5-19) and Raphael's final words
(12:6-10) are series of maxims. And Tobit's and Sara's pleas for death (3:2-6 and
3:11-15), like Tobit's final praise of the God who remembered him (13:1-18), are
moving prayers.

Tobit weaves all these elements into a story based on two folk tales. In "The
Grateful Dead," a dead man rewards the person who provides a decent burial. In
"The Dangerous Bride," potential husbands of a desirable woman perish under
mysterious circumstances. By establishing the characters as exiles in ancient
Nineveh, the author of *Tobit* could transform the "Grateful Dead/Dangerous
Bride" narrative into a vehicle for instruction in Judaism.

Though it embodies many differing features, the story has a notable unity. The
anguish of Sara parallels that of Tobit. Tobit and Raguel have each an only child
and strong concern for the levirate tradition. (See footnote 59 to *Genesis*.) The angel
Raphael is opposed by the demon Asmodeus. The healing power of fish entrails
provides a happy ending for both families. And underlying all the drama and humor
and supernatural magic is the character of Tobit, an exemplary Jew with complete
and active faith in the God of his fathers.

The story of Tobit exists in many versions, some of which differ considerably
from others. Thus, the readings from alternative translations given in the footnotes
may vary a great deal.

TOBIT

TOBIT'S AND SARA'S MISFORTUNES

1 The book od the words of Tobit, son of Tobiel, the son of Ananiel, the son of Aduel, the son of Gabael, of the seed of Asael, of the tribe of Naphtali; 2 Who in the time of Shalmaneser king of the Assyrians was led captive out of Thisbe, which is at the right hand of that city, which is called properly Naphtali in Galilee above Aser.[1]

Tobit's History

3 I Tobit have walked all the days of my life in the way of truth and justice, and I did many almsdeeds to my brethren, and my nation, who came with me to Nineveh, into the land of the Assyrians. 4 And when I was in mine own country, in the land of Israel, being but young, all the tribe of Naphtali my father fell from the house of Jerusalem, which was chosen out of all the tribes of Israel that all the tribes should sacrifice there, where the temple of the habitation of the most High was consecrated and built for all ages. 5 Now all the tribes which together revolted, and the house of my father Naphtali, sacrificed unto the heifer Baal.
6 But I alone went often to Jerusalem at the feasts, as it was ordained unto all the people of Israel by an everlasting decree, having the firstfruits and tenths of increase, with that which was first shorn; and them gave I at the altar to the priests the children of Aaron. 7 The first tenth part of all increase I gave to the sons of Aaron, who ministered at Jerusalem: another tenth part I sold away, and went, and spent it every year at Jerusalem: 8 And the third I gave unto them to whom it was meet, as Debora my father's mother had commanded me, because I was left an orphan by my father.
9 Furthermore, when I was come to the age of a man, I married Anna of mine own kindred, and of her I begat Tobias. 10 And when we were carried away captives to Nineveh, all my brethren and those that were of my kindred did eat of the bread of the Gentiles. 11 But I kept myself from eating; 12 Because I remembered God with all my heart. 13 And the most High gave me grace and favour before Shalmaneser, so that I was his purveyor. 14 And I went into Media, and left in trust with Gabael, the brother of Gabrias, at Rages a city of Media ten talents of silver.[2]
15 Now when Shalmaneser was dead, Sennacherib his son reigned in his stead; whose estate was troubled, that I could not go into Media.

16 And in the time of Shalmaneser I gave many alms to my brethren, and gave my bread to the hungry, 17 And my clothes to the naked: and if I saw any of my nation dead, or cast about the walls of Nineveh, I buried him.[3] 18 And if the king Sennacherib had slain any, when he was come, and fled from Judea, I buried them privily; for in his wrath he killed many; but the bodies were not found, when they were sought for of the king. 19 And when one of the Ninevites went and complained of me to the king, that I buried them, and hid myself; understanding that I was sought for to be put to death, I withdrew myself for fear. 20 Then all my goods were forcibly taken away, neither was there any thing left me, beside my wife Anna and my son Tobias.

21 And there passed not five and fifty days, before two of his sons killed him, and they fled into the mountains of Ararat; and Esarhaddon his son reigned in his stead; who appointed over his father's accounts, and over all his affairs, Ahikar my brother Anael's son. 22 And Ahikar intreating for me, I returned to Nineveh. Now Ahikar was cupbearer, and keeper of the signet, and steward, and overseer of the accounts: and Esarhaddon appointed him next unto him: and he was my brother's son.

2 Now when I was come home again, and my wife Anna was restored unto me, with my son Tobias, in the feast of Pentecost, which is the holy feast of the seven weeks, there was a good dinner prepared me, in the which I sat down to eat. 2 And when I saw abundance of meat, I said to my son, "Go and bring what poor man soever thou shalt find out of our brethren, who is mindful of the Lord; and, lo, I tarry for thee." 3 But he came again, and said, "Father, one of our nation is strangled, and is cast out in the marketplace." 4 Then before I had tasted of any meat, I started

---

1. Samaria, the capital of Israel, was conquered in 722 B.C., and much of its population was transported to Assyria.

2. This sum, about $20,000 in modern currency, was introduced for literary effect, to give Tobias an important reason to travel to Media. It is hard to conceive how Tobit, in his poverty, could suddenly *remember* he had it.

3. The religious obligation to bury the dead, though not specifically enjoined by the Law, was of ancient origin. It derived from an ancient belief that the spirit of a dead person, especially one killed violently, roams homelessly until his corpse is decently buried.

up, and took him up into a room until the going down of the sun. 5 Then I returned, and washed myself, and ate my meat in heaviness, 6 Remembering that prophecy of Amos, as he said,

"Your feasts shall be turned into mourning,

And all your mirth into lamentation." [4]

7 Therefore I wept: and after the going down of the sun I went and made a grave, and buried him. 8 But my neighbours mocked me, and said, "This man is not yet afraid to be put to death for this matter: who fled away; and yet, lo, he burieth the dead again."

9 The same night also I returned from the burial, and slept by the wall of my courtyard, being polluted, and my face was uncovered: 10 And I knew not that there were sparrows in the wall, and mine eyes being open, the sparrows muted warm dung into mine eyes, and a whiteness came in mine eyes; and I went to the physicians, but they helped me not: moreover Ahikar did nourish me, until he went into Elymais.

11 And my wife Anna did take women's works to do.[5] 12 And when she had sent them home to the owners, they paid her wages, and gave her also besides a kid. 13 And when it was in my house, and began to cry, I said unto her, "From whence is this kid? is it not stolen? render it to the owners; for it is not lawful to eat any thing that is stolen." 14 But she replied upon me, "It was given for a gift more than the wages." Howbeit I did not believe her, but bade her render it to the owners: and I was abashed at her. But she replied upon me, "Where are thine alms and thy righteous deeds? behold, thou and all thy works are known." [6]

3 Then I being grieved did weep, and in my sorrow prayed, saying, 2 "O Lord, thou art just, and all thy works and all thy ways are mercy and truth, and thou judgest truly and justly for ever. 3 Remember me, and look on me, punish me not for my sins and ignorances, and the sins of my fathers, who have sinned before thee: 4 For they obeyed not thy commandments: wherefore thou hast delivered us for a spoil, and unto captivity, and unto death, and for a proverb of reproach to all the nations among whom we are dispersed.

5 And now thy judgments are many and true: deal with me according to my sins and my fathers': because we have not kept thy commandments, neither have walked in truth before thee. 6 Now therefore deal with me as seemeth best unto thee, and command my spirit to be taken from me, that I may be dissolved, and become earth: for it is profitable for me to die rather than to live, because I have heard false reproaches, and have much sorrow: command therefore that I may now be delivered out of this distress, and go into the everlasting place; turn not thy face away from me."

Sara's Plight [7]

7 It came to pass the same day, that in Ecbatana a city of Media Sara the daughter of Raguel was also reproached by her father's maids; 8 Because that she had been married to seven husbands, whom Asmodeus the evil spirit had killed, before they had lain with her. "Dost thou not know," said they, "that thou hast strangled thine husbands? thou hast had already seven husbands, neither wast thou named after any of them. 9 Wherefore dost thou beat us for them? if they be dead, go thy ways after them, let us never see of thee either son or daughter." 10 When she heard these things, she was very sorrowful, so that she thought to have strangled herself;[8] and she said, "I am the only daughter of my father, and if I do this, it shall be a reproach unto him, and I shall bring his old age with sorrow unto the grave."

11 Then she prayed toward the window, and said, "Blessed art thou, O Lord my God, and thine holy and glorious name is blessed and honourable for ever: let all thy works praise thee for ever. 12 And now, O Lord, I set mine eyes and my face toward thee, 13 And say, Take me out of the earth, that I may hear no more the reproach. 14 Thou knowest, Lord, that I am pure from all sin with man, 15 And that I never polluted my name, nor the name of my father, in the land of my captivity: I am the only daughter of my father, neither hath he any child to be his heir, neither any near kinsman, nor any son of his alive, to whom I may keep myself for a wife: my seven husbands are already dead; and why should I live? but if it please not thee that I should die, command some regard to be had of

---

4. (2:3-6) Having touched a corpse (presumably that of an executed Jew), Tobit washes himself ceremonially, then recalls lines from *Amos* 8:10.

5. JB: "My wife Anna then undertook woman's work; she would spin wool and take cloth to weave."

6. KNOX finds this passage "much confused," adding "It seems probable that Anna meant, 'Why should you make such a point of being honest, when Providence has given you such a poor reward for being charitable?' "

7. Here, the monologue gives way to a third-person narration.

8. (3:8-10) Asmodeus—the name means "destroyer"—is thought to derive from Persian lore. Beset by this demon-lover, Sara is irritable with her servants and contemplates hanging herself.

me, and pity taken of me, that I hear no more reproach."

16 So the prayers of them both were heard before the majesty of the great God. 17 And Raphael was sent to heal them both, that is, to scale away the whiteness of Tobit's eyes, and to give Sara the daughter of Raguel for a wife to Tobias the son of Tobit; and to bind Asmodeus the evil spirit; because she belonged to Tobias by right of inheritance.[9] The selfsame time came Tobit home, and entered into his house, and Sara the daughter of Raguel came down from her upper chamber.

THE JOURNEY TO RAGES

4 In that day Tobit remembered the money which he had committed to Gabael in Rages of Media, 2 And said with himself, "I have wished for death; wherefore do I not call for my son Tobias, that I may signify to him of the money before I die?" 3 And when he had called him, he said, "My son, when I am dead, bury me; and despise not thy mother, but honour her all the days of thy life,[10] and do that which shall please her, and grieve her not. 4 Remember, my son, that she saw many dangers for thee, when thou wast in her womb; and when she is dead, bury her by me in one grave.

Tobit's Counsel

5 "My son, be mindful of the Lord our God all thy days, and let not thy will be set to sin, or to transgress his commandments: do uprightly all thy life long, and follow not the ways of unrighteousness. 6 For if thou deal truly, thy doings shall prosperously succeed to thee, and to all them that live justly. 7 Give alms of thy substance; and when thou givest alms, let not thine eye be envious, neither turn thy face from any poor, and the face of God shall not be turned away from thee. 8 If thou hast abundance, give alms accordingly: if thou have but a little, be not afraid to give according to that little: 9 For thou layest up a good treasure for thyself against the day of necessity. 10 Because that alms do deliver from death, and suffereth not to come into darkness. 11 For alms is a good gift unto all that give it in the sight of the most High.

12 "Beware of all whoredom, my son, and chiefly take a wife of the seed of thy fathers, and take not a strange woman to wife, which is not of thy father's tribe: for we are the children of the prophets, Noah, Abraham, Isaac, and Jacob: remember, my son, that our fathers from the beginning, even that they all married wives of their own kindred, and were blessed in their children, and their seed shall inherit the land. 13 Now, therefore, my son, love thy brethren, and despise not in thy heart thy brethren, the sons and daughters of thy people, in not taking a wife of them: for in pride is destruction and much trouble, and in lewdness[11] is decay and great want: for lewdness is the mother of famine.

14 "Let not the wages of any man, which hath wrought for thee, tarry with thee, but give him it out of hand: for if thou serve God, he will also repay thee: be circumspect, my son, in all things thou doest, and be wise in all thy conversation. 15 Do that to no man which thou hatest: drink not wine to make thee drunken: neither let drunkenness go with thee in thy journey. 16 Give of thy bread to the hungry, and of thy garments to them that are naked; and according to thine abundance give alms; and let not thine eye be envious, when thou givest alms. 17 "Pour out thy bread on the burial of the just, but give nothing to the wicked. 18 Ask counsel of all that are wise, and despise not any counsel that is profitable. 19 Bless the Lord thy God alway, and desire of him that thy ways may be directed, and that all thy paths and counsels may prosper: for every nation hath not counsel; but the Lord himself giveth all good things, and he humbleth whom he will, as he will; now therefore, my son, remember my commandments, neither let them be put out of thy mind.

20 "And now I signify this to thee, that I committed ten talents to Gabael the son of Gabrias at Rages in Media. 21 And fear not, my son, that we are made poor: for thou hast much wealth, if thou fear God, and depart from all sin, and do that which is pleasing in his sight."

Raphael as Companion

5 Tobias then answered and said, "Father, I will do all things which thou hast commanded me: 2 But how can I receive the money, seeing I know him not?" 3 Then he gave him the handwriting, and said unto him, "Seek thee a man which may go with thee, whiles I yet live, and I will give him wages: and go and receive the money."

4 Therefore when he went to seek a man, he found Raphael that was an angel. 5 But he knew not; and he said unto him, "Canst thou go with

---

9. The levirate law places an obligation on Raguel, Sara's father, and on Tobias, her closest eligible relative.
10. NEB: "do not leave her in the lurch as long as she lives."

11. RSV: "shiftlessness." GOODSPEED: "worthlessness."

me to Rages? and knowest thou those places well?" 6 To whom the angel said, "I will go with thee, and I know the way well: for I have lodged with our brother Gabael." 7 Then Tobias said unto him, "Tarry for me, till I tell my father." 8 Then he said unto him, "Go, and tarry not."

So he went in and said to his father, "Behold, I have found one which will go with me." Then he said, "Call him unto me, that I may know of what tribe he is, and whether he be a trusty man to go with thee."

9 So he called him, and he came in, and they saluted one another. 10 Then Tobit said unto him, "Brother, shew me of what tribe and family thou art." 11 To whom he said, "Dost thou seek for a tribe or family, or an hired man to go with thy son?" Then Tobit said unto him, "I would know, brother, thy kindred and name." 12 Then he said, "I am Azarias, the son of Ananias the great, and of thy brethren." 13 Then Tobit said, "Thou art welcome, brother; be not now angry with me, because I have enquired to know thy tribe and thy family; for thou art my brother, of an honest and good stock: for I know Ananias and Nathan, sons of that great Semelias, as we went together to Jerusalem to worship, and offered the firstborn and the tenths of the fruits; and they were not seduced with the error of our brethren: my brother, thou art of a good stock. 14 But tell me, what wages shall I give thee? wilt thou a drachma a day, and things necessary, as to mine own son? 15 Yea, moreover, if ye return safe, I will add something to thy wages." 16 So they were well pleased. Then said he to Tobias, "Prepare thyself for the journey, and God send you a good journey."

And when his son had prepared all things for the journey, his father said, "Go thou with this man, and God, which dwelleth in heaven, prosper your journey, and the angel of God keep you company." So they went forth both, and the young man's dog with them.[12]

17 But Anna his mother wept, and said to Tobit, "Why hast thou sent away our son? is he not the staff of our hand, in going in and out before us? 18 Be not greedy to add money to money: but let it be as refuse in respect of our child. 19 For that which the Lord hath given us to live with doth suffice us." 20 Then said Tobit to her, "Take no care, my sister; he shall return in safety, and thine eyes shall see him. 21 For the good angel will keep him company, and his jour-

ney shall be prosperous, and he shall return safe." 22 Then she made an end of weeping.

The Fish

6 And as they went on their journey, they came in the evening to the river Tigris, and they lodged there. 2 And when the young man went down to wash himself, a fish leaped out of the river, and would have devoured him.[13] 3 Then the angel said unto him, "Take the fish." And the young man laid hold of the fish, and drew it to land. 4 To whom the angel said, "Open the fish, and take the heart and the liver and the gall, and put them up safely." 5 So the young man did as the angel commanded him; and when they had roasted the fish, they did eat it.

Then they both went on their way, till they drew near to Ecbatana. 6 Then the young man said to the angel, "Brother Azarias, to what use is the heart and the liver and the gall of the fish?" 7 And he said unto him, "Touching the heart and the liver, if a devil or an evil spirit trouble any, we must make a smoke thereof before the man or the woman, and the party shall be no more vexed. 8 As for the gall, it is good to anoint a man that hath whiteness in his eyes, and he shall be healed."

9 And when they were come near to Rages, 10 The angel said to the young man, "Brother, to day we shall lodge with Raguel, who is thy cousin; he also hath one only daughter named Sara; I will speak for her, that she may be given thee for a wife. 11 For to thee doth the right of her appertain, seeing thou only art of her kindred. 12 And the maid is fair and wise: now therefore hear me, and I will speak to her father; and when we return from Rages we will celebrate the marriage: for I know that Raguel cannot marry her to another according to the law of Moses, but he shall be guilty of death, because the right of inheritance doth rather appertain to thee than to any other."

13 Then the young man answered the angel, "I have heard, brother Azarias, that this maid hath been given to seven men, who all died in the marriage chamber. 14 And now I am the only son of my father, and I am afraid, lest, if I go in unto her, I die, as the other before: for a wicked spirit loveth her, which hurteth no body, but those which come unto her: wherefore I also fear lest I die, and bring my father's and my mother's life because of me to the grave with sorrow: for they have no other son to bury them." 15 Then

---

12. William Neil (*Harper's Bible Commentary*, Harper & Row, 1962) writes, "It is pleasant also to find a dog as Tobias' companion, instead of as mostly elsewhere in the Bible being depicted as a scavenger or used as a term of abuse."

13. NAB: "a large fish suddenly leaped out of the water and tried to swallow his foot."

the angel said unto him, "Dost thou not remember the precepts which thy father gave thee, that thou shouldest marry a wife of thine own kindred? wherefore hear me, O my brother; for she shall be given thee to wife; and make thou no reckoning of the evil spirit; for this same night shall she be given thee in marriage. 16 And when thou shalt come into the marriage chamber, thou shalt take the ashes of perfume, and shalt lay upon them some of the heart and liver of the fish, and shalt make a smoke with it: 17 And the devil shall smell it, and flee away, and never come again any more: but when thou shalt come to her, rise up both of you, and pray to God which is merciful, who will have pity on you, and save you: fear not, for she is appointed unto thee from the beginning; and thou shalt preserve her, and she shall go with thee. Moreover I suppose that she shall bear thee children." Now when Tobias had heard these things, he loved her, and his heart was effectually joined to her.

THE MARRIAGE TO SARA

7 And when they were come to Ecbatana, they came to the house of Raguel, and Sara met them: and after they had saluted one another, she brought them into the house. 2 Then said Raguel to Edna his wife, "How like is this young man to Tobit my cousin!" 3 And Raguel asked them, "From whence are ye, brethren?" To whom they said, "We are of the sons of Naphtali, which are captives in Nineveh." 4 Then he said to them, "Do ye know Tobit our kinsman?" And they said, "We know him." Then said he, "Is he in good health?" 5 And they said, "He is both alive, and in good health:" and Tobias said, "He is my father." 6 Then Raguel leaped up, and kissed him, and wept, 7 And blessed him, and said unto him, "Thou art the son of an honest and good man." But when he had heard that Tobit was blind, he was sorrowful, and wept. 8 And likewise Edna his wife and Sara his daughter wept.

Moreover they entertained them cheerfully; and after that they had killed a ram of the flock, they set store of meat on the table. Then said Tobias to Raphael, "Brother Azarias, speak of those things of which thou didst talk in the way, and let this business be dispatched." 9 So he communicated the matter with Raguel: and Raguel said to Tobias, "Eat and drink, and make merry: 10 For it is meet that thou shouldest marry my daughter: nevertheless I will declare unto thee the truth. 11 I have given my daughter in marriage to seven men, who died that night they came in unto her: nevertheless for the pres-

ent be merry." [14] But Tobias said, "I will eat nothing here, till we agree and swear one to another." 12 Raguel said, "Then take her from henceforth according to the manner, for thou art her cousin, and she is thine, and the merciful God give you good success in all things."

13 Then he called his daughter Sara, and she came to her father, and he took her by the hand, and gave her to be wife to Tobias, saying, "Behold, take her after the law of Moses, and lead her away to thy father." And he blessed them; 14 And called Edna his wife, and took paper, and did write an instrument of covenants, and sealed it. 15 Then they began to eat.

16 After Raguel called his wife Edna, and said unto her, "Sister, prepare another chamber, and bring her in thither." 17 Which when she had done as he had bidden her, she brought her thither: and she wept, and she received the tears of her daughter, and said unto her, 18 "Be of good comfort, my daughter; the Lord of heaven and earth give thee joy for this thy sorrow: be of good comfort, my daughter."

8 And when they had supped, they brought Tobias in unto her. 2 And as he went, he remembered the words of Raphael, and took the ashes of the perfumes, and put the heart and the liver of the fish thereupon, and made a smoke therewith. 3 The which smell when the evil spirit had smelled, he fled into the utmost parts of Egypt, and the angel bound him.

4 And after that they were both shut in together, Tobias rose out of the bed, and said, "Sister, arise, and let us pray that God would have pity on us." 5 Then began Tobias to say, "Blessed art thou, O God of our fathers, and blessed is thy holy and glorious name for ever; let the heavens bless thee, and all thy creatures. 6 Thou madest Adam, and gavest him Eve his wife for an helper and stay: of them came mankind: thou hast said, 'It is not good that man should be alone; let us make unto him an aid like unto himself.' 7 And now, O Lord, I take not this my sister for lust, but uprightly: therefore mercifully ordain that we may become aged together." 8 And she said with him, "Amen." 9 So they slept both that night.

And Raguel arose, and went and made a grave, 10 Saying, "I fear lest he also be dead." 11 But when Raguel was come into his house 12 He said unto his wife Edna, "Send one of the maids, and let her see whether he be alive: if he be not,

---

14. There is macabre humor in this line. Raguel rises the next morning and digs a grave for Tobias.

that we may bury him, and no man know it."
13 So the maid opened the door, and went in, and
found them both asleep, 14 And came forth, and
told them that he was alive.

15 Then Raguel praised God, and said, "O
God, thou art worthy to be praised with all pure
and holy praise; therefore let thy saints praise
thee with all thy creatures; and let all thine angels
and thine elect praise thee for ever. 16 Thou art
to be praised, for thou hast made me joyful; and
that is not come to me which I suspected; but
thou hast dealt with us according to thy great
mercy. 17 Thou art to be praised, because thou
hast had mercy of two that were the only
begotten children of their fathers: grant them
mercy, O Lord, and finish their life in health with
joy and mercy." 18 Then Raguel bade his
servants to fill the grave.

19 And he kept the wedding feast fourteen
days. 20 For before the days of the marriage
were finished, Raguel had said unto him by an
oath, that he should not depart till the fourteen
days of the marriage were expired; 21 And then
he should take the half of his goods, and go in
safety to his father; and should have the rest
"when I and my wife be dead."
9 Then Tobias called Raphael, and said unto
him, 2 "Brother Azarias, take with thee a servant, and two camels, and go to Rages of Media
to Gabael, and bring me the money, and bring
him to the wedding.[15] 3 For Raguel hath sworn
that I shall not depart. 4 But my father counteth
the days; and if I tarry long, he will be very
sorry." 5 So Raphael went out, and lodged with
Gabael, and gave him the handwriting: who
brought forth bags which were sealed up, and
gave them to him. 6 And early in the morning
they went forth both together, and came to the
wedding: and Tobias blessed his wife.

THE HOMECOMING

10 Now Tobit his father counted every day: and
when the days of the journey were expired, and
they came not, 2 Then Tobit said, "Are they
detained? or is Gabael dead, and there is no man
to give him the money?" 3 Therefore he was very
sorry. 4 Then his wife said unto him, "My son is
dead, seeing he stayeth long"; and she began to
bewail him, and said, 5 "Now I care for nothing,
my son, since I have let thee go, the light of mine
eyes." 6 To whom Tobit said, "Hold thy peace,
take no care, for he is safe." 7 But she said,
"Hold thy peace and deceive me not; my son is

dead." And she went out every day into the way
which they went, and did eat no meat in the
daytime, and ceased not whole nights to bewail
her son Tobias, until the fourteen days of the
wedding were expired, which Raguel had sworn
that he should spend there.

Then Tobias said to Raguel, "Let me go, for
my father and mother look no more to see me."
8 But his father in law said unto him, "Tarry with
me, and I will send to thy father, and they shall
declare unto him how things go with thee."
9 But Tobias said, "No; but let me go to my
father." 10 Then Raguel arose, and gave him
Sara his wife, and half his goods, servants, and
cattle, and money: 11 And he blessed them, and
sent them away, saying, "The God of heaven give
you a prosperous journey, my children." 12 And
he said to his daughter, "Honour thy father and
thy mother in law, which are now thy parents,
that I may hear good report of thee." And he
kissed her. Edna also said to Tobias, "The Lord
of heaven restore thee, my dear brother, and
grant that I may see thy children of my daughter
Sara before I die, that I may rejoice before the
Lord: behold, I commit my daughter unto thee of
special trust; wherefore do not entreat her evil."

11 After these things Tobias went his way,
praising God that he had given him a prosperous
journey, and blessed Raguel and Edna his wife,
and went on his way till they drew near unto
Nineveh. 2 Then Raphael said to Tobias, "Thou
knowest, brother, how thou didst leave thy father:
3 Let us haste before thy wife, and prepare the
house. 4 And take in thine hand the gall of the
fish." So they went their way, and the dog went
after them.

5 Now Anna sat looking about toward the way
for her son. 6 And when she espied him coming,
she said to his father, "Behold, thy son cometh,
and the man that went with him." 7 Then said
Raphael, "I know, Tobias, that thy father will
open his eyes. 8 Therefore anoint thou his eyes
with the gall, and being pricked therewith, he
shall rub, and the whiteness shall fall away, and
he shall see thee." 9 Then Anna ran forth, and
fell upon the neck of her son, and said unto him,
"Seeing I have seen thee, my son, from henceforth I am content to die." And they wept both.
10 Tobit also went forth toward the door, and
stumbled: but his son ran unto him, 11 And
took hold of his father: and he strake of the gall
on his father's eyes, saying, "Be of good hope, my
father." 12 And when his eyes began to smart,
he rubbed them; 13 And the whiteness pilled
away from the corners of his eyes: and when he
saw his son, he fell upon his neck. 14 And he

---

15. NAB: "the wedding celebration."

wept, and said, "Blessed art thou, O God, and blessed is thy name for ever; and blessed are all thine holy angels: 15 For thou hast scourged, and hast taken pity on me: for, behold, I see my son Tobias." And his son went in rejoicing, and told his father the great things that had happened to him in Media.

16 Then Tobit went out to meet his daughter in law at the gate of Nineveh, rejoicing, and praising God: and they which saw him go marvelled, because he had received his sight. 17 But Tobit gave thanks before them, because God had mercy on him. And when he came near to Sara his daughter in law, he blessed her, saying, "Thou art welcome, daughter: God be blessed, which hath brought thee unto us, and blessed be thy father and thy mother." And there was joy among all his brethren which were at Nineveh. 18 And Ahikar, and Nadab his brother's son, came: 19 And Tobias' wedding was kept seven days with great joy.

Raphael Reveals His Identity

12 Then Tobit called his son Tobias, and said unto him, "My son, see that the man have his wages, which went with thee, and thou must give him more." 2 And Tobias said unto him, "O father, it is no harm to me to give him half of those things which I have brought: 3 For he hath brought me again to thee in safety, and made whole my wife,[16] and brought me the money, and likewise healed thee." 4 Then the old man said, "It is due unto him."

5 So he called the angel, and he said unto him, "Take half of all that ye have brought, and go away in safety." 6 Then he took them both apart, and said unto them, "Bless God, praise him, and magnify him, and praise him for the things which he hath done unto you in the sight of all that live. It is good to praise God, and exalt his name, and honourably to shew forth the works of God; therefore be not slack to praise him. 7 It is good to keep close the secret of a king, but it is honourable to reveal the works of God. Do that which is good, and no evil shall touch you. 8 Prayer is good with fasting and alms and righteousness. A little with righteousness is better than much with unrighteousness. It is better to give alms than to lay up gold: 9 For alms doth deliver from death, and shall purge away all sin. Those that exercise alms and righteousness shall be filled with life: 10 But they that sin are enemies to their own life.

11 "Surely I will keep close nothing from you. For I said, 'It was good to keep close the secret of

a king, but that it was honourable to reveal the works of God.' 12 Now therefore, when thou didst pray, and Sara thy daughter in law, I did bring the remembrance of your prayers before the Holy One: and when thou didst bury the dead, I was with thee likewise. 13 And when thou didst not delay to rise up, and leave thy dinner, to go and cover the dead, thy good deed was not hid from me: but I was with thee. 14 And now God hath sent me to heal thee and Sara thy daughter in law. 15 I am Raphael, one of the seven holy angels,[17] which present the prayers of the saints, and which go in and out before the glory of the Holy One."

16 Then they were both troubled, and fell upon their faces: for they feared. 17 But he said unto them, "Fear not, for it shall go well with you; praise God therefore. 18 For not of any favour of mine, but by the will of our God I came; wherefore praise him for ever. 19 All these days I did appear unto you; but I did neither eat nor drink, but ye did see a vision. 20 Now therefore give God thanks: for I go up to him that sent me; but write all things which are done in a book." 21 And when they arose, they saw him no more. 22 Then they confessed the great and wonderful works of God, and how the angel of the Lord has appeared unto them.

Tobit's Prayer of Joy[18]

13 Then Tobit wrote a prayer of rejoicing, and said,

"Blessed be God that liveth for ever,
And blessed be his kingdom.

2   For he doth scourge, and hath mercy:
He leadeth down to hell, and bringeth up again:
Neither is there any that can avoid his hand.

3   "Confess him before the Gentiles, ye children of Israel;
For he hath scattered us among them.

4   There declare his greatness,
And extol him before all the living;
For he is our Lord,
And he is the God our Father for ever.

5   And he will scourge us for our iniquities,
And will gather us out of all nations,

---

16. JB: "cured my wife." KNOX: "rid her of the fiend's attack."

17. This is among the earliest references to archangels. RSV footnotes: "The growth of angelology was characteristic of the Judaism of this period; this was partly due to an increasing sense of God's transcendence and partly, perhaps, to Persian influences."

18. (13:1-18) This hymn of praise, which is thought to be a later addition to the book, has no particular appropriateness to Tobit's history.

Among whom he hath scattered us.

6   If ye turn to him with your whole heart,
and with your whole mind,
And deal uprightly before him,
Then will he turn unto you,
And will not hide his face from you.
Therefore see what he will do with you,
And confess him with your whole mouth,
And praise the Lord of might, and extol
the everlasting King.
In the land of my captivity do I praise
him,
And declare his might and majesty to a
sinful nation.
O ye sinners, turn and do justice before
him:
Who can tell if he will accept you, and
have mercy on you?

7   "I will extol my God,
And my soul shall praise the King of
heaven,
And shall rejoice in his greatness.

8   Let all men speak,
And let all praise him for his righteousness.

9   "O Jerusalem, the holy city,
He will scourge thee for thy children's
works,
And will have mercy again on the sons of
the righteous.

10   Give praise to the Lord, for he is good:
and praise the everlasting King,
That his tabernacle may be builded in
thee again with joy,
And let him make joyful there in thee
those that are captives,
And love in thee for ever those that are
miserable.

11   Many nations shall come from far to the
name of the Lord God with gifts in
their hands,
Even gifts to the King of heaven; all
generations shall praise thee with great
joy.

12   Cursed are all they which hate thee,
And blessed shall all be which love thee
for ever.

13   Rejoice and be glad for the children of the
just:
For they shall be gathered together,
And shall bless the Lord of the just.

14   O blessed are they which love thee, for
they shall rejoice in thy peace:
Blessed are they which have been sorrowful for all thy scourges;

For they shall rejoice for thee, when they
have seen all thy glory, and shall be
glad for ever.

15   "Let my soul bless God the great King.

16   For Jerusalem shall be built up with
sapphires, and emeralds, and precious
stone;
Thy walls and towers and battlements
with pure gold.

17   And the streets of Jerusalem shall be
paved with beryl and carbuncle and
stones of Ophir.[19]

18   And all her streets shall say, 'Alleluia';
And they shall praise him, saying,
'Blessed be God, which hath extolled it
for ever.' "

TOBIT DIES

14 So Tobit made an end of praising God.
2 And he was eight and fifty years old when he
lost his sight, which was restored to him after
eight years: and he gave alms, and he increased in
the fear of the Lord God, and praised him.

3 And when he was very aged, he called his
son, and the six sons of his son, and said to him,
"My son, take thy children; for, behold, I am
aged, and am ready to depart out of this life.
4 Go into Media, my son, for I surely believe
those things which Nahum the prophet[20] spake of
Nineveh, that it shall be overthrown; and that for
a time peace shall rather be in Media; and that
our brethren shall lie scattered in the earth from
that good land: and Jerusalem shall be desolate,
and the house of God in it shall be burned, and
shall be desolate for a time; 5 And that again
God will have mercy on them, and bring them
again into the land, where they shall build a
temple, but not like to the first, until the time of
that age be fulfilled; and afterward they shall
return from all places of their captivity, and build
up Jerusalem gloriously, and the house of God
shall be built in it for ever with a glorious building, as the prophets have spoken thereof.
6 And all nations shall turn, and fear the Lord
God truly, and shall bury their idols. 7 So shall
all nations praise the Lord, and his people shall
confess God, and the Lord shall exalt his people;
and all those which love the Lord God in truth
and justice shall rejoice, shewing mercy to our
brethren.

19. (13:16-18) This description is echoed in *Revelation* 21:18-21,
which pictures the New Jerusalem.
20. Following a variant reading, RSV writes "Jonah the
prophet." This would refer to the unfulfilled prophecy in
Jonah 3:4.

8 "And now, my son, depart out of Nineveh, because that those things which the prophet Nahum spake shall surely come to pass. 9 But keep thou the law and the commandments, and shew thyself merciful and just, that it may go well with thee. 10 And bury me decently, and thy mother with me; but tarry no longer at Nineveh. Remember, my son, how Nadab handled Ahikar that brought him up, how out of light he brought him into darkness, and how he rewarded him again: yet Ahikar was saved, but the other had his reward: for he went down into darkness. Ahikar gave alms, and escaped the snares of death which they had set for him: but Nadab fell into the snare, and perished. 11 Wherefore now, my son, consider what alms doeth, and how righteousness doth deliver."

When he had said these things, he gave up the ghost in the bed, being an hundred and eight and fifty years old; and he buried him honourably. 12 And when Anna his mother was dead, he buried her with his father. But Tobias departed with his wife and children to Ecbatana, to Raguel his father in law, 13 Where he became old with honour, and he buried his father and mother in law honourably, and he inherited their substance, and his father Tobit's. 14 And he died at Ecbatana in Media, being an hundred and seven and twenty years old. 15 But before he died he heard of the destruction of Nineveh, which was taken by Nebuchadnezzar and Assuerus: and before his death he rejoiced over Nineveh.[21]

21. Nabopolassar, king of Babylon, and Cyaxares conquered Nineveh in 612 B.C. In mentioning Nebuchadnezzar and Assuerus (i.e., Xerxes), the author is calling up great names from the past.

Introduction to
JUDITH

"But the Almighty Lord hath disappointed them by the hand of a woman."

Written about 150 B.C. in Palestine by a pious observer of the Law, *Judith* is didactic fiction. It assured the Jews of God's continuing presence among them and promised they would prevail over all enemies. Probably it referred to a particular threat or persecution of the time, but, if so, no one has established what it was.

In this short story, the threat is the armies commanded by Holofernes, who is conquering the western nations and imposing worship of King Nebuchadnezzar. As the forces draw near Israel, they are thwarted by God, working by the hand of a woman of Bethulia. Judith uses her womanly charms to gain access to Holofernes' bedchamber and then cuts off his head. The tale has proved disturbing to readers who do not like to think of almighty God employing guile, seduction, and a gory murder to effect his purposes.

Judith offers an exciting narrative sustained by vivid characterization. The heroine, whose name means Jewess, is a pious Israelite, a beautiful widow, and an ideal political assassin. One must be impressed by her confidence in her abilities, by the subtlety of her cover story, by her behavior and richly submissive language before Holofernes, and by the careful preparations for the killing and the subsequent escape. The emphasis on her punctilious observance of the Law—prayer, diet, fast days, etc.—seems intended to qualify the worldly competence she demonstrates in her fatal enterprise.

Lesser characters are also well depicted. Holofernes is by no means the bacchanalian brute that tradition has described. There is no evidence he is given to drunkenness or lechery prior to the night of his death. Instead, he is shown to be dutiful to his king, effective as a military officer, and courteous and considerate toward Judith. Eventually, he finds himself facing a gorgeously submissive woman. (Indeed, in the Vulgate, God enhances her beauty to make her irresistible.) When, after several days he seeks to seduce her, he seems more concerned about maintaining his manly reputation than about fulfilling his lust: "We shall be disgraced if we let a woman like this go without knowing her better. If we do not seduce her, everyone will laugh at us!" (JB) On the fatal night, perhaps because of his trepidation concerning Judith, Holofernes drinks "much more wine than he had drunk at any time in one day since he was born" and falls asleep. Instead of being a lecherous, drunken stereotype, the general emerges as a sympathetic human being, vulnerable before temptations which God did not intend he should withstand.

The other figures in the story each receive more than passing characterization. Nebuchadnezzar displays the vengeful petulance of a king who esteems himself a god. Achior, a member of Holofernes' staff, is a student of history whose conversion to Judaism is a result of both knowledge and experience. And Ozias, the governor of Bethulia, is a Jew whose faith wavers under persecution. Probably, it was to Israelites such as Ozias that the book was addressed.

The author of *Judith* devoted seven chapters to circumstances leading up to the appearance of the heroine. He wanted to dramatize the overwhelming threat facing Israel. It is unlikely he used the chapters to give authenticity to the story; there are too many errors and obscurities for the narrative to be considered history. The first verse, for example, shows Nebuchadnezzar, king of the Assyrians, reigning in his capital city Nineveh in the twelfth year of his reign. In fact, Nebuchadnezzar did not rule the Assyrians, and Nineveh was destroyed seven years before he became king. In 2:21, Holofernes and his armies "marched for three days from Nineveh to the plain of Bectileth" (RSV); actually these sites are three hundred miles apart. Many of the named people (Arioch, the Chellians, some of Judith's ancestors) and places (Sur, Ocina, Bethulia, Belmaim, etc.) have never been historically identified. Some scholars have argued that the historical confusion in *Judith* was intended to show the story is fictional and to focus the reader's attention on the religious theme.

Judith is a masterpiece of narrative art. Lacking the quality of rural simplicity found in *Ruth*, the intense personal piety underlying *Tobit*, and the supernatural elements which appear in *Jonah*, it champions passionate nationalism and an active faith. It illustrates Achior's view that the Israelites are invincible as long as they maintain their faith and do not sin against the Lord. And it goes further to suggest a more modern concept: in this world, God's work is performed by human beings.

JUDITH

THE ASSYRIAN CONQUEST

The Defeat of Arphaxad

1 In the twelfth year of the reign of Nebuchadnezzar, who reigned in Nineveh, the great city; in the days of Arphaxad, which reigned over the Medes in Ecbatana, 2 And built in Ecbatana walls round about of stones hewn three cubits broad and six cubits long, and made the height of the wall seventy cubits, and the breadth thereof fifty cubits: 3 And set the towers thereof upon the gates of it, an hundred cubits high, and the breadth thereof in the foundation threescore cubits: 4 And he made the gates thereof, even gates that were raised to the height of seventy cubits, and the breadth of them was forty cubits, for the going forth of his mighty armies, and for the setting in array of his footmen: 5 Even in those days king Nebuchadnezzar made war with king Arphaxad in the great plain, which is the plain in the borders of Ragau, 6 And there came unto him[1] all they that dwelt in the hill country, and all that dwelt by Euphrates, and Tigris, and Hydaspes, and the plain of Arioch the king of the Elams, and very many nations of the sons of Chelod, assembled themselves to the battle.

7 Then Nebuchadnezzar king of the Assyrians sent unto all that dwelt in Persia, and to all that dwelt westward, and to those that dwelt in Cilicia, and Damascus, and Lebanon, and Antilebanon, and to all that dwelt upon the sea coast, 8 And to those among the nations that were of Carmel, and Gilead, and the higher Galilee, and the great plain of Esdraelon, 9 And to all that were in Samaria and the cities thereof, and beyond Jordan unto Jerusalem, and Betane, and Chellus, and Cadesh, and the river of Egypt, and Tahpanhes, and Rameses, and all the land of Goshen, 10 Until ye come beyond Tanis and Memphis, and to all the inhabitants of Egypt, until ye come to the borders of Ethiopia. 11 But all the inhabitants of the land made light of the commandment of Nebuchadnezzar king of the Assyrians, neither went they with him to the battle; for they were not afraid of him: yea, he was before them as one man, and they sent away his ambassadors from them without effect, and with disgrace.

12 Therefore Nebuchadnezzar was very angry with all this country, and sware by his throne and kingdom, that he would surely be avenged upon all those coasts of Cilicia, and Damascus, and Syria, and that he would slay with the sword all the inhabitants of the land of Moab, and the children of Ammon, and all Judea, and all that were in Egypt, till ye come to the borders of the two seas. 13 Then he marched in battle array with his power against king Arphaxad in the seventeenth year, and he prevailed in his battle: for he overthrew all the power of Arphaxad, and all his horsemen, and all his chariots, 14 And became lord of his cities, and came unto Ecbatana, and took the towers, and spoiled the streets thereof, and turned the beauty thereof into shame.[2] 15 He took also Arphaxad in the mountains of Ragau, and smote him through with his darts, and destroyed him utterly that day. 16 So he returned afterward to Nineveh, both he and all his company of sundry nations, being a very great multitude of men of war, and there he took his ease, and banqueted, both he and his army, an hundred and twenty days.

The Campaign against the West

2 And in the eighteenth year, the two and twentieth day of the first month, there was talk in the house of Nebuchadnezzar king of the Assyrians, that he should, as he said, avenge himself on all the earth.[3] 2 So he called unto him all his officers, and all his nobles, and communicated with them his secret counsel, and concluded the afflicting of the whole earth out of his own mouth. 3 Then they decreed to destroy all flesh, that did not obey the commandment of his mouth.

4 And when he had ended his counsel, Nebuchadnezzar king of the Assyrians called Holofernes the chief captain of his army, which was next unto him, and said unto him, 5 "Thus saith the great king, the lord of the whole earth, Behold, thou shalt go forth from my presence, and take with thee men that trust in their own strength, of footmen an hundred and twenty thousand; and the number of horses with their riders twelve thousand. 6 And thou shalt go against all the west country, because they disobeyed my commandment. 7 And thou shalt declare unto them, that they prepare for me earth

---

1. I.e., to King Arphaxad.

2. JB: "he seized its towers and plundered its market places, reducing its former magnificence to a mockery."

3. NEB, RSV: "the whole region."

193

and water:[4] for I will go forth in my wrath against them, and will cover the whole face of the earth with the feet of mine army, and I will give them for a spoil unto them: 8 So that their slain shall fill their valleys and brooks, and the river shall be filled with their dead, till it overflow: 9 And I will lead them captives to the utmost parts of all the earth. 10 Thou therefore shalt go forth, and take beforehand for me all their coasts: and if they will yield themselves unto thee, thou shalt reserve them for me till the day of their punishment. 11 But concerning them that rebel, let not thine eye spare them; but put them to the slaughter, and spoil them wheresoever thou goest. 12 For as I live, and by the power of my kingdom, whatsoever I have spoken, that will I do by mine hand. 13 And take thou heed that thou transgress none of the commandments of thy lord, but accomplish them fully, as I have commanded thee, and defer not to do them."

14 Then Holofernes went forth from the presence of his lord, and called all the governors and captains, and the officers of the army of Assyria; 15 And he mustered the chosen men for the battle, as his lord had commanded him, unto an hundred and twenty thousand, and twelve thousand archers on horseback; 16 And he ranged them, as a great army is ordered for the war. 17 And he took camels and asses for their carriages, a very great number; and sheep and oxen and goats without number for their provision: 18 And plenty of victual for every man of the army, and very much gold and silver out of the king's house. 19 Then he went forth and all his power to go before king Nebuchadnezzar in the voyage, and to cover all the face of the earth westward with their chariots, and horsemen, and their chosen footmen. 20 A great number also of sundry countries came with them like locusts, and like the sand of the earth: for the multitude was without number.

21 And they went forth of Nineveh three days' journey toward the plain of Bectileth, and pitched from Bectileth near the mountain which is at the left hand of the upper Cilicia. 22 Then he took all his army, his footmen, and horsemen, and chariots, and went from thence into the hill country; 23 And destroyed Put and Lud, and spoiled all the children of Rasses, and the children of Ismael, which were toward the wilderness at the south of the land of the Chellians. 24 Then he went over Euphrates, and went through Mesopotamia, and destroyed all the high cities that

were upon the river Arbonai, till ye come to the sea. 25 And he took the borders of Cilicia, and killed all that resisted him, and came to the borders of Japheth, which were toward the south, over against Arabia. 26 He compassed also all the children of Midian, and burned up their tabernacles, and spoiled their sheepcotes. 27 Then Then he went down into the plain of Damascus in the time of wheat harvest, and burnt up all their fields, and destroyed their flocks and herds, also he spoiled their cities, and utterly wasted their countries, and smote all their young men with the edge of the sword. 28 Therefore the fear and dread of him fell upon all the inhabitants of the sea coasts, which were in Sidon and Tyrus, and them that dwelt in Sur and Ocina, and all that dwelt in Jemnaan; and they that dwelt in Azotus and Ascalon feared him greatly.

The Western Nations Submit

3 So they sent ambassadors unto him to treat of peace, saying, 2 "Behold, we the servants of Nebuchadnezzar the great king lie before thee; use us as shall be good in thy sight. 3 Behold, our houses, and all our places, and all our fields of wheat, and flocks, and herds, and all the lodges of our tents, lie before thy face; use them as it pleaseth thee. 4 Behold, even our cities and the inhabitants thereof are thy servants; come and deal with them as seemeth good unto thee."

5 So the men came to Holofernes, and declared unto him after this manner. 6 Then came he down toward the sea coast, both he and his army, and set garrisons in the high cities, and took out of them chosen men for aid. 7 So they and all the country round about received them with garlands, with dances, and with timbrels. 8 Yet he did cast down their frontiers, and cut down their groves: for he had decreed to destroy all the gods of the land, that all nations should worship Nebuchadnezzar only, and that all tongues and tribes should call upon him as god.[5] 9 Also he came over against Esdraelon, near unto Dothan, over against the great strait of Judea. 10 And he pitched between Geba and Scythopolis, and there he tarried a whole month, that he might gather together all the carriages of his army.

THE THREAT TO ISRAEL
Judea Prepares

4 Now the children of Israel, that dwelt in Judea, heard all that Holofernes the chief captain of

---

4. Offering earth and water to a Persian king was a sign of unconditional surrender. Nebuchadnezzar, however, speaks ironically: he plans to fill the land and rivers with dead bodies.

5. Holofernes appears to exceed his original commission. He was ordered to punish the western nations; now he seeks to impose worship of Nebuchadnezzar.

Nebuchadnezzar king of the Assyrians had done to the nations, and after what manner he had spoiled all their temples, and brought them to nought. 2 Therefore they were exceedingly afraid of him, and were troubled for Jerusalem, and for the temple of the Lord their God: 3 For they were newly returned from the captivity, and all the people of Judea were lately gathered together: and the vessels, and the altar, and the house, were sanctified after the profanation. 4 Therefore they sent into all the coasts of Samaria, and the villages, and to Bethoron, and Belmen, and Jericho, and to Choba, and Esora, and to the valley of Salem: 5 And possessed themselves beforehand of all the tops of the high mountains, and fortified the villages that were in them, and laid up victuals for the provision of war: for their fields were of late reaped. 6 Also Joakim the high priest, which was in those days in Jerusalem, wrote to them that dwelt in Bethulia, and Bethomesthaim, which is over against Esdraelon toward the open country, near to Dothan, 7 Charging them to keep the passages of the hill country: for by them there was an entrance into Judea,[6] and it was easy to stop them that would come up, because the passage was strait, for two men at the most. 8 And the children of Israel did as Joakim the high priest had commanded them, with the ancients of all the people of Israel, which dwelt at Jerusalem.

9 Then every man of Israel cried to God with great fervency, and with great vehemency did they humble their souls: 10 Both they, and their wives, and their children, and their cattle, and every stranger and hireling, and their servants bought with money, put sackcloth upon their loins. 11 Thus every man and woman, and the little children, and the inhabitants of Jerusalem, fell before the temple, and cast ashes upon their heads, and spread out their sackcloth before the face of the Lord: also they put sackcloth about the altar, 12 And cried to the God of Israel all with one consent earnestly, that he would not give their children for a prey, and their wives for a spoil, and the cities of their inheritance to destruction, and the sanctuary to profanation and reproach, and for the nations to rejoice at. 13 So God heard their prayers, and looked upon their afflictions: for the people fasted many days in all Judea and Jerusalem before the sanctuary of the Lord Almighty. 14 And Joakim the high priest, and all the priests that stood before the Lord, and they which ministered unto the Lord, had their loins girt with sackcloth, and offered the daily burnt offerings, with the vows and free gifts of the

people, 15 And had ashes on their mitres,[7] and cried unto the Lord with all their power, that he would look upon all the house of Israel graciously.

Achior Identifies the Israelites

5 Then was it declared to Holofernes, the chief captain of the army of Assyria, that the children of Israel had prepared for war, and had shut up the passages of the hill country, and had fortified all the tops of the high hills, and had laid impediments in the champaign countries: 2 Wherewith he was very angry, and called all the princes of Moab, and the captains of Ammon, and all the governors of the sea coast, 3 And he said unto them, "Tell me now, ye sons of Canaan, who this people is, that dwelleth in the hill country, and what are the cities that they inhabit, and what is the multitude of their army, and wherein is their power and strength, and what king is set over them, or captain of their army; 4 And why have they determined not to come and meet me, more than all the inhabitants of the west."

5 Then said Achior, the captain of all the sons of Ammon, "Let my lord now hear a word from the mouth of thy servant, and I will declare unto thee the truth concerning this people, which dwelleth near thee, and inhabiteth the hill countries: and there shall no lie come out of the mouth of thy servant.[8] 6 This people are descended of the Chaldeans: 7 And they sojourned heretofore in Mesopotamia, because they would not follow the gods of their fathers, which were in the land of Chaldea, 8 For they left the way of their ancestors, and worshipped the God of heaven, the God whom they knew: so they cast them out from the face of their gods, and they fled into Mesopotamia, and sojourned there many days. 9 Then their God commanded them to depart from the place where they sojourned, and to go into the land of Canaan: where they dwelt, and were increased with gold and silver, and with very much cattle.

10 "But when a famine covered all the land of Canaan, they went down into Egypt, and sojourned there, while they were nourished, and became there a great multitude, so that one could not number their nation. 11 Therefore the king of Egypt rose up against them, and dealt subtilly with them, and brought them low with labouring in brick, and made them slaves. 12 Then they

---

6. JB: "to occupy the mountain passes, the only means of access to Judaea."

7. NAB, JB: "turbans."
8. (5:5-21) To explain the nature of the Jewish people and their God, Achior surveys Israel's history from the time of Abraham to the return from exile.

cried unto their God, and he smote all the land of Egypt with incurable plagues: so the Egyptians cast them out of their sight. 13 And God dried the Red sea before them, 14 And brought them to mount Sinai and Cadesh-barnea, and cast forth all that dwelt in the wilderness. 15 So they dwelt in the land of the Amorites, and they destroyed by their strength all them of Heshbon, and passing over Jordan they possessed all the hill country. 16 And they cast forth before them the Canaanite, the Perizzite, the Jebusite, and the Schechemite, and all the Girgashites, and they dwelt in that country many days.

17 "And whilst they sinned not before their God, they prospered, because the God that hateth iniquity was with them. 18 But when they departed from the way which he appointed them, they were destroyed in many battles very sore, and were led captives into a land that was not theirs, and the temple of their God was cast to the ground, and their cities were taken by the enemies. 19 But now are they returned to their God, and are come up from the places where they were scattered, and have possessed Jerusalem, where their sanctuary is, and are seated in the hill country; for it was desolate.

20 "Now therefore, my lord and governor, if there be any error in this people, and they sin against their God, let us consider that this shall be their ruin, and let us go up, and we shall overcome them. 21 But if there be no iniquity in their nation, let my lord now pass by, lest their Lord defend them, and their God be for them, and we become a reproach before all the world."

22 And when Achior had finished these sayings, all the people standing round about the tent murmured, and the chief men of Holofernes, and all that dwelt by the sea side, and in Moab, spake that he should kill him. 23 "For," say they, "we will not be afraid of the face of the children of Israel: for, lo, it is a people that have no strength nor power for a strong battle. 24 Now therefore, lord Holofernes, we will go up, and they shall be a prey to be devoured of all thine army."

6 And when the tumult of men that were about the council was ceased, Holofernes the chief captain of the army of Assyria said unto Achior and all the Moabites before all the company of other nations, 2 "And who art thou, Achior, and the hirelings of Ephraim,[9] that thou hast prophesied among us as to day, and hast said, that we should not make war with the people of Israel, because their God will defend them? and who is God but Nebuchadnezzar? 3 He will send his

power, and will destroy them from the face of the earth, and their God shall not deliver them: but we his servants will destroy them as one man; for they are not able to sustain the power of our horses. 4 For with them we will tread them under foot, and their mountains shall be drunken with their blood, and their fields shall be filled with their dead bodies, and their footsteps shall not be able to stand before us, for they shall utterly perish, saith king Nebuchadnezzar, lord of all the earth: for he said, 'None of my words shall be in vain.' 5 And thou, Achior, an hireling of Ammon, which hast spoken these words in the day of thine iniquity, shalt see my face no more from this day, until I take vengeance of this nation that came out of Egypt. 6 And then shall the sword of mine army, and the multitude of them that serve me, pass through thy sides, and thou shalt fall among their slain when I return. 7 Now therefore my servants shall bring thee back into the hill country, and shall set thee in one of the cities of the passages: 8 And thou shalt not perish, till thou be destroyed with them. 9 And if thou persuade thyself in thy mind that they shall not be taken, let not thy countenance fall: I have spoken it, and none of my words shall be in vain."

10 Then Holofernes commanded his servants, that waited in his tent, to take Achior, and bring him to Bethulia, and deliver him into the hands of the children of Israel. 11 So his servants took him, and brought him out of the camp into the plain, and they went from the midst of the plain into the hill country, and came unto the fountains that were under Bethulia. 12 And when the men of the city saw them, they took up their weapons, and went out of the city to the top of the hill: and every man that used a sling kept them from coming up by casting of stones against them. 13 Nevertheless having gotten privily under the hill, they bound Achior, and cast him down, and left him at the foot of the hill, and returned to their lord. 14 But the Israelites descended from their city, and came unto him, and loosed him, and brought him into Bethulia, and presented him to the governors of the city: 15 Which were in those days Ozias the son of Mica, of the tribe of Simeon, and Chabris the son of Gothoniel, and Charmis the son of Melchiel. 16 And they called together all the ancients of the city, and all their youth ran together, and their women, to the assembly, and they set Achior in the midst of all their people. Then Ozias asked him of that which was done. 17 And he answered and declared unto them the words of the council of Holofernes, and all the words that he had spoken in the midst of the princes of Assyria, and whatsoever Holo-

---

9. NEB: "you and your Ammonite mercenaries."

fernes had spoken proudly against the house of Israel. 18 Then the people fell down and worshipped God, and cried unto God, saying, 19 "O Lord God of heaven, behold their pride, and pity the low estate of our nation, and look upon the face of those that are sanctified unto thee this day." 20 Then they comforted Achior, and praised him greatly. 21 And Ozias took him out of the assembly unto his house, and made a feast to the elders; and they called on the God of Israel all that night for help.

The Siege of Bethulia

7 The next day Holofernes commanded all his army, and all his people which were come to take his part, that they should remove their camp against Bethulia, to take aforehand the ascents of the hill country, and to make war against the children of Israel. 2 Then their strong men removed their camps in that day, and the army of the men of war was an hundred and seventy thousand footmen, and twelve thousand horsemen, beside the baggage, and other men that were afoot among them, a very great multitude. 3 And they camped in the valley near unto Bethulia, by the fountain, and they spread themselves in breadth over Dothan, even to Belmaim, and in length from Bethulia unto Cyamon, which is over against Esdraelon. 4 Now the children of Israel, when they saw the multitude of them, were greatly troubled, and said every one to his neighbour, "Now will these men lick up the face of the earth;[10] for neither the high mountains, nor the valleys, nor the hills, are able to bear their weight." 5 Then every man took up his weapons of war, and when they had kindled fires upon their towers, they remained and watched all that night.

6 But in the second day Holofernes brought forth all his horsemen in the sight of the children of Israel which were in Bethulia, 7 And viewed the passages up to the city, and came to the fountains of their waters, and took them, and set garrisons of men of war over them, and he himself removed toward his people. 8 Then came unto him all the chief of the children of Esau, and all the governors of the people of Moab, and the captains of the sea coast, and said, 9 "Let our lord now hear a word, that there be not an overthrow in thine army. 10 For this people of the children of Israel do not trust in their spears, but in the height of the mountains wherein they dwell, because it is not easy to come up to the tops of their mountains. 11 Now therefore, my lord, fight not against them in battle

10. NAB: "devour the whole country."

array, and there shall not so much as one man of thy people perish. 12 Remain in thy camp, and keep all the men of thine army, and let thy servants get into their hands the fountain of water, which issueth forth of the foot of the mountain: 13 For all the inhabitants of Bethulia have their water thence; so shall thirst kill them, and they shall give up their city, and we and our people shall go up to the tops of the mountains that are near, and will camp upon them, to watch that none go out of the city. 14 So they and their wives and their children shall be consumed with famine, and before the sword come against them, they shall be overthrown in the streets where they dwell. 15 Thus shalt thou render them an evil reward; because they rebelled, and met not thy person peaceably."

16 And these words pleased Holofernes and all his servants, and he appointed to do as they had spoken. 17 So the camp of the children of Ammon departed, and with them five thousand of the Assyrians, and they pitched in the valley, and took the waters, and the fountains of the waters of the children of Israel. 18 Then the children of Esau went up with the children of Ammon, and camped in the hill country over against Dothan: and they sent some of them toward the south, and toward the east, over against Egrebel, which is near unto Chus, that is upon the brook Mochmur; and the rest of the army of the Assyrians camped in the plain, and covered the face of the whole land; and their tents and carriages were pitched to a very great multitude.

19 Then the children of Israel cried unto the Lord their God, because their heart failed, for all their enemies had compassed them round about, and there was no way to escape out from among them. 20 Thus all the company of Assyria remained about them, both their footmen, chariots, and horsemen, four and thirty days, so that all their vessels of water failed all the inhabitants of Bethulia. 21 And the cisterns were emptied, and they had not water to drink their fill for one day; for they gave them drink by measure. 22 Therefore their young children were out of heart, and their women and young men fainted for thirst, and fell down in the streets of the city, and by the passages of the gates, and there was no longer any strength in them.

23 Then all the people assembled to Ozias, and to the chief of the city, both young men, and women, and children, and cried with a loud voice, and said before all the elders, 24 "God be judge between us and you: for ye have done us great injury, in that ye have not required peace of the children of Assyria. 25 For now we have no helper: but God hath sold us into their hands,

that we should be thrown down before them with thirst and great destruction. 26 Now therefore call them unto you, and deliver the whole city for a spoil to the people of Holofernes, and to all his army. 27 For it is better for us to be made a spoil unto them, than to die for thirst: for we will be his servants, that our souls may live, and not see the death of our infants before our eyes, nor our wives nor our children to die. 28 We take to witness against you the heaven and the earth, and our God and Lord of our fathers, which punisheth us according to our sins and the sins of our fathers, that he do not according as we have said this day." [11]

29 Then there was great weeping with one consent in the midst of the assembly; and they cried unto the Lord God with a loud voice. 30 Then said Ozias to them, "Brethren, be of good courage, let us yet endure five days, in the which space the Lord our God may turn his mercy toward us; for he will not forsake us utterly. 31 And if these days pass, and there come no help unto us, I will do according to your word." 32 And he dispersed the people, every one to their own charge; and they went unto the walls and towers of their city, and sent the women and children into their houses: and they were very low brought in the city.

JUDITH'S MISSION

8 Now at that time Judith heard thereof, which was the daughter of Merari, the son of Ox, the son of Joseph, the son of Oziel, the son of Helkias, the son of Ananias, the son of Gideon, the son of Raphaim, the son of Ahitub, the son of Elihu, the son of Eliab, the son of Nathanael, the son of Salamiel, the son of Salasadai, the son of Israel. 2 And Manasses was her husband, of her tribe and kindred, who died in the barley harvest. 3 For as he stood overseeing them that bound sheaves in the field, the heat came upon his head, and he fell on his bed, and died in the city of Bethulia: and they buried him with his fathers in the field between Dothan and Balamon. 4 So Judith was a widow in her house three years and four months. 5 And she made her a tent upon the top of her house, and put on sackcloth upon her loins, and ware her widow's apparel. 6 And she fasted all the days of her widowhood, save the eves of the sabbaths, and the sabbaths, and the eves of the new moons, and the new moons, and the feasts and solemn days of the house of Israel. 7 She was also of a goodly countenance, and very

beautiful to behold, and her husband Manasses had left her gold, and silver, and menservants, and maidservants, and cattle, and lands; and she remained upon them. 8 And there was none that gave her an ill word; for she feared God greatly.

Judith before the Elders

9 Now when she heard the evil words of the people against the governor, that they fainted for lack of water; for Judith had heard all the words that Ozias had spoken unto them, and that he had sworn to deliver the city unto the Assyrians after five days; 10 Then she sent her waiting woman, that had the government of all things that she had, to call Ozias and Chabris and Charmis, the ancients of the city.

11 And they came unto her, and she said unto them, "Hear me now, O ye governors of the inhabitants of Bethulia: for your words that ye have spoken before the people this day are not right, touching this oath which ye made and pronounced between God and you, and have promised to deliver the city to our enemies, unless within these days the Lord turn to help you. 12 And now who are ye that have tempted God this day, and stand instead of God among the children of men? 13 And now try the Lord Almighty, but ye shall never know any thing. 14 For ye cannot find the depth of the heart of man, neither can ye perceive the things that he thinketh: then how can ye search out God, that hath made all these things, and know his mind, or comprehend his purpose? Nay, my brethren, provoke not the Lord our God to anger. 15 For if he will not help us within these five days, he hath power to defend us when he will, even every day, or to destroy us before our enemies. 16 Do not bind the counsels of the Lord our God: for God is not as man, that he may be threatened; neither is he as the son of man, that he should be wavering. 17 Therefore let us wait for salvation of him, and call upon him to help us, and he will hear our voice, if it please him.

18 "For there arose none in our age, neither is there any now in these days, neither tribe, nor family, nor people, nor city, among us, which worship gods made with hands, as hath been aforetime. 19 For the which cause our fathers were given to the sword, and for a spoil, and had a great fall before our enemies. 20 But we know none other god, therefore we trust that he will not despise us, nor any of our nation. 21 For if we be taken so, all Judea shall lie waste, and our sanctuary shall be spoiled; and he will require the profanation thereof at our mouth. [12] 22 And the

---

11. JB: "By heaven and earth and by our God, the Lord of our fathers who is punishing us for our sins and the sins of our ancestors, we implore you to take this course now, today."

12. NEB: "God will hold us responsible for its desecration."

slaughter of our brethren, and the captivity of the country, and the desolation of our inheritance, will he turn upon our heads among the Gentiles, wheresoever we shall be in bondage; and we shall be an offence and a reproach to all them that possess us. 23 For our servitude shall not be directed to favour; but the Lord our God shall turn it to dishonour.

24 "Now therefore, O brethren, let us shew an example to our brethren, because their hearts depend upon us, and the sanctuary, and the house, and the altar, rest upon us. 25 Moreover let us give thanks to the Lord our God, which trieth us, even as he did our fathers. 26 Remember what things he did to Abraham, and how he tried Isaac, and what happened to Jacob in Mesopotamia of Syria, when he kept the sheep of Laban his mother's brother. 27 For he hath not tried us in the fire, as he did them, for the examination of their hearts, neither hath he taken vengeance on us: but the Lord doth scourge them that come near unto him, to admonish them."

28 Then said Ozias to her, "All that thou hast spoken hast thou spoken with a good heart, and there is none that may gainsay thy words. 29 For this is not the first day wherein thy wisdom is manifested; but from the beginning of thy days all the people have known thy understanding, because the disposition of thine heart is good. 30 But the people were very thirsty, and compelled us to do unto them as we have spoken, and to bring an oath upon ourselves, which we will not break. 31 Therefore now pray thou for us, because thou art a godly woman, and the Lord will send us rain to fill our cisterns, and we shall faint no more."

32 Then said Judith unto them, "Hear me, and I will do a thing, which shall go throughout all generations to the children of our nation. 33 Ye shall stand this night in the gate, and I will go forth with my waitingwoman: and within the days that ye have promised to deliver the city to our enemies the Lord will visit Israel by mine hand. 34 But enquire not ye of mine act: for I will not declare it unto you, till the things be finished that I do." 35 Then said Ozias and the princes unto her, "Go in peace, and the Lord God be before thee, to take vengeance on our enemies." 36 So they returned from the tent, and went to their wards.

Judith's Prayer

9 Then Judith fell upon her face, and put ashes upon her head, and uncovered the sackcloth wherewith she was clothed; and about the time that the incense of that evening was offered in Jerusalem in the house of the Lord Judith cried with a loud voice, and said, 2 "O Lord God of my father Simeon,[13] to whom thou gavest a sword to take vengeance of the strangers, who loosened the girdle of a maid to defile her, and discovered the thigh to her shame, and polluted her virginity to her reproach; for thou saidst, 'It shall not be so'; and yet they did so: 3 Wherefore thou gavest their rulers to be slain, so that they dyed their bed in blood, being deceived, and smotest the servants with their lords, and the lords upon their thrones; 4 And hast given their wives for a prey, and their daughters to be captives, and all their spoils to be divided among thy dear children; which were moved with thy zeal, and abhorred the pollution of their blood, and called upon thee for aid.

"O God, O my God, hear me also a widow. 5 For thou hast wrought not only those things, but also the things which fell out before, and which ensued after; thou hast thought upon the things which are now, and which are to come. 6 Yea, what things thou didst determine were ready at hand, and said, 'Lo, we are here': for all thy ways are prepared, and thy judgments are in thy foreknowledge.

7 "For, behold, the Assyrians are multiplied in their powers; they are exalted with horse and man; they glory in the strength of their footmen; they trust in shield, and spear, and bow, and sling; and know not that thou art the Lord that breakest the battles: the Lord is thy name. 8 Throw down their strength in thy power, and bring down their force in thy wrath: for they have purposed to defile thy sanctuary, and to pollute the tabernacle where thy glorious name resteth, and to cast down with sword the horn of thy altar. 9 Behold their pride, and send thy wrath upon their heads: give into mine hand, which am a widow, the power that I have conceived. 10 Smite by the deceit of my lips the servant with the prince, and the prince with the servant: break down their stateliness by the hand of a woman.[14] 11 For thy power standeth not in multitude, nor thy might in strong men: for thou art a God of the afflicted, an helper of the oppressed, an upholder of the weak, a protector of the forlorn, a saviour of them that are without hope. 12 I pray thee, I pray thee, O God of my father, and God of the inheritance of Israel, Lord of the heavens and earth, Creator of the waters, King of every crea-

---

13. The reference to "my father Simeon" fits perfectly in a prayer which asks God to preserve the purity of Jewish blood and to further an act of deceit. (See *Genesis* 34:1-30.)
14. The enemy would find it ignominious to be defeated by a woman. This idea recurs in the speech of Bagoas when he finds Holofernes dead (14:18) and particularly in Judith's triumphal song (16:6-7).

ture, hear thou my prayer: 13 And make my speech and deceit to be their wound and stripe, who have purposed cruel things against thy covenant, and thy hallowed house, and against the top of Sion, and against the house of the possession of thy children.   14 And make every nation and tribe to acknowledge that thou art the God of all power and might, and that there is none other that protecteth the people of Israel but thou."

Preparation and Departure

10 Now after that she had ceased to cry unto the God of Israel, and had made an end of all these words,   2 She rose where she had fallen down, and called her maid, and went down into the house, in the which she abode in the sabbath days, and in her feast days,   3 And pulled off the sackcloth which she had on, and put off the garments of her widowhood, and washed her body all over with water, and anointed herself with precious ointment, and braided the hair of her head, and put on a tire[15] upon it, and put on her garments of gladness, wherewith she was clad during the life of Manasses her husband.   4 And she took sandals upon her feet, and put about her her bracelets, and her chains, and her rings, and her earrings, and all her ornaments, and decked herself bravely, to allure the eyes of all men that should see her.[16]   5 Then she gave her maid a bottle of wine, and a cruse of oil, and filled a bag with parched corn, and lumps of figs, and with fine bread; so she folded all these things together, and laid them upon her.

6 Thus they went forth to the gate of the city of Bethulia, and found standing there Ozias, and the ancients of the city, Chabris and Charmis.   7 And when they saw her, that her countenance was altered, and her apparel was changed, they wondered at her beauty very greatly, and said unto her,   8 "The God, the God of our fathers, give thee favour, and accomplish thine enterprizes to the glory of the children of Israel, and to the exaltation of Jerusalem." Then they worshipped God.   9 And she said unto them, "Command the gates of the city to be opened unto me, that I may go forth to accomplish the things whereof ye have spoken with me." So they commanded the young men to open unto her, as she had spoken. 10 And when they had done so, Judith went out,

she, and her maid with her; and the men of the city looked after her, until she was gone down the mountain, and till she had passed the valley, and could see her no more.

Judith before Holofernes

11 Thus they went straight forth in the valley: and the first watch of the Assyrians met her, 12 And took her, and asked her, "Of what people art thou? and whence cometh thou? and whither goest thou?" And she said, "I am a woman of the Hebrews, and am fled from them: for they shall be given you to be consumed: 13 And I am coming before Holofernes the chief captain of your army, to declare words of truth; and I will shew him a way, whereby he shall go, and win all the hill country, without losing the body or life of any one of his men."

14 Now when the men heard her words, and beheld her countenance, they wondered greatly at her beauty, and said unto her,   15 "Thou hast saved thy life, in that thou hast hasted to come down to the presence of our lord: now therefore come to his tent, and some of us shall conduct thee, until they have delivered thee to his hands. 16 And when thou standest before him, be not afraid in thine heart, but shew unto him according to thy word; and he will entreat thee well." 17 Then they chose out of them an hundred men to accompany her and her maid; and they brought her to the tent of Holofernes.

18 Then was there a concourse throughout all the camp: for her coming was noised among the tents, and they came about her, as she stood without the tent of Holofernes, till they told him of her.   19 And they wondered at her beauty and admired the children of Israel because of her, and every one said to his neighbour, "Who would despise this people, that have among them such women? surely it is not good that one man of them be left, who being let go might deceive the whole earth." [17]

20 And they that lay near Holofernes went out, and all his servants, and they brought her into the tent.   21 Now Holofernes rested upon his bed under a canopy, which was woven with purple, and gold, and emeralds, and precious stones. 22 So they shewed him of her; and he came out before his tent with silver lamps going before him. 23 And when Judith was come before him and his servants, they all marvelled at the beauty of her countenance: and she fell down upon her face,

---

15. RSV: "a tiara."
16. In the Vulgate, which differs notably from the present text, God heightened Judith's beauty to further her enterprise. KNOX: "The Lord himself lent grace to her mien; manly resolve, not woman's wantonness, was the occasion of her finery, and he would enhance her beauty till all beholders should vow there was never woman so fair."

17. JB: "let any go and they would twist the whole world round their fingers!"

and did reverence unto him: and his servants took her up.

11 Then said Holofernes unto her, "Woman, be of good comfort, fear not in thine heart: for I never hurt any that was willing to serve Nebuchadnezzar, the king of all the earth. 2 Now therefore, if thy people that dwelleth in the mountains had not set light by me, I would not have lifted up my spear against them: but they have done these things to themselves. 3 But now tell me wherefore thou art fled from them, and art come unto us: for thou art come for safeguard; be of good comfort, thou shalt live this night, and hereafter: 4 For none shall hurt thee, but entreat thee well, as they do the servants of king Nebuchadnezzar my lord."

5 Then Judith said unto him, "Receive the words of thy servant, and suffer thine handmaid to speak in thy presence, and I will declare no lie to my lord this night. 6 And if thou wilt follow the words of thine handmaid, God will bring the thing perfectly to pass by thee; and my lord shall not fail of his purposes. 7 As Nebuchadnezzar king of all the earth liveth, and as his power liveth, who hath sent thee for the upholding of every living thing: for not only men shall serve him by thee, but also the beasts of the field, and the cattle, and the fowls of the air, shall live by thy power under Nebuchadnezzar and all his house.[18] 8 For we have heard of thy wisdom and thy policies, and it is reported in all the earth, that thou only art excellent in all the kingdom, and mighty in knowledge, and wonderful in feats of war.

9 "Now as concerning the matter, which Achior did speak in thy council, we have heard his words; for the men of Bethulia saved him, and he declared unto them all that he had spoken unto thee. 10 Therefore, O lord and governor, reject not his word; but lay it up in thine heart, for it is true: for our nation shall not be punished, neither can the sword prevail against them, except they sin against their God. 11 And now, that my lord be not defeated and frustrate of his purpose, even death is now fallen upon them, and their sin hath overtaken them, wherewith they will provoke their God to anger, whensoever they shall do that which is not fit to be done: 12 For their victuals fail them, and all their water is scant, and they have determined to lay hands upon their cattle, and purposed to consume all those things, that God hath forbidden them to eat by his laws: 13 And are resolved to spend the first fruits of the corn, and the tenths of wine and oil, which they had sanctified, and reserved for the priests that serve in Jerusalem before the face of our God; the which things it is not lawful for any of the people so much as to touch with their hands. 14 For they have sent some to Jerusalem, because they also that dwell there have done the like, to bring them a licence from the senate.[19] 15 Now when they shall bring them word, they will forthwith do it, and they shall be given thee to be destroyed the same day.

16 "Wherefore I thine handmaid, knowing all this, am fled from their presence; and God hath sent me to work things with thee, whereat all the earth shall be astonished, and whosoever shall hear it. 17 For they servant is religious, and serveth the God of heaven day and night: now therefore, my lord, I will remain with thee, and thy servant will go out by night into the valley, and I will pray unto God, and he will tell me when they have committed their sins: 18 And I will come and shew it unto thee: then thou shalt go forth with all thine army, and there shall be none of them that shall resist thee. 19 And I will lead thee through the midst of Judea, until thou come before Jerusalem; and I will set thy throne in the midst thereof; and thou shalt drive them as sheep that have no shepherd, and a dog shall not so much as open his mouth at thee: for these things were told me according to my foreknowledge, and they were declared unto me, and I am sent to tell thee."

20 Then her words pleased Holofernes and all his servants; and they marvelled at her wisdom, and said, 21 "There is not such a woman from one end of the earth to the other, both for beauty of face, and wisdom of words." 22 Likewise Holofernes said unto her, "God hath done well to send thee before the people, that strength might be in our hands, and destruction upon them that lightly regard my lord. 23 And now thou art both beautiful in thy countenance, and witty in thy words: surely if thou do as thou hast spoken, thy God shall be my God, and thou shalt dwell in the house of king Nebuchadnezzar, and shalt be renowned through the whole earth."

12 Then he commanded to bring her in where his plate was set; and bade that they should prepare for her of his own meats, and that she drink of his own wine. 2 And Judith said, "I will not eat thereof, lest there be an offence: but provision shall be made for me of the things that I have brought." 3 Then Holofernes said unto her, "If thy provision should fail, how should we give

---

18. RSV footnotes: "This verse is as obscure in the Greek as in the English."

19. NAB: "They have sent messengers to Jerusalem to bring back to them authorization from the council of the elders; for the inhabitants there have also done these things."

thee the like? for there be none with us of thy nation." 4 Then said Judith unto him, "As thy soul liveth,[20] my lord, thine handmaid shall not spend those things that I have, before the Lord work by mine hand the things that he hath determined."

5 Then the servants of Holofernes brought her into the tent, and she slept till midnight, and she arose when it was toward the morning watch, 6 And sent to Holofernes, saying, "Let my lord now command that thine handmaid may go forth unto prayer." 7 Then Holofernes commanded his guard that they should not stay her: thus she abode in the camp three days, and went out in the night into the valley of Bethulia, and washed herself in a fountain of water by the camp. 8 And when she came out, she besought the Lord God of Israel to direct her way to the raising up of the children of her people. 9 So she came in clean, and remained in the tent, until she did eat her meat at evening.

Holofernes Is Beheaded

10 And in the fourth day Holofernes made a feast to his own servants only, and called none of the officers to the banquet. 11 Then said he to Bagoas the eunuch, who had charge over all that he had, "Go now, and persuade this Hebrew woman which is with thee, that she come unto us, and eat and drink with us. 12 For, lo, it will be a shame for our person, if we shall let such a woman go, not having had her company; for if we draw her not unto us, she will laugh us to scorn." 13 Then went Bagoas from the presence of Holofernes, and came to her, and he said, "Let not this fair damsel fear to come to my lord, and to be honoured in his presence, and drink wine, and be merry with us, and be made this day as one of the daughters of the Assyrians, which serve in the house of Nebuchadnezzar." 14 Then said Judith unto him, "Who am I now, that I should gainsay my lord? surely whatsoever pleaseth him I will do speedily, and it shall be my joy unto the day of my death." 15 So she arose, and decked herself with her apparel and all her woman's attire, and her maid went and laid soft skins on the ground for her over against Holofernes, which she had received of Bagoas for her daily use, that she might sit and eat upon them.

16 Now when Judith came in and sat down, Holofernes his heart was ravished with her, and his mind was moved, and he desired greatly her company; for he waited a time to deceive her, from the day that he had seen her. 17 Then said

Holofernes unto her, "Drink now, and be merry with us." 18 So Judith said, "I will drink now, my lord, because my life is magnified in me this day more than all the days since I was born." 19 Then she took and ate and drank before him what her maid had prepared. 20 And Holofernes took great delight in her, and drank much more wine than he had drunk at any time in one day since he was born.

13 Now when the evening was come, his servants made haste to depart, and Bagoas shut his tent without, and dismissed the waiters from the presence of his lord; and they went to their beds: for they were all weary, because the feast had been long. 2 And Judith was left alone in the tent, and Holofernes lying along upon his bed: for he was filled with wine.

3 Now Judith had commanded her maid to stand without her bedchamber, and to wait for her coming forth, as she did daily: for she said she would go forth to her prayers, and she spake to Bagoas according to the same purpose. 4 So all went forth, and none was left in the bedchamber, neither little nor great. Then Judith, standing by his bed, said in her heart, "O Lord God of all power, look at this present upon the works of mine hands for the exaltation of Jerusalem. 5 For now is the time to help thine inheritance, and to execute mine enterprizes to the destruction of the enemies which are risen against us." 6 Then she came to the pillar of the bed, which was at Holofernes' head, and took down his fauchion from thence, 7 And approached to his bed, and took hold of the hair of his head, and said, "Strengthen me, O Lord God of Israel, this day." 8 And she smote twice upon his neck with all her might, and she took away his head from him, 9 And tumbled his body down from the bed, and pulled down the canopy from the pillars; and anon after she went forth, and gave Holofernes his head to her maid; 10 And she put it in her bag of meat: so they twain went together according to their custom unto prayer: and when they passed the camp, they compassed the valley, and went up the mountain of Bethulia, and came to the gates thereof.

11 Then said Judith afar off to the watchmen at the gate, "Open, open now the gate: God, even our God, is with us, to shew his power yet in Jerusalem, and his forces against the enemy, as he hath even done this day." 12 Now when the men of her city heard her voice, they made haste to go down to the gate of their city, and they called the elders of the city. 13 And then they ran all together, both small and great, for it was strange unto them that she was come: so they opened the

---

20. NEB: "As sure as you live." The phrase adds to the irony of Judith's speech.

gate, and received them, and made a fire for a light, and stood round about them. 14 Then she said to them with a loud voice, "Praise, praise God, praise God, I say, for he hath not taken away his mercy from the house of Israel, but hath destroyed our enemies by mine hands this night." 15 So she took the head out of the bag, and shewed it, and said unto them, "Behold the head of Holofernes, the chief captain of the army of Assyria, and behold the canopy, wherein he did lie in his drunkenness; and the Lord hath smitten him by the hand of a woman. 16 As the Lord liveth, who hath kept me in my way that I went, my countenance hath deceived him to his destruction, and yet hath he not committed sin with me, to defile and shame me."

17 Then all the people were wonderfully astonished, and bowed themselves, and worshipped God, and said with one accord, "Blessed be thou, O our God, which hast this day brought to nought the enemies of thy people." 18 Then said Ozias unto her, "O daughter, blessed art thou of the most high God above all the women upon the earth; and blessed be the Lord God, which hath created the heavens and the earth, which hath directed thee to the cutting off of the head of the chief of our enemies. 19 For this thy confidence shall not depart from the heart of men, which remember the power of God for ever. 20 And God turn these things to thee for a perpetual praise, to visit thee in good things, because thou hast not spared thy life for the affliction of our nation, but hast revenged our ruin, walking a straight way before our God." 21 And all the people said, "So be it, so be it."

ISRAEL TRIUMPHS

14 Then said Judith unto them, "Hear me now, my brethren, and take this head, and hang it upon the highest place of your walls. 2 And so soon as the morning shall appear, and the sun shall come forth upon the earth, take ye every one his weapons, and go forth every valiant man out of the city, and set ye a captain over them, as though ye would go down into the field toward the watch of the Assyrians; but go not down. 3 Then they shall take their armour, and shall go into their camp, and raise up the captains of the army of

Assyria, and they shall run to the tent of Holofernes, but shall not find him: then fear shall fall upon them, and they shall flee before your face. 4 So ye, and all that inhabit the coast of Israel, shall pursue them, and overthrow them as they go. 5 But before ye do these things, call me Achior the Ammonite, that he may see and know him that despised the house of Israel, and that sent him to us, as it were to his death."

6 Then they called Achior out of the house of Ozias; and when he was come, and saw the head of Holofernes in a man's hand in the assembly of the people,[22] he fell down on his face, and his spirit failed. 7 But when they had recovered him, he fell at Judith's feet, and reverenced her, and said, "Blessed art thou in all the tabernacle of Juda, and in all nations, which hearing thy name shall be astonished. 8 Now therefore tell me all the things that thou hast done in these days." Then Judith declared unto him in the midst of the people all that she had done, from the day that she went forth until that hour she spake unto them. 9 And when she had left off speaking, the people shouted with a loud voice, and made a joyful noise in their city. 10 And when Achior had seen all that the God of Israel had done, he believed in God greatly, and circumcised the flesh of his foreskin, and was joined unto the house of Israel unto this day.

11 And as soon as the morning arose, they hanged the head of Holofernes upon the wall, and every man took his weapons, and they went forth by bands unto the straits of the mountain. 12 But when the Assyrians saw them, they sent to their leaders, which came to their captains and tribunes, and to every one of their rulers. 13 So they came to Holofernes' tent, and said to him that had the charge of all his things, "Waken now our lord: for the slaves have been bold to come down against us to battle, that they may be utterly destroyed." 14 Then went in Bagoas, and knocked at the door of the tent; for he thought that he had slept with Judith. 15 But because none answered, he opened it, and went into the bedchamber, and found him cast upon the floor dead, and his head was taken from him. 16 Therefore he cried with a loud voice, with weeping, and sighing, and a mighty cry, and rent his garments. 17 After he went into the tent where Judith lodged: and when he found her not, he leaped out to the people, and cried, 18 "These slaves have dealt treacherously; one woman of the Hebrews hath brought shame upon the house of king Nebuchadnezzar: for, behold, Holofernes

---

21. JB:

"since you did not consider your own life
when our nation was brought to its knees,
but warded off our ruin,
walking undeterred before our God."

Considering Judith's duplicity, the KJV translation sounds like irony.

22. This is intended to recall the promise of Holofernes (6:5).

lieth upon the ground without a head." 19 When the captains of the Assyrians' army heard these words, they rent their coats, and their minds were wonderfully troubled, and there was a cry and a very great noise throughout the camp.

15 And when they that were in the tents heard, they were astonished at the thing that was done. 2 And fear and trembling fell upon them, so that there was no man that durst abide in the sight of his neighbour, but rushing out all together, they fled into every way of the plain, and of the hill country. 3 They also that had camped in the mountains round about Bethulia fled away. Then the children of Israel, every one that was a warrior among them, rushed out upon them. 4 Then sent Ozias to Bethomesthaim, and to Bebai, and Choba, and Chola, and to all the coasts of Israel, such as should tell the things that were done, and that all should rush forth upon their enemies to destroy them. 5 Now when the children of Israel heard it, they all fell upon them with one consent, and slew them unto Choba: likewise also they that came from Jerusalem, and from all the hill country, (for men had told them what things were done in the camp of their enemies,) and they that were in Gilead, and in Galilee, chased them with a great slaughter, until they were past Damascus and the borders thereof. 6 And the residue, that dwelt at Bethulia, fell upon the camp of Assyria, and spoiled them, and were greatly enriched. 7 And the children of Israel that returned from the slaughter had that which remained; and the villages and the cities, that were in the mountains and in the plain, gat many spoils: for the multitude was very great.

8 Then Joakim the high priest, and the ancients of the children of Israel that dwelt in Jerusalem, came to behold the good things that God had shewed to Israel, and to see Judith, and to salute her. 9 And when they came unto her, they blessed her with one accord, and said unto her, "Thou art the exaltation of Jerusalem, thou art the great glory of Israel, thou art the great rejoicing of our nation: 10 Thou hast done all these things by thine hand: thou hast done much good to Israel, and God is pleased therewith: blessed be thou of the Almighty Lord for evermore." And all the people said, "So be it."

11 And the people spoiled the camp the space of thirty days: and they gave unto Judith Holofernes his tent, and all his plate, and beds, and vessels, and all his stuff: and she took it, and laid it on her mule; and made ready her carts, and laid them thereon.

12 Then all the women of Israel ran together to see her, and blessed her, and made a dance among them for her: and she took branches in her hand, and gave also to the women that were with her. 13 And they put a garland of olive upon her and her maid that was with her, and she went before all the people in the dance, leading all the women: and all the men of Israel followed in their armour with garlands, and with songs in their mouths.

Judith's Victory Song [23]

16 Then Judith began to sing this thanksgiving in all Israel, and all the people sang after her this song of praise. 2 And Judith said,
"Begin unto my God with timbrels,
Sing unto my Lord with cymbals:
Tune unto him a new psalm: exalt him, and call upon his name.

3   For God breaketh the battles:
For among the camps in the midst of the people
He hath delivered me out of the hands of them that persecuted me.

4   "Assyria came out of the mountains from the north,
He came with ten thousands of his army,
The multitude whereof stopped the torrents,
And their horsemen have covered the hills.

5   He bragged that he would burn up my borders,
And kill my young men with the sword,
And dash the sucking children against the ground,
And make mine infants as a prey,
And my virgins as a spoil.

6   "But the Almighty Lord hath disappointed them by the hand of a woman.

7   For the mighty one did not fall by the young men,
Neither did the sons of the Titans smite him,
Nor high giants set upon him:
But Judith the daughter of Merari weakened him with the beauty of her countenance.

8   For she put off the garment of her widowhood
For the exaltation of those that were oppressed in Israel,
And anointed her face with ointment,

---

23. (16:1-17) The speaker of the thanksgiving psalm is not Judith, but Israel personified as a woman. In v. 7, Judith is mentioned in the third person.

And bound her hair in a tire,
And took a linen garment to deceive him.

9 Her sandals ravished his eyes,
Her beauty took his mind prisoner,
And the fauchion passed through his neck.

10 "The Persians quaked at her boldness,
And the Medes were daunted at her hardiness.

11 Then my afflicted shouted for joy,
And my weak ones cried aloud;
But they were astonished:
These lifted up their voices,
But they were overthrown.[24]

12 The sons of the damsels have pierced them through,
And wounded them as fugitives' children:
They perished by the battle of the Lord.

13 "I will sing unto the Lord a new song:
O Lord, thou art great and glorious,
Wonderful in strength, and invincible.

14 Let all creatures serve thee:
For thou spakest, and they were made,
Thou didst send forth thy spirit, and it created them,
And there is none that can resist thy voice.

15 For the mountains shall be moved from their foundations with the waters,
The rocks shall melt as wax at thy presence:
Yet thou art merciful to them that fear thee.

16 For all sacrifice is too little for a sweet savour unto thee,
And all the fat is not sufficient for thy burnt offering:

---

24. NEB:
 "Then my oppressed people shouted in triumph, and
  the enemy was afraid;
 my weak ones shouted, and the enemy cowered in fear;
 they raised their voices, and the enemy took to flight."

But he that feareth the Lord is great at all times.

17 "Woe to the nations that rise up against my kindred!
The Lord Almighty will take vengeance of them in the day of judgment,
In putting fire and worms in their flesh;
And they shall feel them, and weep for ever."

18 Now as soon as they entered into Jerusalem, they worshipped the Lord; and as soon as the people were purified, they offered their burnt offerings, and their free offerings, and their gifts. 19 Judith also dedicated all the stuff of Holofernes, which the people had given her, and gave the canopy, which she had taken out of his bedchamber, for a gift unto the Lord. 20 So the people continued feasting in Jerusalem before the sanctuary for the space of three months, and Judith remained with them.

JUDITH'S FAME

21 After this time every one returned to his own inheritance, and Judith went to Bethulia, and remained in her own possession, and was in her time honourable in all the country. 22 And many desired her, but none knew her all the days of her life, after that Manasses her husband was dead, and was gathered to his people. 23 But she increased more and more in honour, and waxed old in her husband's house, being an hundred and five years old, and made her maid free; so she died in Bethulia: and they buried her in the cave of her husband Manasses. 24 And the house of Israel lamented her seven days: and before she died, she did distribute her goods to all them that were nearest of kindred to Manasses her husband, and to them that were the nearest of her kindred. 25 And there was none that made the children of Israel any more afraid in the days of Judith, nor a long time after her death.

Introduction to
THE HISTORY OF SUSANNA

"From that day was Daniel had in great reputation in the sight of the people."

When Shakespeare's Shylock refers to Portia as "A Daniel come to judgment! yea, a Daniel!" he is recalling the clever young man in *The History of Susanna*, the first hero in detective fiction.

Writing about 150 B.C., the anonymous author linked his story to the legendary material surrounding the Daniel of the Babylonian exile (598 B.C.). His tale is part of the cycle of traditions concerning the prophet which were added to the book of *Daniel* when it was translated into Greek. In St. Jerome's *Vulgate* and subsequent Roman Catholic translations of the Bible, the Susanna story appears as *Daniel*, Chapter 13.

Just as he took his hero from the past, the author shaped his mystery story out of two motifs from folklore. The first concerns a virtuous woman falsely accused by a thwarted lover. This appears, for example, in the Jewish legend that the two false prophets denounced in *Jeremiah* 29:21-23 tried to seduce the daughter of Nebuchadnezzar and were burned in the fiery furnace. A variation occurs in the story of Joseph and Potiphar's wife (See *Genesis* 39:7-20). The second motif describes a young rescuer who shows surprising wisdom. This appears in the stories of David and other Judges who in their youth were "raised up" by the Lord to effect his will. According to early exegetical tradition, Daniel is twelve years old when he confounds the elders and saves Susanna.

Commentators agree that *The History of Susanna* is fiction, but there is no consensus regarding the original purpose of the story. Perhaps it was written to add to the laurels of the prophet Daniel. It might have intended to contrast man's law and God's providence. Or it could have been a Pharisaic attack on the Sadducees for their laxity in court procedure. Early Christians identified Susanna as the church and read the story as an allegory concerning baptism and persecution.

The purpose of the story of Susanna remains unknown, as does its author, its original language, and the place of its origin. But in its characters, plot development, climax, and surprise ending, there is no doubt it is an entertaining detective story.

THE HISTORY OF SUSANNA

THE EVIL JUDGES

There dwelt a man in Babylon, called Joacim:
2 And he took a wife, whose name was Susanna,
the daughter of Hilkiah, a very fair woman, and
one that feared the Lord. 3 Her parents also
were righteous, and taught their daughter according to the law of Moses. 4 Now Joacim was a
great rich man, and had a fair garden joining unto
his house: and to him resorted the Jews; because
he was more honourable than all others.

5 The same year were appointed two of the
ancients of the people to be judges, such as the
Lord spake of, that wickedness came from Babylon from ancient judges, who seemed to govern
the people.[1] 6 These kept much at Joacim's
house: and all that had any suits in law came
unto them.

7 Now when the people departed away at noon,
Susanna went into her husband's garden to walk.
8 And the two elders saw her going in every day,
and walking; so that their lust was inflamed
toward her. 9 And they perverted their own
mind, and turned away their eyes, that they might
not look unto heaven, nor remember just judgments. 10 And albeit they both were wounded
with her love, yet durst not one shew another his
grief. 11 For they were ashamed to decalretheir
lust, that they desired to have to do with her.
12 Yet they watched diligently from day to day to
see her.

13 And the one said to the other, "Let us now
go home: for it is dinner time." 14 So when they
were gone out, they parted the one from the
other, and turning back again they came to the
same place; and after that they had asked one
another the cause, they acknowledged their lust:
then appointed they a time both together, when
they might find her alone.

15 And it fell out, as they watched a fit time,
she went in as before with two maids only, and
she was desirous to wash herself in the garden:
for it was hot. 16 And there was no body there
save the two elders, that had hid themselves, and
watched her. 17 Then she said to her maids,
"Bring me oil and washing balls, and shut the
garden doors, that I may wash me." 18 And they
did as she bade them, and shut the garden doors,
and went out themselves at privy doors to fetch

the things that she had commanded them: but
they saw not the elders, because they were hid.
19 Now when the maids were gone forth, the
two elders rose up, and ran unto her, saying,
20 "Behold, the garden doors are shut, that no
man can see us, and we are in love with thee;
therefore consent unto us, and lie with us. 21 If
thou wilt not, we will bear witness against thee,
that a young man was with thee: and therefore
thou didst send away thy maids from thee."
22 Then Susanna sighed, and said, "I am
straitened on every side: for if I do this thing, it is
death unto me: and if I do it not, I cannot escape
your hands.[2] 23 It is better for me to fall into
your hands, and not do it, then to sin in the sight
of the Lord." 24 With that Susanna cried with a
loud voice: and the two elders cried out against
her. 25 Then ran the one, and opened the garden
door.

26 So when the servants of the house heard the
cry in the garden, they rushed in at a privy door,
to see what was done unto her. 27 But when the
elders had declared their matter, the servants
were greatly ashamed: for there was never such a
report made of Susanna.

THE ACCUSATION

28 And it came to pass the next day, when the
people were assembled to her husband Joacim,
the two elders came also full of mischievous
imagination against Susanna to put her to death;
29 And said before the people, "Send for Susanna, the daughter of Hilkiah, Joacim's wife."
And so they sent. 30 So she came with her father
and mother, her children, and all her kindred.

31 Now Susanna was a very delicate woman,
and beauteous to behold.[3] 32 And these wicked
men commanded to uncover her face, (for she
was covered) that they might be filled with her
beauty. 33 Therefore her friends and all that saw
her wept.

34 Then the two elders stood up in the midst of
the people, and laid their hands upon her head.

---

1. "The same year" presumably means the year of Joacim's
wedding to Susanna. The passage about wicked judges may
refer to *Jeremiah* 29:21-23.

2. Susanna's dilemma is founded in Jewish law. If she submits
to the lecherous elders, the Law condemns her to death by
stoning (*Leviticus* 20:10 and *Deuteronomy* 22:22). If she
refuses, the testimony of two witnesses is sufficient for
conviction.

3. (31-32) RSV: "Now Susanna was a woman of great refine-
ment, and beautiful in appearance." In having the elegant
woman remove her veil, the elders are mortifying her,
treating her as if she were guilty of the charge brought
against her.

35 And she weeping looked up toward heaven: for her heart trusted in the Lord. 36 And the elders said, "As we walked in the garden alone, this woman came in with two maids, and shut the garden doors, and sent the maids away. 37 Then a young man, who there was hid, came unto her, and lay with her. 38 Then we that stood in a corner of the garden, seeing this wickedness, ran unto them. 39 And when we saw them together, the man we could not hold: for he was stronger than we, and opened the door, and leaped out. 40 But having taken this woman, we asked who the young man was, but she would not tell us: these things do we testify."

41 Then the assembly believed them, as those that were the elders and judges of the people: so they condemned her to death. 42 Then Susanna cried out with a loud voice, and said, "O everlasting God, that knowest the secrets, and knowest all things before they be: 43 Thou knowest that they have borne false witness against me, and, behold, I must die; whereas I never did such things as these men have maliciously invented against me."

DANIEL SAVES SUSANNA

44 And the Lord heard her voice. 45 Therefore when she was led to be put to death, the Lord raised up the holy spirit of a young youth, whose name was Daniel: 46 Who cried with a loud voice, "I am clear from the blood of this woman." [4] 47 Then all the people turned them toward him, and said, "What mean these words that thou hast spoken?" 48 So he standing in the midst of them said, "Are ye such fools, ye sons of Israel, that without examination or knowledge of the truth ye have condemned a daughter of Israel? 49 Return again to the place of judgment: for they have borne false witness against her."

50 Wherefore all the people turned again in haste, and the elders said unto him, "Come, sit down among us, and shew it us, seeing God hath given thee the honour of an elder." [5] 51 Then said Daniel unto them, "Put these two aside one far from another, and I will examine them." 52 So when they were put asunder one from another, he called one of them, and said unto him, "O thou that art waxen old in wickedness, now thy sins which thou hast committed aforetime are

4. KNOX: "I will be no party to the death of this woman."
5. Probably this is not irony. KNOX: "the elders would have Daniel sit with them, such credit had God given him beyond his years."

come to light: 53 For thou hast pronounced false judgment, and hast condemned the innocent, and hast let the guilty go free; albeit the Lord saith, 'The innocent and righteous shalt thou not slay.' 54 Now then, if thou hast seen her, tell me, Under what tree sawest thou them companying together?" Who answered, "Under a mastick tree." 55 And Daniel said, "Very well; thou hast lied against thine own head; for even now the angel of God hath received the sentence of God to cut thee in two." [6]

56 So he put him aside, and commanded to bring the other, and said unto him, "O thou seed of Canaan, and not of Judah, beauty hath deceived thee, and lust hath perverted thine heart. 57 Thus have ye dealt with the daughters of Israel, and they for fear companied with you: but the daughter of Judah, would not abide your wickedness. [7] 58 Now therefore tell me, Under what tree didst thou take them companying together?" Who answered, "Under an holm tree." 59 Then said Daniel unto him, "Well; thou hast also lied against thine own head: for the angel of God waiteth with the sword to cut thee in two, that he may destroy you." [8]

60 With that all the assembly cried out with a loud voice, and praised God, who saveth them that trust in him. 61 And they arose against the two elders, for Daniel had convicted them of false witness by their own mouth: [9] 62 And according to the law of Moses they did unto them in such sort as they maliciously intended to do to their neighbour: and they put them to death. Thus the innocent blood was saved the same day. 63 Therefore Hilkiah and his wife praised God for their daughter Susanna, with Joacim her husband, and all the kindred, because there was no dishonesty found in her. 64 From that day forth was Daniel had in great reputation in the sight of the people.

6. (54-55) The original text conveyed a pun: the Greek word for "mastic" is similar to the word for "cut." NEB: "He answered, 'Under a clove-tree.' Then Daniel retorted, 'Very good: this lie has cost you your life, for already God's angel has received your sentence from God, and he will cleave you in two.'"
7. The passage reveals the bias of the author toward the southern kingdom. It suggests that women of Judah are less vulnerable than those of Israel.
8. (58-59) The pun recurs, based on the similarity between the word translated "holm tree" and the word translated "cut." (RSV: "evergreen oak" and "saw.") NEB: "'Under a yew-tree,' he replied. Daniel said to him, 'Very good: this lie has cost you your life, for the angel of God is waiting with his sword to hew you down and destroy you both.'"
9. The lie was obvious. A mastic tree is small; a holm tree is a huge oak.

Introduction to
BEL AND THE DRAGON

"Lo, these are the gods ye worship."

Written during the dispersion, a period when the Jews in exile were encouraged to worship local gods, *Bel and the Dragon* is a didactic tale which ridicules idolatry.

Like *The History of Susanna*, this story is an apocryphal addition to the book of *Daniel*. (In Roman Catholic translations, it appears as *Daniel*, Chapter 14.) *Bel and the Dragon* was written about 135 B.C. in a Semitic language, probably Hebrew. All extant manuscripts are in Greek.

With good-humored exaggeration, the anonymous author dismissed the idea of worshipping idols. There is something laughable in King Cyrus' serious concern for his preposterous gods; in the picture of two hundred or more people nightly sneaking into the temple of Bel; in Daniel's slaying a dragon with lumps (RSV: "cakes") made of pitch, fat, and hair; and in Habakkuk's miraculous and reluctant visit to the lion's den. The humor is evident in the food motif which unifies the two parts of the story: this shows an idol which does not eat; a dragon which overeats; and Daniel and the lions who fast until Habakkuk brings the one bread and stew and Cyrus feeds the others Daniel's enemies.

This story of Daniel—faithful to his LORD, scornful of Babylon's gods, skillful in exposing deception, and courageous when threatened—was told and retold among Jews of the first century B.C. When urged to forsake God for an idol, they could recall Daniel's shrewdness and chuckle at the notion.

211

The History of the Destruction of
BEL AND THE DRAGON

THE DESTRUCTION OF BEL

And king Astyages was gathered to his fathers, and Cyrus of Persia received his kingdom. 2 And Daniel conversed with the king, and was honoured above all his friends.

3 Now the Babylonians had an idol, called Bel, and there were spent upon him every day twelve great measures of fine flour, and forty sheep, and six vessels of wine. 4 And the king worshipped it, and went daily to adore it: but Daniel worshipped his own God. And the king said unto him, "Why dost not thou worship Bel?" 5 Who answered and said, "Because I may not worship idols made with hands, but the living God, who hath created the heaven and the earth, and hath sovereignty over all flesh." 6 Then said the king unto him, "Thinkest thou not that Bel is a living God? seest thou not how much he eateth and drinketh every day?" 7 Then Daniel smiled, and said, "O king, be not deceived: for this is but clay within, and brass without, and did never eat or drink any thing."

8 So the king was wroth, and called for his priests, and said unto them, "If ye tell me not who this is that devoureth these expences, ye shall die. 9 But if ye can certify me that Bel devoureth them, then Daniel shall die: for he hath spoken blasphemy against Bel." And Daniel said unto the king, "Let it be according to thy word."

10 Now the priests of Bel were threescore and ten, beside their wives and children. And the king went with Daniel into the temple of Bel. 11 So Bel's priests said, "Lo, we go out: but thou, O king, set on the meat, and make ready the wine, and shut the door fast, and seal it with thine own signet; 12 And to morrow when thou comest in, if thou findest not that Bel hath eaten up all, we will suffer death: or else Daniel, that speaketh falsely against us." 13 And they little regarded it: for under the table they had made a privy entrance, whereby they entered in continually, and consumed those things. 14 So when they were gone forth, the king set meats before Bel. Now Daniel had commanded his servants to bring ashes, and those they strewed throughout all the temple in the presence of the king alone: then went they out, and shut the door, and sealed it with the king's signet, and so departed.

15 Now in the night came the priests with their wives and children, as they were wont to do, and did eat and drink up all.[1] 16 In the morning betime the king arose, and Daniel with him. 17 And the king said, "Daniel, are the seals whole?" And he said, "Yea, O king, they be whole." 18 And as soon as he had opened the door, the king looked upon the table, and cried with a loud voice, "Great art thou, O Bel, and with thee is no deceit at all."

19 Then laughed Daniel, and held the king that he should not go in, and said, "Behold now the pavement, and mark well whose footsteps are these." 20 And the king said, "I see the footsteps of men, women, and children." And then the king was angry, 21 And took the priests with their wives and children, who shewed him the privy doors, where they came in, and consumed such things as were upon the table. 22 Therefore the king slew them, and delivered Bel into Daniel's power, who destroyed him and his temple.

THE DESTRUCTION OF THE DRAGON

23 And in that same place there was a great dragon, which they of Babylon worshipped.[2] 24 And the king said unto Daniel, "Wilt thou also say that this is of brass? lo, he liveth, he eateth and drinketh; thou canst not say that he is no living god: therefore worship him." 25 Then said Daniel unto the king, "I will worship the Lord my God: for he is the living God. 26 But give me leave, O king, and I shall slay this dragon without sword or staff." The king said, "I give thee leave."

27 Then Daniel took pitch, and fat, and hair, and did seethe them together, and made lumps thereof: this he put in the dragon's mouth, and so the dragon burst in sunder: and Daniel said, "Lo, these are the gods ye worship." 28 When they of Babylon heard that, they took great indignation, and conspired against the king, saying, "The king is become a Jew, and he hath destroyed Bel, he hath slain the dragon, and put the priests to death." 29 So they came to the king, and said, "Deliver us Daniel, or else we will destroy thee and thine house." 30 Now when the king saw that they pressed him sore, being constrained, he delivered Daniel unto them: 31 Who cast him

1. The nightly gatherings are festive. RSV and NEB translate the "six vessels of wine" of verse 3 as "fifty gallons of wine."
2. KNOX: "a great serpent." NEB: "a huge snake." JB footnotes, "Nothing is known of a dragon-god in Babylon."

into the lion's den: when he was six days.[3] 32 And in the den there were seven lions, and they had given them every day two carcases, and two sheep: which then were not given to them, to the intent they might devour Daniel.

HABAKKUK RESCUES DANIEL

33 Now there was in Jewry a prophet, called Habakkuk, who had made pottage, and had broken bread in a bowl, and was going into the field, for to bring it to the reapers. 34 But the angel of the Lord said unto Habakkuk, "Go, carry the dinner that thou hast into Babylon unto Daniel, who is in the lions' den." 35 And Habakkuk said, "Lord, I never saw Babylon; neither do I know where the den is." 36 Then the angel of the Lord took him by the crown, and bare him by the hair of his head, and through the vehemency of his spirit set him in Babylon over the den.[4] 37 And Habakkuk cried, saying, "O Daniel, Daniel, take the dinner which God hath sent thee." 38 And Daniel said, "Thou hast remembered me, O God: neither hast thou forsaken them that seek thee and love thee." 39 So Daniel arose, and did eat: and the angel of the Lord set Habakkuk in his own place again immediately.

40 Upon the seventh day the king went to bewail Daniel: and when he came to the den, he looked in, and, behold, Daniel was sitting. 41 Then cried the king with a loud voice, saying, "Great art thou, O Lord God of Daniel, and there is none other beside thee." 42 And he drew him out, and cast those that were the cause of his destruction into the den: and they were devoured in a moment before his face.

---

3. This recalls *Daniel* 6:16-24, where Daniel is put into a lion's den for petitioning God rather than King Darius. JB, NEB, and KNOX specify a lion pit.

4. RSV: "and set him down in Babylon, right over the den, with the rushing sound of the wind itself." NEB: "he swept him to Babylon with the blast of his breath and put him down above the pit." JB: "and carried him off by the hair to Babylon where, with a great thrust of his spirit, he set Habakkuk down on the edge of the pit."

A detail from *The Three Crosses*, fourth state. Rembrandt Harmensz van Ryn, 1653. New York, the Metropolitan Museum of Art.

THE NEW TESTAMENT

Introduction to
THE NEW TESTAMENT

The collective title, "New Testament," emphasizes the relationship of the Christian documents to Hebrew Scripture. For Christians, the appearance of Jesus had divided the world's history into two eras, one of slavery and one of freedom. In *Galatians*, Paul presents the argument and speaks of "the two covenants." "Testament" is the equivalent of "covenant." Consequently, Christian Scripture includes an Old and a New Testament.

The New Testament is deeply rooted in the Old. In fact, the claim of early Christians to an exclusively authentic interpretation of the Old Testament contributed to the Rabbinical Council of Jamnia's decision to close the Hebrew Scripture (A.D. 90). It needed protection from the aggressiveness of Christianity. Throughout, the New Testament reveals dependence on the Old for language, proof-texts, and genres.

For early Christians, the messiah anticipated in Jewish Scripture had appeared as Jesus, the son of God. This dramatic claim justifies the fervor of the writings. In its way, each New Testament book is an affirmation of faith and each author a pamphleteer. This emphasis explains the origin of *gospel* as a genre and the use of prose as the predominant style.

Unlike the Old Testament, whose composition ranged over a thousand years, the New Testament involves barely a century. Most of the books were produced in the six decades from A.D. 50 to 110. The earliest writings were the Pauline epistles, followed by the synoptic gospels, the writings of John, *Revelation*, and finally, about 128, *II Peter*.

For generations, these books and other early Christian writings were shared by the various churches. In time, certain documents were held to be more authentic than others, perhaps because they were considered the work of Jesus' closest disciples. During the second century, most churches came to accept a canon which included the present four Gospels—the *Acts*, thirteen letters of Paul, *I Peter*, and *I John*—while other works lacked general recognition. In his Easter letter of 367, Athanasius, Bishop of Alexandria, listed the twenty-seven books of the New Testament and declared the canon closed.

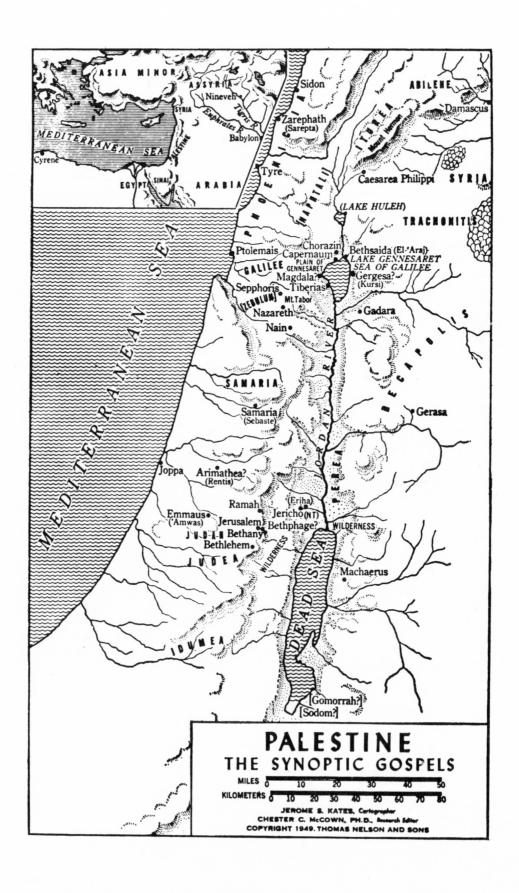

PALESTINE
THE SYNOPTIC GOSPELS

MILES 0 10 20 30 40 50
KILOMETERS 0 10 20 30 40 50 60 70 80

JEROME S. KATES, Cartographer
CHESTER C. McCOWN, PH.D., Research Editor
COPYRIGHT 1949, THOMAS NELSON AND SONS

Introduction to
MARK

"And he saith unto them, 'But whom say ye that I am?' And Peter answereth and saith unto him, 'Thou art the Christ.' And he charged them that they should tell no man of him."

Matthew, Mark, Luke, and *John* make up almost half of the New Testament. Each is a kind of narrative describing the life of Jesus the Messiah and announcing the good news of salvation. *Mark,* dated around 70, is the earliest gospel.

According to tradition, the author is John Mark, a minor figure mentioned in *Acts of the Apostles* as an associate of Peter and a worker in the church at Rome. The attribution is persuasive. The reminiscences of Peter may well have been the background for *Mark.* In the gospel, Peter emerges as the most prominent of the disciples, and events occurring when he is present are described in great detail. Further, the gospel reflects Roman characteristics. Aramaic words are translated and Jewish customs explained: neither would be necessary if Mark's audience were primarily Palestinian or Jewish. Also, the gospel's emphasis on discipleship and martyrdom suggests a period of persecution. Nero's persecution of the Christians in Rome began shortly after the great fire of 64.

One can define Mark's genre only as a *gospel.* There is some biographical structure—the baptism of Jesus, his peripatetic ministry, announcements of his passion, the Passion Narrative—but Mark did not try to shape a realistic biography. (E.g., he grouped his miracle stories in one section and his parables in another; he forced the passion materials into an artificial one-week sequence.) There is some geographical structure—Jesus is shown in Galilee, among the Gadarene Gentiles, on the road to Jerusalem, in Jerusalem—but Mark was often vague about geography (and chronology); his interest lay elsewhere. There is some theological structure—the good news is ratified by Jesus' power exhibited in preaching, exorcising demons, healing, and ordering natural phenomena—but the gospel is not systematic theology. Probably these biographical, geographical, and theological arrangements are handy threads on which the beads of oral tradition and earlier writings were strung.

Practically all scholars believe the gospels are dependent on earlier sources. (The theory helps explain the duplication of materials, arrangement, and vocabulary.) They suggest that Mark based his gospel on writings which came down to him (a Passion Narrative, an apocalypse, some controversy stories, miracle tales, recorded sayings of Jesus) and on oral tradition (the reminiscences of Peter and other Christian witnesses; recollected events, sayings, and parables attributed to Jesus; narratives associated with John the Baptist, etc.). From such sources—passed on, modified, and embellished by four decades of believers—Mark fashioned his gospel. Its purpose: to record events in the life of Jesus and to speak to concerns of the early church.

Four concerns are particularly evident:

Mark—and his sources—wanted to demonstrate Jesus' messianic claim by showing how again and again he fulfilled the prophecies of the Old Testament. In the crucifixion story, for example, Jesus is executed between two thieves, offered vinegar to drink, mocked by passersby, and his clothes are gambled for. Mark took these events from a Passion Narrative where they were included perhaps because they were recollected as facts and perhaps because, if Jesus were in fact the Messiah, they *must* have occurred. D. E. Nineham makes the crucial point: "What God had predicted he would certainly have brought to pass; of that the early Christians had no doubt. If therefore an Old Testament passage referred to the Passion of Christ, the things it predicted must have happened to Jesus, even if there was no other evidence that they had. Old Testament predictions thus became, to a certain extent, a historical source. . . . Accordingly the account of Jesus' end, on which our Gospel accounts are based, was derived from historical reminiscences and Old Testament predictions in a proportion which cannot now be exactly determined." * Fulfilled prophecies were essential for Mark's demonstration concerning "Jesus Christ, the Son of God."

Another purpose evident in the gospel was to explain why neither Jesus nor his disciples actively proclaimed his messianic title during his lifetime. Mark stressed that the disciples, partly because of their "hardness of heart," did not soon comprehend Jesus' identity. And he showed Jesus, time after time, telling those who saw his cures and exorcisms not to reveal the events. Wilhelm Wrede (*Das Messiasgeheimnis in den Evangelien*, 1901) argues that such references were interpolated into the story to claim a status for Jesus which he never claimed for himself. Whether or not this is true, it is apparent that *Mark* lays great emphasis on "the messianic secret."

Another intention of the gospel was to encourage members of the persecuted church at Rome. Giving half of his narrative to introducing and describing the passion of Jesus, Mark reminded his readers that the Lord suffered, that he warned his followers to expect scorn and persecution, and that he promised great and certain rewards to those who remain faithful. In its insistence that nothing which befalls Christians lies outside the providence of God, *Mark* has been called "the martyr gospel."

Probably because Mark wrote at Rome and certainly because the early church met continuing antagonism from Jewish leaders, much of the material in the gospel was intended to condemn the Jews and to absolve Roman authorities. In *Mark*, scribes devour widows' houses; Pharisees cynically demand a sign from heaven; Sadducees approach Jesus with a ludicrous question; the chief priests and elders call up false witnesses and persuade the Jewish citizens to demand his death. Nonscriptural sources make it clear that crucifixion was strictly a Roman punishment, and they describe Pilate as a cruel, inflexible, and corrupt leader. But such facts do not appear in Mark's narration.

Mark is the least sophisticated of the gospels. It contains no charming infancy narrative. It lacks the cherished parables of *Matthew* and *Luke* and the theological symbolism of *John*. It has a nervous twitch as episode is linked to episode by

---

* From D. E. Nineham, *The Gospel of St. Mark* (London: Penguin Books Ltd), 1963. Reprinted by permission of Penguin Books Ltd.

"straightway" and "immediately"—words used more than forty times. Because the loaves-and-fishes story appeared in more than one source, Mark records it as two separate miracles. In a sentence like "And when they had crucified him, they parted his garments, casting lots among them, which every man should take," the Evangelist used six words for the event he believed saved the world and thirteen to a detail of routine spoil.

Nevertheless, *Mark* does display notable literary gifts, particularly in the arrangement of material for dramatic effect. Three times Jesus announces the events of the Passion to come; each announcement is followed by an episode showing the disciples failing to understand his "suffering servant" role. In the midst of the story of saving Jarius' daughter, Jesus cures the hemorrhaging woman. Between cursing the fig tree and finding it dead, Jesus drives the moneychangers from the temple. Between the two trials, he is denied by Peter. In each case, the inserted story comments on the theme of the interrupted narrative. In 8:11-30, after Jesus has performed three major miracles, *Mark* reports the blindness of both the Pharisees and the Apostles; then it shows Jesus curing a blind man, and Peter witnessing the truth.

Mark's style shapes his depiction of Jesus. The rapid succession of cures and exorcisms, the abrupt travels from here to there, the many controversies, the ubiquitous crowds—these render Jesus as an involved human being, busy, frustrated, and compassionate. In *John*, Jesus is introduced as the Word, existing co-eternal with the Father; in *Mark*, he emerges as an active man driven by a personal commitment and his concern for people.

The Gospel According to
MARK

PREPARATION FOR JESUS' MINISTRY

1 The beginning of the gospel of Jesus Christ, the Son of God; 2 As it is written in the prophets,

> "Behold, I send my messenger before thy face, which shall prepare thy way before thee.
>
> 3   The voice of one crying in the wilderness,
>
> 'Prepare ye the way of the Lord,
> Make his paths straight.'" [1]

4 John did baptize in the wilderness, and preach the baptism of repentance for the remission of sins. 5 And there went out unto him all the land of Judea, and they of Jerusalem, and were all baptized of him in the river of Jordan, confessing their sins. 6 And John was clothed with camel's hair, and with a girdle of a skin about his loins; and he did eat locusts and wild honey; 7 And preached, saying, "There cometh one mightier than I after me, the latchet of whose shoes I am not worthy to stoop down and unloose. 8 I indeed have baptized you with water: but he shall baptize you with the Holy Ghost."

9 And it came to pass in those days, that Jesus came from Nazareth of Galilee, and was baptized of John in Jordan. 10 And straightway coming up out of the water, he saw the heavens opened, and the Spirit like a dove descending upon him: 11 And there came a voice from heaven, *saying,*

> "Thou art my beloved Son,
> In whom I am well pleased." [2]

12 And immediately the Spirit driveth him into the wilderness. 13 And he was there in the wilderness forty days tempted of Satan;[3] and was with the wild beasts; and the angels ministered unto him.

---

1. The quotation reflects *Exodus* 23:20, *Isaiah* 40:3, and *Malachi* 3:1. *Mark* uses the preaching (and later the death) of John to show that the time of preparation is over.
2. (1:10-11) GOODSPEED: "And just as he was coming up out of the water he saw the heavens torn open, and the Spirit coming down like a dove to enter into him, and out of the heavens came a voice: 'You are my Son, my Beloved! You are my Chosen!'"
3. The number forty was commonly used to indicate the length of a sacred event: Noah's rain lasted forty days; the Jews wandered in the wilderness for forty years; Moses stayed on Mount Sinai for forty days; Jesus appeared on earth for forty days following his resurrection; etc. See Introduction to *Revelation* (p. 268) for a discussion of number symbolism.

MIRACLES

14 Now after that John was put in prison, Jesus came into Galilee, preaching the gospel of the kingdom of God, 15 And saying, "The time is fulfilled, and the kingdom of God is at hand: repent ye, and believe the gospel." 16 Now as he walked by the sea of Galilee, he saw Simon and Andrew his brother casting a net into the sea: for they were fishers. 17 And Jesus said unto them, "Come ye after me, and I will make you to become fishers of men." 18 And straightway they forsook their nets, and followed him. 19 And when he had gone a little further thence, he saw James the *son* of Zebedee, and John his brother, who also were in the ship mending their nets. 20 And straightway he called them: and they left their father Zebedee in the ship with the hired servants, and went after him.

21 And they went into Capernaum; and straightway on the sabbath day he entered into the synagogue, and taught. 22 And they were astonished at his doctrine: for he taught them as one that had authority, and not as the scribes. 23 And there was in their synagogue a man with an unclean spirit; and he cried out, 24 Saying, "Let *us* alone; what have we to do with thee, thou Jesus of Nazareth? art thou come to destroy us? I know thee who thou art, the Holy One of God." 25 And Jesus rebuked him, saying, "Hold thy peace, and come out of him." 26 And when the unclean spirit had torn him; and cried with a loud voice, he came out of him. 27 And they were all amazed, insomuch that they questioned among themselves, saying, "What thing is this? what new doctrine is this? for with authority commandeth he even the unclean spirits, and they do obey him." 28 And immediately his fame spread abroad throughout all the region round about Galilee. 29 And forthwith, when they were come out of the synagogue, they entered into the house of Simon and Andrew, with James and John. 30 But Simon's wife's mother lay sick of a fever; and anon they tell him of her. 31 And he came and took her by the hand, and lifted her up; and immediately the fever left her, and she ministered unto them.

32 And at even, when the sun did set, they brought unto him all that were diseased, and them that were possessed with devils. 33 And all the city was gathered together at the door.

34 And he healed many that were sick of divers diseases, and cast out many devils: and suffered not the devils to speak, because they knew him.

35 And in the morning, rising up a great while before day, he went out, and departed into a solitary place, and there prayed. 36 And Simon and they that were with him followed after him. 37 And when they had found him, they said unto him, "All *men* seek for thee." 38 And he said unto them, "Let us go into the next towns, that I may preach there also: for therefore came I forth." [4] 39 And he preached in their synagogues throughout all Galilee, and cast out devils.

40 And there came a leper to him, beseeching him, and kneeling down to him, and saying unto him, "If thou wilt, thou canst make me clean." 41 And Jesus, moved with compassion, put forth *his* hand, and touched him, and saith unto him, "I will; be thou clean." 42 And as soon as he had spoken, immediately the leprosy departed from him, and he was cleansed. 43 And he straitly charged him, and forthwith sent him away; 44 And saith unto him, "See thou say nothing to any man: but go thy way, show thyself to the priest, and offer for thy cleansing those things which Moses commanded, for a testimony unto them." 45 But he went out, and began to publish *it* much, and to blaze abroad the matter, insomuch that Jesus could no more openly enter into the city, but was without in desert places: and they came to him from every quarter.

CONTROVERSY STORIES

2 And again he entered into Capernaum after *some* days; and it was noised that he was in the house. 2 And straightway many were gathered together, insomuch that there was no room to receive *them,* no, not so much as about the door: and he preached the word unto them. 3 And they come unto him, bringing one sick of the palsy, which was borne of four. 4 And when they could not come nigh unto him for the press, they uncovered the roof where he was: and when they had broken *it* up, they let down the bed wherein the sick of the palsy lay. 5 When Jesus saw their faith, he said unto the sick of the palsy, "Son, thy sins be forgiven thee." 6 But there were certain of the scribes sitting there, and reasoning in their hearts, 7 "Why doth this *man* thus speak blasphemies? who can forgive sins but God only?" 8 And immediately, when Jesus perceived in his spirit that they so reasoned within themselves, he said unto them, "Why reason ye these things in your hearts? 9 Whether is it easier to say to the sick of the palsy, '*Thy* sins be forgiven thee'; or to say, 'Arise, and take up thy bed, and walk'? 10 But that ye may know that the Son of man hath power on earth to forgive sins," (he saith to the sick of the palsy,) 11 "I say unto thee, Arise, and take up thy bed, and go thy way into thine house." 12 And immediately he arose, took up the bed, and went forth before them all; insomuch that they were all amazed, and glorified God, saying, "We never saw it on this fashion."

13 And he went forth again by the sea side; and all the multitude resorted unto him, and he taught them. 14 And as he passed by, he saw Levi the *son* of Alpheus sitting at the receipt of custom, and said unto him, "Follow me." And he arose and followed him. 15 And it came to pass, that, as Jesus sat at meat in his house, many publicans and sinners sat also together with Jesus and his disciples; for there were many, and they followed him. 16 And when the scribes and Pharisees saw him eat with publicans and sinners, they said unto his disciples, "How is it that he eateth and drinketh with publicans and sinners?" 17 When Jesus heard *it,* he saith unto them, "They that are whole have no need of the physician, but they that are sick: I came not to call the righteous, but sinners to repentance."

18 And the disciples of John and of the Pharisees used to fast: and they come and say unto him, "Why do the disciples of John and of the Pharisees fast, but thy disciples fast not?" 19 And Jesus said unto them, "Can the children of the bridechamber fast, while the bridegroom is with them? as long as they have the bridegroom with them, they cannot fast. 20 But the days will come, when the bridegroom shall be taken away from them, and then shall they fast in those days. 21 No man also seweth a piece of new cloth on an old garment; else the new piece that filled it up taketh away from the old, and the rent is made worse. 22 And no man putteth new wine into old bottles; else the new wine doth burst the bottles, and the wine is spilled, and the bottles will be marred: but new wine must be put into new bottles."

23 And it came to pass, that he went through the corn fields on the sabbath day; and his disciples began, as they went, to pluck the ears of

---

4. (1:37-38) Jesus is frustrated with those who seek his miracles rather than his message. The attitude appears in the following story of the leper, where "moved with compassion" (v. 41) is better translated "with warm indignation."

corn. 24 And the Pharisees said unto him, "Behold, why do they on the sabbath day that which is not lawful?" 25 And he said unto them, "Have ye never read what David did, when he had need, and was ahungered, he, and they that were with him? 26 How he went into the house of God in the days of Abiathar the high priest, and did eat the showbread, which is not lawful to eat but for the priests, and gave also to them which were with him?" 27 And he said unto them, "The sabbath was made for man, and not man for the sabbath: 28 Therefore the Son of man is Lord also of the sabbath."

3 And he entered again into the synagogue; and there was a man there which had a withered hand. 2 And they watched him, whether he would heal him on the sabbath day; that they might accuse him. 3 And he saith unto the man which had the withered hand, "Stand forth." 4 And he saith unto them, "Is it lawful to do good on the sabbath days, or to do evil? to save life, or to kill?" But they held their peace. 5 And when he had looked round about on them with anger, being grieved for the hardness of their hearts, he saith unto the man, "Stretch forth thine hand." And he stretched it out: and his hand was restored whole as the other. 6 And the Pharisees went forth, and straightway took counsel with the Herodians[5] against him, how they might destroy him.

7 But Jesus withdrew himself with his disciples to the sea: and a great multitude from Galilee followed him, and from Judea, 8 And from Jerusalem, and from Idumea, and *from* beyond Jordan; and they about Tyre and Sidon, a great multitude, when they had heard what great things he did, came unto him. 9 And he spake to his disciples, that a small ship should wait on him because of the multitude, lest they should throng him. 10 For he had healed many; insomuch that they pressed upon him for to touch him, as many as had plagues. 11 And unclean spirits, when they saw him, fell down before him, and cried, saying, "Thou art the Son of God." 12 And he straitly charged them that they should not make him known.

13 And he goeth up into a mountain, and calleth *unto him* whom he would: and they came unto him. 14 And he ordained twelve, that they should be with him, and that he might send them forth to preach,[6] 15 And to have power to heal sicknesses, and to cast out devils: 16 And Simon he surnamed Peter; 17 And James the *son* of Zebedee, and John the brother of James; and he surnamed them Boanerges, which is, The sons of thunder: 18 And Andrew, and Philip, and Bartholomew, and Matthew, and Thomas, and James the *son* of Alpheus, and Thaddeus, and Simon the Canaanite, 19 And Judas Iscariot, which also betrayed him: and they went into a house.

20 And the multitude cometh together again, so that they could not so much as eat bread. 21 And when his friends[7] heard *of it,* they went out to lay hold on him: for they said, "He is beside himself." 22 And the scribes which came down from Jerusalem said, "He hath Beelzebub, and by the prince of the devils casteth he out devils." 23 And he called them *unto him,* and said unto them in parables, "How can Satan cast out Satan? 24 And if a kingdom be divided against itself, that kingdom cannot stand. 25 And if a house be divided against itself, that house cannot stand. 26 And if Satan rise up against himself, and be divided, he cannot stand, but hath an end. 27 No man can enter into a strong man's house, and spoil his goods, except he will first bind the strong man; and then he will spoil his house. 28 Verily I say unto you, All sins shall be forgiven unto the sons of men, and blasphemies wherewith soever they shall blaspheme: 29 But he that shall blaspheme against the Holy Ghost hath never forgiveness, but is in danger of eternal damnation": 30 Because they said, "He hath an unclean spirit."

31 There came then his brethren and his mother, and, standing without, sent unto him, calling him. 32 And the multitude sat about him, and they said unto him, "Behold, thy mother and thy brethren without seek for thee." 33 And he answered them, saying, "Who is my mother, or my brethren?" 34 And he looked round about on them which sat about him, and said, "Behold my mother and my brethren! 35 For whosoever shall do the will of God, the same is my brother, and my sister, and mother."

PARABLES

4 And he began again to teach by the sea side: and there was gathered unto him a great multi-

---

5. The Herodians were neither a religious sect nor a political party. They were influential Jews who supported the Roman occupation of Palestine in general and the rule of Herod in particular.

6. Twelve men were chosen to form the new Israel because twelve tribes made up the old Israel. The symbolic character of the number is emphasized by the fact that some of these apostles played little part in the new church.

7. NAB, NEB: "his family."

tude, so that he entered into a ship, and sat in the sea; and the whole multitude was by the sea on the land. 2 And he taught them many things by parables, and said unto them in his doctrine, 3 "Hearken; Behold, there went out a sower to sow: 4 And it came to pass, as he sowed, some fell by the wayside, and the fowls of the air came and devoured it up. 5 And some fell on stony ground, where it had not much earth; and immediately it sprang up, because it had no depth of earth: 6 But when the sun was up, it was scorched; and because it had no root, it withered away. 7 And some fell among thorns, and the thorns grew up, and choked it, and it yielded no fruit. 8 And other fell on good ground, and did yield fruit that sprang up and increased, and brought forth, some thirty, and some sixty, and some a hundred." 9 And he said unto them, "He that hath ears to hear, let him hear."

10 And when he was alone, they that were about him with the twelve asked of him the parable. 11 And he said unto them, "Unto you it is given to know the mystery of the kingdom of God: but unto them that are without, all *these* things are done in parables:

12   That seeing they may see, and not per-
          ceive;
       And hearing they may hear, and not
          understand;
       Lest at any time they should be con-
          verted, and *their* sins should be forgiven
          them." [8]

13 And he said unto them, "Know ye not this parable? and how then will ye know all parables? 14 The sower soweth the word. 15 And these are they by the wayside, where the word is sown; but when they have heard, Satan cometh immediately, and taketh away the word that was sown in their hearts. 16 And these are they likewise which are sown on stony ground; who, when they have heard the word, immediately receive it with gladness; 17 And have no root in themselves, and so endure but for a time: afterward, when affliction or persecution ariseth for the word's sake, immediately they are offended. 18 And these are they which are sown among thorns; such as hear the word, 19 And the cares of this world, and the deceitfulness of riches, and the lusts of other things entering in, choke the word,

and it becometh unfruitful. 20 And these are they which are sown on good ground; such as hear the word, and receive *it*, and bring forth fruit, some thirtyfold, some sixty, and some a hundred."

21 And he said unto them, "Is a candle brought to be put under a bushel, or under a bed? and not to be set on a candlestick? 22 For there is nothing hid, which shall not be manifested; neither was any thing kept secret, but that it should come abroad. 23 If any man have ears to hear, let him hear." 24 And he said unto them, "Take heed what ye hear. With what measure ye mete, it shall be measured to you; and unto you that hear shall more be given. 25 For he that hath, to him shall be given; and he that hath not, from him shall be taken even that which he hath."

26 And he said, "So is the kingdom of God, as if a man should cast seed into the ground; 27 And should sleep, and rise night and day, and the seed should spring and grow up, he knoweth not how. 28 For the earth bringeth forth fruit of herself; first the blade, then the ear, after that the full corn in the ear. 29 But when the fruit is brought forth, immediately he putteth in the sickle, because the harvest is come."

30 And he said, "Whereunto shall we liken the kingdom of God? or with what comparison shall we compare it? 31 *It is* like a grain of mustard seed, which, when it is sown in the earth, is less than all the seeds that be in the earth: 32 But when it is sown, it groweth up, and becometh greater than all herbs, and shooteth out great branches; so that the fowls of the air may lodge under the shadow of it." 33 And with many such parables spake he the word unto them, as they were able to hear *it*. 34 But without a parable spake he not unto them: and when they were alone, he expounded all things to his disciples.

A COLLECTION OF MIRACLES

35 And the same day, when the even was come, he saith unto them, "Let us pass over unto the other side." 36 And when they had sent away the multitude, they took him even as he was in the ship. And there were also with him other little ships. 37 And there arose a great storm of wind, and the waves beat into the ship, so that it was now full. 38 And he was in the hinder part of the ship, asleep on a pillow: and they awake him, and say unto him, "Master, carest thou not that we perish?" 39 And he arose, and rebuked the wind, and said unto the sea, "Peace, be still." And the

---

8. (4:11-12) No satisfactory explanation of this passage exists, largely because the parables of Jesus are obviously intended to be clear and meaningful. In IB, Frederick C. Grant explains: ". . . taking the passage as it stands now in Mark, it must be interpreted as an expression of Mark's theory of the parables, a theory derived partly from early Christian experience in evangelism and partly from the ironic oracle in Isaiah 6:9-10, where the prophet looks back upon his own frustrated ministry and views it as the result of divine intention."

wind ceased, and there was a great calm. 40 And he said unto them, "Why are ye so fearful? how is it that ye have no faith?" 41 And they feared exceedingly, and said one to another, "What manner of man is this, that even the wind and the sea obey him?"

5 And they came over unto the other side of the sea, into the country of the Gadarenes. 2 And when he was come out of the ship, immediately there met him out of the tombs a man with an unclean spirit, 3 Who had *his* dwelling among the tombs; and no man could bind him, no, not with chains: 4 Because that he had been often bound with fetters and chains, and the chains had been plucked asunder by him, and the fetters broken in pieces: neither could any *man* tame him. 5 And always, night and day, he was in the mountains, and in the tombs, crying, and cutting himself with stones. 6 But when he saw Jesus afar off, he ran and worshipped him, 7 And cried with a loud voice, and said, "What have I to do with thee, Jesus, *thou* Son of the most high God? I adjure thee by God, that thou torment me not." 8 For he said unto him, "Come out of the man, *thou* unclean spirit." 9 And he asked him, "What *is* thy name?" And he answered, saying, "My name *is* Legion: for we are many." 10 And he besought him much that he would not send them away out of the country. 11 Now there was there nigh unto the mountains a great herd of swine feeding. 12 And all the devils besought him, saying, "Send us into the swine, that we may enter into them." 13 And forthwith Jesus gave them leave. And the unclean spirits went out, and entered into the swine; and the herd ran violently down a steep place into the sea, (they were about two thousand,) and were choked in the sea. 14 And they that fed the swine fled, and told *it* in the city, and in the country. And they went out to see what it was that was done. 15 And they come to Jesus, and see him that was possessed with the devil, and had the legion, sitting, and clothed, and in his right mind; and they were afraid. 16 And they that saw *it* told them how it befell to him that was possessed with the devil, and *also* concerning the swine. 17 And they began to pray him to depart out of their coasts. 18 And when he was come into the ship, he that had been possessed with the devil prayed him that he might be with him. 19 Howbeit Jesus suffered him not, but saith unto him, "Go home to thy friends, and tell them how great things the Lord hath done for thee, and hath had compassion on thee." 20 And he departed, and began to publish in Decapolis how great things Jesus had done for him: and all *men* did marvel.

21 And when Jesus was passed over again by ship unto the other side, much people gathered unto him; and he was nigh unto the sea. 22 And, behold, there cometh one of the rulers of the synagogue, Jairus by name; and when he saw him, he fell at his feet, 23 And besought him greatly, saying, "My little daughter lieth at the point of death: *I pray thee,* come and lay thy hands on her, that she may be healed; and she shall live." 24 And *Jesus* went with him; and much people followed him, and thronged him.

25 And a certain woman, which had an issue of blood twelve years,[9] 26 And had suffered many things of many physicians, and had spent all that she had, and was nothing bettered, but rather grew worse, 27 When she had heard of Jesus, came in the press behind, and touched his garment. 28 For she said, "If I may touch but his clothes, I shall be whole." 29 And straightway the fountain of her blood was dried up; and she felt in *her* body that she was healed of that plague. 30 And Jesus, immediately knowing in himself that virtue had gone out of him, turned him about in the press, and said, "Who touched my clothes?" 31 And his disciples said unto him, "Thou seest the multitude thronging thee, and sayest thou, 'Who touched me?'" 32 And he looked round about to see her that had done this thing. 33 But the woman fearing and trembling, knowing what was done in her, came and fell down before him, and told him all the truth. 34 And he said unto her, "Daughter, thy faith hath made thee whole; go in peace, and be whole of thy plague."

35 While he yet spake, there came from the ruler of the synagogue's *house certain* which said, "Thy daughter is dead; why troublest thou the Master any further?" 36 As soon as Jesus heard the word that was spoken, he saith unto the ruler of the synagogue, "Be not afraid, only believe." 37 And he suffered no man to follow him, save Peter, and James, and John the brother of James. 38 And he cometh to the house of the ruler of the synagogue, and seeth the tumult, and them that wept and wailed greatly. 39 And when he was come in, he saith unto them, "Why make ye this ado, and weep? the damsel is not dead, but sleepeth." 40 And they laughed him to scorn. But when he had put them all out, he taketh the father and the mother of the damsel, and them that were with him, and entereth in where the damsel was lying. 41 And he took the damsel by the hand, and said unto her, "Talitha cumi":

9. Wherever Mark inserts one story in the midst of another, the two stories make the same point. Here, the daughter of Jairus and the hemorrhaging woman are both beyond medical help, and both are saved by faith.

which is, being interpreted, "Damsel, I say unto thee, arise." 42 And straightway the damsel arose, and walked; for she was *of the age* of twelve years. And they were astonished with a great astonishment. 43 And he charged them straitly that no man should know it; and commanded that something should be given her to eat.

6 And he went out from thence, and came into his own country; and his disciples follow him. 2 And when the sabbath day was come, he began to teach in the synagogue: and many hearing *him* were astonished, saying, "From whence hath this *man* these things? and what wisdom *is* this which is given unto him, that even such mighty works are wrought by his hands? 3 Is not this the carpenter, the son of Mary, the brother of James, and Joses, and of Juda, and Simon? and are not his sisters here with us?" And they were offended at him. 4 But Jesus said unto them, "A prophet is not without honor, but in his own country, and among his own kin, and in his own house." 5 And he could there do no mighty work, save that he laid his hands upon a few sick folk, and healed *them.* 6 And he marveled because of their unbelief.

And he went round about the villages, teaching. 7 And he called *unto him* the twelve, and began to send them forth by two and two; and gave them power over unclean spirits; 8 And commanded them that they should take nothing for *their* journey, save a staff only; no scrip, no bread, no money in *their* purse: 9 But *be* shod with sandals; and not put on two coats. 10 And he said unto them, "In what place soever ye enter into a house, there abide till ye depart from that place. 11 And whosoever shall not receive you, nor hear you, when ye depart thence, shake off the dust under your feet for a testimony against them. Verily I say unto you, It shall be more tolerable for Sodom and Gomorrah in the day of judgment, than for that city." 12 And they went out, and preached that men should repent. 13 And they cast out many devils, and anointed with oil many that were sick, and healed *them.*

14 And king Herod heard *of him*; (for his name was spread abroad;) and he said, "That John the Baptist was risen from the dead, and therefore mighty works do show forth themselves in him." 15 Others said, "That it is Elias." And others said, "That it is a prophet, or as one of the prophets." 16 But when Herod heard *thereof,* he said, "It is John, whom I beheaded: he is risen from the dead." 17 For Herod himself had sent forth and laid hold upon John, and bound him in prison for Herodias' sake, his brother Philip's wife; for he had married her.[10] 18 For John had said unto Herod, "It is not lawful for thee to have thy brother's wife." 19 Therefore Herodias had a quarrel against him, and would have killed him; but she could not: 20 For Herod feared John, knowing that he was a just man and a holy, and observed him; and when he heard him, he did many things, and heard him gladly. 21 And when a convenient day was come, that Herod on his birthday made a supper to his lords, high captains, and chief *estates* of Galilee; 22 And when the daughter of the said Herodias came in, and danced, and pleased Herod and them that sat with him, the king said unto the damsel, "Ask of me whatsoever thou wilt, and I will give *it* thee." 23 And he sware unto her, "Whatsoever thou shalt ask of me, I will give *it* thee, unto the half of my kingdom." 24 And she went forth, and said unto her mother, "What shall I ask?" And she said, "The head of John the Baptist." 25 And she came in straightway with haste unto the king, and asked, saying, "I will that thou give me by and by in a charger the head of John the Baptist." 26 And the king was exceeding sorry; *yet* for his oath's sake, and for their sakes which sat with him, he would not reject her. 27 And immediately the king sent an executioner, and commanded his head to be brought: and he went and beheaded him in the prison, 28 And brought his head in a charger, and gave it to the damsel; and the damsel gave it to her mother. 29 And when the disciples[11] heard *of it,* they came and took up the corpse, and laid it in a tomb.

30 And the apostles gathered themselves together unto Jesus, and told him all things, both what they had done, and what they had taught. 31 And he said unto them, "Come ye yourselves apart into a desert place, and rest a while": for there were many coming and going, and they had no leisure so much as to eat.

32 And they departed into a desert place by ship privately. 33 And the people saw them departing, and many knew him, and ran afoot thither out of all cities, and outwent them, and came together unto him. 34 And Jesus, when he came out, saw much people, and was moved with compassion toward them, because they were as sheep not having a shepherd: and he began to teach them many things. 35 And when the day was now far spent, his disciples came unto him,

10. (6:17-29) This is the only use of the flashback technique in the Gospels.
11. NEB, JB: "John's disciples."

and said, "This is a desert place, and now the time *is* far passed: 36 Send them away, that they may go into the country round about, and into the villages, and buy themselves bread: for they have nothing to eat." 37 He answered and said unto them, "Give ye them to eat." And they say unto him, "Shall we go and buy two hundred pennyworth of bread, and give them to eat?" [12] 38 He saith unto them, "How many loaves have ye? go and see." And when they knew, they say, "Five, and two fishes." 39 And he commanded them to make all sit down by companies upon the green grass. 40 And they sat down in ranks, by hundreds, and by fifties. 41 And when he had taken the five loaves and the two fishes, he looked up to heaven, and blessed, and brake the loaves, and gave *them* to his disciples to set before them; and the two fishes divided he among them all. 42 And they did all eat, and were filled. 43 And they took up twelve baskets full of the fragments, and of the fishes. 44 And they that did eat of the loaves were about five thousand men.

45 And straightway he constrained his disciples to get into the ship, and to go to the other side before unto Bethsaida, while he sent away the people. 46 And when he had sent them away, he departed into a mountain to pray. 47 And when even was come, the ship was in the midst of the sea, and he alone on the land. 48 And he saw them toiling in rowing; for the wind was contrary unto them: and about the fourth watch of the night he cometh unto them, walking upon the sea, and would have passed by them. 49 But when they saw him walking upon the sea, they supposed it had been a spirit, and cried out: 50 For they all saw him, and were troubled. And immediately he talked with them, and saith unto them, "Be of good cheer: it is I; be not afraid." 51 And he went up unto them into the ship; and the wind ceased: and they were sore amazed in themselves beyond measure, and wondered. 52 For they considered not *the miracle* of the loaves; for their heart was hardened.[13]

53 And when they had passed over, they came into the land of Gennesaret, and drew to the shore. 54 And when they were come out of the ship, straightway they knew him, 55 And ran through that whole region round about, and began to carry about in beds those that were sick, where they heard he was. 56 And whithersoever he entered, into villages, or cities, or country, they laid the sick in the streets, and besought him that they might touch if it were but the border of his garment: and as many as touched him were made whole.

CONTROVERSIES

7 Then came together unto him the Pharisees, and certain of the scribes, which came from Jerusalem. 2 And when they saw some of his disciples eat bread with defiled, that is to say, with unwashen hands, they found fault. 3 For the Pharisees, and all the Jews, except they wash *their* hands oft, eat not, holding the tradition of the elders. 4 And *when they come* from the market, except they wash, they eat not. And many other things there be, which they have received to hold, *as* the washing of cups, and pots, brazen vessels, and of tables. 5 Then the Pharisees and scribes asked him, "Why walk not thy disciples according to the tradition of the elders, but eat bread with unwashen hands?" 6 He answered and said unto them, "Well hath Esaias prophesied of you hypocrites, as it is written,

'This people honoreth me with *their* lips,
But their heart is far from me.
7   Howbeit in vain do they worship me,
        teaching *for* doctrines the command-
        ments of men.' [14]

8 For laying aside the commandment of God, ye hold the tradition of men, *as* the washing of pots and cups: and many other such like things ye do." 9 And he said unto them, "Full well ye reject the commandment of God, that ye may keep your own tradition. 10 For Moses said, 'Honor thy father and thy mother'; and, 'Whoso curseth father or mother, let him die the death': 11 But ye say, 'If a man shall say to his father or mother, "*It is* Corban," that is to say, a gift, by whatsoever thou mightest be profited by me; *he shall be free.*' [15] 12 And ye suffer him no more to do aught for his father or his mother; 13 Making the word of God of none effect through your tradition, which ye have delivered: and many such things do ye."

14 And when he had called all the people *unto him,* he said unto them, "Hearken unto me every one *of you,* and understand: 15 There is nothing from without a man, that entering into him can defile him: but the things which come out of him,

---

12. The question is rhetorical. TEV: "Do you want us to go and buy two hundred dollars' worth of bread and feed them?"
13. This is clearly an editorial addition intended to unify the two preceding stories.

14. The original passage (*Isaiah* 29:13) scorned the superficial traditionalism of Judah.
15. "Corban" means "a gift devoted to God." Some Jews thought they could avoid the obligation to care for their parents by pledging money to the temple treasury.

those are they that defile the man. 16 If any man have ears to hear, let him hear." 17 And when he was entered into the house from the people, his disciples asked him concerning the parable. 18 And he saith unto them, "Are ye so without understanding also? Do ye not perceive, that whatsoever thing from without entereth into the man, *it* cannot defile him; 19 Because it entereth not into his heart, but into the belly, and goeth out into the draught, purging all meats?" 20 And he said, "That which cometh out of the man, that defileth the man. 21 For from within, out of the heart of men, proceed evil thoughts, adulteries, fornications, murders, 22 Thefts, covetousness, wickedness, deceit, lasciviousness, an evil eye, blasphemy, pride, foolishness: 23 All these evil things come from within, and defile the man."

MINISTRY TO THE BLIND

Sayings, Miracles, Controversies

24 And from thence he arose, and went into the borders of Tyre and Sidon, and entered into a house, and would have no man know *it:* but he could not be hid. 25 For a *certain* woman, whose young daughter had an unclean spirit, heard of him, and came and fell at his feet: 26 The woman was a Greek, a Syrophenician by nation; and she besought him that he would cast forth the devil out of her daughter. 27 But Jesus said unto her, "Let the children first be filled: for it is not meet to take the children's bread, and to cast *it* unto the dogs." 28 And she answered and said unto him, "Yes, Lord: yet the dogs under the table eat of the children's crumbs." 29 And he said unto her, "For this saying go thy way; the devil is gone out of thy daughter." 30 And when she was come to her house, she found the devil gone out, and her daughter laid upon the bed.[16]

31 And again, departing from the coasts of Tyre and Sidon, he came unto the sea of Galilee, through the midst of the coasts of Decapolis. 32 And they bring unto him one that was deaf, and had an impediment in his speech; and they beseech him to put his hand upon him. 33 And he took him aside from the multitude, and put his

16. (7:24-30) D. E. Nineham writes: "Naturally such a story has presented Christian commentators with something of a puzzle. . . . Briefly, the fact seems to be that Jesus accepted a fairly sharp distinction between Jew and Gentile as part of God's plan, and regarded his commission, and that of his disciples, as being limited to Israel. But he seems to have shared the old Jewish hope that when—through his work as *Jewish* Messiah—the final salvation arrived, large numbers of Gentiles would be called to share in it." (From *The Gospel of St. Mark*, Penguin Books Ltd, 1963. Reprinted by permission of Penguin Books Ltd.)

fingers into his ears, and he spit, and touched his tongue; 34 And looking up to heaven, he sighed, and saith unto him, "Ephphatha," that is, "Be opened." 35 And straightway his ears were opened, and the string of his tongue was loosed, and he spake plain. 36 And he charged them that they should tell no man: but the more he charged them, so much the more a great deal they published *it;* 37 And were beyond measure astonished, saying, "He hath done all things well: he maketh both the deaf to hear, and the dumb to speak."

8 In those days the multitude being very great, and having nothing to eat, Jesus called his disciples *unto him,* and saith unto them, 2 "I have compassion on the multitude, because they have now been with me three days, and have nothing to eat: 3 And if I send them away fasting to their own houses, they will faint by the way: for divers of them came from far." 4 And his disciples answered him, "From whence can a man satisfy these *men* with bread here in the wilderness?" 5 And he asked them, "How many loaves have ye?" And they said, "Seven." 6 And he commanded the people to sit down on the ground: and he took the seven loaves, and gave thanks, and brake, and gave to his disciples to set before *them;* and they did set *them* before the people. 7 And they had a few small fishes: and he blessed, and commanded to set them also before *them.* 8 So they did eat, and were filled: and they took up of the broken *meat* that was left seven baskets. 9 And they that had eaten were about four thousand: and he sent them away. 10 And straightway he entered into a ship with his disciples, and came into the parts of Dalmanutha.

11 And the Pharisees came forth, and began to question with him, seeking of him a sign from heaven, tempting him. 12 And he sighed deeply in his spirit, and saith, "Why doth this generation seek after a sign? verily I say unto you, There shall no sign be given unto this generation." 13 And he left them, and entering into the ship again departed to the other side. 14 Now *the disciples* had forgotten to take bread, neither had they in the ship with them more than one loaf. 15 And he charged them, saying, "Take heed, beware of the leaven of the Pharisees, and *of* the leaven of Herod." 16 And they reasoned among themselves, saying, "*It is* because we have no bread." 17 And when Jesus knew *it,* he saith unto them, "Why reason ye, because ye have no bread? perceive ye not yet, neither understand? have ye your heart yet hardened? 18 Having eyes, see ye not? and having ears, hear ye not?

and do ye not remember? 19 When I brake the five loaves among five thousand, how many baskets full of fragments took ye up?" They say unto him, "Twelve." 20 "And when the seven among four thousand, how many baskets full of fragments took ye up?" And they said, "Seven." 21 And he said unto them, "How is it that ye do not understand?" [17]

22 And he cometh to Bethsaida; and they bring a blind man unto him, and besought him to touch him. 23 And he took the blind man by the hand, and led him out of the town; and when he had spit on his eyes, and put his hands upon him, he asked him if he saw aught. 24 And he looked up, and said, "I see men as trees, walking." 25 After that he put *his* hands again upon his eyes, and made him look up; and he was restored, and saw every man clearly. 26 And he sent him away to his house, saying, "Neither go into the town, nor tell *it* to any in the town."

27 And Jesus went out, and his disciples, into the towns of Cæsarea Philippi: and by the way he asked his disciples, saying unto them, "Whom do men say that I am?" 28 And they answered, "John the Baptist: but some *say* Elias; and others, One of the prophets." 29 And he saith unto them, "But whom say ye that I am?" And Peter answereth and saith unto him, "Thou art the Christ." 30 And he charged them that they should tell no man of him.

"The Son of Man Must Suffer"

31 And he began to teach them, that the Son of man must suffer many things and be rejected of the elders, and *of* the chief priests, and scribes, and be killed, and after three days rise again. 32 And he spake that saying openly. And Peter took him, and began to rebuke him. 33 But when he had turned about and looked on his disciples, he rebuked Peter, saying, "Get thee behind me, Satan: for thou savorest not the things that be of God, but the things that be of men." 34 And

---

17. (8:1-21) The feeding of the 5,000 is a retelling of the earlier loaves-and-fishes story. Some scholars have emphasized that the pattern of 6:34–7:37 is repeated in 8:1-26:
   (1) Feeding the 5,000 (6:34-44)
   (2) Crossing the lake (6:45-56)
   (3) Controversy with Pharisees (7:1-23)
   (4) The children's bread (7:24-30)
   (5) Healing the deaf-dumb man (7:31-37)
      (1) Feeding the 4,000 (8:1-9)
      (2) Crossing the lake (8:10)
      (3) Controversy with Pharisees (8:11-12)
      (4) Sayings about bread (8:13-21)
      (5) Healing the blind man (8:22-26)
   Such repetitions need not be retellings of a single event, but the pairings do reveal how Mark shaped his narrative.

---

when he had called the people *unto him* with his disciples also, he said unto them, "Whosoever will come after me, let him deny himself, and take up his cross, and follow me.[18] 35 For whosoever will save his life shall lose it; but whosoever shall lose his life for my sake and the gospel's, the same shall save it. 36 For what shall it profit a man, if he shall gain the whole world, and lose his own soul? 37 Or what shall a man give in exchange for his soul? 38 Whosoever therefore shall be ashamed of me and of my words, in this adulterous and sinful generation, of him also shall the Son of man be ashamed, when he cometh in the glory of his Father with the holy angels.
9 And he said unto them, "Verily I say unto you, That there be some of them that stand here, which shall not taste of death, till they have seen the kingdom of God come with power."

2 And after six days Jesus taketh *with him* Peter, and James, and John, and leadeth them up into a high mountain apart by themselves: and he was transfigured before them. 3 And his raiment became shining, exceeding white as snow; so as no fuller on earth can white them. 4 And there appeared unto them Elias with Moses:[19] and they were talking with Jesus. 5 And Peter answered and said to Jesus, "Master, it is good for us to be here: and let us make three tabernacles; one for thee, and one for Moses, and one for Elias." 6 For he wist not what to say; for they were sore afraid. 7 And there was a cloud that overshadowed them: and a voice came out of the cloud, saying, "This is my beloved Son: hear him." 8 And suddenly, when they had looked round about, they saw no man any more, save Jesus only with themselves.

9 And as they came down from the mountain, he charged them that they should tell no man what things they had seen, till the Son of man were risen from the dead. 10 And they kept that saying with themselves, questioning one with another what the rising from the dead should mean. 11 And they asked him, saying, "Why say the scribes that Elias must first come?" 12 And he answered and told them, "Elias verily cometh first, and restoreth all things; and how it is written of the Son of man, that he must suffer many things, and be set at nought. 13 But I say unto

---

18. The metaphor—derived from the Roman practice of having a condemned criminal carry part of his own cross to the place of execution—was probably a formulation of the early church. Prior to the crucifixion, it is unlikely that Jesus' audience would understand the allusion.
19. Elias and Moses were expected to appear at the last days. In addition, the Transfiguration relates Jesus to both the prophets (Elijah) and the Law (Moses).

you, That Elias is indeed come, and they have done unto him whatsoever they listed, as it is written of him."

14 And when he came to *his* disciples, he saw a great multitude about them, and the scribes questioning with them. 15 And straightway all the people, when they beheld him, were greatly amazed, and running to *him* saluted him. 16 And he asked the scribes, "What question ye with them?" 17 And one of the multitude answered and said, "Master, I have brought unto thee my son, which hath a dumb spirit; 18 And wheresoever he taketh him, he teareth him; and he foameth, and gnasheth with his teeth, and pineth away: and I spake to thy disciples that they should cast him out; and they could not." 19 He answereth him, and saith, "O faithless generation, how long shall I be with you? how long shall I suffer you? bring him unto me." 20 And they brought him unto him: and when he saw him, straightway the spirit tare him; and he fell on the ground, and wallowed foaming. 21 And he asked his father, "How long is it ago since this came unto him?" And he said, "Of a child. 22 And ofttimes it hath cast him into the fire, and into the waters, to destroy him: but if thou canst do any thing, have compassion on us, and help us." 23 Jesus said unto him, "If thou canst believe, all things *are* possible to him that believeth." [20] 24 And straightway the father of the child cried out, and said with tears, "Lord, I believe; help thou mine unbelief." 25 When Jesus saw that the people came running together, he rebuked the foul spirit, saying unto him, "*Thou* dumb and deaf spirit, I charge thee, come out of him, and enter no more into him." 26 And *the spirit* cried, and rent him sore, and came out of him: and he was as one dead; insomuch that many said, "He is dead." 27 But Jesus took him by the hand, and lifted him up; and he arose. 28 And when he was come into the house, his disciples asked him privately, "Why could not we cast him out?" 29 And he said unto them, "This kind can come forth by nothing, but by prayer and fasting."

30 And they departed thence, and passed through Galilee; and he would not that any man should know *it*. 31 For he taught his disciples, and said unto them, "The Son of man is delivered into the hands of men, and they shall kill him; and after that he is killed, he shall rise the third day." 32 But they understood not that saying, and were afraid to ask him.

33 And he came to Capernaum: and being in the house he asked them, "What was it that ye disputed among yourselves by the way?" 34 But they held their peace: for by the way they had disputed among themselves, who *should be* the greatest. 35 And he sat down, and called the twelve, and saith unto them, "If any man desire to be first, *the same* shall be last of all, and servant of all." 36 And he took a child, and set him in the midst of them: and when he had taken him in his arms, he said unto them, 37 "Whosoever shall receive one of such children in my name, receiveth me; and whosoever shall receive me, receiveth not me, but him that sent me."

38 And John answered him, saying, "Master, we saw one casting out devils in thy name, and he followeth not us; and we forbade him, because he followeth not us." 39 But Jesus said,[21] "Forbid him not: for there is no man which shall do a miracle in my name, that can lightly speak evil of me. 40 For he that is not against us is on our part. 41 For whosoever shall give you a cup of water to drink in my name, because ye belong to Christ, verily I say unto you, he shall not lose his reward. 42 And whosoever shall offend one of *these* little ones that believe in me, it is better for him that a millstone were hanged about his neck, and he were cast into the sea. 43 And if thy hand offend thee, cut it off: it is better for thee to enter into life maimed, than having two hands to go into hell, into the fire that never shall be quenched: 44 Where their worm dieth not, and the fire is not quenched. 45 And if thy foot offend thee, cut it off: it is better for thee to enter halt into life, than having two feet to be cast into hell, into the fire that never shall be quenched: 46 Where their worm dieth not, and the fire is not quenched. 47 And if thine eye offend thee, pluck it out: it is better for thee to enter into the kingdom of God with one eye, than having two eyes to be cast into hell fire: 48 Where their worm dieth not, and the fire is not quenched. 49 For every one shall be salted with fire, and every sacrifice shall be salted with salt. 50 Salt *is* good: but if the salt have lost his saltness, wherewith will ye season it? Have salt in yourselves, and have peace one with another."

10 And he arose from thence, and cometh into the coasts of Judea by the farther side of Jordan:

20. (9:22-23) Jesus' indignation is clearer in PHILLIPS: " 'Ever since he was a child,' he replied. . . . 'But if you can do anything, please take pity on us and help us.' *'If you can do anything!'* retorted Jesus. 'Everything is possible to the man who believes.' "

21. Scholars agree that this speech was constructed from a collection of sayings of Jesus.

and the people resort unto him again; and, as he was wont, he taught them again. 2 And the Pharisees came to him, and asked him, "Is it lawful for a man to put away *his* wife?" tempting him. 3 And he answered and said unto them, "What did Moses command you?" 4 And they said, "Moses suffered to write a bill of divorcement, and to put *her* away." 5 And Jesus answered and said unto them, "For the hardness of your heart he wrote you this precept. 6 But from the beginning of the creation God made them male and female. 7 For this cause shall a man leave his father and mother, and cleave to his wife; 8 And they twain shall be one flesh: so then they are no more twain, but one flesh. 9 What therefore God hath joined together, let not man put asunder." 10 And in the house his disciples asked him again of the same *matter.* 11 And he saith unto them, "Whosoever shall put away his wife, and marry another, committeth adultery against her. 12 And if a woman shall put away her husband, and be married to another, she committeth adultery."

13 And they brought young children to him, that he should touch them; and *his* disciples rebuked those that brought *them.* 14 But when Jesus saw *it,* he was much displeased, and said unto them, "Suffer the little children to come unto me, and forbid them not; for of such is the kingdom of God. 15 Verily I say unto you, Whosoever shall not receive the kingdom of God as a little child, he shall not enter therein." 16 And he took them up in his arms, put *his* hands upon them, and blessed them.

17 And when he was gone forth into the way, there came one running, and kneeled to him, and asked him, "Good Master, what shall I do that I may inherit eternal life?" 18 And Jesus said unto him, "Why callest thou me good? *there is* none good but one, *that is,* God.[22] 19 Thou knowest the commandments, 'Do not commit adultery, Do not kill, Do not steal, Do not bear false witness, Defraud not, Honor thy father and mother.'" 20 And he answered and said unto him, "Master, all these have I observed from my youth." 21 Then Jesus beholding him loved him, and said unto him, "One thing thou lackest: go thy way, sell whatsoever thou hast, and give to the poor, and thou shalt have treasure in heaven: and come, take up the cross, and follow me." 22 And he was sad at that saying, and went away grieved: for he had great possessions. 23 And

Jesus looked round about, and saith unto his disciples, "How hardly shall they that have riches enter into the kingdom of God!" 24 And the disciples were astonished at his words. But Jesus answereth again, and saith unto them, "Children, how hard is it for them that trust in riches to enter into the kingdom of God! 25 It is easier for a camel to go through the eye of a needle, than for a rich man to enter into the kingdom of God." 26 And they were astonished out of measure[23] saying among themselves, "Who then can be saved?" 27 And Jesus looking upon them saith, "With men *it is* impossible, but not with God: for with God all things are possible." 28 Then Peter began to say unto him, "Lo, we have left all, and have followed thee." 29 And Jesus answered and said, "Verily I say unto you, There is no man that hath left house, or brethren, or sisters, or father, or mother, or wife, or children, or lands, for my sake, and the gospel's, 30 But he shall receive a hundredfold now in this time, houses, and brethren, and sisters, and mothers, and children, and lands, with persecutions; and in the world to come eternal life. 31 But many *that are* first shall be last; and the last first."

32 And they were in the way going up to Jerusalem; and Jesus went before them: and they were amazed; and as they followed, they were afraid. And he took again the twelve, and began to tell them what things should happen unto him, 33 *Saying,* "Behold, we go up to Jerusalem; and the Son of man shall be delivered unto the chief priests, and unto the scribes; and they shall condemn him to death, and shall deliver him to the Gentiles: 34 And they shall mock him, and shall scourge him, and shall spit upon him, and shall kill him; and the third day he shall rise again."

35 And James and John, the sons of Zebedee, come unto him, saying, "Master, we would that thou shouldest do for us whatsoever we shall desire." 36 And he said unto them, "What would ye that I should do for you?" 37 They said unto him, "Grant unto us that we may sit, one on thy right hand, and the other on thy left hand, in thy glory." 38 But Jesus said unto them, "Ye know not what ye ask: can ye drink of the cup that I drink of? and be baptized with the baptism that I am baptized with?" 39 And they said unto him, "We can." And Jesus said unto them, "Ye shall indeed drink of the cup that I drink of; and with the baptism that I am baptized withal shall ye be

22. In IB, Frederick C. Grant explains: "The perfect goodness of God was a universal doctrine of Judaism. Jesus has the natural attitude toward God of every pious and devout Jew."

23. The disciples are "astonished out of measure" because they accepted the rabbinic teaching that worldly prosperity is a sign of God's favor.

baptized: 40 But to sit on my right hand and on my left hand is not mine to give; but *it shall be given to them* for whom it is prepared." 41 And when the ten heard *it,* they began to be much displeased with James and John. 42 But Jesus called them *to him,* and saith unto them, "Ye know that they which are accounted to rule over the Gentiles exercise lordship over them; and their great ones exercise authority upon them. 43 But so shall it not be among you: but whosoever will be great among you, shall be your minister: 44 And whosoever of you will be the chiefest, shall be servant of all. 45 For even the Son of man came not to be ministered unto, but to minister, and to give his life a ransom for many."

46 And they came to Jericho: and as he went out of Jericho with his disciples and a great number of people, blind Bartimeus, the son of Timeus, sat by the highway side begging. 47 And when he heard that it was Jesus of Nazareth, he began to cry out, and say, "Jesus, *thou* Son of David, have mercy on me." 48 And many charged him that he should hold his peace: but he cried the more a great deal, "*Thou* Son of David, have mercy on me." 49 And Jesus stood still, and commanded him to be called. And they call the blind man, saying unto him, "Be of good comfort, rise; he calleth thee." 50 And he, casting away his garment, rose, and came to Jesus. 51 And Jesus answered and said unto him, "What wilt thou that I should do unto thee?" The blind man said unto him, "Lord, that I might receive my sight." 52 And Jesus said unto him, "Go thy way; thy faith hath made thee whole." And immediately he received his sight, and followed Jesus in the way.

THE JERUSALEM MINISTRY[24]

11 And when they came nigh to Jerusalem, unto Bethphage and Bethany, at the mount of Olives, he sendeth forth two of his disciples, 2 And saith

unto them, "Go your way into the village over against you: and as soon as ye be entered into it, ye shall find a colt tied, whereon never man sat; loose him, and bring *him.* 3 And if any man say unto you, 'Why do ye this?' say ye that the Lord hath need of him; and straightway he will send him hither." 4 And they went their way, and found the colt tied by the door without in a place where two ways met; and they loose him. 5 And certain of them that stood there said unto them, "What do ye, loosing the colt?" 6 And they said unto them even as Jesus had commanded: and they let them go. 7 And they brought the colt to Jesus, and cast their garments on him; and he sat upon him. 8 And many spread their garments in the way; and others cut down branches off the trees, and strewed *them* in the way. 9 And they that went before, and they that followed, cried, saying,

"Hosanna; Blessed *is* he that cometh in the name of the Lord:[25]

10 Blessed *be* the kingdom of our father David,

That cometh in the name of the Lord: Hosanna in the highest."

11 And Jesus entered into Jerusalem, and into the temple: and when he had looked round about upon all things, and now the eventide was come, he went out unto Bethany with the twelve.

12 And on the morrow, when they were come from Bethany, he was hungry: 13 And seeing a fig tree afar off having leaves, he came, if haply he might find any thing thereon: and when he came to it, he found nothing but leaves; for the time of figs was not *yet.* 14 And Jesus answered and said unto it, "No man eat fruit of thee hereafter for ever." And his disciples heard *it.*[26]

15 And they come to Jerusalem: and Jesus went into the temple, and began to cast out them that sold and bought in the temple, and over-threw the tables of the money changers, and the seats of them that sold doves; 16 And would not suffer that any man should carry *any* vessel through the temple. 17 And he taught, saying unto them, "Is it not written,

'My house shall be called Of all nations the house of prayer'? But ye have made it a den of thieves." [27]

24. (11:1–16:8) Perhaps because the early church was already celebrating an annual Holy Week, Mark compressed the remaining events of Jesus' life into a seven-day period. This artificial arrangement heavily overloads the third and fifth days and contradicts Jesus' statement "I was daily with you in the temple teaching" (14:49). Mark's week takes this form:

Sunday (Palm)—Entry into Jerusalem
Monday—Cursing the fig tree and cleansing the Temple
Tuesday—Temple preaching; the Apocalypse
Wednesday—Anointing in Bethany; Judas' betrayal
Thursday—Preparation for Passover; Last Supper; Geth-semane; arrest; trial before Sanhedrin
Friday—Trial before Pilate; crucifixion, burial
Saturday—Jesus in tomb
Sunday (Easter)—Resurrection

25. See *Psalm* 118:26.

26. (11:12-14, 20-23) It is probable that the story of the fig tree was originally a parable—i.e., the tree is the Jewish nation, but it offers only leaves (laws and ceremonies) rather than fruit (righteousness). Told and retold by early Christians, the parable changed into an episode involving Jesus. (The "money changers" story inserted in the middle ratifies the point of the parable.)

27. The citations are from *Isaiah* 56:7 and *Jeremiah* 7:11.

18 And the scribes and chief priests heard *it,* and sought how they might destroy him: for they feared him, because all the people was astonished at his doctrine. 19 And when even was come, he went out of the city.

20 And in the morning, as they passed by, they saw the fig tree dried up from the roots. 21 And Peter calling to remembrance saith unto him, "Master, behold, the fig tree which thou cursedst is withered away." 22 And Jesus answering saith unto them, "Have faith in God. 23 For verily I say unto you, That whosoever shall say unto this mountain, 'Be thou removed, and be thou cast into the sea'; and shall not doubt in his heart, but shall believe that those things which he saith shall come to pass; he shall have whatsoever he saith. 24 Therefore I say unto you, What things soever ye desire, when ye pray, believe that ye receive *them,* and ye shall have *them.* 25 And when ye stand praying, forgive, if ye have aught against any; that your Father also which is in heaven may forgive you your trespasses. 26 But if ye do not forgive, neither will your Father which is in heaven forgive your trespasses."

Preaching in The Temple

27 And they come again to Jerusalem: and as he was walking in the temple, there come to him the chief priests, and the scribes, and the elders, 28 And say unto him, "By what authority doest thou these things? and who gave thee this authority to do these things?" 29 And Jesus answered and said unto them, "I will also ask of you one question, and answer me, and I will tell you by what authority I do these things. 30 The baptism of John, was *it* from heaven, or of men? answer me." 31 And they reasoned with themselves, saying, "If we shall say, 'From heaven'; he will say, 'Why then did ye not believe him?' 32 But if we shall say, 'Of men' "; they feared the people: for all *men* counted John, that he was a prophet indeed. 33 And they answered and said unto Jesus, "We cannot tell." And Jesus answering saith unto them, "Neither do I tell you by what authority I do these things."

12 And he began to speak unto them by parables. "A *certain* man planted a vineyard, and set a hedge about *it,* and digged *a place for* the winevat, and built a tower, and let it out to husbandmen, and went into a far country. 2 And at the season he sent to the husbandmen a servant, that he might receive from the husbandmen of the fruit of the vineyard. 3 And they caught *him,* and beat

him, and sent *him* away empty. 4 And again he sent unto them another servant; and at him they cast stones, and wounded *him* in the head, and sent *him* away shamefully handled. 5 And again he sent another; and him they killed, and many others; beating some, and killing some. 6 Having yet therefore one son, his well-beloved, he sent him also last unto them, saying, 'They will reverence my son.' 7 But those husbandmen said among themselves, 'This is the heir; come, let us kill him, and the inheritance shall be ours.' 8 And they took him, and killed *him,* and cast *him* out of the vineyard. 9 What shall therefore the lord of the vineyard do? he will come and destroy the husbandmen, and will give the vineyard unto others. 10 And have ye not read this Scripture;

'The stone which the builders rejected
  Is become the head of the corner:
11   This was the Lord's doing,
  And it is marvelous in our eyes?' " [28]

12 And they sought to lay hold on him, but feared the people; for they knew that he had spoken the parable against them: and they left him, and went their way.

13 And they send unto him certain of the Pharisees and of the Herodians, to catch him in *his* words. 14 And when they were come, they say unto him, "Master, we know that thou art true, and carest for no man; for thou regardest not the person of men, but teachest the way of God in truth: Is it lawful to give tribute to Cæsar, or not? [29] 15 Shall we give, or shall we not give?" But he, knowing their hypocrisy, said unto them, "Why tempt ye me? bring me a penny, that I may see *it.*" 16 And they brought *it.* And he saith unto them, "Whose *is* this image and superscription?" And they said unto him, "Cæsar's." 17 And Jesus answering said unto them, "Render to Cæsar the things that are Cæsar's, and to God the things that are God's." And they marveled at him.

18 Then come unto him the Sadducees, which say there is no resurrection; and they asked him, saying, 19 "Master, Moses wrote unto us, 'If a man's brother die, and leave *his* wife *behind him,*

28. (12:10-11) See *Psalm* 118, where the "stone" is Israel. Here, cited in rabbinical argument, it becomes a reference to Jesus.

29. The reference is to an unpopular poll tax which all inhabitants of Judea, Samaria, and Idumea had had to pay since its inception in A.D. 6. Hugh J. Schonfield (*The Passover Plot,* 1965) adds, "The question was loaded, and was all the more dangerous because of its topicality. The year A.D. 34–5 was a census year, and the Roman tax was now due for payment."

and leave no children, that his brother should take his wife, and raise up seed unto his brother.' [30]   20 Now there were seven brethren: and the first took a wife, and dying left no seed. 21 And the second took her, and died, neither left he any seed: and the third likewise.   22 And the seven had her, and left no seed: last of all the woman died also.   23 In the resurrection therefore, when they shall rise, whose wife shall she be of them? for the seven had her to wife."   24 And Jesus answering said unto them, "Do ye not therefore err, because ye know not the Scriptures, neither the power of God?   25 For when they shall rise from the dead, they neither marry, nor are given in marriage; but are as the angels which are in heaven.   26 And as touching the dead, that they rise; have ye not read in the book of Moses, how in the bush God spake unto him, saying, 'I *am* the God of Abraham, and the God of Isaac, and the God of Jacob'?   27 He is not the God of the dead, but the God of the living: ye therefore do greatly err."

28 And one of the scribes came, and having heard them reasoning together, and perceiving that he had answered them well, asked him, "Which is the first commandment of all?" 29 And Jesus answered him, "The first of all the commandments *is,* 'Hear, O Israel; The Lord our God is one Lord: 30 And thou shalt love the Lord thy God with all thy heart, and with all thy soul, and with all thy mind, and with all thy strength': this *is* the first commandment.   31 And the second *is* like, *namely* this, 'Thou shalt love thy neighbor as thyself.' There is none other commandment greater than these."   32 And the scribe said unto him, "Well, Master, thou hast said the truth: for there is one God; and there is none other but he: 33 And to love him with all the heart, and with all the understanding, and with all the soul, and with all the strength, and to love *his* neighbor as himself, is more than all whole burnt offerings and sacrifices."   34 And when Jesus saw that he answered discreetly, he said unto him, "Thou art not far from the kingdom of God." And no man after that durst ask him *any question.*

35 And Jesus answered and said, while he taught in the temple, "How say the scribes that Christ is the son of David?   36 For David himself said by the Holy Ghost,

     'The LORD said to my Lord,
     "Sit thou on my right hand,

     Till I make thine enemies thy foot-
     stool." ' [31]
37 David therefore himself calleth him Lord; and whence is he *then* his son?" And the common people heard him gladly.

38 And he said unto them in his doctrine, "Beware of the scribes, which love to go in long clothing, and *love* salutations in the market places,   39 And the chief seats in the synagogues, and the uppermost rooms at feasts: 40 Which devour widows' houses, and for a pretense make long prayers: these shall receive greater damnation."

41 And Jesus sat over against the treasury, and beheld how the people cast money into the treasury: and many that were rich cast in much. 42 And there came a certain poor widow, and she threw in two mites, which make a farthing. 43 And he called *unto him* his disciples, and saith unto them, "Verily I say unto you, That this poor widow hath cast more in, than all they which have cast into the treasury: 44 For all *they* did cast in of their abundance; but she of her want did cast in all that she had, *even* all her living."

The Apocalypse[32]

13 And as he went out of the temple, one of his disciples saith unto him, "Master, see what manner of stones and what buildings *are here!*" 2 And Jesus answering said unto him, "Seest thou these great buildings? there shall not be left one stone upon another, that shall not be thrown down."   3 And as he sat upon the mount of Olives, over against the temple, Peter and James and John and Andrew asked him privately, 4 "Tell us, when shall these things be? and what *shall be* the sign when all these things shall be fulfilled?"   5 And Jesus answering them began to say, "Take heed lest any *man* deceive you: 6 For many shall come in my name, saying, 'I am *Christ*'; and shall deceive many.   7 And when ye shall hear of wars and rumors of wars, be ye not troubled: for *such things* must needs be; but the end *shall* not *be* yet.   8 For nation shall rise against nation, and kingdom against kingdom: and there shall be earthquakes in divers places,

---

30. See the discussion of the levirate tradition in footnote 59 to *Genesis* 38:8-11.

31. In *Psalm* 110, "The Lord" is Yahweh; and "my Lord" is a king promised victory by God. Here Jesus interprets "my Lord" to be the Messiah. The passage probably derives from the early church and was intended to counter a Jewish objection that Jesus could not be the Messiah because he was not a descendant of David.

32. (13:1-37) See Introduction to *Revelation* (p. 267) concerning the literary characteristics of an apocalypse.

and there shall be famines and troubles: these *are* the beginnings of sorrows.

9 "But take heed to yourselves: for they shall deliver you up to councils; and in the synagogues ye shall be beaten: and ye shall be brought before rulers and kings for my sake, for a testimony against them. 10 And the gospel must first be published among all nations. 11 But when they shall lead *you,* and deliver you up, take no thought beforehand what ye shall speak, neither do ye premeditate: but whatsoever shall be given you in that hour, that speak ye: for it is not ye that speak, but the Holy Ghost. 12 Now the brother shall betray the brother to death, and the father the son; and children shall rise up against *their* parents, and shall cause them to be put to death. 13 And ye shall be hated of all *men* for my name's sake: but he that shall endure unto the end, the same shall be saved.

14 "But when ye shall see the abomination of desolation, spoken of by Daniel the prophet, standing where it ought not, (let him that readeth understand,) then let them that be in Judea flee to the mountains: 15 And let him that is on the housetop not go down into the house, neither enter *therein,* to take any thing out of his house: 16 And let him that is in the field not turn back again for to take up his garment. 17 But woe to them that are with child, and to them that give suck in those days! 18 And pray ye that your flight be not in the winter. 19 For *in* those days shall be affliction, such as was not from the beginning of the creation which God created unto this time, neither shall be. 20 And except that the Lord had shortened those days, no flesh should be saved: but for the elect's sake, whom he hath chosen, he hath shortened the days. 21 And then if any man shall say to you, 'Lo, here *is* Christ'; or, 'lo, *he is* there'; believe *him* not: 22 For false Christs and false prophets shall rise, and shall show signs and wonders, to seduce, if *it were* possible, even the elect. 23 But take ye heed: behold, I have foretold you all things.

24 "But in those days, after that tribulation, the sun shall be darkened, and the moon shall not give her light, 25 And the stars of heaven shall fall, and the powers that are in heaven shall be shaken. 26 And then shall they see the Son of man coming in the clouds with great power and glory. 27 And then shall he send his angels, and shall gather together his elect from the four winds, from the uttermost part of the earth to the uttermost part of heaven. 28 Now learn a parable of the fig tree: When her branch is yet tender, and putteth forth leaves, ye know that summer is near: 29 So ye in like manner, when ye shall see these things come to pass, know that

it is nigh, *even* at the doors. 30 Verily I say unto you, that this generation shall not pass, till all these things be done. 31 Heaven and earth shall pass away: but my words shall not pass away.

32 "But of that day and *that* hour knoweth no man, no, not the angels which are in heaven, neither the Son, but the Father. 33 Take ye heed, watch and pray: for ye know not when the time is. 34 *For the Son of man is* as a man taking a far journey, who left his house, and gave authority to his servants, and to every man his work, and commanded the porter to watch. 35 Watch ye therefore: for ye know not when the master of the house cometh, at even, or at midnight, or at the cockcrowing, or in the morning: 36 Lest coming suddenly he find you sleeping. 37 And what I say unto you I say unto all, Watch."

THE PASSION NARRATIVE

14 After two days was *the feast of* the passover, and of unleavened bread: and the chief priests and the scribes sought how they might take him by craft, and put *him* to death. 2 But they said, "Not on the feast *day,* lest there be an uproar of the people."

3 And being in Bethany, in the house of Simon the leper, as he sat at meat, there came a woman having an alabaster box of ointment of spikenard very precious; and she brake the box, and poured *it* on his head. 4 And there were some that had indignation within themselves, and said, "Why was this waste of the ointment made? 5 For it might have been sold for more than three hundred pence, and have been given to the poor." And they murmured against her. 6 And Jesus said, "Let her alone; why trouble ye her? she hath wrought a good work on me. 7 For ye have the poor with you always, and whensoever ye will ye may do them good: but me ye have not always. 8 She hath done what she could: she is come aforehand to anoint my body to the burying. 9 Verily I say unto you, Wheresoever this gospel shall be preached throughout the whole world, *this* also that she hath done shall be spoken of for a memorial of her."

10 And Judas Iscariot, one of the twelve, went unto the chief priests, to betray him unto them. 11 And when they heard *it,* they were glad, and promised to give him money. And he sought how he might conveniently betray him.

12 And the first day of unleavened bread, when

they killed the passover,[33] his disciples said unto him, "Where wilt thou that we go and prepare that thou mayest eat the passover?" 13 And he sendeth forth two of his disciples, and saith unto them, "Go ye into the city, and there shall meet you a man bearing a pitcher of water: follow him. 14 And wheresoever he shall go in, say ye to the goodman of the house, 'The Master saith, "Where is the guest chamber, where I shall eat the passover with my disciples?"' 15 And he will show you a large upper room furnished *and* prepared: there make ready for us." 16 And his disciples went forth, and came into the city, and found as he had said unto them: and they made ready the passover. 17 And in the evening he cometh with the twelve. 18 And as they sat and did eat, Jesus said, "Verily I say unto you, One of you which eateth with me shall betray me." 19 And they began to be sorrowful, and to say unto him one by one, "*Is* it I?" and another *said,* "*Is* it I?" 20 And he answered and said unto them, "*It is* one of the twelve, that dippeth with me in the dish.[34] 21 The Son of man indeed goeth, as it is written of him: but woe to that man by whom the Son of man is betrayed! good were it for that man if he had never been born."

22 And as they did eat, Jesus took bread, and blessed, and brake *it,* and gave to them, and said, "Take, eat; this is my body." 23 And he took the cup, and when he had given thanks, he gave *it* to them: and they all drank of it. 24 And he said unto them, "This is my blood of the new testament, which is shed for many. 25 Verily I say unto you, I will drink no more of the fruit of the vine, until that day that I drink it new in the kingdom of God."

26 And when they had sung a hymn, they went out into the mount of Olives. 27 And Jesus saith unto them, "All ye shall be offended because of me this night: for it is written, 'I will smite the shepherd, and the sheep shall be scattered.' 28 But after that I am risen, I will go before you into Galilee." 29 But Peter said unto him, "Although all shall be offended, yet *will* not I." 30 And Jesus saith unto him, "Verily I say unto thee, That this day, *even* in this night, before the cock crow twice, thou shalt deny me thrice." 31 But he spake the more vehemently, "If I should die with thee, I will not deny thee in any wise." Likewise also said they all.

32 And they came to a place which was named Gethsemane: and he saith to his disciples, "Sit ye

33. I.e., the Passover lamb.
34. The line does not identify the traitor; it emphasizes the evil of the betrayal. The person has turned against an intimate friend.

here, while I shall pray." 33 And he taketh with him Peter and James and John, and began to be sore amazed, and to be very heavy; 34 And saith unto them, "My soul is exceeding sorrowful unto death: tarry ye here, and watch." 35 And he went forward a little, and fell on the ground, and prayed that, if it were possible, the hour might pass from him. 36 And he said, "Abba, Father, all things *are* possible unto thee; take away this cup from me: nevertheless, not what I will, but what thou wilt." 37 And he cometh, and findeth them sleeping, and saith unto Peter, "Simon, sleepest thou? couldest not thou watch one hour? 38 Watch ye and pray, lest ye enter into temptation. The spirit truly *is* ready, but the flesh *is* weak." 39 And again he went away, and prayed, and spake the same words. 40 And when he returned, he found them asleep again, (for their eyes were heavy,) neither wist they what to answer him. 41 And he cometh the third time, and saith unto them, "Sleep on now, and take *your* rest: it is enough, the hour is come; behold, the Son of man is betrayed into the hands of sinners. 42 Rise up, let us go; lo, he that betrayeth me is at hand."

43 And immediately, while he yet spake, cometh Judas, one of the twelve, and with him a great multitude with swords and staves, from the chief priests and the scribes and the elders. 44 And he that betrayed him had given them a token, saying, "Whomsoever I shall kiss, that same is he; take him, and lead *him* away safely." 45 And as soon as he was come, he goeth straightway to him, and saith, "Master, Master"; and kissed him. 46 And they laid their hands on him, and took him. 47 And one of them that stood by drew a sword, and smote a servant of the high priest, and cut off his ear. 48 And Jesus answered and said unto them, "Are ye come out, as against a thief, with swords and *with* staves to take me? 49 I was daily with you in the temple teaching, and ye took me not: but the Scriptures must be fulfilled." 50 And they all forsook him, and fled.

51 And there followed him a certain young man, having a linen cloth cast about *his* naked *body;* and the young men laid hold on him: 52 And he left the linen cloth, and fled from them naked.

53 And they led Jesus away to the high priest: and with him were assembled all the chief priests and the elders and the scribes. 54 And Peter followed him afar off, even into the palace of the high priest: and he sat with the servants, and warmed himself at the fire. 55 And the chief priests and all the council sought for witness

against Jesus to put him to death; and found none. 56 For many bare false witness against him, but their witness agreed not together. 57 And there arose certain, and bare false witness against him, saying, 58 "We heard him say, 'I will destroy this temple that is made with hands, and within three days I will build another made without hands.'" 59 But neither so did their witness agree together. 60 And the high priest stood up in the midst, and asked Jesus, saying, "Answerest thou nothing? what *is it which* these witness against thee?" 61 But he held his peace, and answered nothing. Again the high priest asked him, and said unto him, "Art thou the Christ, the Son of the Blessed?" 62 And Jesus said, "I am: and ye shall see the Son of man sitting on the right hand of power, and coming in the clouds of heaven." 63 Then the high priest rent his clothes, and saith, "What need we any further witnesses? 64 Ye have heard the blasphemy: what think ye?" And they all condemned him to be guilty of death. 65 And some began to spit on him, and to cover his face, and to buffet him, and to say unto him, "Prophesy":[35] and the servants did strike him with the palms of their hands.

66 And as Peter was beneath in the palace, there cometh one of the maids of the high priest: 67 And when she saw Peter warming himself, she looked upon him, and said, "And thou also wast with Jesus of Nazareth." 68 But he denied, saying, "I know not, neither understand I what thou sayest." And he went out into the porch; and the cock crew. 69 And a maid saw him again, and began to say to them that stood by, "This is *one* of them." 70 And he denied it again. And a little after, they that stood by said again to Peter, "Surely thou art *one* of them: for thou art a Galilean, and thy speech agreeth *thereto*." 71 But he began to curse and to swear, *saying*, "I know not this man of whom ye speak." 72 And the second time the cock crew. And Peter called to mind the word that Jesus said unto him, "Before the cock crow twice, thou shalt deny me thrice." And when he thought thereon, he wept.

15 And straightway in the morning the chief priests held a consultation with the elders and scribes and the whole council, and bound Jesus, and carried *him* away, and delivered *him* to Pilate. 2 And Pilate asked him, "Art thou the King of the Jews?" And he answering said unto him, "Thou

sayest *it*." [36] 3 And the chief priests accused him of many things; but he answered nothing. 4 And Pilate asked him again, saying, "Answerest thou nothing? behold how many things they witness against thee." 5 But Jesus yet answered nothing; so that Pilate marveled. 6 Now at *that* feast he released unto them one prisoner, whomsoever they desired. 7 And there was *one* named Barabbas, *which lay* bound with them that had made insurrection with him, who had committed murder in the insurrection. 8 And the multitude crying aloud began to desire *him to do* as he had ever done unto them. 9 But Pilate answered them, saying, "Will ye that I release unto you the King of the Jews?" 10 For he knew that the chief priests had delivered him for envy. 11 But the chief priests moved the people, that he should rather release Barabbas unto them. 12 And Pilate answered and said again unto them, "What will ye then that I shall do *unto him* whom ye call the King of the Jews?" 13 And they cried out again, "Crucify him." 14 Then Pilate said unto them, "Why, what evil hath he done?" And they cried out the more exceedingly, "Crucify him." 15 And *so* Pilate, willing to content the people, released Barabbas unto them, and delivered Jesus, when he had scourged *him,* to be crucified.

16 And the soldiers led him away into the hall, called Pretorium; and they call together the whole band. 17 And they clothed him with purple, and platted a crown of thorns, and put it about his *head,* 18 And began to salute him, "Hail, King of the Jews!" 19 And they smote him on the head with a reed, and did spit upon him, and bowing *their* knees worshipped him. 20 And when they had mocked him, they took off the purple from him, and put his own clothes on him, and led him out to crucify him.

21 And they compel one Simon a Cyrenian, who passed by, coming out of the country, the father of Alexander and Rufus, to bear his cross. 22 And they bring him unto the place Golgotha, which is, being interpreted, The place of a skull. 23 And they gave him to drink wine mingled with myrrh: but he received *it* not. 24 And when they had crucified him, they parted his garments, casting lots upon them, what every man should take. 25 And it was the third hour, and they crucified him. 26 And the superscription of his

---

35. TEV: "Guess who hit you!"

36. RIEU expresses the cynicism in Pilate's question: "'Are *you*,' he said, 'the King of the Jews?'" Modern translations present Jesus' answer in two different ways. PHILLIPS: "Yes, I am." NAB: "You are the one who is saying it."

accusation was written over,[37] "THE KING OF THE JEWS." 27 And with him they crucify two thieves; the one on his right hand, and the other on his left. 28 And the Scripture was fulfilled, which saith, "And he was numbered with the transgressors." 29 And they that passed by railed on him, wagging their heads, and saying, "Ah, thou that destroyest the temple, and buildest it in three days, 30 Save thyself, and come down from the cross." 31 Likewise also the chief priests mocking said among themselves with the scribes, "He saved others; himself he cannot save. 32 Let Christ the King of Israel descend now from the cross, that we may see and believe." And they that were crucified with him reviled him.

33 And when the sixth hour was come, there was darkness over the whole land until the ninth hour. 34 And at the ninth hour Jesus cried with a loud voice, saying,

"Eloi, Eloi, lama sabachthani?"

which is, being interpreted,

"My God, my God, why hast thou forsaken me?" [38]

35 And some of them that stood by, when they heard it, said, "Behold, he calleth Elias." 36 And one ran and filled a sponge full of vinegar, and put it on a reed, and gave him to drink, saying, "Let alone; let us see whether Elias will come to take him down." 37 And Jesus cried with a loud voice, and gave up the ghost. 38 And the veil of the temple was rent in twain from the top to the bottom. 39 And when the centurion, which stood over against him, saw that he so cried out, and gave up the ghost, he said, "Truly this man was the Son of God."

40 There were also women looking on afar off: among whom was Mary Magdalene, and Mary the mother of James the less and of Joses, and Salome; 41 Who also, when he was in Galilee, followed him, and ministered unto him; and many other women which came up with him unto Jerusalem.

42 And now when the even was come, because it was the preparation, that is, the day before the sabbath, 43 Joseph of Arimathea, an honorable counselor, which also waited for the kingdom of God, came, and went in boldly unto Pilate, and craved the body of Jesus. 44 And Pilate marveled if he were already dead:[39] and calling unto

him the centurion, he asked him whether he had been any while dead. 45 And when he knew it of the centurion, he gave the body to Joseph. 46 And he bought fine linen, and took him down, and wrapped him in the linen, and laid him in a sepulchre which was hewn out of a rock, and rolled a stone unto the door of the sepulchre. 47 And Mary Magdalene and Mary the mother of Joses beheld where he was laid.

THE RESURRECTION

16 And when the sabbath was past, Mary Magdalene, and Mary the mother of James, and Salome, had bought sweet spices, that they might come and anoint him. 2 And very early in the morning, the first day of the week, they came unto the sepulchre at the rising of the sun. 3 And they said among themselves, "Who shall roll us away the stone from the door of the sepulchre?" 4 And when they looked, they saw that the stone was rolled away: for it was very great. 5 And entering into the sepulchre, they saw a young man sitting on the right side, clothed in a long white garment; and they were affrighted. 6 And he saith unto them, "Be not affrighted: ye seek Jesus of Nazareth, which was crucified: he is risen; he is not here: behold the place where they laid him. 7 But go your way, tell his disciples and Peter that he goeth before you into Galilee: there shall ye see him, as he said unto you." 8 And they went out quickly, and fled from the sepulchre; for they trembled and were amazed: neither said they any thing to any man; for they were afraid.[40]

[A 2nd-Century Appendix: Appearances of the Risen Jesus] [41]

9 Now when Jesus was risen early the first day of the week, he appeared first to Mary Magdalene, out of whom he had cast seven devils 10 And she went and told them that had been with him, as they mourned and wept. 11 And they, when they had heard that he was alive, and had been seen of her, believed not. 12 After that he appeared in another form unto two of them, as they walked, and went into the country. 13 And they went and told it unto the residue: neither

---

37. NEB: "and the inscription giving the charge against him read."

38. The cry is taken from Psalm 22:1.

39. Pilate is amazed that Jesus died within six hours. Victims of crucifixion usually died of exhaustion after a day or two.

40. This is the end of Mark's original gospel. Scholars speculate that he did not live to complete his work or that part of his manuscript was lost. However, a persuasive case can be made that this is the ending Mark intended.

41. (16:9-20) This ending was accepted as part of Mark's gospel about A.D. 180. It has been rejected as Marcan on grounds of attestation, style, and content.

believed they them. 14 Afterward he appeared unto the eleven as they sat at meat, and upbraided them with their unbelief and hardness of heart, because they believed not them which had seen him after he was risen. 15 And he said unto them, "Go ye into all the world, and preach the gospel to every creature. 16 He that believeth and is baptized shall be saved; but he that believeth not shall be damned. 17 And these signs shall follow them that believe; In my name shall they cast out devils; they shall speak with new tongues; 18 They shall take up serpents; and if they drink any deadly thing, it shall not hurt them; they shall lay hands on the sick, and they shall recover." 19 So then, after the Lord had spoken unto them, he was received up into heaven, and sat on the right hand of God. 20 And they went forth, and preached every where, the Lord working with *them*, and confirming the word with signs following. Amen.

Introduction to
MATTHEW, LUKE, and JOHN

"And it came to pass, when Jesus had ended these sayings, the people were astonished at his doctrine."

The selections from *Matthew, Luke,* and *John* illustrate the uniqueness of each gospel.

Matthew, written about 85, was addressed to a Jewish audience. The author relied heavily on proof-texts to demonstrate that Jesus is the Messiah, the fulfillment of the glorious promises made to God's people. The Sermon on the Mount, given here in its entirety, contains over two dozen references and allusions to the Old Testament. Though Jesus makes it clear that his requirements concerning adultery, revenge, prayer, fasting, and almsgiving go beyond Jewish regulations, he insists: "Think not that I am come to destroy the law, or the prophets: I am not come to destroy, but to fulfill."

Scholars are in general agreement that the "sermon on the mount" is a dramatic framework used by the author to set forth the preaching and parables given by Jesus on a number of occasions. At times—particularly in Chapter seven—the sayings are grouped so closely that it is difficult to find continuity in them.

Luke, written around 80, presents a body of material which does not appear in *Matthew* or *Mark*. This includes the story of Jesus' birth in a manger at Bethlehem as well as many of the best known parables.

It is generally believed that the author—perhaps Luke the physician, mentioned as a friend of Paul in *Colossians* 4:14, *Philemon* 1:24, and *II Timothy* 4:11—based his gospel on *Mark*, on a collection of the sayings of Jesus (now known as "Q"), and on the oral and written traditions of first-century Christians. Because of their unusually Hebraic style, the birth and infancy narratives are thought to derive from a documentary source. They express the belief of the early Church that the ministry of Jesus was God's great act of deliverance which fulfilled his ancient promises.

The present selection of parables, all delivered by Jesus while traveling from Galilee to Jerusalem, illustrates the teaching effectiveness of the genre. From real-life situations (a man attacked by robbers, a son wasting his inheritance, a servant cheating his master), they develop moral and religious truths. Vivid details, crisp conversations, and believable circumstances contribute to the popularity and effectiveness of the form.

Luke was addressed to a gentile audience; consequently, the parables reject the legalistic attitude of certain Jews (e.g., the Pharisee who scorns the publican, the elder brother who condemns the prodigal son) and affirm the love of God for all men. Jesus does not preach a righteous Yahweh thundering out of Zion. Instead, he tells of a shepherd seeking a lost sheep and of a father who runs to welcome his wayward son.

241

Written about 105, *John* is unlike the synoptic gospels. The author was less concerned with biographical events in the life of Jesus than with their religious import. The first three chapters show this emphasis. The prologue describes the Word, divine from eternity, who enters the world to incarnate both the life and the light of God. Succeeding episodes show early miracles which demonstrate Jesus' divinity: by special revelation, he is made known to John the Baptist; with supernatural insight he reveals facts about Nathanael; at Cana he changes water into wine; in Jerusalem, he performs a number of wonders. The author sets the early events in an artificial six-day period, and he does not even specify what miracles occurred in Jerusalem. His concern is with the significance of the acts, not with the acts themselves. The significance: "these are written, that ye might believe that Jesus is the Christ, the Son of God; and that believing ye might have life through him."

The Gospel According to
MATTHEW

THE SERMON ON THE MOUNT

5 And seeing the multitudes, he went up into a mountain: and when he was set, his disciples came unto him: 2 And he opened his mouth, and taught them, saying,

The Beatitudes

3   "Blessed *are* the poor in spirit:[1] for theirs is the kingdom of heaven.

4   "Blessed *are* they that mourn: for they shall be comforted.

5   "Blessed *are* the meek: for they shall inherit the earth.

6   "Blessed *are* they which do hunger and thirst after righteousness: for they shall be filled.

7   "Blessed *are* the merciful: for they shall obtain mercy.

8   "Blessed *are* the pure in heart:[2] for they shall see God.

9   "Blessed *are* the peacemakers: for they shall be called the children of God.

10   "Blessed *are* they which are persecuted for righteousness' sake: for theirs is the kingdom of heaven.

11   "Blessed are ye, when *men* shall revile you, and persecute *you,* and shall say all manner of evil against you falsely, for my sake. 12 Rejoice, and be exceeding glad: for great *is* your reward in heaven: for so persecuted they the prophets which were before you.

13 "Ye are the salt of the earth: but if the salt have lost his savor, wherewith shall it be salted? it is thenceforth good for nothing, but to be cast out, and to be trodden under foot of men. 14 Ye are the light of the world. A city that is set on a hill cannot be hid. 15 Neither do men light a candle, and put it under a bushel, but on a candlestick; and it giveth light unto all that are in the house. 16 Let your light so shine before men, that they may see your good works, and glorify your Father which is in heaven.

1. (5:3-11) GOODSPEED: "Blessed are those who feel their spiritual need." The Beatitudes contrast the virtue and vulnerability of believers with the reward they will receive in the messianic kingdom.
2. NAB: "the single-hearted." PHILLIPS: "the utterly sincere."

The Old Law and the New

17 "Think not that I am come to destroy the law, or the prophets: I am not come to destroy, but to fulfil. 18 For verily I say unto you, Till heaven and earth pass, one jot or one tittle[3] shall in no wise pass from the law, till all be fulfilled. 19 Whosoever therefore shall break one of these least commandments, and shall teach men so, he shall be called the least in the kingdom of heaven: but whosoever shall do and teach *them,* the same shall be called great in the kingdom of heaven. 20 For I say unto you, That except your righteousness shall exceed *the righteousness* of the scribes and Pharisees,[4] ye shall in no case enter into the kingdom of heaven.

21 "Ye have heard that it was said by them of old time, 'Thou shalt not kill'; and 'Whosoever shall kill shall be in danger of the judgment': 22 But I say unto you, That whosoever is angry with his brother without a cause shall be in danger of the judgment: and whosoever shall say to his brother, 'Raca,' shall be in danger of the council:[5] but whosoever shall say, 'Thou fool,' shall be in danger of hell fire. 23 Therefore if thou bring thy gift to the altar, and there rememberest that thy brother hath aught against thee; 24 Leave there thy gift before the altar, and go thy way; first be reconciled to thy brother, and then come and offer thy gift. 25 Agree with thine adversary quickly, while thou art in the way with him; lest at any time the adversary deliver thee to the judge, and the judge deliver thee to the officer, and thou be cast into prison. 26 Verily I say unto thee, Thou shalt by no means come out thence, till thou hast paid the uttermost farthing.

3. GOODSPEED: "not one dotting of an *i* or crossing of a *t*."
4. In IB, Sherman E. Johnson explains: "There was no finer standard of righteousness in the ancient world than the Pharisaic, with its emphasis on personal holiness and social responsibility. But, like most systems of ethics, it was adjusted to the capabilities of mankind, and it made allowances for the weakness of human nature and the demands made on man by his environment. . . . Jesus, on the contrary, would have men aspire, not to what is socially expedient, but to that righteousness which will be perfectly manifest in the kingdom of God."
5. The phrase "without a cause"—which does not appear in the best ancient manuscripts—is omitted in modern translations. "Raca" is an obscure term of abuse. TEV: "You good-for-nothing!"

27 "Ye have heard that it was said by them of old time, 'Thou shalt not commit adultery': 28 But I say unto you, That whosoever looketh on a woman to lust after her hath committed adultery with her already in his heart. 29 And if thy right eye offend thee, pluck it out, and cast *it* from thee: for it is profitable for thee that one of thy members should perish, and not *that* thy whole body should be cast into hell.[6] 30 And if thy right hand offend thee, cut it off, and cast *it* from thee: for it is profitable for thee that one of thy members should perish, and not *that* thy whole body should be cast into hell. 31 It hath been said, 'Whosoever shall put away his wife, let him give her a writing of divorcement': 32 But I say unto you, That whosoever shall put away his wife, saving for the cause of fornication,[7] causeth her to commit adultery: and whosoever shall marry her that is divorced committeth adultery.

33 "Again, ye have heard that it hath been said by them of old time, 'Thou shalt not forswear thyself, but shalt perform unto the Lord thine oaths': 34 But I say unto you, Swear not at all; neither by heaven; for it is God's throne: 35 Nor by the earth; for it is his footstool: neither by Jerusalem; for it is the city of the great King. 36 Neither shalt thou swear by thy head, because thou canst not make one hair white or black. 37 But let your communication be, 'Yea, yea; Nay, nay':[8] for whatsoever is more than these cometh of evil.

38 "Ye have heard that it hath been said, 'An eye for an eye, and a tooth for a tooth': 39 But I say unto you, That ye resist not evil: but whosoever shall smite thee on thy right cheek, turn to him the other also. 40 And if any man will sue thee at the law, and take away thy coat, let him have *thy* cloak also. 41 And whosoever[9] shall compel thee to go a mile, go with him twain. 42 Give to him that asketh thee, and from him that would borrow of thee turn not thou away.

43 "Ye have heard that it hath been said, 'Thou shalt love thy neighbor, and hate thine enemy.' 44 But I say unto you, Love your enemies, bless them that curse you, do good to them that hate you, and pray for them which despitefully use you, and persecute you; 45 That ye may be the children of your Father which is in heaven: for he maketh his sun to rise on the evil and on the good, and sendeth rain on the just and on the unjust. 46 For if ye love them which love you, what reward have ye? do not even the publicans the same? 47 And if ye salute your brethren only, what do ye more *than others?* do not even the publicans so? 48 Be ye therefore perfect, even as your Father which is in heaven is perfect.

Religious Duties

6 "Take heed that ye do not your alms before men, to be seen of them: otherwise ye have no reward of your Father which is in heaven. 2 Therefore when thou doest *thine* alms, do not sound a trumpet before thee, as the hypocrites do in the synagogues and in the streets, that they may have glory of men. Verily I say unto you, They have their reward. 3 But when thou doest alms, let not thy left hand know what thy right hand doeth: 4 That thine alms may be in secret: and thy Father which seeth in secret himself shall reward thee openly.

5 "And when thou prayest, thou shalt not be as the hypocrites *are:* for they love to pray standing in the synagogues and in the corners of the streets, that they may be seen of men. Verily I say unto you, They have their reward. 6 But thou, when thou prayest, enter into thy closet, and when thou hast shut thy door, pray to thy Father which is in secret; and thy Father which seeth in secret shall reward thee openly. 7 But when ye pray, use not vain repetitions, as the heathen *do:* for they think that they shall be heard for their much speaking. 8 Be not ye therefore like unto them: for your Father knoweth what things ye have need of, before ye ask him.

9 "After this manner therefore pray ye:[10]
   Our Father which art in heaven,
   Hallowed be thy name.
10   Thy kingdom come.
   Thy will be done
   In earth, as *it is* in heaven.
11   Give us this day our daily bread.
12   And forgive us our debts,
   As we forgive our debtors.
13   And lead us not into temptation,
   But deliver us from evil:

---

6. TCNT: "Hell." NAB: "Gehenna." GOODSPEED: "the pit." PHILLIPS: "the rubbish heap."

7. Jesus makes no such exception in *Mark* 10:11. The author is probably reflecting an attitude within the early church.

8. KNOX: "Let your word for Yes be Yes, and No for No."

9. NEB: "If a man in authority." TEV: "And if one of the occupation troops."

10. 6:9-13) A unifying feature of the "Lord's Prayer" is the anticipation of the messianic kingdom. Believers are to pray that God's reign begins soon, that they be fed and blessed until that day comes, and that they be spared during the final tribulation. (NAB: "Subject us not to the trial." TEV: "Do not bring us to hard testing.") The concluding doxology (v. 13c) does not appear in earliest manuscripts.

For thine is the kingdom, and the power,
and the glory, for ever. Amen.

14 For if ye forgive men their trespasses, your
heavenly Father will also forgive you: 15 But if
ye forgive not men their trespasses, neither will
your Father forgive your trespasses.

16 "Moreover when ye fast, be not, as the
hypocrites, of a sad countenance: for they dis-
figure their faces, that they may appear unto men
to fast. Verily I say unto you, They have their
reward. 17 But thou, when thou fastest, anoint
thine head, and wash thy face; 18 That thou
appear not unto men to fast, but unto thy Father
which is in secret: and thy Father which seeth in
secret shall reward thee openly.

True Riches

19 "Lay not up for yourselves treasures upon
earth, where moth and rust doth corrupt, and
where thieves break through and steal: 20 But
lay up for yourselves treasures in heaven, where
neither moth nor rust doth corrupt, and where
thieves do not break through nor steal: 21 For
where your treasure is, there will your heart be
also. 22 The light[11] of the body is the eye: if
therefore thine eye be single, thy whole body shall
be full of light. 23 But if thine eye be evil, thy
whole body shall be full of darkness. If therefore
the light that is in thee be darkness, how great *is*
that darkness! 24 No man can serve two masters: for either he will hate the one, and love the
other; or else he will hold to the one, and despise
the other. Ye cannot serve God and mammon.
25 Therefore I say unto you, Take no thought for
your life, what ye shall eat, or what ye shall drink;
nor yet for your body, what ye shall put on. Is not
the life more than meat, and the body than
raiment? 26 Behold the fowls of the air: for they
sow not, neither do they reap, nor gather into
barns; yet your heavenly Father feedeth them.
Are ye not much better than they? 27 Which of
you by taking thought can add one cubit unto his
stature?[12] 28 And why take ye thought for
raiment? Consider the lilies of the field, how they
grow; they toil not, neither do they spin: 29 And
yet I say unto you, That even Solomon in all his
glory was not arrayed like one of these.
30 Wherefore, if God so clothe the grass of the
field, which to-day is, and to-morrow is cast into
the oven, *shall he* not much more *clothe* you, O ye

of little faith? 31 Therefore take no thought,
saying, 'What shall we eat?' or, 'What shall we
drink?' or, 'Wherewithal shall we be clothed?'
32 (For after all these things do the Gentiles
seek:) for your heavenly Father knoweth that ye
have need of all these things. 33 But seek ye first
the kingdom of God, and his righteousness; and
all these things shall be added unto you. 34 Take
therefore no thought for the morrow: for the
morrow shall take thought for the things of itself.
Sufficient unto the day *is* the evil thereof.

"The Strait Gate"

7 "Judge not, that ye be not judged. 2 For with
what judgment ye judge, ye shall be judged: and
with what measure ye mete, it shall be measured
to you again. 3 And why beholdest thou the
mote that is in thy brother's eye, but considerest
not the beam that is in thine own eye? 4 Or how
wilt thou say to thy brother, 'Let me pull out the
mote out of thine eye'; and, behold, a beam *is* in
thine own eye? 5 Thou hypocrite,[13] first cast out
the beam out of thine own eye; and then shalt
thou see clearly to cast out the mote out of thy
brother's eye. 6 Give not that which is holy unto
the dogs, neither cast ye your pearls before swine,
lest they trample them under their feet, and turn
again and rend you.[14]

7 "Ask, and it shall be given you; seek, and ye
shall find; knock, and it shall be opened unto
you: 8 For every one that asketh receiveth; and
he that seeketh findeth; and to him that knocketh
it shall be opened. 9 Or what man is there of
you, whom if his son ask bread, will he give him a
stone? 10 Or if he ask a fish, will he give him a
serpent? 11 If ye then, being evil, know how to
give good gifts unto your children, how much
more shall your Father which is in heaven give
good things to them that ask him? 12 Therefore
all things whatsoever ye would that men should
do to you, do ye even so to them: for this is the
law and the prophets.

13 "Enter ye in at the strait gate: for wide *is* the
gate, and broad *is* the way, that leadeth to

---

11. (6:22-23) Most translations read "the lamp." If one's eye is
focused on heavenly things, it brings light to his whole
life.

12. WEYMOUTH: "Which of you is able by anxious thought to
add a single foot to his height?" GOODSPEED: "But which of
you for all his worry can add a single hour to his life?"

13. Nowhere else in the gospels are the disciples called hypocrites. It seems certain that this line was originally preached
to a different audience.

14. The metaphor refers to the consecrated meat sacrificed in
the Temple. It probably means that the gospel should not
be preached to gentiles or even to antagonistic Jews. Such a
meaning, however, does not fit this context. J. C. Fenton
(*The Gospel of St. Matthew*, 1963) gives continuity to the
lines by applying them to God: Just as one would not give
holy articles to dogs, so God will not give them to a man
who condemns his neighbor.

destruction, and many there be which go in thereat: 14 Because strait *is* the gate, and narrow *is* the way, which leadeth unto life, and few there be that find it.

15 "Beware of false prophets, which come to you in sheep's clothing, but inwardly they are ravening wolves.   16 Ye shall know them by their fruits. Do men gather grapes of thorns, or figs of thistles?   17 Even so every good tree bringeth forth good fruit; but a corrupt tree bringeth forth evil fruit.   18 A good tree cannot bring forth evil fruit, neither *can* a corrupt tree bring forth good fruit.   19 Every tree that bringeth not forth good fruit is hewn down, and cast into the fire. 20 Wherefore by their fruits ye shall know them. 21 Not every one that saith unto me, 'Lord, Lord,' shall enter into the kingdom of heaven; but he that doeth the will of my Father which is in heaven.   22 Many will say to me in that day, 'Lord, Lord, have we not prophesied in thy name? and in thy name have cast out devils? and in thy name done many wonderful works?'   23 And

then will I profess unto them, 'I never knew you: depart from me, ye that work iniquity.'

24 "Therefore whosoever heareth these sayings of mine, and doeth them, I will liken him unto a wise man, which built his house upon a rock: 25 And the rain descended, and the floods came, and the winds blew, and beat upon that house; and it fell not: for it was founded upon a rock. 26 And every one that heareth these sayings of mine, and doeth them not, shall be likened unto a foolish man, which built his house upon the sand: 27 And the rain descended, and the floods came, and the winds blew, and beat upon that house; and it fell: and great was the fall of it."

28 And it came to pass, when Jesus had ended these sayings, the people were astonished at his doctrine: 29 For he taught them as *one* having authority, and not as the scribes.[15]

15. (7:28-29) The scribes based their teaching on exposition of the Law and the prophets.

The Gospel According to LUKE

1 Forasmuch as many have taken in hand to set forth in order a declaration of those things which are most surely believed among us, 2 Even as they delivered them unto us, which from the beginning were eyewitnesses, and ministers of the word; 3 It seemed good to me also, having had perfect understanding of all things from the very first, to write unto thee in order, most excellent Theophilus, 4 That thou mightest know the certainty of those things, wherein thou hast been instructed.[1]

THE BIRTH NARRATIVE

The Promise of the Birth of John

5 There was in the days of Herod, the king of Judea, a certain priest named Zacharias, of the course of Abia: and his wife *was* of the daughters of Aaron, and her name *was* Elisabeth. 6 And they were both righteous before God, walking in all the commandments and ordinances of the Lord blameless. 7 And they had no child because that Elisabeth was barren; and they both were *now* well stricken in years. 8 And it came to pass, that, while he executed the priest's office before God in the order of his course, 9 According to the custom of the priest's office, his lot was to burn incense when he went into the temple of the Lord. 10 And the whole multitude of the people were praying without at the time of incense. 11 And there appeared unto him an angel of the Lord standing on the right side of the altar of incense. 12 And when Zacharias saw *him*, he was troubled, and fear fell upon him. 13 But the angel said unto him, "Fear not, Zacharias: for thy prayer is heard; and thy wife Elisabeth shall bear thee a son, and thou shalt call his name John. 14 And thou shalt have joy and gladness; and many shall rejoice at his birth. 15 For he shall be great in the sight of the Lord, and shall drink neither wine nor strong drink; and he shall be filled with the Holy Ghost, even from his mother's womb. 16 And many of the children of Israel shall he turn to the Lord their God. 17 And he shall go before him in the spirit and power of Elias, to turn the hearts of the fathers to the children, and the disobedient to the wisdom of the just; to make ready a people prepared for the Lord." 18 And Zacharias said unto the angel, "Whereby shall I know this? for I am an old man, and my wife well stricken in years." 19 And the angel answering said unto him, "I am Gabriel, that stand in the presence of God;[2] and am sent to speak unto thee, and to show thee these glad tidings. 20 And, behold, thou shalt be dumb, and not able to speak, until the day that these things shall be performed, because thou believest not my words, which shall be fulfilled in their season." 21 And the people waited for Zacharias, and marveled that he tarried so long in the temple. 22 And when he came out, he could not speak unto them: and they perceived that he had seen a vision in the temple; for he beckoned unto them, and remained speechless. 23 And it came to pass, that, as soon as the days of his ministration were accomplished, he departed to his own house. 24 And after those days his wife Elisabeth conceived, and hid herself five months, saying, 25 "Thus hath the Lord dealt with me in the days wherein he looked on *me,* to take away my reproach among men." [3]

The Promise of the Birth of Jesus

26 And in the sixth month the angel Gabriel was sent from God unto a city of Galilee, named Nazareth, 27 To a virgin espoused to a man whose name was Joseph, of the house of David; and the virgin's name *was* Mary. 28 And the angel came in unto her, and said, "Hail, *thou that art* highly favored, the Lord *is* with thee: blessed *art* thou among women." 29 And when she saw *him,* she was troubled at his saying, and cast in her mind what manner of salutation this should be. 30 And the angel said unto her, "Fear not, Mary: for thou hast found favor with God. 31 And, behold, thou shalt conceive in thy womb, and bring forth a son, and shalt call his name JESUS. 32 He shall be great, and shall be called the Son of the Highest; and the Lord God shall give unto him the throne of his father David: 33 And he shall reign over the house of Jacob for ever; and of his kingdom there shall be no end." 34 Then said Mary unto the angel, "How shall this be, seeing I know not a man?" 35 And the angel answered and said unto her, "The Holy

---

1. (1:3-4) The tone of deference suggests Theophilus was a man of importance. Perhaps he was a convert to the faith. Perhaps he was an official who had heard adverse reports about Christianity.

2. See *Tobit* 12:15 and footnote.
3. The reproach is childlessness.

Ghost shall come upon thee, and the power of the Highest shall overshadow thee: therefore also that holy thing which shall be born of thee shall be called the Son of God. 36 And, behold, thy cousin Elisabeth, she hath also conceived a son in her old age; and this is the sixth month with her, who was called barren. 37 For with God nothing shall be impossible." 38 And Mary said, "Behold the handmaid of the Lord; be it unto me according to thy word." And the angel departed from her.

The Visit of Mary to Elisabeth [4]

39 And Mary arose in those days, and went into the hill country with haste, into a city of Juda; 40 And entered into the house of Zacharias, and saluted Elisabeth. 41 And it came to pass, that, when Elisabeth heard the salutation of Mary, the babe leaped in her womb; and Elisabeth was filled with the Holy Ghost: 42 And she spake out with a loud voice, and said, "Blessed *art* thou among women, and blessed *is* the fruit of thy womb. 43 And whence *is* this to me, that the mother of my Lord should come to me? 44 For, lo, as soon as the voice of thy salutation sounded in mine ears, the babe leaped in my womb for joy. 45 And blessed *is* she that believed: for there shall be a performance of those things which were told her from the Lord." 46 And Mary said,

"My soul doth magnify the Lord,
47 And my spirit hath rejoiced in God my Saviour.
48 For he hath regarded the low estate of his handmaiden:
For, behold, from henceforth all generations shall call me blessed.
49 For he that is mighty hath done to me great things;
And holy *is* his name.
50 And his mercy *is* on them that fear him
From generation to generation.
51 He hath showed strength with his arm;
He hath scattered the proud in the imagination of their hearts.
52 He hath put down the mighty from *their* seats,
And exalted them of low degree.
53 He hath filled the hungry with good things;
And the rich he hath sent empty away.
54 He hath holpen his servant Israel,
In remembrance of *his* mercy;

55 As he spake to our fathers,
To Abraham, and to his seed for ever." [5]
56 And Mary abode with her about three months, and returned to her own house.

The Birth of John the Baptist

57 Now Elisabeth's full time came that she should be delivered; and she brought forth a son. 58 And her neighbors and her cousins heard how the Lord had showed great mercy upon her; and they rejoiced with her. 59 And it came to pass, that on the eighth day they came to circumcise the child; and they called him Zacharias, after the name of his father. 60 And his mother answered and said, "Not *so;* but he shall be called John." 61 And they said unto her, "There is none of thy kindred that is called by this name." 62 And they made signs to his father, how he would have him called. 63 And he asked for a writing table, and wrote, saying, "His name is John." And they marveled all. 64 And his mouth was opened immediately, and his tongue *loosed,* and he spake, and praised God. 65 And fear came on all that dwelt round about them: and all these sayings were noised abroad throughout all the hill country of Judea. 66 And all they that heard *them* laid *them* up in their hearts, saying, "What manner of child shall this be?" And the hand of the Lord was with him. 67 And his father Zacharias was filled with the Holy Ghost, and prophesied, saying,

68 "Blessed *be* the Lord God of Israel;
For he hath visited and redeemed his people,
69 And hath raised up a horn of salvation [6] for us
In the house of his servant David;
70 As he spake by the mouth of his holy prophets,
Which have been since the world began:
71 That we should be saved from our enemies,
And from the hand of all that hate us;
72 To perform the mercy *promised* to our fathers,
And to remember his holy covenant;
73 The oath which he sware to our father Abraham,

4. (1:39-45) The Visitation is important in unifying the birth narratives. Here the Jesus story and the John story are joined.

5. (1:46-55) G. B. Caird (*Saint Luke*, 1963) writes: "Mary's song is called the Magnificat and, like the Benedictus and the Nunc Dimittis which follow [1:68-79 and 2:29-32], gets its name from the first word of the Vulgate version. All three are a mosaic of Old Testament texts, and the Magnificat is based largely on the Song of Hannah." (See *I Samuel* 2:1-10.)

6. GOODSPEED: "a mighty Savior." NEB: "a deliverer of victorious power." In the Old Testament, the horn is a common metaphor for strength.

74   That he would grant unto us, that we,
      being delivered out of the hand of our
      enemies,
   Might serve him without fear,

75   In holiness and righteousness before him,
   All the days of our life.

76   And thou, child, shalt be called the
      prophet of the Highest:
   For thou shalt go before the face of the
      Lord
   To prepare his ways;

77   To give knowledge of salvation unto his
      people
   By the remission of their sins,

78   Through the tender mercy of our God;
   Whereby the dayspring from on high hath
      visited us,

79   To give light to them that sit in darkness
      and *in* the shadow of death,
   To guide our feet into the way of peace."

80 And the child grew, and waxed strong in spirit, and was in the deserts till the day of his showing unto Israel.

The Birth of Jesus

2 And it came to pass in those days, that there went out a decree from Cæsar Augustus, that all the world should be taxed.[7] 2 (*And* this taxing was first made when Cyrenius was governor of Syria.) 3 And all went to be taxed, every one into his own city. 4 And Joseph also went up from Galilee, out of the city of Nazareth, into Judea, unto the city of David, which is called Bethlehem, (because he was of the house and lineage of David,) 5 To be taxed with Mary his espoused wife, being great with child. 6 And so it was, that, while they were there, the days were accomplished that she should be delivered. 7 And she brought forth her firstborn son, and wrapped him in swaddling clothes, and laid him in a manger; because there was no room for them in the inn.

8 And there were in the same country shepherds abiding in the field, keeping watch over their flock by night. 9 And, lo, the angel of the Lord came upon them, and the glory of the Lord shone round about them; and they were sore afraid. 10 And the angel said unto them, "Fear not: for, behold, I bring you good tidings of great joy, which shall be to all people. 11 For unto you is born this day in the city of David a Saviour, which is Christ the Lord. 12 And this *shall be* a sign unto you; Ye shall find the babe wrapped in swaddling clothes, lying in a manger." 13 And suddenly there was with the angel a multitude of the heavenly host praising God, and saying,

14   "Glory to God in the highest,
   And on earth peace,
   Good will toward men."

15 And it came to pass, as the angels were gone away from them into heaven, the shepherds said one to another, "Let us now go even unto Bethlehem, and see this thing which is come to pass, which the Lord hath made known unto us." 16 And they came with haste, and found Mary and Joseph, and the babe lying in a manger. 17 And when they had seen *it,* they made known abroad the saying which was told them concerning this child. 18 And all they that heard *it* wondered at those things which were told them by the shepherds. 19 But Mary kept all these things, and pondered *them* in her heart. 20 And the shepherds returned, glorifying and praising God for all the things that they had heard and seen, as it was told unto them.

The Presentation in the Temple

21 And when eight days were accomplished for the circumcising of the child, his name was called Jesus, which was so named of the angel before he was conceived in the womb. 22 And when the days of her purification according to the law of Moses were accomplished, they brought him to Jerusalem, to present *him* to the Lord; 23 (As it is written in the law of the Lord, Every male that openeth the womb shall be called holy to the Lord;) [8] 24 And to offer a sacrifice according to that which is said in the law of the Lord, A pair of turtledoves, or two young pigeons. 25 And, behold, there was a man in Jerusalem, whose name *was* Simeon; and the same man *was* just and devout, waiting for the consolation of Israel: and the Holy Ghost was upon him. 26 And it was revealed unto him by the Holy Ghost, that he should not see death, before he had seen the Lord's Christ. 27 And he came by the Spirit into the temple: and when the parents brought in the child Jesus, to do for him after the custom of the law, 28 Then took he him up in his arms, and blessed God, and said,

29   "Lord, now lettest thou thy servant depart
      In peace, according to thy word:

30   For mine eyes have seen thy salvation,

31   Which thou hast prepared before the face
      of all people;

32   A light to lighten the Gentiles,
   And the glory of thy people Israel."

33 And Joseph and his mother marveled at those things which were spoken of him. 34 And Simeon blessed them, and said unto Mary his mother, "Behold, this *child* is set for the fall and rising

---

7. NAB: "ordering a census of the whole world."

8. See *Exodus* 13:1-2 and footnote 32 to *Genesis* 22:1-13.

again of many in Israel; and for a sign which shall be spoken against;[9] 35 (Yea, a sword shall pierce through thy own soul also;) that the thoughts of many hearts may be revealed." 36 And there was one Anna, a prophetess, the daughter of Phanuel, of the tribe of Aser: she was of a great age, and had lived with a husband seven years from her virginity; 37 And she *was* a widow of about fourscore and four years, which departed not from the temple, but served *God* with fastings and prayers night and day. 38 And she coming in that instant gave thanks likewise unto the Lord, and spake of him to all them that looked for redemption in Jerusalem. 39 And when they had performed all things according to the law of the Lord, they returned into Galilee, to their own city Nazareth.

The Boy Jesus in the Temple

40 And the child grew, and waxed strong in spirit, filled with wisdom; and the grace of God was upon him. 41 Now his parents went to Jerusalem every year at the feast of the passover. 42 And when he was twelve years old, they went up to Jerusalem after the custom of the feast.[10] 43 And when they had fulfilled the days, as they returned, the child Jesus tarried behind in Jerusalem; and Joseph and his mother knew not *of it*. 44 But they, supposing him to have been in the company, went a day's journey; and they sought him among *their* kinsfolk and acquaintance. 45 And when they found him not, they turned back again to Jerusalem, seeking him. 46 And it came to pass, that after three days they found him in the temple, sitting in the midst of the doctors, both hearing them, and asking them questions. 47 And all that heard him were astonished at his understanding and answers. 48 And when they saw him, they were amazed: and his mother said unto him, "Son, why hast thou thus dealt with us? behold, thy father and I have sought thee sorrowing." 49 And he said unto them, "How is it that ye sought me? wist ye not that I must be about my Father's business?"[11] 50 And they understood not the saying which he spake unto them. 51 And he went down with them, and came to Nazareth, and was subject unto them: but his mother kept all these sayings in her heart. 52 And Jesus increased in wisdom and stature, and in favor with God and man.

---

9. PHILLIPS: "and to set up a standard which many will attack."
10. When he became twelve years old, a Jewish boy assumed a man's obligations concerning feasts and worship. He became *bar mitzvah,* a son of the Law.
11. RSV, PHILLIPS, TEV, NEB: "in my Father's house."

*   *   *

PARABLES
The Good Samaritan

10

25 And, behold, a certain lawyer stood up, and tempted him, saying, "Master, what shall I do to inherit eternal life?" 26 He said unto him, "What is written in the law? how readest thou?" 27 And he answering said, "Thou shalt love the Lord thy God with all thy heart, and with all thy soul, and with all thy strength, and with all thy mind; and thy neighbor as thyself."[12] 28 And he said unto him, "Thou hast answered right: this do, and thou shalt live." 29 But he, willing to justify himself,[13] said unto Jesus, "And who is my neighbor?" 30 And Jesus answering said, "A certain *man* went down from Jerusalem to Jericho, and fell among thieves, which stripped him of his raiment, and wounded *him,* and departed, leaving *him* half dead. 31 And by chance there came down a certain priest that way; and when he saw him, he passed by on the other side. 32 And likewise a Levite, when he was at the place, came and looked *on him,* and passed by on the other side. 33 But a certain Samaritan,[14] as he journeyed, came where he was; and when he saw him, he had compassion *on him,* 34 And went to *him,* and bound up his wounds, pouring in oil and wine, and set him on his own beast, and brought him to an inn, and took care of him. 35 And on the morrow when he departed, he took out two pence, and gave *them* to the host, and said unto him, 'Take care of him: and whatsoever thou spendest more, when I come again, I will repay thee.' 36 Which now of these three, thinkest thou, was neighbor unto him that fell among the thieves?" 37 And he said, "He that showed mercy on him." Then said Jesus unto him, "Go, and do thou likewise."

*   *   *

The Rich Fool

12

13 And one of the company said unto him, "Master, speak to my brother, that he divide the

---

12. In *Mark* 12:28-31, when a scribe asks concerning "the first commandment of all," Jesus gives this response. The lines reflect *Deuteronomy* 6:4 and *Leviticus* 19:18.
13. KINGDOM: "wanting to prove himself righteous." GOODSPEED: "wishing to justify his question."
14. (10:31-33) While a priest and a Levite represent ranking religious figures, a Samaritan—derived from Jews and foreign peoples—was despised as a kind of mongrel.

inheritance with me." [15] 14 And he said unto him, "Man, who made me a judge or a divider over you?" 15 And he said unto them, "Take heed, and beware of covetousness: for a man's life consisteth not in the abundance of the things which he possesseth." [16] 16 And he spake a parable unto them, saying, "The ground of a certain rich man brought forth plentifully: 17 And he thought within himself, saying, 'What shall I do, because I have no room where to bestow my fruits?' 18 And he said, 'This will I do: I will pull down my barns, and build greater; and there will I bestow all my fruits and my goods. 19 And I will say to my soul, Soul, thou hast much goods laid up for many years; take thine ease, eat, drink, *and* be merry.' 20 But God said unto him, '*Thou* fool, this night thy soul shall be required of thee: then whose shall those things be, which thou hast provided?' 21 So *is* he that layeth up treasure for himself, and is not rich toward God."

*   *   *

The Lost Sheep and the Lost Coin

15 Then drew near unto him all the publicans and sinners for to hear him. 2 And the Pharisees and scribes murmured, saying, "This man receiveth sinners, and eateth with them." 3 And he spake this parable unto them, saying, 4 "What man of you, having a hundred sheep, if he lose one of them, doth not leave the ninety and nine in the wilderness, and go after that which is lost, until he find it? [17] 5 And when he hath found *it,* he layeth *it* on his shoulders, rejoicing. 6 And when he cometh home, he calleth together *his* friends and neighbors, saying unto them, 'Rejoice with me; for I have found my sheep which was lost.' 7 I say unto you, that likewise joy shall be in heaven over one sinner that repenteth, more than over ninety and nine just persons, which need no repentance.

8 "Either what woman having ten pieces of silver, if she lose one piece, doth not light a candle, and sweep the house, and seek diligently till she find *it?* 9 And when she hath found *it,* she calleth *her* friends and *her* neighbors together,

---

15. The request is not unreasonable: rabbis were considered experts on the civil regulations of the Law. The speaker seems to be a younger son, who, according to *Deuteronomy* 21:17, should receive half as much as the older brother.
16. GOODSPEED: "for a man's life does not belong to him, no matter how rich he is."
17. Because a single sheep could give wool for seven or eight years, its loss would be significant. Similarly, the lost silver coin, in the following parable, had sufficient purchasing power in Jesus' day to make the woman's search reasonable.

saying, 'Rejoice with me; for I have found the piece which I had lost.' 10 Likewise, I say unto you, there is joy in the presence of the angels of God over one sinner that repenteth."

The Prodigal Son

11 And he said, "A certain man had two sons: 12 And the younger of them said to *his* father, 'Father, give me the portion of goods that falleth *to me.*' [18] And he divided unto them *his* living. 13 And not many days after the younger son gathered all together, and took his journey into a far country, and there wasted his substance with riotous living. 14 And when he had spent all, there arose a mighty famine in that land; and he began to be in want. 15 And he went and joined himself to a citizen of that country; and he sent him into his fields to feed swine.[19] 16 And he would fain have filled his belly with the husks that the swine did eat: and no man gave unto him. 17 And when he came to himself, he said, 'How many hired servants of my father's have bread enough and to spare, and I perish with hunger! 18 I will arise and go to my father, and will say unto him, "Father, I have sinned against heaven, and before thee, 19 And am no more worthy to be called thy son: make me as one of thy hired servants." ' 20 And he arose, and came to his father. But when he was yet a great way off, his father saw him, and had compassion, and ran, and fell on his neck, and kissed him. 21 And the son said unto him, 'Father, I have sinned against heaven, and in thy sight, and am no more worthy to be called thy son.' 22 But the father said to his servants, 'Bring forth the best robe, and put *it* on him; and put a ring on his hand, and shoes on *his* feet: 23 And bring hither the fatted calf, and kill *it;* and let us eat, and be merry: 24 For this my son was dead, and is alive again; he was lost, and is found.' And they began to be merry. 25 Now his elder son was in the field: and as he came and drew nigh to the house, he heard music and dancing. 26 And he called one of the servants, and asked what these things meant. 27 And he said unto him, 'Thy brother is come; and thy father hath killed the fatted calf, because he hath received him safe and sound.' 28 And he was angry, and would not go in: therefore came his father out, and entreated him. 29 And he answering said to *his* father, 'Lo, these many years do I serve thee, neither transgressed I at any time thy commandment; and yet thou never gavest me a kid, that I might make merry with my

---

18. (15:11-12) See footnote 13 to *Luke* 12:13.
19. For a Jew, tending swine would be a particularly degrading job.

friends: 30 But as soon as this thy son[20] was come, which hath devoured thy living with harlots, thou hast killed for him the fatted calf.' 31 And he said unto him, 'Son, thou art ever with me, and all that I have is thine. 32 It was meet that we should make merry, and be glad: for this thy brother was dead, and is alive again; and was lost, and is found.' "

The Prudent Steward

16 And he said also unto his disciples, "There was a certain rich man, which had a steward; and the same was accused unto him that he had wasted his goods. 2 And he called him, and said unto him, 'How is it that I hear this of thee? give an account of thy stewardship; for thou mayest be no longer steward.' 3 Then the steward said within himself, 'What shall I do? for my lord taketh away from me the stewardship: I cannot dig; to beg I am ashamed. 4 I am resolved what to do, that, when I am put out of the stewardship, they may receive me into their houses.' 5 So he called every one of his lord's debtors *unto him,* and said unto the first, 'How much owest thou unto my lord?' 6 And he said, 'A hundred measures of oil.' And he said unto him, 'Take thy bill, and sit down quickly, and write fifty.' 7 Then said he to another, 'And how much owest thou?' And he said, 'A hundred measures of wheat.' And he said unto him, 'Take thy bill, and write fourscore.' 8 And the lord commended the unjust steward, because he had done wisely: for the children of this world are in their generation wiser than the children of light.[21] 9 And I say unto you, Make to yourselves friends of the mammon of unrighteousness; that, when ye fail, they may receive you into everlasting habitations.[22] 10 He that is faithful in that which is least is faithful also in much: and he that is unjust in the least is unjust also in much. 11 If therefore ye have not been faithful in the unrighteous mammon, who will commit to your trust the true *riches?* 12 And if ye have not been faithful in that which is another man's, who shall give you that which is your own? 13 No servant can serve two masters: for either he will hate the one, and love the other; or else he will hold to the one, and despise the other. Ye cannot serve God and mammon."

* * *

Lazarus and Dives

16 19 "There was a certain rich man, which was clothed in purple and fine linen, and fared sumptuously every day.[23] 20 And there was a certain beggar named Lazarus, which was laid at his gate, full of sores, 21 And desiring to be fed with the crumbs which fell from the rich man's table: moreover the dogs came and licked his sores. 22 And it came to pass, that the beggar died, and was carried by the angels into Abraham's bosom:[24] the rich man also died, and was buried; 23 And in hell he lifted up his eyes, being in torments, and seeth Abraham afar off, and Lazarus in his bosom. 24 And he cried and said, 'Father Abraham, have mercy on me, and send Lazarus, that he may dip the tip of his finger in water, and cool my tongue; for I am tormented in this flame.' 25 But Abraham said, 'Son, remember that thou in thy lifetime receivedst thy good things, and likewise Lazarus evil things: but now he is comforted, and thou art tormented. 26 And beside all this, between us and you there is a great gulf fixed: so that they which would pass from hence to you cannot; neither can they pass to us, that *would come* from thence.' 27 Then he said, 'I pray thee therefore, father, that thou wouldest send him to my father's house: 28 For I have five brethren; that he may testify unto them, lest they also come into this place of torment.' 29 Abraham saith unto him, 'They have Moses and the prophets; let them hear them.' 30 And he said, 'Nay, father Abraham: but if one went unto them from the dead, they will repent.' 31 And he said unto him, 'If they hear not Moses and the prophets, neither will they be persuaded, though one rose from the dead.' "

* * *

The Persistent Widow

18 And he spake a parable unto them *to this end,* that men ought always to pray, and not to faint;[25] 2 Saying, "There was in a city a judge, which feared not God, neither regarded man: 3 And there was a widow in that city; and she came unto

---

20. RSV, JB, TEV: "this son of yours." In v. 32, the father challenges the scornful tone of the eldest son by reminding him of the good fortune of "thy brother."

21. TEV: "The master of this dishonest manager praised him for doing such a shrewd thing; for the people of this world are much more shrewd in handling their affairs than the people who belong to the light."

22. JB: "use money, tainted as it is, to win you friends, and thus make sure that when it fails you, they will welcome you into the tents of eternity." Believers are urged to practice charity and almsgiving and thus to merit heavenly reward.

23. The story of Dives (Latin for "rich man") echoes the theme of the unjust steward parable. Dives did not use his earthly wealth in a manner which would win him heavenly blessings.

24. A traditional phrase meaning "gathered to his fathers."

25. TEV: "and never become discouraged." The story is addressed to those who might despair while waiting for the messianic age to begin.

him,[26] saying, 'Avenge me of mine adversary.' 4 And he would not for a while: but afterward he said within himself, 'Though I fear not God, nor regard man; 5 Yet because this widow troubleth me, I will avenge her, lest by her continual coming she weary me.' " 6 And the Lord said, "Hear what the unjust judge saith. 7 And shall not God avenge his own elect, which cry day and night unto him, though he bear long with them? 8 I tell you that he will avenge them speedily. Nevertheless, when the Son of man cometh, shall he find faith on the earth?"

The Pharisee and the Publican

9 And he spake this parable unto certain which trusted in themselves that they were righteous, and despised others: 10 "Two men went up into the temple to pray; the one a Pharisee, and the other a publican.[27] 11 The Pharisee stood and prayed thus with himself, 'God, I thank thee, that I am not as other men *are,* extortioners, unjust, adulterers, or even as this publican. 12 I fast twice in the week, I give tithes of all that I possess.' 13 And the publican, standing afar off, would not lift up so much as *his* eyes unto heaven, but smote upon his breast, saying, 'God be merciful to me a sinner.' 14 I tell you, this man went down to his house justified *rather* than the other: for every one that exalteth himself shall be abased; and he that humbleth himself shall be exalted."

*   *   *

The Foolish Servant

19

11 And as they heard these things, he added and spake a parable, because he was nigh to Jerusalem, and because they thought that the kingdom of God should immediately appear. 12 He said therefore, "A certain nobleman went into a far country to receive for himself a kingdom.[28] and to return. 13 And he called his ten servants, and delivered them ten pounds, and said unto them, 'Occupy till I come.' 14 But his citizens hated him, and sent a message after him, saying, 'We will not have this *man* to reign over us.' 15 And it came to pass, that when he was returned, having received the kingdom, then he commanded these servants to be called unto him, to whom he had given the money, that he might know how much every man had gained by trading. 16 Then came the first, saying, 'Lord, thy pound hath gained ten pounds.' 17 And he said unto him, 'Well, thou good servant: because thou hast been faithful in a very little, have thou authority over ten cities.' 18 And the second came, saying, 'Lord, thy pound hath gained five pounds.' 19 And he said likewise to him, 'Be thou also over five cities.' 20 And another came, saying, 'Lord, behold, *here is* thy pound, which I have kept laid up in a napkin: 21 For I feared thee, because thou art an austere man: thou takest up that thou layedst not down, and reapest that thou didst not sow.' 22 And he saith unto him, 'Out of thine own mouth will I judge thee, *thou* wicked servant. Thou knewest that I was an austere man, taking up that I laid not down, and reaping that I did not sow: 23 Wherefore then gavest not thou my money into the bank, that at my coming I might have required mine own with usury?' 24 And he said unto them that stood by, 'Take from him the pound, and give *it* to him that hath ten pounds.' 25 (And they said unto him, 'Lord, he hath ten pounds.') 26 'For I say unto you, That unto every one which hath shall be given; and from him that hath not, even that he hath shall be taken away from him. 27 But those mine enemies, which would not that I should reign over them, bring hither, and slay *them* before me.' " 28 And when he had thus spoken, he went before, ascending up to Jerusalem.

26. Modern translations emphasize the widow's persistence. TEV: "kept coming to him." TCNT: "went to him again and again."

27. This Pharisee is particularly pious. He fasts two days a week, when the Law requires only one day. He gives one-tenth of all his goods, not just of his agricultural products as the Law requires. Publicans are tax collectors, commonly scorned as thieves and as traitorous collaborators with Rome.

28. I.e., to be made king over the country he already lives in. (The parable probably derives from an historical event. In 4 B.C., after the death of Herod the Great, Archelaus sailed to Rome to ask Augustus to appoint him king. A delegation of fifty Jews vigorously opposed his petition.)

The Gospel According to
JOHN

THE PROLOGUE

1 In the beginning was the Word,[1] and the Word was with God, and the Word was God. 2 The same was in the beginning with God. 3 All things were made by him; and without him was not any thing made that was made. 4 In him was life; and the life was the light of men. 5 And the light shineth in darkness; and the darkness comprehended it not.

6 There was a man sent from God, whose name *was* John. 7 The same came for a witness, to bear witness of the Light, that all *men* through him might believe. 8 He was not that Light, but *was sent* to bear witness of that Light. 9 *That* was the true Light, which lighteth every man that cometh into the world. 10 He was in the world, and the world was made by him, and the world knew him not. 11 He came unto his own, and his own received him not. 12 But as many as received him, to them gave he power to become the sons of God, *even* to them that believe on his name: 13 Which were born, not of blood, nor of the will of the flesh, nor of the will of man, but of God.

14 And the Word was made flesh, and dwelt among us, (and we beheld his glory, the glory as of the only begotten of the Father,) full of grace and truth. 15 John bare witness of him, and cried, saying, "This was he of whom I spake, 'He that cometh after me is preferred before me; for he was before me.' "[2] 16 And of his fulness have all we received, and grace for grace. 17 For the law was given by Moses, *but* grace and truth came by Jesus Christ. 18 No man hath seen God at any time; the only begotten Son, which is in the bosom of the Father, he hath declared *him.*

TESTIMONIES CONCERNING JESUS

John the Baptist

19 And this is the record of John, when the Jews sent priests and Levites from Jerusalem to ask him, "Who art thou?" 20 And he confessed, and denied not; but confessed, "I am not the Christ." 21 And they asked him, "What then? Art thou Elias?" And he saith, "I am not." "Art thou that Prophet?" And he answered, "No." 22 Then said they unto him, "Who art thou? that we may give an answer to them that sent us. What sayest thou of thyself?" 23 He said, "I *am*

The voice of one crying in the wilderness,
'Make straight the way of the Lord,'

as said the prophet Esaias."[3] 24 And they which were sent were of the Pharisees. 25 And they asked him, and said unto him, "Why baptizest thou then, if thou be not that Christ, nor Elias, neither that Prophet?" 26 John answered them, saying, "I baptize with water: but there standeth one among you, whom ye know not; 27 He it is, who coming after me is preferred before me, whose shoe-latchet I am not worthy to unloose." 28 These things were done in Bethabara beyond Jordan, where John was baptizing.

29 The next day John seeth Jesus coming unto him, and saith, "Behold the Lamb of God, which taketh away the sin of the world! 30 This is he of whom I said, 'After me cometh a man which is preferred before me; for he was before me.' 31 And I knew him not: but that he should be made manifest to Israel, therefore am I come baptizing with water." 32 And John bare record, saying, "I saw the Spirit descending from heaven like a dove, and it abode upon him. 33 And I knew him not: but he that sent me to baptize with water, the same said unto me, 'Upon whom thou shalt see the Spirit descending, and remaining on him, the same is he which baptizeth with the Holy Ghost.' 34 And I saw, and bare record that this is the Son of God."

The First Disciples

35 Again the next day after, John stood, and two of his disciples; 36 And looking upon Jesus as he walked, he saith, "Behold the Lamb of God!" 37 And the two disciples heard him speak, and they followed Jesus. 38 Then Jesus turned, and saw them following, and saith unto them, "What seek ye?" They said unto him, "Rabbi, (which is to say, being interpreted, Master,) where dwellest thou?" 39 He saith unto them, "Come and see." They came and saw where he dwelt, and abode with him that day: for it was about the tenth hour. 40 One of the two

---

1. PHILLIPS: "At the beginning God expressed himself." Jesus is seen as the Word, i.e., an expression of the creative power of God.
2. NEB: "This is the man I meant when I said, 'He comes after me, but takes rank before me'; for before I was born, he already was." The paradox is repeated in vv. 27 and 30.

3. To identify himself, John quotes *Isaiah* 40:3.

which heard John *speak,* and followed him, was Andrew, Simon Peter's brother. 41 He first findeth his own brother Simon, and saith unto him, "We have found the Messias," which is, being interpreted, the Christ. 42 And he brought him to Jesus. And when Jesus beheld him, he said, "Thou art Simon the son of Jona: thou shalt be called Cephas," which is by interpretation, A stone.

43 The day following Jesus would go forth into Galilee, and findeth Philip, and saith unto him, "Follow me." 44 Now Philip was of Bethsaida, the city of Andrew and Peter. 45 Philip findeth Nathanael, and saith unto him, "We have found him, of whom Moses in the law, and the prophets, did write, Jesus of Nazareth, the son of Joseph." 46 And Nathanael said unto him, "Can there any good thing come out of Nazareth?" [4] Philip saith unto him, "Come and see." 47 Jesus saw Nathanael coming to him, and saith of him, "Behold an Israelite indeed, in whom is no guile!" 48 Nathanael saith unto him, "Whence knowest thou me?" Jesus answered and said unto him, "Before that Philip called thee, when thou wast under the fig tree, I saw thee." 49 Nathanael answered and saith unto him, "Rabbi, thou art the Son of God; thou art the King of Israel." 50 Jesus answered and said unto him, "Because I said unto thee, 'I saw thee under the fig tree,' believest thou? thou shalt see greater things than these." 51 And he saith unto him, "Verily, verily, I say unto you, Hereafter ye shall see heaven open, and the angels of God ascending and descending upon the Son of man." [5]

JESUS IN CANA AND JERUSALEM

The Wedding Feast

2 And the third day there was a marriage in Cana of Galilee; and the mother of Jesus was there: 2 And both Jesus was called, and his disciples, to the marriage. 3 And when they wanted wine, the mother of Jesus saith unto him, "They have no wine." 4 Jesus saith unto her, "Woman, what have I to do with thee? [6] mine hour is not yet come." 5 His mother saith unto the servants, "Whatsoever he saith unto you, do

it." 6 And there were set there six waterpots of stone, after the manner of the purifying of the Jews, containing two or three firkins apiece.[7] 7 Jesus saith unto them, "Fill the waterpots with water." And they filled them up to the brim. 8 And he saith unto them, "Draw out now, and bear unto the governor of the feast." And they bare *it.* 9 When the ruler of the feast had tasted the water that was made wine, and knew not whence it was (but the servants which drew the water knew), the governor of the feast called the bridegroom, 10 And saith unto him, "Every man at the beginning doth set forth good wine; and when men have well drunk, then that which is worse: *but* thou hast kept the good wine until now." 11 This beginning of miracles did Jesus in Cana of Galilee, and manifested forth his glory; and his disciples believed on him.

Cleaning the Temple

12 After this he went down to Capernaum, he, and his mother, and his brethren, and his disciples; and they continued there not many days. 13 And the Jews' passover was at hand, and Jesus went up to Jerusalem, 14 And found in the temple those that sold oxen and sheep and doves, and the changers of money sitting:[8] 15 And when he had made a scourge of small cords, he drove them all out of the temple, and the sheep, and the oxen; and poured out the changers' money, and overthrew the tables; 16 And said unto them that sold doves, "Take these things hence; make not my Father's house a house of merchandise." 17 And his disciples remembered that it was written, "The zeal of thine house hath eaten me up." 18 Then answered the Jews and said unto him, "What sign showest thou unto us, seeing that thou doest these things?" 19 Jesus answered and said unto them, "Destroy this temple, and in three days I will raise it up." 20 Then said the Jews, "Forty and six years was this temple in building, and wilt thou rear it up in three days?" 21 But he spake of the temple of his body. 22 When therefore he was risen from the dead, his disciples remembered that he had said this unto them; and they believed the Scripture, and the word which Jesus had said.

23 Now when he was in Jerusalem at the passover, in the feast *day,* many believed in his

---

4. (1:45-46) Nathanael, who is probably the person called Bartholomew in the other gospels, is from Cana and does not like to think that the hope of Israel would come from the neighboring village of Nazareth.

5. This recalls Jacob's vision. See *Genesis* 28:12.

6. Many efforts have been made to explain away the seeming abruptness of this line. One explanation is that, while Jesus intends no disrespect toward his mother, he cannot admit that his actions are dependent upon any human authority. TEV: "You must not tell me what to do, woman." GOODSPEED: "Do not try to direct me."

7. RSV: "Now six stone jars were standing there, for the Jewish rites of purification, each holding twenty or thirty gallons."

8. In the outer court of the Temple was a virtual marketplace where visitors could buy the unblemished animals needed for sacrifice and could change their money for Tyrian shekels and half-shekels, the only acceptable religious coins.

name, when they saw the miracles which he did. 24 But Jesus did not commit himself unto them, because he knew all *men,* 25 And needed not that any should testify of man; for he knew what was in man.

JESUS AND NICODEMUS

3 There was a man of the Pharisees, named Nicodemus, a ruler of the Jews: 2 The same came to Jesus by night, and said unto him, "Rabbi, we know that thou art a teacher come from God: for no man can do these miracles that thou doest, except God be with him." 3 Jesus answered and said unto him, "Verily, verily, I say unto thee, Except a man be born again, he cannot see the kingdom of God." 4 Nicodemus saith unto him, "How can a man be born when he is old? can he enter the second time into his mother's womb, and be born?" 5 Jesus answered, "Verily, verily, I say unto thee, Except a man be born of water and *of* the Spirit, he cannot enter into the kingdom of God. 6 That which is born of the flesh is flesh; and that which is born of the Spirit is spirit. 7 Marvel not that I said unto thee, 'Ye must be born again.' 8 The wind bloweth where it listeth, and thou hearest the sound thereof, but canst not tell whence it cometh, and whither it goeth: so is every one that is born of the Spirit." 9 Nicodemus answered and said unto him, "How can these things be?" 10 Jesus answered and said unto him, "Art thou a master of Israel, and knowest not these things? 11 Verily, verily, I say unto thee, We speak that we do know, and testify that we have seen; and ye receive not our witness. 12 If I have told you earthly things, and ye believe not, how shall ye believe, if I tell you *of* heavenly things? 13 And no man hath ascended up to heaven, but he that came down from heaven, *even* the Son of man which is in heaven. 14 And as Moses lifted up the serpent in the wilderness, even so must the Son of man be lifted up: 15 That whosoever believeth in him should not perish, but have eternal life."

16 For God so loved the world, that he gave his only begotten Son, that whosoever believeth in him should not perish, but have everlasting life.[9] 17 For God sent not his Son into the world to condemn the world; but that the world through him might be saved. 18 He that believeth on him is not condemned: but he that believeth not is condemned already, because he hath not believed in the name of the only begotten Son of God. 19 And this is the condemnation, that light is come into the world, and men loved darkness rather than light, because their deeds were evil. 20 For every one that doeth evil hateth the light, neither cometh to the light, lest his deed should be reproved. 21 But he that doeth truth cometh to the light, that his deeds may be made manifest, that they are wrought in God.

JOHN BEARS WITNESS
TO JESUS

22 After these things came Jesus and his disciples into the land of Judea; and there he tarried with them, and baptized. 23 And John also was baptizing in Ænon near to Salim, because there was much water there: and they came, and were baptized. 24 For John was not yet cast into prison.

25 Then there arose a question between *some* of John's disciples and the Jews about purifying. 26 And they came unto John, and said unto him, "Rabbi, he that was with thee beyond Jordan, to whom thou barest witness, behold, the same baptizeth, and all *men* come to him." 27 John answered and said, "A man can receive nothing, except it be given him from heaven. 28 Ye yourselves bear me witness, that I said, I am not the Christ, but that I am sent before him. 29 He that hath the bride is the bridegroom: but the friend of the bridegroom, which standeth and heareth him, rejoiceth greatly because of the bridegroom's voice: this my joy therefore is fulfilled. 30 He must increase, but I *must* decrease."

31 He that cometh from above is above all:[10] he that is of the earth is earthly, and speaketh of the earth: he that cometh from heaven is above all. 32 And what he hath seen and heard, that he testifieth; and no man receiveth his testimony. 33 He that hath received his testimony hath set to his seal that God is true. 34 For he whom God hath sent speaketh the words of God: for God giveth not the Spirit by measure *unto him.* 35 The Father loveth the Son, and hath given all things into his hand. 36 He that believeth on the Son hath everlasting life: and he that believeth not the Son shall not see life; but the wrath of God abideth on him.

9. (3:16-21) In IB, Wilbert F. Howard clarifies: "These verses are a reflection of the evangelist rather than part of a conversation. By this time Nicodemus has faded out of the picture, and John is pondering over the mystery of grace by which law and judgment have been superceded by gospel and forgiveness." However, several modern translations (e.g., MOFFATT, NEB, JB) include these verses as part of Jesus' speech.

10. (3:31-36) These verses resume the evangelist's meditation begun in vv. 16-21.

Introduction to
THE LETTERS OF PAUL

"for if righteousness come by the law, then Christ is dead in vain."

GALATIANS

The epistle to the Galatians has been called the Magna Carta of Christian liberty. It repudiates all institutions, laws, and customs which might separate an individual from the grace of God.

Though scholarship relating to the issues is both extensive and complex, it is probable that Paul wrote the letter from Ephesus, that his message was for the churches of North Galatia, and that the date was between A.D. 53 and 57. *Galatians* is among the earliest Christian documents.

Of all literary forms, a letter is perhaps the most personal and often the most perplexing. It is personal because the writer expresses his immediate thoughts and emotions concerning a current experience. It can be perplexing because it is but one-half of a dialogue. The author and his audience have shared experiences which the letter need not explain. Later readers of the document, however, may find the audience unknown, the context uncertain, and the allusions obscure. They must work to reconstruct the background against which the letter was written.

It is not difficult to establish the context for *Galatians*. Paul had learned that a body of Jewish Christians—perhaps emissaries from Jerusalem, perhaps simply local converts—were seeking to persuade his Galatian converts that circumcision and the practices of the Mosaic law were obligatory for Christians of pagan origin. To effect this, they had to undermine Paul's ministry. The Judaizers emphasized that Paul had never seen Jesus, that he was merely a disciple of the disciples of Christ. They accused him of currying favor by preaching circumcision among the Jews and opposing it among Gentiles. They said he contributed to license by promising salvation through grace rather than by conformity to the Law.

Recognizing that these teachers would reduce Christianity to a sect of Judaism, Paul responded with vigorous eloquence. In a letter, presumably to be read aloud at meetings of the church, he insists that his gospel came directly from God: "For I neither received it of man, neither was I taught it, but by the revelation of Jesus Christ." Knowing that the divine experience at Damascus could never be proved, Paul offers himself—his total change from being a persecuting Pharisee; his labors in spreading the faith; his co-equal relations with Peter, James, and John; his intense conviction; his oath—to demonstrate the authenticity of his ministry. Answering charges that he practiced hypocrisy and promoted license, Paul lays a curse on the Judaizers, then challenges: "do I now persuade men or God; or do I seek to please men?" He insists that the Mosaic law was satisfied by the sacrifice of

Jesus and that those responding to the sacrifice will live moral lives: "the fruit of the Spirit is love, joy, peace, long-suffering, gentleness, goodness, faith, meekness, temperance."

Urging the Galatians not to give up the "liberty we·have in Christ Jesus," Paul employs a range of emotional and logical arguments. He reminds them of his sufferings on their behalf and recalls the time when they would have given their very eyes for him. He scorns the Jewish teachers as "false brethren" seeking only their own glory and recommends that those preaching circumcision castrate themselves like Cybele worshipers in nearby Phrygia. He offers close readings from Scripture (promises were made to Abraham and his "seed," not his "seeds") and extends them by analogy (the Mosaic law is no more than a codicil to God's prior contract with Abraham) and allegorical interpretation (Hagar and Sarah represent the old and new covenants). Paul combines paradox

> "For I through the law am dead to the law"   [2:19]

> "Christ hath redeemed us from the curse of the law, being made a curse for us"   [3:13]

and richly meaningful imagery

> "I am crucified with Christ"   [2:20]

> "For as many of you as have been baptized into Christ have put on Christ"   [3:27]

with straightforward deductive argument defending himself and his gospel:

> "If I yet preach circumcision, why do I yet suffer persecution?"   [5:11]

> "if righteousness comes by the law, then Christ is dead in vain."   [2:21]

He assures the Galatians there is no need for them to observe Jewish regulations: they are already "the children of promise," members of "the Israel of God."

An author's immediate feelings appear in his letters, and Paul's seem magnified by his eloquence. He is so involved with his message and with his audience that he cannot always express the gentleness and long-suffering which are fruits of the spirit. He begins his letter abruptly, omitting the customary thanksgiving for the achievements and prospects of the church. He closes it without the usual expressions of good will toward individual church members. He marvels at the weak faith of the Galatians and calls them foolish, bewitched, and spiritually proud. Though he urges that erring brothers be restored "in the spirit of meekness," Paul has only outrage and sarcasm to offer the Jewish teachers. He does not consider the possibility that they might be holy men with sincere motives (though such might be inferred from his warning against even "an angel from heaven" who preaches a contrary gospel). He assails them as false Christians, self-seeking troublemakers who would pervert the truth of Christ.

Yet the intemperateness in *Galatians* reveals Paul's greatest strength: his transcendent commitment to the person he had never seen in the flesh—"our Lord Jesus Christ, by whom the world is crucified unto me, and I unto the world"—and his parallel commitment to the erring people of God.

II CORINTHIANS

This selection from the letter to the Greek Christians at Corinth echoes the ideas and emotions expressed in *Galatians*. Again Paul recounts his own history, defending himself against Jewish charges that he is not an authentic apostle. Again he reveals his vigorous commitment to the gospel and his passionate antagonism toward those who would lead astray the children of God. Perhaps the most revealing lines in Paul occur in this letter, where he describes the many sufferings he has endured for the faith, then adds one more:

> Besides those things that are without, that which cometh upon
> me daily, the care of all the churches. Who is weak, and I am not
> weak? who is offended, and I burn not?

The Letter of Paul to the
GALATIANS

PAUL'S APOSTOLATE

1 Paul, an apostle, (not of men, neither by man, but by Jesus Christ, and God the Father, who raised him from the dead;) 2 And all the brethren which are with me, unto the churches of Galatia: 3 Grace *be* to you, and peace, from God the Father, and *from* our Lord Jesus Christ, 4 Who gave himself for our sins, that he might deliver us from this present evil world,[1] according to the will of God and our Father: 5 To whom *be* glory for ever and ever. Amen.

6 I marvel that ye are so soon removed from him that called you into the grace of Christ unto another gospel: 7 Which is not another; but there be some that trouble you, and would pervert the gospel of Christ. 8 But though we, or an angel from heaven, preach any other gospel unto you than that which we have preached unto you, let him be accursed. 9 As we said before, so say I now again, "If any *man* preach any other gospel unto you than that ye have received, let him be accursed." 10 For do I now persuade men, or God? or do I seek to please men? for if I yet pleased men, I should not be the servant of Christ.

11 But I certify you, brethren, that the gospel which was preached of me is not after man. 12 For I neither received it of man, neither was I taught *it,* but by the revelation of Jesus Christ.[2]

13 For ye have heard of my conversation in time past in the Jews' religion, how that beyond measure I persecuted the church of God, and wasted it: 14 And profited in the Jews' religion above many my equals in mine own nation, being more exceedingly zealous of the traditions of my fathers. 15 But when it pleased God, who separated me from my mother's womb, and called *me* by his grace,[3] 16 To reveal his Son in me, that I might preach him among the heathen; immediately I conferred not with flesh and blood: 17 Neither went I up to Jerusalem to them which were apostles before me; but I went into Arabia, and returned again unto Damascus.

18 Then after three years I went up to Jerusalem to see Peter, and abode with him fifteen days.[4] 19 But other of the apostles saw I none, save James the Lord's brother. 20 Now the things which I write unto you, behold, before God, I lie not.

21 Afterward I came into the regions of Syria and Cilicia; 22 And was unknown by face unto the churches of Judea which were in Christ: 23 But they had heard only, That he which persecuted us in times past now preacheth the faith which once he destroyed. 24 And they glorified God in me.

PAUL AND THE OTHER APOSTLES

2 Then fourteen years after I went up again to Jerusalem with Barnabas, and took Titus with *me* also. 2 And I went up by revelation, and communicated unto them that gospel which I preach among the Gentiles, but privately to them which were of reputation, lest by any means I should run, or had run, in vain. 3 But neither Titus, who was with me, being a Greek, was compelled to be circumcised: 4 And that because of false brethren unawares brought in, who came in privily to spy out our liberty which we have in Christ Jesus, that they might bring us into bondage: 5 To whom we gave place by subjection, no, not for an hour; that the truth of the gospel might continue with you. 6 But of those who seemed to be somewhat, (whatsoever they were, it maketh no matter to me: God accepteth no man's person:) for they who seemed *to be somewhat* in conference added nothing to me: 7 But contrariwise, when they saw that the gospel of the uncircumcision was committed unto me, as *the gospel* of the circumcision *was* unto Peter; 8 (For he that wrought effectually in Peter to the apostleship of the circumcision, the same was mighty in me toward the Gentiles;)[5] 9 And when James, Cephas, and John, who seemed to be pillars,[6] perceived the grace that was given unto me,

---

1. NEB: "this present age of wickedness."
2. This refers to the conversion experience described in *Acts of the Apostles.*
3. TEV: "But God, in his grace, chose me even before I was born, and called me to serve him."
4. PHILLIPS: "It was not until three years later that I went up to Jerusalem to see Cephas, and I only stayed with him just over a fortnight." Paul is stressing his independence from the Jerusalem church.
5. NEB: "For God whose action made Peter an apostle to the Jews, also made me an apostle to the Gentiles."
6. James seems to have been the authoritative figure in the Jerusalem church. Cephas is another name for Peter.

they gave to me and Barnabas the right hands of fellowship; that we *should go* unto the heathen, and they unto the circumcision. 10 Only *they would* that we should remember the poor; the same which I also was forward to do.

11 But when Peter was come to Antioch, I withstood him to the face, because he was to be blamed. 12 For before that certain came from James, he did eat with the Gentiles: but when they were come, he withdrew and separated himself, fearing them which were of the circumcision. 13 And the other Jews dissembled likewise with him; insomuch that Barnabas also was carried away with their dissimulation. 14 But when I saw that they walked not uprightly according to the truth of the gospel, I said unto Peter before *them* all, "If thou, being a Jew, livest after the manner of Gentiles, and not as do the Jews, why compellest thou the Gentiles to live as do the Jews?" [7] 15 We *who are* Jews by nature, and not sinners of the Gentiles, 16 Knowing that a man is not justified by the works of the law, but by the faith of Jesus Christ, even we have believed in Jesus Christ, that we might be justified by the faith of Christ, and not by the works of the law: for by the works of the law shall no flesh be justified. 17 But if, while we seek to be justified by Christ, we ourselves also are found sinners, *is* therefore Christ the minister of sin? God forbid. 18 For if I build again the things which I destroyed, I make myself a transgressor.[8] 19 For I through the law am dead to the law, that I might live unto God. 20 I am crucified with Christ: nevertheless I live; yet not I, but Christ liveth in me: and the life which I now live in the flesh I live by the faith of the Son of God, who loved me, and gave himself for me. 21 I do not frustrate the grace of God: for if righteousness *come* by the law, then Christ is dead in vain.

THE LAW OR THE PROMISE

3 O foolish Galatians, who hath bewitched you, that ye should not obey the truth, before whose eyes Jesus Christ hath been evidently set forth, crucified among you? 2 This only would I learn of you, Received ye the Spirit by the works of the law, or by the hearing of faith? 3 Are ye so foolish? having begun in the Spirit, are ye now made perfect by the flesh? 4 Have ye suffered so many things in vain? [9] if *it be* yet in vain. 5 He therefore that ministereth to you the Spirit, and worketh miracles among you, *doeth he it* by the works of the law, or by the hearing of faith?

6 Even as Abraham "believed God, and it was accounted to him for righteousness." 7 Know ye therefore that they which are of faith, the same are the children of Abraham. 8 And the Scripture, foreseeing that God would justify the heathen through faith, preached before the gospel unto Abraham, *saying,* "In thee shall all nations be blessed." [10] 9 So then they which be of faith are blessed with faithful Abraham.

10 For as many as are of the works of the law are under the curse: for it is written, "Cursed *is* every one that continueth not in all things which are written in the book of the law to do them." 11 But that no man is justified by the law in the sight of God, *it is* evident: for, "The just shall live by faith." 12 And the law is not of faith: but, "The man that doeth them shall live in them."[11]

13 Christ hath redeemed us from the curse of the law, being made a curse for us: for it is written, "Cursed *is* every one that hangeth on a tree":[12] 14 That the blessing of Abraham might come on the Gentiles through Jesus Christ; that we might receive the promise of the Spirit through faith.

15 Brethren, I speak after the manner of men; Though *it be* but a man's covenant, yet *if it be* confirmed, no man disannulleth, or addeth thereto. 16 Now to Abraham and his seed were the promises made. He saith not, "And to seeds," as of many; but as of one, "And to thy seed," which is Christ. 17 And this I say, *that* the covenant, that was confirmed before of God in Christ, the law, which was four hundred and thirty years after, cannot disannul, that it should make the promise of none effect. 18 For if the

---

7. Most modern translations close Paul's speech to Peter at v. 14 and read these following verses as his elaboration on the subject. However, JB and SCHONFIELD close Paul's speech at v. 21.

8. JB: "If I were to return to a position I had already abandoned, I should be admitting I had done something wrong."

9. NEB: "Have all your great experiences been in vain?" This probably recalls the initial joy in their conversion.

10. (3:-8) Paul uses *Genesis* 15:6 and 12:3 as support for his argument.

11. (3: 10-12) NEB: "On the other hand those who rely on obedience to the law are under a curse; for Scripture says, 'A curse is on all who do not persevere in doing everything that is written in the Book of the Law.' It is evident that no one is ever justified before God in terms of law; because we read, 'he shall gain life who is justified through faith.' Now law is not all a matter of having faith: we read, 'he who does this shall gain life by what he does.'" Paul quotes from *Deuteronomy* 27:26, *Habakkuk* 2:4, and *Leviticus* 18:5.

12. The reference is to *Deuteronomy* 21:23: "for he that is hanged is accursed of God." The requirement was that after a man was executed, his body should be hanged (impaled) on a tree to mark his extreme disgrace. (See *Genesis* 40:18-19.)

inheritance *be* of the law, *it is* no more of promise: but God gave *it* to Abraham by promise.

19 Wherefore then *serveth* the law? It was added because of transgressions, till the seed should come to whom the promise was made; *and it was* ordained by angels in the hand of a mediator. 20 Now a mediator is not *a mediator* of one, but God is one.[13] 21 *Is* the law then against the promises of God? God forbid: for if there had been a law given which could have given life, verily righteousness should have been by the law. 22 But the Scripture hath concluded all under sin, that the promise by faith of Jesus Christ might be given to them that believe.

23 But before faith came, we were kept under the law, shut up unto the faith which should afterward be revealed. 24 Wherefore the law was our schoolmaster *to bring us* unto Christ, that we might be justified by faith. 25 But after that faith is come, we are no longer under a schoolmaster. 26 For ye are all the children of God by faith in Christ Jesus. 27 For as many of you as have been baptized into Christ have put on Christ. 28 There is neither Jew nor Greek, there is neither bond nor free, there is neither male nor female: for ye are all one in Christ Jesus. 29 And if ye *be* Christ's, then are ye Abraham's seed, and heirs according to the promise.

SONS OF GOD

4 Now I say, *That* the heir, as long as he is a child, differeth nothing from a servant, though he be lord of all; 2 But is under tutors and governors until the time appointed of the father. 3 Even so we, when we were children, were in bondage under the elements of the world:[14] 4 But when the fulness of the time was come, God sent forth his Son, made of a woman, made under the law, 5 To redeem them that were under the law, that we might receive the adoption of sons. 6 And because ye are sons, God hath sent forth the Spirit of his Son into your hearts, crying, "Abba, Father." 7 Wherefore thou art no more a servant, but a son; and if a son, then an heir of God through Christ.

8 Howbeit then, when ye knew not God, ye did service unto them which by nature are no gods. 9 But now, after that ye have known God, or rather are known of God, how turn ye again to the weak and beggarly elements, whereunto ye desire again to be in bondage? 10 Ye observe days, and months, and times, and years. 11 I am afraid of you, lest I have bestowed upon you labor in vain.

12 Brethren, I beseech you, be as I *am;* for I *am* as ye *are:* ye have not injured me at all.[15] 13 Ye know how through infirmity of the flesh I preached the gospel unto you at the first. 14 And my temptation which was in my flesh ye despised not, nor rejected;[16] but received me as an angel of God, *even* as Christ Jesus. 15 Where is then the blessedness ye spake of? for I bear you record, that, if *it had been* possible, ye would have plucked out your own eyes, and have given them to me. 16 Am I therefore become your enemy, because I tell you the truth? 17 They zealously affect you, *but* not well; yea, they would exclude you, that ye might affect them. 18 But *it is* good to be zealously affected always in *a* good *thing,* and not only when I am present with you. 19 My little children, of whom I travail in birth again until Christ be formed in you, 20 I desire to be present with you now, and to change my voice; for I stand in doubt of you.

21 Tell me, ye that desire to be under the law, do ye not hear the law? 22 For it is written, that Abraham had two sons, the one by a bondmaid, the other by a free woman.[17] 23 But he *who was* of the bondwoman was born after the flesh; but he of the free woman *was* by promise. 24 Which things are an allegory: for these are the two covenants; the one from the mount Sinai, which gendereth to bondage, which is Agar. 25 For this Agar is mount Sinai in Arabia, and answereth to Jerusalem which now is, and is in bondage with her children. 26 But Jerusalem which is above is free, which is the mother of us all. 27 For it is written,

"Rejoice, thou barren that bearest not;
Break forth and cry, thou that travailest not:

13. (3:19-20) There are said to be 300 different interpretations of this. An acceptable one is that the old law was a kind of contract, under which man did certain things and God responded. (The mediator between the two parties was Moses.) The new covenant expresses itself in the free, unmerited gift of divine grace: God is the sole agent.

14. Modern translations differ in expressing this passage. The word *stoicheia* ("elements") can refer to the letters of the alphabet, i.e., to simple rudimentary truths. (KNOX: "we toiled away at the school-room tasks which the world gave us.") It can also refer to the elements thought to control human destiny: spirits, demons, the astrological sway of the stars, etc. (NEB: "we were slaves to the elemental spirits of the universe.")

15. WILLIAMS: "I beg you, brothers, take my point of view, just as I took yours. You did me no injustice then."

16. BECK: "Though my sick body was a test to you, you didn't despise or scorn me." Commentators speculate the repulsive disease may have been epilepsy or malaria.

17. (4:22-31) In these verses Paul recalls the accounts of Abraham, Sarah and Hagar (*Genesis* 16:1-12 and 21:1-21) and gives them an allegorical interpretation. Much early Christian use of the Old Testament was allegorical.

For the desolate hath many more children
Than she which hath a husband." [18]
28 Now we, brethren, as Isaac was, are the
children of promise. 29 But as then he that was
born after the flesh persecuted him *that was born*
after the Spirit, even so *it is* now. 30 Nevertheless
what saith the Scripture? "Cast out the bondwoman and her son: for the son of the bondwoman shall not be heir with the son of the
free woman." 31 So then, brethren, we are not
children of the bondwoman, but of the free.

THE FRUIT OF THE SPIRIT

5 Stand fast therefore in the liberty wherewith
Christ hath made us free, and be not entangled
again with the yoke of bondage. 2 Behold, I Paul
say unto you, that if ye be circumcised, Christ
shall profit you nothing. 3 For I testify again to
every man that is circumcised, that he is a debtor
to do the whole law. 4 Christ is become of no
effect unto you, whosoever of you are justified by
the law; ye are fallen from grace. 5 For we
through the Spirit wait for the hope of righteousness by faith. 6 For in Jesus Christ neither
circumcision availeth any thing, nor uncircumcision; but faith which worketh by love. 7 Ye did
run well; who did hinder you that ye should not
obey the truth? 8 This persuasion *cometh* not of
him that calleth you. 9 A little leaven leaveneth
the whole lump. 10 I have confidence in you
through the Lord, that ye will be none otherwise
minded: but he that troubleth you shall bear his
judgment, whosoever he be. 11 And I, brethren,
if I yet preach circumcision, why do I yet suffer
persecution? then is the offense of the cross
ceased. 12 I would they were even cut off which
trouble you. [19]

13 For, brethren, ye have been called unto
liberty; only *use* not liberty for an occasion to the
flesh, but by love serve one another. 14 For all
the law is fulfilled in one word, *even* in this;
"Thou shalt love thy neighbor as thyself." 15 But
if ye bite and devour one another, take heed that
ye be not consumed one of another.
16 *This* I say then, Walk in the Spirit, and ye
shall not fulfil the lust of the flesh. 17 For the
flesh lusteth against the Spirit, and the Spirit

against the flesh: and these are contrary the one
to the other; so that ye cannot do the things that
ye would. 18 But if ye be led of the Spirit, ye are
not under the law. 19 Now the works of the flesh
are manifest, which are *these,* Adultery, fornication, uncleanness, lasciviousness, 20 Idolatry,
witchcraft, hatred, variance, emulations, wrath,
strife, seditions, heresies, 21 Envyings, murders,
drunkenness, revelings, and such like: of the
which I tell you before, as I have also told *you* in
time past, that they which do such things shall not
inherit the kingdom of God. 22 But the fruit of
the Spirit is love, joy, peace, long-suffering, gentleness, goodness, faith, 23 Meekness, temperance: against such there is no law. 24 And they
that are Christ's have crucified the flesh with the
affections and lusts. 25 If we live in the Spirit, let
us also walk in the Spirit. 26 Let us not be
desirous of vainglory, provoking one another,
envying one another.

6 Brethren, if a man be overtaken in a fault, ye
which are spiritual, restore such a one in the spirit
of meekness; considering thyself, lest thou also be
tempted. 2 Bear ye one another's burdens, and
so fulfil the law of Christ. 3 For if a man think
himself to be something, when he is nothing, he
deceiveth himself. 4 But let every man prove his
own work, and then shall he have rejoicing in
himself alone, and not in another. 5 For every
man shall bear his own burden.
6 Let him that is taught in the word communicate unto him that teacheth in all good things.[20]
7 Be not deceived; God is not mocked: for
whatsoever a man soweth, that shall he also reap.
8 For he that soweth to his flesh shall of the flesh
reap corruption; but he that soweth to the Spirit
shall of the Spirit reap life everlasting. 9 And let
us not be weary in well doing: for in due season
we shall reap, if we faint not. 10 As we have
therefore opportunity, let us do good unto all
men, especially unto them who are of the household of faith.

CONCLUSION

11 Ye see how large a letter I have written unto
you with mine own hand.[21] 12 As many as desire
to make a fair show in the flesh, they constrain
you to be circumcised; only lest they should

---

18. JB: "Break into shouts of joy and gladness, you who were
never in labour. For there are more sons of the forsaken one
than sons of the wedded wife." The idea is that the Jews had
a husband (i.e., an established order), but that the Christians would be desolate (i.e., dispersed) only for a short
time. The metaphor, taken from *Genesis* and from *Isaiah*
54:1, cannot bear scrutiny.
19. NEB: "As for these agitators, they had better go the whole
way and make eunuchs of themselves!"

20. WILLIAMS: "Those who are taught the truth should share all
their goods with the man who teaches them."
21. GOODSPEED: "See what large letters I make, when I write to
you with my own hand!" Usually, Paul only added his sig-
nature to a letter dictated to a scribe. Here he shows his personal concern for the Galatians by writing the whole last
paragraph.

suffer persecution for the cross of Christ. 13 For neither they themselves who are circumcised keep the law; but desire to have you circumcised, that they may glory in your flesh. 14 But God forbid that I should glory,[22] save in the cross of our Lord Jesus Christ, by whom the world is crucified unto me, and I unto the world. 15 For in Christ Jesus neither circumcision availeth any thing, nor uncircumcision, but a new creature. 16 And as many as walk according to this rule, peace *be* on them, and mercy, and upon the Israel of God.

17 From henceforth let no man trouble me: for I bear in my body the marks of the Lord Jesus.

18 Brethren, the grace of our Lord Jesus Christ *be* with your spirit. Amen.

22. Paul, too, could boast of his converts.

The Second Letter of Paul to the
CORINTHIANS

PAUL'S APOSTOLIC CREDENTIALS

11 Would to God ye could bear with me a little in *my* folly: and indeed bear with me.[1] 2 For I am jealous over you with godly jealousy: for I have espoused you to one husband, that I may present *you as* a chaste virgin to Christ. 3 But I fear, lest by any means, as the serpent beguiled Eve through his subtilty, so your minds should be corrupted from the simplicity that is in Christ. 4 For if he that cometh preacheth another Jesus, whom we have not preached, or *if* ye receive another spirit, which ye have not received, or another gospel, which ye have not accepted, ye might well bear with *him.* 5 For I suppose I was not a whit behind the very chiefest apostles. 6 But though *I be* rude in speech, yet not in knowledge; but we have been thoroughly made manifest among you in all things.

7 Have I committed an offense in abasing myself that ye might be exalted, because I have preached to you the gospel of God freely? 8 I robbed other churches, taking wages *of them,* to do you service. 9 And when I was present with you, and wanted, I was chargeable to no man: for that which was lacking to me the brethren which came from Macedonia supplied: and in all *things* I have kept myself from being burdensome unto you, and *so* will I keep *myself.* 10 As the truth of Christ is in me, no man shall stop me of this boasting in the regions of Achaia. 11 Wherefore? because I love you not? God knoweth. 12 But what I do, that I will do, that I may cut off occasion from them which desire occasion; that wherein they glory, they may be found even as we. 13 For such *are* false apostles, deceitful workers, transforming themselves into the apostles of Christ. 14 And no marvel; for Satan himself is transformed into an angel of light. 15 Therefore *it is* no great thing if his ministers also be transformed as the ministers of righteousness; whose end shall be according to their works.

16 I say again, Let no man think me a fool; if otherwise, yet as a fool receive me, that I may boast myself a little. 17 That which I speak, I speak *it* not after the Lord, but as it were foolishly, in this confidence of boasting.

18 Seeing that many glory after the flesh, I will glory also. 19 For ye suffer fools gladly, seeing ye *yourselves* are wise.[2] 20 For ye suffer, if a man bring you into bondage, if a man devour *you,* if a man take *of you,* if a man exalt himself, if a man smite you on the face.

21 I speak as concerning reproach, as though we had been weak. Howbeit, whereinsoever any is bold, (I speak foolishly,) I am bold also. 22 Are they Hebrews? so *am* I. Are they Israelites? so *am* I. Are they the seed of Abraham? so *am* I. 23 Are they ministers of Christ? (I speak as a fool,) I *am* more; in labors more abundant, in stripes above measure, in prisons more frequent, in deaths oft. 24 Of the Jews five times received I forty *stripes* save one. 25 Thrice was I beaten with rods, once was I stoned, thrice I suffered shipwreck, a night and a day I have been in the deep; 26 *In* journeyings often, *in* perils of waters, *in* perils of robbers, *in* perils by *mine own* countrymen, *in* perils by the heathen, *in* perils in the city, *in* perils in the wilderness, *in* perils in the sea, *in* perils among false brethren; 27 In weariness and painfulness, in watchings often, in hunger and thirst, in fastings often, in cold and nakedness. 28 Beside those things that are without, that which cometh upon me daily, the care of all the churches. 29 Who is weak, and I am not weak? who is offended, and I burn not?

30 If I must needs glory, I will glory of the things which concern mine infirmities. 31 The God and Father of our Lord Jesus Christ, which is blessed for evermore, knoweth that I lie not. 32 In Damascus the governor under Aretas the king kept the city of the Damascenes with a garrison, desirous to apprehend me: 33 And through a window in a basket was I let down by the wall, and escaped his hands.

A MAN IN CHRIST

12 It is not expedient for me doubtless to glory. I will come to visions and revelations of the Lord. 2 I knew a man in Christ above fourteen years ago, (whether in the body, I cannot tell; or whether out of the body, I cannot tell: God knoweth;) such a one caught up to the third

---

1. TEV: "I wish you would tolerate me, even when I am a bit foolish. Please do!"

2. The irony is clearer in PHILLIPS: "From your heights of superior wisdom I am sure you can smile tolerantly on a fool."

heaven.[3] 3 And I knew such a man, (whether in the body, or out of the body, I cannot tell: God knoweth;) 4 How that he was caught up into paradise, and heard unspeakable words, which it is not lawful for a man to utter. 5 Of such a one will I glory: yet of myself I will not glory, but in mine infirmities. 6 For though I would desire to glory, I shall not be a fool; for I will say the truth: but *now* I forbear, lest any man should think of me above that which he seeth me *to be,* or *that* he heareth of me. 7 And lest I should be exalted above measure through the abundance of the revelations, there was given to me a thorn in the flesh, the messenger of Satan to buffet me, lest I should be exalted above measure. 8 For this thing I besought the Lord thrice, that it might depart from me. 9 And he said unto me, "My grace is sufficient for thee: for my strength is made perfect in weakness." Most gladly therefore will I rather glory in my infirmities, that the power of Christ may rest upon me. 10 Therefore I take pleasure in infirmities, in reproaches, in necessities, in persecutions, in distresses for Christ's sake: for when I am weak, then am I strong.

11 I am become a fool in glorying; ye have compelled me: for I ought to have been commended of you: for in nothing am I behind the very chiefest apostles, though I be nothing.[4]

12 Truly the signs of an apostle were wrought among you in all patience, in signs, and wonders, and mighty deeds. 13 For what is it wherein ye were inferior to other churches, except *it be* that I myself was not burdensome to you? [5] forgive me this wrong.

14 Behold, the third time I am ready to come to you; and I will not be burdensome to you: for I seek not yours, but you: for the children ought not to lay up for the parents, but the parents for the children. 15 And I will very gladly spend and be spent for you; though the more abundantly I love you, the less I be loved. 16 But be it so, I did not burden you: nevertheless, being crafty, I caught you with guile.[6] 17 Did I make a gain of you by any of them whom I sent unto you? 18 I desired Titus, and with *him* I sent a brother. Did Titus make a gain of you? walked we not in the same spirit? *walked we* not in the same steps?

19 Again, think ye that we excuse ourselves unto you? we speak before God in Christ: but *we do* all things, dearly beloved, for your edifying. 20 For I fear, lest, when I come, I shall not find you such as I would, and *that* I shall be found unto you such as ye would not: lest *there be* debates, envyings, wraths, strifes, backbitings, whisperings, swellings, tumults: 21 *And* lest, when I come again, my God will humble me among you, and *that* I shall bewail many which have sinned already, and have not repented of the uncleanness and fornication and lasciviousness which they have committed.

---

3. PHILLIPS: "I know a man in Christ who, fourteen years ago, had the experience of being caught up into the third Heaven. I don't know whether it was an actual physical experience; only God knows that." V. 7 suggests that Paul is describing his own experience.

4. In context, the irony is powerful. BERKELEY: "In fact, though I am nobody, I am not in the least inferior to these super-apostles."

5. NEB: "I never sponged upon you."

6. TEV: "You will agree, then, that I was not a burden to you. But, someone will say, I was tricky and trapped you with lies."

Introduction to
REVELATION

"And the seventh angel poured out his vial into the air; and there came a great voice out of the temple of heaven, from the throne, saying, 'It is done.'"

The book of *Revelation* impresses all readers with its vivid imagery, its intense conviction, and its puzzling symbolism. At first reading, the difficulties seem insuperable. The faithful at Pergamos are promised "a white stone, and in the stone a new name written, which no man knoweth saving he that receiveth it." The throne of God is attended by four beasts resembling a lion, a calf, a man, and a flying eagle. At the sound of a third trumpet, a star named Wormwood falls and contaminates the freshwater rivers and springs. Seven thunders make a revelation which John is forbidden to utter. Satan appears as "a great red dragon, having seven heads and ten horns," and he delegates authority to two beasts, one of which is identified by the number 666. Facing such language, a famous commentator once concluded that study of *Revelation* either finds a man mad or leaves him mad.

Nevertheless, though many of the details remain obscure, the central message of *Revelation* is notably clear. Writing toward the end of the reign of Emperor Domitian (81–96), a time of persecution and frustration for Christians, a leader named John wrote in an established literary form to urge his people to persevere and to assure them of ultimate victory.

Christians had lived through events which challenged their faith. They had expected Jesus to return in "a little while," but sixty years had passed since the crucifixion. They suffered cruel persecution following the fire in Rome in 64. They saw the Jewish revolt of 67–70 end with the fall of Jerusalem and the destruction of the Temple. They endured cruel penalties for opposing the compulsory Caesar worship imposed under Domitian. And instead of hearing of the return of Christ, they met continuing rumors that Nero was not dead, that he would return with hordes of Parthian troops to continue his reign of evil. John wrote Revelation to strengthen the infant Church at a time when members suffered repression, lack of faith, and temptation to despair. His message: We *are* the new Israel, the chosen people; Christ will return *soon*; we will overcome.

To express this, John used a literary form, the apocalypse, which Jewish writers had made familiar during the preceding centuries. In the *Book of Enoch*, the *Secrets of Enoch*, the *Sybilline Oracles*, the *Apocalypse of Baruch*, the so-called *Fourth Book of Esdras*, and other works, authors assured a suffering people of the golden age which would come when God had made all things new. The genre had these characteristics: the use of visions with an angelic guide to provide explanations; a detailed description of the future bliss of the faithful and the horrible suffering of their enemies; and the use of figurative language (stylized phraseology, animal and astral imagery, symbolic numbers, etc.). Taking *Ezekiel*, *Isaiah*, and *Daniel* as his particular models, John described the vengeance awaiting the Roman oppressors and the triumphant return of the Lord Jesus Christ.

Many of the apocalyptic images related to Rome and the practice of emperor worship. Under Domitian, a worldwide organization was established to compel every Roman citizen once a year to burn incense and profess "Caesar is Lord." This was a political rather than a religious act; once one had done homage to the emperor, he could worship any god he chose. Christians who refused were punished not as heretics but as traitors. Hence, John described a beast from the sea (the Roman Empire) with seven heads (seven emperors), ten crowns (the seven emperors plus three brief claimants), blasphemous names on the heads (terms like "divine," "son of God," and "savior of the world"—used in Caesar worship), and one head bearing a deadly wound now healed (the belief that Nero might return to power). The beast from the land (the institution of emperor worship) has a number (666, usually translated as NERON CAESAR) and causes men to receive a mark (a sign they had made annual sacrifice to the emperor). Facing such adversaries, John urged Christians not to accommodate the present powers at the expense of future glory. The white stone with a new name is reserved for "him that overcometh," for "witnesses" (i.e., martyrs) who preserve the faith. The many warnings against "fornication" routinely refer to idolatry: the Church is "the bride, the Lamb's wife"; the "great whore" is Rome.

Such language was part of the apocalyptic tradition, and John's readers could recognize particular images and even specific language he borrowed from his sources. The four beasts before the throne of God resemble the "four living creatures" in *Ezekiel* (1:5-11) and the six-winged seraphim in *Isaiah* (6:2-3). The number of the angels—"ten thousand times ten thousand, and thousands of thousands"—appeared in *Daniel* (7:10). With the opening of the sixth seal, the sun becomes black as sackcloth (as in *Isaiah* 50:3), the moon becomes as blood (*Joel* 2:31), the mountains move (*Jeremiah* 4:24), the heavens roll up like a scroll (*Isaiah* 34:4), and terrified people beg mountains and hills to fall upon them (*Hosea* 10:8). John's dirge over fallen "Babylon" (i.e., Rome) invoked the language of *Jeremiah* on Babylon, *Isaiah* on Tyre, *Nahum* on Ninevah, and *Ezekiel* on Samaria and Jerusalem.

John also employed the kind of number symbolism which appeared in Jewish apocalypses. For example, he used 7 and 12 (and their multiples) to signify plenitude or perfection. The Lamb has 7 horns and 7 eyes; there are seven churches, spirits, seals, trumpets, thunders, and vials; as well as 7 blessings, 7 appearances of the name of Christ, 7 uses of the promise "I come quickly," etc. Similarly, there are 24 elders around the throne of God and 144,000 faithful servants sealed. The New Jerusalem measures 12,000 furlongs in length, height, and breadth; its wall is 144 cubits high; and it has 12 gates, 12 foundations, and 12 manners of fruit. The number 6 (which falls short of 7) signifies imperfection: the second beast is identified as 666. And $3\frac{1}{2}$ (one-half of 7) appears in various forms, representing the limited period during which God's enemies can prosper. Power is given to the first beast for 42 months (i.e., $3\frac{1}{2}$ years); Gentiles tread the holy city for 42 months; the two witnesses prophesy for 1260 days; they die and their bodies lie unburied for $3\frac{1}{2}$ days. The woman fleeing from the dragon hides in a wilderness for 1260 days, a period also described as "a time, and times, and half a time."

John's first readers would never have taken the apocalyptic images and numbers as literal description. They would have recognized the seven seals, the seven trumpets, and the seven vials not as sequential occurrences, but as cyclic descriptions of the same event. When the four trumpets announce the destruction of a "third part" of the trees, the sea, the sun, and the stars, they would have interpreted this as a vast and general devastation and would perhaps have recognized the indebtedness to *Ezekiel* (5:12). They would have taken the church of Smyrna's tribulation for "ten days" to signify a very short ordeal. And they would have read the martyr's reign of "a thousand years" to mean a long time. They would not permit such detailed symbolism to obscure the message of the work.

In *Revelation*, John assured an isolated, scorned, and suffering people that their faith would be rewarded. In a new Jerusalem, they would walk on streets of gold, eat from the tree of life, and reign before the throne of God: "He that overcometh shall inherit all things." In contrast, their all-powerful enemies would die in horrible agony and suffer thereafter in "the lake which burneth with fire and brimstone." And, considering the unrelenting imagery, one cannot mask the fact that John and his followers cherished the latter prospect at least as much as the first. Commenting on this vindictiveness, William Barclay makes an essential point about the book as a whole. Comparing passages of *Revelation* with similar expressions in *Isaiah, Zephaniah*, and *Jeremiah*, he concludes:

> In spite of their grim foretelling of ruin these passages are all great poetry, for they are the poetry of passion and of intensity of heart and spirit. They are the poetry of men who in their desperate plight are confidently awaiting the avenging hand of God on their oppressors. It may be that here we are far from the Christian doctrine of forgiveness; but we are very close to the beating of the human heart.*

* From *The Revelation of John*, Volume 2. Translated and interpreted by William Barclay. Published in the U.S.A. by The Westminster Press, 1961. Used by permission.

REVELATION

THE CALL TO PROPHECY

1 The Revelation of Jesus Christ, which God gave unto him, to show unto his servants things which must shortly come to pass; and he sent and signified *it* by his angel unto his servant John: 2 Who bare record of the word of God, and of the testimony of Jesus Christ, and of all things that he saw. 3 Blessed *is* he that readeth, and they that hear the words of this prophecy, and keep those things which are written therein: for the time *is* at hand.

4 JOHN to the seven churches which are in Asia: Grace *be* unto you, and peace, from him which is, and which was, and which is to come; and from the seven Spirits which are before his throne; 5 And from Jesus Christ, *who is* the faithful witness, *and* the first-begotten of the dead, and the prince of the kings of the earth. Unto him that loved us, and washed us from our sins in his own blood, 6 And hath made us kings and priests unto God and his Father; to him *be* glory and dominion for ever and ever. Amen. 7 Behold, he cometh with clouds; and every eye shall see him, and they *also* which pierced him: and all kindreds of the earth shall wail because of him. Even so, Amen.

8 "I am Alpha and Omega, the beginning and the ending," saith the Lord, which is, and which was, and which is to come, the Almighty.

9 I John, who also am your brother, and companion in tribulation, and in the kingdom and patience of Jesus Christ, was in the isle that is called Patmos, for the word of God, and for the testimony of Jesus Christ.[1] 10 I was in the Spirit on the Lord's day, and heard behind me a great voice, as of a trumpet, 11 Saying, "I am Alpha and Omega, the first and the last": and, "What thou seest, write in a book, and send *it* unto the seven churches which are in Asia; unto Ephesus, and unto Smyrna, and unto Pergamos, and unto Thyatira, and unto Sardis, and unto Philadelphia, and unto Laodicea."

12 And I turned to see the voice that spake with me. And being turned, I saw seven golden candlesticks; 13 And in the midst of the seven candlesticks *one* like unto the Son of man, clothed with a garment down to the foot, and girt about the paps with a golden girdle. 14 His head and *his* hairs *were* white like wool, as white as snow; and his eyes *were* as a flame of fire; 15 And his feet like unto fine brass, as if they burned in a furnace; and his voice as the sound of many waters. 16 And he had in his right hand seven stars: and out of his mouth went a sharp two-edged sword: and his countenance *was* as the sun shineth in his strength.

17 And when I saw him, I fell at his feet as dead. And he laid his right hand upon me, saying unto me, "Fear not; I am the first and the last: 18 *I am* he that liveth, and was dead; and, behold, I am alive for evermore, Amen; and have the keys of hell and of death.[2] 19 Write the things which thou hast seen, and the things which are, and the things which shall be hereafter; 20 The mystery of the seven stars which thou sawest in my right hand, and the seven golden candlesticks. The seven stars are the angels of the seven churches: and the seven candlesticks which thou sawest are the seven churches."

LETTERS TO THE CHURCHES[3]

Ephesus

2 "Unto the angel of the church of Ephesus write; 'These things saith he that holdeth the seven stars in his right hand, who walketh in the midst of the seven golden candlesticks;

2 "'I know thy works, and thy labor, and thy patience, and how thou canst not bear them which are evil: and thou hast tried them which say they are apostles, and are not, and hast found them liars: 3 And hast borne, and hast patience, and for my name's sake hast labored, and hast not fainted. 4 Nevertheless I have *somewhat* against thee, because thou hast left thy first love. 5 Remember therefore from whence thou art fallen, and repent, and do the first works; or else I will come unto thee quickly, and will remove thy candlestick out of his place, except thou repent. 6 But this thou hast, that thou hatest the deeds of the Nicolaitans, which I also hate. 7 He that

---

1. TEV: "I was put on the island called Patmos because I had proclaimed God's word and the truth that Jesus revealed."

2. Here, as in 6:8 and 20:14, hell is not a place of punishment but a realm where the dead stay until the general resurrection. NEB: "the keys of Death and Death's domain." PHILLIPS: "the keys of death and the grave."

3. Because these messages lack the usual epistolary form, scholars suggest they were not real letters, only a literary device to convey the author's ideas. The content is general, probably intended for any Christian "that hath an ear."

hath an ear, let him hear what the Spirit saith unto the churches; To him that overcometh will I give to eat of the tree of life, which is in the midst of the paradise of God.'

Smyrna

8 "And unto the angel of the church in Smyrna write; 'These things saith the first and the last, which was dead, and is alive;

9 " 'I know thy works, and tribulation, and poverty, (but thou art rich) and *I know* the blasphemy of them which say they are Jews, and are not, but *are* the synagogue of Satan. 10 Fear none of those things which thou shalt suffer: behold, the devil shall cast *some* of you into prison, that ye may be tried; and ye shall have tribulation ten days: be thou faithful unto death, and I will give thee a crown of life. 11 He that hath an ear, let him hear what the Spirit saith unto the churches; He that overcometh shall not be hurt of the second death.'

Pergamos

12 "And to the angel of the church in Pergamos write; 'These things saith he which hath the sharp sword with two edges;

13 " 'I know thy works, and where thou dwellest, *even* where Satan's seat *is:* and thou holdest fast my name, and hast not denied my faith, even in those days wherein Antipas *was* my faithful martyr, who was slain among you, where Satan dwelleth. 14 But I have a few things against thee, because thou hast there them that hold the doctrine of Balaam, who taught Balak to cast a stumbling block before the children of Israel, to eat things sacrificed unto idols, and to commit fornication. 15 So hast thou also them that hold the doctrine of the Nicolaitans, which thing I hate. 16 Repent; or else I will come unto thee quickly, and will fight against them with the sword of my mouth. 17 He that hath an ear, let him hear what the Spirit saith unto the churches; To him that overcometh will I give to eat of the hidden manna, and will give him a white stone, and in the stone a new name written, which no man knoweth saving he that receiveth *it*.'

Thyatira

18 "And unto the angel of the church in Thyatira write; 'These things saith the Son of God, who hath his eyes like unto a flame of fire, and his feet *are* like fine brass;

19 " 'I know thy works, and charity, and service, and faith, and thy patience, and thy works;

and the last *to be* more than the first. 20 Notwithstanding I have a few things against thee, because thou sufferest that woman Jezebel, which calleth herself a prophetess, to teach and to seduce my servants to commit fornication; and to eat things sacrificed unto idols.[4] 21 And I gave her space to repent of her fornication; and she repented not. 22 Behold, I will cast her into a bed,[5] and them that commit adultery with her into great tribulation, except they repent of their deeds. 23 And I will kill her children with death; and all the churches shall know that I am he which searcheth the reins and hearts: and I will give unto every one of you according to your works. 24 But unto you I say, and unto the rest in Thyatira, as many as have not this doctrine, and which have not known the depths of Satan, as they speak; I will put upon you none other burden. 25 But that which ye have *already,* hold fast till I come. 26 And he that overcometh, and keepeth my works unto the end, to him will I give power over the nations: 27 And he shall rule them with a rod of iron; as the vessels of a potter shall they be broken to shivers: even as I received of my Father. 28 And I will give him the morning star. 29 He that hath an ear, let him hear what the Spirit saith unto the churches.'

Sardis

3 "And unto the angel of the church in Sardis write; 'These things saith he that hath the seven Spirits of God, and the seven stars;

" 'I know thy works, that thou hast a name that thou livest, and art dead. 2 Be watchful, and strengthen the things which remain, that are ready to die: for I have not found thy works perfect before God. 3 Remember therefore how thou hast received and heard, and hold fast, and repent. If therefore thou shalt not watch, I will come on thee as a thief, and thou shalt not know what hour I will come upon thee. 4 Thou hast a few names even in Sardis which have not defiled their garments; and they shall walk with me in white: for they are worthy. 5 He that overcometh, the same shall be clothed in white raiment; and I will not blot out his name out of the book of life, but I will confess his name before my Father, and before his angels. 6 He that hath

---

4. It is reasonable to conclude that "Jezebel" is a description rather than a name and that "fornication" refers to some form of idolatry. GOODSPEED: "But I hold it against you that you tolerate that Jezebel of a woman who claims to be inspired and who is misleading my slaves and teaching them to practice immorality and to eat meat that has been sacrificed to idols."

5. TCNT: "upon a bed of sickness."

an ear, let him hear what the Spirit saith unto the churches.'

Philadelphia

7 "And to the angel of the church in Philadelphia write; 'These things saith he that is holy, he that is true, he that hath the key of David, he that openeth, and no man shutteth; and shutteth, and no man openeth;
8 " 'I know thy works: behold, I have set before thee an open door, and no man can shut it: for thou hast a little strength, and hast kept my word, and hast not denied my name. 9 Behold, I will make them of the synagogue of Satan, which say they are Jews, and are not, but do lie; behold, I will make them to come and worship before thy feet, and to know that I have loved thee. 10 Because thou hast kept the word of my patience, I also will keep thee from the hour of temptation, which shall come upon all the world, to try them that dwell upon the earth. 11 Behold, I come quickly: hold that fast which thou hast, that no man take thy crown. 12 Him that overcometh will I make a pillar in the temple of my God, and he shall go no more out: and I will write upon him the name of my God, and the name of the city of my God, *which is* new Jerusalem, which cometh down out of heaven from my God: and *I will write upon him* my new name. 13 He that hath an ear, let him hear what the Spirit saith unto the churches.'

Laodicea

14 "And unto the angel of the church of the Laodiceans write; 'These things saith the Amen, the faithful and true witness, the beginning of the creation of God;[6]
15 " 'I know thy works, that thou art neither cold nor hot: I would thou wert cold or hot. 16 So then because thou art lukewarm, and neither cold nor hot, I will spew thee out of my mouth. 17 Because thou sayest, "I am rich, and increased with goods, and have need of nothing"; and knowest not that thou art wretched, and miserable, and poor, and blind, and naked: 18 I counsel thee to buy of me gold tried in the fire, that thou mayest be rich; and white raiment, that thou mayest be clothed, and *that* the shame of thy nakedness do not appear; and anoint thine eyes with eyesalve, that thou mayest see. 19 As many as I love, I rebuke and chasten: be zealous therefore, and repent. 20 Behold, I stand at the door, and knock: if any man hear my voice, and open

the door, I will come in to him, and will sup with him, and he with me. 21 To him that overcometh will I grant to sit with me in my throne, even as I also overcame, and am set down with my Father in his throne. 22 He that hath an ear, let him hear what the Spirit saith unto the churches.' "

THE VISION OF HEAVEN

4 After this I looked, and, behold, a door *was* opened in heaven: and the first voice which I heard *was* as it were of a trumpet talking with me; which said, "Come up hither, and I will show thee things which must be hereafter." 2 And immediately I was in the Spirit: and, behold, a throne was set in heaven, and *one* sat on the throne. 3 And he that sat was to look upon like a jasper and a sardine stone: and *there was* a rainbow round about the throne, in sight like unto an emerald.[7] 4 And round about the throne *were* four and twenty seats: and upon the seats I saw four and twenty elders sitting, clothed in white raiment; and they had on their heads crowns of gold.[8] 5 And out of the throne proceeded lightnings and thunderings and voices: and *there were* seven lamps of fire burning before the throne, which are the seven Spirits of God. 6 And before the throne *there was* a sea of glass like unto crystal:

And in the midst of the throne, and round about the throne, *were* four beasts full of eyes before and behind. 7 And the first beast *was* like a lion, and the second beast like a calf, and the third beast had a face as a man, and the fourth beast *was* like a flying eagle.[9] 8 And the four beasts had each of them six wings about *him;* and *they were* full of eyes within: and they rest not day and night, saying,

"Holy, holy, holy, Lord God Almighty,
Which was, and is, and is to come."
9 And when those beasts give glory and honor and thanks to him that sat on the throne, who liveth for ever and ever, 10 The four and twenty elders fall down before him that sat on the throne, and worship him that liveth for ever and ever, and cast their crowns before the throne, saying,

---

6. JB:"the ultimate source of God's creation." See footnote 1 to *John* 1:1.

7. (4:3-11) Rather than seek to identify each symbolic feature of this scene, one should recognize the overall meaning. The author is depicting a heavenly court that is totally nonanthropomorphic. There is nothing on earth like it.

8. The speculation that the twenty-four elders are the twelve patriarchs and the twelve apostles is reinforced by 21:12-14.

9. (4:6-7) Like the four creatures in *Ezekiel* 1:5, the beasts resembling a lion, a calf, a man, and a flying eagle, presumably reflect God's majesty, strength, knowledge, and retributive omnipresence. Most translations read "ox" or "bull" instead of "calf."

11 "Thou art worthy, O Lord, to receive glory and honor and power: for thou hast created all things, and for thy pleasure they are and were created."

5 And I saw in the right hand of him that sat on the throne a book written within and on the back side, sealed with seven seals. 2 And I saw a strong angel proclaiming with a loud voice, "Who is worthy to open the book, and to loose the seals thereof?" 3 And no man in heaven, nor in earth, neither under the earth, was able to open the book, neither to look thereon. 4 And I wept much, because no man was found worthy to open and to read the book, neither to look thereon. 5 And one of the elders saith unto me, "Weep not: behold, the Lion of the tribe of Juda, the Root of David, hath prevailed to open the book, and to loose the seven seals thereof."

6 And I beheld, and, lo, in the midst of the throne and of the four beasts, and in the midst of the elders, stood a Lamb as it had been slain, having seven horns and seven eyes, which are the seven Spirits of God sent forth into all the earth. 7 And he came and took the book out of the right hand of him that sat upon the throne. 8 And when he had taken the book, the four beasts and four *and* twenty elders fell down before the Lamb, having every one of them harps, and golden vials full of odors, which are the prayers of saints. 9. And they sung a new song, saying,

"Thou art worthy to take the book, and to open the seals thereof:
For thou wast slain, and hast redeemed us to God by thy blood
Out of every kindred, and tongue, and people, and nation;
10 And hast made us unto our God kings and priests:
And we shall reign on the earth."

11 And I beheld, and I heard the voice of many angels round about the throne, and the beasts, and the elders: and the number of them was ten thousand times ten thousand, and thousands of thousands; 12 Saying with a loud voice,

"Worthy is the Lamb that was slain to receive power, and riches, and wisdom, and strength, and honor, and glory, and blessing."

13 And every creature which is in heaven, and on the earth, and under the earth, and such as are in the sea, and all that are in them, heard I saying,

"Blessing, and honor, and glory, and power, *be* unto him that sitteth upon the throne, and unto the Lamb for ever and ever."

14 And the four beasts said, "Amen." And the four *and* twenty elders fell down and worshipped him that liveth for ever and ever.

THE SEVEN SEALS

6 And I saw when the Lamb opened one of the seals, and I heard, as it were the noise of thunder, one of the four beasts saying, "Come and see." 2 And I saw, and behold a white horse: and he that sat on him had a bow; and a crown was given unto him: and he went forth conquering, and to conquer.

3 And when he had opened the second seal, I heard the second beast say, "Come and see." 4 And there went out another horse *that was* red: and *power* was given to him that sat thereon to take peace from the earth, and that they should kill one another: and there was given unto him a great sword.

5 And when he had opened the third seal, I heard the third beast say, "Come and see." And I beheld, and lo a black horse; and he that sat on him had a pair of balances in his hand. 6 And I heard a voice in the midst of the four beasts say, "A measure of wheat for a penny, and three measures of barley for a penny; and *see* thou hurt not the oil and the wine." 10

7 And when he had opened the fourth seal, I heard the voice of the fourth beast say, "Come and see." 8 And I looked, and behold a pale horse: and his name that sat on him was Death, and Hell followed with him. And power was given unto them over the fourth part of the earth, to kill with sword, and with hunger, and with death, and with the beasts of the earth.

9 And when he had opened the fifth seal, I saw under the altar the souls of them that were slain for the word of God, and for the testimony which they held: 10 And they cried with a loud voice, saying, "How long, O Lord, holy and true, dost thou not judge and avenge our blood on them that dwell on the earth?" 11 And white robes were given unto every one of them; and it was said unto them, that they should rest yet for a little season, until their fellow servants also and their brethren, that should be killed as they *were,* should be fulfilled.

12 And I beheld when he had opened the sixth

10. TEV: "A quart of wheat for a whole day's wages . . ." This predicts a famine during which most people can barely afford to feed themselves, but during which the rich continue to live in unfeeling luxury.

seal, and, lo, there was a great earthquake; and the sun became black as sackcloth of hair, and the moon became as blood; 13 And the stars of heaven fell unto the earth, even as a fig tree casteth her untimely figs, when she is shaken of a mighty wind. 14 And the heaven departed as a scroll when it is rolled together; and every mountain and island were moved out of their places. 15 And the kings of the earth, and the great men, and the rich men, and the chief captains, and the mighty men, and every bondman, and every free man, hid themselves in the dens and in the rocks of the mountains; 16 And said to the mountains and rocks, "Fall on us, and hide us from the face of him that sitteth on the throne, and from the wrath of the Lamb: 17 For the great day of his wrath is come; and who shall be able to stand?"

THE SERVANTS OF GOD PROTECTED

7 And after these things I saw four angels standing on the four corners of the earth, holding the four winds of the earth, that the wind should not blow on the earth, nor on the sea, nor on any tree. 2 And I saw another angel ascending from the east, having the seal of the living God: and he cried with a loud voice to the four angels, to whom it was given to hurt the earth and the sea, 3 Saying, "Hurt not the earth, neither the sea, nor the trees, till we have sealed the servants of our God in their foreheads." 4 And I heard the number of them which were sealed: *and there were* sealed a hundred *and* forty *and* four thousand of all the tribes of the children of Israel. 5 Of the tribe of Juda *were* sealed twelve thousand. Of the tribe of Reuben *were* sealed twelve thousand. Of the tribe of Gad *were* sealed twelve thousand. 6 Of the tribe of Aser *were* sealed twelve thousand. Of the tribe of Nephthalim *were* sealed twelve thousand. Of the tribe of Manasses *were* sealed twelve thousand. 7 Of the tribe of Simeon *were* sealed twelve thousand. Of the tribe of Levi *were* sealed twelve thousand. Of the tribe of Issachar *were* sealed twelve thousand. 8 Of the tribe of Zabulon *were* sealed twelve thousand. Of the tribe of Joseph *were* sealed twelve thousand. Of the tribe of Benjamin *were* sealed twelve thousand.

9 After this I beheld, and, lo, a great multitude, which no man could number, of all nations, and kindreds, and people, and tongues, stood before the throne, and before the Lamb, clothed with white robes, and palms in their hands; 10 And cried with a loud voice, saying,

"Salvation to our God which sitteth upon the throne, and unto the Lamb."

11 And all the angels stood round about the throne, and *about* the elders and the four beasts, and fell before the throne on their faces, and worshipped God, 12 Saying,

"Amen: Blessing, and glory, and wisdom, and thanksgiving, and honor, and power, and might, *be* unto our God for ever and ever. Amen."

13 And one of the elders answered, saying unto me, "What are these which are arrayed in white robes? and whence came they?" 14 And I said unto him, "Sir, thou knowest." And he said to me, "These are they which came out of great tribulation, and have washed their robes, and made them white in the blood of the Lamb. 15 Therefore are they before the throne of God, and serve him day and night in his temple: and he that sitteth on the throne shall dwell among them. 16 They shall hunger no more, neither thirst any more; neither shall the sun light on them, nor any heat. 17 For the Lamb which is in the midst of the throne shall feed them, and shall lead them unto living fountains of waters: and God shall wipe away all tears from their eyes."

THE SEVEN TRUMPETS

8 And when he had opened the seventh seal, there was silence in heaven about the space of half an hour.[11] 2 And I saw the seven angels which stood before God; and to them were given seven trumpets. 3 And another angel came and stood at the altar, having a golden censer; and there was given unto him much incense, that he should offer *it* with the prayers of all saints upon the golden altar which was before the throne. 4 And the smoke of the incense, *which came* with the prayers of the saints, ascended up before God out of the angel's hand. 5 And the angel took the censer, and filled it with fire of the altar, and cast *it* into the earth: and there were voices, and thunderings, and lightnings, and an earthquake. 6 And the seven angels which had the seven trumpets prepared themselves to sound.

7 The first angel sounded, and there followed hail and fire mingled with blood, and they were cast upon the earth: and the third part of trees was burnt up, and all green grass was burnt up.

8 And the second angel sounded, and as it were a great mountain burning with fire was cast into the sea: and the third part of the sea became blood; 9 And the third part of the creatures

---

11. This puzzling line is best clarified in PHILLIPS: "there was utter silence in Heaven for what seemed to me half an hour." In context, this is an intensely dramatic pause.

which were in the sea, and had life, died; and the third part of the ships were destroyed.

10 And the third angel sounded, and there fell a great star from heaven, burning as it were a lamp, and it fell upon the third part of the rivers, and upon the fountains of waters; 11 And the name of the star is called Wormwood: and the third part of the waters became wormwood; and many men died of the waters, because they were made bitter.

12 And the fourth angel sounded, and the third part of the sun was smitten, and the third part of the moon, and the third part of the stars; so as the third part of them was darkened, and the day shone not for a third part of it, and the night likewise.

13 And I beheld, and heard an angel [12] flying through the midst of heaven, saying with a loud voice, "Woe, woe, woe, to the inhabiters of the earth by reason of the other voices of the trumpet of the three angels, which are yet to sound!"

9 And the fifth angel sounded, and I saw a star fall from heaven unto the earth: and to him was given the key of the bottomless pit.[13] 2 And he opened the bottomless pit; and there arose a smoke out of the pit, as the smoke of a great furnace; and the sun and the air were darkened by reason of the smoke of the pit. 3 And there came out of the smoke locusts upon the earth: and unto them was given power, as the scorpions of the earth have power. 4 And it was commanded them that they should not hurt the grass of the earth, neither any green thing, neither any tree; but only those men which have not the seal of God in their foreheads. 5 And to them it was given that they should not kill them, but that they should be tormented five months: and their torment *was* as the torment of a scorpion, when he striketh a man. 6 And in those days shall men seek death, and shall not find it; and shall desire to die, and death shall flee from them.

7 And the shapes of the locusts *were* like unto horses prepared unto battle; and on their heads *were* as it were crowns like gold, and their faces *were* as the faces of men. 8 And they had hair as the hair of women, and their teeth were as *the teeth* of lions. 9 And they had breastplates, as it were breastplates of iron; and the sound of their wings *was* as the sound of chariots of many horses running to battle. 10 And they had tails like unto scorpions, and there were stings in their tails: and

their power *was* to hurt men five months. 11 And they had a king over them, *which is* the angel of the bottomless pit, whose name in the Hebrew tongue *is* Abaddon, but in the Greek tongue hath *his* name Apollyon.

12 "One woe is past; *and,* behold, there come two woes more hereafter."

13 And the sixth angel sounded, and I heard a voice from the four horns of the golden altar which is before God, 14 Saying to the sixth angel which had the trumpet, "Loose the four angels which are bound in the great river Euphrates." 15 And the four angels were loosed, which were prepared for an hour, and a day, and a month, and a year, for to slay the third part of men.[14] 16 And the number of the army of the horsemen *were* two hundred thousand thousand: and I heard the number of them. 17 And thus I saw the horses in the vision, and them that sat on them, having breastplates of fire, and of jacinth, and brimstone: and the heads of the horses *were* as the heads of lions; and out of their mouths issued fire and smoke and brimstone. 18 By these three was the third part of men killed, by the fire, and by the smoke, and by the brimstone, which issued out of their mouths. 19 For their power is in their mouth, and in their tails: for their tails *were* like unto serpents, and had heads, and with them they do hurt.

20 And the rest of the men which were not killed by these plagues yet repented not of the works of their hands, that they should not worship devils, and idols of gold, and silver, and brass, and stone, and of wood; which neither can see, nor hear, nor walk: 21 Neither repented they of their murders, nor of their sorceries, nor of their fornication, nor of their thefts.

THE BITTER BOOK
OF THINGS TO COME

10 And I saw another mighty angel come down from heaven, clothed with a cloud: and a rainbow *was* upon his head, and his face *was* as it were the sun, and his feet as pillars of fire: 2 And he had in his hand a little book open: and he set his right foot upon the sea, and *his* left *foot* on the earth, 3 And cried with a loud voice, as *when* a lion roareth: and when he had cried, seven thunders uttered their voices. 4 And when the seven thunders had uttered their voices, I was about to write: and I heard a voice from heaven saying unto me, "Seal up those things which the seven

---

12. For "angel," all modern translations read "eagle." The creature repeats its message of woe in 9:12 and 11:14.

13. The star is probably the same angelic servant mentioned in 20:1.

14. The dramatic effect is stronger in NEB: "They had been held ready for this moment, for this very year and month, day and hour."

thunders uttered, and write them not." 5 And the angel which I saw stand upon the sea and upon the earth lifted up his hand to heaven, 6 And sware by him that liveth for ever and ever, who created heaven, and the things that therein are, and the earth, and the things that therein are, and the sea, and the things which are therein, that there should be time no longer: 7 But in the days of the voice of the seventh angel, when he shall begin to sound, the mystery of God should be finished,[15] as he hath declared to his servants the prophets.

8 And the voice which I heard from heaven spake unto me again, and said, "Go *and* take the little book which is open in the hand of the angel which standeth upon the sea and upon the earth." 9 And I went unto the angel, and said unto him, "Give me the little book." And he said unto me, "Take *it*, and eat it up; and it shall make thy belly bitter, but it shall be in thy mouth sweet as honey." 10 And I took the little book out of the angel's hand, and ate it up; and it was in my mouth sweet as honey: and as soon as I had eaten it, my belly was bitter. 11 And he said unto me, "Thou must prophesy again before many peoples, and nations, and tongues, and kings."

THE TWO WITNESSES

11 And there was given me a reed like unto a rod: and the angel stood, saying, "Rise, and measure the temple of God, and the altar, and them that worship therein. 2 But the court which is without the temple leave out, and measure it not; for it is given unto the Gentiles: and the holy city shall they tread under foot forty *and* two months.[16] 3 And I will give *power* unto my two witnesses, and they shall prophesy a thousand two hundred *and* threescore days, clothed in sackcloth."

4 These are the two olive trees, and the two candlesticks standing before the God of the earth. 5 And if any man will hurt them, fire proceedeth out of their mouth, and devoureth their enemies: and if any man will hurt them, he must in this manner be killed. 6 These have power to shut heaven, that it rain not in the days of their prophecy: and have power over waters to turn them to blood, and to smite the earth with all

plagues, as often as they will. 7 And when they shall have finished their testimony, the beast that ascendeth out of the bottomless pit shall make war against them, and shall overcome them, and kill them. 8 And their dead bodies *shall lie* in the street of the great city, which spiritually is called Sodom and Egypt, where also our Lord was crucified.[17] 9 And they of the people and kindreds and tongues and nations shall see their dead bodies three days and a half, and shall not suffer their dead bodies to be put in graves. 10 And they that dwell upon the earth shall rejoice over them, and make merry, and shall send gifts one to another; because these two prophets tormented them that dwelt on the earth. 11 And after three days and a half the Spirit of life from God entered into them, and they stood upon their feet; and great fear fell upon them which saw them. 12 And they heard a great voice from heaven saying unto them, "Come up hither." And they ascended up to heaven in a cloud; and their enemies beheld them. 13 And the same hour was there a great earthquake, and the tenth part of the city fell, and in the earthquake were slain of men seven thousand: and the remnant were affrighted, and gave glory to the God of heaven.

14 "The second woe is past; *and*, behold, the third woe cometh quickly."

15 And the seventh angel sounded; and there were great voices in heaven, saying,

> "The kingdoms of this world are become *the kingdoms* of our Lord, and of his Christ; and he shall reign for ever and ever."

16 And the four and twenty elders, which sat before God on their seats, fell upon their faces, and worshipped God, 17 Saying,

> "We give thee thanks, O Lord God Almighty, which art, and wast, and art to come; because thou hast taken to thee thy great power, and hast reigned. 18 And the nations were angry, and thy wrath is come, and the time of the dead, that they should be judged, and that thou shouldest give reward unto thy servants the prophets, and to the saints, and them that fear thy name, small and great; and shouldest destroy them which destroy the earth."

19 And the temple of God was opened in heaven, and there was seen in his temple the ark of his testament: and there were lightnings, and voices, and thunderings, and an earthquake, and great hail.

---

15. PHILLIPS: "the mysterious purpose of God shall be completed." KNOX: "God's secret design . . . would be accomplished."

16. Besides its numerical symbolism as one-half of 7, the 3½ figure (42 months; 1260 days; a time, and times, and half a time) probably relates to the 3½-year persecution which the Jewish people suffered under Antiochus Epiphanes, King of Syria (168–165 B.C.).

17. Though this seems to describe Jerusalem, most scholars identify the city as Rome. There are seven other references to "the great city" in *Revelation*; in each case, it means Rome.

THE WOMAN AND THE DRAGON

12 And there appeared a great wonder in heaven; a woman clothed with the sun, and the moon under her feet, and upon her head a crown of twelve stars: 2 And she being with child cried, travailing in birth, and pained to be delivered.[18] 3 And there appeared another wonder in heaven; and behold a great red dragon, having seven heads and ten horns, and seven crowns upon his heads. 4 And his tail drew the third part of the stars of heaven, and did cast them to the earth: and the dragon stood before the woman which was ready to be delivered, for to devour her child as soon as it was born. 5 And she brought forth a man child, who was to rule all nations with a rod of iron: and her child was caught up unto God, and *to* his throne. 6 And the woman fled into the wilderness, where she hath a place prepared of God, that they should feed her there a thousand two hundred *and* threescore days.

7 And there was war in heaven: Michael and his angels fought against the dragon; and the dragon fought and his angels, 8 And prevailed not; neither was their place found any more in heaven. 9 And the great dragon was cast out, that old serpent, called the Devil, and Satan, which deceiveth the whole world: he was cast out into the earth, and his angels were cast out with him. 10 And I heard a loud voice saying in heaven,

> "Now is come salvation, and strength, and the kingdom of our God, and the power of his Christ: for the accuser of our brethren is cast down, which accused them before our God day and night. 11 And they overcame him by the blood of the Lamb, and by the word of their testimony; and they loved not their lives unto the death. 12 Therefore rejoice, *ye* heavens, and ye that dwell in them. Woe to the inhabiters of the earth and of the sea! for the devil is come down unto you, having great wrath, because he knoweth that he hath but a short time."

13 And when the dragon saw that he was cast unto the earth, he persecuted the woman which brought forth the man *child.* 14 And to the woman were given two wings of a great eagle, that she might fly into the wilderness, into her place, where she is nourished for a time, and times, and half a time, from the face of the

serpent. 15 And the serpent cast out of his mouth water as a flood after the woman, that he might cause her to be carried away of the flood. 16 And the earth helped the woman; and the earth opened her mouth, and swallowed up the flood which the dragon cast out of his mouth. 17 And the dragon was wroth with the woman, and went to make war with the remnant of her seed, which keep the commandments of God, and have the testimony of Jesus Christ.

THE TWO BEASTS

13 And I stood upon the sand of the sea, and saw a beast rise up out of the sea, having seven heads and ten horns, and upon his horns ten crowns, and upon his heads the name of blasphemy. 2 And the beast which I saw was like unto a leopard, and his feet were as *the feet* of a bear, and his mouth as the mouth of a lion: and the dragon gave him his power, and his seat, and great authority. 3 And I saw one of his heads as it were wounded to death; and his deadly wound was healed: and all the world wondered after the beast. 4 And they worshipped the dragon which gave power unto the beast: and they worshipped the beast, saying, "Who *is* like unto the beast? who is able to make war with him?"

5 And there was given unto him a mouth speaking great things and blasphemies; and power was given unto him to continue forty *and* two months. 6 And he opened his mouth in blasphemy against God, to blaspheme his name, and his tabernacle, and them that dwell in heaven. 7 And it was given unto him to make war with the saints, and to overcome them: and power was given him over all kindreds, and tongues, and nations. 8 And all that dwell upon the earth shall worship him, whose names are not written in the book of life of the Lamb slain from the foundation of the world. 9 If any man have an ear, let him hear. 10 He that leadeth into captivity shall go into captivity: he that killeth with the sword must be killed with the sword. Here is the patience and the faith of the saints.

11 And I beheld another beast coming up out of the earth; and he had two horns like a lamb, and he spake as a dragon. 12 And he exerciseth all the power of the first beast before him, and causeth the earth and them which dwell therein to worship the first beast, whose deadly wound was healed. 13 And he doeth great wonders, so that he maketh fire come down from heaven on the earth in the sight of men, 14 And deceiveth them that dwell on the earth by *the means of* those miracles which he had power to do in the sight of

---

18. The woman symbolizes the Hebrew people, who brought forth the Messiah. The birth pangs refer to periods of messianic tribulation and expectation.

the beast; saying to them that dwell on the earth, that they should make an image to the beast, which had the wound by a sword, and did live. 15 And he had power to give life unto the image of the beast, that the image of the beast should both speak, and cause that as many as would not worship the image of the beast should be killed. 16 And he causeth all, both small and great, rich and poor, free and bond, to receive a mark in their right hand, or in their foreheads: 17 And that no man might buy or sell, save he that had the mark, or the name of the beast, or the number of his name. 18 Here is wisdom. Let him that hath understanding count the number of the beast: for it is the number of a man; and his number *is* Six hundred three-score *and* six.

THE LAMB AND HIS REDEEMED HOST

14 And I looked, and, lo, a Lamb stood on the mount Sion, and with him a hundred forty *and* four thousand, having his Father's name written in their foreheads. 2 And I heard a voice from heaven, as the voice of many waters, and as the voice of a great thunder: and I heard the voice of harpers harping with their harps: 3 And they sung as it were a new song before the throne, and before the four beasts, and the elders: and no man could learn that song but the hundred *and* forty *and* four thousand, which were redeemed from the earth. 4 These are they which were not defiled with women; for they are virgins.[19] These are they which follow the Lamb whithersoever he goeth. These were redeemed from among men, *being* the firstfruits unto God and to the Lamb. 5 And in their mouth was found no guile: for they are without fault before the throne of God.

6 And I saw another angel fly in the midst of heaven, having the everlasting gospel to preach unto them that dwell on the earth, and to every nation, and kindred, and tongue, and people, 7 Saying with a loud voice, "Fear God, and give glory to him; for the hour of his judgment is come: and worship him that made heaven, and earth, and the sea, and the fountains of waters." 8 And there followed another angel, saying, "Babylon is fallen, is fallen, that great city, because she made all nations drink of the wine of the wrath of her fornication." 9 And the third angel followed them, saying with a loud voice, "If any man worship the beast and his image, and

receive *his* mark in his forehead, or in his hand, 10 The same shall drink of the wine of the wrath of God, which is poured out without mixture into the cup of his indignation; and he shall be tormented with fire and brimstone in the presence of the holy angels, and in the presence of the Lamb: 11 And the smoke of their torment ascendeth up for ever and ever: and they have no rest day nor night, who worship the beast and his image, and whosoever receiveth the mark of his name."

12 Here is the patience of the saints: here *are* they that keep the commandments of God, and the faith of Jesus.

13 And I heard a voice from heaven saying unto me, "Write, Blessed *are* the dead which die in the Lord from henceforth": "Yea," saith the Spirit, "that they may rest from their labors; and their works do follow them."

14 And I looked, and behold a white cloud, and upon the cloud *one* sat like unto the Son of man, having on his head a golden crown, and in his hand a sharp sickle. 15 And another angel came out of the temple, crying with a loud voice to him that sat on the cloud, "Thrust in thy sickle, and reap: for the time is come for thee to reap; for the harvest of the earth is ripe." 16 And he that sat on the cloud thrust in his sickle on the earth; and the earth was reaped. 17 And another angel came out of the temple which is in heaven, he also having a sharp sickle. 18 And another angel came out from the altar, which had power over fire; and cried with a loud cry to him that had the sharp sickle, saying, "Thrust in thy sharp sickle, and gather the clusters of the vine of the earth; for her grapes are fully ripe." 19 And the angel thrust in his sickle into the earth, and gathered the vine of the earth, and cast *it* into the great winepress of the wrath of God. 20 And the winepress was trodden without the city, and blood came out of the winepress, even unto the horse bridles, by the space of a thousand *and* six hundred furlongs.

THE LAST PLAGUES

15 And I saw another sign in heaven, great and marvelous, seven angels having the seven last plagues; for in them is filled up the wrath of God.

The Hymn of the Saints

2 And I saw as it were a sea of glass mingled with fire: and them that had gotten the victory

---

19. The sentence is most intelligible and consistent if interpreted as a reference to spiritual adultery, i.e., idolatry.
However, this probably distorts the author's meaning. The
tendency to glorify celibacy and virginity was present in the
early church.

over the beast, and over his image, and over his mark, *and* over the number of his name, stand on the sea of glass, having the harps of God. 3 And they sing the song of Moses the servant of God, and the song of the Lamb, saying,

> "Great and marvelous *are* thy works,
> Lord God Almighty;
> Just and true *are* thy ways,
> Thou King of saints.
> 4 Who shall not fear thee, O Lord, and
>   glorify thy name?
> For *thou* only *art* holy:
> For all nations shall come and worship
>   before thee;
> For thy judgments are made manifest."

5 And after that I looked, and, behold, the temple of the tabernacle of the testimony in heaven was opened: 6 And the seven angels came out of the temple, having the seven plagues, clothed in pure and white linen, and having their breasts girded with golden girdles. 7 And one of the four beasts gave unto the seven angels seven golden vials[20] full of the wrath of God, who liveth for ever and ever. 8 And the temple was filled with smoke from the glory of God, and from his power; and no man was able to enter into the temple, till the seven plagues of the seven angels were fulfilled.

The Seven Vials

16 And I heard a great voice out of the temple saying to the seven angels, "Go your ways, and pour out the vials of the wrath of God upon the earth." 2 And the first went, and poured out his vial upon the earth; and there fell a noisome and grievous sore upon the men which had the mark of the beast, and *upon* them which worshipped his image.

3 And the second angel poured out his vial upon the sea; and it became as the blood of a dead *man:* and every living soul died in the sea.

4 And the third angel poured out his vial upon the rivers and fountains of waters; and they became blood. 5 And I heard the angel of the waters say,

> "Thou art righteous, O Lord, which art,
> and wast, and shalt be, because thou hast
> judged thus. 6 For they have shed the
> blood of saints and prophets, and thou
> hast given them blood to drink; for they
> are worthy."

7 And I heard another out of the altar say,
> "Even so, Lord God Almighty, true and
> righteous *are* thy judgments."

8 And the fourth angel poured out his vial upon the sun; and power was given unto him to scorch men with fire. 9 And men were scorched with great heat, and blasphemed the name of God, which hath power over these plagues: and they repented not to give him glory.

10 And the fifth angel poured out his vial upon the seat of the beast; and his kingdom was full of darkness; and they gnawed their tongues for pain, 11 And blasphemed the God of heaven because of their pains and their sores, and repented not of their deeds.

12 And the sixth angel poured out his vial upon the great river Euphrates; and the water thereof was dried up, that the way of the kings of the east might be prepared. 13 And I saw three unclean spirits like frogs *come* out of the mouth of the dragon, and out of the mouth of the beast, and out of the mouth of the false prophet.[21] 14 For they are the spirits of devils, working miracles, *which* go forth unto the kings of the earth and of the whole world, to gather them to the battle of that great day of God Almighty. 15 "Behold, I come as a thief. Blessed *is* he that watcheth, and keepeth his garments, lest he walk naked, and they see his shame." 16 And he gathered them together into a place called in the Hebrew tongue Armageddon.[22]

17 And the seventh angel poured out his vial into the air; and there came a great voice out of the temple of heaven, from the throne, saying, "It is done." 18 And there were voices, and thunders, and lightnings; and there was a great earthquake, such as was not since men were upon the earth, so mighty an earthquake, *and* so great. 19 And the great city was divided into three parts, and the cities of the nations fell: and great Babylon came in remembrance before God,[23] to give unto her the cup of the wine of the fierceness of his wrath. 20 And every island fled away, and the mountains were not found. 21 And there fell upon men a great hail out of heaven, *every stone* about the weight of a talent: and men blas-

---

20. Almost all modern translations read "bowls." Probably the reference is to the kind of bronze basins used by priests in sacrificial rituals.

21. The false prophet seems identical with the "beast coming up out of the earth" (13:11-18). See 1920 and 20:10.

22. Megiddo and the plain of Esdraelon was the site of many decisive battles. It was the scene of Sisera's defeat (See *Judges* 5:19-20) and of Josiah's death (*II Kings* 23:29).

23. NEB makes the irony clearer: "And God did not forget Babylon the great."

phemed God because of the plague of the hail; for the plague thereof was exceeding great.

THE PUNISHMENT OF BABYLON
The Great Whore

17 And there came one of the seven angels which had the seven vials, and talked with me, saying unto me, "Come hither; I will show unto thee the judgment of the great whore that sitteth upon many waters; 2 With whom the kings of the earth have committed fornication, and the inhabitants of the earth have been made drunk with the wine of her fornication." 3 So he carried me away in the spirit into the wilderness: and I saw a woman sit upon a scarlet-colored beast, full of names of blasphemy, having seven heads and ten horns. 4 And the woman was arrayed in purple and scarlet color, and decked with gold and precious stones and pearls, having a golden cup in her hand full of abominations and filthiness of her fornication: 5 And upon her forehead *was* a name written "MYSTERY, BABYLON THE GREAT,[24] THE MOTHER OF HARLOTS AND ABOMINATIONS OF THE EARTH." 6 And I saw the woman drunken with the blood of the saints, and with the blood of the martyrs of Jesus:

And when I saw her, I wondered with great admiration. 7 And the angel said unto me, "Wherefore didst thou marvel? I will tell thee the mystery of the woman, and of the beast that carrieth her, which hath the seven heads and ten horns. 8 The beast that thou sawest was, and is not; and shall ascend out of the bottomless pit, and go into perdition: and they that dwell on the earth shall wonder, whose names were not written in the book of life from the foundation of the world, when they behold the beast that was, and is not, and yet is. 9 And here *is* the mind which hath wisdom.[25] The seven heads are seven mountains, on which the woman sitteth. 10 And there are seven kings: five are fallen, and one is, *and* the other is not yet come; and when he cometh, he must continue a short space. 11 And the beast that was, and is not, even he is the eighth, and is of the seven, and goeth into perdition. 12 And the ten horns which thou sawest are ten kings, which have received no kingdom as yet; but receive power as kings one hour with the beast.[26] 13 These have one mind, and shall give their

power and strength unto the beast. 14 These shall make war with the Lamb, and the Lamb shall overcome them: for he is Lord of lords, and King of kings: and they that are with him *are* called, and chosen, and faithful."

15 And he saith unto me, "The waters which thou sawest, where the whore sitteth, are peoples, and multitudes, and nations, and tongues. 16 And the ten horns which thou sawest upon the beast, these shall hate the whore, and shall make her desolate and naked, and shall eat her flesh, and burn her with fire. 17 For God hath put in their hearts to fulfil his will, and to agree, and give their kingdom unto the beast, until the words of God shall be fulfilled. 18 And the woman which thou sawest is that great city, which reigneth over the kings of the earth."

The Fall of Babylon

18 And after these things I saw another angel come down from heaven, having great power; and the earth was lightened with his glory. 2 And he cried mightily with a strong voice, saying,

"Babylon the great is fallen, is fallen,
And is become the habitation of devils,
And the hold of every foul spirit,
And a cage of every unclean and hateful bird.

3   For all nations have drunk of the wine of the wrath of her fornication,
And the kings of the earth have committed fornication with her,
And the merchants of the earth are waxed rich through the abundance of her delicacies."

4 And I heard another voice from heaven, saying, "Come out of her, my people,
That ye be not partakers of her sins,
And that ye receive not of her plagues.

5   For her sins have reached unto heaven,
And God hath remembered her iniquities.

6   Reward her even as she rewarded you,
And double unto her double according to her works:
In the cup which she hath filled, fill to her double.

7   How much she hath glorified herself, and lived deliciously,
So much torment and sorrow give her:
For she saith in her heart, 'I sit a queen,
And am no widow, and shall see no sorrow.'

8   Therefore shall her plagues come in one day,
Death, and mourning, and famine;
And she shall be utterly burned with fire:

---

24. PHILLIPS: "On her forehead is written a name with a secret meaning—BABYLON THE GREAT."
25. GOODSPEED: "Here is a problem for a profound mind."
26. (17:12-17) Barclay comments: "Who the ten kings are is not certain. But it is likely that they are the satraps and authorities of the East and of Parthia whom the resurrected Nero, the Antichrist, is to lead against Rome."

For strong *is* the Lord God who judgeth
her."

9 And the kings of the earth, who have committed fornication and lived deliciously with her,
shall bewail her, and lament for her, when they
shall see the smoke of her burning, 10 Standing
afar off for the fear of her torment, saying,
  "Alas, alas, that great city
  Babylon, that mighty city!
  For in one hour is thy judgment come."

11 And the merchants of the earth shall weep
and mourn over her; for no man buyeth their
merchandise any more: 12 The merchandise of
gold, and silver, and precious stones, and of
pearls, and fine linen, and purple, and silk, and
scarlet, and all thyine wood, and all manner
vessels of ivory, and all manner vessels of most
precious wood, and of brass, and iron, and
marble, 13 And cinnamon, and odors, and
ointments, and frankincense, and wine, and oil,
and fine flour, and wheat, and beasts, and sheep,
and horses, and chariots, and slaves, and souls of
men.[27]
14   "And the fruits that thy soul lusted after
        are departed from thee,
      And all things which were dainty and
        goodly are departed from thee,
      And thou shalt find them no more at all."
15 The merchants of these things, which were
made rich by her, shall stand afar off for the fear
of her torment, weeping and wailing, 16 And
saying,
      "Alas, alas, that great city,
      That was clothed in fine linen, and purple,
        and scarlet,
      And decked with gold, and precious
        stones, and pearls!
17   For in one hour so great riches is come to
        nought."

And every shipmaster, and all the company in
ships, and sailors, and as many as trade by sea,
stood afar off, 18 And cried when they saw the
smoke of her burning, saying, "What *city is* like
unto this great city!"
19 And they cast dust on their heads, and cried,
weeping and wailing, saying,
      "Alas, alas, that great city,
      Wherein were made rich all that had ships
        in the sea by reason of her costliness!
      For in one hour is she made desolate.
20   Rejoice over her, *thou* heaven,
      And *ye* holy apostles and prophets;
      For God hath avenged you on her."

21 And a mighty angel took up a stone like a
great millstone, and cast *it* into the sea, saying,
      "Thus with violence shall that great city
        Babylon be thrown down,
      And shall be found no more at all.
22   And the voice of harpers, and musicians,
        and of pipers, and trumpeters,
      Shall be heard no more at all in thee;
      And no craftsman, of whatsoever craft *he
        be,*
      Shall be found any more in thee;
      And the sound of a millstone
      Shall be heard no more at all in thee;
23   And the light of a candle shall shine no
        more at all in thee;
      And the voice of the bridegroom and of
        the bride
      Shall be heard no more at all in thee:
      For thy merchants were the great men of
        the earth;
      For by thy sorceries were all nations
        deceived.
24   And in her was found the blood of
        prophets, and of saints,
      And of all that were slain upon the earth."

SONGS OF TRIUMPH IN HEAVEN

19 And after these things I heard a great voice of
much people in heaven, saying,
      "Alleluia; Salvation, and glory, and
        honor, and power, unto the Lord our
        God:
2   For true and righteous *are* his judgments;
      For he hath judged the great whore,
        which did corrupt the earth with her
        fornication,
      And hath avenged the blood of his ser-
        vants at her hand."
3 And again they said, "Alleluia. And her smoke
rose up for ever and ever."

4 And the four and twenty elders and the four
beasts fell down and worshipped God that sat on
the throne, saying, "Amen; Alleluia." 5 And a
voice came out of the throne, saying,
      "Praise our God, all ye his servants,
      And ye that fear him, both small and
        great."

6 And I heard as it were the voice of a great
multitude, and as the voice of many waters, and
as the voice of mighty thunderings, saying,
      "Alleluia: for the Lord God omnipotent
        reigneth.
7   Let us be glad and rejoice, and give honor
        to him:

---

27. Lattimore: "and bodies and souls of men."

For the marriage of the Lamb is come,
And his wife hath made herself ready.

8   And to her was granted that she should be
         arrayed in fine linen, clean and white":
for the fine linen is the righteousness of saints.

9 And he saith unto me, "Write, 'Blessed *are*
they which are called unto the marriage supper of
the Lamb.' " And he saith unto me, "These are
the true sayings of God." 10 And I fell at his feet
to worship him. And he said unto me, "See *thou
do it* not: I am thy fellow servant, and of thy
brethren that have the testimony of Jesus: worship God":[28] for the testimony of Jesus is the
spirit of prophecy.

THE FINAL VICTORIES
The First Battle

11 And I saw heaven opened, and behold a
white horse; and he that sat upon him *was* called
Faithful and True, and in righteousness he doth
judge and make war. 12 His eyes *were* as a flame
of fire, and on his head *were* many crowns; and
he had a name written, that no man knew, but he
himself. 13 And he *was* clothed with a vesture
dipped in blood: and his name is called The
Word of God. 14 And the armies *which were* in
heaven followed him upon white horses, clothed
in fine linen, white and clean. 15 And out of his
mouth goeth a sharp sword, that with it he should
smite the nations; and he shall rule them with a
rod of iron: and he treadeth the winepress of the
fierceness and wrath of Almighty God. 16 And
he hath on *his* vesture and on his thigh a name
written, "KING OF KINGS, AND LORD OF LORDS."
17 And I saw an angel standing in the sun; and
he cried with a loud voice, saying to all the fowls
that fly in the midst of heaven, "Come and gather
yourselves together unto the supper of the great
God; 18 That ye may eat the flesh of kings, and
the flesh of captains, and the flesh of mighty men,
and the flesh of horses, and of them that sit on
them, and the flesh of all *men, both* free and bond,
both small and great." 19 And I saw the beast,
and the kings of the earth, and their armies,
gathered together to make war against him that
sat on the horse, and against his army. 20 And
the beast was taken, and with him the false
prophet that wrought miracles before him, with
which he deceived them that had received the
mark of the beast, and them that worshipped his
image. These both were cast alive into a lake of
fire burning with brimstone. 21 And the remnant
were slain with the sword of him that sat upon the
horse, which *sword* proceeded out of his mouth:
and all the fowls were filled with their flesh.

The Thousand-Year Reign

20 And I saw an angel come down from heaven,
having the key of the bottomless pit and a great
chain in his hand. 2 And he laid hold on the
dragon, that old serpent, which is the Devil, and
Satan, and bound him a thousand years, 3 And
cast him into the bottomless pit, and shut him up,
and set a seal upon him, that he should deceive
the nations no more, till the thousand years
should be fulfilled: and after that he must be
loosed a little season.

4 And I saw thrones, and they sat upon them,
and judgment was given unto them: and *I saw* the
souls of them that were beheaded for the witness
of Jesus, and for the word of God, and which had
not worshipped the beast, neither his image,
neither had received *his* mark upon their foreheads, or in their hands; and they lived and
reigned with Christ a thousand years.[29] 5 But the
rest of the dead lived not again until the thousand
years were finished. This *is* the first resurrection.
6 Blessed and holy *is* he that hath part in the first
resurrection: on such the second death hath no
power, but they shall be priests of God and of
Christ, and shall reign with him a thousand
years.

The Second Battle

7 And when the thousand years are expired,
Satan shall be loosed out of his prison, 8 And
shall go out to deceive the nations which are in
the four quarters of the earth, Gog and Magog, to
gather them together to battle: the number of
whom *is* as the sand of the sea. 9 And they went
up on the breadth of the earth, and compassed
the camp of the saints about, and the beloved
city: and fire came down from God out of
heaven, and devoured them. 10 And the devil
that deceived them was cast into the lake of fire
and brimstone, where the beast and the false
prophet *are,* and shall be tormented day and
night for ever and ever.

---

28. Most modern translations end the angel's speech at this
point. However, GOODSPEED and NEB close the quotation
at the end of the verse. The final phrase is clearest in KNOX:
"It is the truth concerning Jesus that inspires all prophecy."

29. Through most of their history, the Jewish people had no expectation of an afterlife; they thought the Lord would inter-
vene and create a new age of righteousness on earth. Later,
the concept of resurrection led many to contemplate an
ideal eternity in heaven. John offers the best of both worlds.
Before the redeemed find new life in the heavenly realm, the
martyrs will reign over an earthly kingdom.

The Last Judgment

11 And I saw a great white throne, and him that sat on it, from whose face the earth and the heaven fled away; and there was found no place for them. 12 And I saw the dead, small and great, stand before God; and the books were opened: and another book was opened, which is *the book* of life: and the dead were judged out of those things which were written in the books, according to their works. 13 And the sea gave up the dead which were in it; and death and hell delivered up the dead which were in them: and they were judged every man according to their works. 14 And death and hell were cast into the lake of fire. This is the second death. 15 And whosoever was not found written in the book of life was cast into the lake of fire.

THE NEW JERUSALEM

21 And I saw a new heaven and a new earth: for the first heaven and the first earth were passed away; and there was no more sea. 2 And I John saw the holy city, new Jerusalem, coming down from God out of heaven, prepared as a bride adorned for her husband. 3 And I heard a great voice out of heaven saying, "Behold, the tabernacle of God *is* with men, and he will dwell with them, and they shall be his people, and God himself shall be with them, *and be* their God. 4 And God shall wipe away all tears from their eyes; and there shall be no more death, neither sorrow, nor crying, neither shall there be any more pain: for the former things are passed away."

5 And he that sat upon the throne said, "Behold, I make all things new." And he said unto me, "Write: for these words are true and faithful." 6 And he said unto me, "It is done. I am Alpha and Omega, the beginning and the end. I will give unto him that is athirst of the fountain of the water of life freely. 7 He that overcometh shall inherit all things; and I will be his God, and he shall be my son. 8 But the fearful, and unbelieving, and the abominable, and murderers, and whoremongers, and sorcerers, and idolaters, and all liars, shall have their part in the lake which burneth with fire and brimstone: which is the second death."

9 And there came unto me one of the seven angels which had the seven vials full of the seven last plagues, and talked with me, saying, "Come hither, I will show thee the bride, the Lamb's wife." 10 And he carried me away in the spirit to a great and high mountain, and showed me that great city, the holy Jerusalem, descending out of heaven from God, 11 Having the glory of God: and her light *was* like unto a stone most precious, even like a jasper stone, clear as crystal; 12 And had a wall great and high, *and* had twelve gates, and at the gates twelve angels, and names written thereon, which are *the names* of the twelve tribes of the children of Israel: 13 On the east three gates; on the north three gates; on the south three gates; and on the west three gates. 14 And the wall of the city had twelve foundations, and in them the names of the twelve apostles of the Lamb.

15 And he that talked with me had a golden reed to measure the city, and the gates thereof, and the wall thereof. 16 And the city lieth foursquare, and the length is as large as the breadth: and he measured the city with the reed, twelve thousand furlongs. The length and the breadth and the height of it are equal. 17 And he measured the wall thereof, a hundred *and* forty *and* four cubits, *according to* the measure of a man, that is, of the angel.[30] 18 And the building of the wall of it was *of* jasper: and the city *was* pure gold, like unto clear glass. 19 And the foundations of the wall of the city *were* garnished with all manner of precious stones. The first foundation *was* jasper; the second, sapphire; the third, a chalcedony; the fourth, an emerald; 20 The fifth, sardonyx; the sixth, sardius; the seventh, chrysolite; the eighth, beryl; the ninth, a topaz; the tenth, a chrysoprasus; the eleventh, a jacinth; the twelfth, an amethyst. 21 And the twelve gates *were* twelve pearls; every several gate was of one pearl: and the street of the city *was* pure gold, as it were transparent glass.

22 And I saw no temple therein: for the Lord God Almighty and the Lamb are the temple of it. 23 And the city had no need of the sun, neither of the moon, to shine in it: for the glory of God did lighten it, and the Lamb *is* the light thereof. 24 And the nations of them which are saved shall walk in the light of it: and the kings of the earth do bring their glory and honor into it. 25 And the gates of it shall not be shut at all by day: for there shall be no night there. 26 And they shall bring the glory and honor of the nations into it. 27 And there shall in no wise enter into it any thing that defileth, neither *whatsoever* worketh abomination, or *maketh* a lie: but they which are written in the Lamb's book of life.

30. (21:16-17) TEV: "it was fifteen hundred miles long, and was as wide and as high as it was long. The angel also measured the wall, and it was two hundred and sixteen feet high, according to the normal unit of measure, which he was using."

22 And he showed me a pure river of water of life, clear as crystal, proceeding out of the throne of God and of the Lamb. 2 In the midst of the street of it, and on either side of the river, *was there* the tree of life, which bare twelve *manner of* fruits, *and* yielded her fruit every month: and the leaves of the tree *were* for the healing of the nations. 3 And there shall be no more curse: but the throne of God and of the Lamb shall be in it; and his servants shall serve him:[31] 4 And they shall see his face; and his name *shall be* in their foreheads. 5 And there shall be no night there; and they need no candle, neither light of the sun; for the Lord God giveth them light: and they shall reign for ever and ever.

EPILOGUE[32]

6 And he said unto me, "These sayings *are* faithful and true: and the Lord God of the holy prophets sent his angel to show unto his servants the things which must shortly be done. 7 Behold, I come quickly."

Blessed *is* he that keepeth the sayings of the prophecy of this book.

8 And I John saw these things, and heard *them.* And when I had heard and seen, I fell down to worship before the feet of the angel which showed me these things. 9 Then saith he unto me, "See *thou do it* not: for I am thy fellow servant, and of thy brethren the prophets, and of them which

---

31. In IB, Martin Rist notes, "in the new age the distinction between Christ and God will not be important or even clear."

32. (22:6-21) The material in the Epilogue is repetitive and disconnected. It is possible that John was deliberately repeating important themes from the book. It is more likely that he did not edit the last chapter and that it exists in unfinished form.

keep the sayings of this book: worship God."

10 And he saith unto me, "Seal not the sayings of the prophecy of this book: for the time is at hand. 11 He that is unjust, let him be unjust still: and he which is filthy, let him be filthy still: and he that is righteous, let him be righteous still: and he that is holy, let him be holy still.

12 "And, behold, I come quickly; and my reward *is* with me, to give every man according as his work shall be. 13 I am Alpha and Omega, the beginning and the end, the first and the last."

14 Blessed *are* they that do his commandments, that they may have right to the tree of life, and may enter in through the gates into the city. 15 For without *are* dogs, and sorcerers, and whoremongers, and murderers, and idolaters, and whosoever loveth and maketh a lie.

16 "I Jesus have sent mine angel to testify unto you these things in the churches. I am the root and the offspring of David, *and* the bright and morning star." 17 And the Spirit and the bride say, "Come." And let him that heareth say, "Come." And let him that is athirst come. And whosoever will, let him take the water of life freely.

18 For I testify unto every man that heareth the words of the prophecy of this book, If any man shall add unto these things, God shall add unto him the plagues that are written in this book: 19 And if any man shall take away from the words of the book of this prophecy, God shall take away his part out of the book of life, and out of the holy city, and *from* the things which are written in this book.

20 He which testifieth these things saith, "Surely I come quickly": Amen. Even so, come, Lord Jesus.

21 The grace of our Lord Jesus Christ *be* with you all. Amen.

APPENDIX

GLOSSARY

Alexandrian Codex. A fifth-century Greek manuscript of the Bible.

Allegory. A narrative in which abstract qualities are made concrete in order to convey a moral.

Anthropomorphism. The ascription of human characteristics to deity.

Aphorism. A succinct generalization.

Apocalypse. A prophetic description of the cataclysmic end of history and of the new age to follow.

Apocrypha. The fourteen books of the Vulgate Old Testament which are not in the Hebrew canon. These are writings produced and used by Alexandrian Jews.

Apostle. One of the twelve main disciples of Jesus.

Ark of the Covenant. A chest or shrine symbolizing the presence of Yahweh among the Hebrews.

Armageddon. Literally, the mountains of Megiddo; the prophetic battlefield where the kings of the earth are to gather during the last days.

Baal. Canaanite deity; god of the storm and male fertility figure.

Babylonian Exile. The separation of Jews from Palestine following the Babylonian deportations beginning in 597 B.C. After Persia conquered Babylon in 539 B.C., many Jews were allowed to return home.

Canon. The books chosen to be included in Scripture.

Charismatic. A person seized with the spirit of God and thus able to lead and inspire others.

Chērem. A ban under which a conquered city is sacrificed to God. It is a sacrilege to take booty or to fail to kill every living creature.

Codex. A manuscript consisting of folded sheets sewn together; it replaced the scroll form.

Concubine. A secondary wife in a polygamous family.

Covenant. An agreement or compact between God and men.

Covenant Code. The collection of laws found in *Exodus* 20:23–23:33.

Dead Sea Scrolls. The library of a monastic community living on the western side of the Dead Sea around the time of Jesus. The first documents were discovered in 1947.

Decalogue. The Ten Commandments.

Diaspora. The body of Jews living outside Palestine after the Babylonian captivity.

Disciple. A follower or student of Jesus.

Doublet. Two versions of a single story, presumably included because an editor thought they concerned two separate events.

Doxology. A hymn of praise.

E. The Elohist, the northern kingdom source of Pentateuchal material.

Elegy. A song of lament and praise for the dead.

Elohim. An Old Testament name for deity; translated "God" in the KJV.

Enuma Elish. Ancient Babylonian story of creation.

Epic. A long narrative poem in which a great hero performs acts contributing to the development of a race or nation.

Eponym. A person from whom a tribe, place, or institution is thought to take its name.

Epistle. A letter. The term is applied to the messages of Paul.

Exodus. The deliverance of Israel from Egyptian bondage.

Folklore. Songs, tales, and semihistorical accounts cherished and passed on by common people.

Gehenna. A valley outside Jerusalem used for burning refuse. At one time, children were sacrificed there to the fire god Moloch. Jesus used the name to describe a place of hellish punishment.

Gospel. A narrative form announcing the "good news" concerning the life and mission of Jesus.

Hellenism. The presence and influence of Greek language and thought.

Israel. The northern kingdom during the period of the divided monarchies (922–722 B.C.). The southern kingdom was Judah.

J. The Yahwist, the earliest contributor(s) to the Pentateuch.

Jamnia. Site of the Rabbinic Assembly which defined the canon of the Old Testament (A.D. 90).

Judah. The southern kingdom during the period of the divided monarchies (922–722 B.C.). The northern kingdom was Israel.

Judges. Charismatic leaders who rallied the Jews against foreign oppressors during the period of the tribal confederacy (ca. 1200–1000 B.C.).

Koinē. Familiar, colloquial Greek; the language of the New Testament.

The Law. The first five books of the Hebrew canon.

Legend. An unverifiable tradition about past events, usually transmitted orally.

Levirate marriage. A Hebrew requirement that a man marry the widow of his brother or nearest of kin, if the deceased has left no sons.

LXX. Abbreviation for the Septuagint.

Maxim. A direct injunction concerning moral conduct.

Messiah. The expected king who would come to establish Jewish world domination and rule with peace and righteousness.

Messianic Secret. The fact that Jesus, particularly in *Mark*, deliberately sought to conceal his role as Messiah. This has occasioned a body of speculation.

Midrash. A commentary on Scripture.

Myth. A story about supernatural beings, often explaining the origin of natural phenomena or religious practice.

Nicolaitans. This group taught that Christians could continue to engage in heathen practices, e.g., eat meat sacrificed to idols.

Number symbolism. A literary technique which uses numbers, not as literal units of measurement, but as terms possessing symbolic value.

Oracle. A prophetic declaration.

P. The authors and editors of the Priestly school who contributed to the Pentateuch.

Papyri. The many papyrus fragments unearthed, mainly in Egypt, since the closing years of the nineteenth century. They offer Biblical scholars examples of ordinary language used by contemporaries of Jesus.

Parable. A story from ordinary experience which illustrates a moral or religious point.

Passion Narrative. A unified account of the last days of Jesus, which the Evangelists used in shaping their gospels.

Passover. The annual feast commemorating the delivery of Israel from Egyptian bondage.

Patriarchs. The eponyms of *Genesis* regarded as the fathers of Israel and of mankind.

Pentateuch. The first five books of the Old Testament.

Pharisees. A popular sect in Judaism which emphasized strict observance of the Law.

Philistines. Non-Semitic sea people who settled on the southern coast of Palestine around 1100 B.C.

The Prophets. The second division of the Hebrew canon.

Psalter. The collection of 150 psalms in the Old Testament.

Publican. A tax collector. Commonly one who used the office for personal gain; an extortionist.

Sadducees. An aristocratic sect of Judaism which held exclusively to the Torah and rejected later concepts such as resurrection.

Saga. The traditional history of an important family.

Samaritans. Inhabitants of the district of Samaria in central Palestine. They were scorned by the Jews as descendants of foreigners who intermarried with Israelites after the fall of Samaria in 721 B.C.

Sanhedrin. The highest ecclesiastical and judicial body of postexilic Judaism.

Scribes. Scholars, interpreters of the Law. Applying the Law to matters of daily life, they are also called "lawyers."

Septuagint. The Greek translation of the Hebrew Scriptures, begun in Alexandria in the third century B.C.

Sheol. The place of the dead, thought to be a subterranean land of gloom.

Sinaitic Codex. The manuscript of a fourth century Greek Bible. This is the earliest extant manuscript providing a complete New Testament.

Suffering Servant. The subject of several poems in *Isaiah*, a man who suffers vicariously for the nations of the earth.

Superscription. An introductory note to a Biblical book or poem.

Synoptic Gospels. The first three Gospels, which share the same subjects, stories, and language.

The Temple. This could refer to the Temple of Solomon (965–587 B.C.); the Temple of Zerubbabel (516–20 B.C.); or the Temple of Herod (20 B.C. to A.D. 70).

Testament. The Latin equivalent of covenant.

Torah. The Hebrew word for the Law, the first five books of the Old Testament.

Vatican Codex. The manuscript of a fourth-century Greek Bible.

Vulgate. The Latin translation of the Bible made by Jerome in the fourth century A.D.

Wisdom literature. Works which meditate on the mysteries of life: the nature of God, the fate of man, etc.

The Writings. After the Law and the Prophets, the third division of Hebrew Scripture.

Yahweh. Distinctive name for God in the Old Testament, translated "Lord" in the KJV.

Zealots. The militaristic faction in Judaism which favored open revolt against Rome.

Zion. Either the eastern hill of Jerusalem on which the Temple was built or the city of Jerusalem itself.